Figures available in three downloadable sizes (resolutions)

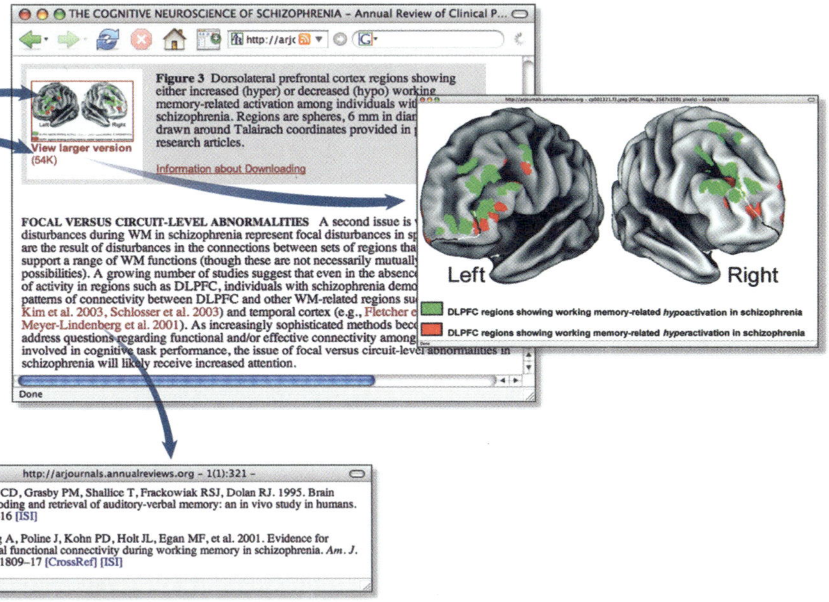

Citations in text link to references in bibliography

References in Annual Reviews article bibliography link out to sources of cited articles online

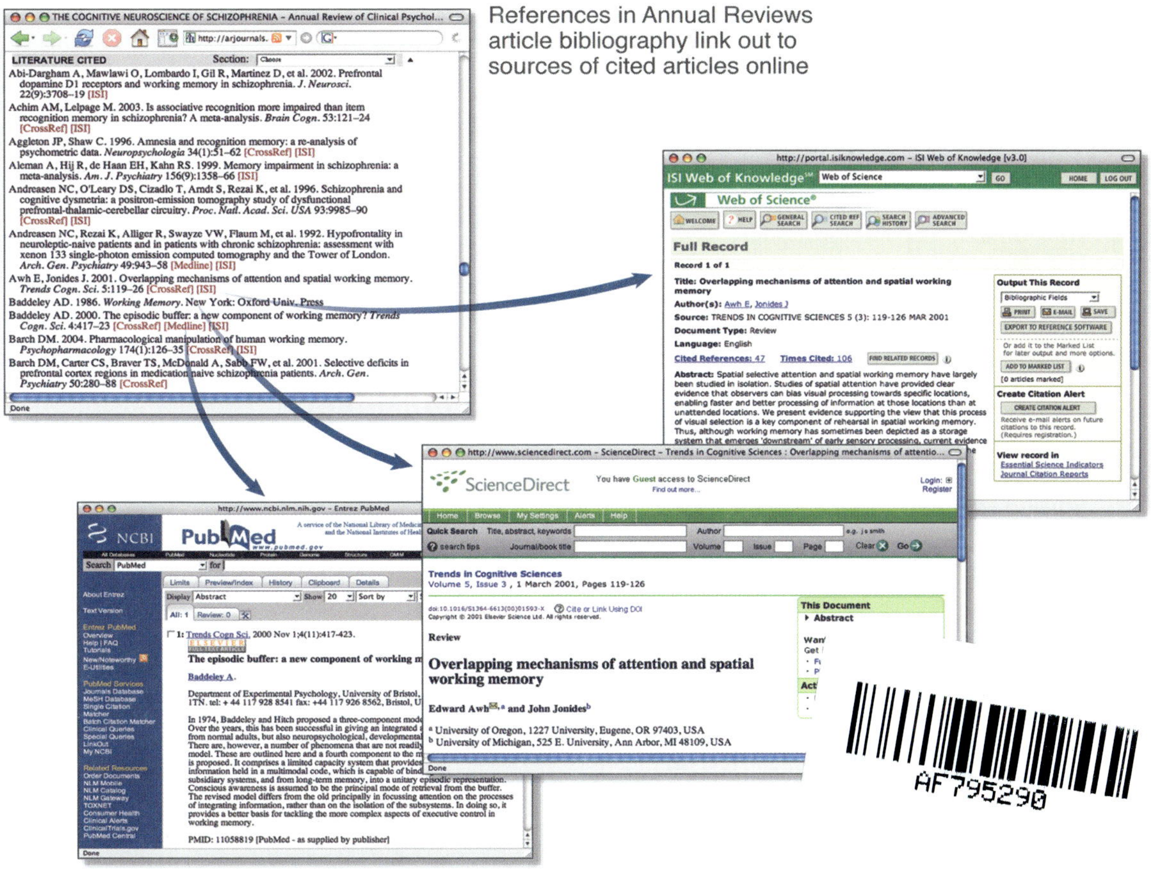

AF795290

Annual Review of Clinical Psychology

Production Editor: Lisa Dean
Managing Editor: Veronica Dakota Padilla
Bibliographic Quality Control: Mary A. Glass
Electronic Content Coordinator: Suzanne K. Moses

Annual Review of Clinical Psychology

Volume 3, 2007

Susan Nolen-Hoeksema, *Editor*
Yale University

Tyrone D. Cannon, *Associate Editor*
University of California, Los Angeles

Thomas Widiger, *Associate Editor*
University of Kentucky

www.annualreviews.org • science@annualreviews.org • 650-493-4400

Annual Reviews
4139 El Camino Way • P.O. Box 10139 • Palo Alto, California 94303-0139

Annual Reviews
Palo Alto, California, USA

International Standard Serial Number: 1548-5943
International Standard Book Number: 978-0-8243-3903-6

TYPESET BY APTARA, INC., FALLS CHURCH, VIRGINIA
PRINTED AND BOUND BY MALLOY INCORPORATED, ANN ARBOR, MICHIGAN

Preface

Clinical psychology in the twenty-first century is an entirely different enterprise than it was 50, or even 20, years ago. Our theorizing about the etiology of mental disorders has evolved over several generations, fueled by advancements in our basic understanding of cognition, emotion, and biology. Methodologically, the buzzword is "interdisciplinary," and researchers are attempting to integrate approaches from multiple disciplines. And the standard that assessments and treatments, old and new, must meet is rigorous empirical support.

The foci of our theories, research, and treatments are different now as well. We are attempting to understand mental health issues in populations that were previously ignored or shunned. The Internet brings new opportunities both for conducting research and for delivering treatment in innovative ways to populations that might not otherwise access treatment.

The chapters in Volume 3 of the *Annual Review of Clinical Psychology* reflect the modern enterprise of clinical psychology in several ways. There are chapters on mechanisms of change in psychotherapy research and in eating disorder prevention programs, and on evidence-based assessment. There are chapters on the use of the Internet to deliver treatment and on the development of new drug treatments specifically targeted to improve cognition in schizophrenia. Separate chapters are concerned with drug abuse in African American and Hispanic adolescents, and in mental health in sexual minorities. Two chapters discuss the application of basic research in other areas of psychology (i.e., cognitive and social psychology) to mental health issues (i.e., children's testimony in abuse cases and coping processes, respectively). The remaining chapters review the leading-edge research on a variety of other critical topics.

Our not-so-distant ancestors in clinical psychology could not have dreamed of a volume with the range of topics represented in Volume 3 of *Annual Review of Clinical Psychology*, because many of the methods or treatments represented in these chapters did not exist even 30 years ago, and several of the issues addressed in these chapters were not of concern then. It is interesting to ponder what our descendents in clinical psychology will be writing about for Volume 33 of the *Annual Review of Clinical Psychology*.

Susan Nolen-Hoeksema, New Haven
Tyrone Cannon, Los Angeles
Tom Widiger, Lexington

Annual Review of Clinical Psychology
Volume 3, 2007

Contents

Indexes

Errata

An online log of corrections to *Annual Review of Clinical Psychology* chapters (if any) may be found at http://clinpsy.AnnualReviews.org

Related Articles

From the ***Annual Review of Anthropology***, Volume 35, 2006

Diet in Early Homo: A Review of the Evidence and a New Model of Adaptive Versatility
Peter S. Ungar, Frederick E. Grine, and Mark F. Teaford

Alcohol: Anthropological/Archaeological Perspectives
Michael Dietler

Obesity in Biocultural Perspective
Stanley J. Ulijaszek and Hayley Lofink

Food and Memory
Jon D. Holtzman

Evolution of the Size and Functional Areas of the Human Brain
P. Thomas Schoenemann

From the ***Annual Review of Law and Social Science***, Volume 2, 2006

Law and Social Movements: Contemporary Perspectives
Michael McCann

From the ***Annual Review of Medicine***, Volume 58, 2007

The Drug Development Crisis: Efficiency and Safety
C. Thomas Caskey

Schizophrenia: New Pathological Insights and Therapies
L. Fredrik Jarskog, Seiya Miyamoto, and Jeffrey A. Lieberman

From the ***Annual Review of Neuroscience***, Volume 29, 2006

Deep Brain Stimulation
Joel S. Perlmutter and Jonathan W. Mink

Brain Work and Brain Imaging
Marcus E. Raichle and Mark A. Mintun

Neural Mechanisms of Addiction: The Role of Reward-Related Learning and Memory
Steven E. Hyman, Robert C. Malenka, and Eric J. Nestler

From the ***Annual Review of Psychology***, Volume 58, 2007

Research on Attention Networks as a Model for the Integration of Psychological Science
Michael I. Posner and Mary K. Rothbart

The Development of Coping
Ellen A. Skinner and Melanie J. Zimmer-Gembeck

The Neurobiology of Stress and Development
Megan R. Gunnar and Karina Quevedo

An Interactionist Perspective on the Socioeconomic Context of Human Development
Rand D. Conger and M. Brent Donnellan

Race, Race-Based Discrimination, and Health Outcomes Among African Americans
Vickie M. Mays, Susan D. Cochran, and Namdi W. Barnes

Assessment and Diagnosis of Personality Disorder: Perennial Issues and an Emerging Reconceptualization
Lee Anna Clark

Social Cognitive Neuroscience: A Review of Core Processes
Matthew D. Lieberman

Motivational and Emotional Aspects of the Self
Mark R. Leary

Moral Emotions and Moral Behavior
June Price Tangney, Jeff Stuewig, and Debra J. Mashek

The Experience of Emotion
Lisa Feldman Barrett, Batja Mesquita, Kevin N. Ochsner, and James J. Gross

The Close Relationships of Lesbians and Gay Men
Letitia Anne Peplau and Adam W. Fingerhut

Health Psychology: Psychological Adjustment to Chronic Disease
Annette L. Stanton, Tracey A. Revenson, and Howard Tennen

Mediation Analysis
David P. MacKinnon, Amanda J. Fairchild, and Matthew S. Fritz

Analysis of Nonlinear Patterns of Change with Random Coefficient Models
Robert Cudeck and Jeffrey R. Harring

From the ***Annual Review of Public Health***, Volume 28, 2007

Assessing Public Health Emergency Preparedness: Concepts, Tools, and Challenges
Christopher Nelson, Nicole Lurie, and Jeffrey Wasserman

Church-Based Health Promotion Interventions: Evidence and Lessons Learned
Marci Kramish Campbell, Marlyn Allicock Hudson, Ken Resnicow, Natasha Blakeney, Amy Paxton, and Monica Baskin

Delivery of Health Services to Migrant and Seasonal Farmworkers
Thomas A. Arcury and Sara A. Quandt

First Responders: Mental Health Consequences of Natural and Human-Made Disasters for Public Health and Public Safety Workers
David M. Benedek, Carol Fullerton, and Robert J. Ursano

Health Impact Assessment: A Tool to Help Policy Makers Understand Health Beyond Healthcare
Brian L. Cole and Jonathan E. Fielding

How Can We Increase Translation of Research into Practice? Types of Evidence Needed
Russell E. Glasgow and Karen M. Emmons

Lessons from Cost-Effectiveness Research for United States Public Health Policy
Scott D. Grosse, Steven M. Teutsch, and Anne C. Haddix

Managed Behavioral Health Care Carve-Outs: Past Performance and Future Prospects
Richard G. Frank and Rachel L. Garfield

Methods for Improving Regression Analysis for Skewed Continuous or Counted Responses
Abdelmonem A. Afifi, Jenny B. Kotlerman, Susan L. Ettner, and Marie Cowan

Physical Activity and Weight Management Across the Lifespan
Jennifer H. Goldberg and Abby C. King

Quality Improvement in Public Health Emergency Preparedness
Michael Seid, Debra Lotstein, Valerie L. Williams, Christopher Nelson, Kristin J. Leuschner, Allison Diamant, Stefanie Stern, Jeffrey Wasserman, and Nicole Lurie

Rationale and Public Health Implications of Changing CHD Risk Factor Definitions
Robert M. Kaplan and Michael Ong

Risk Communication for Public Health Emergencies
Deborah C. Glik

The Epidemiology of Autism Spectrum Disorders
Craig J. Newschaffer, Lisa A. Croen, Julie Daniels, Ellen Giarelli, Judith K. Grether, Susan E. Levy, David S. Mandell, Lisa A. Miller, Jennifer Pinto-Martin, Judy Reaven, Ann M. Reynolds, Catherine E. Rice, Diana Schendel, and Gayle C. Windham

The Hitchhiker's Guide to Tobacco Control: A Global Assessment of Harms, Remedies, and Controversies
Ronald M. Davis, Melanie Wakefield, Amanda Amos, and Prakash C. Gupta

Youth Violence Prevention Comes of Age: Research, Training, and Future Directions
Kara Williams, Lourdes Rivera, Robert Neighbours, and Vivian Reznik

From the ***Annual Review of Sociology***, Volume 32, 2006

Sociological Theories of Human Emotions
Jonathan H. Turner and Jan E. Stets

Problems and Prospects in the Study of Physician-Patient Interaction: 30 Years of Research
John Heritage and Douglas W. Maynard

Sons, Daughters, and Family Processes: Does Gender of Children Matter?
Sara Raley and Suzanne Bianchi

Annual Reviews is a nonprofit scientific publisher established to promote the advancement of the sciences. Beginning in 1932 with the *Annual Review of Biochemistry*, the Company has pursued as its principal function the publication of high-quality, reasonably priced *Annual Review* volumes. The volumes are organized by Editors and Editorial Committees who invite qualified authors to contribute critical articles reviewing significant developments within each major discipline. The Editor-in-Chief invites those interested in serving as future Editorial Committee members to communicate directly with him. Annual Reviews is administered by a Board of Directors, whose members serve without compensation.

Annual Reviews of

Anthropology
Astronomy and Astrophysics
Biochemistry
Biomedical Engineering
Biophysics and Biomolecular Structure
Cell and Developmental Biology
Clinical Psychology
Earth and Planetary Sciences
Ecology, Evolution, and Systematics
Entomology
Environment and Resources
Fluid Mechanics
Genetics
Genomics and Human Genetics
Immunology
Law and Social Science
Materials Research
Medicine
Microbiology
Neuroscience
Nuclear and Particle Science
Nutrition
Pathology: Mechanisms of Disease
Pharmacology and Toxicology
Physical Chemistry
Physiology
Phytopathology
Plant Biology
Political Science
Psychology
Public Health
Sociology

SPECIAL PUBLICATIONS
Excitement and Fascination of Science, Vols. 1, 2, 3, and 4

Mediators and Mechanisms of Change in Psychotherapy Research

Alan E. Kazdin

Department of Psychology, Yale University, New Haven, Connecticut 06520-8205; email: alan.kazdin@yale.edu

Annu. Rev. Clin. Psychol. 2007. 3:1–27

First published online as a Review in Advance on October 11, 2006

The *Annual Review of Clinical Psychology* is online at http://clinpsy.annualreviews.org

This article's doi:
10.1146/annurev.clinpsy.3.022806.091432

1548-5943/07/0427-0001$20.00

Key Words

mediators, moderators, mechanisms of psychotherapy, processes and outcomes of therapy, randomized controlled trials, mediation analyses, treatment evaluation

Abstract

There has been enormous progress in psychotherapy research. This has culminated in recognition of several treatments that have strong evidence in their behalf. Even so, after decades of psychotherapy research, we cannot provide an evidence-based explanation for how or why even our most well studied interventions produce change, that is, the mechanism(s) through which treatments operate. This chapter presents central requirements for demonstrating mediators and mechanisms of change and reviews current data-analytic and designs approaches and why they fall short of meeting these requirements. The role of the therapeutic alliance in psychotherapy and cognitive changes in cognitive therapy for depression are highlighted to illustrate key issues. Promising lines of work to identify mediators and mechanisms, ways of bringing to bear multiple types of evidence, recommendations to make progress in understanding how therapy works, and conceptual and research challenges in evaluating mediators and mechanisms are also presented.

Contents

INTRODUCTION

Several forms of psychotherapy for children, adolescents, and adults produce therapeutic change, as demonstrated in scores of controlled treatment studies (Kazdin & Weisz 2003, Lambert 2004, Nathan & Gorman 2007). The changes can encompass social, emotional, cognitive, behavioral, educational, and physical spheres of functioning. We know well that therapy "works," i.e., is responsible for change, but have little knowledge of why or how it works.

Discussions and theory about why psychotherapy changes people are plentiful, but supportive evidence is quite rare. The American humorist and writer, Mark Twain (1835–1910) noted that, "everybody talks about the weather but nobody does anything about it."[1] Mechanism is the weather of psychotherapy research. The focus of this review is on why treatment works, through what processes, and

[1] Mark Twain (Samuel L. Clemens) is credited with this quote but some suggest that his coauthor A. Charles Dudley Warner wrote the statement (Twain & Warner 1874).

how change comes about, or more succinctly, on the mechanism(s) of therapeutic change. This review also discusses the importance of studying mediators and mechanisms of therapy, examines the limitations of existing data evaluation and design strategies, and provides recommendations for changes needed in research.

CONCEPTUAL AND DEFINITIONAL ISSUES

Several related concepts are important to delineate in part because of their confusion but also because they are relevant to elaborating mechanisms (please see **Table 1**). It is useful to begin with cause or causal relation. A randomized controlled trial (RCT) may show that treatment compared to no treatment leads to therapeutic change. From the demonstration, we can say that the treatment *caused* the change, as the term "cause" is used in science.

Demonstrating a cause does not say *why* the intervention led to change or how the change came about. To evaluate how change comes about, research often looks at mediators. As noted in the table, mediator is a construct that shows important statistical relations between an intervention and outcome, but may not explain the precise process through which change comes about. The term "mechanism" refers to a greater level of specificity than does the term "mediator" and reflects the steps or processes through which therapy (or some independent variable) actually unfolds and produces the change. Mechanism explains how the intervention translates into events that lead to the outcome. This is easily confused with the notion of mediation. For example, cognitions may be shown to mediate change in therapy, an important lead perhaps. However, this does not explain specifically how the change came about, i.e., what are the intervening steps between cognitive change and reduced stress or anxiety. In this review, the primary focus is on mediators and mechanisms. The goal is to understand the mechanisms of change; the study of mediators is often a first step, as is illustrated below.

Moderator refers to some characteristic that influences the direction or magnitude of the relation between the intervention and outcome. If treatment outcome varies as a function of characteristics of the patient or therapist (e.g., sex, ethnicity, temperament), treatment delivery (e.g., individual versus group treatment), or cohort (e.g., so-called generation X versus baby boomers), these latter variables are moderators. I return to moderators below because they have important bearing on mediators and mechanisms.

REASONS FOR STUDYING MEDIATORS AND MECHANISMS

Evaluating mediators and mechanisms of therapeutic change is important for several reasons. First, there is an embarrassing

Table 1 Key terms and concepts

Cause: a variable or intervention that leads to and is responsible for the outcome or change.

Mediator: an intervening variable that may account (statistically) for the relationship between the independent and dependent variable. Something that mediates change may not necessarily explain the processes of how change came about. Also, the mediator could be a proxy for one or more other variables or be a general construct that is not necessarily intended to explain the mechanisms of change. A mediator may be a guide that points to possible mechanisms but is not necessarily a mechanism.

Mechanism: the basis for the effect, i.e., the processes or events that are responsible for the change; the reasons why change occurred or how change came about.

Moderator: a characteristic that influences the direction or magnitude of the relationship between and independent and dependent variable. If the relationship between variable x and y varies is different for males and females, sex is a moderator of the relation. Moderators are related to mediators and mechanisms because they suggest that different processes might be involved (e.g., for males or females).

wealth of treatments in use. For example, in the context of child and adolescent therapy alone, 550+ psychotherapies can be delineated (Kazdin 2000). Some of these are known to produce change; it is not likely that the different treatments produce change for different reasons. Understanding the mechanisms of change can bring order and parsimony to the current status of multiple interventions.

Second, therapy can have quite broad outcome effects, beyond the familiar benefits of reducing social, emotional, and behavioral problems (e.g., suicidal ideation, depression, and panic attacks). Therapy also alters physical conditions (e.g., pain, blood pressure), improves recovery from surgery or illness, and increases the quality of life (see Kazdin 2000). How do these effects come about? Elaborating mechanisms of therapy will clarify the connections between what is done (treatment) and the diverse outcomes.

Third, by understanding the processes that account for therapeutic change one ought to be better able to optimize therapeutic change. Indeed, without understanding what is critical to treatment and how it operates, we are at a bit of a loss. Should we focus on more practice, catharsis, chatting, homework—what leads to change and why? If we know how changes come about, perhaps we can direct better, stronger, different, or more strategies that trigger the critical change process(es).

Fourth, extending treatments from research to clinic or "real world" settings will be difficult without understanding how treatment works. We enter the clinical arena with one hand tied beyond our back if we apply an unspecified and possibly low dose of some treatment that we do not understand. To optimize the generality of treatment effects from research to practice we want to know what is needed to make treatment work, what are the optimal conditions, and what components must not be diluted to achieve change.

Fifth, understanding how therapy works can help identify moderators of treatment, i.e., variables on which the effectiveness of a given treatment may depend. Understanding the processes through which treatment operates can help sort through those facets that might be particularly influential in treatment outcome and permit better selection of suitable patients. For example, if changes in cognitive processes account for therapeutic change, this finding might draw attention to the pretreatment status of related processes (abstract reasoning, problem-solving, attributions) that might moderate who responds or fails to respond to treatment.

Finally, understanding the mechanisms through which change takes place is important beyond the context of psychotherapy. Many interventions or experiences in everyday life improve adjustment and adaptive functioning, ameliorate problems of mental and physical health, help people manage and cope with stress and crises, and more generally navigate the shoals of life. As examples, participating in religion, chatting with friends, exercising, undergoing hypnosis, and writing about sources of stress all have evidence in their behalf. Mechanisms that elaborate how therapy works might have generality for understanding human functioning beyond the context of therapy. The other side is also true. Mechanisms that explain how other change methods work might well inform therapy. Basic psychological processes (e.g., learning, memory, perception, persuasion, social interaction) and their biological pathways (e.g., changes in neurotransmitters) may be common to many types of interventions, including psychotherapy.

REQUIREMENTS FOR DEMONSTRATING MEDIATORS AND MECHANISMS OF CHANGE

Multiple Criteria

Establishing a mediator or mechanism has several requirements. The requirements are highlighted because they provide the background for why changes are needed in research. I focus on mediation because this is an important interim step between demonstrating a causal relation and understanding concretely the mechanism of action through which the effect occurs. Also, mediation is the primary focus of contemporary research.

Strong association. Demonstration of a strong association between the psychotherapeutic (A) intervention and the hypothesized mediator of change (B) is an initial requirement. Then of course, there ought to be an association between the proposed mediator (B) and therapeutic change (C). Indeed, if these three variables are not related, the case for the operation of a mediator is greatly weakened, if not eliminated.

Specificity. The second criterion refers to the demonstration of the specificity of the association between the intervention, proposed mediator, and outcome. We would not want multiple mediators to account for the change, but rather show a more specific connection. A demonstration that many plausible constructs do not account for therapeutic change, with the exception of one, strengthens the argument that the proposed construct mediates change.

Consistency. Replication of an observed result across studies, samples, and conditions, i.e., consistency in the relation, contributes to inferences about mediators. We expect the relations among A, B, and C not to be sample specific. Inconsistency across two or more demonstrations does not necessarily mean that the proposed mediator is not involved. The relation between a proposed mediator and outcome might be perfectly consistent but moderated by a variable we have not yet identified. Yet, when consistency across studies is obtained, this greatly facilitates drawing inferences about whether a particular mediator may be involved.

Experimental manipulation. Direct manipulation through an experiment obviously makes a strong case between therapy and outcome (A and C). This type of demonstration (e.g., RCT) is common and demonstrates cause. However, uncommon are experiments that manipulate the proposed mediator or mechanism (B) and show the impact on outcome (C). Experimental evidence strengthens the case that a proposed mediator is responsible for a change in the outcome of interest.

Timeline. A timeline must be established to infer a causal relation or mediator of change. Causes and mediators must temporally precede the effects and outcomes. Demonstrating a timeline between cause and an effect, albeit obvious, is the Achilles' heel of treatment studies, as I elaborate below.

Gradient. Showing a gradient in which stronger doses or greater activation of the proposed mediator is associated with greater change in the outcome can help make the case for a particular mediator. A common analysis in medicine, epidemiology, and public health is showing a dose-response relation. For example, there is a dose-response (and linear) relation between passive cigarette smoke (i.e., exposure to secondhand smoke) and coronary heart disease (He et al. 1999). Demonstrating a dose-response relation increases the plausibility of an agent being causally involved and may point to likely mechanisms as well. Of course, it is possible that there is no dose-response relation (e.g., a qualitative or on-off gradient) or that the relation is not linear. Such relations do not mean a particular construct is not causally related, but may make inferences more difficult or require supplementary information.

Plausibility or coherence. Plausibility or coherence of an explanation of how a mediator or mechanism operates and integration of findings with the broader scientific knowledge base contribute to the inferences. In medicine, pathophysiology often is invoked to meet this criterion. That is, in light of the findings, is there a plausible, coherent, and reasonable process (e.g., buildup of plaque) through which the disorder (e.g., atherosclerosis and heart attack) might be explained? An explanation is plausible because it invokes other information and steps in some process-outcome relation that are reasonable or supported by other research.

The use of plausibility and coherence to elaborate mechanisms is poignantly illustrated in child abuse. Occasionally, parents bring their very injured and pained child to an emergency room for treatment and tell the physician that the child has been injured. Three examples from my own experience include a child who allegedly fell off a bicycle, another who fell down the five front stairs of a cement porch at home, and a child who got into a fistfight with a seven-year-old sibling. In each case, the physician (a different person for each case) was suspicious because the injuries consisted of large and deep bruise marks across the back (with lines resembling a belt) and a mark that could resemble a belt buckle on the upper shoulder (child 1); three or possibly four round burn marks on the child's back in the size of the end of a cigarette (child 2); and a black eye and open scalp wound under the hair (child 3). The physician in each case was suspicious primarily based on the criterion of plausibility and coherence of the "mechanisms" or process involved leading to these outcomes. In light of how a child is likely to fall off a bicycle or down the stairs or to be hit by young sibling, respectively, the injuries were not very likely (plausible, coherent). However, the injuries were very plausible by invoking another process or mechanism, namely, parent abuse of their children. (One could use the term "parsimonious" here, but I use "plausible" and "coherent" to focus on a greater level of specificity, namely, looking at the operation of a mechanism and how it unfolds to produce an outcome.)

In relation to psychotherapy, plausibility and coherence convey the importance of theoretically based investigation of mediators and mechanisms of change. Here we need more than a global construct that can be used to explain onset of a clinical problem or therapeutic change. We need a plausible account of how the construct works and leads (in a testable way) to the outcomes.

General Comments

Drawing inferences about a mediator of change requires convergence of multiple criteria because they act in concert. Interpretation of what accounts for or explains a particular relation (mediator, mechanism) is not likely to come from a single investigation. By the very nature of one of the criteria (consistency), replication is required. Yet, apart from that criterion, the case for a mediator is built by a sequence of studies that may vary in the set of criteria they address and the clarity of the demonstration. After several studies, and when all or most of the criteria are met, one can state that some intervening process accounts for change.

CURRENT STATUS OF RESEARCH ON MEDIATORS AND MECHANISMS

Mechanisms of treatment are increasingly discussed, a likely precursor to more empirical work on the topic (e.g., Brent & Kolko 1998, Grawe 2004, Hofmann 2000, Kazdin 2006, Kazdin & Nock 2003, Weersing & Weisz 2002). I believe this has fostered the view that we know about key processes leading to change and are using suitable methodological, statistical, and design tools. Few empirical studies are available that meet even two or three of the criteria mentioned previously. Consider briefly two therapy areas where mediators and mechanisms of action are often discussed.

Examples Where Mediators and Mechanisms are Discussed But Not Well Established

Therapeutic alliance and treatment outcome. The therapeutic alliance refers to the collaborative nature of the patient-therapist interaction, their agreement on goals, and the personal bond that emerges in treatment. A consistent finding is that the stronger the alliance the greater the therapeutic change (Horvath & Bedi 2002, Orlinsky et al. 2004). Studies that evaluate alliance during (e.g., early, middle) treatment often show that alliance predicts improvement in symptoms at the end of treatment. Showing that alliance predicts later symptom change by itself does not show that alliance plays a causal role, leaving aside the more specific matter of reflecting a potential mediator. Merely because symptoms are not assessed in the middle of treatment, does not mean they have not already changed. Perhaps very early in treatment clients get a little better (some symptom improvement) and *as a result* form a positive alliance with the therapist.

For example, a study of psychodynamically oriented supportive therapy showed that changes in alliance early in treatment predicted symptom change at the end of treatment, in keeping with a large body of evidence (Barber et al. 2000). However, a critical addition was included. Both symptom change and alliance were assessed at multiple points. Symptom changes early in treatment predicted alliance and that alliance also predicted further symptom change. Thus, the familiar alliance-outcome correlation in part reflects the relation of early and later symptom change, and the timeline is symptom change to alliance as well as the reverse. Assessment of both symptom change and alliance were completed at multiple points during the course of treatment to identify these interesting relations. Other studies with assessments at multiple points have shown that a positive alliance may follow improvements in symptoms (DeRubeis & Feeley 1990, Tang & DeRubeis 1999).

From these examples, I do not wish to assert that alliance is invariably the effect rather than a cause. Indeed, the correlational evidence does not permit statements about cause or mediation. The reciprocal or bidirectional relations of symptoms and alliance are interesting to pursue. The broader point is more pertinent here, to wit, in the vast majority of studies the timeline between alliance and symptom change has not been established.

Cognitions in cognitive therapy for depression. There are very few forms of psychotherapy as well established as cognitive therapy (CT) for unipolar depression among adults (American Psychiatric Association 2000, Hollon & Beck 2004). This treatment is evidence based, and then some, in light of the range of trials. But why does CT work, i.e., through what mediators or mechanisms? In fact, little can be stated as to why treatment works. In the development of this treatment, the basis of therapeutic change was thought to be changes in key cognitive processes (negative triad) that characterize many depressed patients. CT is designed to change these cognitions and in the process change depression. The relation of cognitions and cognitive change in treatment to therapeutic change has been studied in different ways by assessing symptom change and cognitive change at the end of treatment and showing that one shares variance with the other, or by evaluating whether cognitions assessed early or in the middle of treatment correlate with subsequent therapeutic change (e.g., DeRubeis et al. 1990, Kwon & Oei 2003). In both of these methods, the timeline problem is unresolved, i.e., we do not know the ordering of cognitive change and symptom change. This issue is similar to the concern raised in relation to alliance, namely, in the vast majority of studies, symptom change may have preceded or occurred concurrently with cognitive changes. From research as currently designed and discussed, it is not possible to say that cognitive processes serve as the mediators of therapeutic change.

Actually, unlike the research on alliance, perhaps one can say a bit more about mediators and mechanisms of cognitive therapy. The research permits one to say more about what is *not* a likely mediator of the effects of CT. Tests of mediation and evaluation of therapeutic changes quite early in the course of treatment suggest that improvements can readily occur without changes in cognitions or in advance of implementing cognitive-change strategies in treatment (e.g., Burns & Spangler 2001, Tang & DeRubeis 1999). Challenges to the cognitive bases of change in CT for depression are not new (Ilardi & Craighead 1994, Whisman 1999). Perhaps we can state more confidently now than before that whatever may be the basis of changes with CT, it does not seem to be the cognitions as originally proposed.

General Comments

I have highlighted two areas that are often discussed as if we know the basis for the effect, i.e., the mechanism involved. In both alliance and cognitive therapy literatures, the timeline problem is a methodological shroud that covers most studies. Without clearly establishing that the putative basis for the effect invariably comes before symptom change, conclusions about mediation are in question. Of course, it follows that more specific statements about mechanisms are premature.

The two examples are intended to convey how a key criterion, establishing a timeline, is not met in otherwise well-studied areas where mechanisms are discussed. The examples were used to illustrate this single point rather than to review comprehensively the respective literatures. Although I focused on the timeline problem, other concerns in relation to these literatures could be illustrated by applying all of the criteria. Let me mention one to note that this is not a vacuous claim.

We do not have a clear picture or set of studies that test how the putative mechanism unfolds in such a way as to alter symptoms. In relation to plausibility and coherence of the mechanism-outcome relation, precisely what happens that leads to symptom change? For example, through what process or sequence of events along any dimensions (cognitive processes, neurotransmitters, stress) does alliance lead to reductions in depression, anxiety, or feelings that life is meaningless? The time sequence problem is more basic, but how does one get from "my therapist and I are bonding" to "my marriage, anxiety, and tics are better"? This is a leap with the intervening steps unspecified or untested, at least to my knowledge. The steps are not academic. If we could identify the steps, there may be other ways to activate them than through alliance alone. Also, we might identify novel moderators related to the mechanisms that help us select individuals likely to vary in responsiveness to the intervention.

OVERVIEW OF METHODS FOR STUDYING MEDIATORS AND MECHANISMS IN PSYCHOTHERAPY

Dominant methods of evaluating mediators in therapy research have limited what can be concluded in large part because critical conditions mentioned previously are not met. I highlight current methods and discuss why we have not been able to learn very much about mediators or mechanisms from them.

Statistical Techniques

Tests of mediation. Statistical evaluation can play a central role in addressing whether a particular construct accounts for change. Multiple regression techniques, path analysis, structural equation modeling, and bootstrap methods are prominent options (Baron & Kenny 1986, Holmbeck 2002, Hoyle & Smith 1994, Kenny et al. 1998, MacKinnon et al. 2002, Shrout & Bolger 2002). Multiple regression analyses have been the most commonly used techniques, and an overview of the logic conveys the benefits as well as the problems. Consider a hypothetical outcome study in which we evaluate the following components:

- A = an intervention (the treatment)
- B = a mediator or intervening variable
- C = an outcome (therapeutic change)

The interrelations of A, B, and C, as evaluated statistically, are used to infer whether B can explain why treatment works. In demonstrating mediation statistically, four conditions and tests are usually proposed:

- The treatment or intervention (A) must be related to therapeutic change (C);
- The treatment (A) must be related to the proposed mediator (B);
- The proposed mediator (B) must be related to therapeutic change (C); and
- The relation between the intervention (A) and therapeutic change (C) must be reduced after statistically controlling for the proposed mediator (B).

The logic seems compelling because the many conditions, if met, suggest that the impact of treatment (A) on therapeutic change (C) really depends on some intervening processes (B). My simple description ignores many nuances. For example, the extent to which the A-C relationship is reduced by controlling for B is a matter of degree, and there is no cut point (beyond statistical significance [e.g., Sobel test]) to decide whether there is or is not support for a particular mediational view. Also, the various statistical analyses are not free from controversy or challenge (e.g., Kraemer et al. 2001, 2002). I merely wish to convey that the statistical analyses highlighted here are used to evaluate mediators of change in therapy.

As is so often the case in statistical analyses, the concerns here are not about the statistics per se but about their use and interpretation. A key interpretive limitation is the fact that the timeline between the mediator and the outcome is not necessarily established. Most psychotherapy studies of mediation evaluate the mediator and symptoms at pre and post or evaluate the mediator but not the symptoms during treatment. Change in the mediator is shown to correlate, predict, and account for variance in relation to the outcome. The statistical analysis alone cannot establish that one influence preceded, and therefore possibly mediated, the other.

Even when the timeline is established, mediation does not necessarily suggest the mechanism of action. If, for example, some cognitions are shown to come before symptom change and statistically explain the intervention-outcome (A-C) relation that by itself does not show the construct is the mechanism. What precisely is the process of change, what are the steps from the construct to the change, and are other variables embedded in the measure? One might say that cognitions as a mediator might be a first step to move to more fine-grained analyses, a defensible position. But one must also say that cognitions might not be the variable at all or at least the cognitions of interest to the investigator. Cognitions might be a proxy variable for some other construct or be a global construct that includes multiple distinguishable components (Kraemer et al. 2001).

In cross-sectional studies, the language used to describe the data-analytic strategies and the findings lends itself to misconception in relation to the timeline. For instance, regression analyses identify variables as "predictors" or independent variables and others as "outcomes" or dependent variables. Yet, the timeline is only established by the experimental design. The distinction between antecedent (independent) and outcome (dependent) variables, from the standpoint of the steps of the statistical analyses (and printouts) is arbitrary. Similarly, the accompanying diagrams of the results with a flow chart of some kind to convey the authors' views of mediation (e.g., a structural equation model with arrows pointing to the right) may lead the author or reader to conclude erroneously that there is a timeline.

Percentage of variance. Occasionally, researchers focus on the notion of percentage of variance accounted for, or "explained by," a variable and consider this as proof that a critical process or the critical explanation has been identified. If two variables are correlated (r), then one can identify the proportion of common or shared influence (r^2). For example, therapeutic processes (e.g., alliance) "predict" therapeutic change. Researchers often note that alliance accounts for a significant proportion of variance and sometimes even more variance than other influences (e.g., treatment technique). Further interpretation is often added to suggest this must mean that the alliance is why treatment leads to change or is the most significant/important influence in therapy.

Nothing in the measure of percentage of variance speaks to mediators or mechanisms. First, shared variance of alliance and outcome could be huge, but that could be due to symptom change occurring before alliance. Second, the therapeutic alliance can "account for" treatment outcome variance but itself be explained by one or more other variables, such as common method variance in the alliance outcome measures or even characteristics of the patients before they came to treatment (e.g., Kazdin & Whitley 2006, Zigler & Glick 1986). In short, amount variance may or may not point toward mediators or mechanisms. Whether the relation (any correlation) provides meaningful leads will stem from the conditions required for establishing mediators, as enumerated above.

Biases in the data analysis. The way the data analyses are completed occasionally can foster the view that a critical influence or mediator has been identified. An example in psychotherapy research pertains to integrity or fidelity of treatment, that is, the notion that treatment was carried out as intended. Investigators evaluate whether clients who received the treatment as intended show greater change than those who did not (for a review see Perepletchikova & Kazdin 2005). Obviously, if critical procedures of treatment are responsible for change, adherence to these procedures ought to make a difference in outcome. A measure of treatment integrity may allow the investigator to delineate the extent to which clients received the full dose or proper implementation of treatment. (Related to this article, but not this section, many studies that assess integrity do so at the end of treatment, at the same time that symptom change is evaluated, raising some timeline issues we can forego here.) The investigator may analyze the data with only those clients who received the intervention as intended or who received some minimal dose or by including all the data and showing a correlation between how well treatment was implemented and the degree of therapeutic change. Receiving the appropriate levels of treatment is not randomly distributed and may well be confounded with client or client *x* therapist characteristics. For example, getting more, better, or more carefully implemented treatment may relate to the personality of the client (or therapist), severity of his or her problems, match of values and interests between the therapist and patient, and more.

The example is on treatment integrity but the broader point is critical. In studying any intervening process or construct of therapy, the investigator may wish to include in the data analyses only those individuals for whom the putative mediator was invoked or occurred. After random assignment of cases to different groups, keeping or using only cases where the mediator was effectively manipulated changes the equality of the sample and introduces other constructs that are likely to be confounded with the variable (mediator) of interest.

Design Methods for Studying Mediators and Mechanisms

Randomized controlled trials. RCTs remain the primary method of demonstrating a causal relation between treatment and therapeutic change. The most common limitation of RCTs pertinent to this discussion is the failure to establish a timeline between a proposed mediator or mechanism and outcome, as I illustrated above. Assessing the proposed mediator during treatment is necessary but not sufficient to show the timeline between the mediator and outcome. The assessment of symptom change is required during treatment as well. Changes in assessment and design of treatment trials, noted later in the chapter, can address this concern.

Component analyses of treatment techniques. One way that investigators attempt to get at mediators and mechanisms is by analyzing a treatment that is known to be effective. In this context, treatment is considered a "package," i.e., several distinguishable ingredients or components (e.g., *x*, *y*, and *z*). Dismantling studies provide all the components of the package to one group and variations without all of the components to one or more other groups. The complementary approach is the constructive strategy in which one begins with one component and adds others (to other groups or individuals in a crossover design) (see Kazdin 2003). The idea behind each strategy is to identify necessary, sufficient, and facilitative ingredients for treatment to achieve change. Under ideal circumstances there is a theory underlying the package with a more specific statement that some ingredient (e.g., focus on specific activities or exercises) is essential for therapeutic change. If a component is shown to contribute greatly to change and little or no change occurs without that component, investigators often interpret this as evidence for a mediator or mechanism.

Identifying a critical component of treatment, while valuable for many reasons (e.g., for extending abbreviated versions of treatment to clinical work), does not provide direct support for a mediator or mechanism. A component might achieve its effects for all sorts of reasons (processes) that must be assessed. Investigators might note that dismantling is a first step—true in principle. In practice, there are scores of very informative dismantling studies that have not moved to the next steps to understand why a component might be important.

General Comments

In demonstrating causal relations and identifying candidates that might be mediators or mechanisms of change, one ought to begin with the criteria or requirements mentioned above. Statistical analyses and experimental designs (arrangements) are tools to address these requirements. One completes the statistical analysis and then reverts to one of the criteria to ask, "Was this criterion met?" Whether the timeline of a supposed mediator or mechanism of change or whether a construct is a plausible and coherent explanation of therapeutic change are not questions about statistical analyses per se but about interpretation of those analyses.

PATHS TO IDENTIFYING AND ELABORATING MEDIATORS AND MECHANISMS

Understanding mediators and then mechanisms is not a matter of one study but is a matter of creeping up on the process that draws on a series of projects often seemingly unrelated or from different disciplines or types of research. It is useful to think of the search for mechanisms as a chess game. Even though there might be a final winning move (checkmate), the game is won on multiple fronts, an integrated sequence of actions, and converging moves that make checkmate possible. Critical to a chess game is that there is movement toward a goal; whether psychotherapy research shows this movement, at least in relation to understanding mechanisms, is not so clear. By movement, I refer to a progression that reflects depth or type of understanding of the factors that produce therapeutic change.

Consider the progression in understanding based on the concepts of correlate, risk factor, and cause (Kraemer et al. 1997) in relation to the familiar example of cigarette smoking and lung cancer. The connection between the characteristic and outcome began as a correlate (e.g., cross-sectional study findings that people with lung cancer reported a higher rate of smoking) and moved to a risk factor or a correlate where one characteristic clearly precedes another (e.g., longitudinal study findings that those who smoked had higher mortality rates for lung cancer). Then the connection moved to being identified as a causal factor. Both quasi experiments with humans and true experiments with animals showed that the amount of smoking altered the outcome. The dose-response relation of the findings as well as direct experimentation supported the causal role of smoking and disease. Once a causal role is demonstrated, one can ask more analytically how, or through what mechanism, does the cause operate?

Much of research on treatment, but also on psychiatric disorders, identifies correlates and risk factors (predictors) of the outcome. A difficulty is that the work rarely progresses to the next step that would provide a more in-depth evaluation of how the factor operates. Research on heart disease and cholesterol illustrates the progress and more in-depth evaluation. Cholesterol has been known to be a risk factor and predictor of heart disease. Research progressed to evaluate whether cholesterol is causally involved, and indeed, it is. Changing (reducing) cholesterol, in fact, alters the subsequent risk for heart disease.

Psychological research often moves from risk factor to causal risk factor casually and without actual tests. In the usual instance, a study identifies, let us say, two risk factors for some deleterious outcome. The investigator then suggests that we ought to change, address, or in someway attend to these risk factors to make people better. This is a non sequitur. We do not know that the risk factors bear any causal relation to the outcome. The practice of identifying a risk factor and then discussing an intervention to alter that risk factor is so common that one looks for system issues that might foster it (e.g., journals or funding agencies that insist on clinical implications on what might [merely] be a basic critical finding).

Psychological research rarely moves the evaluation from correlate, to risk factor, to causal agent. A usual reason given is that one cannot experimentally manipulate critical variables in humans (e.g., child-rearing practices, attachment style), and therefore we are confined to correlation. The problem is elsewhere, namely, little theory about key constructs (mediators) and how they could be studied, little effort to identify steps or processes (mechanisms) by which the construct leads to an outcome, and little use of convergent lines of inquiry that could strengthen inferences about causes, mediators, and mechanisms. One does not need true experiment necessarily. One needs to build the case by meeting the requirements outlined above. There are many strategies to understand mechanisms or at least to move the ball forward significantly beyond correlation, as I address below.

Meticulous Description

Understanding mechanisms is readily framed as an explanation of some phenomenon of interest. In research (and life) one can readily distinguish description (what is happening) from explanation (why it is happening or through what forces, processes, or mechanisms). This is a helpful distinction to learn and to teach but for this discussion to blur. In many instances in science, one can conceive of description and explanation as related and as opposite ends of a continuum. Depending on the detail, level of analysis, and sequence of moving from one to the other, description can become explanation. Let us continue the example of cigarette smoking and lung cancer.

Spanning decades, cross-sectional and longitudinal studies and research with humans and animals have established a causal role between cigarette smoking and lung cancer, which is where we left off in the comments above. Establishing a causal relation does not automatically explain the mechanisms, i.e., the process(es) through which lung cancer comes about. The mechanism has been uncovered by describing what happens in a sequence from smoking to mutation of cells into cancer (Denissenko et al. 1996). A chemical (benzo[*a*]pyrene) found in cigarette smoke induces genetic mutation at specific regions of the gene's DNA that is identical to the damage evident in lung cancer cells. This finding is considered to convey precisely how cigarette smoking leads to cancer at the molecular level. This is an example of where the "what" (description) can be sufficiently fine grained to convey the "how."

In therapy, proposed mechanisms might encompass such constructs as the therapeutic relationship. Research needs to go beyond the demonstrated correlation and even the predictive portion (i.e., on the assumption that the timeline can be firmly established). One way to move closer to understanding mechanisms would be to describe social interaction outside of the context of therapy in relation to neurological or other biological indices (e.g., Adolphs 2003, Meyer-Lindenberg et al. 2005). What changes take place in social interaction? There is still a huge leap between these descriptions and explaining how a relation in therapy leads to symptom change, but this is a start and moves beyond where we are today in the therapy literature.

Moderators as a Path to Identifying Mediators and Mechanisms

Moderators refer to characteristics that influence the direction or strength of the relation between an intervention and outcome. For example, we know that childhood signs of antisocial behavior predict later delinquency in adolescence for boys but not for girls, i.e., sex moderates the relationship (Tremblay et al. 1992). This suggests that different mediators and mechanisms are likely to be involved in the onset of delinquency for boys and girls. The finding is very useful indeed, because any search for mediators that combined boys and girls might not find an effect; a clear effect for boys might be diluted or nullified by the absence of any effect among girls.

Moderators can play a more direct role in elaborating mediators and mechanisms of action, and these have yet to be exploited. Consider an example of the effect of experience during childhood on subsequent criminal behavior, where a genetic characteristic is a moderator. As is well known, children with a history of physical abuse are at risk for later antisocial behavior. Most people who are abused as children do not engage in antisocial behavior. A genetic characteristic moderates the relationship. Abused children with a genetic polymorphism (related to the metabolism of serotonin) have much higher rates of antisocial behaviors than those without this polymorphism (Caspi et al. 2002). Among boys with the allele and maltreatment, 85% developed some form of antisocial behavior (diagnosis of conduct disorder, personality assessment of aggression, symptoms of adult personality disorder, or court conviction of violent crime) by the age of 26. Individuals with the combined allele and maltreatment constituted only 12% of the sample, but accounted for 44% of the cohort's violent convictions. Further research has replicated and extended the finding by noting that parent neglect as well as abuse in conjunction with the polymorphism increase risk for conduct problems and violence (Foley et al. 2004, Jaffee et al. 2005).

So far, this is a fascinating illustration of moderation. However, closer scrutiny is helpful here because it hints at mechanism. Caspi and colleagues (2002) looked at the allele for monoamine oxidase A (MAO-A) because:

- The gene that encodes the MAO-A enzyme that metabolizes neurotransmitters is linked with maltreatment victimization and aggressive behavior;
- A rare mutation causing a null allele at the MAO-A locus in human males is associated with increased aggression;
- Animal gene knockout studies show that deleting this gene increases aggression; and
- Restoring this gene expression decreases aggression.

In one sense we have identified a moderator—the influence of an independent variable (abuse in the home) and outcome (antisocial behavior years later) is influenced by some other characteristic or variable (MAO-A allele). Clearly, we have much more

because the work and the results it generated are beginning to point to the genetic and molecular underpinnings. We do not know how the allele and abuse traverse specific steps from *a* to *z* in which aggression emerges, but we are getting close. For example, recent findings show the neural mechanisms through which the genetic influence is likely to operate (Meyer-Lindenberg et al. 2006). The MAO-A allele is associated with diminished brain circuitry related to impulse control that would promote aggression.

The type of moderator work illustrated here has some characteristics uncommon in the usual moderator research in relation to therapy. In the illustration, the moderator was identified based on considering mechanisms that might be involved. Theory about potential mechanisms, prior correlational evidence (abuse and victimization), and other studies indirectly related served as background. In much of treatment research and moderator research in clinical psychology more generally, moderators of convenience are used, such as information routinely obtained and global indices (e.g., socioeconomic class, ethnicity, comorbidity). There is little sound theory behind the research or predictions that derive from proposing precisely what facets of the moderator might be important in explaining the relation. Thus, there is a vast literature with analyses showing boys and girls, younger versus older, and this ethnic group versus that ethnic group differ. This is fine as a start, but much of the research never gets past the "start." Moderation can lead to insights about mediation, as the example of aggression shows, but it requires tests of ideas about what the mechanisms are or could be.

Direct Intervention and Manipulation

Direct manipulation of a proposed mechanism is of course a powerful way to move our understanding forward. Consider the work on fear conditioning and psychotherapy. There have been decades of research on Pavlovian conditioning of fear in humans and animals. Conditioning as an explanation of fear acquisition and extinction as an explanation of fear reduction or elimination are useful paradigms for the processes that might be involved in treatment. Research has suggested that extinction is not merely unlearning (elimination of a previously established connection) because the connection is not erased or lost, but rather is actively suppressed through relearning of an acquired inhibition (Myers & Davis 2002).

Understanding the neurological underpinnings of extinction has moved to intervention research. Conditioning and extinction of fear depend on a particular receptor in the amygdala (N-methyl-D-aspartate) (see Davis et al. 2006). Chemically blocking the receptor shortly before extinction training blocks extinction in animal research, a finding that shows a dose-response relation. Blocking the receptor after extinction training also blocks extinction, which suggests that the consolidation process can be interrupted. A compound (D-cycloserine) binds to the receptor and makes the receptor work better, i.e., enhances extinction when given before or soon after extinction training.

The laboratory research has moved to therapy trials where exposure therapy, based on an extinction model, was evaluated to test whether enhancing a mechanism of extinction would improve treatment outcome. An initial controlled trial was completed with individuals who suffered acrophobia (fear of heights) (Ressler et al. 2004). Exposure therapy, one of the most well demonstrated treatments for anxiety, was used as the treatment. The goal was to extinguish fear; exposure to heights was provided in presentations via virtual reality. Presumably, activation of the critical receptor (with D-cycloserine) would improve the effects of exposure therapy (i.e., augment extinction). Indeed, that was found. Participants who received the drug (oral administration two to four hours before each session) showed greater improvements than those who received a placebo. The results were reflected on several measures of avoidance, anxiety, global improvement, and self-exposures to real-world heights as well as skin conductance, as a measure of anxiety during and after treatment. The effects were evident one week and three months after treatment. The enhanced outcome effects (with D-cycloserine) have been replicated for the treatment of social anxiety (Hofmann et al. 2006).

The model of the research program, i.e., movement from moderators and mediators to mechanisms and from basic to applied research, more than two outcome studies needs to be replicated. Understanding mechanisms of learning and extinction, but also memory, belief, persuasion, control, stress alleviation, anticipation, and so on are within empirical reach in a similar way. Once such mechanisms are studied, potential targets can be identified, with a similar paradigm of manipulating the mechanisms. Manipulation might be through psychological interventions as well as biological ones.

Converging Lines of Work

The prior examples emphasize key elements of the demonstrations such as studying moderators or intervening directly on an intended mechanism. Actually, the emphases are useful but the examples are part of a broader strategy. Multiple lines of evidence are likely to be needed to converge on precisely what the mechanism is. The examples I have provided focus on moderators and mechanisms and underpinnings that are biological. This is not a coincidence; the technological advances for studying biological processes are astounding and in some cases, processes (e.g., neurotransmitter or synapse activity) can be observed in real time. Studying mediators and mechanisms and key theses of this review have nothing inherently to do with biology. The focus on mechanisms and the convergence of multiple lines of work can be gleaned from studying psychological processes and human interaction, as illustrated in research on parenting practices in the homes of young children.

In the 1960s, Patterson and his colleagues began an extensive research program designed to understand the emergence and maintenance of aggressive child behavior (Patterson 1982, Patterson et al. 1992). The studies included directly observing child and parent interaction in the home in a detailed fashion (29 different behaviors and interactions occurring from moment to moment including such behaviors as attending to and unwittingly reinforcing child deviant behavior, using commands, delivering harsh punishment, and failing to attend to appropriate child behavior). Among the many interaction patterns, those involving coercion have received the greatest attention (Patterson et al. 1992, Snyder & Stoolmiller 2002). Coercion refers to a sequence of parent and child actions and reactions that increase the frequency and amplitude of angry, hostile, and aggressive behaviors. The sequence may begin with an argument over some action that has or has not been performed. This intensifies through verbal statements (e.g., yelling, screaming) to more intensive actions (e.g., hitting, shoving). Ultimately, a high-intensity action of one person (usually the child) ends the aversive behavior of the other person (usually the parent). Thus through negative reinforcement (increase in likelihood of a behavior that terminates an aversive condition), children are inadvertently rewarded for their aggressive interactions. Their escalation of coercive behavior is increased in the process, and children are likely to be more aggressive (more often, higher intensity) in the future. The parent behaviors are part of the discipline practices that sustain aggressive behavior. The interaction does not place a single-unidirectional causal relation between the parent and child. Rather, a dynamic interaction exists in which aversive behavior on the part of both parties escalates and does so in a way that systematically programs, fosters, and develops greater deviance in the child.

The parent-child interaction does not necessarily determine the next behavior but increases the probability that the behavior would move in one direction and toward some end rather than another. Given *x* (behavior of the parent), *y* (behavior of the child) is much more likely to occur and so on in the sequence. Conditional probabilities of behaviors were used to describe the interactions leading to aggression. I mentioned previously that there is a way in which meticulous description can blend with and become an explanation. Much of the sequence of interactions was of this type, namely, showing that the interactions fostered aggression and that the timeline was clear.

The studies showing that specific inept child-rearing practices contributed to aggressive behavior served as a model for intervention (Reid et al. 2002). Several studies have shown that changing parent-child interactions (via parent management training) significantly reduces aggressive behavior and related conduct problems (see Kazdin 2005, Reid et al. 2002 for reviews). Thus, a converging set of studies showed a sequence of coercive parent-child interactions leading to escalation, support for a model that explains the interaction (coercion theory and reinforcement leading to escalated aggression), and an intervention that changes putatively critical parenting processes that controvert aggressive child behavior. The unfolding of coercive behavior and effective intervention go very far to suggest the mechanisms involved in onset and elimination of aggression in the home, at least for some children.

General Comments

The discussion highlights examples of treatment-related research that moves from causal relations toward understanding mediators and mechanisms. I have omitted studies on mediation, which have become relatively common. The reason for omitting these was explained in the discussion of statistical tests of mediation, namely, the studies rarely establish the critical conditions for establishing a timeline and a mediator is not necessarily a mechanism. When the timeline is not established, it is even too much of a leap to imply there is a mediation relation beyond a statistical connection in which the mediator and outcome could be reversed.

Table 2 Recommendations for research

1. Use theory as a guide
2. Include measures of potential mediators in treatment studies
3. Establish the timeline of the proposed mediator or mechanism and outcome
4. Assess more than one mediator or mechanism
5. Use designs that can evaluate mediators and mechanisms
6. Examine consistencies across different types of studies
7. Intervene to change the proposed mediator or mechanism

RECOMMENDATIONS FOR RESEARCH

Psychotherapy research has a long history of discussing processes of therapy, but little research has addressed the conditions necessary to establish mediators or mechanisms. In general, the investigation of mediators and mechanisms of therapy can be improved in several ways. **Table 2** lists recommendations to enhance our understanding of therapeutic change.

Use Theory as a Guide

The guiding question for treatment research is how does treatment achieve change? The answer may involve basic psychological processes (e.g., memory, learning, information processing) or a broader theory (e.g., motivation). It is no longer sufficient to provide global conceptual views (e.g., psychodynamic, cognitive, or familial) that foster a treatment approach or orientation toward what to do in the sessions. Rather, to ensure progress, specific conceptual models are needed to explain those processes that are responsible for therapeutic change. What is needed further is greater specificity in conceptualizing not only the critical construct but also how that operates to produce symptom change. We need more than tests of mediation to understand mechanisms. Mediation tests of plausible constructs can provide a screening device of sorts to identify potential avenues to be pursued in a fine-grained fashion.

It would be helpful for intervention research to identify "candidate mediators" and mechanisms or plausible constructs that would explain or account for (statistically) therapeutic change, manipulate the proposed mechanism, assess to ensure it has been manipulated, and then evaluate change. For example, in relation to tobacco use among teenagers, several mediators that may serve as useful targets have been identified, including coping skills of the youth, peer influences, and availability of tobacco, among others (MacKinnon et al. 2002). The targets can be the focus of intervention. If one of these targets leads to change in tobacco use, this would serve as an excellent basis for further work to understand exactly how the influence produces change. We need next-step research that begins with theory but tests directly how the proposed mediator operates.

In research training, there is often a strong demand of the investigator to begin with a theory or conceptual model. The study that follows is a test of that theory. However, the goal of research is to end up with an understanding of how therapy works. This goal can be achieved by research that generates hypotheses and theories in addition to research that tests hypotheses. There is far too little research that focuses on generating hypotheses from careful observation and on building theory that can be tested (Kazdin 2003, McGuire 1997).

Include Measures of Potential Mediators in Treatment Studies

The mediator or mechanism ought to be specified so it can be measured. Studies occasionally include such measures (Hofmann 2000, Weersing & Weisz 2002), although their administration has not allowed evaluation of timelines. Yet, measures are available. More fine-grained analyses will be needed to study the unfolding of processes over time and how a change in some process results in symptom change. As a prerequisite to understanding, assessments of potential mediators ought to be included in treatment studies.

Establish the Timeline of the Proposed Mediator or Mechanism and Outcome

It is important to establish that the proposed mediator is changing before the outcome. The timeline has two requirements: (*a*) the proposed mediator must be assessed before the proposed outcome, and (*b*) the "outcome" must also be assessed early to ensure the mediator has in fact changed before the outcome. Even during the middle of treatment, long before the investigator may be interested in therapeutic change, it is quite possible that improvements occur in the client and these improvements come before change in the putative mediator.

Assessment is the main change needed in research. Assessment on multiple occasions during treatment can provide information on the timeline of mediators and mechanisms and outcomes and the possibility of bidirectional changes, i.e., each one influences the other in some way and at different points. Assessment on a session-by-session basis (i.e., every occasion over the course of treatment) permits evaluation of the mediator of change and symptom reduction and considers individual differences in the course of these changes.

Assess More than One Mediator or Mechanism

The accumulation of evidence would profit from the assessment of more than one mediator in a given study. It is rare that one mediator is studied, and hence there may be little value in raising the bar even higher by recommending the assessment of two or more mediators. Recommending the assessment of more than one mediator during treatment means that the assessment battery (e.g., how many measures) will increase as each mediator is added to the design. In laboratory (efficacy) studies of therapy, the addition of one or two measures during the course of treatment may not be particularly onerous.

The assessment of multiple mediators in a given study has enormous benefits. If two or more mediators are studied, one can identify if one is more plausible or makes a greater contribution to the outcome. In addition, the assessment of multiple potential mediators within individual studies is economically efficient, given the tremendous amount of time and resources needed for any treatment investigation. Across many studies, some mediators may repeatedly emerge as possible contenders while others fall by the wayside.

Use Designs that Can Evaluate Mediators and Mechanisms

Table 3 lists five designs that vary in the assessment of potential mediators or mechanisms of change and treatment outcome. Assume all to be RCTs in which treatment is compared with no treatment. The first and most commonly used design variation omits assessment of potential mediators. RCTs are excellent in demonstrating a causal relation between the intervention and therapeutic change. Yet, the designs that resemble the first variation can say nothing about mediators or mechanisms, even though we as authors often do. In the second design variation, symptoms and possible mediators are assessed at the same time at pre- and post-treatment. With this variation, conclusions cannot be reached about whether improvements in symptoms influenced the proposed mediator or vice versa, or whether both were altered by another variable.

The third design variation assesses symptoms at pre- and post-treatment, but during the course of treatment (on one or more occasions) the proposed mediator is assessed. The data analyses then evaluate whether the process during treatment contributes to (predicts, accounts for) treatment outcome. This research gives a strong but misleading impression that a timeline is established between some process (e.g., cognitions, alliance) and therapeutic change. The failure to measure symptoms at the same time or indeed before the mid-assessment of the supposed mediator precludes conclusions about whether the mediator comes before symptom change. Just because symptoms were not assessed in the middle of treatment does not mean they did not improve or indeed even improve before the putative process variable.

The fourth design variation improves on the prior designs by including assessment of the proposed mediator and the outcome (symptoms) during treatment. Ideally, there will be more than one assessment occasion during treatment. This variation can evaluate the time sequence, i.e., whether changes in the mediator preceded symptom change and whether symptom change preceded change in

Table 3 Outcome study designs and evaluation of mediators or mechanisms

	Mechanism assessment			Outcome assessment		
Design variation	**Pre**	**During**	**Post**	**Pre**	**During**	**Post**
1. Usual outcome design	N	N	N	Y	N	Y
2. Concurrent study of mechanisms and outcomes	Y	N	Y	Y	N	Y
3. Assessment of mechanism during treatment	N	Y	N	Y	N	Y
4. Assessment of mechanisms and outcomes during treatment	Y	Y	Y	Y	Y	Y
5. Assessment of mechanisms and outcomes all or most sessions	Y	Y, Y, Y, . . .	Y	Y	Y, Y, Y, . . .	Y

Y = yes, assessment is conducted; N = no assessment.

the putative mediator (which may make the mediator an effect rather than a cause). However, if the assessment is only on one occasion during treatment, it is possible that both the proposed mediator and symptom change occurred or appear to have occurred at the same time. Their relation might not be easy to discern and the possibility exists that a third variable led to both changes in the mediator and symptoms.

A disadvantage of the fourth design variation is that it presumes that the course of change for both the mediator and outcome is captured by measuring each of these at only one (or even two) fixed points during treatment. There could be great variation in when the change is made among patients receiving the same treatment. Both the mediator and symptoms may change at different points among a set of patients. The fifth design variation, an extension of the prior design, provides a more fine-grained analysis of change in mediator and symptoms and overcomes this concern. Assessments are made so that one can examine the course of change of the mediator and symptoms and can take into account individual differences in when the changes occur.

Examine Consistencies Across Different Types of Studies

Understanding mediators and mechanisms through which therapeutic change occurs could profit from different types of studies, beyond those that might be construed as therapy research. Conclusions from these studies may be consistent and converge in making a particular process plausible.

Animal laboratory research. Granted, many of proposed mediators of therapy may not be amenable to mouse or zebra fish models. Yet, some of the mediators and mechanisms of therapy might be studied in the lab, and we ought not to be shy about them or shy away from them. I mentioned above the work on fear conditioning and how understanding key mechanisms of extinction has already improved the effectiveness of extinction-based treatment (Davis et al. 2005). Therapeutically relevant phenomena (e.g., attachment, separation, social support) can be studied in animal research to identify processes (e.g., changes in the structure or function of the brain) and their consequences in behavior. These in turn might direct research to plausible underpinnings to support a conceptual view of the mechanism of therapeutic change. Such tests, far removed from therapy settings, provide important tests of principle. For example, maternal caregiving behaviors (e.g., nursing, licking, grooming) among rats influence the responsiveness to stress in the offspring; the effects can be seen in behavioral as well as from the neurological and endocrine responses of the offspring (e.g., Champagne et al. 2003, Pruessner et al. 2004). This might well be pertinent to understanding stress, coping with stress, and interventions designed to ameliorate stress.

Naturalistic studies. If one is proposing a mediator of change, is there a sample, population, or setting in which this mediator may be expected to vary naturally, i.e., without investigator intervention? For example, if changing parenting style is proposed to explain why a parent- or family-based treatment of a child clinical problem is effective, naturalistic studies examining families with and without these practices and the short- and long-term child behaviors with which these are associated are relevant. Among naturally occurring instances of the process or construct, is there a dose-response relation?

As an example and following up on the prior example of maternal caregiving among rats, naturalistic studies of "normal" mothering have revealed that stress reactivity in human infants is influenced by maternal caregiving (e.g., sensitivity, availability, lack of intrusiveness) during routine activities (e.g., feeding, meal preparation) very much in keeping with the animal research highlighted above (Hume & Fox 2006). Low-quality caregiving was associated with greater stress reactivity of their infants (e.g., fearfulness, more right frontal brain asymmetry), an effect that could not be explained by infant temperament. Caregiving in relation to stress response and reactivity "behaves" in a similar way across different research paradigms and draws attention to mediators or mechanisms that might be pertinent to therapy (e.g., trauma, stress, coping).

Naturalistic studies by themselves may not permit strong causal conclusions. Yet, such evidence can be enormously helpful. Many advances in understanding cancer, heart disease, and stroke began by looking for variation in putative mediators (e.g., in health habits, diet) among individuals with varied outcomes (e.g., morbidity, mortality). Observing processes that may be operative in the natural environment and their short- and long-term correlates can be very useful, for both generating and testing hypotheses about mediators and mechanisms.

Qualitative research. Qualitative research is an approach to the subject matter of human experience and focuses on narrative accounts, description, interpretation, context, and meaning. Among the key characteristics is the in-depth study of the phenomena of interest. Individual participants or cases are focused on intensely to examine processes, meaning, characteristics, and contexts. Qualitative research is a rigorous, verifiable, empirical, and replicable set of methodologies that encompasses many different disciplines and diverse design, assessment, and data-analytic strategies (Berg 2001, Denzin & Lincoln 2005). In the context of the present discussion, qualitative research might study the process of therapy, how the patient and therapist experience that process, and what might be critical actions or cognitions and how they relate to improvements outside of treatment. Qualitative research can provide a fine-grained analysis by intensively evaluating the richness and details of the process, including who changes and how change unfolds, and who does not change and what might be operative there.

Laboratory studies of therapeutic processes. Such studies are viewed with ambivalence because they do not show whether treatment works in "real-life settings." Controlled studies of therapy in research rather than clinical settings are more important now than ever before. The careful control afforded such research is precisely what is needed to identify mediators and mechanisms. Translational research without knowing what to translate will have a checkered yield in clinical applications of treatment.

Intervene to Change the Proposed Mediator or Mechanism

An excellent strategy is to conduct an experiment in which the proposed mediator is in fact altered or varied across groups, as illustrated in the treatment study cited above on extinction of fear (Davis et al. 2005). Groups randomly composed might be assigned to low, high, and medium levels of a proposed mediator (as a general concept) or mechanism (as a more specific set of steps expected to lead directly to the outcome). Strong support would be evident from findings that outcome varies directly as a function of levels of the manipulated dose.

Intervening to change a mediator is an excellent strategy. Here, too, assessing more than one mediator would be helpful in understanding why change occurred. Intervening to alter the mediator and assessing the level of that mediator (as a check on the manipulation) and two or more plausible, other mediators that are not manipulated would be an elegant way to evaluate mechanisms. In such a study, one can rule out or make implausible some mediators while providing evidence on behalf of another mediator.

A variation of the intervention approach is worth distinguishing, and I refer to this here as "therapy knockout studies." The term draws from genetic work (e.g., gene knockout studies with mice) where a particular gene is omitted or altered and the effects are evident on behavior or some other facet suspected to be controlled by the gene. The general model of this research would be a wonderful extension to psychotherapy mechanisms. More specifically, if the investigator believes or theory predicts that a specific mechanism accounts for change, it would be useful to provide the therapy with an added intervention that is designed to "knock out" (inactivate) the mechanism. If role-play, practice, or warm fuzzy relations are critical to the technique, give two variations of the treatment: the original and the original with an effort to inactivate the mechanism. As with any single study, supportive evidence that treatment worked wonders only when the mechanism was allowed to operate could be explained in multiple ways. Even so, this evidence would be a superb addition to accumulating evidence.

SPECIAL CHALLENGES AND OBSTACLES

There are multiple challenges in considering mediators and mechanisms that extend beyond a few changes in designs or measurement strategies. Consider some of the key challenges briefly.

Mechanism-Outcome Relations

The discussion has implied a simple model in which a single mechanism leads to a single outcome or the effects are strong, simple, and linear. Yet multiple variants have implications for conceptualizing, designing, and interpreting research.

Single agent (influence), multiple outcomes. One complexity occurs when a single influence produces multiple outcomes. For example, cigarette smoking leads to several physical and psychological conditions. In some of these, we know there is a causal relation and have identified the mechanism; in others, we know of increased risk. The pervasiveness of the influence of smoking on so many conditions can introduce complexities in the search for mechanisms because so many biological systems are involved. There may be multiple and different mechanisms for the single agent but different outcomes. On the other hand, some common pathways may exist that help focus research.

Multiple influences, single outcomes. Similar outcomes may be reached through multiple paths. Thus, we do not expect to see all people with a particular characteristic (high kindness, bipolar disorder) to have reached these delineations through the same path. There are multiple paths. The paths may reflect similar mechanisms activated by different experiences or different mechanisms. For example, low IQ could result from genetic, prenatal, cultural, and postnatal toxic (e.g., lead) influences. This "single outcome" has many paths. Essential to work on mediators and mechanisms is distinguishing different courses or paths and moderating influences. Looking for one explanation or mechanism for one group, one therapy, or one outcome may yield little. Conceptual work on possible moderators and exploratory studies (and yes, fishing expeditions) followed by conceptual work will be critical to look for subgroups.

Nonlinear relations. We are trained to think, love statistics that generate, and perhaps even are victims of a cognitive heuristic (I call it slippery-slope thinking) that attracts us to linear relations. Many critical relations are nonlinear. For example, cholesterol and risk for heart disease is positive and linear; higher cholesterol increases risk. Cholesterol and stroke are U shaped, i.e., nonlinear so that low and high cholesterol increase risk. Nonlinear relations propose a challenge in the sense that dose-response relation (as a linear function) is one clue on the path toward mechanisms, although it is not essential. Looking at means of groups and using statistics that evaluate and search for linear relations can speed or delay progress. We may find a weak relation or no relation between an agent and outcome (e.g., cholesterol and stroke) for the sample as a whole. Analyses of subgroups and tests of nonlinear relations to identify reliable patterns of mediator-outcome relations are a starting point.

Timing of Change. Assume for a moment that 10 patients receive identical treatment over the course of 20 sessions and that treatment works for each of them for the identical reason, i.e., the same mechanism is responsible for change. It is not likely that the process of change will follow the identical time course so that by session 8, for example, the mechanism has changed in a critical way and symptom change is underway. Indeed, apparently the timeline of therapeutic change can be altered by what patients are told about the duration of treatment prior to beginning treatment (Barkham et al. 1996).

Some patients may make rapid or sudden gains at a particular point in treatment (e.g., Tang & DeRubeis 1999). One could say that at a given point, some have and some have not made change in some qualitative or categorical fashion. Alternatively, one could consider that the point of therapeutic change for all individuals is normally distributed with a mean and standard deviation. In either scenario (sudden gains but not at the identical point or normally distributed changes across several points), assessment of the mechanism is a challenge. Assessment of the mechanism at any one or two points in a study may not capture when change in the mechanism has occurred. A challenge for research is ensuring that one can evaluate mechanism and change that may vary in course among individuals.

Everything in Moderation

The effects of an intervention may be moderated in ways that exert enormous impact. For example, a "standard" dose of psychotropic medication (e.g., for clinical depression) can be an overdose or underdose for people of different ethnicities and countries (Lin et al. 1993). Medication effects are moderated by ethnicity. Among the intriguing issues, would medication effects operate similarly if doses were adjusted to each group, or is this not merely a matter of dose? Either way, evaluating or analyzing data for an overall (main) effect of medication and ignoring ethnicity would lead to a weak effect and not encourage pursuit of mechanisms.

It is possible that the mediator or mechanism of change in psychotherapy varies as a function of a moderator variable. Searching for moderators (a priori or post hoc), testing them (statistical power from dividing of the sample into subgroups), and interpreting them (e.g., is the moderator a proxy for some other variable?) have their own special challenges. Rather than looking for main effects of an intervention and a uniform mechanism of change, we may need to identify and characterize subgroups, very much in the way that genetic researchers often profit from looking at special groups and individual outliers.

Measurement Development

Mediators and mechanisms in therapy are often discussed but validated measures of key constructs are not readily available. Many advances in biotechnology as represented by the continued advances in neuroimaging have had enormous impact on the search for neurological mechanisms, although these assessments have nontrivial interpretive challenges. If by mediators or mechanisms, we will be searching for psychological explanations of action, we will need valid measures. In the parent training literature, mentioned above, behavioral observations were used to show that parent-child interactions unfolded in a sequence leading to (conditional probabilities) child aggressive behavior. Among the many virtues of this work was the assessment of observable actions and charting a sequence that promotes aggression.

Presumably, many mediators of change begin as broad constructs (e.g., changes in cognition). We need valid measures of such constructs and then demonstration of how the constructs operate. There are promising leads. For example, break down of coping skills in high-risk situations is associated with cocaine and other substance abuse. Treatment often targets coping skills as the critical mediator of change in reducing substance use. A role-play measure (Cocaine Risk Response Test) has been developed, evaluated, and integrated into controlled treatment research to evaluate the mediator (Carroll et al. 1999, 2005). Assessment of mediators and mechanisms raises all of the usual questions in measurement development. The topic has not been accorded sufficient attention.

CONCLUSIONS

Enormous progress has been made in psychotherapy research. This has culminated in recognition of several treatments that have strong evidence in their behalf. Despite this progress, research advances are sorely needed in studying the mediators and mechanisms of therapeutic change. It is remarkable that after decades of psychotherapy research, we cannot provide an evidence-based explanation for how or why even our most well studied interventions produce change.

Many researchers might regard the rather large body of research on the therapeutic relationship as a potential exception. Yet, the vast majority of studies rarely rule out the possibility that the relationship is the result of symptom change or some other variable rather than a mechanism responsible for it. I am not challenging the importance of relationships—in everyday life, I have tried one or two myself. This is a quarrel about the necessary assessment and design requirements that are infrequently included in research. In addition, assuming the timeline were unequivocally established, we need "next-step" research that clarifies how a relationship in therapy leads to symptom change, i.e., through what specific steps. These steps need to be evaluated.

Prior research has provided important groundwork on which future studies could build. For instance, an increasing number of studies are including assessments during the course of treatment (e.g., Beauchaine et al. 2005, Eddy & Chamberlain 2000, Kolko et al. 2000, Kwon & Oei 2003). The designs used in these investigations represent a great improvement over prior studies and signal progress in research on mechanisms of change. Yet, existing studies have attempted to evaluate only a handful of potential mediators and mechanisms of change.

The scientific study of mechanisms of change is certainly not an easy path on which to embark. A given treatment might work for multiple reasons. Just as there is no simple and single path to many diseases, disorders, or social, emotional, and behavioral problems (e.g., lung cancer, attention-deficit/hyperactivity disorder), there may be analogous complexity in mechanisms for a given treatment technique or therapeutic outcome. Two patients in the same treatment conceivably could respond for different reasons. The complexities are critically important to understand because of a point made above, namely, the best patient care will come from ensuring that the optimal variation of treatment is provided. Understanding mechanisms of treatment is the path toward improved treatment.

ACKNOWLEDGMENT

Completion of this chapter was facilitated by support from the National Institute of Mental Health (MH59029).

LITERATURE CITED

Adolphs R. 2003. Cognitive neuroscience of human social behavior. *Nat. Rev. Neurosci.* 4:165–178

American Psychiatric Association. 2000. Practice guideline for the treatment of patients with major depressive disorder (revision). *Am. J. Psychiatry* 157(Suppl. 4):1–45

Barber JP, Connolly MB, Crits-Christoph P, Gladis L, Siqueland L. 2000. Alliance predicts patients' outcome beyond in-treatment change in symptoms. *J. Consult. Clin. Psychol.* 68:1027–32

Barkham M, Rees A, Stiles WB, Shapiro DA, Hardy GE, Reynolds S. 1996. Dose-effect relations in time-limited psychotherapy for depression. *J. Consult. Clin. Psychol.* 64:927–35

Baron RM, Kenny DA. 1986. The moderator-mediator variable distinction in social psychological research: conceptual, strategic, and statistical considerations. *J. Personal. Soc. Psychol.* 51:1173–82

Beauchaine TP, Webster-Stratton C, Reid MJ. 2005. Mediators, moderators, and predictors of 1-year outcomes among children treated for early-onset conduct problems: a latent growth curve analysis. *J. Consult. Clin. Psychol.* 73:371–88

Berg BL. 2001. *Qualitative Research Methods for the Social Sciences.* Needham Heights, MA: Allyn & Bacon. 4th ed.

Brent DA, Kolko DJ. 1998. Psychotherapy: definitions, mechanism of action, and relationship to etiological models. *J. Abnorm. Child Psychol.* 26:17–25

Burns DD, Spangler DL. 2001. Do changes in dysfunctional attitudes mediate changes in depression and anxiety in cognitive behavioral therapy? *Behav. Ther.* 32:337–69

Carroll KM, Nich C, Ball SA. 2005. Practice makes progress? Homework assignments and outcome in treatment of cocaine dependence. *J. Consult. Clin. Psychol.* 73:749–55

Carroll KM, Nich C, Frankforter TL, Bisighini RM. 1999. Do patients change in ways we intend? Assessing acquisition of coping skills among cocaine-dependent patients. *Psychol. Assess.* 11:77–85

Caspi A, McClay J, Moffitt TE, Mill J, Martin J, et al. 2002. Role of genotype in the cycle of violence in maltreated children. *Science* 297:851–54

Champagne FA, Francis DD, Mar A, Meaney M. 2003. Variations in maternal care in the rat as a mediating influence for the effects of development on behavior. *Physiol. Behav.* 79:359–71

Davis M, Myers KM, Chhatwal J, Ressler KJ. 2006. Pharmacological treatments that facilitate extinction of fear: relevance to psychotherapy. *NeuroRx* 3:82–96

Davis M, Myers KM, Ressler KJ, Rothbaum BO. 2005. Facilitation of extinction of conditioned fear by D-cycloserine. *Curr. Direct. Psychol. Sci.* 14:214–19

Denissenko MF, Pao A, Tang M, Pfeifer GP. 1996. Preferential formation of benzo[*a*]pyrene adducts at lung cancer mutational hotspots in *P53*. *Science* 274:430–32

Denzin NK, Lincoln YS, eds. 2005. *The SAGE Handbook of Qualitative Research.* Thousand Oaks, CA: Sage. 3rd ed.

DeRubeis RJ, Evans MD, Hollon SD, Garvey MJ, Grove WM, Tuason VB. 1990. How does cognitive therapy work? Cognitive change and symptom change in cognitive therapy and pharmacotherapy for depression. *J. Consult. Clin. Psychol.* 58:862–69

DeRubeis RJ, Feeley M. 1990. Determinants of change in cognitive therapy for depression. *Cogn. Ther. Res.* 14:469–82

Eddy JM, Chamberlain P. 2000. Family management and deviant peer association as mediators of the impact of treatment condition on youth antisocial behavior. *J. Consult. Clin. Psychol.* 68:857–63

Foley D, Wormley B, Silberg J, Maes H, Hewitt J, et al. 2004. Childhood adversity, MAOA genotype, and risk for conduct disorder. *Arch. Gen. Psychiatry* 61:738–44

Grawe K. 2004. *Psychological Therapy*. Cambridge, MA: Hogrefe & Huber

He J, Vupputuri S, Allen K, Prerost MR, Hughes J, Whelton PK. 1999. Passive smoking and the risk of coronary heart disease—a meta-analysis of epidemiologic studies. *New Engl. J. Med.* 340:920–26

Hofmann SG. 2000. Treatment of social phobia: potential mediators and moderators. *Clin. Psychol. Sci. Pract.* 7:3–16

Hofmann SG, Meuret AE, Smits JA, Simon NM, Pollack MH, et al. 2006. Augmentation of exposure therapy with D-cycloserine for social anxiety disorder. *Arch. Gen. Psychiatry* 63:298–304

Hollon SD, Beck AT. 2004. Cognitive and cognitive behavioral therapies. In *Bergin and Garfield's Handbook of Psychotherapy and Behavior Change*, ed. MJ Lambert, pp. 447–92. New York: Wiley. 5th ed.

Holmbeck GN. 2002. Post-hoc probing of significant moderational and mediational effects in studies of pediatric populations. *J. Pediatr. Psychol.* 27:87–96

Horvath AO, Bedi RP. 2002. The alliance. In *Psychotherapy Relationships That Work: Therapist Contributions and Responsiveness to Patients*, ed. JC Norcross, pp. 37–69. New York: Oxford Univ. Press

Hoyle RH, Smith GT. 1994. Formulating clinical research hypotheses as structural equation models: a conceptual overview. *J. Consult. Clin. Psychol.* 62:429–40

Hume AA, Fox NA. 2006. Ordinary variations in maternal caregiving influence human infants' stress reactivity. *Psychol. Sci.* 17:550–56

Ilardi SS, Craighead WE. 1994. The role of nonspecific factors in cognitive-behavior therapy for depression. *Clin. Psychol. Sci. Pract.* 1:138–56

Jaffee SR, Caspi A, Moffitt TE, Dodge K, Rutter M, et al. 2005. Nature x nurture: genetic vulnerabilities interact with physical maltreatment to promote behavior problems. *Dev. Psychopathol.* 17:67–84

Kazdin AE. 2000. *Psychotherapy for Children and Adolescents: Directions for Research and Practice*. New York: Oxford Univ. Press

Kazdin AE. 2003. *Research Design in Clinical Psychology*. Needham Heights, MA: Allyn & Bacon. 4th ed.

Kazdin AE. 2005. *Parent Management Training: Treatment for Oppositional, Aggressive, and Antisocial Behavior in Children and Adolescents*. New York: Oxford Univ. Press

Kazdin AE. 2006. Mechanisms of change in psychotherapy: advances, breakthroughs, and cutting-edge research (do not yet exist). In *Strengthening Research Methodology: Psychological Measurement and Evaluation*. ed. RR Bootzin, PM McKnight, pp. 77–101. Washington, DC: Am. Psychol. Assoc.

Kazdin AE, Nock MK. 2003. Delineating mechanisms of change in child and adolescent therapy: methodological issues and research recommendations. *J. Child Psychol. Psychiatry* 44:1116–29

Kazdin AE, Weisz JR, eds. 2003. *Evidence-Based Psychotherapies for Children and Adolescents*. New York: Guilford

Kazdin AE, Whitley MK. 2006. Pretreatment social relations, therapeutic alliance, and improvements in parenting practices in parent management training. *J. Consult. Clin. Psychol.* 74:346–55

Kenny DA, Kashy DA, Bolger N. 1998. Data analysis in social psychology. In *Handbook of Social Psychology*, ed. D Gilbert, ST Fiske, G Lindzey, Vol. 1, pp. 233–65. New York: McGraw-Hill. 4th ed.

Kolko DJ, Brent DA, Baugher M, Bridge J, Birmaher B. 2000. Cognitive and family therapies for adolescent depression: treatment specificity, mediation, and moderation. *J. Consult. Clin. Psychol.* 68:603–14

Kraemer HC, Kazdin AE, Offord DR, Kessler RC, Jensen PS, Kupfer DJ. 1997. Coming to terms with the terms of risk. *Arch. Gen. Psychiatry* 54:337–43

Kraemer HC, Stice E, Kazdin AE, Offord DR, Kupfer DJ. 2001. How do risk factors work together? Mediators, moderators, independent, overlapping, and proxy-risk factors. *Am. J. Psychiatry* 158:848–56

Kraemer HC, Wilson GT, Fairburn CG, Agras WS. 2002. Mediators and moderators of treatment effects in randomized clinical trials. *Arch. Gen. Psychiatry* 59:877–83

Kwon S, Oei TPS. 2003. Cognitive processes in a group cognitive behavior therapy of depression. *J. Behav. Ther. Exp. Psychiatry* 34:73–85

Lambert MJ, ed. 2004. *Bergin and Garfield's Handbook of Psychotherapy and Behavior Change*. New York: Wiley. 5th ed.

Lin K, Poland RE, Nagasaki G, eds. 1993. *Psychopharmacology and Psychobiology of Ethnicity*. Washington, DC: Am. Psychiatr. Press

MacKinnon DP, Lockwood CM, Hoffman JM, West SG, Sheets V. 2002. A comparison of methods to test mediation and other intervening variable effects. *Psychol. Methods* 7:83–104

MacKinnon DP, Taborga MP, Morgan-Lopez AA. 2002. Mediation designs in tobacco prevention research. *Drug Alcohol Depend.* 68:S69–83

McGuire WJ. 1997. Creative hypothesis generating in psychology: some useful heuristics. *Annu. Rev. Psychol.* 48:1–30

Meyer-Lindenberg A, Buckholtz JW, Kolachana B, Ahmad R, Hariri AR, et al. 2006. Neural mechanisms of genetic risk for impulsivity and violence in humans. *Proc. Natl. Acad. Sci. USA* 103:6269–74

Meyer-Lindenberg A, Hariri AR, Munoz KE, Mervis CB, Mattay VS, et al. 2005. Neural correlates of genetically abnormal social cognition in Williams syndrome. *Nat. Neurosci.* 8:991–93

Myers KM, Davis M. 2002. Behavioral and neural analysis of extinction: a review. *Neuron* 36:567–84

Nathan PE, Gorman JM, eds. 2007. *Treatments That Work*. New York: Oxford Univ. Press. 3rd ed. In press

Orlinsky DE, Rønnestad MH, Willutzki U. 2004. Fifty years of psychotherapy process-outcome research: continuity and change. In *Bergin and Garfield's Handbook of Psychotherapy and Behavior Change*, ed. MJ Lambert, pp. 307–89. New York: Wiley. 5th ed.

Patterson GR. 1982. *Coercive Family Process*. Eugene, OR: Castalia

Patterson GR, Reid JB, Dishion TJ. 1992. *Antisocial Boys*. Eugene, OR: Castalia

Perepletchikova F, Kazdin AE. 2005. Treatment integrity and therapeutic change: issues and research recommendations. *Clin. Psychol. Sci. Pract.* 12:365–83

Pruessner JC, Champagne F, Meaney MJ, Dagher A. 2004. Dopamine release in response to a psychological stress in humans and its relationship to early maternal care: a positron emission tomography study using [C]raclopride. *J. Neurosci.* 24:2825–31

Reid JB, Patterson GR, Snyder J, eds. 2002. *Antisocial Behavior in Children and Adolescents: A Developmental Analysis and Model for Intervention*. Washington, DC: Am. Psychol. Assoc.

Ressler KJ, Rothbaum BO, Tannenbaum L, Anderson P, Graap K, et al. 2004. Cognitive enhancers as adjuncts to psychotherapy. Use of D-cycloserine in phobic individuals to facilitate extinction of fear. *Arch. Gen. Psychiatry* 61:1136–44

Shrout PE, Bolger N. 2002. Mediation in experimental and nonexperimental studies: new procedures and recommendations. *Psychol. Methods* 7:422–45

Snyder J, Stoolmiller M. 2002. Reinforcement and coercion mechanisms in the development of antisocial behavior: the family. In *Antisocial Behavior in Children and Adolescents: A Developmental Analysis and Model for Intervention*, ed. JB Reid, GR Patterson, J Snyder, pp. 65–100. Washington, DC: Am. Psychol. Assoc.

Tang TZ, DeRubeis RJ. 1999. Sudden gains and critical sessions in cognitive-behavioral therapy for depression. *J. Consult. Clin. Psychol.* 67:894–904

Tremblay RE, Masse B, Perron D, LeBlanc M, Schwartzman AE, Ledingham JE. 1992. Early disruptive behavior, poor school achievement, delinquent behavior, and delinquent personality: longitudinal analyses. *J. Consult. Clin. Psychol.* 60:64–72

Twain M, Warner ACD. 1874. *The Gilded Age: A Tale of Today*. Hartford, CT: Am. Publ.

Weersing VR, Weisz JR. 2002. Mechanisms of action in youth psychotherapy. *J. Child Psychol. Psychiatry* 43:3–29

Whisman MA. 1999. The importance of the cognitive theory of change in cognitive therapy of depression. *Clin. Psychol. Sci. Pract.* 6:300–4

Zigler E, Glick MA. 1986. *A Developmental Approach to Adult Psychopathology*. New York: Wiley

Evidence-Based Assessment

John Hunsley[1] and Eric J. Mash[2]

[1]School of Psychology, University of Ottawa, Ottawa, Ontario, K1N 6N5 Canada; email: hunch@uottawa.ca

[2]Department of Psychology, University of Calgary, Calgary, Alberta T2N 1N4 Canada; email: mash@ucalgary.ca

Annu. Rev. Clin. Psychol. 2007. 3:29–51

First published online as a Review in Advance on October 12, 2006

The *Annual Review of Clinical Psychology* is online at http://clinpsy.annualreviews.org

This article's doi:
10.1146/annurev.clinpsy.3.022806.091419

1548-5943/07/0427-0029$20.00

Key Words

psychological assessment, incremental validity, clinical utility

Abstract

Evidence-based assessment (EBA) emphasizes the use of research and theory to inform the selection of assessment targets, the methods and measures used in the assessment, and the assessment process itself. Our review focuses on efforts to develop and promote EBA within clinical psychology. We begin by highlighting some weaknesses in current assessment practices and then present recent efforts to develop EBA guidelines for commonly encountered clinical conditions. Next, we address the need to attend to several critical factors in developing such guidelines, including defining psychometric adequacy, ensuring appropriate attention is paid to the influence of comorbidity and diversity, and disseminating accurate and up-to-date information on EBAs. Examples are provided of how data on incremental validity and clinical utility can inform EBA. Given the central role that assessment should play in evidence-based practice, there is a pressing need for clinically relevant research that can inform EBAs.

Contents

INTRODUCTION

Over the past decade, attention to the use of evidence-based practices in health care services has grown dramatically. Developed first in medicine (Sackett et al. 1996), a number of evidence-based initiatives have been undertaken in professional psychology, culminating with the American Psychological Association policy statement on evidence-based practice in psychology (Am. Psychol. Assoc. Presid. Task Force Evid.-Based Pract. 2006). Although the importance of assessment has been alluded to in various practice guidelines and discussions of evidence-based psychological practice, by far the greatest attention has been on intervention. However, without a scientifically sound assessment literature, the prominence accorded evidence-based treatment has been likened to constructing a magnificent house without bothering to build a solid foundation (Achenbach 2005). In their recent review of clinical assessment, Wood et al. (2002) advanced the position that it is necessary for the field to have assessment strategies that are clinically relevant, culturally sensitive, and scientifically sound. With these factors in mind, the focus of our review is on recent efforts to develop and promote evidence-based assessment (EBA) within clinical psychology.

From our perspective, EBA is an approach to clinical evaluation that uses research and theory to guide the selection of constructs to be assessed for a specific assessment purpose, the methods and measures to be used in the assessment, and the manner in which the assessment process unfolds. It involves the recognition that, even with data from psychometrically strong measures, the assessment process is inherently a decision-making task in which the clinician must iteratively formulate and test hypotheses by integrating data that are often incomplete or inconsistent. A truly evidence-based approach to assessment, therefore, would involve an evaluation of the accuracy and usefulness of this complex decision-making task in light of potential errors in data synthesis and interpretation, the costs associated with the assessment process and, ultimately, the impact the assessment had on clinical outcomes for the person(s) being assessed.

In our review of EBA, we begin by briefly illustrating some current weaknesses and lacunae in clinical assessment activities that underscore why a renewed focus on the evidence base for clinical assessment instruments and activities is necessary. We then present recent efforts to operationalize EBA for specific disorders and describe some of the challenges in developing and disseminating EBA. Finally, we illustrate how a consideration of incremental validity and clinical utility can contribute to EBAs.

EXAMPLES OF CURRENT PROBLEMS AND LIMITATIONS IN CLINICAL ASSESSMENT

In this section, we illustrate some of the ways in which current clinical assessment practices may be inconsistent with scientific evidence. Our brief illustrations are not intended as a general indictment of the value of clinical assessments. Rather, by focusing on some frequently used instruments and common assessment activities, our intent is to emphasize that clients involved in assessments may not always be receiving services that are optimally informed by science. As recipients of psychological services, these individuals deserve, of course, nothing less than the best that psychological science has to offer them.

Problems with Some Commonly Taught and Used Tests

Over the past three decades, numerous surveys have been conducted on the instruments most commonly used by clinical psychologists and taught in graduate training programs and internships. With some minor exceptions, the general patterns have remained remarkably consistent and the relative rankings of specific instruments have changed very little over time (e.g., Piotrowski 1999). Unfortunately, many of the tools most frequently taught and used have either limited or mixed supporting empirical evidence. In the past several years, for example, the Rorschach inkblot test has been the focus of a number of literature reviews (e.g., Hunsley & Bailey 1999, 2001; Meyer & Archer 2001; Stricker & Gold 1999; Wood et al. 2003). There appears to be general agreement that the test (*a*) must be administered, scored, and interpreted in a standardized manner, and (*b*) has appropriate reliability and validity for at least a limited set of purposes. Beyond this minimal level of agreement, however, there is no consensus among advocates and critics on the evidence regarding the clinical value of the test.

The Rorschach is not the only test for which clinical use appears to have outstripped empirical evidence. In this regard, it is illuminating to contrast the apparent popularity of the Thematic Apperception Test (TAT; Murray 1943) and various human figure drawings tasks, both of which usually appear among the ten most commonly recommended and used tests in these surveys, with reviews of these tests' scientific adequacy. There is evidence that some apperceptive measures can be both reliable and valid (e.g., Spangler 1992): This is not the case with the TAT itself. Decades of research have documented the enormous variability in the manner in which the test is administered, scored, and interpreted. As a result, Vane's (1981) conclusion that no cumulative evidence supports the test's reliability and validity still holds today (Rossini & Moretti 1997). In essence, it is a commonly used test that falls well short of professional standards for psychological tests. The same set of problems besets the various types of projective drawing tests. In a recent review, Lally (2001) concluded that the most frequently researched and used approaches to scoring projective drawings fail to meet legal standards for a scientifically valid technique. Scoring systems for projective drawings emphasizing the frequency of occurrence of multiple indicators of psychopathology fared somewhat better, with Lally (2001) suggesting that "[a]lthough their validity is weak, their conclusions are limited in scope, and they appear to offer no additional information over other psychological tests, it can

Evidence-based assessment (EBA): the use of research and theory to inform the selection of assessment targets, the methods and measures to be used, and the manner in which the assessment process unfolds and is, itself, evaluated

Evidence-based psychological practice: the use of best available evidence to guide the provision of psychological services, while taking into account both a clinician's expertise and a client's context and values

Assessment purposes: psychological assessment can be conducted for a number of purposes (e.g., diagnosis, treatment evaluation), and a measure's psychometric properties pertaining to one purpose may not generalize to other purposes

Incremental validity: the extent to which additional data contribute to the prediction of a variable beyond what is possible with other sources of data

at least be argued that they cross the relatively low hurdle of admissibility" (p. 146).

Clinical utility: the extent to which the use of assessment data leads to demonstrable improvements in clinical services and, accordingly, results in improvements in client functioning

TAT: Thematic Apperception Test

IQ: intelligence quotient

Problems in Test Selection and Inadequate Assessment

The results of clinical assessments can often have a significant impact on those being assessed. Nowhere is this more evident than in evaluations conducted for informing child custody decisions. As a result, numerous guidelines have been developed to assist psychologists in conducting sound child custody evaluations (e.g., Am. Psychol. Assoc. 1994). It appears, however, that psychologists often fail to follow these guidelines or to heed the cautions contained within them. For example, a survey of psychologists who conduct child custody evaluations found that projective tests were often used to assess child adjustment (Ackerman & Ackerman 1997). As we described above, apperceptive tests, projective drawings, and other projectives often do not possess evidence of their reliability and validity. Moving beyond self-report information of assessment practices, Horvath et al. (2002) conducted content analyses of child custody evaluation reports included in court records. They found considerable variability in the extent to which professional guidelines were followed. For example, evaluators often failed to assess general parenting abilities and the ability of each parent to meet his/her child's needs. The assessment of potential domestic violence and child abuse was also frequently found to be neglected by evaluators.

Problems in Test Interpretation

Because of the care taken in developing norms and establishing reliability and validity indices, the Wechsler intelligence scales are typically seen as among the psychometrically strongest psychological instruments available. Interpretation of the scales typically progresses from a consideration of the full-scale IQ score, to the verbal and performance IQ scores, and then to the factor scores (e.g., Groth-Marnat 2003). The availability of representative norms and supporting validity studies provide a solid foundation for using these scores to understand a person's strengths and weaknesses in the realm of mental abilities.

It is also common, however, for authorities to recommend that the next interpretive step involve consideration of the variability between and within subtests (e.g., Flanagan & Kaufman 2004, Kaufman & Lichtenberger 1999). There are, however, a number of problems with this practice. First, the internal consistency of each subtest is usually much lower than that associated with the IQ and factor scores. This low reliability translates into reduced precision of measurement, which leads directly to an increased likelihood of false positive and false negative conclusions about the ability measured by the subtest. Second, there is substantial evidence over several decades that the information contained in subtest profiles adds little to the prediction of either learning behaviors or academic achievement once the IQ scores and factor scores are taken into account (Watkins 2003). An evidence-based approach to the assessment of intelligence would indicate that nothing is to be gained, and much is to be potentially lost, by considering subtest profiles.

Limited Evidence for Treatment Utility of Commonly Used Tests

In test development and validation, the primary foci have been determining the reliability and validity of an instrument. For example, Meyer et al. (2001) provided extensive evidence that many psychological tests have substantial validity when used for clinically relevant purposes. Assessment, however, is more than the use of one or two tests: It involves the integration of a host of data sources, including tests, interviews, and clinical observations. Unfortunately, despite the compelling psychometric evidence for the validity of many psychological tests, almost no research addresses the accuracy (i.e., validity) or the usefulness (i.e., utility) of psychological assessments (Hunsley 2002, Smith 2002).

In particular, as numerous authors have commented over the years (e.g., Hayes et al. 1987), surprisingly little attention has been paid to the treatment utility of commonly used psychological instruments and methods. Although diagnosis has some utility in determining the best treatment options for clients, there is a paucity of evidence on the degree to which clinical assessment contributes to beneficial treatment outcomes (Nelson-Gray 2003). A recent study by Lima et al. (2005) illustrates the type of utility information that can and should be obtained about assessment tools. These researchers had clients complete the Minnesota Multiphasic Personality Inventory-2 (MMPI-2) prior to commencing treatment; half the treating clinicians received feedback on their client's MMPI-2 data, half did not. Clients presented with a range of diagnoses, with the most common being mood disorders, anxiety disorders, substance-related disorders, adjustment disorders, eating disorders, and personality disorders. Between-group comparisons were conducted on variables related to treatment outcome. In sum, the researchers found that providing clinicians with these results as a potential aid in treatment planning had no positive impact on variables such as improvement ratings or premature termination rates. These data provide evidence that utility, even from an instrument as intensively researched as the MMPI-2, should not be assumed.

DEFINING EVIDENCE-BASED ASSESSMENT OF SPECIFIC DISORDERS/CONDITIONS

In light of the frequent discrepancies between the research base of an assessment instrument and the extent and manner of its use in clinical practice, the need for evidence-based assessment practices is obvious. From our perspective, three critical aspects should define EBA (Hunsley & Mash 2005, Mash & Hunsley 2005). First, research findings and scientifically viable theories on both psychopathology and normal human development should be used to guide the selection of constructs to be assessed and the assessment process. Second, as much as possible, psychometrically strong measures should be used to assess the constructs targeted in the assessment. Specifically, these measures should have replicated evidence of reliability, validity, and, ideally, clinical utility. Given the range of purposes for which assessment instruments can be used (e.g., screening, diagnosis, treatment monitoring) and the fact that psychometric evidence is always conditional (based on sample characteristics and assessment purpose), supporting psychometric evidence must be available for each purpose for which an instrument or assessment strategy is used. Psychometrically strong measures must also possess appropriate norms for norm-referenced interpretation and/or replicated supporting evidence for the accuracy (i.e., sensitivity, specificity, predictive power, etc.) of cut-scores for criterion-referenced interpretation. Third, although at present little evidence bears on the issue, it is critical that the entire process of assessment (i.e., selection, use, and interpretation of an instrument, and integration of multiple sources of assessment data) be empirically evaluated. In other words, a critical distinction must be made between evidence-based assessment methods and tools, on the one hand, and evidence-based assessment processes, on the other.

In 2005, special sections in two journals, *Journal of Clinical Child and Adolescent Psychology* and *Psychological Assessment*, were devoted to developing EBA guidelines, based on the aforementioned principles, for commonly encountered clinical conditions. As many authors in these special sections noted, despite the voluminous literature on psychological tests relevant to clinical conditions, few concerted attempts have been made to draw on the empirical evidence to develop assessment guidelines, and even fewer evaluations of the utility of assessment guidelines. In the following sections we summarize key points authors

Treatment utility: the extent to which assessment methods and measures contribute to improvement in the outcomes of psychological treatments

MMPI-2: Minnesota Multiphasic Personality Inventory-2

raised about the evidence-based assessment of disorders usually first diagnosed in youth, anxiety disorders, mood disorders, personality disorders, and couple distress.

ADHD: attention-deficit/hyperactivity disorder

Disorders Usually First Diagnosed in Youth

Pelham et al. (2005) addressed the assessment of attention-deficit/hyperactivity disorder (ADHD). Based on their literature review, they contended that data obtained from symptom rating scales, completed by both parent and teacher, provide the best information for diagnostic purposes. Despite the widespread use of structured and semistructured interviews, the evidence indicates that they have no incremental validity or utility once data from brief symptom rating scales are considered. Moreover, the authors argued that the diagnostic assessment itself has little treatment utility, especially as the correlation between ADHD symptoms and functional impairment is modest. Accordingly, they suggested that a full assessment of impairments and adaptive skills should be the priority once diagnosis is established. This would involve assessment of (*a*) functioning in specific domains known to be affected by the disorder (peer relationships, family environment, and school performance) and (*b*) specific target behaviors that will be directly addressed in any planned treatment.

Drawing on extensive psychopathology research on externalizing behaviors such as oppositional behavior, aggression, physical destructiveness, and stealing, McMahon & Frick (2005) recommended that the evidence-based assessment of conduct problems focus on (*a*) the types and severity of the conduct problems and (*b*) the resulting impairment experienced by the youth. Clinicians should also obtain information on the age of onset of severe conduct problems. Compared with an onset after the age of 10 years, onset before the age of 10 is associated with more extreme problems and a greater likelihood of subsequent antisocial and criminal acts. The influence of temperament and social environment may also differ in child- versus adolescent-onset conduct problems. Many other conditions may co-occur, especially ADHD, depression, and anxiety disorders. Screening for these conditions, therefore, typically is warranted. A range of behavior rating scales, semistructured interviews, and observational systems are available to obtain data on primary and associated features of youth presenting with conduct problems and, as with most youth disorders, obtaining information from multiple informants is critical. However, as McMahon & Frick (2005) indicated, many of these of measures are designed for diagnostic and case conceptualization purposes—few have been examined for their suitability in tracking treatment effects or treatment outcome.

Based on recent assessment practice parameters and consensus panel guidelines, Ozonoff et al. (2005) outlined a core battery for assessing autism spectrum disorders. The battery consisted of a number of options for assessing key aspects of the disorders, including diagnostic status, intelligence, language skills, and adaptive behavior. As with the assessment of many disorders, some excellent measurement tools developed in research settings have yet to find their way into clinical practice. Moreover, the authors noted that there has been little attempt to conduct research that directly compares different instruments that assess the same domain, thus leaving clinicians with little guidance about which instrument to use. Ozonoff et al. (2005) also made suggestions for the best evidence-based options for assessing additional domains commonly addressed in autism spectrum disorders evaluations, including attention, executive functions, academic functioning, psychiatric comorbidities, environmental context (i.e., school, family, and community), and response to treatment. Importantly, though, they noted that there was no empirical evidence on whether assessing these domains adds meaningfully to the information available from the recommended core battery.

In their analysis of the learning disabilities assessment literature, Fletcher et al.

(2005) emphasized that approaches to classifying learning disabilities and the measurement of learning disabilities are inseparably connected. Accordingly, rather than focus on specific measures used in learning disability evaluations, these authors highlighted the need to evaluate the psychometric evidence for different models of classification/measurement. Four models were reviewed, including models that emphasized (*a*) low achievement, (*b*) discrepancies between aptitude and achievement, (*c*) intraindividual differences in cognitive functioning, and (*d*) responsiveness to intervention. On the basis of the scientific literature, Fletcher and colleagues concluded that (*a*) the low-achievement model suffers from problems with measurement error and, thus, reliability, (*b*) the discrepancy model has been shown in recent meta-analyses to have very limited validity, (*c*) the intraindividual-differences model also suffers from significant validity problems, and (*d*) the response-to-intervention model has demonstrated both substantial reliability and validity in identifying academic underachievers, but is insufficient for identifying learning disabilities. As a result, they recommended that a hybrid model, combining features of the low-achievement and response-to-treatment models, be used to guide the assessment of learning disabilities. Regardless of the ultimate validity and utility of this hybrid model, Fletcher and colleagues' analysis is extremely valuable for underscoring the need to consider and directly evaluate the manner in which differing assumptions about a disorder may influence measurement.

Anxiety Disorders

Two articles in the special sections dealt with a broad range of anxiety disorders. Silverman & Ollendick (2005) reviewed the literature on the assessment of anxiety and anxiety disorder in youth, and Antony & Rowa (2005) reviewed the comparable literature in adults. Both reviews noted that, regardless of age, the high rates of comorbidity among anxiety disorders pose a significant challenge for clinicians attempting to achieve an accurate and complete assessment. Additionally, because substantial evidence suggests that individuals diagnosed with an anxiety disorder and another psychiatric disorder (such as ADHD or a mood disorder) are more severely impaired than are individuals presenting with either disorder on its own, assessing for the possible presence of another disorder must be a key aspect of any anxiety disorder evaluation.

Comorbidity: the co-occurrence of multiple disorders or clinically significant patterns of dysfunction

Silverman & Ollendick (2005) provided an extensive review of instruments available for youth anxiety disorders, including numerous diagnostic interviews, self-report symptom scales, informant symptom-rating scales (including parent, teacher, and clinician), and observational tasks. Although psychometrically sound instruments are available, many obstacles face clinicians wishing to conduct an evidence-based assessment. For example, the authors reported that efforts to accurately screen for the presence of an anxiety disorder may be hampered by the fact that scales designed to measure similar constructs have substantially different sensitivity and specificity properties. Another obstacle noted by the authors is that all of the measures used to quantify symptoms and anxious behaviors rely on an arbitrary metric (cf. Blanton & Jaccard 2006, Kazdin 2006). As a result, we simply do not know how well scores on these measures map on to actual disturbances and functional impairments. A final example stems from the ubiquitous research finding that youth and their parents are highly discordant in their reports of anxiety symptoms. In light of such data, it is commonly recommended that both youth and parent reports be obtained, but, as Silverman & Ollendick (2005) cautioned, care must be exercised to ensure that neither is treated as a gold standard when diagnosing an anxiety disorder.

Antony & Rowa (2005) emphasized the importance of assessing key dimensions that cut across anxiety disorders in their review of the adult anxiety disorder literature. Based on diagnostic criteria, anxiety disorders research, and expert consensus statements, they recommended that evidence-based assessment for anxiety disorders should target anxiety cues and triggers, avoidance behaviors, compulsions and overprotective behaviors, physical symptoms and responses, comorbidity, skills deficits, functional impairment, social environment factors, associated health issues, and disorder development and treatment history. To illustrate how these dimensions could be assessed, the authors presented an assessment protocol to be used for assessing treatment outcome in the case of panic disorder with agoraphobia. The literature on the assessment of anxiety problems in adults has an abundance of psychometrically strong interviews and self-report measures, and numerous studies have supported the value of obtaining self-monitoring data and using behavioral tests to provide observable evidence of anxiety and avoidance. Nevertheless, Antony & Rowa (2005) cautioned that, even for well-established measures, little validity data exist beyond evidence of how well one measure correlates with another. Echoing the theme raised by Silverman & Ollendick (2005), they emphasized that little is currently known about how well an instrument correlates with responses in anxiety-provoking situations.

Mood Disorders

Three articles in the special sections dealt with mood disorders. Klein et al. (2005) addressed the assessment of depression in youth, Joiner et al. (2005) dealt with the assessment of depression in adults, and Youngstrom et al. (2005) discussed initial steps toward an evidence-based assessment of pediatric bipolar disorder. With respect to the assessment of depression, both sets of authors recommended that the best assessment practice would be to use a validated semistructured interview to address diagnostic criteria, comorbidity, disorder course, family history, and social environment. Additionally, these authors stressed the critical need to include a sensitive and thorough assessment of suicidal ideation and the potential for suicidal behavior in all depression-related assessments.

Klein et al. (2005) reported that psychometrically strong semistructured interviews are available for the assessment of depression in youth. The need for input from multiple informants is especially important, as younger children may not be able to comment accurately on the time scale associated with depressive experiences or on the occurrence and duration of previous episodes. As with anxiety disorders, there is consistent evidence regarding the limited agreement between youth and parent reports of depression, although recent evidence shows that youth, parent, and teacher reports can all contribute uniquely to the prediction of subsequent outcomes. On the other hand, Klein and colleagues (2005) cautioned that depressed parents have been found to have a lower threshold, relative to nondepressed parents, in identifying depression in their children. Ratings scales, for both parents and youth, were described as especially valuable for the assessment purposes of screening, treatment monitoring, and treatment evaluation. Unfortunately, most such rating scales have rather poor discriminant validity, especially with respect to anxiety disorders. The authors also indicated that, because so little research exists on the assessment of depression in preschool-age children, it is not possible to make strong recommendations for clinicians conducting such assessments.

Based on extensive research, Joiner et al. (2005) concluded that depression can be reliably and validly assessed, although they cautioned that attention must be paid to the differential diagnosis of subtypes of depression, such as melancholic-endogenous depression, atypical depression, and seasonal affective disorder. The authors noted that there is no strong evidence of gender or ethnicity biases in depression assessment instruments and, although there is some concern about inflated scores on self-report measures among older adults (primarily due to items dealing with somatic and vegetative symptoms), good measures are available for use with older adults. Psychometrically strong measures exist for both screening and treatment monitoring purposes; for this latter purpose, some research has indicated that clinician ratings are more sensitive to treatment changes than are client ratings. Nevertheless, Joiner and colleagues emphasized that the methods and measures currently available to assess depression have yet to demonstrate their value in the design or delivery of intervention services to depressed adults.

Because of the relative recency of the research literature on bipolar disorder in youth and the ongoing debate about the validity of the diagnosis in children and adolescents, Youngstrom et al. (2005) focused on providing guidance on how evidence-based assessment might develop for this disorder. The paucity of psychometrically adequate interviews and self-report instruments led the authors to address foundational elements that should be included in an assessment. For example, they stressed the need to carefully consider family history: Although an average odds ratio of 5 has been found for the risk of the disorder in a child if a parent has the disorder, approximately 95% of youth with a parent who has bipolar disorder will not, themselves, meet diagnostic criteria. They also emphasized the importance of attending to symptoms that are relatively specific to the disorder (e.g., elevated mood, grandiosity, pressured speech, racing thoughts, and hypersexuality) and to evidence of patterns such as mood cycling and distinct spontaneous changes in mood states. Because of the likely lack of insight or awareness in youth of possible manic symptoms, collateral information from teachers and parents has been shown to be particularly valuable in predicting diagnostic status. Finally, due to the need to identify patterns of mood shifts and concerns about the validity of retrospective recall, Youngstrom and colleagues (2005) strongly recommended that an assessment for possible bipolar disorder should occur over an extended period, thus allowing the clinician an opportunity to obtain data from repeated evaluations.

Personality Disorders

In their review of the literature on the assessment of personality disorders, Widiger & Samuel (2005) described several scientifically sound options for both semistructured interviews and self-report measures, although they did note that not all instruments have normative data available. To maximize accuracy and minimize the burden on the clinician, they recommended a strategy whereby a positive response on a self-report instrument is followed up with a semistructured interview. Concerns about limited self-awareness and inaccuracies in self-perception among individuals being assessed for a personality disorder raise the issue of relying on self-report, whether on rating scales or interviews. Moreover, given the potential for both gender and ethnicity biases to occur in these instruments, clinicians must be alert to the possibility of diagnostic misclassification. As with youth disorders, the use of collateral data is strongly encouraged, especially as research has indicated that both client and informant provide data that contribute uniquely to a diagnostic assessment. Widiger & Samuel (2005) also underscored the need for the development of measures to track treatment-related changes in maladaptive personality functioning.

Couple Distress

Snyder et al. (2005) presented a conceptual framework for assessing couple functioning that addresses both individual and dyadic characteristics. Drawing on extensive studies of intimate relationships, they highlighted the need to assess relationship behaviors (e.g., communication, handling conflict), relationship cognitions (e.g., relationship-related standards, expectations, and attributions), relationship affect (e.g., rates, duration, and reciprocity of both negative and positive affect), and individual distress. Much valuable information on these domains can be obtained from psychometrically sound rating scales; however, the authors concluded that most self-report measures have not undergone sufficient psychometric analysis to warrant their clinical use. Moreover, the authors noted that very little progress had been made in developing interview protocols that demonstrate basic levels of reliability and validity. They also stressed the unique contribution afforded by the use of analog behavior observation in assessing broad classes of behavior such as communication, power, problem solving, and support/intimacy. Thus, rather than recommending a specific set of measures to be used in assessing couples, Snyder and colleagues (2005) suggested that their behavior/cognition/affect/distress framework be used to guide the selection of constructs and measures as the assessment process progressed from identifying broad relationship concerns to specifying elements of these concerns that are functionally linked to the problems in couple functioning.

CHALLENGES IN DEVELOPING AND DISSEMINATING EVIDENCE-BASED ASSESSMENT

Based on the foregoing analysis of EBA for commonly encountered clinical conditions, many scientific and logistic challenges must be addressed. In this section, we focus on some of the more pressing issues stemming from efforts to develop a truly evidence-based approach to assessment in clinical psychology. We begin with the basic question of what constitutes "good enough" psychometric criteria, then move on to examine issues such as comorbidity, attention to diversity parameters, and the promotion of EBA in clinical practice. Additional potential challenges in EBA, such as the use of multiple measures and multiple informants and the integration of assessment data, are discussed below in a section on incremental validity.

Defining Psychometric Adequacy

In their presentation on the assessment of depression in youth, Klein and colleagues (2005) queried what constitutes an acceptable level of reliability or validity in an instrument. After many decades of research on test construction and evaluation, it would be tempting to assume that the criteria for what constitutes "good enough" evidence to support the clinical use of an instrument have been clearly established: Nothing could be further from the case. The *Standards for Educational and Psychological Testing* (Am. Educ. Res. Assoc., Am. Psychol. Assoc., Natl. Counc. Meas. Educ. 1999) set out generic standards to be followed in developing and using tests, and these standards are well accepted by psychologists. In essence, for an instrument to be psychometrically sound, it must be standardized, have relevant norms, and have appropriate levels of reliability and validity (cf. Hunsley et al. 2003). The difficulty comes in defining what standards should be met when considering these characteristics.

As we and many others have stressed in our work on psychological assessment, psychometric characteristics are not properties of an instrument per se, but rather are properties of an instrument when used for a specific purpose with a specific sample. For this reason, many assessment scholars and psychometricians are understandably reluctant to provide precise standards for the psychometric properties that an instrument or strategy must have in order to be used for assessment purposes (e.g., Streiner & Norman 2003). On the other hand, both researchers and clinicians are constantly faced with the decision of whether an instrument is good enough for the assessment task at hand.

Some attempts have been made over the past two decades to delineate criteria for measure selection and use. Robinson, Shaver & Wrightsman (1991) developed evaluative criteria for the adequacy of attitude and personality measures, covering the domains of theoretical development, item development, norms, interitem correlations, internal consistency, test-retest reliability, factor analytic results, known groups validity, convergent validity, discriminant validity, and freedom from response sets. Robinson and colleagues (1991) also used specific criteria for many of these domains. For example, a coefficient α of 0.80 was deemed exemplary, as was the availability of three or more studies showing the instrument had results that were independent of response biases. More recently, efforts have been made to establish general psychometric criteria for determining disability in speech-language disorders (Agency Healthc. Res. Qual. 2002) and reliability criteria for a multinational measure of psychiatric services (Schene et al. 2000). Taking a different approach, expert panel ratings were used by the Measurement and Treatment Research to Improve Cognition in Schizophrenia Group to develop a consensus battery of cognitive tests to be used in clinical trials in schizophrenia (MATRICS 2006). Rather than specify precise psychometric criteria, panelists were asked to rate, on a nine-point scale, each proposed test's characteristics, including test-retest reliability, utility as a repeated measure, relation to functional outcome, responsiveness to treatment change, and practicality/tolerability.

In a recent effort to promote the development of EBA in clinical assessment, we developed a rating system for instruments that was intended to embody a "good enough" principle across psychometric categories with clear clinical relevance (Hunsley & Mash 2006). We focused on nine categories: norms, internal consistency, interrater reliability, test-retest reliability, content validity, construct validity, validity generalization, sensitivity to treatment change, and clinical utility. Each of these categories is applied in relation to a specific assessment purpose (e.g., case conceptualization) in the context of a specific disorder or clinical condition (e.g., eating disorders, self-injurious behavior, and relationship conflict). For each category, a rating of acceptable, good, excellent, or not applicable is possible. The precise nature of what constitutes acceptable, good, and excellent varied, of course, from category to category. In general, though, a rating of acceptable indicated that the instrument meets a minimal level of scientific rigor, good indicated that the instrument would generally be seen as possessing solid scientific support, and excellent indicated there was extensive, high-quality supporting evidence. When considering the clinical use of a measure, it would be desirable to use only those measures that would meet, at a minimum, our criteria for good. However, as measure development is an ongoing process, we felt it was important to provide the option of the acceptable rating in order to fairly evaluate (*a*) relatively newly developed measures and (*b*) measures for which comparable levels of research evidence are not available across all psychometric categories in our rating system.

To illustrate this rating system, we focus on the internal consistency category. Although a number of indices of internal consistency are available, α is the most widely used index (Streiner 2003). Therefore, even though concerns have been raised about the potential for undercorrection of measurement error with this index (Schmidt et al. 2003), we established criteria for α in our system. Across all three possible ratings in the system, we encouraged attention to the preponderance of research results. Such an approach allows a balance to be maintained between (*a*) the importance of having replicated results and (*b*) the recognition that variability in samples and sampling strategies will yield a range of reliability values for any measure. Ideally, meta-analytic indices of effect size could be used to provide precise estimates from the research literature. Recommendations for what constitutes good internal consistency vary from author to author, but most authorities seem to view 0.70 as the minimum acceptable value (cf. Charter 2003). Accordingly, our rating of adequate is appropriate when the preponderance of evidence indicated values of 0.70–0.79. For a rating of good, we required that the preponderance of evidence indicated values of 0.80–0.89. Finally, because of cogent arguments that an α value of at least 0.90 is highly desirable in clinical assessment contexts (Nunnally &

Bernstein 1994), we required that the preponderance of evidence indicated values ≥ 0.90 for an instrument to be rated as having excellent internal consistency. That being said, it is also possible for α to be too (artificially) high, as a value close to unity typically indicates substantial redundancy among items.

Addressing Comorbidity

As stressed by all contributors to the special sections on EBA described above, the need to assess accurately comorbid conditions is a constant clinical reality. Simply put, people seen in clinical settings, across the age span, frequently meet diagnostic criteria for more than one disorder or have symptoms from multiple disorders even if they occur at a subclinical level (Kazdin 2005). Indeed, recent nationally representative data on comorbidity in adults indicated that 45% of those meeting criteria for an anxiety, mood, impulse control, or substance disorder also met criteria for one or two additional diagnoses (Kessler et al. 2005). At present, it is not possible to disentangle the various factors that may account for this state of affairs. True heterogeneity among the patterns of presenting symptoms, poor content validity within some symptom measures, limitations inherent in current diagnostic categories, and the use of mixed-age samples to estimate lifetime prevalence of comorbidity, singly or together, can contribute to the high observed rates of comorbidity (Achenbach 2005, Kraemer et al. 2006).

However, evidence is emerging that observed comorbidity is at least partially due to the presence of core pathological processes that underlie the overt expression of a seemingly diverse range of symptoms (Krueger & Markon 2006, Widiger & Clark 2000). In particular, the internalizing and externalizing dimensions first identified as relevant to childhood disorders appear to have considerable applicability to adult disorders. In a cross-cultural study examining the structure of psychiatric comorbidity in 14 countries, Krueger et al. (2003) found that a two-factor (internalizing and externalizing) model accurately represented the range of commonly reported symptoms. Moreover, there is evidence that individuals diagnosed with comorbid conditions are more severely impaired in daily life functioning, are more likely to have a chronic history of mental health problems, have more physical health problems, and use more health care services than do those with a single diagnosable condition (Newman et al. 1998). Hence, for numerous reasons, the evidence-based assessment of any specific disorder requires that the presence of commonly encountered comorbid conditions, as defined by the results of extant psychopathology research, be evaluated.

Fortunately, viable options exist for conducting such an evaluation. Conceptualizing the assessment process as having multiple, interdependent stages, it is relatively straightforward to have the initial stage address more general considerations such as a preliminary broadband evaluation of symptoms and life context. As indicated by many contributors to the special sections, some semistructured interviews provide such information, for both youth and adults. However, time constraints and a lack of formal training, among other considerations, may leave may clinicians disinclined to use these instruments. Good alternatives do exist, including multidimensional screening tools and brief symptom checklists for disorders most frequently comorbid with the target disorder (Achenbach 2005, Mash & Hunsley 2005). Additionally, it may be worthwhile to ensure that the assessment includes an evaluation of common parameters or domains that cut across the comorbid conditions. For example, regardless of the specific diagnoses being evaluated, situational triggers and avoidance behaviors are particularly important in the EBA of anxiety disorders in adults (Antony & Rowa 2005).

Addressing Diversity

When considering the applicability and potential utility of assessment instruments for a particular clinical purpose with a specific individual, clinicians must attend to diversity parameters such as age, gender, and ethnicity. Dealing with developmental differences, throughout the life span, requires measures that are sensitive to developmental factors and age-relevant norms. Unfortunately, it is often the case that measures for children and adolescents are little more than downward extensions of those developed for use with adults (Silverman & Ollendick 2005). On the other hand, relevant research often is available to guide the clinician's choice of variables to assess. For example, research indicating that girls are more likely to use indirect and relational forms of aggression than they are physical aggression may point to different assessment targets for girls and boys when assessing youth suspected of having a conduct disorder (Crick & Nelson 2002). Likewise, the literature is rapidly expanding on ethnic and cultural variability in symptom expression and the psychometric adequacy of commonly used self-report measures in light of this variability (e.g., Achenbach et al. 2005, Joneis et al. 2000).

Presentations of the conceptual and methodological requirements and challenges involved in translating a measure into a different language and determining the appropriateness of a measure and its norms to a specific cultural group are also widely available (e.g., Geisinger 1994, van Widenfelt et al. 2005). As described succinctly by Snyder et al. (2005), four main areas need to be empirically evaluated in using or adapting instruments cross-culturally. These are (*a*) linguistic equivalence of the measure, (*b*) psychological equivalence of items, (*c*) functional equivalence of the measure, including predictive and criterion validity, and (*d*) scalar equivalence, including regression line slope and comparable metrics. Addressing these areas provides some assurance that cultural biases have been minimized or eliminated from a measure. However, many subtle influences may impede efforts to develop culturally appropriate measures. For example, investigations into the associations between ethnicity/culture and scores on a measure must be sensitive to factors such as subgroup differences in cultural expression and identity, socioeconomic status, immigration and refugee experiences, and acculturation (Alvidrez et al. 1996).

Notwithstanding the progress made in developing assessment methods and measures that are sensitive to diversity considerations, a very considerable challenge remains in developing EBAs that are sensitive to aspects of diversity. As cogently argued by Kazdin (2005), the number of potential moderating variables is so large that it is simply not realistic to expect that we will be able to develop an assessment evidence base that fully encompasses the direct and interactional influences these variables have on psychological functioning. Therefore, in addition to attending to diversity parameters in designing, conducting, and interpreting assessment research, psychologists need to be able to balance knowledge of instrument norms with an awareness of an individual's characteristics and circumstances. The availability, for commonly used standardized instruments, of nationally representative norms that are keyed to gender and age has great potential for aiding clinicians in understanding client functioning (Achenbach 2005). Such data must, however, be augmented with empirically derived principles that can serve as a guide in determining which elements of diversity are likely to be of particular importance for a given clinical case or situation.

Dissemination

For those interested in advancing the use of EBAs, the situation is definitely one in which the "glass" can either be seen as "half full" or as "half empty." Recent surveys of clinical psychologists indicate that a relatively limited amount of professional time is devoted to psychological assessment activities (Camara et al. 2000) and that relatively few clinical psychologists routinely formally evaluate treatment outcome (Cashel 2002, Hatfield &

Ogles 2004). Despite mounting pressure for the use of outcome assessment data in developing performance indicators and improving service delivery (e.g., Heinemann 2005), one recent survey found that, even when outcome assessments were mandatory in a clinical setting, most clinicians eschewed the available data and based their practices on an intuitive sense of what they felt clients needed (Garland et al. 2003). Furthermore, the assessment methods and measures typically taught in graduate training programs and those most frequently used by clinical psychologists bear little resemblance to the methods and measures involved in EBAs (Hunsley et al. 2004). On the other hand, an increasing number of assessment volumes wholeheartedly embrace an evidence-based approach (e.g., Antony & Barlow 2002, Hunsley & Mash 2006, Mash & Barkley 2006, Nezu et al. 2000).

In 2000, the American Psychiatric Association published the *Handbook of Psychiatric Measures*, a resource designed to offer information to mental health professionals on the availability of self-report measures, clinician checklists, and structured interviews that may be of value in the provision of clinical services. This compendium includes reviews of both general (e.g., health status, quality of life, family functioning) and diagnosis-specific assessment instruments. For each measure, there is a brief summary of its intended purpose, psychometric properties, likely clinical utility, and the practical issues encountered in using the measure. Relatedly, in their continuing efforts to improve the quality of mental health assessments, the American Psychiatric Association just released the second edition of its *Practice Guideline for the Psychiatric Evaluation of Adults* (2006). Drawing from both current scientific knowledge and the realities of clinical practice, this guideline addresses both the content and process of an evaluation. Despite the longstanding connection between psychological measurement and the profession of clinical psychology, no comparable concerted effort has been made to develop assessment guidelines in professional psychology. From a purely professional perspective, this absence of leadership in the assessment field seems unwise, but only time will tell whether the lack of involvement of organized psychology proves detrimental to the practice of psychological assessment.

Indications are growing that, across professions, clinicians are seeking assessment tools they can use to determine a client's level of pretreatment functioning and to develop, monitor, and evaluate the services received by the client (Barkham et al. 2001, Bickman et al. 2000, Hatfield & Ogles 2004); in other words, exactly the type of data encompassed by EBAs. Assuming, therefore, that at least a sizeable number of clinical psychologists might be interested in adopting EBA practices, what might be some of the issues that must be confronted if widespread dissemination is to occur? There must be some consensus on the psychometric qualities necessary for an instrument to merit its use in clinical services and, ideally, there should be consensus among experts about instruments that possess those qualities when used for a specific assessment purpose (Antony & Rowa 2005). Although some clinicians may simply be unwilling to adopt new assessment practices, it is imperative that the response cost for those willing to learn and use EBAs be relatively minimal. It would be ideal if most measures used in EBAs were brief, inexpensive to use, had robust reliability and validity characteristics across client groups, and were straightforward to administer, score, and interpret. To enhance the value of any guideline developed for EBAs, guidelines would need to be succinct, employ presentational strategies to depict complex psychometric data in a straightforward manner, be easily accessible (e.g., downloadable documents on a Web site), and be regularly updated as warranted by advances in research (Mash & Hunsley 2005). The strategies, methods, and technologies needed to develop and maintain such guidelines are all readily available. For example, meta-analytic summaries using data across studies can provide accurate estimates of the psychometric characteristics of a measure. The challenge is to pull together all the requisite components in a scientifically rigorous and sustainable fashion.

One final point is also clear: Simply doing more of the same in terms of the kind of assessment research typically conducted will not advance the use of EBAs. At present, there continues to be a proliferation of measures, the usual study focuses on a measure's concurrent validity with respect to other similar measures, and relatively little attention is paid to the prediction of clients' real-world functioning or to the clinical usefulness of the measure (Antony & Rowa 2005, Kazdin 2005, McGrath 2001). All of these mitigate against the likelihood of clinicians having access to scientifically solid assessment tools that are both clinically feasible and useful. In the sections below, we turn to the clinical features necessary to the uptake of EBAs—namely, incremental validity and utility.

INCREMENTAL VALIDITY AND EVIDENCE-BASED ASSESSMENT

Incremental validity is essentially a straightforward concept that addresses the question of whether data from an assessment tool add to the prediction of a criterion beyond what can be accomplished with other sources of data (Hunsley & Meyer 2003, Sechrest 1963). Nested within this concept, however, are a number of interrelated clinical questions that are crucial to the development and dissemination of EBA. These include questions such as whether it is worthwhile, in terms of both time and money, to (*a*) use a given instrument, (*b*) obtain data on the same variable using multiple methods, (*c*) collect parallel information from multiple informants, and (*d*) even bother collecting assessment data beyond information on diagnostic status, as most evidence-based treatments are keyed to diagnosis.

Ideally, incremental validity research should be able to provide guidance to clinicians on what could constitute the necessary scope for a given assessment purpose. Such guidance is especially important in the realm of clinical services to children and adolescents, as the norm for many years has been to collect data on multiple measures from multiple informants. In reality, however, there is little replicated evidence in the clinical literature on which to base such guidance (cf. Garb 2003, Johnston & Murray 2003). This is primarily due to the extremely limited use of research designs and analyses relevant to the question of incremental validity of instruments or data sources. Haynes & Lench (2003) reported, for example, that over a five-year period, only 10% of manuscripts submitted for possible publication in the journal *Psychological Assessment* considered a measure's incremental validity.

Nevertheless, in the literature some important incremental validity data are available that have direct relevance to the practice of clinical assessment. Moreover, a renewed focus on the topic (e.g., Haynes & Lench 2003, McFall 2005) and the availability of guidelines for interpreting what constitutes clinically meaningful validity increments (Hunsley & Meyer 2003) may lead to greater attention to conducting incremental validity analyses. In the following sections, we provide some examples of the ways in which incremental validity research has begun to address commonly encountered challenges in clinical assessment. We begin with research on using data from multiple informants and then turn to the use of data from multiple instruments.

Data from Multiple Informants

As we indicated, in assessing youth, it has been a longstanding practice for clinicians to obtain assessment data from multiple informants such as parents, teachers, and the youths themselves. It is now commonly accepted that, because of differing perspectives, these informant ratings will not be interchangeable but can each provide potentially valuable assessment data (e.g., De Los Reyes & Kazdin 2005). Of course, in usual clinical services, only a very limited amount of time is available to obtain initial assessment data. The obvious issue, therefore, is determining which informants are optimally placed to provide data most relevant to the assessment question at hand. Several distinct approaches to integrating data from multiple sources can be found in the literature. As summarized by Klein et al. (2005), these include the "or" rule (assuming that the feature targeted in the assessment is present if any informant reports it), the "and" rule (requiring two or more informants to confirm the presence of the feature), and the use of statistical regression models to integrate data from the multiple sources. In the following examples, we focus on the issue of obtaining multiple informant data for the purposes of clinical diagnosis.

Several research groups have been attempting to determine what could constitute a minimal set of assessment activities required for the assessment of ADHD in youth (e.g., Power et al. 1998, Wolraich et al. 2003). Focusing on instruments that are both empirically supported and clinically relevant, Pelham and colleagues (2005) recently synthesized the results of this line of research and drew several conclusions of direct clinical value. First, they concluded that diagnosing ADHD is most efficiently accomplished by relying on data from parent and teacher ADHD rating scales. Structured diagnostic interviews do not possess incremental validity over rating scales and, therefore, are likely to have little value in clinical settings. Second, clinical interviews and/or other rating scales are important for gaining information about the onset of the disorder and ruling out other conditions. Such information can be invaluable in designing intervention services and, consistent with diagnostic criteria, confirmatory data from both teachers and parents are necessary for the diagnosis of ADHD. However, in ruling out an ADHD diagnosis, it is not necessary to use both parent and teacher data: If either informant does not endorse rating items that possess strong negative predictive power, the youth is unlikely to have a diagnosis of ADHD.

Youngstrom et al. (2004) compared the diagnostic accuracy of six different instruments designed to screen for youth bipolar disorder. Three of these instruments involved parent reports, two involved youth self-reports, and one relied on teacher reports. Parent-based measures consistently outperformed measures based on youth self-report and teacher report in identifying bipolar disorder among youth (as determined by a structured diagnostic interview of the youth and parent). Additionally, the researchers found that no meaningful increment in prediction occurred when data from all measures were combined. Although none of the measures studied was designed to be a diagnostic instrument, and none was sufficient on its own for diagnosing the condition, the clinical implications from these findings are self-evident.

Data from Multiple Instruments

Within the constraints of typical clinical practice, there are perennial concerns regarding which instruments are critical for a given purpose and whether including multiple instruments will improve the accuracy of the assessment. In the research on the clinical assessment of adults, a growing number of studies address these concerns. We have chosen to illustrate what can be learned from this literature by focusing on two high-stakes assessment issues: detecting malingering and predicting recidivism.

The detection of malingering has become an important task in many clinical and forensic settings. Researchers have examined the ability of both specially developed malingering measures and the validity scales included in broadband assessment measures to identify accurately individuals who appear to be feigning clinically significant distress. In this context, Bagby et al. (2005) recently evaluated the incremental validity of several MMPI-2 validity scales to detect those faking depressive symptoms. Data from the Malingering Depression scale were compared to the F scales in a sample of MMPI-2 protocols that included depressed patients and mental health professionals instructed to feign depression. All validity scales had comparable results in detecting feigned depression, with no one scale being substantially better than any other scale. The Malingering Depression scale was found to have slight, but statistically significant, incremental validity over the other scales. However, the researchers reported that this statistical advantage did not translate into a meaningful clinical advantage: Very few additional "malingering" protocols were accurately identified by the scale beyond what was achieved with the generic validity scales.

The development of actuarial risk scales has been responsible for significant advances in the accurate prediction of criminal recidivism. Seto (2005) examined the incremental validity of four well-established actuarial risk scales, all with substantial empirical support, in predicting the occurrence among adult sex offenders of both serious violent offenses and sexual offense involving physical contact with the victims.

As some variability existed among the scales in terms of their ability to predict accurately both types of criminal offenses, Seto (2005) examined the predictive value of numerous strategies for combining data from multiple scales. These included both the "or" and "and" rules described above, along with strategies that used the average results across scales and statistical optimization methods derived via logistic regression and principal component analysis. Overall, Seto found that no combination of scales improved upon the predictive accuracy of the single best actuarial scale for the two types of criminal offenses. Accordingly, he suggested that evaluators should simply select the single best scale for the assessment purpose, rather than obtaining the information necessary for scoring and interpreting multiple scales.

CLINICAL UTILITY AND EVIDENCE-BASED ASSESSMENT

OQ-45: Outcome Questionnaire-45

The concept of clinical utility has received a great deal of attention in recent years. Although definitions vary, an emphasis on garnering evidence regarding actual improvements in both decisions made by clinicians and service outcomes experienced by patients and clients is at the heart of clinical utility, whether the focus is on diagnostic systems (First et al. 2004, Kendell & Jablensky 2003), assessment tools (Hunsley & Bailey 1999, McFall 2005), or intervention strategies (Am. Psychol. Assoc. Presid. Task Force Evid.-Based Pract. 2006).

Without a doubt, recent decades have witnessed considerable advances in the quality and quantity of assessment tools available for studying both normal and abnormal human functioning. On the other hand, despite thousands of studies on the reliability and validity of psychological instruments, very little evidence exists that psychological assessment data have any functional relation to the enhanced provision and outcome of clinical services. Indeed, the Lima et al. (2005) study described above is one of the few examples in which an assessment tool has been examined for evidence of utility. However, a truly evidence-based approach to clinical assessment requires not only psychometric evidence of the soundness of instruments and strategies, but also data on the fundamental question of whether or not the assessment enterprise itself makes a difference with respect to the accuracy, outcome, or efficiency of clinical activities.

One exception to this general state of affairs can be found in the literature on the Outcome Questionnaire-45 (OQ-45). The OQ-45 measures symptoms of distress, interpersonal relations, and social functioning, and has been shown repeatedly to have good psychometric characteristics, including sensitivity to treatment-related change (Vermeersch et al. 2000, 2004). Lambert et al. (2003) conducted a meta-analysis of three large-scale studies (totaling more than 2500 adult clients) in which feedback on session-by-session OQ-45 data from clients receiving treatment was obtained and then, depending on the experimental condition, was either provided or not provided to the treating clinicians. In the clinician feedback condition, the extent of the feedback was very limited, involving simply an indication of whether clients, based on normative data, were making adequate treatment gains, making less-than-adequate treatment gains, or experiencing so few benefits from treatment that they were at risk for negative treatment outcomes. By the end of treatment, in the no-feedback/treatment-as-usual condition, based on OQ-45 data, 21% of clients had experienced a deterioration of functioning and 21% had improved in their functioning. In contrast, in the feedback condition, 13% had deteriorated and 35% had improved. In other words, compared with usual treatment, simply receiving general feedback on client functioning each session resulted in 38% fewer clients deteriorating in treatment and 67% more clients improving in treatment. Such data provide promising evidence of the clinical utility of the OQ-45 for treatment monitoring purposes and, more broadly, of the value of conducting utility-relevant research.

CONCLUSIONS

In this era of evidence-based practice, there is a need to re-emphasize the vital importance of using science to guide the selection and use of assessment methods and instruments. Assessment is often viewed as a clinical activity and service in its own right, but it is important not to overlook the interplay between assessment and intervention that is at the heart of providing evidence-based psychological treatments. This assessment-intervention dialectic, involving the use of assessment data both to plan treatment and to modify the treatment in response to changes in a client's functioning and goals (Weisz et al. 2004), means that EBA has relevance for a broad range of clinical services. Regardless of the purpose of the assessment, the central focus within EBA on the clinical application of assessment strategies makes the need for research on incremental validity and clinical utility abundantly clear. Moreover, although it is fraught with potential problems, the process of establishing criteria and standards for EBA has many benefits, including providing (*a*) useful information to clinicians on assessment options, (*b*) indications of where gaps in supporting scientific evidence may exist for currently available instruments, and (*c*) concrete guidance on essential psychometric criteria for the development and clinical use of assessment instruments.

SUMMARY POINTS

1. Evidence-based assessment (EBA) is a critical, but underappreciated, component of evidence-based practice in psychology.
2. Based on existing research, initial guidelines for EBAs have been delineated for many commonly encountered clinical conditions.
3. Researchers and clinicians are frequently faced with the decision of whether an instrument is good enough for the assessment task at hand. Thus, despite the challenges involved, steps must be taken to determine the psychometric properties that make a measure "good enough" for clinical use.

4. More research is needed on the influence of diversity parameters, such as age, gender, and ethnicity, on assessment methods and measures. Additionally, empirically derived principles that can serve as a guide in determining which elements of diversity are likely to be of particular importance for a given clinical case or situation.
5. A growing body of research addresses the optimal manner for combining data from multiple instruments and from multiple sources. Such research can inform the optimal use of assessment data for various clinical purposes.
6. Clinical utility is emerging as a key consideration in the development of diagnostic systems, assessment, and intervention. The utility of psychological assessment, and of EBA itself, requires much greater empirical attention than has been the case to date.
7. Although a challenging enterprise due to the scope of the assessment literature, the strategies, methods, and technologies needed to develop and maintain EBA guidelines are available and can be used to advance the evidence-based practice of psychology.

LITERATURE CITED

Achenbach TM. 2005. Advancing assessment of children and adolescents: commentary on evidence-based assessment of child and adolescent disorders. *J. Clin. Child Adolesc. Psychol.* 34:541–47

Achenbach TM, Rescorla LA, Ivanova MY. 2005. International cross-cultural consistencies and variations in child and adolescent psychopathology. In *Comprehensive Handbook of Multicultural School Psychology*, ed. CL Frisby, CR Reynolds, Cecil R, pp. 674–709. Hoboken, NJ: Wiley

Ackerman MJ, Ackerman MC. 1997. Custody evaluation practices: a survey of experienced professionals (revisited). *Prof. Psychol. Res. Pract.* 28:137–45

Agency Healthc. Res. Qual. 2002. Criteria for determining disability in speech-language disorders. *AHRQ Publ. No. 02-E009*. Rockville, MD: AHRQ

Alvidrez J, Azocar F, Miranda J. 1996. Demystifying the concept of ethnicity for psychotherapy researchers. *J. Consult. Clin. Psychol.* 64:903–8

Am. Educ. Res. Assoc., Am. Psychol. Assoc., Natl. Counc. Meas. Educ. 1999. *Standards for Educational and Psychological Testing*. Washington, DC: Am. Educ. Res. Assoc. 194 pp.

Am. Psychiatr. Assoc. 2000. *Handbook of Psychiatric Measures*. Washington, DC: Am. Psychiatr. Publ. 848 pp.

Am. Psychiatr. Assoc. 2006. *Practice Guideline for the Psychiatric Evaluation of Adults*. 2nd ed. **http://www.psych.org/psych_pract/treatg/pg/PsychEval2ePG_04–28–06.pdf**

Am. Psychol. Assoc. 1994. Guidelines for child custody evaluations in divorce proceedings. *Am. Psychol.* 49:677–80

Am. Psychol. Assoc. Presid. Task Force Evid.-Based Pract. 2006. Evidence-based practice in psychology. *Am. Psychol.* 61:271–85

States how evidence-based practices can be operationalized within professional psychology.

Antony MM, Barlow DH, eds. 2002. *Handbook of Assessment and Treatment Planning for Psychological Disorders*. New York: Guilford

Antony MM, Rowa K. 2005. Evidence-based assessment of anxiety disorders in adults. *Psychol. Assess.* 17:256–66

Bagby RM, Marshall MD, Bacchiochi JR. 2005. The validity and clinical utility of the MMPI-2 Malingering Depression scale. *J. Personal. Assess.* 85:304–11

Barkham M, Margison F, Leach C, Lucock M, Mellor-Clark J, et al. 2001. Service profiling and outcomes benchmarking using the CORE-OM: toward practice-based evidence in the psychological therapies. *J. Consult. Clin. Psychol.* 69:184–96

Bickman L, Rosof-Williams J, Salzerm MS, Summerfelt WT, Noser K, et al. 2000. What information do clinicians value for monitoring adolescent client progress and outcomes? *Prof. Psychol. Res. Pract.* 31:70–74

Blanton H, Jaccard J. 2006. Arbitrary metrics in psychology. *Am. Psychol.* 61:27–41

Camara WJ, Nathan JS, Puente AE. 2000. Psychological test usage: implications in professional psychology. *Prof. Psychol. Res. Pract.* 31:141–54

Cashel ML. 2002. Child and adolescent psychological assessment: current clinical practices and the impact of managed care. *Prof. Psychol. Res. Pract.* 33:446–53

Charter RA. 2003. A breakdown of reliability coefficients by test type and reliability method, and the clinical implications of low reliability. *J. Gen. Psychol.* 130:290–304

Crick NR, Nelson DA. 2002. Relational and physical victimization within friendships: Nobody told me there'd be friends like these. *J. Abnorm. Child Psychol.* 30:599–607

De Los Reyes A, Kazdin AE. 2005. Informant discrepancies in the assessment of childhood psychopathology: a critical review, theoretical framework, and recommendations for further study. *Psychol. Bull.* 131:483–509

Summarizes research on differences in data provided by multiple informants and provides guidance on how to conceptualize and use these different perspectives.

First MB, Pincus HA, Levine JB, Williams JBW, Ustun B, Peele R. 2004. Clinical utility as a criterion for revising psychiatric diagnoses. *Am. J. Psychiatry* 161:946–54

Presents the case for attending to clinical utility in the development and use of diagnostic criteria.

Flanagan DP, Kaufman AS. 2004. *Essentials of WISC-IV Assessment.* New York: Wiley

Fletcher JM, Francis DJ, Morris RD, Lyon GR. 2005. Evidence-based assessment of learning disabilities in children and adolescents. *J. Clin. Child Adolesc. Psychol.* 34:506–22

Garb HN. 2003. Incremental validity and the assessment of psychopathology in adults. *Psychol. Assess.* 15:508–20

Garland AF, Kruse M, Aarons GA. 2003. Clinicians and outcome measurement: What's the use? *J. Behav. Health Serv. Res.* 30:393–405

Geisinger KF. 1994. Cross-cultural normative assessment: translation and adaptation issues influencing the normative interpretation of assessment instruments. *Psychol. Assess.* 6:304–12

Groth-Marnat G. 2003. *Handbook of Psychological Assessment.* Hoboken, NJ: Wiley. 4th ed.

Hatfield DR, Ogles BM. 2004. The use of outcome measures by psychologists in clinical practice. *Prof. Psychol. Res. Pract.* 35:485–91

Hayes SC, Nelson RO, Jarrett RB. 1987. The treatment utility of assessment: a functional approach to evaluating treatment quality. *Am. Psychol.* 42:963–74

Discusses the importance of evaluating the value of assessment data in terms of their impact on the outcomes of psychological services.

Haynes SN, Lench HC. 2003. Incremental validity of new clinical assessment measures. *Psychol. Assess.* 15:456–66

Heinemann AW. 2005. Putting outcome measurement in context: a rehabilitation psychology perspective. *Rehab. Psychol.* 50:6–14

Horvath LS, Logan TK, Walker R. 2002. Child custody cases: a content analysis of evaluations in practice. *Prof. Psychol. Res. Pract.* 33:557–63

Hunsley J. 2002. Psychological testing and psychological assessment: a closer examination. *Am. Psychol.* 57:139–40

Hunsley J, Bailey JM. 1999. The clinical utility of the Rorschach: unfulfilled promises and an uncertain future. *Psychol. Assess.* 11:266–77

Hunsley J, Bailey JM. 2001. Whither the Rorschach? An analysis of the evidence. *Psychol. Assess.* 13:472–85

Hunsley J, Crabb R, Mash EJ. 2004. Evidence-based clinical assessment. *Clin. Psychol.* 57(3):25–32

Presents the case for why evidence-based assessment is needed in clinical psychology and some of the training-related challenges in ensuring the provision of evidence-based assessments.

Hunsley J, Lee CM, Wood J. 2003. Controversial and questionable assessment techniques. In *Science and Pseudoscience in Clinical Psychology*, ed. SO Lilienfeld, SJ Lynn, J Lohr, pp. 39–76. New York: Guilford

Hunsley J, Mash EJ. 2005. Introduction to the special section on developing guidelines for the evidence-based assessment (EBA) of adult disorders. *Psychol. Assess.* 17:251–55

Hunsley J, Mash EJ, eds. 2006. *A Guide to Assessments That Work*. New York: Oxford Univ. Press. In press

Hunsley J, Meyer GJ. 2003. The incremental validity of psychological testing and assessment: conceptual, methodological, and statistical issues. *Psychol. Assess.* 15:446–55

Provides an overview of numerous considerations in testing for, and using information about, incremental validity.

Johnston C, Murray C. 2003. Incremental validity in the psychological assessment of children and adolescents. *Psychol. Assess.* 15:496–507

Joiner TE, Walker RL, Pettit JW, Perez M, Cukrowicz KC. 2005. Evidence-based assessment of depression in adults. *Psychol. Assess.* 17:267–77

Joneis T, Turkheimer E, Oltmanns TF. 2000. Psychometric analysis of racial differences on the Maudsley Obsessional Compulsive Inventory. *Assessment* 7:247–58

Kaufman AS, Lichtenberger EO. 1999. *Essentials of WAIS-III Assessment*. New York: Wiley

Kazdin AE. 2005. Evidence-based assessment for children and adolescents: issues in measurement development and clinical applications. *J. Clin. Child Adolesc. Psychol.* 34:548–58

Kazdin AE. 2006. Arbitrary metrics: implications for identifying evidence-based treatments. *Am. Psychol.* 61:42–49

Kendell R, Jablensky A. 2003. Distinguishing between the validity and utility of psychiatric diagnoses. *Am. J. Psychiatry* 160:4–12

Kessler RC, Chiu WT, Demler O, Walters EE. 2005. Prevalence, severity, and Comorbidity of 12-month DSM-IV disorders in the National Comorbidity Survey Replication. *Arch. Gen. Psychiatry* 62:617–27

Klein DN, Dougherty LR, Olino TM. 2005. Toward guidelines for evidence-based assessment of depression in children and adolescents. *J. Clin. Child Adolesc. Psychol.* 34:412–32

Kraemer HC, Wilson KA, Hayward C. 2006. Lifetime prevalence and pseudocomorbidity in psychiatric research. *Arch. Gen. Psychiatry* 63:604–8

Krueger RF, Chentsova-Dutton YE, Markon KE, Goldberg D, Ormel J. 2003. A cross-cultural study of the structure of comorbidity among common psychopathological syndromes in the general health care setting. *J. Abnorm. Psychol.* 112:437–47

Krueger RF, Markon KE. 2006. Reinterpreting comorbidity: a model-based approach to understanding and classifying psychopathology. *Annu. Rev. Clin. Psychol.* 2:111–33

Lally SJ. 2001. Should human figure drawings be admitted into the court? *J. Personal. Assess.* 76:135–49

Lambert MJ, Whipple JL, Hawkings EJ, Vermeersch D, Nielsen SL, Smart DW. 2003. Is it time to track patient outcome on a routine basis? A meta-analysis. *Clin. Psychol. Sci. Pract.* 10:288–301

Presents meta-analytic data illustrating the value of treatment monitoring data in improving psychotherapy services.

Lima EN, Stanley S, Kaboski B, Reitzel LR, Richey JA, et al. 2005. The incremental validity of the MMPI-2: When does therapist access not enhance treatment outcome? *Psychol. Assess.* 17:462–68

Mash EJ, Barkley RA, eds. 2006. *Assessment of Childhood Disorders*. New York: Guilford. 4th ed. In press

Mash EJ, Hunsley J. 2005. Evidence-based assessment of child and adolescent disorders: issues and challenges. *J. Clin. Child Adolesc. Psychol.* 34:362–79

Discusses key considerations in the development of guidelines for evidence-based assessment.

MATRICS. 2006. Results of the MATRICS RAND panel meeting: average medians for the categories of each candidate test. **http://www.matrics.ucla.edu/matrics-psychometrics-frame.htm**

McFall RM. 2005. Theory and utility—key themes in evidence-based assessment: comment on the special section. *Psychol. Assess.* 17:312–23
McGrath RE. 2001. Toward more clinically relevant assessment research. *J. Personal. Assess.* 77:307–32
McMahon RJ, Frick PJ. 2005. Evidence-based assessment of conduct problems in children and adolescents. *J. Clin. Child Adolesc. Psychol.* 34:477–505
Meyer GJ, Archer RP. 2001. The hard science of Rorschach research: What do we know and where do we go? *Psychol. Assess.* 13:486–502
Meyer GJ, Finn SE, Eyde L, Kay GG, Moreland KL, et al. 2001. Psychological testing and psychological assessment: a review of evidence and issues. *Am. Psychol.* 56:128–65
Murray HA. 1943. *Thematic Apperception Test Manual.* Cambridge, MA: Harvard Univ. Press
Nelson-Gray RO. 2003. Treatment utility of psychological assessment. *Psychol. Assess.* 15:521–31

Summarizes evidence on the extent to which assessment data meaningfully influence the provision of psychological treatments.

Newman DL, Moffitt TE, Caspi A, Silva PA. 1998. Comorbid mental disorders: implications for treatment and sample selection. *J. Abnorm. Psychol.* 107:305–11
Nezu AM, McClure KS, Ronan GR, Meadows EA. 2000. *Practitioner's Guide to Empirically Based Measures of Depression*. Hingham, MA: Kluwer Plenum
Nunnally JC, Bernstein IH. 1994. *Psychometric Theory*. New York: McGraw-Hill. 752 pp. 3rd ed.
Ozonoff S, Goodlin-Jones BL, Solomon M. 2005. Evidence-based assessment of autism spectrum disorders in children and adolescents. *J. Clin. Child Adolesc. Psychol.* 34:523–40
Pelham WE, Fabiano GA, Massetti GM. 2005. Evidence-based assessment of attention deficit hyperactivity disorder in children and adolescents. *J. Clin. Child Adolesc. Psychol.* 34:449–76
Piotrowski C. 1999. Assessment practices in the era of managed care: current status and future directions. *J. Clin. Psychol.* 55:787–96
Power TJ, Andrews TJ, Eiraldi RB, Doherty BJ, Ikeda MJ, et al. 1998. Evaluating attention deficit hyperactivity disorder using multiple informants: the incremental utility of combining teach with parent reports. *Psychol. Assess.* 10:250–60
Robinson JP, Shaver PR, Wrightsman LS. 1991. Criteria for scale selection and evaluation. In *Measures of Personality and Social Psychological Attitudes*, ed. JP Robinson, PR Shaver, LS Wrightsman, pp. 1–16. New York: Academic
Rossini ED, Moretti RJ. 1997. Thematic Apperception Test (TAT) interpretation: practice recommendations from a survey of clinical psychology doctoral programs accredited by the American Psychological Association. *Prof. Psychol. Res. Pract.* 28:393–98
Sackett DL, Rosenberg WMC, Gray JAM, Haynes RB, Richardson WS. 1996. Evidence based medicine: what it is and what it isn't. *Br. Med. J.* 312:71–72
Schene AH, Koeter M, van Wijngaarden B, Knudsen HC, Leese M, et al. 2000. Methodology of a multi-site reliability study. *Br. J. Psychiatry* 177(Suppl. 39):15–20
Schmidt FL, Le H, Ilies R. 2003. Beyond alpha: an empirical examination of the effects of different sources of measurement error on reliability estimates for measures of individual differences constructs. *Psychol. Methods* 8:206–24
Sechrest L. 1963. Incremental validity: a recommendation. *Educ. Psychol. Meas.* 23:152–58
Seto MC. 2005. Is more better? Combining actuarial risk scales to predict recidivism among adult sex offenders. *Psychol. Assess.* 17:156–67
Silverman WK, Ollendick TH. 2005. Evidence-based assessment of anxiety and its disorders in children and adolescents. *J. Clin. Child Adolesc. Psychol.* 34:380–411
Smith DA. 2002. Validity and values: monetary and otherwise. *Am. Psychol.* 57:136–37
Snyder DK, Heyman RE, Haynes SN. 2005. Evidence-based approaches to assessing couple distress. *Psychol. Assess.* 17:288–307

Spangler WD. 1992. Validity of questionnaire and TAT measures of need for achievement: two meta-analyses. *Psychol. Bull.* 112:140–54
Streiner DL. 2003. Starting at the beginning: an introduction to coefficient alpha and internal consistency. *J. Personal. Assess.* 80:99–103
Streiner DL, Norman GR. 2003. *Health Measurement Scales: A Practical Guide to Their Development and Use*. New York: Oxford Univ. Press. 283 pp. 3rd ed.
Stricker G, Gold JR. 1999. The Rorschach: towards a nomothetically based, idiographically applicable configural model. *Psychol. Assess.* 11:240–50
Vane JR. 1981. The Thematic Apperception Test: a review. *Clin. Psychol. Rev.* 1:319–36
van Widenfelt BM, Treffers PDA, de Beurs E, Siebelink BM, Koudijs E. 2005. Translation and cross-cultural adaptation of assessment instruments used in psychological research with children and families. *Clin. Child Fam. Psychol. Rev.* 8:135–47
Vermeersch DA, Lambert MJ, Burlingame GM. 2000. Outcome Questionnaire: item sensitivity to change. *J. Personal. Assess.* 74:242–61
Vermeersch DA, Whipple JL, Lambert MJ, Hawkins EJ, Burchfield CM, Okiishi JC. 2004. Outcome Questionnaire: Is it sensitive to changes in counseling center clients? *J. Counsel. Psychol.* 51:38–49
Watkins MW. 2003. IQ subtest analysis: clinical acumen or clinical illusion? *Sci. Rev. Mental Health Pract.* 2:118–41
Weisz JR, Chu BC, Polo AJ. 2004. Treatment dissemination and evidence-based practice: strengthening intervention through clinician-researcher collaboration. *Clin. Psychol. Sci. Pract.* 11:300–7
Widiger TA, Clark LA. 2000. Toward DSM-V and the classification of psychopathology. *Psychol. Bull.* 126:946–63
Widiger TA, Samuel DB. 2005. Evidence-based assessment of personality disorders. *Psychol. Assess.* 17:278–87
Wolraich ML, Lambert W, Doffing MA, Bickman L, Simmons T, Worley K. 2003. Psychometric properties of the Vanderbilt ADHD diagnostic parent rating scale in a referred population. *J. Pediatr. Psychol.* 28:559–68
Wood JM, Garb HN, Lilienfeld SO, Nezworski MT. 2002. Clinical assessment. *Annu. Rev. Psychol.* 53:519–43
Wood JM, Nezworski MT, Lilienfeld SO, Garb HN. 2003. *What's Wrong with the Rorschach?* San Francisco: Jossey-Bass
Youngstrom EA, Findling RL, Calabrese JR, Gracious BL, Demeter C, et al. 2004. Comparing the diagnostic accuracy of six potential screening instruments for bipolar disorder in youths aged 5 to 17 years. *J. Am. Acad. Child Adolesc. Psychiatry* 43:847–58
Youngstrom EA, Findling RL, Youngstrom JK, Calabrese JR. 2005. Toward an evidence-based assessment of pediatric bipolar disorder. *J. Clin. Child Adolesc. Psychol.* 34:433–48

Internet Methods for Delivering Behavioral and Health-Related Interventions (eHealth)

Victor Strecher

Center for Health Communications Research, University of Michigan, Ann Arbor, Michigan 48109-0471, and HealthMedia, Inc., Ann Arbor, Michigan 48104; email: strecher@umich.edu

Annu. Rev. Clin. Psychol. 2007. 3:53–76

First published online as a Review in Advance on January 2, 2007

The *Annual Review of Clinical Psychology* is online at http://clinpsy.annualreviews.org

This article's doi:
10.1146/annurev.clinpsy.3.022806.091428

1548-5943/07/0427-0053$20.00

Key Words

World Wide Web, tailored, interactive health communication, health behavior

Abstract

Emerging communications technologies allow us to potentially reach more individuals with effective health-related advice and information at a very low cost. As we begin a new era of "personalized medicine," advances in consumer health informatics will parallel and eventually merge with those being made in bioinformatics (e.g., genomic information), medical informatics (e.g., electronic medical records), and public health informatics (e.g., disease surveillance). This article discusses access, use, quality, and types of eHealth programming with a focus on the Internet as the initial instantiation of this programming. Also discussed are criteria relevant to the dissemination of eHealth programming in real-world settings. Finally, possible directions for future eHealth research are presented.

Contents

INTRODUCTION

In 1995, former U.S. Surgeon General C. Everett Koop stated, "Cutting-edge technology, especially in communication and information transfer, will enable the greatest advances yet in public health. Eventually, we will have access to health information 24 hours a day, 7 days a week, encouraging personal wellness and prevention, and leading to better informed decisions about health care" (Koop 1995). Nearly a decade later, an emerging "eHealth" field is charting the course predicted by Dr. Koop.

Although eHealth has been defined in numerous ways (Oh et al. 2005), a generally accepted definition proposed by Eng (2001) focuses on the use of emerging interactive technologies (such as the Internet, CD-ROM, personal digital assistants, interactive voice response, and computer kiosks) to enable disease prevention and disease management. For the purposes of this review, we focus largely on Internet-based eHealth programming. The Internet appears to have the greatest near-term potential as an eHealth tool for health-related behavior change and decision-making. The variety of multimedia, interactivity, and connectivity formats offered by the Internet is extensive. Reasons for delivering Internet-based interventions include reduced delivery costs, convenience to users, timeliness, reduction of stigma, increased user and supplier control of the intervention, and reduction of geographically based as well as time- and mobility-based isolation barriers (Griffiths et al. 2006).

This article examines current evidence for, and the promise of, Internet methods for delivering behavioral and health-related interventions. Internet-based eHealth is considered in terms of its reach, ability to collect valid information, and effectiveness. Since Internet-based eHealth interventions must interact, by Eng's (2001) definition, in some manner with the user, different models of interaction are discussed. Barriers to disseminating eHealth interventions are also examined. Finally, future directions for eHealth are explored, with a focus on improvements in content, data collection, and emerging intersections with medical informatics, public health informatics, and bioinformatics systems.

Table 1 Health topics searched online (reproduced from Fox 2005)

Health topic	Percentage of Internet users who have searched for information on the topic	
	2002	2004
Specific disease or medical problem	63	66
Certain medical treatment or procedure	47	51
Diet, nutrition, vitamins, or nutritional supplements	44	51
Exercise or fitness	36	42
Prescription or over-the-counter drugs	34	40
Health insurance	25	31
Alternative treatments or medicines	28	30
Depression, anxiety, stress, or mental health issues	21	23
Experimental treatments or medicines	18	23
Environmental health hazards	17	18
Immunizations or vaccinations	13	16
Sexual health information	10	11
Problems with drugs or alcohol	8	8
How to quit smoking	6	7

Source: Pew Internet & American Life Project December 2002 Survey (N = 1220) and November 2004 Survey (N = 537); **http://www.pewinternet.org.** Margin of error for comparing the two samples is +/− 4.6%.

THE REACH OF INTERACTIVE HEALTH COMMUNICATIONS

Probably the most compelling support for Dr. Koop's prediction is the growth of Internet access and its use for health purposes. The proportion of adults in the United States with Web access now exceeds 78% (Center for the Digital Future 2005). The number of Americans using the Internet at home has increased from 47% in 2000 to 66% in 2005 (Center for the Digital Future 2005). The largest increases in Internet access are among low-income and older Americans. The University of Southern California Annenberg School's Center for the Digital Future (2005) reported that 61% of respondents with incomes of less than $30,000 and 75% of respondents aged 56–65 were using the Internet in 2005.

The Pew Internet and American Life Project 2004 survey of American adults with access to the Internet found that 79% of respondents (roughly 95 million) reported using the Web to obtain health information (Fox 2005). **Table 1** presents percentages of Internet users searching for specific health topics.

Individuals seeking health information on the Internet were far more likely than in the past to have higher-speed broadband Internet access. High-speed access is increasing rapidly: In 2006, 72% of active Internet users in the United States were connected via broadband, up from 57% in 2005 (Nielsen/NetRatings 2006).

Use of the Web for prevention is lower than for treatment issues but is nonetheless significant: 51% of respondents with Internet access reported using the Web for information about diet, nutrition, vitamins, or nutritional supplements; 42% for information about exercise or fitness; and 7% for information about how to quit smoking. Although 7% of all adult Internet users may seem to be a small proportion, this amounts to more than 10 million individuals and compares favorably with the estimate that 800,000 smokers in the United States call quitlines each year for cessation advice (Ossip-Klein & McIntosh 2003).

In all of these areas, more females than males sought Web-based information. Seekers of Web-based health information, in comparison with nonseekers, were more likely to be better educated, to have higher incomes, and to be younger. Yet elderly patients, even those without Internet experience, appear to participate readily in Internet-based self-management programs (Feil et al. 2000, Gustafson et al. 1998, McTavish et al. 1995). Many senior centers around the country now possess Internet-based information and resource programming that allows requests for information delivered via email; in addition, these facilities provide access to Web pages, online databases, document downloads, Web links, bulletin boards, and chat rooms. Organizations such as Never 2 Late and ClickSilver provide Internet access and training for seniors. Programs to teach cancer patients to use the Internet have had a very positive reception, with significant rates of subsequent use (Edgar et al. 2002).

In a study examining cancer information source use over time (Satterlund et al. 2003), 40% of breast cancer patients cited the Internet as a source of information 16 months after diagnosis. The Internet was used more frequently at this period than were books, videos, volunteers, support groups, and telephone information services. Specifically, participants in the Satterland et al. (2003) study reported using the Internet at least four times more than they used support groups and at least five times more than the National Cancer Institute's Cancer Information Service to obtain cancer information.

Internet access and use is exceptionally high among teens (U.S. Census Bureau 2001) and is now considered an important method of reaching teens with health-related information (Griffiths et al. 2006). Popular subjects among both upper-income and ethnically diverse and disadvantaged high school girls, for example, include disease-related information, diet and nutrition, exercise and fitness, sex, alcohol and drug abuse, mental health, medicines, and violence (Borzekowski & Rickert 2000). Most girls in this survey felt it was particularly important to have access to contraceptive and diet/nutrition information. Yet Internet access statistics belie some significant barriers to teens seeking important health information. A lack of privacy, not necessarily of an Internet site, but rather of the physical surrounding of the computer that is used to access the Internet, poses a barrier to finding sensitive information (Skinner et al. 2003). Other barriers to access identified by Skinner and colleagues (2003) include Internet filtering software, which often removes access to sensitive health information (such as human sexuality) (Richardson et al. 2002), an insufficient amount of time allocated to Internet use in schools, and low bandwidth.

Why do people use the Internet rather than other sources of health information? A Pew Foundation study (Rainie & Packel 2001) found that 93% of those using the Internet for health information thought it was important to obtain the information at any hour. Despite concerns about the cold nature of computer technology (e.g., Gregorc 1985), a very important advantage of eHealth programs appears to be their impersonal qualities. Eighty percent of respondents in the Pew study (Rainie & Packel 2001) found the Internet particularly useful because they could obtain health information anonymously, without having to talk with anyone. Cigarette smokers who use the Web have also described the desire for anonymity and a discomfort in speaking with human counselors (Frisby et al. 2002). As a participant in the Frisby et al. (2002) study stated, "You don't have to speak to people who make you feel bad." Similarly, a subject in the Skinner et al. (2003) study reported, ". . . especially if it's something very personal like it avoids confrontation and you don't have to be like talking to a public health nurse or doctor about it, you can just like [find it]."

A prerequisite for interactivity is the ability to understand the needs of the user, and now more than a decade of studies have demonstrated that well-designed computer-based assessments can at least rival the validity of assessments using paper-and-pencil methods, trained interviewers, or clinicians (e.g., Alemi et al. 1994, Hasley 1995, Johnson et al. 2001). In many studies, eHealth assessments identify a greater proportion of individuals reporting unsafe sexual behavior (e.g., Kissinger et al. 1999, Locke et al. 1992, Metzger et al. 2000, Turner et al. 1998), drug use, and drug-related behaviors (e.g., Gribble et al. 2000, Metzger et al. 2000). For example, sexually active women were 9 times as likely to report having had anal sex to an audio computer-assisted self-interview (A-CASI) than to a trained human interviewer. In their responses to an A-CASI versus a traditional self-administered questionnaire, adolescent males were more than 9 times as likely to report having ever shared a needle for street drug use, more than 13 times as likely to report having had sex with someone who shoots drugs, and nearly 8 times as likely to report having had receptive anal sex with another male (Turner et al. 1998). Blood donors were more than 30 times more likely to receive a positive screening for HIV-related factors through a computer interview than through standard Red Cross elicitation procedures, which included both written questionnaires and face-to-face interviews (Locke et al. 1992).

Participants in such studies generally report greater preference for computer-based questionnaires (e.g., Bernhardt et al. 2001, Paperny et al. 1990). Acceptability of computer-based methods of data collection appears to be high among patient (Velikova et al. 1999) and low-income populations (e.g., Bernhardt et al. 2001, Bock et al. 1999). Moreover, in a general population survey of HIV risk behaviors, internal consistency between questionnaire items was found to be higher with computer-assisted than paper-and-pencil interviews, and item nonresponse was found to be lower (Johnson et al. 2001).

Although many reasons exist for using the Internet for advice and assistance in changing health-related behaviors, high attrition rates from Internet-based behavior change programs are well documented (Tate & Zabinski 2004). Lack of program use, however, may not necessarily be an indicator of failure. Individuals who are successfully changing their behavior may correctly believe that program use is no longer relevant or important. For example, smokers who have successfully quit may not wish to be reminded of their smoking behavior. In other behaviors, continued program use may be critical. Clarke and colleagues (2005) found that adding reminders (either postcards or brief telephone calls) to an Internet-based depression skills program resulted in significant, positive effects of the program, whereas a previous trial with no reminders found no program effect.

The results reported in this section suggest the need for further research examining the types of individuals who use the Internet for health-behavior change and decision-making assistance, their patterns of use, outcomes based on these use patterns, and methods of enhancing use.

THE QUALITY AND EFFECTIVENESS OF INTERACTIVE HEALTH COMMUNICATIONS

During the "dot-com boom" (roughly 1997–1999), 85% of online health-information seekers were concerned about the reliability of information obtained through the Internet (Fox & Rainie 2000). This concern was well founded. In a review of 55 studies examining the quality of online health information for consumers, Eysenbach and colleagues (2002) found quality to be a consistent problem. For example, in their study of the quality of online information related to Ewing's sarcoma, Biermann and colleagues (1999) found tremendous variation in reported survival rates (5% to 85%)—information that could dramatically alter the treatment decisions of the patients' parents. Noteworthy is their finding of clearly erroneous information even in what are normally considered credible sources, such as Encyclopaedia

Britannica's Web page. It has been reported that patients have to sort through a "staggering" amount of misinformation related to complementary and alternative cancer treatments (Matthews et al. 2003), some of which could lead to premature death (see, e.g., Hainer et al. 2000).

The impression of the Internet as a useful source of health information reached its nadir when a Cochrane meta-analysis of interventions using interactive health communication applications (IHCAs) reported an overall negative effect of IHCAs among users with chronic diseases (Murray et al. 2004). This meta-analysis turned out to be blatantly flawed, with at least 8 of the 11 study outcomes reversed after careful review (Eysenbach & Kummervold 2005), and the initial finding of a negative effect of IHCAs was reversed to an overall positive effect. Within 13 days of a press release campaign by the Cochrane publication, the authors retracted the review. In fact, the revised version of the Cochrane publication concludes that IHCAs improve knowledge, social support, self-efficacy, health behaviors, and clinical outcomes of users with chronic disease (Murray et al. 2006).

The damage of the initial review, however, appeared to be done when headlines, including "Internet Makes Us Sick," "Is Cybermedicine Killing You?" and "Click to Get Sick?" emerged in major media channels. These headlines, by and large, were not retracted or corrected by the press (Rada 2005). Moreover, media channels either reported press release statements verbatim, such as "People who use their computers to find health information often wind up in worse condition than if they had listened to their doctor," or condensed them into even stronger tones, including, "Some people with chronic health problems who seek online advice would be better off just listening to their doctors," or "Patient, don't try to heal thyself" (cited in Eysenbach & Kummervold 2005). These statements were particularly disturbing to eHealth experts, who generally have considered the Internet to be a potentially empowering tool for consumers and patients (Eysenbach & Kummervold 2005).

Although randomized trials of Internet-based programs still represent an emerging area of research, positive results have been demonstrated for smoking cessation (Etter & Laszlo 2005, Strecher et al. 2005, Swartz et al. 2006), hazardous drinking (Kypri et al. 2004), weight management (Rothert et al. 2006, Tate et al. 2001, Williamson et al. 2005), diabetes (Glasgow et al. 2003), asthma (Krishna et al. 2003), tinnitus (Andersson & Kaldo 2004), stress (Hasson et al. 2005), anxiety and depression (Christensen et al. 2006, Clarke et al. 2005, Marks et al. 2003), complicated grief (Wagner et al. 2006), encopresis (Ritterband et al. 2003), chronic back pain (Buhrman et al. 2004), HIV (Gustafson et al. 1999), insomnia (Strom et al. 2004), headache (Strom et al. 2000), and multiple risk factors (Kypri & McAnally 2005). These trials represent a mix of Internet-only and counselor-mediated interventions. A detailed discussion of the relative advantages and disadvantages of these delivery modalities can be found in Tate & Zabinski (2004).

Some well-designed evaluations of well-conceived Internet-based interventions have found no effect (e.g., Marks et al. 2006, Patten et al. 2006). Nonetheless, the majority of Internet-based interventions for health behavior change and health-related decision-making have found positive psychological, behavioral, and clinical outcomes (Cavanagh & Shapiro 2004, Murray et al. 2006, Tate & Zabinski 2004).

Although the effectiveness of many interactive health communications programs has been demonstrated in randomized controlled trials, significant room for improvement exists in real-world interventions. In a systematic analysis of the content, quality, and usability of smoking cessation treatments on the Internet, Bock and colleagues (2004) found that 80% of such sites failed to cover one or more key components of recommended cessation treatment guidelines, with the interactive nature of the Internet generally ignored. A review of 24 Web sites designed to promote physical activity (Doshi et al. 2003) found very low utilization of health behavior change theory and a lack of attention to assessment or feedback tailored to characteristics of the user.

During the dot-com boom, individuals with limited understanding of behavior change research and practice launched portals containing vast amounts of digitized information (often called "pamphletware" or "shovelware"). Most of these sites have gone out of business, but digital "pamphlet racks" persist as the most common and easily constructed form of Internet health site. It is unfortunate that even many of the Internet-based interventions used in research continue to be focused on these simple information-transfer models. As Cline & Haynes (2001) state in their appraisal of the field, "Much of the literature reviewed here focuses on the Internet as a high-tech conveyor in the rapid diffusion of information or health lessons. However, to do so is to ignore the very nature of the Internet." The Internet offers far more potential than simply that of a clearinghouse of health information or another form of mass media (Cassel et al. 1998, Neuhauser & Kreps 2003). Evaluation of the Internet's efficacy must be predicated on an understanding and classification of interventions that can be created from the interactive technologies.

One starting point is to consider the ways that the Internet can interact with the user. Four types of interactivity seem relevant: (*a*) user navigation, (*b*) collaborative filters, (*c*) expert systems, and (*d*) human-to-human interaction.

User Navigation (a Vast Library at Your Fingertips)

The interactive strategy most commonly employed on the Internet requires the user to search through the Internet, identifying what he or she considers the most relevant sites and information within those sites. Once in a site, the user searches for the information relevant to his or her needs and interests. A library is a relevant metaphor to this form of navigation. Similar to a library, the Internet has methods of searching for the large amount of available health information. Also like a library, however, the Internet doesn't automatically make available the best information or advice that an individual needs at a particular time. An expectation that users will create their own educational experiences is common on the Internet, but just as in a library, users might not know precisely what to search for or may fail to search in the right places (Eveland & Dunwoody 2002).

A number of studies in the educational literature have found that, when compared with fixed sequencing of instructional material, user control results in deviations from important information or methods of instruction (see Clark 1982 for a review) and subsequent lower performance (Coldevin et al. 1993, Steinberg 1977). For example, in an instructional math program, Ross & Rakow (1981) found that students who did not have control of the program performed better on the post-test than those who did have control. Similarly, in a study of biology students, Gay (1986) found that students who did not have control over sequencing or pace of instructional material performed better on the post-test than those who had control. Additionally, Gay found that those under the user-tailored environment avoided unfamiliar topics.

Users who begin a program with low levels of knowledge or ability appear to perform even more poorly in user-navigated environments (Gay 1986, Ross & Morrison 1989, Steinberg 1977). As Ross & Morrison (1989, p. 29) state, "In general, while high achievers seem capable of using most forms of learner control effectively, low achievers seem much less able to benefit from forms that require them to make decisions about instructional properties of a lesson (i.e., what, how and how much information is being taught)."

When these findings are applied to the area of IHC, it seems plausible that users with little prior knowledge or experience might experience less success with user-navigated IHC programming. Bhavnani and colleagues (2002) found that domain expertise is a critical factor in the use of the Web. Expert Web shoppers were far less efficient or accurate in obtaining medical information than were medical librarians when both groups were asked to find the individuals who should and should not get the flu vaccine. Medical librarians, on the other hand, were far less efficient in finding a low-priced digital camera on the Web.

The experiment by Bhavnani and colleagues (2002) described above demonstrated that search strategies are specific to question domains. Beyond competent use of comprehensive search engines and portals, knowledge of how to search the Web is critical for efficient, accurate information acquisition. Bhavnani and colleagues (2006) therefore developed and pilot tested a prototypic system to deliver such strategic knowledge to novice users. This new class of Web site, entitled "strategy hub," is intended to provide the factual and procedural information used by experts to search for material in a specific domain such as health care.

The strategy hub prototype, built to develop knowledge of skin cancer prevention and treatment, allows a user to specify a question type by selecting a topic and type of cancer. This portal was developed after a taxonomy of real-world questions related to skin cancer was identified. The strategy hub provides users with strategies that are tailored to specific question types.

Future research in this area will include the development of similar taxonomies of real-world questions for other cancers, identification of commonalities in these taxonomies across different cancers, and identification of strategies that are specific to question types in the taxonomy. Tests are being conducted of the hypothesis that the factual and procedural knowledge provided by strategy portals will enable novice health care searchers, in comparison with searchers using general-purpose search engines, to more effectively obtain health care information.

Encouraging and teaching users to create their own experience has clear advantages. Users who have greater control will likely build self-efficacy from positive experiences. Moreover, users are likely to best understand their own needs. There is a reason, however, that individuals look to others, including laypeople and experts, for information and advice. IHC programming that provides guidance tailored to an assessment of needs and interests may help the user become more effective and efficient in this search process.

Collaborative Filtering (What Others Like You Are Doing)

It is common to use the actions and subsequent outcomes of peers to inform one's own decisions. A local bookseller may say, "I know six other customers like you who enjoy John Le Carré mysteries . . . they're now reading this new Tom Clancy novel." Using a similar approach, a collaborative filtering system on the Internet is able to inform you, "We have *six hundred thousand* other customers who, like you, enjoy John Le Carré mysteries . . . many of them are now reading this new Tom Clancy novel." Greater discrimination in filtering is possible with larger numbers of individuals, along with the potential for creating more useful advice.

Collaborative filtering in the health area could match the coping strategies, medical decisions, and preferences of similar others with the specific needs and interests of the user. Let us take, for example, an individual with a body mass index of 32 (obese). The person's physician suggests he goes on a diet. While the physician might normally say, "A couple of my patients have found that diet strategy X is worthwhile," a Web site using a collaborative filter could assess the patient's taste preferences and match them to a diet strategy found useful among others with similar taste preferences who are successfully managing their weight. This method of interaction could readily be developed to create dynamic, global communities that provide useful health advice and information.

Collaborative filtering programs, however, will also face a number of challenges (Claypool et al. 1999). First, early users have very few others with whom they can compare. Predictions of what the user needs will likely be inaccurate when only a few similar users exist. Second, it may be difficult to find other users matching in more than just a few domains. Finally, individuals who do not consistently agree or disagree with anyone else (so-called gray sheep in collaborative filtering; Claypool et al. 1999) will fail to receive consistently useful information from a collaborative filter.

Expert Systems (When You Need a Counselor)

A third interactive approach, closely approximating a counseling experience, is termed an "expert system." These systems, which have undergone more experimental research than any other computer-based system for health behavior change, attempt to apply an expert's assessment, decision rules, and feedback strategies to software. The expert systems tested in the health behavior area typically require (*a*) a collection of characteristics, at an individual level, relevant to the targeted behavior change (or movement through stages of change), (*b*) an algorithm that uses these data to generate messages tailored to the specific needs of the user, and (*c*) a feedback protocol that combines these messages in a clear, vivid manner. The inferences made from the data are an attempt to reflect standards of a human expert (Negotia 1985, Velicer 1993).

An expert system attempts to create an educational experience using methods similar to a real-world clinical encounter. A program participant may be asked to answer questions about issues such as personal and family health history, behavior triggers, barriers to success, readiness to change, and intrinsic and extrinsic motives for change (among many others). Selection of tailoring factors is based on two criteria: what is most important (predictive of behavior and behavior change) and what is most changeable (Green & Kreuter 1991). Selection of factors on which to tailor feedback to the user is one of the most important steps in the development of an expert system. As a result, expert systems are more likely to utilize a conceptual model of behavior change. A high proportion of recently developed, effective Internet-based programs, for example, utilize some form of cognitive-behavioral programming (e.g., Cavanagh & Shapiro 2004, Clarke et al. 2005, Proudfoot et al. 2004, Rothert et al. 2006, Strecher et al. 2005, Wagner et al. 2005).

Over the past ten years, expert-tailored print interventions for a variety of health-related behaviors have been developed and evaluated in diverse settings. A rapidly growing number of research studies have demonstrated that tailored expert system interventions are more effective than generic health education materials, even among underserved populations. These studies cover a range of topics, including smoking cessation, weight management, dietary fat reduction, fruit and vegetable intake, physical activity, and cancer screening (Brug 1999, Lancaster & Stead 2000, Skinner et al. 1999, Strecher 1999).

A generally positive body of evidence demonstrates the efficacy of print-based computer-tailored smoking cessation interventions in adults (Lancaster & Stead 2000, Strecher 1999, Velicer et al. 1999). In a Cochrane meta-analysis of smoking cessation materials developed by expert systems, Lancaster & Stead (2000) found an average odds ratio of 1.41 (CI: 1.14–1.75) for such materials compared with untailored or stage-matched materials.

A review of eight published studies assessing the impact of print-based expert systems concluded that these materials were more likely to be read, remembered, and experienced as more personally relevant than were standard, untailored print materials (Brug et al. 1999). Six of these studies found a significant effect on the reduction of fat intake, one on weight reduction, one on increased fiber intake, and two on fruit and vegetable intake. Two reported no significant effect on vegetable and fruit intake.

A commonly asked question is whether underserved individuals, particularly those with low literacy skills, will respond to tailored materials. A noteworthy study by Lipkus and colleagues (1999) found a significantly higher cessation rate among low-income and indigent African American smokers who received tailored smoking cessation materials plus provider advice versus those who received provider advice alone. These results were supported by Skinner and colleagues (1994), who found the greatest difference between tailored and untailored materials for mammography screening among African American women and women with low levels of education.

With their increasing reach and a greater prospect for interactivity and lower cost, expert systems delivered via the Internet offer significant potential for health-related behavior change and decision-making. Most print-based tailored interventions developed for research studies used little more than the mail merge feature available with most word processing software. Yet experts rarely respond in the simple, rote fashion of asking a question, then providing a static response to that question. A human expert would be more likely to attempt summarization and integration before addressing specific problems. For example, if a person cites many barriers to changing, an expert might initially say, "It sounds like you have lots of things keeping you from making this change. Let's look at them one by one." On the other hand, a person may have only one barrier that stands out significantly from any other barrier. This might elicit a summary comment of "It sounds like you have one thing that's really holding you back. Let's focus on this barrier."

Relational skills such as empathy, social dialogue, and nonverbal immediacy behaviors can also be integrated into Internet-based interfaces. Bickmore and colleagues (2005) found that the inclusion of relational behaviors in an automated longitudinal health behavior change intervention produced significant improvements in perceived trust, understanding, liking, respect, concern, and caring after 27 days of use. Moreover, the inclusion of relational behaviors enhanced the desire to continue working with the program. This finding may have significant implications for reducing attrition in Internet-based programs.

Human-to-Human Interaction (a Channel for Social Support)

Online support groups allow patients a convenient way to provide and receive informational and emotional support (Brennan & Fink 1997, Shaw et al. 2000, Tate & Zabinski 2004). The 24/7 accessibility to online support is considered a significant advantage to patients who, because of stress, pain, or the cancer treatment itself, have irregular sleeping habits. Patients report frequent use of discussion groups late at night (Shaw et al. 2000). Again, anonymity is a frequently cited benefit of computer-mediated groups. As one person in the Shaw et al. (2000) study states: "It's a gift to be able to tell people as much or as little as you want about yourself." Use of computer-mediated support services, however, has been found to be somewhat low among underserved populations, including minority and elderly patients (Gustafson et al. 1998).

In a review of ten studies of online cancer support groups, Klemm et al. (2003) found significant support for improved patient coping. However, Smaglik and colleagues (1998) found that, when given a menu of online discussion group and informational services, HIV+ individuals used the discussion group services more frequently than the information services but benefited from them less in terms of quality-of-life improvements. The researchers suggest, "Although discussion groups or chat-line functions are easy to provide, are often enormously popular, and can stimulate interest and user loyalty, they may not be sufficient to achieve many needed changes. Systems should probably also include a mix of information tools to help individuals take control of and improve their quality of life" (p. 67).

All of the published studies focused on the support of patients through computer-mediated groups. Many of these studies lacked controlled experimental designs. Many were conducted among small, homogeneous groups of patients, mainly white women (Klemm et al. 2003). Although it is an important issue to program developers, published research also has not examined the differential influence of peer-moderated versus professionally moderated groups (Till 2003).

No study could be found that examined the reach or effectiveness of online discussion groups for health-related behaviors (e.g., smoking cessation, dietary changes, or physical activity). One might expect low reach, similar to that found in face-to-face group programs (Chapman 1985), although the anonymity and convenience of online groups might encourage many who would not normally utilize a face-to-face group.

Another human-to-human interaction relevant to the Internet is with online therapists. This approach is similar to telephone hotlines with counselors or information specialists and could presumably (though this has not been examined in the literature) be proactive or reactive. Tate and colleagues (2003) found that an online counselor plus an Internet-based weight loss program had a significant impact on 12-month weight loss in comparison with the Internet program alone. The combination of minimal email therapy with an Internet-administered self-help program has also produced a significant effect on panic disorder when compared to an applied relaxation program (Carlbring et al. 2003). This study, however, did not include an Internet self-help-only group and therefore could not evaluate the independent effect of the email therapist.

Online Internet interactions with therapists offer significant convenience to both the user and the therapist. Although this issue has not yet been examined, online therapy may offer an added degree of anonymity and therefore the possibility of a more honest expression of behaviors, attitudes, and emotions. As is the case with telecounseling services, however, proactive online therapy could be difficult and expensive to scale with high quality to large populations.

Which Interactive Strategy to Use?

An exciting area for future research will be to tailor interactive strategy to specific characteristics of the user. Burger (1985) states, "The matching of the teaching style of the specific computer program and the learning style of the student must be considered" (p. 21). For example, in a study of computer-assisted instruction (CAI), Ross & Schulz (1999) found that subjects characterized as being "highly focused on the world of feeling and emotion... sensitive, spontaneous, attuned, person oriented" performed quite poorly in the structured CAI environment. These individuals, however, may still benefit from human-to-human interactions on the computer (Shaw et al. 2000). Beyond learning style, other individual characteristics that moderate the impact of different interactive strategies may include previous experience, perceived competence, actual ability, age, cultural factors, self-efficacy, need for cognition, motivation, and locus of control.

Hybrid models could combine expert system (e.g., identifying current ability and barriers to tailor food cooking and shopping skills messages), user navigation (e.g., an information library with accurate, timely information regarding obesity and diabetes), collaborative filtering (e.g., a personalized recipe book based on recommendations of similar users), and human-to-human (e.g., an online support group) interactions in the same program. For example, the Comprehensive Health Enhancement Support System (CHESS) is an organization of information services (e.g., a user-navigated "Instant Library" and "Resource Directory" interactions), communication services (e.g., human-to-human "Discussion Groups" and "Ask an Expert" interactions), and analysis services (e.g., expert system "Assessments" and "Decisions-Decisions" interactions) (Gustafson et al. 1998, 1999; Smaglik et al. 1998). CHESS has been developed to address a range of health issues, including those affecting patients with breast cancer, prostate cancer, and HIV/AIDS, and for caregivers of patients with Alzheimer's. CHESS is notable for the extensive formative and outcomes evaluation conducted on the program for a broad range of health conditions and populations. Current research is evaluating the impact of specific CHESS components.

THE DISSEMINATION OF INTERACTIVE HEALTH COMMUNICATIONS

Until the past couple of years, there were very few randomized controlled trials of Internet-based interventions for health-related behavior change and decision-making. Neither eHealth experts nor the marketplace had a basis of evidence for confidently selecting Internet-based programs. With the advent of new randomized controlled trials, the gap between what is currently available and what could be available to the public is clearly evident. The next five years will likely see a significant growth in evidence-based Internet programming available on a large scale. The health care industry has lagged significantly behind other industries in embracing and effectively utilizing interactive communications technologies. Currently, one can be exposed to far more sophisticated information technology and tailored advice when purchasing a book online than when asking a clinician the best way to quit smoking.

Adoption, implementation, and maintenance of high-quality IHCs through clinical practices, health maintenance organizations, voluntary health organizations, state and federal agencies, and employers will evolve only when such programming has been demonstrated to have (*a*) high reach to the population in need, (*b*) high efficacy in achieving desired outcomes, and (*c*) low cost. Decision makers will require a greater understanding of the importance of theoretically and empirically informed programming in achieving desired outcomes. Without this understanding, shovelware will be adopted that has little value to the user; this will ultimately undermine the adoption process. The value of the data collected from users will need to be demonstrated. For example, computerized prompting of clinicians to perform preventive care activities has demonstrated clear improvements in these activities and has been readily accepted by clinicians (Balas et al. 2000, Harris et al. 1990, Knight et al. 1987). Extending the concept of prompting to the provision of feedback about patients using an Internet-based intervention to lose weight and displaying collective and individual patient data regarding success, barriers to changing, and motives for changing is likely to be motivational and educational to the clinician. Using the data to examine the relationship between body mass index and weight loss by outpatient utilization is likely to motivate and educate health care administrators.

In addition to understanding the benefits of such systems, decision makers must view the costs of implementation and maintenance as low. Internet-based programming must be turnkey—able to switch on and off easily. Although many larger health organizations typically prefer to create their own health education materials, they are beginning to understand that custom Web sites that extend beyond the digitization of their pamphlets involve significant expertise, effort, and expense. An analogous situation would be an organization that attempted to build its own word-processing program from scratch.

With any appreciable efficacy, Internet-based interventions should be more cost effective than other commonly used alternatives. Ultimately, these interventions involve the movement of electrons, which should be very inexpensive. Licensing existing software, possibly with appropriate branding and customizations, may be a more appropriate model for large-scale implementation. Innovative financial models for such dissemination are evolving away from per-user fees toward capitated plans allowing use from an entire target population for a fixed fee. This approach encourages the organization to promote the programming to the largest number of individuals, lowering the per-user fee with every new participant.

It should go without saying that IHC programming must run without significant problems, work for a variety of user interfaces (e.g., operating systems and connection speeds), and work well under extreme loads, which is often the case when a new Internet-based intervention is promoted. Conformance with regulatory bodies and preventive guidelines is also essential. The notion of flipping a switch to allow broadscale use of Internet-based interventions developed in a research laboratory is frankly naïve. Crossing the chasm (Moore 1999) from research prototype to real-world product is a huge endeavor. It is therefore suggested that partnerships with the eHealth industry use models similar to those developed between biomedical research and the pharmaceutical and medical device industries.

FUTURE DIRECTIONS FOR INTERNET-BASED HEALTH COMMUNICATIONS

The eHealth field continues to change rapidly in terms of information technologies, access to these technologies, and consumer attitudes toward the technologies and associated interventions. This gives researchers in this area a tremendous challenge to remain timely and relevant (Cline & Haynes 2001). Note the proportion of articles cited in this review that were published within the past three years. Many studies published before then employed what are now dated information technologies among subjects with different attitudes toward the technology. For example, early research on even crudely tailored print materials may have found positive outcomes due to central processing of information considered more novel and interesting to the user. The novelty has worn off. We are in fact tired of receiving countless "Hello <your name>!" materials through the Internet and conventional mail. Researchers are encouraged to consider innovative intervention approaches and new research paradigms in studying the active ingredients of the Internet (Abrams et al. 1999, Kreps 2003, Lepper & Gurtner 1989, Neuhauser & Kreps 2003). Some of the more interesting research within this field includes (*a*) the exploration of characteristics of the individual that moderate the impact of Internet-based intervention components, (*b*) the use of technologies that allow more refined methods of data collection and feedback, and (*c*) the integration of consumer health informatics with other informatics fields. These directions are considered below.

Identifying the Active Ingredients of Tailoring

The Internet allows us to adapt or tailor to specific needs and interests of the individual user. Tailoring seeks to improve the efficacy of interventions by varying aspects of the intervention according to observable characteristics of the individual. The assignment of particular treatment components is based on characteristics of the individual that are expected to moderate the effect of the intervention component (Collins et al. 2004, 2005). Research examining how users differentially respond to intervention components therefore becomes highly relevant. Williams-Piehota and colleagues (2003), for example, found that an individual's need for cognition moderated the impact of mammography screening messages and that tailoring the message to the subject's need for cognition produced a positive effect on mammography screening behavior at six-month follow-up. Similarly, Bakker (1999) found that an HIV prevention message in comic format best influenced the attitudes of subjects with a low need for cognition, whereas a text format of the message best influenced subjects with a high need for cognition. Again, examining the moderating effects of individual characteristics on the impact of messages and the presentation of messages will more likely lead to a systematic progression of this field.

Emerging Technologies

eHealth communications that adapt an intervention to the specific needs and interests of the user must rely on high-quality assessment (Collins et al. 2004). As stated above, the similarity and, in some cases, superiority of computer-assessed versus paper-and-pencil or interviewer-assessed psychosocial and health data has been well established.

New interactive technologies are demonstrating clear advantages over standard survey techniques and may provide useful tools for tailored feedback. Ecological momentary assessment (EMA, Stone & Shiffman 1994) typically uses portable monitoring devices to collect multiple data points in the relevant environment, in real time (Stone & Shiffman 1994). Sampling strategies can vary according to the type of information collected (Wheeler & Reis 1991). For example, event-contingent recording can track the details of specific behavioral events, smoking or dietary behavior, episodes of nausea, or precipitants of pain. Other assessments might require information collected at specific intervals or at random, for example when assessing cigarette or food cravings during particular times of the day or night.

Collection of data in real time, from a real-world environment, offers the possibility of providing tailored feedback in real time, in the same environment. It is not difficult to envision a handheld device that periodically collects both event-based and signal-contingent data from a smoker who has recently quit and provides the following feedback: "The last three times you've been in a bar you had a very strong urge to smoke. Your urge to smoke increased with the number of alcoholic drinks you had. Since you're in a bar again now you might want to limit your drinking."

A particularly interesting direction for EMA is the involvement of microelectromechanical systems technologies. Microsystem "labs on chips" (larger than nanoscale technologies) are currently being developed to regularly assess blood glucose, cholesterol, and other physiological data. Larger-scale physiological data collection devices (e.g., glucometers, instrumented inhalers, ambulatory blood pressure monitors) already collect parallel streams of psychological and physiological data (e.g., Guyll & Contrada 1998, Kamarck et al. 2005). These technologies will continue to become more portable and nearly invisible to the user, embedded in clothing, shoes, product containers (e.g., soft drink cans, sunscreen bottles), and many other objects of daily use. Still other proteomic and genomic assessment tools will offer interesting and doubtless controversial intervention strategies.

Integration of Consumer and Medical Informatics Systems

More difficult to predict will be the emergent interactions between the types of eHealth interventions discussed in this chapter, often termed "consumer health informatics," and other informatics systems of clinical medicine, biology, and public health. With organizations such as the Veterans Administration taking a lead in demonstrating the effectiveness and efficiency of electronic medical records (EMR) systems (Murphy 2002), large managed care systems—including Kaiser Permanente and Group Health Cooperative—are beginning to integrate tools to prompt and record cancer-related screening, counseling, and decision support activities.

In the Veterans Administration system, proportions of patients receiving cancer screening and counseling for alcohol abuse and smoking have increased between 130% and 500% since the inception of an EMR system (Murphy 2002). Using an administrative database (billing system) to regularly assess smoking status, Group Health Cooperative increased the documentation of tobacco use and intervention by more than threefold (McAfee et al. 2002). A challenge to this integration, however, will likely be clinicians' perceptions that administrative databases have little clinical relevance to their clinical interactions with patients (Bentz et al. 2002, Curry et al. 2002). This is an important issue since expert data collection and data management are the bases of eHealth programming.

A logical progression in medical informatics programming is to integrate electronic medical record information with consumer health portals. Patient-sanctioned transactions (through opt-in approaches) that allow dietary, physical activity, smoking cessation, medication adherence, and other health-related information collected at home (through a variety of technologies) to be transferred to the EMR may significantly improve the quality and efficiency of the provider-patient interaction.

Online communication between clinicians and patients would seem, on the face of it, to be another logical extension of the medical-consumer informatics integration. Such interactions, however, have yielded mixed results (Katz et al. 2003), with both physicians and patients expressing preferences for some types of email interactions (e.g., simpler clinical issues and requests for normal lab results) over others (e.g., complex or sensitive issues such as mental health or pain management). Moreover, we must recognize the fundamental transitions in the structure and process of clinical practice that are likely to occur as a result of the integration of online communications systems (Katz & Moyer 2004). Although various reimbursement models are being explored, payment for online communication has not yet been readily adopted. Other significant steps toward a systematic integration would be an effective triage (e.g., physician/nurse/Web site) of patient questions and complete documentation of online communication in the EMR (Katz et al. 2003).

Unfortunately, embodiments of medical/consumer health informatics integration appear to focus on patient-held medical records combined with a library of health information, with little attention paid to the importance of tailored behavior-change tools. This may reflect a locus of power residing among the EMR developers, many of whom are clinicians with traditional views of health behavior change and decision-making. For nearly four decades, researchers have found that knowledge is generally unrelated to health behavior and that simple information transmission fails to change health-related behaviors. Yet the concept of the pamphlet rack outside of the doctor's office, even in electronic form, endures. Successful integration of these fields of informatics can probably yield outcomes greater than the sums of their parts, but a scientific, theoretically grounded understanding of both fields will be required to achieve success.

Integration of Consumer and Public Health Informatics Systems

Excellent epidemiological data are a prerequisite for effective population-based health programming. The application of information technologies to public health research and practice allows us to link geographically specific disease patterns with environmental, behavioral, demographic, and eventually, genetic data (Kopp et al. 2002). Data sources can include reportable diseases, diagnostic information for inpatients and outpatients, intensive care unit admissions, Medicare or Medicaid claims, poison information calls, Internet hits for medical information, road and transit usage, weather records, and school and work absenteeism records (Pavlin et al. 2003). Efforts to better integrate multiple sources of data through information technology infrastructures will occur only through governmental and intergovernmental cooperation (Kun 2001). The rewards of this multilevel integration will be deeper understanding of the incidence, prevalence, distribution, and multifactor etiologies of disease.

Integration of Consumer and Bioinformatics Systems

The application of statistical and computational methods to understanding the human genome should yield tremendous benefits in our understanding of disease susceptibility, responsiveness to prevention efforts, chronic disease management, and long-term survivorship. To date, estimates of an individual's health risk are calculated from population-based data (Beery et al. 1986). In other words, we currently use population-based mortality data to calculate a "risk age" on the basis of an individual's demographic characteristics and health habits (Beery et al. 1986). Feedback from such health risk assessments can provide only averaged, usually bland, feedback regarding risk and generally has very little impact on behavior change (Kreuter & Strecher 1996, Strecher & Kreuter 1995). The significant amount of variation in an individual's actual risk is based on the individual's genetic susceptibility. Assessing an individual's risk using genotypic, environmental, and behavioral data will ultimately allow far more accurate, detailed, and personalized feedback to that individual. Interactive health communications will play an important role in creating very personalized feedback tailored to the abilities and preferences of the individual. Once this feedback is provided, genetic information could be used in combination with behavioral, psychosocial, and environmental data to create a far more tailored intervention plan. For example, genetic data could inform the type and dosing of pharmacotherapy for smoking cessation in combination with a tailored behavioral treatment plan (Lerman & Berrettini 2003).

Whether or not to get genetic testing in the first place is a current frontier for IHCs. Genetic counselors are trained to convey the risks and benefits of a genetic screening decision in an unbiased manner. However, with the advent of rapid, easier tests for genetic conditions, our traditional genetic counseling facilities may rapidly be overwhelmed (Wang et al. 2005). Interactive health communication technologies may have a role in addressing this issue but must demonstrate capability of conveying genetic screening information with the same unbiased, highly informed qualities of genetic counselors. Initial trials of CD-ROM-based and tailored print-based IHC for genetic counseling have been promising and warrant further research of risk communication and informed decision-making outcomes using IHC (Skinner et al. 2002, Wang et al. 2005).

CONCLUSION

From this review of Internet-based health interventions, it is evident that some, but not all, of Dr. Koop's predictions have come true. The Internet now reaches the majority of the North American, European, and Australian populace. Internet penetration in developing countries, however, lags far behind and continues to grow slowly. Use of the Internet for prevention has been lower than its use for treatment. This finding is not surprising and remains an important challenge that is familiar to prevention researchers: encouraging the use of preventive health services and improving health-related behaviors.

Users of Internet-based programs find them attractive because of their convenience, availability, and anonymity. Collection of health behavior and psychosocial data using the Internet can be efficient in comparison with other data collection methods, and the data collected are generally at least as valid as the data collected using paper-and-pencil or human interview methods.

As the IHC field develops, researchers and practitioners would benefit from more careful consideration of what it means for a program to be interactive. This review presents different approaches to Internet-based interactivity, approaches that likely will be differentially effective based on an individual's health and behavioral issues, optimal (but not necessarily preferred) learning style, need for cognition, ability, perceived competence, and many other characteristics. Unfortunately, the Internet interaction approach most commonly employed, which requires the user to navigate through an electronic library of information (pamphletware), may be the least effective among individuals who are low in ability, perceived competence, or prior knowledge.

Controlled trials comparing the impact of different interactivity approaches, media, content, and message frequency, among other factors, with characteristics of the individual would likely improve the quality and understanding of the Internet. One of the most egregious sins of this field has been to generalize Internet-based programs into one class of intervention. Asking, "Is the Internet effective?" is like asking, "Do movies entertain?" Clearly, some movies do and some do not. Our challenge is to determine the optimal fit of Internet programming to individual needs and preferences. This question is completely consistent with the adaptive potential of the Internet.

We should also recognize that Internet-based health programming is still in its infancy. Access, content, and technology will continue to improve. EMA through MEMS and eventually nanotechnologies will challenge researchers to develop equally immediate, relevant feedback tailored to the assessment. Linkages between consumer health informatics programming and EMRs, public health databases, and eventually, genetic data will allow a new generation of more finely tuned and systematic behavioral and health-related interventions. Researchers will be challenged to remain abreast of these advances while developing and evaluating programs that can effectively and efficiently reach larger numbers of individuals in need.

DISCLOSURE STATEMENT

The author is founder and chairman of HealthMedia, Inc., a company that develops Internet-based health programs for the marketplace.

LITERATURE CITED

Abrams DB, Mills S, Bulger D. 1999. Challenges and future directions for tailored communication research. *Ann. Behav. Med.* 21(4):299–306

Alemi F, Stephens R, Parran T, Llorens S, Bhatt P, et al. 1994. Automated monitoring of outcomes: application to treatment of drug abuse. *Med. Decis. Making* 14(2):180–87

Andersson G, Kaldo V. 2004. Internet-based cognitive behavioral therapy for tinnitus. *J. Clin. Psychol.* 60(2):171–78

Bakker AB. 1999. Persuasive communication about AIDS prevention: need for cognition determines the impact of message format. *AIDS Educ. Prev.* 11(2):150–62

Balas EA, Weingarten S, Garb CT, Blumenthal D, Boren SA, Brown GD. 2000. Improving preventive care by prompting physicians. *Arch. Intern. Med.* 160(3):301–8

Beery WL, Schoenbach VJ, Wagner EH, Graham R, Karon J, Pezzullo S. 1986. Health risk appraisal: methods and programs with annotated bibliography. *Department of Health and Human Services Publication No. (PHS) 86-3396*. Washington, DC: Natl. Cent. Health Serv. Res. Health Care Technol.

Bentz CJ, Davis N, Bayley B. 2002. The feasibility of paper-based tracking codes and electronic medical record systems to monitor tobacco-use assessment and intervention in an individual practice association (IPA) model health maintenance organization (HMO). *Nicotine Tob. Res.* 4(Suppl. 1):S9–17

Bernhardt JM, Strecher VJ, Bishop KR, Potts P, Madison EM, Thorp J. 2001. Handheld computer-assisted self-interviews: user comfort level and preferences. *Am. J. Health Behav.* 25(6):557–63

Bhavnani SK, Bichakjian CK, Johnson TM, Little RJ, Peck FA, et al. 2006. Strategy hubs: domain portals to help find comprehensive information. *J. Am. Soc. Inform. Sci. Technol.* 57(1):4–24

Bhavnani SK, Bichakjian CK, Schwartz JL, Strecher VJ, Dunn RL, et al. 2002. Getting patients to the right healthcare sources: from real-world questions to Strategy Hubs. *Proc. AMIA Symp.*, pp. 51–55

Bickmore T, Gruber A, Picard R. 2005. Establishing the computer-patient working alliance in automated health behavior change interventions. *Patient Educ. Counsel.* 59(1):21–30

Biermann JS, Golladay GJ, Greenfield ML, Baker LH. 1999. Evaluation of cancer information on the Internet. *Cancer* 86(3):381–90

Bock B, Graham A, Sciamanna C, Krishnamoorthy J, Whiteley J, et al. 2004. Smoking cessation treatment on the Internet: content, quality, and usability. *Nicotine Tob. Res.* 6(2):207–19

Bock B, Niaura R, Fontes A, Bock F. 1999. Acceptability of computer assessments among ethnically diverse, low-income smokers. *Am. J. Health Promot.* 13(5):299–304

Borzekowski DL, Rickert VI. 2000. Urban girls, Internet use, and accessing health information. *J. Pediatr. Adolesc. Gynecol.* 13(2):94–95

Brennan P, Fink S. 1997. Health promotion, social support, and computer networks. In *Health Promotion and Interactive Technology*, ed. R Street, W Gold, T Manning, pp. 157–70. Mahwah, NJ: Erlbaum

Brug J, Campbell M, van Assema P. 1999. The application and impact of computer-generated personalized nutrition education: a review of the literature. *Patient Educ. Counsel.* 36:145–56

Buhrman M, Faltenhag S, Strom L, Andersson G. 2004. Controlled trial of Internet-based treatment with telephone support for chronic back pain. *Pain* 111(3):368–77

Burger K. 1985. Computer-assisted instruction: learning style and academic achievement. *J. Computer-Based Instruct.* 12(1):21–22

Carlbring P, Ekselius L, Andersson G. 2003. Treatment of panic disorder via the Internet: a randomized trial of CBT vs. applied relaxation. *J. Behav. Ther. Exp. Psychiatry* 34(2):129–40

Cassel MM, Jackson C, Cheuvront B. 1998. Health communication on the Internet: an effective channel for health behavior change? *J. Health Comm.* 3:71–79

Cavanagh K, Shapiro DA. 2004. Computer treatment for common mental health problems. *J. Clin. Psychol.* 60(3):239–51

Center for the Digital Future Project. 2005. *Digital Future Report.* **http://www.digitalcenter.org**

Chapman S. 1985. Stop Smoking Clinics: a case for their abandonment. *Lancet* 1:918–20

Christensen H, Leach LS, Barney L, Mackinnon AJ, Griffiths KM. 2006. The effect of Web-based depression interventions on self-reported help seeking: randomized controlled trial. *BMC Psychiatry* 6:13

Clark RE. 1982. Antagonism between achievement and enjoyment in ATI studies. *Educ. Psychol.* 17:92–101

Clarke G, Eubanks D, Reid E, Kelleher C, O'Connor E, et al. 2005. Overcoming Depression on the Internet (ODIN) (2): a randomized trial of a self-help depression skills program with reminders. *J. Med. Internet Res.* 7(2):e16

Claypool M, Gokhale A, Miranda T, Murnikov P, Netes D, Sartin M. 1999. *Combining content-based and collaborative filters in an online newspaper. Paper presented at ACM*

SIGIR Workshop on Recommended Systems—Implementation and Evaluation, Berkeley, CA. **http://citeseer.ist.psu.edu/article/claypool99combining.html**

Cline RJ, Haynes KM. 2001. Consumer health information seeking on the Internet: the state of the art. *Health Educ. Res.* 16(6):671–92

Coldevin G, Tovar M, Brauer A. 1993. Influence of instructional control and learner characteristics on factual recall and procedural learning from interactive video. *Can. J. Educ. Communication* 22(2):113–30

Collins LM, Murphy SA, Bierman KL. 2004. A conceptual framework for adaptive preventive interventions. *Prevent. Sci.* 5:185–96

Collins LM, Murphy SA, Nair VN, Strecher VJ. 2005. A strategy for optimizing and evaluating behavioral interventions. *Ann. Behav. Med.* 30(1):65–73

Curry SJ, Fiore MC, Orleans CT, Keller P. 2002. Addressing tobacco in managed care: documenting the challenges and potential for systems-level change. *Nicotine Tob. Res.* 4(Suppl. 1):S5–7

Doshi A, Patrick K, Sallis JF, Calfas K. 2003. Evaluation of physical activity Web sites for use of behavior change theories. *Ann. Behav. Med.* 25(2):105–11

Edgar L, Greenberg A, Remmer J. 2002. Providing Internet lessons to oncology patients and family members: a shared project. *Psychooncology* 11(5):439–46

Eng TR. 2001. *The eHealth Landscape: A Terrain Map of Emerging Information and Communication Technologies in Health and Health Care.* Princeton, NJ: Robert Wood Johnson Found.

Etter JF, Laszlo E. 2005. Evaluation of a poster campaign against passive smoking for World No-Tobacco Day. *Patient Educ. Counsel.* 57(2):190–98

Eveland WP, Dunwoody S. 2002. An investigation of elaboration and selective scanning as mediators of learning from the Web versus print. *J. Broadcast. Electron. Media* 46(1):34–53

Eysenbach G, Kummervold PE. 2005. "Is Cybermedicine Killing You?" The story of a Cochrane disaster. *J. Med. Internet Res.* 7(2):e21

Eysenbach G, Powell J, Kuss O, Sa ER. 2002. Empirical studies assessing the quality of health information for consumers on the World Wide Web: a systematic review. *JAMA* 287(20):2691–700

Feil EG, Glasgow RE, Boles SM, McKay HG. 2000. Who participates in Internet-based self-management programs? A study among novice computer users in a primary care setting. *Diabetes Educator* 26(5):806–11

Fox S. 2005. *Health information online. May 17. Pew Internet and American Life Project.* **http://www.pewinternet.org**

Fox S, Fallows D. 2003. *Internet health resources. July 16. Pew Internet and American Life Project.* **http://www.pewinternet.org**

Fox S, Rainie L. 2000. *The online health care revolution: how the Web helps Americans take better care of themselves. Pew Internet and American Life Project.* **http://www.pewinternet.org**

Frisby G, Bessell TL, Borland R, Anderson JN. 2002. Smoking cessation and the Internet: a qualitative method examining online consumer behavior. *J. Med. Internet Res.* 4(2):E8

Gay G. 1986. Interaction of learner control and prior understanding in computer-assisted video instruction. *J. Educ. Psychol.* 78(3):225–27

Glasgow RE, Boles SM, McKay HG, Feil EG, Barrera MJ. 2003. The D-Net diabetes self-management program: long-term implementation, outcomes, and generalization results. *Prevent. Med.* 36(4):410–19

Green LW, Kreuter MW. 1991. *Health Promotion Planning: An Educational and Environmental Approach.* Mountain View, CA: Mayfield. 2nd ed.

Gregorc AF. 1985. *Inside Style: Beyond the Basics.* Columbia, CT: Gregorc Assoc. Inc.

Gribble JN, Miller HG, Cooley PC, Catania JA, Pollack L, Turner CF. 2000. The impact of T-ACASI interviewing on reported drug use among men who have sex with men. *Subst. Use Misuse* 35(6–8):869–90

Griffiths F, Lindenmeyer A, Powell J, Lowe P, Thorogood M. 2006. Why are health care interventions delivered over the Internet? A systematic review of the published literature. *J. Med. Internet Res.* 8(2):e10

Gustafson DH, Hawkins R, Boberg E, Pingree S, Serlin RE, et al. 1999. Impact of a patient-centered, computer-based health information/support system. *Am. J. Prevent. Med.* 16(1):1–9

Gustafson DH, McTavish F, Hawkins RP, Pingree S, Arora NK, et al. 1998. Computer support for elderly women with breast cancer: results of a population-based intervention. *JAMA* 280(15):1305

Guyll M, Contrada RJ. 1998. Trait hostility and ambulatory cardiovascular activity: responses to social interaction. *Health Psychol.* 17(1):30–39

Hainer MI, Tsai N, Komura ST, Chiu CL. 2000. Fatal hepatorenal failure associated with hydrazine sulfate. *Ann. Intern. Med.* 133(11):877–80

Harris RP, O'Malley MS, Fletcher SW, Knight BP. 1990. Prompting physicians for preventive procedures: a five-year study of manual and computer reminders. *Am. J. Prev. Med.* 6(3):145–52

Hasley S. 1995. A comparison of computer-based and personal interviews for the gynecologic history update. *Obstet Gynecol.* 85(4):494–98

Hasson D, Anderberg UM, Theorell T, Arnetz BB. 2005. Psychophysiological effects of a Web-based stress management system: a prospective, randomized controlled intervention study of IT and media workers. *BMC Public Health* 5:78

Johnson AM, Copas AJ, Erens B, Mandalia S, Fenton K, et al. 2001. Effect of computer-assisted self-interviews on reporting of sexual HIV risk behaviours in a general population sample: a methodological experiment. *AIDS* 15(1):111–15

Kamarck TW, Schwartz JE, Shiffman S, Muldoon MF, Sutton-Tyrrell K, Janicki DL. 2005. Psychosocial stress and cardiovascular risk: What is the role of daily experience? *J. Personal.* 73(6):1–26

Katz SJ, Moyer CA. 2004. The emerging role of online communication between patients and their providers. *J. Gen. Internet Med.* 19(9):978–83

Katz SJ, Moyer CA, Cox DT, Stern DT. 2003. Effect of a triage-based E-mail system on clinic resource use and patient and physician satisfaction in primary care: a randomized controlled trial. *J. Gen. Intern. Med.* 18(9):736–44

Kissinger P, Rice J, Farley T, Trim S, Jewitt K, et al. 1999. Application of computer-assisted interviews to sexual behavior research. *Am. J. Epidemiol.* 149(10):950–54

Klemm P, Bunnell D, Cullen M, Soneji R, Gibbons P, Holecek A. 2003. Online cancer support groups: a review of the research literature. *Comput. Inform. Nurs.* 21(3):136–42

Knight BP, O'Malley MS, Fletcher SW. 1987. Physician acceptance of a computerized health maintenance prompting program. *Am. J. Prev. Med.* 3(1):19–24

Koop CE. 1995. A personal role in health care reform. *Am. J. Publ. Health* 85:759–60

Kopp S, Shuchman R, Strecher V, Gueye M, Ledlow J, et al. 2002. Public health applications. *Telemed. J. e-Health* 8(1):35–48

Kreps GL. 2003. The impact of communication on cancer risk, incidence, morbidity, mortality, and quality of life. *Health Commun.* 15:2:163–71

Kreuter MW, Strecher VJ. 1996. Do tailored behavior change messages enhance the effectiveness of health risk appraisal? Results from a randomized trial. *Health Educ. Res.* 11:97–105

Krishna S, Francisco BD, Balas EA, Konig P, Graff GR, Madsen RW. 2003. Randomized trial. Internet-enabled interactive multimedia asthma education program: a randomized trial. *Pediatrics* 111(3):503–10

Kunn LG. 2001. Telehealth and global health network in the 21st century. From homecare to public health informatics. *Computer Methods Prog. Biomed.* 64:155–67

Kypri K, McAnally HM. 2005. Randomized controlled trial of a Web-based primary care intervention for multiple health risk behaviors. *Prevent. Med.* 41(3–4):761–66

Kypri K, Saunders JB, Williams SM, McGee RO, Langley JD, et al. 2004. Web-based screening and brief intervention for hazardous drinking: a double-blind randomized controlled trial. *Addiction* 99(11):1410–17

Lancaster T, Stead LF. 2000. Self-help interventions for smoking cessation. *Cochrane Database Syst. Rev.* CD001118

Lepper MR, Gurtner J. 1989. Children and computers: child development and education approaching the twenty-first century. *Am. Psychol.* 44:170–78

Lerman C, Berrettini W. 2003. Elucidating the role of genetic factors in smoking behavior and nicotine dependence. *Am. J. Med. Genet. B Neuropsychiatr. Genet.* 118(1):48–54

Lipkus IM, Lyna PR, Rimer BK. 1999. Using tailored interventions to enhance smoking cessation among African-Americans at a community health center. *Nicotine Tob. Res.* 1(1):77–85

Locke SE, Kowaloff HB, Hoff RG, Safran C, Popovsky MA, et al. 1992. Computer-based interview for screening blood donors for risk of HIV transmission. *JAMA* 268(10):1301–5

Marks IM, Mataix-Cols D, Kenwright M, Cameron R, Hirsch S, Gega L. 2003. Pragmatic evaluation of computer-aided self-help for anxiety and depression. *Br. J. Psychiatry* 183:57–65

Marks JT, Campbell MK, Ward DS, Ribisl KM, Wildemuth BM, Symons MJ. 2006. A comparison of Web and print media for physical activity promotion among adolescent girls. *J. Adolesc. Health* 39(1):96–104

Matthews SC, Camacho A, Mills PJ, Dimsdale JE. 2003. The Internet for medical information about cancer: help or hindrance? *Psychosomatics* 44(2):100–3

McAfee T, Grossman R, Dacey S, McClure J. 2002. Capturing tobacco status using an automated billing system: steps toward a tobacco registry. *Nicotine Tob. Res.* 4(Suppl. 1):S31–37

McTavish FM, Gustafson DH, Owens BH, Hawkins RP, Pingree S, et al. 1995. CHESS: an interactive computer system for women with breast cancer piloted with an underserved population. *J. Ambul. Care Manage.* 18(3):35–41

Metzger DS, Koblin B, Turner C, Navaline H, Valenti F, et al. 2000. Randomized controlled trial of audio computer-assisted self-interviewing: utility and acceptability in longitudinal studies. HIVNET Vaccine Preparedness Study Protocol Team. *Am. J. Epidemiol.* 152(2):99–106

Moore G. 1999. *Crossing the Chasm*. New York: HarperCollins

Murphy F. 2002. *Department of Veterans Affairs: Information Technology Can Improve Health Care Quality. Health Legacy Conference and eHealth Initiative Annual Meeting*. Washington, DC: Natl. Press Club

Murray E, Burns J, See TS, Lai R, Nazareth I. 2004. Interactive health communication applications for people with chronic disease. *Cochrane Database Syst. Rev.* (4):CD004274

Murray E, Burns J, Tai S, Lai R, Nazareth I. 2006. Interactive health communication applications for people with chronic disease. *Cochrane Database Syst. Rev.* Issue 2

Negotia UN. 1985. *Expert Systems and Fuzzy Systems*. Menlo Park, CA: Benjamin-Cummings

Neuhauser L, Kreps GL. 2003. Rethinking communication in the e-health era. *J. Health Psychol.* 8(1):7–23

Nielsen/NetRatings. 2006. *U.S. broadband composition reaches 72 percent at home, a 15-point year-over-year increase.* **http://www.nielsen-netratings.com**

Oh H, Rizo C, Enkin M, Jadad A. 2005. What is eHealth (3): a systematic review of published definitions. *J. Med. Internet Res.* 7(1):e1

Ossip-Klein DJ, McIntosh S. 2003. Quitlines in North America: evidence base and applications. *Am. J. Med. Sci.* 326(4):201–5

Paperny DM, Aono JY, Lehman RM, Hammar SL, Risser J. 1990. Computer-assisted detection and intervention in adolescent high-risk health behaviors. *J. Pediatr.* 116(3):456–62

Patten CA, Croghan IT, Meis TM, Decker PA, Pingree S, et al. 2006. Randomized clinical trial of an Internet-based versus brief office intervention for adolescent smoking cessation. *Patient Educ. Counsel.* 64(1–3):249–58

Pavlin JA. 2003. Investigation of disease outbreaks detected by "syndromic" surveillance systems. *J. Urban Health* 80(2 Suppl. 1):i107–14

Proudfoot J, Ryden C, Everitt B, Shapiro DA, Goldberg D, et al. 2004. Clinical efficacy of computerised cognitive-behavioural therapy for anxiety and depression in primary care: randomised controlled trial. *Br. J. Psychiatry* 185:46–54

Rada R. 2005. A case study of a retracted systematic review on inactive health communication applications: impact on media, scientists, and patients. *J. Med. Internet Res.* 7(2):e18

Rainie L, Packel D. 2001. *More online, doing more: the Pew Internet & American Life Project.* **http://www.pewinternet.org**

Richardson CR, Resnick PJ, Hansen DL, Derry HA, Rideout VJ. 2002. Does pornography-blocking software block access to health information on the Internet? *JAMA* 288(22):2887–94

Ritterband LM, Cox DJ, Walker LS, Kovatchev B, McKnight L, et al. 2003. An Internet intervention as adjunctive therapy for pediatric encopresis. *J. Consult. Clin. Psychol.* 71(5):910–17

Ross J, Schulz R. 1999. Can computer-aided instruction accommodate all learners equally? *Br. J. Educ. Technol.* 30(1):5–24

Ross S, Morrison G. 1989. In search of a happy medium in instructional technology research: issues concerning external validity, media replications, and learner control. *Educ. Technol. Res. Dev.* 37(1):19–33

Ross S, Rakow E. 1981. Learner control as adaptive strategies for selection of instructional support on math rules. *Educ. Psychol.* 73(5):745–53

Rothert K, Strecher VJ, Doyl LA, Caplan WM, Joyce JS, et al. 2006. Web-based weight management programs in an integrated health care setting: a randomized, controlled trial. *Obes. Res.* 14(2):266–72

Satterlund MJ, McCaul KD, Sandgren AK. 2003. Information gathering over time by breast cancer patients. *J. Med. Internet Res.* 5(3):e15

Shaw BR, McTavish F, Hawkins R, Gustafson DH, Pingree S. 2000. Experiences of women with breast cancer: exchanging social support over the CHESS computer network. *J. Health Comm.* 5:135–59

Skinner CS, Campbell MK, Rimer BK, Curry S, Prochaska JO. 1999. How effective is tailored print communication? *Ann. Behav. Med.* 21(4):290–98

Skinner CS, Schildkraut JM, Berry D, Calingaert B, Marcom PK, et al. 2002. Pre-counseling education materials for BRCA testing: Does tailoring make a difference? *Genet Test.* 6(2):93–105

Skinner CS, Strecher VJ, Hospers H. 1994. Physicians' recommendations for mammography: Do tailored messages make a difference? *Am. J. Public Health* 84:43–49

Skinner H, Biscope S, Poland B, Goldberg E. 2003. How adolescents use technology for health information: implications for health professionals from focus group studies. *J. Med. Internet Res.* 5(4):e32
Smaglik P, Hawkins RP, Pingree S, Gustafson DH, Boberg E, Bricker E. 1998. The quality of interactive computer use among HIV-infected individuals. *J. Health Commun.* 3(1):53–68
Steinberg ER. 1977. Review of student control in computer-assisted instruction. *J. Computer-Based Instr.* 3:84–90
Stone AA, Shiffman S. 1994. Ecological momentary assessment (EMA) in behavioral medicine. *Ann. Behav. Med.* 16:199–202
Strecher VJ. 1999. Computer-tailored smoking cessation materials: a review and discussion. *Patient Educ. Counsel.* 36:107–17
Strecher VJ, Kreuter MW. 1995. The psychosocial and behavioral impact of health risk appraisals. In *Psychosocial Effects of Screening for Disease Prevention and Detection*, ed. RT Croyle, pp. 144–84. New York: Oxford Univ. Press
Strecher VJ, Shiffman S, West R. 2005. Randomized controlled trial of a Web-based computer-tailored smoking cessation program as a supplement to nicotine patch therapy. *Addiction* 100(5):682–88
Strom L, Pettersson R, Andersson G. 2000. A controlled trial of self-help treatment of recurrent headache conducted via the Internet. *J. Consult. Clin. Psychol.* 68(4):722–27
Strom L, Pettersson R, Andersson G. 2004. Internet-based treatment for insomnia: a controlled evaluation. *J. Consult. Clin. Psychol.* 72(1):113–20
Swartz LHG, Noell JW, Schroeder SW, Ary DV. 2006. A randomized control study of a fully automated Internet-based smoking cessation program. *Tob. Control* 15:7–12
Tate DF, Jackvony EH, Wing RR. 2003. Effects of Internet behavioral counseling on weight loss in adults at risk for type 2 diabetes: a randomized trial. *JAMA* 289(14):1833–36
Tate DF, Wing RR, Winett RA. 2001. Using Internet technology to deliver a behavioral weight loss program. *JAMA* 285(9):1172–77
Tate DF, Zabinski MF. 2004. Computer and Internet applications for psychological treatment: update for clinicians. *J. Consult. Clin. Psychol.* 60(2):209–20
Till JE. 2003. Evaluation of support groups for women with breast cancer: importance of the navigator role. *Health Qual. Life Outcomes* 1(1):16
Turner CF, Ku L, Rogers SM, Lindberg LD, Pleck JH, Sonenstein FL. 1998. Adolescent sexual behavior, drug use, and violence: increased reporting with computer survey technology. *Science* 280(5365):867–73
U.S. Census Bureau. 2001. *Home computers and Internet use in the United States.* Aug. 2000, Sept. 2001. **http://www.census.gov/population/www/socdemo/computer.html**
Velicer WF, Prochaska JO, Bellis JM, DiClemente CC, Rossi JS, et al. 1993. An expert system intervention for smoking cessation. *Addict. Behav.* 18:269–90
Velicer WF, Prochaska JO. 1999. An expert system intervention for smoking cessation. *Patient Educ. Counsel.* 36(2):119–29
Velikova G, Wright EP, Smith AB, Cull A, Gould A, et al. 1999. Automated collection of quality-of-life data: a comparison of paper and computer touch-screen questionnaires. *J. Clin. Oncol.* 17(3):998–1007
Wagner B, Knaevelsrud C, Maercker A. 2006. Internet-based cognitive-behavioral therapy for complicated grief: a randomized controlled trial. *Death Stud.* 30(5):429–53
Wang C, Gonzalez R, Milliron KJ, Strecher VJ, Merajver SD. 2005. Genetic counseling for BRCA1/2: a randomized controlled trial of two strategies to facilitate the education and counseling process. *Am. J. Med. Genet. A* 134(1):66–73

Wheeler L, Reis HT. 1991. Self-recording of everyday life events: origins, types, and uses. *J. Personal.* 59(3):339–54

Williamson DA, Martin PD, White MA, Newton R, Walden H, et al. 2005. Efficacy of an Internet-based behavioral weight loss program for overweight adolescent African-American girls. *Eat. Weight Disord.* 10(3):193–203

Williams-Piehota P, Schneider TR, Pizarro J, Mowad L, Salovey P. 2003. Matching health messages to information processing styles: need for cognition and mammography utilization. *Health Commun.* 15(4):375–92

Drug Abuse* in African American and Hispanic Adolescents: Culture, Development, and Behavior

José Szapocznik,[1] Guillermo Prado,[2] Ann Kathleen Burlew,[3] Robert A. Williams,[4] and Daniel A. Santisteban[1]

[1]Center for Family Studies, Department of Psychiatry and Behavioral Sciences, Miller School of Medicine, University of Miami, Miami, Florida 33136; email: JSzapocz@med.miami.edu

[2]Department of Epidemiology and Biostatistics, Stempel School of Public Health, Florida International University, Miami, Florida 33199

[3]Department of Psychology, University of Cincinnati, Cincinnati, Ohio 45221

[4]Department of Counseling, San Francisco State University, San Francisco, California 94312

Annu. Rev. Clin. Psychol. 2007. 3:77–105

First published online as a Review in Advance on January 18, 2007

The *Annual Review of Clinical Psychology* is online at http://clinpsy.annualreviews.org

This article's doi:
10.1146/annurev.clinpsy.3.022806.091408

1548-5943/07/0427-0077$20.00

*The term "abuse" is used to denote the use of illicit drugs or the use of nonprescribed licit drugs.

Key Words

drugs, prevention, treatment, adolescents, culture, family

Abstract

An understanding of African American and Hispanic adolescent drug abuse occurs at the intersection of context, development, and behavior. The focus of this review is on the impact of racial/ethnic culture as one of the important contexts that influence adolescent development toward or away from prosocial behaviors. Because family plays a major role in both African American and Hispanic cultures, it is also a centerpiece of any discussion of adolescent development in these groups. This review on the state of the science in drug abuse for African American and Hispanic adolescents focuses on epidemiology, culturally specific risk and protective processes, and prevention and treatment research. From the perspective of a broad lens, specific minority groups such as African Americans and Hispanics would appear to have more in common than not. However, each of these groups encompasses considerable genetic, historical, social, and cultural heterogeneity. Investigation across such diversity will yield a more complete picture of the human condition.

Contents

INTRODUCTION

Risk and protective processes: a naturally occurring or designed sequence of changes in a system or across systems that increases or diminishes the likelihood of occurrence of an undesirable outcome (e.g., drug use)

Drug use is a significant public health problem that is widespread among American youths of all ages and ethnicities. Drug use has severe physical and social consequences. For example, according to the National Vital Statistics Report, more than 74.5% of all deaths among 15- to 24-year-olds are attributed to accidents, assaults/homicides, intentional harm/suicides, HIV/AIDS, and chronic lower respiratory disease, all of which have been associated with drug use (Arias et al. 2003). These health statistics do not encompass other important long-term consequences of adolescent drug use into adulthood, including criminal activity (Ellickson et al. 2003, Newcomb 1997), cancer of the respiratory tract (Hall & MacPhee 2002), and psychiatric disorders in adulthood described in the DSM-IV-TR (Am. Psychiatr. Assoc. 1994), such as substance abuse and dependence, affective disorders, anxiety disorders, and antisocial disorders (Gil et al. 2004).

In addition, minority adolescent drug use is associated with dropping out of school (Brook et al. 1996), delinquency (Mensch & Kandel 1988), and risky sexual behaviors (Cook et al. 2002). This article focuses on African Americans and Hispanics because these are the two largest racial/ethnic minority groups in the United States, accounting for approximately 12% and 14% of the U.S. population, respectively (U.S. Census Bureau 2005). Moreover, a focus on adolescents in these groups is important because both groups have large youthful populations (defined as under the age of 19), accounting for 34.6% for African Americans (Marotta & Garcia 2003) and 37.4% for Hispanics (Marotta & Garcia 2003).

ETHNICITY, RACE, AND CULTURE

Adolescent development is embedded in a complex set of contexts. These contexts influence and are influenced by developmental trajectories as they interact and develop over time (Szapocznik & Coatsworth 1999). A number of theorists have suggested that culture is an important aspect of context that affects development (e.g., Bronfenbrenner 1979, 1986). An interest in the "cultural patterns" that may be found in African American and Hispanic[1] youths and their families stems

[1]The term "Hispanic" is used to be consistent with the U.S. Census Bureau's terminology. However, it is intended to include individuals living in the United States or Puerto Rico from a vast variety of backgrounds, some of whom may identify themselves as Latino(a) or Chicano(a).

from the belief that beyond race and ethnicity, an understanding of cultural processes that are proximal to daily life is needed. Culture can be described as knowledge, skills, attitudes, and behaviors that are shared by a group of people and may be transmitted from one generation to another (Carter 1995). Elements of culture may be expressed through "familial roles, communication patterns, affective styles and values regarding personal control, individualism, collectivism, spirituality and religiosity" (Betancourt & Lopez 1993, p. 630). Because culture is learned, one important task of the family is to socialize children into its identified culture. An appreciation of the unique cultural patterns of racial/ethnic groups such as African Americans and Hispanics can considerably enrich understanding of these groups, the emergence of symptoms, the buffering of stress, and responses to prevention and treatment interventions.

There are costs and benefits to using such broad terms as Hispanic, Latino(a), African American, or black families. For example, although much can be gained by focusing on cultural patterns evident across "Hispanics" (e.g., common linguistic and value orientations), it must be acknowledged that much is also lost by using this wide-angle lens rather than zooming more closely into the unique and more specific cultural patterns evident in Mexican migrant workers in South Florida or third-generation, moderately educated Puerto Rican youths in the Bronx. In fact, this process of zooming closer to people of a specific national background would begin to reveal cultural differences within that national group (e.g., Puerto Rican) that may result from Spanish, African, or indigenous ancestry. With an understanding of these shortcomings, we present information that can be gleaned from research on broad categorizations such as Hispanic and African American youths and families, and we note when some of the finer distinctions become evident in research.

PREVALENCE

Data from the Monitoring the Future survey reveal interesting subgroup differences: Contrary to popular belief, African American eighth, tenth, and twelfth graders historically have reported the lowest rates of use (relative to non-Hispanic white and Hispanic eighth, tenth, and twelfth graders) of alcohol, cigarette, and any illicit drugs (Johnston et al. 2006). In the most recent survey, when all classes of illicit drugs are examined, the data indicate that African American adolescents report less use of most illicit drugs for eighth graders (including cocaine, crack cocaine, and hallucinogens), and all illicit drugs for tenth and twelfth graders, than do their non-Hispanic white and Hispanic counterparts (Johnston et al. 2006). Hence, in the last survey, annual drug use among eighth grade African American adolescents has slightly increased. Specifically, "annual prevalence for any illicit drug use" and "lifetime cigarette use," although still considerably lower than that reported by Hispanics, is now slightly higher than that of white Americans.

Citing possible shortcomings of school-based surveys (e.g., Monitoring the Future survey for African Americans), some researchers have challenged the accuracy of findings that suggest African American adolescents are using alcohol, cigarettes, and illicit drugs less frequently than are their non-Hispanic white and Hispanic counterparts (Wallace & Bachman 1993). However, different methods of data collection such as in-person surveys (National Household Survey on Drug Use and Health; Subst. Abuse Mental Health Serv. Admin. 2005) resulted in similar low rates of alcohol, cigarette, and illicit drug use among African American adolescents. Moreover, attempts to statistically and methodologically correct for possible confounds have not helped explain the lower rates of alcohol, cigarette, and illicit drug use among African American adolescents. In fact, investigators from the Monitoring

Context: typically refers to the social or cultural environment of a child or family

Culture: knowledge, skills, attitudes, and behaviors that are shared by a group of people and may be transmitted from one generation to another

Development: typically refers to the psychological, social, and biological trajectory across the life span. Trajectories can occur toward prosocial or antisocial adjustment

Family: a network of mutual commitments

the Future survey have investigated several explanations for the historically lower rates of use and found that none diminished the racial and ethnic differences in rates or adequately explained the lower prevalence rates among African American adolescents (Wallace & Bachman 1993). Thus, despite early concerns, there does appear to be validity to the evidence suggesting that African American adolescents have historically had the lowest usage rates of alcohol, cigarette, and most illicit drugs for eighth, tenth, and twelfth graders, when compared with non-Hispanic whites and Hispanics.

It should be noted, however, that the most recent trends show an increase in cigarette and illicit drug use for eighth graders, and these rates are now slightly higher than rates for white Americans. These trends should be watched to determine whether there is a new wave of increased use in this population, which would cause the trend to become evident in tenth and twelfth grade, as the children mature.

In contrast to the lower rates of drug use by African American adolescents, Hispanic eighth and tenth graders report the highest lifetime, annual, and 30-day prevalence rates of alcohol, cigarette, and licit or illicit drug use (all classes of illicit drugs with the exception of amphetamines) of any racial/ethnic groups studied (Johnston et al. 2006). For example, among eighth graders, the annual prevalence rate of any illicit drug use is 14.6, 14.9, and 20.9 for African Americans, non-Hispanic whites, and Hispanics, respectively (Johnston et al. 2005). Of particular concern is a rapidly increasing rate of prescription drug abuse, which now affects 21% of Hispanic adolescents. Interestingly, the relatively high prevalence rates among Hispanic eighth and tenth graders are reversed by the twelfth grade for most major drugs. That is, the data indicate that the rates of drug use among Hispanic twelfth graders fall between those of African American and non-Hispanic white twelfth graders (Johnston et al. 2006). Several explanations have been posited for this change in ranking between the tenth and twelfth grade. One possible explanation may be that Hispanic adolescents have considerably higher dropout rates. Thus, in comparison with African American and white adolescents, a larger percentage of the drug-prone segment of Hispanics may drop out before twelfth grade (U.S. Census Bureau 2003). However, evidence from nonschool-based surveys may contradict the high school dropout hypothesis. Specifically, the National Household Survey on Drug Use and Health (Subst. Abuse Mental Health Serv. Admin. 2005) has found that during late adolescence and emerging-adulthood, non-Hispanic whites have the highest rates of drug use, followed by Hispanics. So, if the large percentages of high school dropouts may not explain the change in drug use rankings in Hispanics, then what may?

One explanation could be that the higher rates of drug use among Hispanic eighth and tenth graders represent a new wave of heightened drug use among Hispanics. If so, we would expect that the rates of drug use would increase for twelfth-grade Hispanics in the future. However, arguing against this hypothesis is that Hispanic eighth and tenth graders historically have had higher drug use rates in comparison with the two other racial/ethnic groups. Another explanation could be that Hispanics initiate their drug use earlier, but by twelfth grade, non-Hispanic whites have surpassed the Hispanic rates (Johnston et al. 2004). Research is needed to understand the reasons for the very high rates of drug use among Hispanics in eighth and tenth grade as well as the reported drop in ranking by the twelfth grade.

Although Hispanics as a whole have elevated rates of drug use, considerable variation exists in use within the Hispanic adolescent population. Two primary contextual sources of this variation have been identified in the literature: country of origin and U.S.-born versus foreign-born adolescents (Alegria et al. 2006). A study by Delva et al. (2005) compared eighth-grade Cuban Americans, Mexican Americans, Puerto Ricans, and other Latin Americans on use of marijuana and cocaine and on heavy drinking using Monitoring the Future survey data for the two most recent periods (1997–1999 and 2000–2002) in which these comparisons were made. The findings demonstrate that Cuban American eighth graders had the highest rates of marijuana and cocaine use and heavy drinking, compared with Mexican American, Puerto Rican, and other Latin American eighth-grade adolescents living in the United States. Systematic differences in drug use patterns have also been observed when comparing U.S.-born and foreign-born Hispanics. A population-based study by Vega et al. (2002) revealed that U.S.-born Hispanic adolescents report higher drug use rates than do foreign-born Hispanics. These findings have been replicated (Turner et al. 2006) and are consistent with findings on a variety of health problems (e.g., Gordon-Larsen et al. 2003). Future research is needed to further explain variations in drug use among Hispanic subgroups (see, e.g., Prado et al. 2006b).

If the findings of higher rates of drug use among younger Hispanics are viewed in the context of the increasing number of U.S.-born Hispanics, it could be suggested that a new wave of U.S.-born Hispanics—with higher drug use—are driving the high prevalence rates in younger youths.

It would appear that the developmental outcomes for African American and Hispanic adolescents vary, and that within Hispanic adolescents substantial differences exist in developmental outcomes across national groups. As noted above, there is likely to be important contextual heterogeneity along genetic, historical, social, and cultural dimensions across and within each of these groups. It would not be surprising, then, that such diversity of contexts gave rise to different developmental trajectories with their corresponding course of drug use, related problem behaviors, and their consequences.

CULTURALLY SPECIFIC RISK AND PROTECTIVE PROCESSES

Adolescent drug use often represents one facet of a cluster of problematic adolescent behaviors, referred to as problem behavior syndrome (Jessor et al. 1995) or general deviancy (McGee & Newcomb 1992). Early or severe adolescent drug use tends to co-occur with other problem behaviors, such as unsafe sexual behavior (Tubman et al. 1996), conduct problems and delinquency (Barnes et al. 2005), and academic failure (Guagliardo et al. 1998). Not surprisingly, drug use and related problem behaviors share common risk and protective processes.

The various elements of the problem behavior syndrome have been found to result from a common set of antecedents (e.g., Griffin et al. 2003). The risk and protective factors paradigm (Hawkins et al. 1992) is one of the most widely accepted frameworks for organizing the contexts that predispose adolescents of all ethnic groups, including African Americans and Hispanics, toward or away from drug use. Risk and protective processes can be grouped into domains that include individual, family, peer, school, neighborhood, and societal and cultural processes. More contemporary views of risk, such as Ecodevelopmental Theory (Szapocznik & Coatsworth 1999), take into consideration the complex set of contexts, their interaction, and the developmental trajectory of these processes over time as they reciprocally influence each other and behavior. Among the many contexts prominent in Ecodevelopmental Theory is culture. Although predictors of drug use in African American and Hispanic adolescents cut across multiple psychosocial domains, below we review studies that have shed light on culturally specific processes that are particularly important for African Americans and Hispanics in drug use and related

Ecodevelopmental theory: explains the role of multiple social contexts and their interrelationships, both over time, in risk and protection for adolescent developmental trajectories—toward or away from drug use and related problem behaviors

problem behaviors. For rigor, this review only reports on longitudinal studies, unless otherwise indicated.

Racial identity: "a sense of collective identity based on one's perception that he or she shares a common heritage with a particular racial group" (Helms 1990, p. 3)

Acculturation: a unidimensional or bidimensional process by which a person's psychological state(s), behaviors, and worldviews change as a result of contact with a new culture

Risk and Protection for African Americans

Racial identity is a culturally specific factor that has been found to be protective of a wide array of negative consequences in African Americans, including racial discrimination, psychological functioning, and drug use (Caldwell et al. 2006, Hughes & Demo 1989, Rowley et al. 1997). Racial identity is broadly defined as "a sense of collective identity based on one's perception that he or she shares a common heritage with a particular racial group" (Helms 1990, p. 3). Adolescence is considered to be an important period in the development of racial identity because the adolescent is transitioning from childhood, a time when racial identity is more a reflection of parental attitudes, to a more cognitively complex identity in adulthood (White & Parham 1996). A strong racial identity has been demonstrated to be associated with more favorable outcomes in African American adolescents (e.g., Chavous 2003, Sellers et al. 2006). Cross-sectional studies examining the association between racial identity and substance abuse suggest that African American adolescents who endorse positive attitudes about being African American report more antidrug attitudes (Belgrave 2002, Belgrave et al. 1997, Resnicow et al. 1999) and less substance use (Caldwell et al. 2006).

Racial identity can be enhanced by communicating messages to adolescents, a process known as racial socialization (Fischer & Shaw 1999, Hughes 2003). The communication of messages that define racial socialization can occur via the parent or the broader social context. Stevenson (1994) identified several themes that are important in racial socialization: promotion of black heritage and culture through an appreciation for spirituality, religion, extended family involvement, and the importance of child rearing, as well as an awareness of racism in society and survival skills for successfully managing oneself in the context of racism. Despite the fact that most of the studies to date on racial socialization have been cross-sectional, the findings from the broader literature suggest that parents and other family members are the primary agents of racial socialization among African Americans (Coard et al. 2004, Hughes & Johnson 2001). Further, parental racial socialization is associated with favorable family interactions (Frabutt et al. 2002) as well as positive adolescent outcomes (Caughy et al. 2002, Constantine & Blackmon 2002, Miller 1999). These findings suggest it might be useful to include racial socialization in the construction of interventions for African American adolescents.

Risk and Protection for Hispanics

The most consistent culture-specific finding in the risk and protection literature on Hispanic adolescents is the relationship between drug use and acculturation-related processes. Acculturation, defined as a unidimensional or bidimensional process, occurs when the individual interacts with a host cultural-social context (Szapocznik & Kurtines 1993). Youths born in the United States, youths who have lived more years in the United States, and youths with higher levels of acculturation (typically represented by preference for English language use and/or endorsement of interests and values of the host culture) show higher rates of delinquency and substance use (Fridrich & Flannery 1995, Gil et al. 2000, Turner et al. 2006, Warner et al. 2006).

This finding regarding risk for drug use is part of a larger pattern often referred to as the immigrant paradox in many health domains. This immigrant paradox (Burnam et al. 1987, Vega et al. 1998) refers to the fact that foreign-born Hispanics who would be expected to show poorer signs of health due to immigration, acculturation stress, and life disruptions tend to report better health indicators than do U.S.-born Hispanics. It also refers to the fact that recent Hispanic immigrants have better health than Hispanic immigrants who have been in the United States longer. This relationship is paradoxical only in terms of the expectations that birth and life in the United States should be beneficial, but are not.

Identification of the factors that contribute to this paradoxical relationship promises to shed light on important risk and protective processes for Hispanic youths, and it has been the focus of recent research. For example, deterioration in Hispanic family values, attitudes, and familistic behaviors has been found to affect the relationship between acculturation and acculturation stress on the one hand, and alcohol use on the other (Gil et al. 2000). Although Gil et al. (1998) found that accumulation of family risk (i.e., low family pride, family cohesion, ineffective parenting, family communication, and high family drug problems and parent derogation) was highly predictive of drug use initiation in both immigrant and U.S.-born Hispanics, Turner et al. (2006) found that cumulative stress exposure within and outside of the family was highly predictive of drug initiation among Hispanics. Similarly, Turner et al. (2006) found that recent immigrants tended to report lower levels of stress exposure when compared with U.S.-born Hispanics, which suggests another possible explanation for the immigrant paradox. These studies imply that family processes commonly suggested to create risk for drug abuse (e.g., inconsistent and unpredictable parenting practices, family conflict, poor parent-child relationships) could be exacerbated by acculturation-related processes. Finally, discrepancies in acculturation have been found to be related to drug use. These discrepancies in acculturation, known as differential acculturation, tend to occur when adolescents from immigrant families are more likely than are their parents to master English and to adopt host country behaviors and values (Szapocznik & Kurtines 1993). Differential acculturation promotes risk for drug abuse (and other problem behaviors) in Hispanic immigrant adolescents because it creates additional familial conflict that undermines adolescent bonding to the family and erodes parental authority (De la Rosa et al. 2000, Szapocznik & Kurtines 1993). Acculturation stress associated with the conflict of values between the old culture and those of the new culture have been shown to influence drug use among Hispanics (Strait 1999). In a recent study, Martinez (2006) showed that the relationship between discrepancies in acculturation and risk are mediated by family stress and parenting practices.

Differential acculturation: discrepancies in retention of culture of origin or in adoption of host culture that occur when adolescents from immigrant families master the host culture more quickly than their parent figures and/or other extended family members

PREVENTION AND TREATMENT INTERVENTIONS

A growing body of evidence supports the efficacy of behavioral interventions for both drug abuse prevention (Nation et al. 2003) and treatment (Volkow 2003). Unfortunately, the literature on African American and Hispanic adolescents is rather limited. The objective of this section is to present efficacious drug abuse intervention models for both African American and Hispanic adolescents, to identify commonalities and differences among these models, to discuss culture-specific interventions and cultural adaptations to generic intervention models, and to review studies on mediation and moderation, as well as studies on initial (referred to as engagement) and continued (referred to as retention) participation in an intervention. To identify prevention and treatment intervention models with efficacy for African American or Hispanic adolescents, we conducted a search of the *PsychINFO* and *MEDLINE* databases from 1985–2006 using the keywords "drug or drugs" and "prevention or preventive or treatment" and "Hispanic, Latino(a), African American, or black." Included in this review are studies that met the following criteria: (*a*) randomized controlled trials, (*b*) adolescents ages 12–17, and (*c*) primarily African American or Hispanic sample (i.e., 70% or greater) or reported separate results for either African Americans or Hispanics.

Ten drug abuse preventive intervention models were identified: Six demonstrated efficacy with African American adolescents and four with Hispanic adolescents. The number of drug abuse treatment studies with African American and Hispanic adolescents was more limited: One intervention demonstrated efficacy with African American adolescents and one intervention demonstrated efficacy for Hispanic adolescents. A summary, including sample demographics, research design, intervention description, and results for each of the 12 intervention models can be found in **Table 1**. To avoid redundancy, we do not summarize each of the studies listed in **Table 1** in the narrative of the article.

Similarities: Family

One of the most striking similarities across nine of the twelve preventive and treatment models is the inclusion of parents or families in the intervention. Seven of the ten prevention programs involve the family in at least one of the intervention sessions, with the majority involving the family in multiple intervention sessions. Furthermore, two of the Hispanic preventive programs (i.e., Familias Unidas and Nuestras Familias) have demonstrated that it is possible to improve adolescent outcomes by working primarily with the parent and minimally involving the target adolescent. Both of the treatment interventions make family their centerpiece. The nine interventions involving the family also target risk and protective processes in the family domain. In fact, the studies on these programs assess and report on family-level outcomes including positive parental extent of involvement, parenting, family support, family functioning, parent-adolescent communication, and general parent-adolescent affective quality.

The fact that most of the efficacious interventions are family based and target risk and protective family processes may not be coincidental. A substantial literature has established that the family is the most important and fundamental social system influencing human development (e.g., Bronfenbrenner 1979, 1986; Perrino et al. 2000; Szapocznik & Coatsworth 1999). This may be especially true among African Americans and Hispanics (Santisteban et al. 2002), for whom familism (e.g., use of family network as a source of emotional social support, likelihood to reside in close proximity to family) is an integral part of the culture. Therefore, it is not surprising that these interventions target some aspect of family functioning, such as parental behavior.

Although there are a multiplicity of risk and protective targets for intervention including individual, family, peer, school, and neighborhood, each prevention and treatment model and its theoretical framework makes a decision with regard to the most strategic point of intervention. Remarkably, for most of the models found to be efficacious with our two target populations, the strategic point of entry for behavioral change was the family. Is it something about the population, the state of the field, or the set of tools available to the developers? Is it because developers believe that family plays a central role in adolescent development and behavior in these populations, or is it that those interventions that were found efficacious tended to be family based? This last question juxtaposes belief and empirical evidence. It is not possible to unconfound these variables from the available research. That is, it is not possible to determine if other nonfamily interventions would have been as efficacious with our two target populations, had they been tested. However, it should be noted that even outside of minority group research, family has played a crucial role in evidence-based prevention and treatment interventions for drug abuse. For example, in adolescent drug abuse treatment, family interventions have typically been found to be more efficacious than other treatment modalities (Szapocznik et al. 2006).

Similarities: Culture

Another theme across many of the models in **Table 1** is the prominent role of culture. Although no clear consensus exists about the relative efficacy of generic versus culturally

Table 1 Summary of drug abuse preventive and treatment intervention models for African American and Hispanic adolescents

Source	Participants	Research design	Experimental condition	Results
	Prevention interventions for African Americans			
Strong African American Families (SAAF) Program Initial study: Brody et al. (2006a) Follow-up study: Brody et al. (2006b)	• 150 African American parents and their adolescent children • Age: $M = 11.2$ • Families living in the rural South	• Randomized counties to SAAF or to a control condition in which parents received 3 mailings about development in early adolescence, stress management, and techniques to encourage children to exercise • Data collected at pretest, post-test (8 months after pretest), and follow-up (29 months after the pretest)	• Modification of Strong Families Program Curriculum (Kumpfer et al. 1989) • Theoretical orientation: Social Ecological Model (Bronfenbrenner & Morris 1998) and Cognitive Model of Adolescent Health Risk Behavior (Gibbons et al. 2003) • Format: parent, adolescent, and combined parent-adolescent sessions • Number of possible sessions: 7 • Aim of intervention: to reduce alcohol and other drug use, delinquent activity, aggression, and other problem behaviors by enhancing parent and youth competence	Adolescent outcomes: compared with control group, adolescents in SAAF intervention at post-test reported less initiation of risk behaviors (alcohol and other drug use, sexual intercourse) and slower increase in alcohol use over time among those who used alcohol. Adolescents in SAAF reported less initiation of alcohol use at 29-month follow-up than did controls. Parent outcomes: compared with controls, SAAF parents reported more use of communicative parenting behaviors and adolescents reported more positive parenting. Mediator effects: changes in parenting behaviors (regulated, communicative parenting, and positive parental behaviors) mediated the relationship between group assignment and adolescent participation in high-risk behaviors. At the 29-month follow-up, an increase in youth protective factors (e.g., goal-directed future orientation, negative attitudes about alcohol, images of drinkers, and resistance efficacy) mediated the relationship between group assignment and alcohol use.

(Continued)

Table 1 *(Continued)*

Source	Participants	Research design	Experimental condition	Results
Strengthening Families Program: For Parents and Youth 10–14 (SFP 10–14) Spoth et al. (2003)	• 119 African American families • Age: M = 10.5	• Randomized families to intervention or wait-list control • Pre- and post-test data collected[a]	• Modified version of generic Iowa Strengthening Families Program (SFP; Molgaard et al. 2000) • Theoretical orientation: social ecological model (Bronfenbrenner & Morris 1998) • Format: parent, adolescent, and family sessions • Number of possible sessions: 6 • Aim of intervention: to reduce adolescent substance abuse and other problem behaviors by enhancing social skills in youths, improving parenting behaviors, and improving relationships among family members	Adolescent outcomes: relative to the wait-list control, the SFP 10–14 adolescents reported improved scores on behavior problems. Parent caregivers of SFP 10–14 participants reported a higher level of adolescent participation in family meetings (outside of intervention session). The two groups did not differ on alcohol-related peer resistance, general peer resistance, or alcohol refusal. Parent and family outcomes: the two groups did not differ on intervention-targeted parent behaviors, the number of family meetings held, or parent-child affective quality.
Life Skills Training (LST) Program Botvin et al. (1989)	• 603 participants (87% African American) • Age: seventh graders	• Randomized nine inner-city schools to either the LST intervention or to a control condition that only included ongoing educational activities available at the school • Pre- and post-test data collected	• Modified version of generic LST Program (Botvin & Griffin 2004) • Theoretical rationale: cognitive-behavioral • Format: teacher-led groups • Number of possible sessions: 12 • Aim of intervention: to reduce tobacco use by using cognitive strategies to enhance self esteem, demonstrating techniques to resist advertising appeals, strengthening coping techniques, improving verbal and nonverbal communication, improving social skills, and improving assertive skills	Adolescent outcomes: fewer smokers in LST at follow-up than in control group.

Classroom Centered (CC)[b] Family School Partnership (FSP)[b] Storr et al. (2002)	• 653 adolescents • Sample is 86.6% African American • Recruited in first grade and followed until seventh grade. • Age: $M = 6.2$, $SD = 0.4$	• Randomized children and teachers to either one of the two intervention conditions (CC or FSP) or to the control group (usual curriculum) • Data collected at pretest, first and second grades, and again six years after the intervention, when participants were in the seventh grade	• Theoretical orientation: life course/social field theory (Kellam & Rebok 1992) • Format: classroom centered or combined family and school activities in the FSP • Number of possible sessions: FSP, 7 weekly; CC, school year • Aim of intervention: both aimed at reducing harmful factors assumed to increase risk for later problem behaviors. CC aimed at reducing aggressive and shy behaviors and academic achievement. FSP sought to address the same risk factors by increasing family–school communication and parenting practices	Adolescent outcomes: participants in CC and FSP were less likely than controls to have initiated tobacco use by seventh grade.
Multidimensional Family Prevention (MDFP) Hogue et al. (2002)	• 124 adolescents and their families • Sample is 97% African American • Age: $M =$ 12.5 years, $SD = 0.90$	• Randomized families to either MDFP or a no-contact control • Pre- and post-test data collected	• Theoretical orientation: developmental-ecological family-based prevention • Format: conducted with individual families. Separate adolescent and family modules but also a combined interactional and an extrafamilial module • Possible number of sessions: 15–20 over 3- to 4-month period • Aim of intervention: to prevent or delay substance abuse by strengthening the attachment to parents and family and by helping adolescent to build positive connections to schools, prosocial peer groups, and recreational and religious institutions	Adolescent outcomes: MDFP participants demonstrated more improvement than did controls on self-concept, school bonding, and antisocial behaviors of peers. No group differences on drug use attitudes, parental monitoring, school grades, school antisocial behavior, and prosocial activities. Family outcomes: MDFP group demonstrated more positive outcomes on family cohesion but no group differences on parental monitoring.

(Continued)

Table 1 *(Continued)*

Source	Participants	Research design	Experimental condition	Results
	Prevention interventions for Hispanics			
Familias Unidas Pantin et al. (2003)	• 167 Hispanic adolescents (and their primary caregivers) • Grade range: 6–7 • Age range: 10.69–14.89, (M = 12.40, SD = 0.80)	• Randomized families to Familias Unidas or to no-contact control • Data collected at baseline, 3, 6, 9, and 12 months post-baseline	• Theoretical orientation: ecodevelopmental theory (Coatsworth, Pantin, & Szapocznik 2002; Szapocznik & Coatsworth 1999) • Format: parent group intervention • Aim of intervention: improve adolescent behaviors by promoting parental investment and fostering parenting skills	Adolescent outcomes: Familias Unidas was more efficacious than control group in decreasing behavior problems. No group differences on school bonding. Parent outcomes: increases in parental investment were not significantly different at 6 months. However, Familias Unidas participants were more likely to maintain parental investment increases at the 12-month follow-up. Mediator (process) effects: although classic mediation (cf. Baron & Kenny 1986) was not found, changes in parental investment between consecutive assessments intervals was significantly related to subsequent levels of adolescent behavior problems.
Nuestras Familias Martinez & Eddy (2005)	• 73 adolescents (and their parents) • Age: M = 12.74, SD = 1.05	• Parents randomized to Nuestras Familias or no-contact control • Pre- and post-intervention approximately 6 months post-baseline	• Theoretical orientation: social interaction learning theory (Reid et al. 2002) and ecodevelopmental theory (Szapocznik & Coatsworth 1999) • Format: parent groups • Possible number of sessions: 12 • Aim of intervention: reduce youth problems (e.g., substance use, police contacts, out-of-home placements, number of days institutionalized, difficulties with peers and teachers, and depression) by influencing parenting practices and family environmental variables	Adolescent outcomes: adolescents in Nuestra Familias demonstrated fewer behavior problems (aggression and externalizing) and less tobacco use than did the control group. The two groups did not differ on alcohol or marijuana use, depression, or academic success. Parent outcomes: in comparison with the control group, parents in Nuestra Familias demonstrated more effective and better use of effective parenting strategies during past month and contingent positive reinforcement in response to youth prosocial behavior. Moderator effects: the outcomes on youth aggression and externalizing behaviors was similar for U.S.-born and foreign-born youths who participated in Nuestras Familias. However, the outcomes for the no-contact control

				were more favorable for foreign-born than U.S.-born participants. Depression was also more evident among adolescents of U.S.-born participants than among foreign-born participants.
Keepin' it REAL Kulis et al. (2005)	• 3402 youths of Mexican heritage • Age: seventh graders • Age range: *M* = 12.52, SD = 0.64	• Randomized 35 middle schools to either one of the three versions of the intervention or to a control condition that received a course selected by the schools to meet state-mandated substance abuse prevention programming • Data collected at baseline and again at 14 months after program completion	• Theoretical orientation: ecological risk and resilience approach (Bogenschneider 1996) • Format: school based (classroom activities, videos, and homework assignments) • Number of possible sessions: 10-lesson curriculum • Aim of intervention: to reduce substance use by enhancing cultural identification, promoting personal antidrug norms, and to develop decision-making and resistance skills • Three versions of the curriculum: Mexican American, European and African American, and multicultural	Adolescent outcomes: in comparison with controls, youths in the Latino version reported less recent alcohol use and recent marijuana use, stronger intentions to refuse substances, greater confidence they could do so, and lower estimates of substance-using peers. Compared with controls, youths in the multicultural version reported less recent alcohol use, marijuana use, and substance use.
Family Effectiveness Training (FET) Szapocznik et al. (1989)	• 79 Hispanic youths (and their families) • Age range: 6–12 (*M* = 9.44)	• Randomized families to either the FET intervention or a minimal contact control • Solomon four-group design. Half within each condition had a pretest assessment and the other half did not. Data collected from all groups at post-test	• Theoretical orientation: Strategic Structural Systems (Szapocznik & Kurtines 1989) approach • Format: family sessions • Possible number of sessions: 13 • Aim of intervention: reduce problem behaviors by improving family functioning	Adolescent outcomes: FET adolescents had lower behavior problem scores than did the control adolescents overall and in these areas: conduct problems, personality problems, and inadequacy-immaturity. FET adolescents reported more gains in self-concept than did control adolescents. The two groups did not differ on a measure of social delinquency. Family outcomes: FET families reported more improvement in family relations overall and in the following specific areas: conflict resolution, structure, resonance, and developmental stage. More improvement reported in fathers' perception of expressiveness among FET families than among control families.

(Continued)

Table 1 (*Continued*)

Source	Participants	Research design	Experimental condition	Results
	Treatment interventions for African Americans			
Multisystemic Therapy (MST) Henggeler et al. (1991)	• 47 adolescents • 74% African American • Age: M = 15.7 years	• Adolescents randomly assigned to MST or to usual juvenile justice services • Data collected at pre- and post-test	• Theoretical orientation: Family Systems Theory (Haley 1976, Minuchin 1974) and Social Ecological Theory (Bronfenbrenner & Morris 1998) • Treatment setting: family home or alternative community setting • Mean hours of treatment: M: 36, SD = 34 • Aim of intervention: reduce delinquent behavior by targeting dysfunctional interactions within the family as well as multisystemic factors in the youth's environment	Adolescent outcomes: MST adolescents reported less alcohol and marijuana use in comparison with controls.
	Treatment interventions for Hispanics			
Brief Strategic Family Therapy (BSFT) Santisteban et al. (2003)	• 126 behavior problem Hispanic adolescents (and their families) • Age range: 12–18 years (M = 15.6)	• Randomized families to BSFT or to a group control condition • Pre- and post-test data collected	• Theoretical orientation: Strategic Structural Systems (Szapocznik & Kurtines 1989) • Treatment setting: family sessions at the clinic or home • Number of sessions: M = 11.2, SD = 3.8 • Aim of intervention: improve adolescent behavior by transforming family interaction patterns	Adolescent outcomes: In comparison with controls, BSFT adolescents reported less marijuana use but not less alcohol use. Parents reported fewer conduct problems and peer-based delinquency in BSFT adolescents than did parents of controls. Family outcomes: BSFT adolescents reported more improvement in cohesion scores than did controls. No group differences were evident for parent-reported cohesion scores. Moderator effects: for families entering treatment with relatively poor family functioning, BSFT improved family functioning, whereas the group condition did not. For families entering treatment with relatively good family functioning, BSFT maintained good family functioning, whereas the group condition deteriorated.

[a]Although a follow-up (Time 3) data collection was included, only the post-test (Time 2) outcomes are described here.
[b]Note that two interventions were tested in a single study.

specific interventions (see Castro et al. 2004), a number of arguments have been made to support the role of culture in both understanding racial/ethnic minority group behavior (e.g., Belgrave 2002, Gil et al. 2000) and its prevention and treatment (see Castro et al. 2004, Miranda et al. 2005). One important argument in support of culturally specific interventions is that differences in the type of exposure to risk and protection exist between ethnic groups (e.g., racial identity for African Americans, acculturation for Hispanics). A second argument is that specific groups (by gender, by race/ethnicity, by age, by psychiatric morbidity) may respond better to interventions that are specific to their preferred views, attitudes, customs, or needs. Szapocznik and colleagues (Szapocznik et al. 1978, 1990), for example, used empirical strategies to match characteristics and problems of particular subpopulations to specific interventions.

In the models listed in **Table 1**, several were developed for particular populations with specific characteristics and target problems. For example, Familias Unidas, Family Effectiveness Training, and Brief Strategic Family Therapy™ were initially developed for very specific Hispanic subpopulations, each confronting a set of very well-defined risk and protective processes (e.g., acculturation gap/intergenerational conflict and other acculturation stressors) and/or problem behaviors. Interestingly, however, all three of these models were developed using universal principles derived from broad theoretical frameworks (e.g., Ecodevelopmental Theory) that ensure their integration with a larger body of research as well as facilitate their generalizability (Coatsworth et al. 2002, Szapocznik & Williams 2000). In contrast, adaptations from generic interventions include Nuestras Familias (developed from Parenting Management Training; Reid et al. 1999), the Strong African American Families Program (developed from the Strong Families Program; Kumpfer et al. 1989), Life Skills Training (developed from Life Skills Training; Botvin & Griffin 2004), and the Strengthening Families Program (developed from the Iowa Strengthening Families Program; Molgaard et al. 2000).

Yet, other interventions, such as Multidimensional Family Prevention and Multisystemic Family Therapy, were not specifically developed or adapted for work with the target minority population, African Americans. However, Multidimensional Family Prevention's predecessor, Multidimensional Family Therapy, as well as Multisystemic Therapy have been amply used with African Americans, although no separate analyses for African Americans have been published.

Some Considerations About Adaptations from Generic to Culture-Specific Interventions

Resnicow et al. (2000) describe two strategies for adapting generic interventions. An example of the first strategy, referred to as surface modifications, was used in the adaptation of the Strengthening Families. The name of the intervention was changed to be more Africentric (i.e., Harambee). In addition, the racial composition of the videotape actors and staff was African American, and sessions were modified based on the team's understanding that African American adolescents prefer more active sessions. The second strategy described by Resnicow and colleagues involves the modification of the actual content and process of the intervention to incorporate the cultural norms and social realities of the ethnic group into the intervention. This approach is referred to as deep structure, and the modifications are seen as more substantive than the surface approach. A deep structural approach was used to modify the Strong Families Program for the Strong African Americans Program. Specifically, the basis for the modification of the generic curriculum was the team's earlier research (Brody et al. 2002) that identified specific competence-promoting parenting practices that protect African American youths, such as racial socialization activities aimed at bolstering ethnic pride and communicating that African American adolescents can achieve their goals despite societal obstacles.

The Role of Context in Minority Interventions

In recognition of the systemic nature of the relationship among the many processes that are likely to precede, be concurrent, or to occur as a consequence of drug use, many of the systemic and developmental theoretical approaches undergirding drug abuse prevention and treatment interventions recognize a complex set of interacting antecedents as potential targets, even when the interventions themselves are more limited in scope. For example, most interventions target far more than just drug use. As noted above, deviant adolescent developmental trajectories often comprise a wide array of problem behaviors, including drug and alcohol use, as well as problems with school adjustment, conduct, delinquency, and risk-taking sexual behavior, among others. Efficacious interventions are likely to address multiple targets, ranging from family functioning through school bonding and achievement, conduct problems, association with antisocial peers, and delinquency.

As might occur in complex systemic processes, some processes, such as family functioning, are typically labeled as antecedents to problem behavior, although Santisteban et al. (2003) found that some families with problem-behavior adolescents entered treatment with relatively good family functioning. Hence, maladaptive family functioning may precede, be concurrent, or even occur as a result of adolescent drug abuse. Similarly, other processes, such as school adjustment and bonding and associating with antisocial peers, can both precede problem behavior including drug use and can be exacerbated by drug use. The complex, systemic nature of ecodevelopmental processes and the recognition of such complexity in many interventions are true of the field in general as well as of interventions that target minorities.

Some of the culturally specific interventions might appear to be unique in their attention to specific cultural or other contextual conditions. For example, Brief Strategic Family Therapy (Szapocznik et al. 2003) was initially developed specifically to adapt to the value orientations of the target population and to address the intergenerational conflict that arose from acculturation differences between adolescents and their parents. It is possible that all interventions, minority-specific or not, are responsive to the cultural and contextual conditions in which they are designed and delivered. Thus, it is possible that mainstream interventions are responding to mainstream culture and other contextual conditions, even though the developer may not pay particular attention to the relationship between culture and intervention. What may be truly unique is that developers of minority-specific interventions are more likely to identify those aspects of the intervention that are culture specific than are developers of mainstream interventions.

Mediation and Moderation

An important observation is that a small number of the studies reviewed presented analyses on mediation. Mediation explains how interventions have their effects. Typically, mediation is hypothesized to operate through theoretical mechanisms, and as such, evidence for mediation lends credence to the theory underlying the intervention. Brody et al. (2006) demonstrated that the Strong African American Families Program had its impact on adolescents by increasing parent-reported parental involvement, discipline, and parental monitoring as well as adolescent-reported positive parental involvement. Although Pantin et al. (2003) did not find classic mediation (cf. Baron & Kenny 1986), in part as a function of the quadratic nature of the trajectory of Hispanic behavior problems, changes in parental investment between consecutive assessments intervals was significantly related to subsequent levels of adolescent behavior problems. An understanding of the processes by which these interventions have their impact on minority adolescents can provide guidance on how interventions can be streamlined or strengthened.

In addition to understanding the processes by which interventions have their effect, it is important to understand for whom specific drug use preventive and treatment interventions are efficacious and for whom they are not. Two of the eleven published interventions reported such analyses, revealing that intervention effects varied by U.S.- versus foreign-born participants (Nuestra Familias; Martinez & Eddy 2005) and levels of behavior problems (Storr et al. 2002). These findings support the need to consider within-group heterogeneity in the design of future studies. As noted above, the terms "Hispanic" and "African American" reflect extremely broad groupings. When the lens is zoomed in on these groups, their within-group diversity may become evident.

Not surprisingly, none of the prevention or treatment interventions summarized in **Table 1** reported separate analyses for girls. Adolescent girls generally use drugs less than do adolescent boys (Johnston et al. 2005). Nevertheless, it has been suggested that girls in drug treatment tend to have much higher levels of severity of psychopathology and family conflict (e.g., Dakof 2000). African American and Hispanic adolescent females are double minorities, and as such, less attention has been paid to these groups. Although prevention studies listed in **Table 1** have tended to include an adequate number of girls in their samples, treatment studies listed in **Table 1** have not, in large part because the majority of adolescents referred to these studies were boys. Although most studies are not powered for separate analyses by gender, it is recommended that future studies with these minority groups at least report separate effect sizes for boys and girls.

A final and obvious finding from **Table 1** is the overall limited number of existing published drug abuse preventive and treatment interventions for African American and Hispanic adolescents. The small number of interventions is especially disconcerting considering the elevated levels of drug use among Hispanics and the severe consequences of drug use among African Americans. Research findings have typically suggested that African Americans and Hispanics receive less drug treatment than do their non-Hispanic white counterparts (Wells et al. 2001).

ENGAGEMENT AND RETENTION

Access to care can be understood from the perspective of the barriers or facilitators that occur in a community, an agency, an interventionist, or the client. There is a substantial literature on the impact of community and agency characteristics that might affect access to care (e.g., Alegria et al. 2004). Similarly, an extensive literature examines the role of pre-existing client variables (e.g., socioeconomic status, social support, motivation) as predictors of engagement (e.g., Perrino et al. 2001) and retention (e.g., Coatsworth et al. 2006). It has been suggested that the latter type of research may blame the minority client (e.g., "They don't come because they are unmotivated"). Consistent with Surgeon General Satcher's emphasis (U.S. Dept. Health Human Serv. 2001), we review studies that do not blame the client, but rather explore how interventions can be changed to be more efficacious in engaging and retaining African American and Hispanic clients. Like the studies reviewed in this section reveal, this approach to engagement and retention of minority clients has considerable potential for improving the quality of care.

Prevention and treatment interventions are based on the assumption that clients receive the intervention. Failure to receive services often results from an inability to engage and retain the adolescent in services. Thus, adequate dosage is essential for efficacious interventions. Attainment of efficacy, hence, assumes that it is possible to facilitate engagement and retention in an intervention.

BSFT: Brief Strategic Family Therapy™

For interventions involving the family, including most of the interventions summarized in **Table 1**, engagement may be even more challenging because of the complexities involved in obtaining the participation of adolescents, parent figures, and/or any other family members that is needed to successfully deliver the intervention (e.g., DeMarsh & Kumpfer 1986, Gorman-Smith et al. 2002). This section reviews studies focusing on engagement and retention of efficacious intervention models with Hispanic or African American adolescents. Because of the growing literature focusing on this topic, we limit our discussion on published engagement and retention studies to one of the eleven efficacious intervention models with African Americans or Hispanics summarized in **Table 1**.

Engagement and retention prevention process studies. Two published process studies focus on engagement and retention in Familias Unidas. Coatsworth et al. (2006) found that participant leadership in the group and group cohesion (i.e., positive alliances with other group members) significantly predicted retention. In the second study, Prado et al. (2006a) established that parent-facilitator relationship quality measured as therapeutic alliance at initial contact, which occurred before the first group intervention session, was found to be the strongest predictor of engagement, accounting for over 36% of the engagement variance. Similarly, group cohesion, participant involvement in the group, and participant working toward achieving her/his goals positively predicted retention. These studies point to possible targets for improving engagement and retention of Hispanic families in prevention interventions, including strategies to improve parent-group and parent-facilitator alliances, group cohesion, and encouraging involvement in group as well as participant work toward achievement of goals. Attending to intraintervention processes moves the focus away from the minority client characteristics and toward the identification of strategies that facilitators can use to increase engagement and retention in this specific minority subgroup.

Engagement and retention treatment outcome studies. A challenge in adolescent drug treatment has been to engage adolescents and their families in treatment (Santisteban et al. 2005). Three randomized studies evaluated the efficacy of Brief Strategic Family Therapy™ (BSFT™)-Engagement, a set of specialized engagement procedures ranging from establishing strategic alliances with powerful members of the family to conducting home-based services when appropriate (Coatsworth et al. 2001, Santisteban et al. 1996, Szapocznik et al. 1988). Participants randomized to BSFT plus the specialized BSFT-Engagement module engaged at significantly higher rates than did the control families in both studies. Although Szapocznik et al. (1988) had significantly greater retention in the BSFT + BSFT-Engagement module, Santisteban et al. (1996) did not. In a third study (Coatsworth et al. 2001), BSFT-Engagement was fully integrated into BSFT. Coatsworth et al. (2001) found that families randomized to BSFT (with BSFT-Engagement) had significantly higher rates of engagement and retention than did participants randomized to a family-oriented, community-based treatment agency.

The engagement and retention process and outcome studies reviewed share commonalities that have important implications. First, the studies highlight the critical importance of the parent-interventionist relationship quality and interventionists' skills at the initial contact (cf. Prado et al. 2006a, Szapocznik et al. 1988). It is vitally important that facilitators/therapists develop a positive alliance with the participant at the initial contact. Second, the retention studies found that intervention processes are important predictors of continued attendance. Identification of in-sessions processes that predict retention is important given that these processes, just as therapeutic alliance at first contact, are malleable to interventionist training. Finally, the 80% to 90% engagement in the three treatment-engagement studies and the 90% engagement rates observed by Prado et al. (2006a) suggest that integrating specialized engagement modules that focus on changing therapist/clinician behavior as a way of engaging families is highly promising. Given the considerable literature on the difficulties Hispanics experience in accessing treatment, these engagement studies demonstrate that changes in interventionist behaviors have considerable potential for improving access. Of course, many barriers were removed in these studies for both the specialized engagement and control conditions, such as employing fully Spanish-speaking interventionists who were trained to work with families. Nevertheless, the changes in interventionist behaviors were responsible for significantly better outcomes in engagement and retention, above and beyond those that resulted in the control condition when structural barriers were removed. Finally, as suggested by these studies, the specific changes in the interventionist behaviors need to be guided through use of a manual, yet remain sufficiently flexible to permit approaching families in ways that uniquely respond to each family's circumstances.

CONCLUSIONS AND IMPLICATIONS

An understanding of African American and Hispanic adolescent drug abuse occurs at the intersection of context, development, and behavior. The focus of this review is on the impact of racial/ethnic culture as one of the important contexts that influence adolescent development toward or away from prosocial behaviors. Because family plays a major role in both African American and Hispanic cultures, it is also a centerpiece of any discussion of adolescent development in these groups.

Culture is central to the understanding of adolescent developmental trajectories. All youths develop within complex cultural contexts. Socialization, racial or otherwise, is the task of families and societies across the racial/ethnic/nationality spectrum. Not unlike the case of racial socialization, socialization in general includes elements that help youths cope with their social context. Similarly, the struggle with cultural change is pervasive in a modern society in which modernization is shaping culture at unprecedented speed. Acculturation is a response to cultural change. More specifically, acculturation is the individual's response to a special case of exposure to an environment that is changing for the individual as the individual travels across geography, time, and sociocultural context. Acculturation, however, affects not only immigrants. It affects all individuals exposed to changes in culture, regardless of whether these changes come about through migration or exposure to modernization over time. Findings on Hispanic adolescent drug use reveal that acculturation has led to increases in drug use. In these studies, acculturation took place toward U.S. mainstream culture. It is also the case that during the last half of the twentieth century, a period during which the United States suffered a bout of cultural modernization, drug use among all adolescents increased. Is it possible that that the acculturation effects measured in Hispanics are only a special case of acculturation that may have occurred for all U.S. adolescents during the last half century?

An understanding of drug abuse among African American and Hispanic adolescents then requires attention to universal principles. As predicted by a number of theories (e.g., Ecodevelopmental, Social-Ecological), context influences development. Context is both social and cultural, and as such the sociocultural context of the two racial/ethnic groups will define elements of adolescent development. Particularly important aspects of context for these two groups are culture, the specific protective cultural processes (e.g., racial socialization), and cultural risk processes (e.g., acculturation). Context defines development and development will define the adolescent's behavior, including drug use.

From the perspective of a broad lens, specific minority groups such as African Americans and Hispanics would appear to have more in common than not. However, each of these groups encompasses considerable genetic, historical, social, and cultural heterogeneity. The study of the human condition is incomplete without the study of the full range of variability along these variables. Paradoxically, the study of any one racial/ethnic group is equally incomplete without the study of the full range of variability for that group on these same four variables.

With two handfuls of efficacious interventions, the danger is to assume that one size fits all: that each of these interventions may be generalizable to all adolescents in the specific racial/ethnic group. Although the 11 efficacious interventions described in **Table 1** represent an enormous leap forward in knowledge for these two racial/ethnic groups, a master strategic plan might start by systematically mapping all the domains of risk and protection, ranging from genetic to cultural. From the multiple risk and protective processes within each domain and their interaction and consequences, strategic targets for intervention must be selected. Subsequently, interventions might be designed to impact these strategic targets. If such a plan were followed, might family emerge as the strategic target, as it appears to have emerged as the target of choice by intervention developers? Considerable theoretical and empirical research suggests that it might. However, little research has been sufficiently comprehensive to permit assessment of the multiple processes at work, and in such broad context identify the crucial targets for potential intervention. Most studies have tended to include a relatively small number of variables, and it has been necessary to put together a patchwork quilt of findings in efforts to imagine what the larger picture might be. This challenge is ever more serious with minorities, for whom we know so much less.

Finally, given the small number of interventions that have provided information about their usefulness for either African Americans or Hispanics, it is essential that future intervention studies that include even small samples of a racial/ethnic minority group provide sample analyses of the efficacy or effectiveness of the intervention for a specific racial/ethnic group.

Selected Research Priorities

African Americans. The drug use rates of African American adolescents tend to be lower than rates of their Hispanic and white counterparts. However, the consequences of drug use among African Americans are more severe than those of the other two groups, both in terms of HIV/AIDS contraction (particularly for women) and criminal justice involvement (particularly for men) (cf. Wallace et al. 2002). For African American adolescents, it is critical to prevent drug use, given its potential dire consequences; and when drug use occurs, it is essential to prevent further penetration into addiction and its social and health consequences. Structural interventions that improve broad contextual conditions should also be considered. Culturally specific mechanisms, such as racial socialization, appear to exist for African American parents, and knowledge of these mechanisms would greatly benefit their children.

Hispanics. Although much of the prevention research has focused on recent Hispanic immigrant families and their acculturating adolescents, based on the well-documented concerns about the impact of acculturation stressors, epidemiological research now suggests that U.S.-born Hispanics are at higher risk for drug use. Consequently, there is a need to increase research efforts to develop and evaluate prevention interventions for U.S.-born Hispanics and their families. Similarly, additional etiologic research is needed regarding the mechanism through which drug use rates are increased in U.S.-born adolescents. For example, as already noted, the accumulation of family risk processes such as low family cohesion and poor family communication may play a role in the increased drug use rates among U.S.-born Hispanics. Might this be, at least in part, a function of foreign-born parents who were exposed to acculturation as recent adolescent immigrants? Is there a multigenerational transmission of the impact of acculturation? If so, should prevention of drug abuse in the next generation start by intervening with immigrants or foreign-born parents who will bear children in this country?

With 27% drug use rates occurring among eighth-grade Hispanic adolescents, perhaps prevention efforts should be targeted earlier than eighth grade. Moreover, considering that Hispanic eighth- and tenth-grade adolescents have a greater likelihood of reporting drug use than do their African American or white counterparts, large-scale, potentially structural interventions might be considered with this population. For example, Hispanic parents can be encouraged to improve their communication with their children, including speaking with their children about drug use. Thus, large-scale interventions to encourage Hispanic parents to speak with their children about drug use may be beneficial. However, it has been argued (Pantin et al. 2003), at least for Hispanic parents in South Florida, that parents must establish broad channels of communication with their children in order for communication about drug use to be effective.

The intervention trials reported to date bring attention to important aspects of research on interventions, including the study of mechanisms by which interventions have their effects, and the identification of subgroups for which specific interventions are most efficacious. Moreover, research has emerged on a partial solution to problems that the health services literature have reported are particularly recalcitrant: studies on intervention processes and strategies that increase engagement and retention. The next step for the programs of research reported is an effort to replicate findings or, in the case of the BSFT engagement findings, to conduct effectiveness trials. Future replications and effectiveness study should attend to the considerable heterogeneity of the populations under study.

Given the size of the African American and Hispanic populations in the United States, the high rates of drug use among Hispanic adolescents, and the very severe consequences of drug use among African Americans, there continues to be an urgent need to develop, test, and disseminate prevention and treatment interventions to work with these populations. Research is needed to determine if a focus on the unique cultural processes that influence African American and Hispanic adolescent drug use increases the efficacy of interventions.

SUMMARY POINTS

1. African American and Hispanic adolescent drug abuse occurs at the intersection of context, development, and behavior.
2. African American eighth, tenth, and twelfth graders historically have reported the lowest rates of alcohol, cigarette, and illicit drug use (relative to non-Hispanic white and Hispanic eighth, tenth, and twelfth graders).
3. Relative to non-Hispanic whites and African Americans, Hispanic eighth and tenth graders report the highest lifetime, annual, and 30-day prevalence rates of alcohol, cigarette, and licit or illicit drug use, except amphetamines.
4. Racial identity is a culturally specific process that is protective of a wide array of negative consequences in African Americans, including racial discrimination, psychological functioning, and drug use.

5. Hispanic youth have higher rates of drug use when they (*a*) are born in the United States, (*b*) have lived longer in the United States, and (*c*) have higher levels of acculturation.
6. Six drug abuse preventive intervention models have demonstrated efficacy for African American adolescents, and four have demonstrated efficacy for Hispanic adolescents.
7. One drug abuse treatment intervention has demonstrated efficacy with African American adolescents, and one has demonstrated efficacy for Hispanic adolescents.
8. The majority of the preventive and treatment models demonstrating efficacy for African American and Hispanic adolescents have conceptualized the important role of family in the interventions. Consistent with this conceptualization, parents or families were included in some aspect of the intervention, with the majority of models including parents or families intensely.
9. Culture is a prominent theme in most of the preventive and treatment intervention models found to be efficacious with African American and Hispanic adolescents.

FUTURE ISSUES

1. A master strategic plan is needed to systematically map domains of risk and protection for African American and Hispanic adolescents drug use, ranging from genetic to cultural.
2. Structural interventions that improve contextual conditions for African American and Hispanic adolescents should be developed and evaluated.
3. Given the evidence that U.S.-born Hispanics are at higher risk for drug use than foreign-born Hispanics, there is a need to increase research efforts to develop and evaluate prevention interventions for U.S.-born Hispanics and their families.
4. For African American adolescents, it is critical to prevent drug use, given its potential dire consequences; and when drug use occurs, preventing further penetration into addiction as well as its social and health consequences is essential.
5. For the efficacious intervention models reported, replications are needed. In the case of BSFT, Familias Unidas, and LST (which have been replicated), effectiveness trials are needed.
6. Researchers conducting efficacy and effectiveness trials are encouraged to report separate analyses by race/ethnicity, and when appropriate use small sample statistics.
7. Researchers conducting efficacy and effectiveness trials with racial/ethnic minorities are encouraged to report separate analyses by gender, and when appropriate use small sample statistics.
8. For the interventions described in this article, research is needed to understand (*a*) for whom the interventions work and (*b*) the processes by which the interventions have their effect.

ACKNOWLEDGMENTS

Preparation of this manuscript was supported by NIH NIDA grants DA13720, DA19101, DA13732, and DA13104.

LITERATURE CITED

Alegria M, Canino G, Stinson FS, Grant BF. 2006. Nativity and DSM-IV psychiatric disorders among Puerto Ricans, Cuban Americans, and non-Latino whites in the United Status: results from the National Epidemiologic Survey on Alcohol and Related Conditions. *J. Clin. Psychiatry* 67(1):56–65

Alegria M, Takeuchi D, Canino G, Duan N, Shrout P, et al. 2004. Considering context, place and culture: the National Latino and Asian American Study. *Int. J. Methods Psychiatr. Res.* 13(4):208–20

Am. Psychiatr. Assoc. 1994. *Diagnostic and Statistical Manual of Mental Disorders IV-TR*. Washington, DC: Am. Psychiatr. Assoc. 4th ed., text rev.

Arias E, Anderson RN, Kung H, Murphy SL, Kochanek KD. 2003. *Deaths: Final Data for 2001. National Vital Statistics Reports, Vol. 52, No. 3*. Washington, DC: Cent. Disease Control Prev.

Barnes GM, Welte JW, Hoffman JH, Dintcheff BA. 2005. Shared predictors of youthful gambling, substance use and delinquency. *Psychol. Addict. Behav.* 19(2):165–74

Baron RM, Kenny DA. 1986. The moderator-mediator variable distinction in social psychological research: conceptual, strategic, and statistical considerations. *J. Personal. Soc. Psychol.* 52:1173–82

Belgrave FZ. 2002. Relational theory and cultural enhancement interventions for African American adolescent girls. *Public Health Rep.* 117:76–81

Belgrave FZ, Townsend T, Cherry V, Cunningham D. 1997. The influence of an Africentric worldview and demographic variables on drug knowledge, attitudes, and use among African American youth. *J. Community Psychol.* 25:421–33

Bernal G, Scharron-del-Rio M. 2001. Are empirically supported treatments valid for ethnic minorities? Toward an alternative approach for treatment research. *Cultur. Divers. Ethnic Minor. Psychol.* 7:328–42

Bersamin M, Paschall MJ, Flewelling RL. 2005. Ethnic differences in relationships between risk factors and adolescent binge drinking: a national study. *Prev. Sci.* 6(2):127–37

Betancourt H, Lopez SR. 1993. The study of culture, ethnicity, and race in American psychology. *Am. Psychol.* 48(6):629–37

Biafora FA, Warheit GJ, Vega WA, Gil AG. 1994. Stressful life events and changes in substance use among a multiracial/ethnic sample of adolescent boys. *J. Community Psychol.* 22:296–311

Bogenschneider K. 1996. An ecological risk/protective theory for building prevention programs, policies and community capacity to support youth. *Fam. Relat.* 45(2):127–38

Botvin G, Batson H, Witts-Vitale S, Bess V, Baker E, Dusenbury L. 1989. A psychosocial approach to smoking prevention for urban black youth. *Public Health Rep.* 104:573–82

Botvin G, Griffin K. 2004. Life skills training: empirical findings and future directions. *J. Primary Prev.* 25:211–23

Brody GH, McBride MV, Murry V, Kim S, Brown A. 2002. Longitudinal pathways to competence and psychological adjustment among African American children living in rural single-parent households. *Child Dev.* 73:1505–16

Brody GH, Murry VM, Gerrard M, Gibbons FX, McNari L, et al. 2006a. The strong African American families program: prevention of youths' high-risk behavior and a test of a model of change. *J. Fam. Psychol.* 20(1):1–11

Brody GH, Murry VM, Kogan SM, Gerrard M, Gibbons FX, et al. 2006b. The strong African American families program: a cluster-randomized prevention trial of long-term effects and a mediational model. *J Consult. Clin. Psychol.* 74(2):356–66

Bronfenbrenner U. 1979. Contexts of child rearing: problems and prospects. *Am. Psychol.* 34(10):844–50

Bronfenbrenner U. 1986. Ecology of the family as a context for human development: research perspectives. *Dev. Psychol.* 22(6):723–42

Bronfenbrenner U, Morris P. 1998. The ecology of developmental processes. In *Handbook of Child Psychology. Theoretical Models of Human Development*, ed. RM Lerner, W Damon, 1:993–1028. New York: Wiley

Discusses the influence of multiple social contexts on human development.

Brook JS, Whiteman M, Finch SJ, Cohen P. 1996. Young adult drug use and delinquency: childhood antecedents and adolescent mediators. *J. Am. Acad. Child Adolesc. Psychiatry* 35(12):1584–92

Burnam MA, Hough RL, Karno M, Escobar JI. 1987. Acculturation and lifetime prevalence of psychiatric disorders among Mexican Americans in Los Angeles. *J. Health Soc. Behav.* 28(1):89–102

Caldwell C, Sellers R, Bernat D, Zimmerman M. 2006. Racial identity, parental support, and alcohol use in a sample of at-risk African American high school students. *Am. J. Community Psychol.* 34:71–82

Carter JH. 1995. Psychosocial/cultural issues in medicine and psychiatry: treating African Americans. *J. Natl. Med. Assoc.* 87(12):857–60

Castro FG, Barrera M, Martinez CR. 2004. The cultural adaptation of prevention interventions: resolving tensions between fidelity and fit. *Prev. Sci.* 5(1):41–45

Caughy M, O'Campo P, Randolph S, Nickerson K. 2002. The influence of racial socialization practices on the cognitive and behavioral competence of African American preschoolers. *Child Dev.* 73:1611–25

Chavous T, Bernat D, Schmeelk-Cone K, Cadwell C, Kohn-Wood L, Zimmerman M. 2003. Racial identity and academic attainment among African American adolescents. *Child Dev.* 74:1076–90

Coard S, Wallace S, Stevenson H, Brotman L. 2004. Towards culturally relevant preventive interventions: the consideration of racial socialization in training with African American families. *J. Child Fam. Stud.* 13:277–93

Coatsworth JD, Duncan L, Pantin H, Szapocznik J. 2006. Retaining ethnic minority parents in a preventive intervention: the quality of group process. *J. Primary Prev.* 27(2):171–93

Coatsworth JD, Pantin H, Szapocznik J. 2002. Familias Unidas: a family-centered ecodevelopmental intervention to reduce risk for problem behavior among Hispanic adolescents. *Clin. Child Fam. Psychol. Rev.* 5(2):113–32

Explains the Familias Unidas intervention model, weaving together intervention process, social context, and culture.

Coatsworth JD, Santisteban DA, McBride C, Szapocznik J. 2001. Brief Strategic Family Therapy versus community control: engagement, retention, and an exploration of the moderating role of adolescent symptom severity. *Fam. Proc.* 40(3):313–32

Constantine M, Blackmon S. 2002. Black adolescents' racial socialization experiences: their relations to home, school, and peer esteem. *J. Black Stud.* 32:322–35

Cook RL, Pollock NK, Rao AK, Clark DB. 2002. Increased prevalence of herpes simplex virus type 2 among adolescent women with alcohol use disorders. *J. Adolesc. Health* 30(3):169–74

Dakof GA. 2000. Understanding gender differences in adolescent drug abuse: issues of comorbidity and family functioning. *J. Psychoactive Drugs* 32(1):25–32

De la Rosa M, Vega R, Radisch MA. 2000. The role of acculturation in the substance abuse behavior of African-American and Latino adolescents: advances, issues, and recommendations? *J. Psychoactive Drugs* 32:33–42

Delva J, Wallace JM, O'Malley PM, Bachman JG, Johnston LD, Schulenberg JE. 2005. The epidemiology of alcohol, marijuana, and cocaine use among Mexican American, Puerto Rican, Cuban American and other Latin American eighth-grade students in the United States: 1991–2002. *Am. J. Public Health* 95(4):696–702

DeMarsh J, Kumpfer KL. 1986. Family-oriented interventions for the prevention of chemical dependency in children and adolescents. *J. Child. Contemp. Soc.* 18(1–2):117–51

Ellickson PL, Tucker JS, Klein DJ. 2003. Ten-year prospective study of public health problems associated with early drinking. *Pediatrics* 111(5):949–55

Fischer A, Shaw C. 1999. African Americans' mental health and perceptions of racist discrimination: the moderating effects of racial socialization experiences and self esteem. *J. Couns. Psychol.* 46:395–407

Frabutt J, Walker A, MacKinnon-Lewis C. 2002. Racial socialization messages and the quality of mother/child interaction in African American families. *J. Early Adolesc.* 22:200–17

Fridrich A, Flannery DJ. 1995. The effects of ethnicity and acculturation on early adolescent delinquency. *J. Child Fam. Stud.* 4(1):69–87

Gasch H, Poulson DM, Fullilove RE, Fullilove MT. 1991. Shaping AIDS education and prevention programs for African Americans amid community decline. *J. Negro Educ.* 60:85–96

Gibbons FX, Gerrard M, Lane DJ. 2003. A social reaction model of adolescent health risk. In *Social Psychological Foundations of Health and Illness*, ed. JM Suls, KA Wallston, pp. 107–36. Malden, MA: Blackwell Sci.

Gil AG, Vega WA, Biafora F. 1998. Temporal influences of family structure and family risk factors on drug use initiation in a multiethnic sample of adolescent boys. *J. Youth Adolesc.* 27(3):373–93

Gil AG, Wagner EF, Tubman JG. 2004. Culturally sensitive substance abuse intervention for Hispanic and African-American adolescents: empirical examples from the Alcohol Treatment Targeting Adolescents in Need (ATTAIN) Project. *Addiction* 99(12):40–150

Gil AG, Wagner EF, Vega WA. 2000. Acculturation, familism, and alcohol use among Latino adolescent males: longitudinal relations. *J. Community Psychol.* 28(4):443–58

Gordon-Larsen P, Harris KM, Ward DS, Popkin DS. 2003. Acculturation and overweight-related behaviors among Hispanic immigrants to the U.S.: the National Longitudinal Study of Adolescent Health. *Soc. Sci. Med.* 57:2023–34

Gorman-Smith D, Tolan PH, Henry DB, Leventhal A, Schoeny M, Lutovsky K. 2002. Predictors of participation in a family-focused preventive intervention for substance use. *Psychol. Addict. Behav.* 16:S55-64

Griffin KW, Botvin GJ, Scheier LM, Doyle MM, Williams C. 2003. Common predictors of cigarette smoking, alcohol use, aggression, and delinquency among inner-city minority youth. *Addict. Behav.* 28(6):1141–48

Guagliardo MF, Huang Z, Hicks JD, Angelo L. 1998. Increased drug use among old-for-grade and dropout urban adolescents. *Am. J. Prev. Med.* 15(1):42–48

Haley J. 1976. *Problem Solving Therapy*. San Francisco, CA: Jossey-Bass

Hall W, MacPhee D. 2002. Cannabis use and cancer. *Addiction* 97:243–47

Hawkins JD, Catalano RF, Miller JY. 1992. Risk and protective factors for alcohol and other drug problems in adolescence and early adulthood: Implications for substance abuse prevention. *Psychol. Bull.* 112(1):64–105

Reports greater drug use, psychopathology, and family dysfunction among drug treatment referred girls than boys.

Provides a framework for understanding antecedents to adolescent alcohol and drug use.

Helms J. 1990. *Black and White Racial Identity: Theory, Research, and Practice*. Westport, CT: Greenwood

Henggeler SW, Borduin CM, Melton BG, Mann BJ, Smith L, et al. 1991. Effects of multisystemic therapy on drug use and abuse in serious juvenile offenders: a progress report from two outcome studies. *Fam. Dyn. Addict. Q.* 1:40–51

Hogue A, Liddle HA, Becker D, Johnson-Leckrone J. 2002. Family-based prevention counseling for high-risk young adolescents: immediate outcomes. *J. Community Psychol.* 30(1):1–22

Hughes D. 2003. Correlates of African American and Latino parents' messages to children about ethnicity and race: a comparative study of racial socialization? *Am. J. Community Psychol.* 31:15–33

Hughes M, Demo D. 1989. Self-perceptions of black Americans: self-esteem and personal efficacy. *Am. J. Sociol.* 95:132–59

Hughes D, Johnson D. 2001. Correlates in children's experiences of parents' racial socialization behaviors. *J. Marriage Fam.* 63:981–95

Jessor R, Van-Den-Bos J, Vanderryn J, Costa FM, Turbin MS. 1995. Protective factors in adolescent problem behavior: moderator effects and developmental change. *Dev. Psychol.* 31(6):923–33

Johnston LD, O'Malley PM, Bachman JG, Schulenberg JE. 2004. *Monitoring the Future: National Survey Results on Drug Use*. Rockville, MD: Natl. Inst. Drug Abuse

Johnston LD, O'Malley PM, Bachman JG, Schulenberg JE. 2005. *Monitoring the Future: National Survey Results on Drug Use*. Rockville, MD: Natl. Inst. Drug Abuse

Johnston LD, O'Malley PM, Bachman JG, Schulenberg JE. 2006. *Monitoring the Future: National Results on Adolescent Drug Use. Overview of Key Findings, 2005*. Bethesda, MD: Natl. Inst. Drug Abuse

Kellam S, Rebok G. 1992. Building developmental and ecological theory through epidemiologically based preventive intervention trials. In *Preventing Antisocial Behavior: Interventions from Birth Through Adolescence*, ed. J McCord, R Trembblay, pp. 162–95. New York: Guilford

Kulis S, Marsiglia FF, Elek E, Dustman P, Wagstaff DA, Hecht ML. 2005. Mexican/Mexican American adolescents and Keepin' it REAL: an evidence-based substance abuse prevention program. *Child. Schools* 27:133–45

Kumpfer KL, DeMarsh JP, Child W. 1989. *Strengthening Families Program: Children's Skills Training Curriculum Manual, Parent Training Manual, Children's Skills Training Manual, and Family Skills Training Manual*. Salt Lake City, UT: Univ. Utah, Soc. Res. Inst., Grad. School Soc. Work

Marotta SA, Garcia JG. 2003. Latinos in the United States in 2000. *Hisp. J. Behav. Sci.* 25(1):13–34

Martinez CR. 2006. Effects of differential family acculturation on Latino adolescent substance use. *Fam. Relat.* 55(3):306–17

Martinez CR, Eddy JM. 2005. Effects of culturally adapted parent management training on Latino youth behavioral outcomes. *J. Consult. Clin. Psychol.* 73(4):841–51

McGee L, Newcomb MD. 1992. General deviance syndrome: expanded hierarchical evaluations at four ages from early adolescence to adulthood. *J. Consult. Clin. Psychol.* 60:766–76

Mensch BS, Kandel DB. 1988. Dropping out of high school and drug involvement. *Soc. Educ.* 61(2):95–113

Miller D. 1999. Racial socialization and racial identity: Can they promote resiliency for African American adolescents? *Adolescent* 32:493–501

Minuchin S. 1974. *Families and Family Therapy*. Cambridge, MA: Harvard Univ. Press

Miranda J, Bernal G, Lau A, Kohn L, Hwang WC, La Fromboise T. 2005. State of the science on psychosocial interventions for ethnic minorities. *Annu. Rev. Clin. Psychol.* 1:113–42

Molgaard VM, Spoth R, Redmond C. 2000. Competency training: the Strengthening Families Program for parents and youth 10–14. *OJJDP Juv. Just. Bull.* (NCJ 182208). Washington, DC: U.S. Dept. Just., Off. Juv. Just. Delinq. Prev. (PF 48)

Nation NM, Crusto C, Wandersman A, Kumpfer KL, Seybolt D, et al. 2003. What works in prevention: Principles of effective prevention programs. *Am. Psychol.* 58:449–56

Newcomb MD. 1997. Psychological predictors and consequences of drug use: a developmental perspective within a prospective study. *J. Addict. Dis.* 16(1):51–89

Pantin H, Coatsworth JD, Feaster DJ, Newman FL, Briones E, et al. 2003a. Familias Unidas: the efficacy of an intervention to increase parental investment in Hispanic immigrant families. *Prev. Sci.* 4:189–201

Pantin H, Schwartz SJ, Sullivan S, Coatsworth J, Szapocznik J. 2003b. Preventing substance abuse in Hispanic immigrant adolescents: an ecodevelopmental, parent-centered approach. *Hisp. J. Behav. Sci.* 25:469–500

Perrino T, Coatsworth JD, Briones E, Pantin H, Szapocznik J. 2001. Initial engagement in parent-centered interventions: a family systems perspective. *J. Primary Prev.* 22(1):21–44

Perrino T, Gonzalez-Soldevilla A, Pantin H, Szapocznik J. 2000. The role of families in adolescent HIV prevention: a review. *Clin. Child Fam. Psychol. Rev.* 3(2):81–96

Prado G, Pantin H, Schwartz SJ, Lupei NS, Szapocznik J. 2006a. Predictors of engagement and retention into a parent-centered, ecodevelopmental HIV preventive intervention for Hispanic adolescents and their families. *J. Pediatr. Psychol.* 31(9):874–90

Reports that therapeutic alliance accounts for the largest percentage of variance and thus is more important than client characteristics in predicting engagement to a preventive intervention.

Prado G, Schwartz SJ, Pattatucci-Aragon A, Clatts M, Pantin H, et al. 2006b. The prevention of HIV transmission in Hispanic adolescents. *Drug Alcohol Depend.* 84S:S43-53

Reid JB, Eddy JM, Fetrow RA, Stoolmiller M. 1999. Description and immediate impacts of a preventive intervention for conduct problems. *Am. J. Community Psychol.* 27:483–517

Reid JB, Patterson GR, Snyder J. 2002. *Antisocial Behavior in Children and Adolescents: A Developmental Analysis and Model for Intervention.* Washington, DC: Am. Psychol. Assoc.

Resnicow K, Soler R, Braithwaite R, Ahluwalia J, Butler J. 2000. Cultural sensitivity in substance use prevention. *J. Community Psychol.* 28:271–90

Resnicow K, Soler R, Braithwaite R, Selassie M, Smith M. 1999. Development of a racial and ethnic identity scale for African American adolescents: the survey of Black Life. *J. Black Psychol.* 25:171–88

Rowley S, Sellers RM, Chavous TM, Smith MA. 1997. The relationship between racial identity and self-esteem in African American college and high school students. *J. Personal. Soc. Psychol.* 74:715–24

Santisteban DA, Coatsworth JD, Perez-Vidal A, Kurtines WM, Schwartz S, et al. 2003. Efficacy of brief strategic family therapy in modifying Hispanic adolescent behavior problems and substance use. *J. Fam. Psychol.* 17:121–31

Santisteban DA, Dillon F, Mena MP, Estrada Y, Vaughan EL. 2005. Psychiatric, family, and ethnicity-related factors that can impact treatment utilization among Hispanic substance abusing adolescents. *J. Soc. Work Pract. Addict.* 5(1–2):133–55

Santisteban DA, Muir-Malcolm JA, Mitrani VB, Szapocznik J. 2002. Integrating the study of ethnic culture and family psychology intervention science. In *Family Psychology: Science-Based Interventions*, ed. HA Liddle, DA Santisteban, RF Levant, JH Bray, pp. 331–51. Washington, DC: Am. Psychol. Assoc.

Discusses the role of cultural factors in family-based treatments of adolescents.

Santisteban DA, Szapocznik J, Perez-Vidal A, Kurtines WM, Murray EJ, Laperriere A. 1996. Efficacy of intervention for engaging youth and families into treatment and some variables that may contribute to differential effectiveness. *J. Fam. Psychol.* 10(1):35–44

Sellers R, Copeland-Linder N, Martin P, Lewis L, Heureux R. 2006. Racial identity matters: the relationship between racial discrimination and psychological functioning in African American adolescents. *J. Res. Adolesc.* 16:187–216

Reports on the significant role of racial identity in predicting the positive development of African American adolescents.

Spoth R, Guyll M, Chao W, Molgaard V. 2003. Exploratory study of preventive intervention with general population African American families. *J. Early Adolesc.* 23:435–58

Stevenson H. 1994. Validation of the scale of racial socialization from African American adolescents: steps toward multidimensionality. *J. Black Psychol.* 20:445–68

Storr CL, Ialongo NS, Kellam SG, Anthony JC. 2002. A randomized control trial of two primary school intervention strategies to prevent early onset tobacco smoking. *Drug Alcohol Depend.* 66:51–60

Strait SC. 1999. Drug use among Hispanic youth: examining common and unique contributing factors. *Hisp. J. Behav. Sci.* 21(2):89–103

Subst. Abuse Mental Health Serv. Admin. 2005. *National Household Survey on Drug Use and Health*

Szapocznik J, Coatsworth JD. 1999. An ecodevelopmental framework for organizing the influences on drug abuse: a developmental model of risk and protection. In *Drug Abuse: Origins and Interventions*, ed. M Glantz, C Hartel, pp. 331–66. Washington, DC: Am. Psychol. Assoc.

Provides an integrated framework for understanding adolescent development as a function of multiple interacting contexts as they evolve over time.

Szapocznik J, Hervis OE, Schwartz S. 2003. *Brief Strategic Family Therapy for Adolescent Drug Abuse*. Rockville, MD: Natl. Inst. Drug Abuse

Szapocznik J, Kurtines WM. 1989. *Breakthroughs in Family Therapy with Drug Abusing and Problem Youth*. New York: Springer. 205 pp.

Szapocznik J, Kurtines WM. 1993. Family psychology and cultural diversity: opportunities for theory, research and application. *Am. Psychol.* 48(4):400–7

Szapocznik J, Kurtines WM, Santisteban DA, Rio AT. 1990. The interplay of advances among theory, research, and application in treatment interventions aimed at behavior problem children and adolescents. *J. Consult. Clin. Psychol.* 58(6):696–703

Szapocznik J, Lopez B, Prado G, Schwartz SJ, Pantin H. 2006. Outpatient drug abuse treatment for Hispanic adolescents. *Drug Alcohol Depend.* 84S:S54-63

Reviews research on outpatient drug abuse treatment for Hispanic adolescents.

Szapocznik J, Perez-Vidal A, Brickman A, Foote FH, Santisteban D, et al. 1988. Engaging adolescent drug abusers and their families into treatment: a strategic structural systems approach. *J. Consult. Clin. Psychol.* 56(4):552–57

Reports the first study to develop a treatment intervention module to successfully increase family involvement in adolescent drug treatment.

Szapocznik J, Santisteban S, Rio A, Perez-Vidal A, Kurtines WM. 1989. Family Effectiveness Training: an intervention to prevent drug abuse and problem behaviors in Hispanic adolescents. *Hisp. J. Behav. Sci.* 11:4–27

Szapocznik J, Scopetta MA, King OE. 1978. Theory and practice in matching treatment to the special characteristics and problems of Cuban immigrants. *J. Community Psychol.* 6:112–22

Szapocznik J, Williams RA. 2000. Brief Strategic Family Therapy: twenty-five years of interplay among theory, research and practice in adolescent behavior problems and drug abuse. *Clin. Child. Fam. Psychol. Rev.* 3(2):117–35

Tubman JG, Windle M, Windle RC. 1996. Cumulative sexual intercourse patterns among middle adolescents: problem behavior precursors and concurrent health risk behaviors. *J. Adolesc. Health* 18(3):182–91

Turner RJ, Lloyd DA, Taylor LJ. 2006. Stress burden, drug dependence and the nativity paradox among U.S. Hispanics. *Drug Alcohol Depend.* 28:79–89

U.S. Census Bureau. 2003. *Child Trends' Calculations of U.S. Census Bureau. School Enrollment—Social and Economic Characteristics of Students: October 2003.* **http://www.census.gov/population/www/socdemo/school/cps2003.html**
U.S. Census Bureau. 2005. *Population of the United States by Race and Hispanic/Latino Origin: Census 2000 and July 1, 2005. National Population Estimates.* **http://www.infoplease.com/ipa/A0762156.html**
U.S. Dept. Health Human Serv. 2001. Mental health and children. In *Mental Health: A Report of the Surgeon General.* **http://www.surgeongeneral.gov/library/mentalhealth/pdfs/c3.pdf**
Vega WA, Aguilar-Gaxiola S, Andrade L, Bijl R, Borges G, et al. 2002. Prevalence and age of onset for drug use in seven international sites: results from the International Consortium of Psychiatric Epidemiology. *Drug Alcohol Depend.* 68(3):285–97
Vega WA, Kolody B, Aguilar-Gaxiola S, Alderete E, Catalano R, Caraveo-Anduaga J. 1998. Lifetime prevalence of DSM-III-R psychiatric disorders among urban and rural Mexican Americans in California. *Arch. Gen. Psychiatry* 55(9):771–78
Volkow ND. 2003. Foreword. In *Brief Strategic Family Therapy for Adolescent Drug Abuse*, ed. J Szapocznik, OE Hervis, S Schwartz, p. iii. Rockville, MD: Natl. Inst. Drug Abuse
Wallace JM Jr, Bachman JG. 1993. Validity of self-reports in student based studies on minority populations: issues and concerns. In *Drug Abuse Among Minority Youth: Advances in Research and Methodology*, ed. M De La Rosa, JL Andrados, pp. 167–200. Rockville, MD: Natl. Inst. Drug Abuse
Wallace JM Jr, Bachman JG, O'Malley PM, Johnston LD, Schulenberg JE, Cooper SM. 2002. Tobacco, alcohol, and illicit drug use: racial and ethnic differences among U.S. high school seniors, 1976–2000. *Public Health Rep.* 117S:S67-75
Warner LA, Valdez A, Vega WA, de la Rosa M. 2006. Hispanic drug abuse in an evolving cultural context: an agenda for research. *Drug Alcohol Depend.* 84(1):8–16
Wells KB, Klap R, Koike A, Sherbourne CD. 2001. Ethnic disparities in unmet need for alcoholism, drug abuse, and mental health care. *Am. J. Psychiatry* 158(12):2027–32
White JL, Parham TA. 1996. The struggle for identity congruence in African Americans. In *Passages Beyond the Gate: A Jungian Approach to Understanding the Nature of American Psychology at the Dawn of the New Millenium*, ed. GH Jennings, pp. 246–53. Needham Heights, MA: Simon & Schuster. 352 pp.

RELATED RESOURCES

Amaro H, Iguchi MY. 2006. Supplement: scientific opportunities in Hispanic drug abuse research. *Drug Alcohol Depend.* 84S:S1–101
Monitoring the Future. **http://www.monitoringthefuture.org**
National Clearinghouse for Alcohol and Drug Information. **http://ncadi.samhsa.gov/**
National Hispanic Science Network on Drug Abuse. **http://www.hispanicscience.org**
National Household Study of Drug Use and Health. **http://www.oas.samhsa.gov/nsduh.htm**
National Institute on Drug Abuse. **http://www.nida.nih.gov**
Youth Risk Behavior Surveillance System. **http://www.cdc.gov/HealthyYouth/yrbs/index.htm**
Special Issue on Substance Abuse in the African American Community. 2000. *J. Black Psychol.* 26(4):Entire issue
Supplement to the Surgeon General Report (1999) on Mental Health: culture, race, ethnicity. **http://mentalhealth.samhsa.gov/cre/default.asp**

Depression in Mothers

Sherryl H. Goodman

Department of Psychology, Emory University, Atlanta, Georgia 30322;
email: psysg@emory.edu

Annu. Rev. Clin. Psychol. 2007. 3:107–35

The *Annual Review of Clinical Psychology* is online at http://clinpsy.annualreviews.org

This article's doi:
10.1146/annurev.clinpsy.3.022806.091401

1548-5943/07/0427-0107$20.00

Key Words

developmental psychopathology, risk, prevention, transactional, vulnerability

Abstract

Whether one takes a biological, psychological, or psychosocial perspective, depression in mothers raises concerns about risks for the development of psychopathology in the children. This review addresses the complexity of that risk and the essential role of development in a model that explains processes of transmission. This article addresses the following aims: (*a*) to provide convincing evidence that depression in mothers is an important topic for clinical psychologists; (*b*) to summarize current theoretical models of mechanisms of risk for the development of psychopathology in children of depressed mothers and the status of empirical support for those models; (*c*) to examine the theoretical bases and current status of evidence for moderators of this risk; (*d*) to argue for the advantages to be gained from a developmental psychopathology perspective on this topic; and (*e*) to point to future directions for theory, research, and practice.

Contents

WHY IS DEPRESSION IN MOTHERS AN IMPORTANT TOPIC FOR CLINICAL PSYCHOLOGISTS?

Prevalence of Depression in Women

Between 6% and 17% of women experience a major depressive episode (MDE) at some point in their lifetimes, a rate that is one-and-a-half to three times higher than in men (Kessler 2006). Rates of MDE are strikingly similar in women during pregnancy, the postpartum period, and overall through the child-bearing years (Evans et al. 2001, O'Hara & Swain 1996, Regier et al. 1993, Somerset et al. 2006). Rates of subsyndromal depression or elevated depressed mood are even higher than rates of MDE and, similarly, are consistently found to be higher in women than in men (Almeida & Kessler 1998, Lennon 1987). The available data show that the pattern holds true for African Americans (although rates are higher in single African American men relative to women), some but not all Asian American groups, and both Cuban Americans and Mexican Americans (Jackson & Williams 2006).

Other epidemiological data raise further concerns. In particular, depression is a highly recurrent disorder, with the recurrence now understood to be at least partly due to the consequences of the prior episode(s) (Lewinsohn et al. 1999). More than 80% of depressed individuals have more than one episode, with about 50% of those who recover from an MDE experiencing a reoccurrence within two years (Belsher & Costello 1988) and relapse rates increasing with the number of previous episodes (Keller et al. 1992). Further, although depression is not likely to be more chronic in women in comparison with men, women are more likely than men to have recurring short depressive episodes, whether endogenous or stress-provoked (Kessler 2006).

Effects of Maternal Depression on Children's Psychological Development

A detailed review of the range of outcomes in children that have been found to be associated with depression in mothers is beyond the scope of this chapter and has been the subject of recent reviews (e.g., Goodman & Tully 2006). A strong consensus from this literature is that from the earliest ages when depression can reliably be measured in children, rates of depression are significantly higher in children with depressed mothers relative to a range of groups to which they have been compared. Overall, rates of depression in the school-aged and adolescent children of depressed mothers have been reported to be between 20% and 41%, with the variability within that range explained by the severity or impairment of the parent's depression, whether the father is also depressed, and a number of other sociodemographic variables. Not only are rates of depression higher, but depression in children of depressed parents, relative to depression in same-age children of nondepressed parents, has an earlier age of onset, longer duration, and is associated with greater functional impairment and a higher likelihood of recurrence (Hammen et al. 1990a, 2003; Keller et al. 1986; Warner et al. 1992).

Depression is not the only adverse outcome associated with maternal depression. Beginning in infancy and then throughout development, depression in mothers is associated with children's other emotional and behavioral problems and also with wide-ranging problems in affective, cognitive, interpersonal, neuroendocrine, and brain functioning (Goodman & Tully 2006). Specifically, infants of depressed mothers show more negative affect and more self-directed regulatory behaviors (Field 1992, Tronick & Gianino 1986), toddlers show more dysregulated aggression and heightened emotionality (Zahn-Waxler et al. 1984), and adolescents (particularly girls) display more dysphoric and less happy affect (Hops et al. 1990). Maternal depression is also associated with anxiety (social phobia, separation anxiety, and other anxiety disorders) in children, and with dysregulated aggression and more externalizing problems (attention deficit disorders and disruptive behavior disorders) beginning in the preschool period, although some researchers find the latter to be specific to daughters (Biederman et al. 2001, Luoma et al. 2001, Orvaschel et al. 1988, Weissman et al. 1984, Zahn-Waxler et al. 1990). Although depression in both mothers and fathers has been shown to affect children's psychological functioning, a meta-analysis of 134 samples, with a total of more than 60,000 parent-child dyads, showed that both internalizing and externalizing problems in children are more strongly associated with depression in mothers relative to depression in fathers (Connell & Goodman 2002).

Children of depressed mothers show early signs of cognitive vulnerability to depression, including being more likely than controls to blame themselves for negative outcomes, having a more negative attributional style, being less likely to recall positive self-descriptive adjectives, and having lower self-concept. Further, children of depressed mothers have been found to score lower on measures of intelligence and also to have poorer academic performance overall (Anderson & Hammen 1993, Hammen & Brennan 2001, Hay & Kumar 1995, Jaenicke et al. 1987).

Studies of interpersonal functioning have identified a range of variables on which children of depressed mothers show problems relative to controls. Infants show less secure attachment relationships (van IJzendoorn et al. 1992), preschool-aged children interacting with their depressed mothers engage in excessive compliance (Zahn-Waxler et al. 1992), kindergarten-aged children are more often excluded by peers (Cummings et al. 2005), and sons, but not daughters, display more

MAJOR DEPRESSIVE EPISODE

As defined by the DSM-IV, a major depressive episode includes at least five symptoms that present during the same two-week period and represent a change from previous functioning. At least one of the symptoms is either depressed mood (most of the day, nearly every day) or loss of interest or pleasure in all or most activities most of the day nearly every day. Other symptoms (which also must occur nearly every day) include significant weight loss or gain or decrease or increase in appetite, insomnia or hypersomnia, psychomotor agitation or retardation, fatigue or loss of energy, feelings of worthlessness or guilt, trouble thinking or concentrating or indecisiveness, recurrent thoughts of death or suicidal ideation or attempt. The diagnosis also requires evidence of impairment.

EEG: electroencephalogram

HPA: hypothalamic pituitary adrenal

aggressive behavior during interactions with friends (the latter effect was mediated by the children's exposure to interparental conflict) (Hipwell et al. 2005). In addition, adolescent daughters of depressed mothers may be more likely than adolescent sons to show depression (Davies & Windle 1997, Fergusson et al. 1995, Hops 1996), which may be a function of gender-specific socialization of social behaviors such as relationship orientation and low instrumentality (Sheeber et al. 2002).

In studies of neurobiological or neuroendocrine functioning, researchers have found significant associations between maternal depression and two psychobiological systems in children that have been found to play a role in emotion regulation and expression: (*a*) stress responses measured in either autonomic activity (higher heart rate and lower vagal tone) or in stress hormonal levels [higher cortisol as an index of hypothalamic pituitary adrenal (HPA) axis activity] and (*b*) cortical activity in the prefrontal cortex [greater relative right frontal electroencephalogram (EEG) asymmetries]. These abnormalities in neurobiological or neuroendocrine functioning in infants are sometimes specifically found to be associated with face-to-face interaction with their depressed mothers (Field 1992) and with harsh parenting in particular (Hertsgaard et al. 1995), but others find them to reflect a more general trait (Dawson et al. 2001). These general patterns also show remarkable stability from as early as one week of age to three years old, suggesting that the early measures are reliably detecting an individual difference pattern (Dawson et al. 1997, 2003; Fox 1994; Jones et al. 1997).

In sum, a broad range of aspects of psychological functioning has been found to be associated with maternal depression. The early-identified psychopathology is a particular concern because in general population samples, early-identified problems are strongly predictive of psychopathology in later years (Campbell 1995). The other problems may be early signs of (or markers for) depression or other disorders or may represent vulnerabilities to the later development of psychopathology.

THEORIZED MECHANISMS: EVIDENCE THAT THEY ARE ASSOCIATED WITH DEPRESSION IN MOTHERS AND EVIDENCE THAT THEY FUNCTION AS MEDIATORS

The Integrative Model for the Transmission of Risk to Children of Depressed Mothers (Goodman & Gotlib 1999) serves to organize the individual and interacting mechanisms proposed to explain associations between maternal depression and the development of psychopathology and other disorders in children and is the basis for organizing the critical analysis of the current state of knowledge in this section. As shown in **Figure 1**, my colleague Ian Gotlib and I proposed four mechanisms: heritability; innate dysfunctional neuroregulatory mechanisms; exposure to mother's negative and/or maladaptive cognitions, behaviors, and affect; and exposure to stressful environments. In this model, the term "mechanism" is used consistently with the statistical concept of mediation. Mechanisms are conceptualized as intervening or causal variables by which maternal depression has its effects on the development of psychopathology in the children (Baron & Kenny 1986, Holmbeck 1997, Kraemer et al. 2001). The identification of mechanisms is thus central to understanding the processes by which maternal depression has its effects. Although there is ongoing debate on this topic, mediation is basically understood to have been supported if, first, the initial variable (in this case, maternal depression) is significantly correlated with the mediator (e.g., maladaptive parenting) and if, second, the mediator is significantly correlated with the outcome variable (e.g., depression in the children) after controlling for the initial variable (Kenny et al. 1998). In the following sections, I summarize the status of support for each of the mechanisms by addressing these two criteria where the data allow.

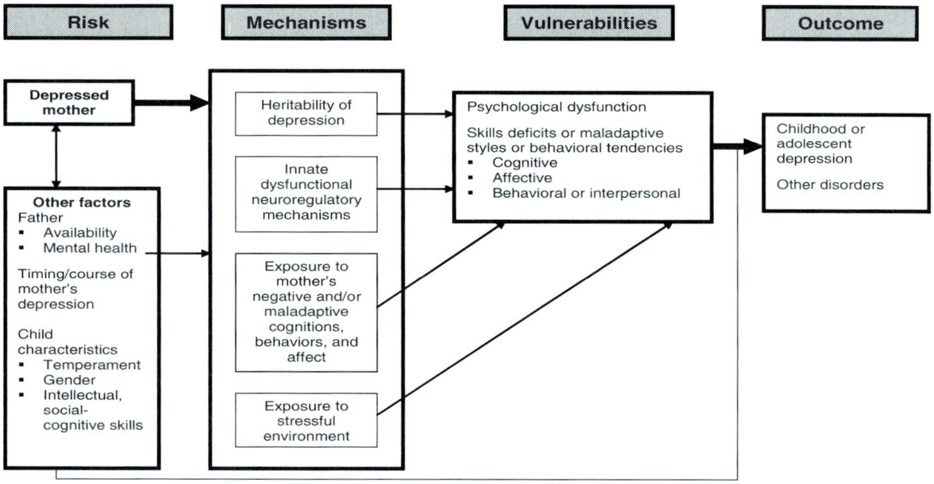

Figure 1

Integrative Model for the Transmission of Risk to Children of Depressed Mothers (Goodman & Gotlib 1999).

Heredity

Genetic effects on major depression in adults account for between 26% and 42% of the variance (Sullivan et al. 2000). Estimates of heritability of depression in children have been more variable, probably due to problems in reliability of child reports and reliance on mother reports. In addition, most studies of heritability of depression in children have relied on depression symptom scales rather than clinical diagnoses. In general, there is no single estimate of genetic effects on depression in children, and existing estimates vary by severity of symptoms, maternal versus child report, and children's age and gender. In addition, because heritability of depression is likely to not be specific to depression, heritability likely contributes to the risk for other disorders that are identified in higher rates in children of depressed mothers relative to controls (Moldin 1999, Tsuang & Faraone 1990).

Although several possibilities have been proposed, no particular genes have been definitively associated with major depression and thus might be implicated in the transmission of risk for depression from mothers to their children. Published findings provide support for a region of chromosome 2 containing the CREB1 gene as a susceptibility gene for unipolar depression in women (Levinson et al. 2003). CREB1 is a highly plausible candidate gene in depression because of its role in the pathway that mediates many aspects of serotonin- and catecholamine-mediated neurotransmission thought to be relevant to depressive symptoms. Also generating interest is the serotonin transporter (5HTTLPR) gene, given the accumulating evidence for the role of the serotonin system in major depression and in the effectiveness of serotonin reuptake-inhibitor drugs in the treatment of depression (Ressler & Nemeroff 2000). In an intriguing test of the stress-diathesis model, Caspi et al. (2003) found that a functional polymorphism of this gene moderated the prospective association between stressful life events and depression in a birth-cohort sample of young adults. The importance of identifying susceptibility genes for major depression is tied to the promise of revealing the biological mechanisms regulated by these genes, which may increase vulnerability to the development of depression in children who inherit these gene variations.

CREB1: cyclic nucleotide response element-binding protein

5HTTLPR: serotonin transporter gene

CRF: corticotrophin-releasing factor

In addition to the notion that children with depressed mothers inherit the likelihood for depression per se is the idea that heritability contributes significantly to vulnerabilities to depression, such as those proposed in the Goodman & Gotlib (1999) model. In particular, high levels of heritability are found for individual differences in behavioral inhibition and shyness (Cherny et al. 1994), low self-esteem (Loehlin & Nichols 1976), neuroticism (Tellegen et al. 1988), sociability (Plomin et al. 1993), subjective well-being (Lykken & Tellegen 1996), expression of negative emotion (Plomin et al. 1993), and frontal EEG asymmetry (Anokhin et al. 2006). High levels of heritability are even found for individual differences in the autonomic processes related to reactivity to emotional stimuli, such as heart-rate variability and vagal tone (Davidson et al. 1990, Healy 1992, Porges 2001) and at least basal levels of indices of HPA axis activity (if not reactivity) (Bartels et al. 2003, Wust et al. 2005, Young et al. 2000). This body of research suggests possible genetic transmission of affective, cognitive, interpersonal, and psychobiological vulnerability for depression.

Other Biological Concerns

Innate dysfunctional neuroregulatory mechanisms. The second proposed mechanism of the Goodman & Gotlib (1999) model is that children of depressed mothers are born with dysfunctional neuroregulatory mechanisms that interfere with emotional regulation processes and consequently increase vulnerability to depression. The theory is that whether through genetics or adverse prenatal experiences, children of depressed mothers may enter the world with psychobiological systems that contribute to the development of psychopathology. As noted earlier, prenatal depression is at least as common as, if not more common than, postnatal depression, occurring in about 10% to 15% of women (Evans et al. 2001, Green & Murray 1994, O'Hara et al. 1990). Thus, children of depressed mothers may be exposed prenatally to conditions that impair their psychobiological systems. Few studies of infants with depressed mothers have begun during pregnancy, and thus we know little about the consequences to infants of fetal exposure to maternal depression. Evidence is just beginning to suggest that antenatal maternal mood can have lasting effects on the psychological development of a child, and several recent and ongoing studies are working to explain those associations (Goodman 2006, Goodman & Gotlib 1999, Jones et al. 2004, O'Connor et al. 2003).

Theories of depression and research with animals suggest that depression during pregnancy is likely to expose fetuses to a number of risks for problems in development. These risks might include neuroendocrine alterations associated with the mother's depression or stress [hypersecretion of corticotrophin-releasing factor (CRF)], constricted blood flow, poor health behaviors (e.g., smoking, drinking, inadequate nutrition), and exposure to antidepressant medications (Diego et al. 2004, Gitau et al. 2001, Handley et al. 1980, Smith et al. 1990).

Both the human and animal literatures on stress and anxiety during pregnancy (two common correlates of depression) point to their influence on reactivity of the HPA system and the emergence of children's behavioral or emotional problems later in development (Graham et al. 1999, Huizink et al. 2004, O'Connor et al. 2002, Sanchez et al. 2001, Wadhwa et al. 2002). Very few studies have examined the neurobiology of pregnant, depressed women. Studies from Field's lab show that depression during pregnancy increases the woman's level of cortisol (Field 2002). Further, there is some suggestion that maternal cortisol crosses the placenta in that maternal levels of cortisol account for 50% of the variance in fetal levels of cortisol (Gitau et al. 2001, Glover 1997).

Elevated stress hormone levels in pregnant women are of concern because they have been associated with impaired neurodevelopment in the fetus (Wadhwa et al. 2002). Women's prenatal levels of cortisol predict newborns' cortisol levels (Lundy et al. 1999), and the number of months a woman is depressed during pregnancy predicts her preschool-aged children's baseline cortisol levels (Ashman & Dawson 2002). Stress-related physiological dysregulation in children may index children's sensitivity to stress, suggesting a particular pathway by which maternal depression during pregnancy may increase children's later development of depression (Sanchez et al. 2001). These infants may not only show elevations in cortisol in response to stress, but also may demonstrate EEG asymmetries and have a predilection to experience negative or "withdrawal" emotions. In addition, they may exhibit other early signs of vulnerability to the development of stress-related psychopathology. However, research is needed to show that the dysfunctions and disorders found in the children of depressed mothers are, at least partially, sequelae of innate dysfunctional neuroregulatory mechanisms.

More broadly, more studies are needed with prospective data on prenatal exposure to clinically significant levels of depression in mothers before conclusions can be drawn that differences in prenatal experiences or exposures associated with maternal depression at least partially mediate the development of psychopathology in the children. Preliminary findings from a study of women at risk for perinatal depression given a history of past major depressive episodes are showing associations between fetal exposure to maternal depression and neuroregulatory dysfunctions not only in newborns but also across the first year of life (Goodman 2006).

Early life stress. Brain development continues at a rapid pace at least for two years postnatally (Chugani & Phelps 1986), and early life stress can have lasting consequences. To the extent that having a mother with depression can be considered an early life stressor, we must examine potential early postnatal life influences on neuroregulatory mechanisms. That is, not only prenatal but also postnatal experiences might influence aspects of hormonal functioning and of brain development, each of which may increase vulnerability to depression (Ashman & Dawson 2002).

Postnatal exposure to stressors associated with maternal depression may disrupt HPA processes (Ashman & Dawson 2002). In particular, depressed mothers' insensitive or unresponsive behavior may mediate the association between maternal depression and children's neuroregulatory abilities, which in turn increases risk for the development of depression that may emerge in childhood or adolescence. Although not direct tests of mediation, three studies of children exposed to postnatal depression provide evidence consistent with mediation. One found that those who had early exposure had a stronger association between maternal stress and the children's basal cortisol at age 4 years, and both children's cortisol and maternal stress predicted children's internalizing and externalizing problems (Essex et al. 2002). Another found that 13-year-olds who had been exposed to their mothers' postnatal depression, compared with those with no such exposure, showed higher and more variable morning basal cortisol, the pattern that has been associated with depression (Halligan et al. 2004). Although these findings were strongly consistent with the model of altered cortisol levels serving as a mechanism linking depression in mothers and their children, these authors did not directly test the role of the abnormal HPA functioning in the association between exposure to postnatal depression and the adolescents' development of depression. In the third such study, Dawson and colleagues found that although mothers' postnatal depression predicted children's cortisol at age 3 years (Hessl et al. 1998), it no longer was a significant predictor when the children reached the age of 7 years (Ashman et al. 2002).

Abnormal brain development (frontal lobe activity) is a second biological mechanism implicated in the development of depression in children of depressed mothers. Of particular interest is the abnormal EEG pattern of relatively greater baseline right frontal activation, which is a stable individual difference factor by adolescence (Tomarken et al. 1992) and has been associated with the tendency in children to experience withdrawal emotions such as sadness or fear (Davidson & Fox 1989) and with depression in adolescents and adults (Davidson et al. 1990). Particularly strong evidence for this mechanism in children of depressed mothers comes from Dawson and colleagues' findings showing associations between frontal lobe activity and affective expressions in infants of depressed mothers (Dawson et al. 1992), and further, that 3-year-olds' frontal brain activation mediated the relation between maternal depression and the children's level of behavior problems (Dawson et al. 2003). Further research is needed to reveal the extent to which genetics and fetal or early postnatal experiences contribute to the abnormal brain activation patterns.

Qualities of Parenting

Weissman & Paykel (1974) and Brown & Harris (1978) were among the first to call attention to the lives of women suffering from depression. They suggested that the same social processes that elicit and maintain depression in women would cause them difficulties in relating to children, and that the children in families of depressed women were likely to be exposed to a range of interpersonal deficits in their mothers. These interpersonal deficits would serve both as models of maladaptive social functioning and also as stressors to the children (Hammen 2002).

Depression in mothers is associated with maladaptive cognitions, affect, and behaviors and, more specifically, negative parenting practices. In addition, researchers are finding that living with a parent with depression is stressful both in relation to and beyond the problems with parenting (Hammen 2002), and children struggle to cope with these stressors (Compas et al. 2002). Several chapters and articles have reviewed this now-large literature, including a meta-analysis (Lovejoy et al. 2000). For this article, I take a different approach and organize the review around the theorized mechanisms by which parenting may explain associations between maternal depression and the development of psychopathology in children.

Modeling of cognitive, affective, and behavioral aspects of depression. Through social learning processes such as modeling, observational learning, and reinforcement, children of depressed mothers may acquire cognitions, behaviors, and affect that resemble those of the depressed parent. These acquired depressotypic cognitions, behaviors, and affect may place the children at elevated risk for developing depression.

Much evidence supports the different processes involved in this mechanism. First, children have ample opportunities to be exposed to negative cognitions, behaviors, and affect associated with depression in their mothers. A meta-analysis of 46 observational studies revealed that maternal depression is strongly associated with negative (hostile/coercive) parenting behavior, moderately associated with parenting characterized as disengagement, and shows a small association with lower levels of positive behavior (Lovejoy et al. 2000). Further, depression in mothers is likely to result in ample opportunities for children to model problems with emotion regulation and emotion expression (Garber et al. 1991). The negatively biased cognitions associated with depression in adults (Gotlib et al. 2000) emerge in depressed mothers' parenting, which, relative to controls, is characterized by (*a*) more negative views of themselves as a parent (Gelfand & Teti 1990, Goodman et al. 1993b), (*b*) less confidence in being able to positively influence their children (Kochanska et al. 1987), and (*c*) more negative, critical perceptions of their children (Goodman et al. 1994) relative to controls.

Second, these aspects of depression in mothers are associated with the development of both vulnerabilities to depression and depression per se in children and adolescent offspring of depressed mothers. Depressed mothers' negative, critical perceptions of their children are associated with children's self-blaming attributions for negative events and with lowered perceived self-worth (Goodman et al. 1994, Jaenicke et al. 1987, Radke-Yarrow et al. 1990). That is, children seem to be internalizing their depressed mother's negative views of them, thereby acquiring a cognitive vulnerability to depression (Beck et al. 1979). Depressed mothers' displays of depressive interpersonal behaviors and poor problem-solving and coping skills (Compas et al. 1988, Garber et al. 1991, Kashani et al. 1988) are associated with children's less active strategies for responding to negative affect (Garber et al. 1991, Nolen-Hoeksema et al. 1995). Depressed mothers' greater criticism and hostility (Frye & Garber 2005, Webster-Stratton & Hammond 1988) also may contribute to the emergence of coercive processes similar to those implicated in the development of externalizing behavior problems in particular, and also of depression (Davis et al. 2002, Hops et al. 1990). However, family coercion was not found to mediate associations between maternal depression in the early school years and adolescent boys' or girls' depression (Compton et al. 2003). Further support for social learning processes comes from findings based on extensive observational coding and analyses of sequences of interactions revealing that depression in mothers reduces other family members' aversive behaviors (Dumas & Gibson 1990, Hops et al. 1990).

Some researchers find support for direct tests of mediation between depressed mothers' cognitions, affect, and behavior and children's depression vulnerability. Dysfunctional communication in the mother mediates the association between maternal depression and children's negative self-concept (Hammen et al. 1990b). Also, mothers' affective attitudes toward their child (measured by the criticism component of expressed emotion) partially mediated the relationship between maternal depression (both past and current) and externalizing problems in a community sample of 15-year-olds (Nelson 2001). Similarly, mothers' critical expressed emotion was associated with children's depression symptoms even after controlling for mothers' history of and current depression and children's depressive symptoms one year previously (Hilsman 2001). Maternal social skills mediated the association between mothers' depression and children's social competence, although only for girls (Prinstein & LaGreca 1999). Finally, in one of our studies we found the negative attitudes mothers expressed toward their children moderated the association between maternal depression and children's lower global self-worth (Goodman et al. 1994).

Inadequate parenting. Interpersonal theories emphasize interpersonal processes such as the depressed mother being an inadequate social partner for the child, and the mother being unable to meet the child's stage-salient social and emotional needs (Cicchetti & Toth 1998). This inadequate parenting would, in turn, negatively affect the child's development of social and cognitive skills. Depressed mothers' parenting of infants and young children may also serve as an early life stressor (Caldji et al. 2000, Newport et al. 2002, Sanchez et al. 2001). Evidence consistent with this model comes from multiple sources ranging from studies showing less responsive parenting of infants by women with depression relative to women without depression to studies of depressed parents of adolescents providing less structure, monitoring, and discipline.

Several studies have tested whether maternal parenting mediates the association between maternal depression and children's depression and other outcomes. Most of the studies, summarized in **Table 1**, relied on structural equation modeling to determine support for at least partial mediation, and the number of studies finding support for parenting as a mediator is impressive and growing. A few contradictory findings have also been reported in that some qualities of

Table 1 Empirical support for parenting as a mediator of the association between maternal depression and outcomes in children

Citation	Children's age	Mediator	Outcome
Lundy 2002	6 months	Synchrony in mother-infant interactions	Quality of mother-infant attachment
Dawson et al. 2003	14 months	Insensitivity	Reduced left frontal brain activity
Snyder 1991	4–5 years	Harsh, inconsistent, or ineffective discipline	Conduct problems
Ghodsian et al. 1984	Infant through 4 years	Frequency of physical punishment	Child behavior problems
Murray et al. 1993	2 months	Maternal speech characterized by negative affect and not infant focused	Cognitive development at 18 months
Kam 2001	Second grade	Warmth	Emotion regulation skills
Harnish et al. 1995	First grade	Mother-child interaction quality	Externalizing problems (but not in African Americans)
McCarty & McMahon 2003	11–12 years	Cold, hostile, or difficult mother-child relationship	Disruptive behavior problems
McCarty & McMahon 2003	11–12 years	Less maternal social support	Internalizing problems
Hammen et al. 1990	8–16 years	Dysfunctional communication	Negative self-concept
Nelson 2001	15 years	Critical attitudes toward the child	Externalizing problems
Hilsman 2001	12–14 years	Parental criticism	Depressive disorder
Prinstein & LaGreca 1999	5–6 years	Maternal social skills	Social competence (girls only)

parenting such as mothers' ability to maintain stability and routines in their children's activities and family coercion failed to mediate the association between maternal depression and children's concurrent or later psychopathology (Compton et al. 2003, Dawson et al. 2003, Roderick 2002). Other studies relied on interventions as experimental tests of mediation. Interventions designed to improve the quality of parenting and parent-child relationships in families with a depressed parent are demonstrating effectiveness in minimizing the consequences to children, from infancy through adolescence (Gladstone & Beardslee 2002). On the other hand, although a home-visiting service targeted to women at high social risk (owing to a combination of maternal depression, poverty, and inadequate caretaking) was associated with infants' significant improvement in mental and physical development and in attachment security, these changes were not associated with changes in mothers' increased involvement or decreased hostility/intrusiveness with their infants (Lyons-Ruth et al. 1990).

Stress

The fourth mechanism in the Goodman & Gotlib (1999) model refers to the role of stressors in the association between maternal depression and adverse child outcomes. Hammen (2002) has taken the lead in suggesting that maternal depression increases children's exposure to stress in several ways. The stressfulness for children of depressed mothers may include the inadequate parenting as reviewed above, the symptoms and episodic course of the mothers' depression (Compas et al. 2002), the chronic and episodic stressors that are often the context for depression (Monroe & Hadjiyannakis 2002), and the stress generation (e.g., marital conflict) found to be associated with depression (Hammen 1991).

Support is beginning to emerge for the role of stressors as a mediator of the association between maternal depression and children's depression. Both episodic and chronic stressors are associated with depression symptoms and depressive disorders in children and adolescents (Grant et al. 2003). Further, depression in adolescent offspring of depressed parents was found to be more strongly associated with chronic and episodic social stressors relative to depression in adolescents of parents who had not suffered from depression (Hammen et al. 2003). Stress is also implicated in the development of many of the proposed vulnerabilities, as in Dawson's premise that the stressfulness of infants' interaction with an insensitive depressed mother is associated with the development of the infants' pattern of brain activity characterized by reduced activity in the left frontal region (Dawson et al. 2003). Finally, some studies provide empirical support for stressors such as contextual risk factors, poverty, and chronic family stress mediating the association between maternal depression and depression or other behavioral problems in children ranging in age from 20 months to 14 years old (Brennan et al. 2002, Cicchetti et al. 1998, Dawson et al. 2003, Eamon & Zuehl 2001). In contrast, measures of social disadvantage did not explain the association between postnatal depression and 11-year old children's IQ scores (Hay & Pawlby 2001).

Given the common co-occurrence of depression and marital discord, and the known stressfulness for children of marital discord itself, it is important to understand how they interact in predicting the development of psychopathology in children. One study of this question found that depression and marital discord work together in different manners to predict children's externalizing and internalizing problems. Although marital distress mediated the association between maternal depressive symptoms and adolescents' externalizing symptoms, maternal depressive symptoms mediated the effects of marital distress on adolescents' depressive symptoms (Davies & Dumenci 1999). The latter supports a pathway from marital distress through maternal depression to adolescents' depression. Further, the specific nature of the marital conflict matters. For example, parents' use of observable conflict strategies involving depressive behaviors such as physical distress, withdrawal, sadness, and fear mediated the association between depressive symptoms in mothers and their children's internalizing symptoms, whereas destructive and constructive marital conflict strategies did not serve as mediators (Du Rocher Schudlich & Cummings 2003). These latter studies suggest the need to further consider the roles of maternal depression and marital discord in relation to each other and the risk for the development of psychopathology in children.

Similar concerns are raised by the common association between depression and alcohol or drug use. In one study addressing this potential set of interacting mediators, maternal depression symptoms mediated the relation between parents' problematic drinking and 6- to 12-year-old children's internalizing problems (El-Sheikh & Flanagan 2001). More work is needed along these lines.

Interacting Etiological Mechanisms

Complicating the model of risk for depression in offspring of depressed mothers, the individual mechanisms of risk interact in complex ways to create diverse pathways to disorder. Diverse pathways may lead to the same outcome, a concept termed "equifinality," and similar developmental pathways may lead to diverse outcomes, a concept termed "multifinality" (Cicchetti & Rogosch 1996, Harrington 1996). Transactional models are particularly helpful for understanding these individual, complex pathways. Transactional models emphasize the interaction of genetic, neurobiological, biochemical, psychological, and sociological factors that, through mutual exchange between characteristics of the child and the environment, result in the development of psychopathology (Cicchetti & Toth 1995).

Researchers have proposed several theoretical models of the interface between two or more mechanisms, and empirical support for these models is beginning to appear (reviewed in Goodman 2003). These include passive, reactive, and active gene-environment correlation or covariation (Goldsmith et al. 1997b, Rutter et al. 1997), gene-environment interactions such as stress-diathesis models (Caspi et al. 2003, Monroe & Simons 1991), genetic vulnerabilities interacting with other biological vulnerabilities or cognitive vulnerabilities (Coccaro et al. 1994), genes interacting with other genes (Goldsmith et al. 1997b), stress-diathesis models with diatheses other than genetics (such as temperament) (Cicchetti & Toth 1998, Goldsmith et al. 1997a, Sameroff 1995), and child qualities evoking environmental qualities (Field et al. 1990, Teti & Gelfand 1991). Genetic factors are likely to play a role in the model that best explains associations among maternal depression, stressors, and the emergence of depression in children. For example, Silberg et al. (2001) found support for an environmentally mediated effect of independent, negative life events on adolescent depression only in the presence of parental emotional disorder. At the same time, the twin design showed that genetic factors are significant in influencing individual differences in susceptibility to environmentally mediated risk.

Other data suggest the importance of interactions involving parenting and stress mediators. For example, in one study, maternal depression was found to mediate the association between the stressor of neighborhood safety and mothers' consistent discipline (Hill & Herman-Stahl 2002). The next steps in this line of study would be to extend the model to explain the development of psychopathology in the children.

MODERATORS

Maternal Characteristics

Sameroff and colleagues (1982) were among the first to suggest that severity and chronicity may be at least as important as diagnosis in the transmission of psychopathology from parents to children (Keller et al. 1986). For example, the pattern of mothers' depression symptoms (mean, maximum, minimum, and variability in numbers of symptoms per month) over children's ages from 14 to 30 months predicted observed children's functioning even after controlling for diagnostic status (Seifer et al. 2001).

Chronicity and course are particularly salient given the known episodic and recurrent nature of depression, as reviewed above, and the compelling concern for children exposed to the resulting unpredictability of their mothers. The actual timing of episodes may also be important. Most studies of children with depressed parents have been cross-sectional, which does not allow for examining of chronicity, course, or timing. However, of those with longitudinal designs, some findings are consistent with this expectation. For example, postnatal depression that lasted into infants' sixth month of age, but not short-lived depression (through two months of age) predicted mothers' qualities of interaction with their infants (Campbell et al. 1995). In addition, Field (1992) reported that of mothers who had been depressed early in the postpartum period, 75% of the women continued to have symptoms at six months postpartum, but of the others who were no longer depressed when the infants were six months old, the infants did not display a "depressed" style of interaction or have lower Bayley mental and motor scale scores at one year of age (Field 2002).

In their large Australian sample, Brennan and colleagues (2002) found that both severity and chronicity of maternal depression symptoms from pregnancy through child age 5 years, as well as their statistical interaction, predicted 5-year-olds' higher levels of behavior problems, as did timing (more recent timing was associated with more behavior problems). In a study of those children at age 15, severity was a stronger predictor of children's depression than was chronicity, but chronicity was the stronger predictor of psychopathology other than depression (Hammen & Brennan 2003). In a prospective study of infants followed through age five, timing was also found to be important in that it predicted differentially to outcomes in the children (Essex et al. 2001). Specifically, children who had been exposed to maternal depression as infants had higher levels of internalizing symptoms co-occurring with externalizing symptoms relative to children who were not first exposed to their mothers depression until they were toddlers or preschool-aged. Later initial exposure was associated with increased risk of externalizing symptoms not co-occurring with internalizing symptoms, especially among girls. Finally, Hammen and colleagues (1991) reported a synchrony between maternal and child depression in that children of depressed mothers tended to have their depressive episodes in close proximity in time following their mothers' episodes.

Comorbidity is another key characteristic of depression. Depression, especially in women, is often comorbid with anxiety (Clark 1989, Kessler 2006) and with personality disorders (Shea et al. 1987, Widiger et al. 2006). Research on comorbidity that predicts children's outcomes is limited and mixed. In one study, major depression in parents was associated a range of internalizing and externalizing disorders in children regardless of the parents' comorbid panic disorder, but panic disorder and major depression individually and comorbidly predicted children's separation anxiety disorder and children having two or more anxiety disorders (Biederman et al. 2001). The presence of personality disorders among women with depression increased the likelihood of associations between maternal depression and qualities of their parenting of their nine-year-old children, but children's outcomes were not reported (DeMulder et al. 1995).

Fathers

Several theoretical models suggest that fathers will play at least a moderating role in the association between maternal depression and children's development, if not an independent role. Genetic models suggest fathers will contribute to children's risk for depression as much as mothers, albeit potentially through different mechanisms (Kendler et al. 2001). Parenting models of transmission have most often considered fathers in a moderating role in that mothers' parenting is expected to be more positive in the presence of available and supportive fathers (Crnic et al. 1983, Crockenberg 1986, Tamis-LeMonda & Cabrera 2002, Teti & Gelfand 1991) and fathers are expected to be more involved in the context of good marital relationships (Shannon et al. 2005). Stress models also ascribe a role to fathers in that fathers may either exacerbate or ameliorate stress in women with depression. Assortative mating, in particular the selection of a mate who also has a mood disorder, is known to be a significant factor in mate selection for women with affective disorders, although not as much as for men (Matthews & Reus 2001). Thus, children whose mothers are depressed have a higher-than-average likelihood of having a father who has depression or another disorder.

Fathers' depression contributes to the prediction of child psychopathology beyond that explained by maternal depression (Eiden & Leonard 1986, Goodman et al. 1993a, Thomas & Forehand 1991, Weissman et al. 1984). Results may differ for male and female offspring and for the specific child outcome. For example, in a large Australian sample, depression in mothers and fathers had additive effects on externalizing disorders in adolescents, whereas adolescent depression was best predicted by an interaction of maternal depression with paternal depression (and paternal substance abuse) (Brennan et al. 2002). It is therefore critical to examine transmission of putative risk alleles from fathers (as well as mothers) to probands. Other support for roles of fathers includes a finding from retrospective interviews of adolescent and young adult daughters of psychiatrically disturbed mothers (not just depression) that abuse by fathers predicted psychopathology in the daughters independently of psychiatric disorder in mothers (Andrews et al. 1990).

Child Characteristics

The Integrative Model for the Transmission of Risk (Goodman & Gotlib 1999) proposed a third set of moderators: child characteristics. In particular, the model suggested that children's temperament, gender, and intellectual and social-cognitive skills might moderate associations between maternal depression and the development of psychopathology. Although each of these child characteristics other than gender might also be conceptualized as outcomes, their proposed roles as moderators are based on the tradition of the competence construct in developmental psychopathology (Masten et al. 1995). Although definitions vary, competence is typically defined in terms of individuals' qualities or characteristics that enhance positive adaptation, especially in the context of adversity.

Temperament is sometimes (Rosenbaum et al. 2000, Sugawara et al. 1999), but not always (Austin et al. 2005, Whiffen & Gotlib 1989), found to be directly associated with maternal depression. A few studies found that prenatal anxiety, but not necessarily depression, predicted difficult temperament (Austin et al. 2005, Huizink et al. 2002), and another found a significant interaction of panic disorder and major depression in predicting behavioral inhibition (Rosenbaum et al. 2000). Also provocative are findings that patterns of fetal movement, which may be associated with depression or anxiety during pregnancy, predict infant temperament up to two years later (DiPietro et al. 2002). In an early exploration of this set of associations, pregnancy-depressed mood predicted infant temperament, which subsequently was concurrently associated with postpartum depressed mood (Cutrona & Troutman 1986). Infant irritability, scored from the Brazelton, predicted the onset of depression by eight weeks postpartum but did not predict the quality of mother-infant interaction (Murray et al. 1996).

Studies of temperament as a moderator of associations between maternal depression and child psychopathology are rare, despite thoughtful considerations of the manners in which temperament and maternal depression are likely to interact (Crockenberg 1986). Maternal hopelessness (the cognitive component of depression) significantly interacted with infant negative emotionality to predict lower levels of mothers' sensitivity while interacting with their babies, but the authors did not report any child functioning measures per se (Pauli-Pott et al. 2000). Consistent with the Goodman & Gotlib (1999) model, Rubin & Mills (1991) suggested that child temperament would interact with maternal depression (and attachment) to predict child outcomes. In a recent study of trajectories in the development of internalizing and externalizing behavior problems from ages 5 to 17, temperament by maternal depression interactions were not significant for girls, but for boys, maternal depression predicted increases in externalizing behavior only when the temperament construct of impulsivity was low (Leve et al. 2005). Thus, despite strong theoretical grounding and supportive corroborating data, more research is needed before we can draw conclusions about the moderating role of infant temperament in associations between maternal depression and children's problems in development.

Researchers have found support for gender as a moderator of three of the four proposed mechanisms in Goodman & Gotlib's (1999) model, namely heritability of depression, exposure to negative maternal cognitions, behaviors, and affect, and the stressful context of living with a depressed mother. Heritability estimates for depression have been found to be higher for girls than boys (Eley & Stevenson 1999, Murray & Sines 1996). Girls may also be more likely than boys to model the behavioral vulnerabilities displayed by depressed mothers given both gender stereotyping that would increase the salience of those behaviors to girls and the greater power of same-sex parents as models (Bandura 1986). Additionally, maternal depression's association with poor parenting may be a specific risk to girls through (*a*) impaired mother-daughter relationships, which are already characterized by high levels of conflict during adolescence (Hill et al. 1985, Steinberg 1987), and (*b*) adolescent girls developing a sense of responsibility for the family and taking on the role of parenting other children and caring for the depressed mother, a burden that increases the risk for depression (Stephens et al. 1987). Finally, girls may be particularly sensitive to heightened levels of stress (e.g., marital discord, economic hardships), and maternal depression is a nonspecific stressor that may exacerbate the risk already posed to girls, increasing the likelihood of developing internalizing symptoms (Compas et al. 2002, Conger et al. 1999).

Beyond gender and temperament, some theory and research considers the role of other child characteristics such as social-cognitive or cognitive-intellectual skills (Masten et al. 1999). For example, Compas and colleagues (2002) found that in coping with the stressors associated with having a depressed mother, children who report using volitional coping responses have fewer emotional and behavior problems. Among adolescents whose parents were depressed, having more advanced social-cognitive skills was associated with better adaptation (Beardslee et al. 1987). In fact, Gladstone & Beardslee (2002) have had success with interventions including a component of enhancing adolescent offspring's perspective-taking and other skills to prevent their development of psychopathology.

IMPLICATIONS AND FUTURE DIRECTIONS

The major challenge facing clinical researchers in this field of study is dealing with the complexities inherent in transactional models and multifinality and understanding that there are multiple alternative pathways that the children of depressed mothers will follow. These difficulties begin with challenges in generating hypotheses and progress quickly to measurement issues, study design (typically requiring multiple data points in longitudinal studies), statistical approaches (latent variable analyses, complex modeling of developmental trajectories, etc.), and interpretation of findings. The reviewed literature shows much of the support for various components of the theoretical model relying on cross-sectional designs rather than experiments or even the longitudinal designs that would elucidate the developmental processes theorized. Although there will always be a role for cross-sectional studies, most of the pressing unresolved questions will not be answered with these designs. Longitudinal studies minimize (although they do not eliminate) the likelihood of errors in cause-effect assumptions (Forehand & McCombs 1988, Marchand & Hock 1998).

Other issues facing researchers in this field center on measurement. In particular, it is essential to move beyond a single reporter of both risk (maternal depression) and outcome (child vulnerability or disorder) (Kraemer et al. 2003). Following the helpful writing of Richters (1992) on how to think about concerns about depression influencing mothers' reports on their children, researchers with well-designed studies to address this question continue to find small to moderate support for an association between higher maternal depression and mothers' tendency to overreport child behavior problems, relative to a latent criterion variable (Boyle & Pickles 1997, Fergusson et al. 1993). There remain important unresolved questions, which are beyond the scope of this chapter, about how to interpret this association. Also, many of our constructs are complex and require multiple measures regardless of the source.

The approach taken to measuring depression in mothers is clearly most essential for this area of study. Ideally, theory drives considerations of whether to measure symptom levels relative to diagnostic status. For example, we might want to ask questions about associations with severity of depression across the full range of scores in the population studied or, alternatively, ask questions specific to the presence or absence of depression that meets diagnostic criteria. A middle ground, which is commonly used and is less clear in terms of generalizing findings, is the approach of using symptom scales with their established cut-scores to designate mothers as depressed or not. In a review of epidemiological and adult outcome differences between depression as a mood feature and depression as a diagnostic category, Harrington, Rutter, and Fombonne (1996) found this distinction to be important for a number of different aspects of clinical functioning. In a meta-analysis being completed in my lab, we are finding that studies relying on diagnosis of mothers' depression found significantly larger effect sizes for associations between maternal depression and a range of outcomes in the children relative to studies relying on symptom ratings of mothers' depression (Goodman et al. 2003). The commonality of comorbidity, especially anxiety, also needs to be tackled by researchers, given known associations (from animal and human studies) between stress and anxiety during pregnancy and early life and the development of behavior problems. More work is needed to sort out the independent and interacting influences of the two disorders. Also needing attention are issues of culture and race/ethnicity and the extent to which these influences may act as moderators given different cultures' views on depression, emotion expression, emotion regulation, etc.

Researchers also face difficult decisions in selecting the population from which to sample. Many of the studies relied on samples of families in poverty, those with adolescent mothers, single-parent families, those experiencing marital conflict, and families in other situations that enhance the risk for psychopathology in the children. Although it is undeniable that these are important populations to study, it is also essential to be able to distinguish the effects of depression and the likely direct and interacting effects of the context variables. Similar concerns follow from design decisions such as studying women from clinical versus community samples, a narrow rather than a broad age range of children, and being able to address potential gender differences. Greater use of designs that allow for tests of moderation with these variables has the potential to inform future refinement of theoretical models of the effects of maternal depression. For instance, findings may highlight subgroups of children or families that appear to be at greater risk (i.e., infants/toddlers, children in single-parent families, or low-socioeconomic-status families), pointing to the need for future studies examining the mechanisms underlying such heightened risk in detail.

Implications for Practice and Policy

Although researchers in this field of study are motivated to contribute to the understanding of the nature and extent of effects of maternal depression on children and the mechanisms for those effects, undoubtedly much of our motivation also stems from the expectation of being able to contribute to the treatment, if not prevention, of those effects. Thus, it may come as a surprise that few clinical research studies target children of depressed mothers for tests of prevention or treatment. On the other hand, an understanding of the complexities of the nature of the risk (having a mother with depression), mechanisms, moderators, and transactional processes provides a sober reminder of the challenges faced by designers of intervention studies.

Gladstone & Beardslee (2002) provide a helpful review of this limited literature that takes a developmental perspective. Stage-salient issues that are expected to be or are known to be affected by depression in mothers, such as those reviewed in this article, are used as guides to evaluate the extent to which intervention studies have addressed these issues. That review continues to serve as a source of empirically based suggestions for interventions targeted to particular ages of children. The broader notion of patient-treatment matching might also benefit interventions designed for children of depressed mothers, even though the children are not likely to be "patients" and the "treatment" is likely to be preventive. Rather than strictly characteristics of patients, the focus might be on implications for intervention based on tailored risk assessments of the child, the mother, and relevant contextual variables. With due respect for limitations in applying knowledge of risk factors to the design of preventive interventions (Howe 2003, Silberg & Rutter 2002), I end this article with a list of conclusions one might draw from the literature reviewed here and that might serve as beginning considerations for the development of guidelines for preventive interventions or treatments for children whose mothers have suffered from depression.

1. Employ a transactional perspective, including systemic notions of interplay within families such that any encounter with depression in a mother will lead to a developmentally sensitive assessment of the children (ideally the spouse/partner as well), the quality of parenting, and stressors in the environment.
2. Include fathers as both a source of information and potential target of intervention.
3. Screen children not only for indices of psychopathology but also for symptoms that may not yet be impairing and for vulnerabilities to the later development of psychopathology. Good examples are affect regulation and stress reactivity in addition to the social cognitive skills that Beardslee's work has revealed to be protective.
4. Design age-appropriate interventions that enhance children's understanding of depression in parents (Beardslee et al. 1993), coping skills (Compas et al. 2002), affect regulation abilities, and other social-cognitive competencies that have been found to be protective. Also, consider training in physiological stress reactivity.
5. Reduce marital conflict and other stressors found to be important in both direct and moderating roles (Cummings et al. 2005). Teach depressed mothers how to resolve conflicts and enhance their problem-solving skills. Instruct them in ways to help their children learn to solve problems and resolve conflicts. Teach husbands and partners how to cope with depression in a loved one, and educate them in their role in reducing marital conflict.
6. Consider behavioral family therapy, given the findings on children's tendencies to reinforce depressive behaviors in their parents and their emotional reliance on their parents, and parents' tendency to reinforce their children's (especially daughters') depressive behaviors (Sheeber et al. 2002). The latter socialization practices might make a reasonable approach for universal prevention, beginning with parents of young children.
7. Enhance qualities of parenting that have been found to be disrupted with depression. Consider tailoring the parenting intervention to the particular parenting difficulties or interactional style of the mother (Field 2002).
8. Target interventions to other aspects of the depressed mother's behavior that may contribute to the high-risk environment for her child (Hammen 2002).
9. Inform depressed women and their partners about the role of cognitions in enhancing vulnerability to depression in their children and design interventions to minimize depressed parents' criticism and other mechanisms identified in the research (Garber & Martin 2002).
10. Begin efforts early, including considering designing interventions for pregnant women who experience or are at risk for depression.

11. Treat the comorbid disorders in the mothers. Findings are particularly strong with regard to the importance of co-occurring anxiety disorders and personality disorders.
12. For policy makers—require screening of depression in pregnancy, postpartum, and throughout parenting. Pediatricians and obstetricians/gynecologists as well as teachers play critical roles as gatekeepers.
13. Remember that not all children of depressed mothers will develop psychopathology. Use the knowledge on moderators to target those children who are most at risk for adverse outcomes associated with their mothers having depression.

SUMMARY POINTS

1. Depression in mothers is an important topic for clinical psychologists, regardless of whether one's research or practice is primarily concerned with children or adults.
2. Goodman & Gotlib (1999) developed a theoretical model of mechanisms of risk for the development of psychopathology in children of depressed mothers that has strong empirical support for some aspects of the model and pinpoints areas that need further study.
3. Not all children of depressed mothers will develop psychological problems. More knowledge is needed of moderators of this risk, which informs whom and under what circumstances children are more or less at risk.
4. A developmental psychopathology perspective offers useful concepts and methods for further advances in this field of study.
5. Several suggestions are offered for future directions for theory, research, and practice.

LITERATURE CITED

Almeida DM, Kessler RC. 1998. Everyday stressors and gender differences in daily distress. *J. Personal. Soc. Psychol.* 75:670–80

Anderson CA, Hammen CL. 1993. Psychosocial outcomes of children of unipolar depressed, bipolar, medically ill, and normal women: a longitudinal study. *J. Consult. Clin. Psychol.* 61:448–54

Andrews B, Brown GW, Creasey L. 1990. Intergenerational links between psychiatric disorder in mothers and daughters: the role of parenting experiences. *J. Child Psychiatry* 31:1115–29

Anokhin AP, Heath AC, Myers E. 2006. Genetic and environmental influences on frontal EEG asymmetry: a twin study. *Biol. Psychol.* 71:289–95

Ashman SB, Dawson G. 2002. Maternal depression, infant psychobiological development, and risk for depression. In Goodman & Gotlib 2002, pp. 37–58

Ashman SB, Dawson G, Panagiotides H, Yamada E, Wilkinson CW. 2002. Stress hormone levels of children of depressed mothers. *Dev. Psychopathol.* 14:333–49

Austin MP, Hadzi-Pavlovic D, Leader L, Saint K, Parker G. 2005. Maternal trait anxiety, depression and life event stress in pregnancy: relationships with infant temperament. *Early Hum. Dev.* 81:183–90

Bandura A. 1986. *Social Foundations of Thought and Action: A Social Cognitive Theory*. Englewood Cliffs, NJ: Prentice-Hall

Baron RM, Kenny DA. 1986. The moderator-mediator variable distinction in social psychological research: conceptual, strategic, and statistical considerations. *J. Personal. Soc. Psychol.* 51:1173–82

Bartels M, Van den Berg M, Sluyter F, Boomsma DI, de Geus EJ. 2003. Heritability of cortisol levels: review and simultaneous analysis of twin studies. *Psychoneuroendocrinology* 28:121–37

Beardslee WR, Salt P, Porterfield K, Rothberg PC, van de Velde P, et al. 1993. Comparison of preventive interventions for families with parental affective disorder. *J. Am. Acad. Child Adolesc. Psychiatry* 32:254–63

Beardslee WR, Schultz LH, Selman RL. 1987. Level of social-cognitive development, adaptive functioning, and DSM-III diagnoses in adolescent offspring of parents with affective disorders: implications for the development of the capacity for mutuality. *Dev. Psychol.* 23:807–15

Beck AT, Rush AJ, Shaw BF, Emery G. 1979. *Cognitive Therapy of Depression*. New York: Guilford

Belsher G, Costello CG. 1988. Relapse after recovery from unipolar depression: a critical review. *Psychol. Bull.* 104:84–96

Biederman J, Rosenbaum JF, Faraone SV, Hirshfeld-Becker DR, Friedman D, et al. 2001. Patterns of psychopathology and dysfunction in high-risk children of parents with panic disorder and major depression. *Am. J. Psychiatry* 158:49–57

Boyle MH, Pickles AR. 1997. Influence of maternal depressive symptoms on ratings of childhood behavior. *J. Abnorm. Child Psychol.* 25:399–412

Brennan PA, Hammen C, Anderson MJ, Bor W, Najman JM, Williams GM. 2000. Chronicity, severity, and timing of maternal depressive symptoms: relationships with child outcomes at age five. *Dev. Psychol.* 36:759–66

Brennan PA, Hammen C, Katz AR, Le Brocque RM. 2002. Maternal depression, paternal psychopathology, and adolescent diagnostic outcomes. *J. Consult. Clin. Psychol.* 70:1075–85

Brown GW, Harris TO. 1978. *Social Origins of Depression: A Study of Psychiatric Disorder in Women*. New York: Free Press

Caldji C, Diorio J, Meaney MJ. 2000. Variations in maternal care in infancy regulate the development of stress reactivity. *Biol. Psychiatry* 48:1164–74

Campbell SB. 1995. Behavior problems in preschool children: a review of recent research. *J. Child Psychol. Psychiatry* 36:113–49

Campbell SB, Cohn J, Meyers T. 1995. Depression in first-time mothers: mother-infant interaction and depression chronicity. *Dev. Psychol.* 31:349–57

Caspi A, Sugden K, Moffitt TE, Taylor A, Craig IW, et al. 2003. Influence of life stress on depression: moderation by a polymorphism in the 5-HTT gene. *Science* 301:386–89

Cherny SS, Fulker DW, Corley RP, Plomin R, DeFries JC. 1994. Continuity and change in infant shyness from 14 to 20 months. *Behav. Genet.* 24:365–79

Chugani HT, Phelps ME. 1986. Maturational changes in cerebral function in infants determined by 18FDG positron emission tomography. *Science* 231:840–43

Cicchetti D, Rogosch FA. 1996. Equifinality and multifinality in developmental psychopathology. *Dev. Psychopathol.* 8:597–600.

Presents definitions and rationale for key concepts in developmental psychopathology.

Cicchetti D, Rogosch FA, Toth SL. 1998. Maternal depressive disorder and contextual risk: contributions to the development of attachment insecurity and behavior problems in toddlerhood. *Dev. Psychopathol.* 10:283–300

Cicchetti D, Toth SL. 1995. Developmental psychopathology and disorders of affect. In *Developmental Psychopathology*, ed. D Cicchetti, DJ Cohen, pp. 369–420. Oxford: Wiley

Cicchetti D, Toth SL. 1998. The development of depression in children and adolescents. *Am. Psychol.* 53:221–41

Clark LA. 1989. The anxiety and depressive disorders: descriptive psychopathology and differential diagnoses. In *Anxiety and Depression: Distinctive and Overlapping Features*, ed. PC Kendall, D Watson, pp. 83–129. San Diego, CA: Academic

Coccaro EF, Silverman JM, Klar HM, Horvath TB, Siever LJ. 1994. Familial correlates of reduced central serotonergic system function in patients with personality disorders. *Arch. Gen. Psychiatry* 51:318–24

Compas BE, Langrock AM, Keller G, Merchant MJ, Copeland ME. 2002. Children coping with parental depression: processes of adaptation to family stress. In Goodman & Gotlib 2002, pp. 227–52

Compas BE, Malcarne VL, Fondacaro KM. 1988. Coping with stressful events in older children and young adolescents. *J. Consult. Clin. Psychol.* 56:405–11

Compton K, Snyder J, Schrepferman L, Bank L, Shortt JW. 2003. The contribution of parents and siblings to antisocial and depressive behavior in adolescents: a double jeopardy coercion model. *Dev. Psychopathol.* 15:163–82

Conger RD, Conger KD, Matthews LS, Elder GHJ. 1999. Pathways of economic influence on adolescent adjustment. *Am. J. Community Psychol.* 27:519–41

Connell AM, Goodman SH. 2002. The association between psychopathology in fathers versus mothers and children's internalizing and externalizing behavior problems: a meta-analysis. *Psychol. Bull.* 128:746–73.

Addresses the issue of relative influence of mothers' and fathers' psychopathology on children's psychopathology.

Crnic KA, Greenberg MT, Ragozin AS, Robinson NM, Basham RB. 1983. Effects of stress and social support on mothers and premature and full-term infants. *Child Dev.* 54:209–17

Crockenberg SB. 1986. Are temperamental differences in babies associated with predictable differences in care giving? *New Direct. Child Dev.* 31:52–73

Cummings EM, Keller PS, Davies PT. 2005. Towards a family process model of maternal and paternal depressive symptoms: exploring multiple relations with child and family functioning. *J. Child Psychol. Psychiatry* 46:479–89

Cutrona DE, Troutman BR. 1986. Social support, infant temperament, and parenting self-efficacy: a mediational model of postpartum depresion. *Child Dev.* 57:1507–18

Davidson RJ, Ekman P, Saron C, Senulis R, Friesen WV. 1990. Approach-withdrawal and cerebral asymmetry: emotional expression and brain physiology I. *J. Personal. Soc. Psychol.* 58:330–41.

This key work describes the importance of brain asymmetry as measured by EEG for the development of psychopathology.

Davidson RJ, Fox NA. 1989. Frontal brain asymmetry predicts infants' response to maternal separation. *J. Abnorm. Psychol.* 98:127–31

Davies PT, Dumenci L. 1999. The interplay between maternal depressive symptoms and marital distress in the prediction of adolescent adjustment. *J. Marriage Fam.* 61:238–54

Davies PT, Windle M. 1997. Gender-specific pathways between maternal depressive symptoms, family discord, and adolescent adjustment. *Dev. Psychol.* 33:657–68

Davis B, Sheeber L, Hops H. 2002. Coercive family processes and adolescent depression. In *Antisocial Behavior in Children and Adolescents: Developmental Analysis and the Oregon Model for Intervention*, ed. JB Reid, GR Patterson, JJ Snyder, pp. 173–94. Washington, DC: Am. Psychol. Assoc.

Dawson G, Ashman SB, Hessl D, Spieker S, Frey K, et al. 2001. Autonomic and brain electrical activity in securely and insecurely attached infants of depressed mothers. *Infant Behav. Dev.* 24:135–49

Dawson G, Ashman SB, Panagiotides H, Hessl D, Self J, et al. 2003. Preschool outcomes of children of depressed mothers: role of maternal behavior, contextual risk, and children's brain activity. *Child Dev.* 74:1158–75

Dawson G, Frey K, Panagiotides H, Osterling J, Hessl D. 1997. Infants of depressed mothers exhibit atypical frontal brain activity: a replication and extension of previous findings. *J. Child Psychol. Psychiatry* 38:179–86
Dawson G, Grofer Klinger L, Panagiotides H, Hill D, Spieker S. 1992. Frontal lobe activity and affective behavior of infants of mothers with depressive symptoms. *Child Dev.* 63(3):725–37
DeMulder EK, Tarulla LB, Klimes-Dougan B, Free K. 1995. Personality disorders of affectively ill mothers: links to maternal behavior. *J. Personal. Disord.* 9:199–212
Diego MA, Field T, Hernandez-Reif M, Cullen C, Schanberg S, Kuhn C. 2004. Prepartum, postpartum, and chronic depression effects on newborns. *Psychiatry* 67:63–80
DiPietro JA, Bornstein MH, Costigan KA, Pressman EK, Hahn CS, et al. 2002. What does fetal movement predict about behavior during the first two years of life? *Dev. Psychobiol.* 40:358–71
Du Rocher Schudlich TD, Cummings EM. 2003. Parental dysphoria and children's internalizing symptoms: marital conflict styles as mediators of risk. *Child Dev.* 74:1663–81
Dumas JE, Gibson JA. 1990. Behavioral correlates of maternal depressive symptomatology in conduct disorder children II. Systemic effects involving fathers and siblings. *J. Consult. Clin. Psychol.* 58:877–81
Eamon MK, Zuehl RM. 2001. Maternal depression and physical punishment as mediators of the effect of poverty on socioemotional problems of children in single-mother families. *Am. J. Orthopsychiatry* 71:218–26
Eiden RD, Leonard KE. 1986. Paternal alcohol use and the mother-infant relationship. *Dev. Psychopathol.* 8:307–23
El-Sheikh M, Flanagan E. 2001. Parental problem drinking and children's adjustment: family conflict and parental depression as mediators and moderators of risk. *J. Abnorm. Child Psychol.* 29:417–32
Eley TC, Stevenson J. 1999. Exploring the covariation between anxiety and depression symptoms: a genetic analysis of the effect of age and sex. *J. Child Psychol. Psychiatry* 40:1273–84
Essex MJ, Klein MH, Cho E, Kalin NH. 2002. Maternal stress beginning in infancy may sensitize children to later stress exposure: effects on cortisol and behavior. *Biol. Psychiatry* 52:776–84
Essex MJ, Klein MH, Miech R, Smider NA. 2001. Timing of initial exposure to maternal major depression and children's mental health symptoms in kindergarten. *Br. J. Psychiatry* 179:151–56
Evans J, Heron J, Francomb H, Oke S, Golding J, Team TALSPCS. 2001. Cohort study of depressed mood during pregnancy and after childbirth. *Br. Med. J.* 323:257–60
Fergusson DM, Horwood LJ, Lynskey MT. 1995. Maternal depressive symptoms and depressive symptoms in adolescents. *J. Child Psychol. Psychiatry* 36:1161–78
Fergusson DM, Lynskey MT, Horwood LJ. 1993. The effect of maternal depression on maternal ratings of child behavior. *J. Abnorm. Child Psychol.* 21:245–69
Field T. 1992. Infants of depressed mothers. *Dev. Psychopathol.* 4:49–66
Field T. 2002. Prenatal effects of maternal depression. In Goodman & Gotlib 2002, pp. 59–88
Field T, Healy B, Goldstein S, Guthertz M. 1990. Behavior-state matching and synchrony in mother-infant interactions of nondepressed versus depressed dyads. *Dev. Psychol.* 26:7–14
Forehand R, McCombs A. 1988. Unraveling the antecedent-consequence conditions in maternal depression and adolescent functioning. *Behav. Res. Ther.* 26:399–405
Fox NA. 1994. *The Development of Emotion Regulation: Biological and Behavioral Considerations.* Chicago: Univ. Chicago Press
Frye A, Garber J. 2005. The relations among maternal depression, maternal criticism, and adolescents' externalizing and internaling symptoms. *J. Abnorm. Child Psychol.* 33:1–11

Provides an excellent source on the key construct of emotion regulation as related to the development of psychopathology.

Garber J, Braafladt N, Zeman J. 1991. The regulation of sad affect: an information-processing perspective. In *The Development of Emotion Regulation and Dysregulation*, ed. J Garber, KA Dodge, pp. 208–42. Cambridge, UK: Cambridge Univ. Press

Garber J, Martin NC. 2002. Negative cognitions in offspring of depressed parents: mechanisms of risk. In Goodman & Gotlib 2002, pp. 121–54

Gelfand DM, Teti DM. 1990. The effects of maternal depression on children. *Clin. Psychol. Rev.* 10:329–53

Ghodsian M, Zayicek E, Wolkind S. 1984. A longitudinal study of maternal depression and child behavior problems. *J. Child Psychol. Psychiatry* 25:91–109

Gitau R, Fisk NM, Teixeira JM, Cameron A, Glover V. 2001. Fetal hypothalamic-pituitary-adrenal stress responses to invasive procedures are independent of maternal responses. *J. Clin. Endocrinol. Metab.* 86:104–9

Gladstone TRG, Beardslee WR. 2002. Treatment, intervention, and prevention with children of depressed parents: a developmental perspective. In Goodman & Gotlib 2002, pp. 277–305.

Offers a survey of the evidence-based approaches to prevention and treatment for children of depressed mothers.

Glover V. 1997. Maternal stress or anxiety in pregnancy and emotional development of the child. *Br. J. Psychiatry* 171:105–6

Goldsmith HH, Buss KA, Lemery KS. 1997a. Toddler and childhood temperament: expanded content, stronger genetic evidence, new evidence for the importance of environment. *Dev. Psychol.* 33:891–905

Goldsmith HH, Gottesman II, Lemery KS. 1997b. Epigenetic approaches to developmental psychopathology. *Dev. Psychopathol.* 9:365–87

Goodman SH. 2003. Genesis and epigenesis of psychopathology in children with depressed mothers: toward an integrative biopsychosocial perspective. In *Neurodevelopmental Mechanisms in the Genesis and Epigenesis of Psychopathology: Future Research Directions*, ed. D Cicchetti, E Walker, pp. 428–60. New York: Cambridge Univ. Press

Goodman SH. 2006. *Prenatal mood disturbance predicts infant behavior*. Tenth World Congress World Assoc. Infant Mental Health. Paris, France

Goodman SH, Adamson LB, Riniti J, Cole S. 1994. Mothers' expressed attitudes: associations with maternal depression and children's self-esteem and psychopathology. *J. Am. Acad. Child Adolesc. Psychiatry* 33:1265–74

Goodman SH, Brogan D, Lynch ME, Fielding B. 1993a. Social and emotional competence in children of depressed mothers. *Child Dev.* 64:516–31

Goodman SH, Connell AM, Broth MR, Hall CM. 2003. The association between behavior problems and competence in children and depression in mothers: a meta-analysis. Poster presented at Soc. Res. Child Develop., Tampa, FL

Goodman SH, Gotlib IH. 1999. Risk for psychopathology in the children of depressed mothers: a developmental model for understanding mechanisms of transmission. *Psychol. Rev.* 106:458–90

Presents the key theoretical model for mechanism of transmission and provides evidence.

Goodman SH, Gotlib IH, eds. 2002. *Children of Depressed Parents: Mechanisms of Risk and Implications for Treatment*. Washington, DC: Am. Psychol. Assoc.

Discusses each of the core components of the model for the transmission of psychopathology from depressed mothers to their children.

Goodman SH, Sewell DR, Cooley EL, Leavitt N. 1993b. Assessing levels of adaptive functioning: the Role Functioning Scale. *Community Ment. Health J.* 29:119–31

Goodman SH, Tully EC. 2006. Depression in women who are mothers: an integrative model of risk for the development of psychopathology in their sons and daughters. In *Women and Depression: A Handbook for the Social, Behavioral, and Biomedical Sciences*, ed. CLM Keyes, SH Goodman, pp. 241–82. New York: Cambridge Univ. Press

Gotlib IH, Gilboa E, Sommerfeld BK. 2000. Cognitive functioning in depression: nature and origins. In *Wisconsin Symposium on Emotion*, Vol. 1, ed. RJ Davidson, pp. 133–63. New York: Oxford Univ. Press

Graham YP, Heim C, Goodman SH, Miller AH, Nemeroff CB. 1999. The effects of neonatal stress on brain development: implications for psychopathology. *Dev. Psychopathol.* 11:545–65

Grant KE, Compas BE, Stuhlmacher AF, Thurm AE, McMahon SD, Halpert JA. 2003. Stressors and child and adolescent psychopathology: moving from markers to mechanisms of risk. *Psychol. Bull.* 129:447–66

Green JM, Murray D. 1994. The use of the Edinburgh Postnatal Depression Scale in research to explore the relationship between antenatal and postnatal dysphoria. In *Perinatal Psychiatry: Use and Misuse of the Edinburgh Postnatal Depression Scale*, ed. J Cox, J Holden, pp. 180–98. London: Gaskell

Halligan SL, Herbert J, Goodyer IM, Murray L. 2004. Exposure to postnatal depression predicts elevated cortisol in adolescent offspring. *Biol. Psychiatry* 55:376–81

Hammen C. 1991. Generation of stress in the course of unipolar depression. *J. Abnorm. Psychol.* 100:555–61

Hammen C. 2002. Context of stress in families of children with depressed parents. In Goodman & Gotlib 2002, pp. 175–202

Hammen C, Brennan PA. 2001. Depressed adolescents of depressed and nondepressed mothers: tests of an interpersonal impairment hypothesis. *J. Consult. Clin. Psychol.* 69:284–94

Hammen C, Brennan PA. 2003. Severity, chronicity, and timing of maternal depression and risk for adolescent offspring diagnoses in a community sample. *Arch. Gen. Psychiatry* 60:253–58

Hammen C, Burge D, Adrian C. 1991. Timing of mother and child depression in a longitudinal study of children at risk. *J. Consult. Clin. Psychol.* 59:341–45

Hammen C, Burge D, Burney E, Adrian C. 1990a. Longitudinal study of diagnoses in children of women with unipolar and bipolar affective disorder. *Arch. Gen. Psychiatry* 47:1112–17

Hammen C, Burge D, Stansbury K. 1990b. Relationship of mother and child variables to child outcomes in a high risk sample: a causal modeling analysis. *Dev. Psychol.* 26:24–30

Hammen C, Shih J, Altman T, Brennan PA. 2003. Interpersonal impairment and the prediction of depressive symptoms in adolescent children of depressed and nondepressed mothers. *J. Am. Acad. Child Adolesc. Psychiatry* 42:571–77

Handley SL, Dunn TL, Waldron G, Baker JM. 1980. Tryptophan, cortisol and puerperal mood. *Br. J. Psychiatry* 136:498–508

Harnish JD, Dodge KA, Valente E. 1995. Mother-child interaction quality as a partial mediator of the roles of maternal depressive symptomatology and socioeconomic status in the development of child behavior problems. *Child Dev.* 66:739–53

Harrington R. 1996. Family-genetic findings in child and adolescent depressive disorders. *Int. Rev. Psychiatry* 8:355–68

Harrington R, Rutter M, Frombonne E. 1996. Developmental pathways in depression: multiple meanings, antecedents, and endpoints. *Dev. Psychopathol.* 8:601–16

Hay DF, Kumar R. 1995. Interpreting the effects of mothers' postnatal depression on children's intelligence: a critique and reanalysis. *Child Psychiatry Hum. Dev.* 25:165–81

Hay DF, Pawlby S. 2001. Intellectual problems shown by 11-year-old children whose mothers had postnatal depression. *J. Child Psychol. Psychiatry* 42:871–89

Healy BT. 1992. The heritability of autonomic nervous system processes. In *Stress and Coping in Infancy and Childhood. Stress and Coping*, ed. TM Field, PM McCabe, pp. 69–82. Hillsdale, NJ: Erlbaum

Hertsgaard L, Gunnar M, Erickson M, Nachmias M. 1995. Adrenocortical response to the strange situation in infants with disorganized/disoriented attachment relationships. *Child Dev.* 66:1100–6

Hessl D, Dawson G, Frey K, Panagiotides H, Self H, et al. 1998. A longitudinal study of children of depressed mothers: psychobiological findings related to stress. In *Advancing Research on Developmental Plasticity: Integrating the Behavioral Sciences and the Neurosciences of Mental Health*, ed. DM Hann, LC Huffman, KK Lederhendler, D Minecke, p. 256. Bethesda, MD: Natl. Inst. Ment. Health

Hill JP, Holmbeck GN, Marlow L, Green TM, Lynch ME. 1985. Menarcheal status and parent-child relations in families of seventh-grade girls. *J. Youth Adolesc.* 14:301–16

Hill NE, Herman-Stahl MA. 2002. Neighborhood safety and social involvement: associations with parenting behaviors and depressive symptoms among African-American and Euro-American mothers. *J. Fam. Psychol.* 16:209–19

Hilsman R. 2001. Maternal expressed emotion, child of self-cognitions, and psychopathology in children of depressed and nondepressed mothers. *Dissert. Abstr. Int. Sect. B: Sci. Eng.* 62(2-B):1082

Hipwell AE, Murray L, Ducournau P, Stein A. 2005. The effects of maternal depression and parental conflict on children's peer play. *Child Care Health Dev.* 31:11–23

Holmbeck G. 1997. Toward terminological, conceptual, and statistical clarity in the study of mediators and moderators: examples from the child-clinical and pediatric psychology literatures. *J. Consult. Clin. Psychol.* 65:599–610

Hops H. 1996. Intergenerational transmission of depressive symptoms: gender and developmental considerations. In *Interpersonal Factors in the Origin and Course of Affective Disorders*, ed. C Mundt, MJ Goldstein, K Hahlweg, P Fiedler, pp. 113–28. London: Gaskell/R. Coll. Psychiatr.

Hops H, Sherman L, Biglan A. 1990. Maternal depression, marital discord, and children's behavior: a developmental perspective. In *Depression and Aggression in Family Interaction*, ed. GR Patterson, pp. 185–208. Hillsdale, NJ: Erlbaum

Howe GW. 2003. Next-generation trials for the prevention of depression: lessons from longitudinal epidemiology and developmental psychopathology. *Prevent. Treat.* 6 (article 16)

Huizink AC, Mulder EJH, Buitelaar JK. 2004. Prenatal stress and risk for psychopathology: specific effects of induction of general susceptibility? *Psychol. Bull.* 130:115–42

Huizink AC, Robles de Medina PG, Mulder EJH, Visser GHA, Buitelaar JK. 2002. Psychological measures of prenatal stress as predictors of infant temperament. *J. Am. Acad. Child Adolesc. Psychiatry* 41:1078–85

Jackson PB, Williams DR. 2006. Culture, race/ethnicity, and depression. In *Women and Depression: A Handbook for the Social, Behavioral, and Biomedical Sciences*, ed. CLM Keyes, SH Goodman, pp. 328–59. New York: Cambridge Univ. Press

Jaenicke C, Hammen CL, Zupan B, Hiroto D, Gordon D, et al. 1987. Cognitive vulnerability in children at risk for depression. *J. Abnorm. Child Psychol.* 15:559–72

Jones NA, Field T, Davalos M, Pickens J. 1997. EEG stability in infants/children of depressed mothers. *Child Psychiatry Hum. Dev.* 28:59–70

Jones NA, McFall BA, Diego M. 2004. Patterns of brain electrical activity in infants of depressed mothers who breastfeed and bottle feed: the mediating role of infant temperament. *Biol. Psychol.* 67:103–24

Kam C-M. 2001. Effects of maternal depression on children's social and emotional functioning during early school year. *Dissert. Abstr. Int. Sect. B Sci. Eng.* 62(5-B):2516

Kashani JH, Burbach DJ, Rosenberg TK. 1988. Perception of family conflict resolution of depressive symptomatology in adolescents. *J. Am. Acad. Child Adolesc. Psychiatry* 27:42–48

Keller MB, Beardslee WR, Dorer DJ, Lavori PW, Samuelson H, Klerman GR. 1986. Impact of severity and chronicity of parental affective illness on adaptive functioning and psychopathology in children. *Arch. Gen. Psychiatry* 43:930–37

Keller MB, Lavori PW, Mueller TI, Endicott J, Coryell W, et al. 1992. Time to recovery, chronicity, and levels of psychopathology in major depression: a 5-year prospective follow-up of 431 subjects. *Arch. Gen. Psychiatry* 49:809–16

Kendler KS, Gardner CO, Neale MC, Prescott CA. 2001. Genetic risk factors for major depression in men and women: similar or different heritabilities and same or partly distinct genes? *Psychol. Med.* 31:605–16

Kenny DA, Kashy DA, Bolger N. 1998. Data analysis in social psychology. In *The Handbook of Social Psychology*, ed. D Gilbert, S Fiske, G Lindzey, pp. 233–65. Boston, MA: McGraw-Hill

Kessler RC. 2006. The epidemiology of depression among women. In *Women and Depression: A Handbook for the Social, Behavior, and Biomedical Sciences*, ed. CLM Keyes, SH Goodman, pp. 22–40. New York: Cambridge Univ. Press

Kochanska G, Radke-Yarrow M, Kuczynski L, Friedman S. 1987. Normal and affectively ill mothers' beliefs about their children. *Am. J. Orthopsychiatry* 57:345–50

Kraemer HC, Measelle JR, Ablow JC, Essex MJ, Boyce W, Kupfer DJ. 2003. A new approach to integrating data from multiple informants in psychiatric assessment and research: mixing and matching contexts and perspectives. *Am. J. Psychiatry* 160:1566–77

Kraemer HC, Stice E, Kazdin A, Offord D, Kupfer DJ. 2001. How do risk factors work together? Mediators, moderators, and independent, overlapping, and proxy risk factors. *Am. J. Psychiatry* 158:848–56.

Clearly defines and persuasively argues for the importance of developing interventions based on understanding of various constructs.

Lennon MC. 1987. Sex differences in distress: the impact of gender and work roles. *J. Health Soc. Behav.* 28:290–305

Leve LD, Kim HK, Pears KC. 2005. Childhood temperament and family environment as predictors of internalizing and externalizing trajectories from ages 5 to 17. *J. Abnorm. Child Psychol.* 33:505–20

Levinson DF, Zubenko GS, Crowe RR, DePaulo RJ, Scheftner WS, et al. 2003. Genetics of recurrent early-onset depression (GenRED): design and preliminary clinical characteristics of a repository sample for genetic linkage studies. *Am. J. Med. Genet.* 119B:118–30

Lewinsohn PM, Allen NB, Seeley JR, Gotlib IH. 1999. First onset versus recurrence of depression: differential processes of psychosocial risk. *J. Abnorm. Psychol.* 108:483–89

Loehlin JC, Nichols RC. 1976. *Heredity, Environment, and Personality*. Austin: Univ. Texas Press

Lovejoy MC, Graczyk PA, O'Hare E, Neuman G. 2000. Maternal depression and parenting behavior: a meta-analytic review. *Clin. Psychol. Rev.* 20:561–92.

Provides a meta-analysis of degree of association between qualities of parenting behavior and depression in mothers.

Lundy B. 2002. Paternal socio-psychological factors and infant attachment: the mediating role of synchrony in father-infant interactions. *Infant Behav. Dev.* 25:221–36

Lundy B, Jones N, Field T, Pietro P, Nearing G, et al. 1999. Prenatal depression effects on neonates. *Infant Behav. Dev.* 22:119–29

Luoma I, Tamminen T, Kaukonen P, Laippala P, Puura K, et al. 2001. Longitudinal study of maternal depressive symptoms and child well-being. *J. Am. Acad. Child Adolesc. Psychiatry* 40:1367–74

Lykken DT, Tellegen A. 1996. Happiness is a stochatic phenomenon. *Psychol. Sci.* 7:186–89

Lyons-Ruth K, Connell DB, Grunebaum HU, Botein S. 1990. Infants at social risk: maternal depression and family support as mediators of infant development and security of attachment. *Child Dev.* 61:85–98

Marchand JF, Hock E. 1998. The relation of problem behaviors in preschool children to depressive symptoms in mothers and fathers. *J. Genet. Psychol.* 159:353–66
Masten AS, Coastworth JD, Neeman J, Gest SD, Tellegen A, Garmezy N. 1995. The structure and coherence of competence from childhood through adolescence. *Child Dev.* 66:1635–59.

Presents the construct of competence in developmental psychopathology.

Masten AS, Hubbard JJ, Gest SD, Tellegen A, Garmezy N, Ramirez M. 1999. Competence in the context of adversity: pathways to resilience and maladaptation from childhood to late adolescence. *Dev. Psychopathol.* 11:143–69
Matthews CA, Reus VI. 2001. Assortative mating in the affective disorders: a systematic review and meta-analysis. *Compr. Psychiatry* 42:257–62
McCarty CA, McMahon RJ. 2003. Mediators of the relation between maternal depressive symptoms and child internalizing and disruptive behavior disorders. *J. Fam. Psychol.* 17(4):545–56
Moldin SO. 1999. Report of the NIMH's Genetic Workgroups: summary of research. *Biol. Psychiatry* 45:559–602
Monroe SM, Hadjiyannakis K. 2002. The social environment and depression: focusing on severe life stress. In *Handbook of Depression*, ed. IH Gotlib, CL Hammen, pp. 314–40. New York: Guilford
Monroe SM, Simons AD. 1991. Diathesis-stress theories in the context of life-stress research: implications for depressive disorders. *Psychol. Bull.* 110:406–25
Murray KT, Sines JO. 1996. Parsing the genetic and nongenetic variance in children's depressive behavior. *J. Affect. Disord.* 38:23–34
Murray LC, Kempton C, Woolgar M, Hooper R. 1993. Depressed mothers' speech to their infants and its relation to infant gender and cognitive development. *J. Child Psychol. Psychiatry* 34:1083–101
Murray L, Stanley C, Hooper R, King F, Fiori-Cowley A. 1996. The role of infant factors in postnatal depression and mother-infant interactions. *Dev. Med. Child Neurol.* 38:109–19
Nelson DR. 2001. Children of depressed mothers: the role of expressed emotion. *Dissert. Abstr. Int. Sect. B: Sci. Eng.* 62(2-B):1093
Newport DJ, Stowe AN, Nemeroff CB. 2002. Parental depression: animal models of an adverse life event. *Am. J. Psychiatry* 159:1265–83
Nolen-Hoeksema S, Wolfson A, Mumme D, Guskin K. 1995. Helplessness in children of depressed and nondepressed mothers. *Dev. Psychol.* 31:377–87
O'Connor TG, Heron J, Golding J, Beveridge M, Glover V. 2002. Maternal antenatal anxiety and children's behavioural/emotional problems at 4 years: report from the Avon Longitudinal Study of Parents and Children. *Br. J. Psychiatry* 180:502–8
O'Connor TG, Heron J, Golding J, Glover V. 2003. Maternal antenatal anxiety and behavioural/emotional problems in children: a test of a programming hypothesis. *J. Child Psychol. Psychiatry* 44:1025–36
O'Hara MW, Swain AM. 1996. Rates and risk of postpartum depression: a meta-analysis. *Int. Rev. Psychiatry* 8:37–54
O'Hara MW, Zekoski EM, Philipps LH, Wright EJ. 1990. A controlled, prospective study of postpartum mood disorders: comparison of childbearing and nonchildbearing women. *J. Abnorm. Psychol.* 99:3–15
Orvaschel H, Walsh-Allis G, Ye W. 1988. Psychopathology in children of parents with recurrent depression. *J. Abnorm. Child Psychol.* 16:17–28
Pauli-Pott U, Mertesacker B, Bade U, Bauer C, Beckmann D. 2000. Contexts of relations of infant negative emotionality to caregiver's reactivity/sensitivity. *Infant Behav. Dev.* 23:23–29

Plomin R, Emde RN, Braungart JM, Campos J, Corley RP, et al. 1993. Genetic change and continuity from fourteen to twenty months: the MacArthur Longitudinal Twin Study. *Child Dev.* 64:1354–76
Porges SW. 2001. The Polyvagal Theory: phylogenetic substrates of a social nervous system. *Int. J. Psychophysiol.* 42:123–46
Prinstein MJ, LaGreca AM. 1999. Links between mothers' and children's social competence and associations with maternal adjustment. *J. Clin. Child Psychol.* 28:197–210
Radke-Yarrow M, Belmont B, Nottelman E, Bottomly L. 1990. Young children's self-conceptions: origins in the natural discourse of depressed and normal mothers and their children. In *The Self in Transition: Infancy to Childhood*, ed. D Cicchetti, M Beeghly, pp. 345–61. Chicago: Univ. Chicago Press
Regier DA, Narrow WE, Rae DS, Manderscheid RW, Locke BZ, Goodwin FK. 1993. The de facto US mental and addictive disorders service system: Epidemiologic Catchment Area prospective 1-year prevalence rates of disorders and services. *Arch. Gen. Psychiatry* 50:85–94
Ressler KJ, Nemeroff CB. 2000. Role of serotonergic and noradrenergic systems in the pathophysiology of depression and anxiety disorders. *Depress. Anxiety* 12(Suppl. 1):2-19
Richters JE. 1992. Depressed mothers as informants about their children: a critical review of the evidence for distortion. *Psychol. Bull.* 112:485–99
Roderick HA. 2002. *Family Stability as a Mediator of the Relationship Between Maternal Attributes and Child Psychosocial Adjustment*. Doctoral dissert., State Univ. Albany, NY
Rosenbaum J, Biederman J, Hirshfeld-Becker DR, Kagan J, Snidman N, et al. 2000. A controlled study of behavioral inhibition in children of parents with panic disorder and depression. *Am. J. Psychiatry* 157(12):2002–10
Rubin KH, Mills RS. 1991. Conceptualizing developmental pathways to internalizing disorders in childhood. *Can. J. Behav. Sci.* 23:300–17
Rutter M, Dunn J, Plomin R, Simonoff E, Pickles A, et al. 1997. Integrating nature and nurture: implications of person-environment correlations and interactions for developmental psychopathology. *Dev. Psychopathol.* 9:335–64
Sameroff AJ. 1995. General systems theories and developmental psychopathology. In *Developmental Psychopathology, Vol. 1: Theory and Methods*, ed. D Cicchetti, DJ Cohen, pp. 659–95. New York: Wiley
Sameroff AJ, Seifer R, Zax M. 1982. Early development of children at risk for emotional disorder. *Monogr. Soc. Res. Child Dev.* 47:1–82
Sanchez MM, Ladd CO, Plotsky PM. 2001. Early adverse experience as a developmental risk factor for later psychopathology: evidence from rodent and primate models. *Dev. Psychopathol.* 13:419–49
Seifer R, Dickstein S, Sameroff AJ, Magee KD, Hayden LC. 2001. Infant mental health and variability of parental depression symptoms. *J. Am. Acad. Child Adolesc. Psychiatry* 40:1375–82
Shannon JD, Tamis-LeMonda CS, Margolin A. 2005. Father involvement in infancy: influences of past and current relationships. *Infancy* 8:21–41
Shea MT, Glass DR, Pilkonis PA, Watkins J, Docherty JP. 1987. Frequency and implications of personality disorders in a sample of depressed outpatients. *J. Personal. Disord.* 1:27–42
Sheeber L, Davis B, Hops H. 2002. Gender-specific vulnerability to depression in children of depressed mothers. In Goodman & Gotlib 2002, pp. 253–74
Silberg J, Pickles A, Rutter M, Hewitt J, Simonoff E, et al. 2001. The influence of genetic factors and life stress on depression among adolescent girls. *Arch. Gen. Psychiatry* 56:225–32

Silberg J, Rutter M. 2002. Nature-nurture interplay in the risks associated with parental depression. In Goodman & Gotlib 2002, pp. 13–36
Smith R, Cubis J, Brinsmead M, Lewin T, Singh B, et al. 1990. Mood changes, obstetrical experience and alterations in plasma cortisol, beta-endorphin and corticotrophin releasing hormone during pregnancy and the puerperium. *J. Psychosom. Res.* 34:53–69
Snyder J. 1991. Discipline as a mediator of the impact of maternal stress and mood on child conduct problems. *Dev. Psychopathol.* 3:263–76
Somerset W, Newport DJ, Ragan K, Stowe ZN. 2006. Depressive disorders in women: from menarche to beyond the menopause. In *Women and Depression: A Handbook for the Social, Behavioral, and Biomedical Sciences*, ed. CLM Keyes, SH Goodman, pp. 62–88. New York: Cambridge Univ. Press
Steinberg L. 1987. Recent research on the family at adolescence: the extent and nature of sex differences. *J. Youth Adolesc.* 16:191–97
Stephens RS, Hokanson JE, Welker R. 1987. Responses to depressed interpersonal behavior: mixed reactions in a helping role. *J. Personal. Soc. Psychol.* 52:1274–82
Sugawara M, Kitamura T, Toda MA, Shima S. 1999. Longitudinal relationship between maternal depression and infant temperament in a Japanese population. *J. Clin. Psychol.* 55:869–80
Sullivan PF, Neale MC, Kendler KS. 2000. Genetic epidemiology of major depression: review and meta-analysis. *Am. J. Psychiatry* 157:1552–62
Tamis-LeMonda CS, Cabrera N. 2002. *Handbook of Father Involvement: Multidisciplinary Perspectives*. Mahwah, NJ: Erlbaum
Tellegen A, Lykken DT, Bouchard TJ, Wilcox KJ, Segal NL, Rich S. 1988. Personality similarity in twins reared apart and together. *J. Personal. Soc. Psychol.* 54:1031–39
Teti DM, Gelfand DM. 1991. Behavioral competence among mothers of infants in the first year: the mediational role of maternal self-efficacy. *Child Dev.* 62:918–29
Thomas AM, Forehand R. 1991. The relationship between paternal depressive mood and early adolescent functioning. *J. Fam. Psychol.* 4:43–52
Tomarken AJ, Davidson RJ, Wheeler RE, Kinney L. 1992. Psychometric properties of resting anterior EEG asymmetry: temporal stability and internal consistency. *Psychophysiology* 29:576–92
Tronick EZ, Gianino AF Jr. 1986. The transmission of maternal disturbance to the infant. In *Maternal Depression and Infant Disturbance*, ed. EZ Tronick, T Field, pp. 5–11. San Francisco: Jossey-Bass
Tsuang MT, Faraone SV. 1990. *The Genetics of Mood Disorders*. Baltimore, MD: Johns Hopkins Univ. Press
van IJzendoorn MH, Goldberg S, Kroonenberg PM, Frenkel OJ. 1992. The relative effects of maternal and child problems on the quality of attachment: a meta-analysis of attachment in clinical samples. *Child Dev.* 63:840–58
Wadhwa PD, Glynn L, Hobel CJ, Garite TJ, Porto M, et al. 2002. Behavioral perinatology: biobehavioral processes in human fetal development. *Regul. Pept.* 108:149–57
Warner V, Weissman MM, Fendrich M, Wickramaratne P, Moreau D. 1992. The course of major depression in the offspring of depressed parents: incidence, recurrence, and recovery. *Arch. Gen. Psychiatry* 49:795–801
Webster-Stratton C, Hammond M. 1988. Maternal depression and its relationship to life stress, perceptions of child behavior problems, parenting behaviors, and child conduct problems. *J. Abnorm. Child Psychol.* 16:299–315
Weissman MM, Paykel ES. 1974. *The Depressed Woman: A Study of Social Relationships*. Chicago: Univ. Chicago Press

Weissman MM, Prusoff B, Gammon GD, Merikangagas KR, Leckman JF, Kidd KK. 1984. Psychopathology in the children (ages 6–18) of depressed and normal parents. *J. Am. Acad. Adolesc. Psychiatry* 23:78–84

Whiffen VE, Gotlib IH. 1989. Infants of postpartum depressed mothers: temperament and cognitive status. *J. Abnorm. Psychol.* 98:274–79

Widiger TA, Mullins-Sweatt W, Anderson KG. 2006. Personality and depression in women. In *Women and Depression: A Handbook for the Social, Behavioral, and Biomedical Sciences*, ed. CLM Keyes, SH Goodman, pp. 176–98. New York: Cambridge Univ. Press

Wust S, Federenko S, van Rossum EFC, Koper JW, Hellhammer DH. 2005. Habituation of cortisol responses to repeated psychosocial stress—further characterization and impact of genetic factors. *Psychoneuroendocrinology* 30:199–211

Young EA, Aggen SH, Prescott CA, Kendler KS. 2000. Similarity in saliva cortisol measures in monozygotic twins and the influence of part major depression? *Biol. Psychiatry* 48:70–74

Zahn-Waxler C, Cummings EM, Iannotti RJ, Radke-Yarrow M. 1984. Young children of depressed parents: a population at risk for affective problems. In *Childhood Depression. New Directions for Child Development*, ed. D Cicchetti, pp. 81–105. San Francisco:Jossey-Bass

Zahn-Waxler C, Iannotti RJ, Cummings EM, Denham S. 1990. Antecedents of problem behaviors in children of depressed mothers. *Dev. Psychopathol.* 2:271–91

Zahn-Waxler C, Radke-Yarrow M, Wagner E, Chapman M. 1992. Development of concern for others. *Dev. Psychol.* 28:126–36

Prevalence, Comorbidity, and Service Utilization for Mood Disorders in the United States at the Beginning of the Twenty-first Century

Ronald C. Kessler,[1] Kathleen R. Merikangas,[2] and Philip S. Wang[3]

[1]Department of Health Care Policy, Harvard Medical School, Boston, Massachusetts 02115, [2]Intramural Research Program, Section on Developmental Genetic Epidemiology, National Institute of Mental Health, Bethesda, Maryland 20892, [3]Division of Services and Intervention Research, National Institute of Mental Health, Bethesda, Maryland 20892; email: Kessler@hcp.med.harvard.edu

Annu. Rev. Clin. Psychol. 2007. 3:137–58

First published online as a Review in Advance on December 6, 2006

The *Annual Review of Clinical Psychology* is online at http://clinpsy.annualreviews.org

This article's doi:
10.1146/annurev.clinpsy.3.022806.091444

1548-5943/07/0427-0137$20.00

Key Words

bipolar disorder, depression, manic-depression, major depressive disorder

Abstract

The results of recent community epidemiological research are reviewed, documenting that major depressive disorder (MDD) is a highly prevalent, persistent, and often seriously impairing disorder, and that bipolar disorder (BPD) is less prevalent but more persistent and more impairing than MDD. The higher persistence and severity of BPD results in a substantial proportion of all seriously impairing depressive episodes being due to threshold or subthreshold BPD rather than to MDD. Although the percentage of people with mood disorders in treatment has increased substantially since the early 1990s, a majority of cases remain either untreated or undertreated. An especially serious concern is the misdiagnosis of depressive episodes due to BPD as due to MDD because the majority of depression treatment involves medication provided by primary care doctors in the absence of psychotherapy. The article closes with a discussion of future directions for research.

Contents

INTRODUCTION

Although community surveys of mental disorders have been carried out in the United States since the end of World War II (Comstock & Helsing 1976, Helgason 1964, Lin 1953), it was not until the early 1980s that the development of fully structured diagnostic interviews made it possible to estimate the prevalence of specific mental disorders in these surveys (Robins et al. 1981, Robins & Regier 1991). Although a number of large-scale surveys using fully structured diagnostic interviews have been carried out since that time, changes in the criteria for mood disorders in successive editions of the American Psychiatric Association's *Diagnostic and Statistical Manual of Mental Disorders* (DSM) have hampered efforts to replicate results. The most recent nationally representative population data on the prevalence and correlates of mood disorders come from the National Comorbidity Survey Replication (NCS-R) (Kessler & Merikangas 2004). The current report presents an overview of NCS-R results on the prevalence, comorbidity, and treatment of mood disorders.

Fully structured diagnostic interviews: interviews based on respondent answers to largely structured questions and do not require interview clinical judgments of responses

NCS-R: National Comorbidity Survey Replication

Comorbidity: the joint occurrence of two or more disorders in the same person either at a specified point in time or over a specified interval of time

Prevalence: the proportion of the population that has a given disorder at a point either in time or at some point in an interval of time

The term "prevalence" refers to the proportion of the population that has a disorder in some specified interval of time (Susser et al. 2006). The two most commonly studied prevalence estimates in the literature are lifetime prevalence (the proportion of the population that has a history of the disorder as of the point in time of the assessment) and 12-month prevalence (the proportion of the population that had the disorder at some time in the 12 months before the assessment). The ratio of 12-month to lifetime prevalence has been used as a rough indirect indicator of disorder persistence (Kessler et al. 2005), but this ratio is difficult to interpret because it does not take into consideration time since first onset. The latter is a joint function of age at onset and age at interview. Age at onset is typically assessed retrospectively in surveys of mood disorders in an effort to calculate the age-of-onset (AOO) distribution (Burke et al. 1991), a curve that shows the increase in the lifetime prevalence of the disorder with increasing age. The AOO curve is of interest both because it allows us to make projections of lifetime risk and because it helps us understand variation in onset risk across the life course.

Few surveys of mental illness tell us much about the persistence of mood disorders over the life course, although as noted in the previous paragraph, attempts have been made to make inferences about persistence by comparing 12-month and lifetime prevalence estimates. In addition to the difficulty with this approach being a joint function of age at onset and age at interview, it is also problematic because recall bias is likely in reports about AOO (Simon & VonKorff 1992). A number of recent surveys have consequently attempted to improve on this approach by asking explicit questions about course (Kessler & Ustun 2004). A small number of longitudinal studies also exist that have examined persistence directly either in community samples (Mattisson et al. 2005, Murphy et al. 2004) or in clinical samples (Judd et al. 2000). Recent findings from the NCS-R are reviewed that extend our findings in this area.

We also review evidence regarding the seriousness of mood disorders in the general population both in terms of clinical severity and in terms of severity of role impairment. A good deal is known about the severity of mood disorders among people who seek treatment (Judd et al. 2002, Paykel et al. 2006). Little is known, though, about whether untreated cases of mood disorder are similarly severe. This is an important issue in estimating the societal burden of mood disorders for purposes of policy planning. The main approach to making such estimates up to now has been to use information about clinical cases to make inferences about the severity of community cases (Morrow et al. 1998). This approach is almost certainly flawed. The NCS-R took a different approach to this problem by building into the community survey fully structured versions of the standard clinical severity measures used in treatment studies. As described in the body of the paper, surprising results about the severity of mood disorders in the community emerged from the analysis of these data.

Comorbidity is known to be a common feature of mood disorders (Goodwin & Jamison 1990, Kessler 1995) and has been studied in order to investigate the underlying processes leading to the joint occurrence of multiple disorders (Khan et al. 2005) as well as to investigate the effects of temporally primary disorders on secondary disorders (Hettema et al. 2003). However, only a limited amount of work has been done to investigate the comorbidity of mood disorders with a wide range of other conditions in large representative community surveys (Kessler et al. 1996). Recent results in this area are reviewed below.

Finally, we review the most recent NCS-R data on patterns of treatment of mood disorders in the United States. We know from tracking administrative databases that the number of people seeking treatment for mental disorders increased dramatically in the 1990s (Olfson et al. 2002b, 2004). Much less is known, though, about correlates of that trend or about adequacy of the increased treatment. Important trend results based on comparison of the baseline NCS and the subsequent NCS-R are reviewed here.

METHODS

The NCS-R is a psychiatric epidemiological survey of English-speaking adult household residents of the continental United States. Interviews were carried out with 9282 respondents between February 2001 and April 2003. Informed consent was obtained prior to data collection. The response rate was 70.9%. Respondents were given a $50 incentive for participation. In addition, a probability subsample of hard-to-recruit predesignated respondents was selected for a brief telephone nonrespondent survey, the results of which were used to weight the main sample for nonresponse bias. Nonrespondent survey participants were given a $100 incentive. A series of clinical reappraisal studies was carried out in various NCS-R subsamples in which clinical interviewers contacted respondents subsequent to their participation in the NCS-R and evaluated these respondents for the presence of various DSM-IV (Am. Psychiatr. Assoc. 1994) disorders blinded to the diagnostic assessments in the main survey. Separate consent was obtained and financial incentive provided for participation in clinical reappraisal interviews. The Human Subjects Committees of Harvard Medical School and the University of Michigan both approved these recruitment and consent procedures.

The NCS-R interview was administered in two parts. Part I included a core diagnostic assessment of all respondents. Part II included questions about correlates and additional disorders administered to all Part I respondents who met lifetime criteria for any core disorder plus a roughly one-in-three probability subsample of other respondents ($n = 5692$). An assessment of work performance, which we discuss below, was included in Part II in the subsample of 3378 respondents were either employed or self-employed 20 hours or more per week in the month before the interview. The records for Part II respondents were

AOO (age-of-onset) curve: a curve that shows the cumulative lifetime probability of occurrence of a given disorder as a function of age

CIDI: World Health Organization's Composite International Diagnostic Interview

MDD: major depressive disorder

BPD: bipolar disorder

MDE: major depressive episode (due to either BPD or MDD)

weighted to adjust for differential probability of selection into Part II and for differential nonresponse. A more detailed discussion of NCS-R sampling and weighting is presented elsewhere (Kessler et al. 2004a).

NCS-R diagnoses are based on Version 3.0 of the World Health Organization's Composite International Diagnostic Interview (CIDI) (Kessler & Ustun 2004), a fully structured lay-administered diagnostic interview. DSM-IV criteria were used to define all disorders. Both lifetime and 12-month prevalence were assessed. The core disorders assessed in addition to mood disorders include anxiety disorders (panic disorder, generalized anxiety disorder, phobias, obsessive-compulsive disorder, and posttraumatic stress disorder), impulse-control disorders (oppositional-defiant disorder, conduct disorder, attention-deficit/hyperactivity disorder, and intermittent explosive disorder), and substance disorders (alcohol and drug abuse with or without dependence). Organic exclusion rules were used in making all diagnoses. As detailed elsewhere (Kessler et al. 2004a, 2005), blinded clinical reinterviews using the nonpatient version of the Structured Clinical Interview for DSM-IV (SCID) (First et al. 2002) with a probability subsample of NCS-R respondents found generally good concordance between CIDI/DSM-IV diagnoses of anxiety and substance disorders and independent clinical assessments. Impulse-control disorder diagnoses were not validated, as the SCID clinical reappraisal interviews did not include an assessment of these disorders.

The DSM-IV mood disorders assessed in the NCS-R include major depressive disorder (MDD) and bipolar disorder (BPD). Diagnosis of BPD required separate assessments of major depressive episode (MDE), mania, and hypomania. Respondents were classified as having lifetime MDD if they ever had MDE and never had either mania or hypomania. They were classified as having lifetime bipolar I disorder (BP-I) if they ever had a manic episode. They were classified as having lifetime bipolar II disorder (BP-II) if they ever had a hypomanic episode (in the absence of a lifetime manic episode) and ever had MDE. Mixed episodes and rapid cycling subtypes of bipolar disorder were not assessed, leading to a likely overestimation of number of lifetime episodes of mania/hypomania and MDE due to double counting. Organic exclusions were made in making diagnoses.

We also investigated subthreshold BPD, which was defined as occurring in any of three situations: (*a*) if the respondent had a history of recurrent (two or more lifetime episodes) subthreshold hypomania (at least two DSM-IV Criterion B symptoms along with all other criteria for hypomania) in the presence of intercurrent MDE; (*b*) if the respondent had a history of recurrent hypomania in the absence of recurrent MDE with or without subthreshold MDE; or (*c*) if the respondent had a history of recurrent subthreshold hypomania in the absence of intercurrent MDE with or without subthreshold MDE. The reduction in number of required symptoms for a determination of subthreshold hypomania was confined to two Criterion B symptoms (from the DSM-IV requirement of three—four if the mood is only irritable) in order to retain the core features of hypomania in the subthreshold definition. Recurrent hypomania or subthreshold hypomania in the absence of intercurrent MDE was included in the definition because it is part of the DSM-IV definition of BPD not otherwise specified. For purposes of this review, we define the bipolar spectrum as a lifetime history of BP-I, BP-II, or subthreshold BPD as specified above. All diagnoses excluded cases with plausible organic causes.

As described in more detail elsewhere (Haro et al. 2007, Kessler et al. 2004a, 2005), a comparison of CIDI and SCID diagnoses in a clinical reappraisal sample showed good concordance at the individual level for lifetime prevalence of MDE ($\kappa = 0.59$), with 78% of CIDI lifetime cases confirmed by the SCID. At the aggregate level, the CIDI lifetime MDE prevalence estimate was significantly lower than the SCID estimate ($\chi^2{}_1 = 8.1$,

$p = 0.004$). CIDI-SCID concordance was also excellent for any BPD (i.e., BP-I, BP-II, or subthreshold BPD; $\kappa = 0.94$), with 88% of CIDI cases confirmed by the SCID and an insignificant difference in CIDI versus SCID prevalence estimates ($\chi^2{}_1 = 0.6$, $p = 0.45$) (Kessler et al. 2007). Concordance (κ) for individual BPD diagnoses was lower, but still acceptable: 0.88 for BP-I, 0.50 for BP-II, and 0.51 for subthreshold BPD, and 0.89 for either BP-II or subthreshold BPD, with CIDI versus SCID prevalence differences consistently insignificant ($\chi^2{}_1 = 0.1$–0.3, $p = 0.56$–0.75). The much lower κ values for BP-II and subthreshold BPD than for BP-I reflects the fact that the CIDI distinguishes respondents with these disorders with good accuracy in comparison to respondents without BPD, but has difficulty distinguishing between BP-II and subthreshold BPD.

AOO of MDE, mania, hypomania, and subthreshold hypomania was assessed with retrospective self-reports at the syndrome level. Respondents with lifetime MDD were defined as 12-month cases if they were in an episode at any time in the 12 months before interview. Respondents with lifetime BPD were defined as 12-month cases if they had an episode of MDE, mania, hypomania, or subthreshold hypomania at any time in the 12 months before interview. Persistence was assessed by asking respondents to estimate the number of years in their life when they had a major depressive episode and, separately, the number of years when they had a manic or hypomanic episode.

Clinical severity was assessed among 12-month cases using a fully structured self-report version of the Quick Inventory of Depressive Symptoms Self-Report (Q-IDS-SR) (Rush et al. 2003) for MDE and the Young Mania Rating Scale (YMRS) (Young et al. 1978) for mania/hypomania. The structured YMRS was based on a fully structured respondent report version developed for parent reports (Gracious et al. 2002). Standard QIDS and YMRS cut-points were used to define episodes as severe (including original QIDS and YMRS ratings of very severe, with ratings in the range 16+ on the QIDS and 25+ on the YMRS), moderate (11–15 on the QIDS; 15–24 on the YMRS), mild (6–10 on the QIDS; 9–14 on the YMRS), or not clinically significant (0–5 on the QIDS; 0–8 on the YMRS). Severity was assessed for the most severe month in the past year. No data were collected on the accuracy of these retrospective reports.

Severity of role impairment among 12-month cases was assessed with the Sheehan Disability Scales (SDS; Leon et al. 1997). As with the YMRS and QIDS, the SDS scales asked respondents to focus on the one month in the past year when their mania/hypomania or MDE symptoms were most severe. The SDS questions asked respondents to rate separately how much the condition interfered during that month with their home management, work, social life, and personal relationships using a 0–10 visual analogue scale of none (0), mild (1–3), moderate (4–6), severe (7–9), and very severe (10).

Questions were asked about lifetime and 12-month treatment that distinguished treatment by a psychiatrist, other mental health professional, general medical provider, human services professional (e.g., minister, social worker in a welfare agency), and complementary-alternative treatment provider (e.g., native healer, relaxation therapist). Questions about 12-month treatment also assessed medication. Antidepressants were classified as the only appropriate medications for MDD, while mood stabilizers, anticonvulsants, and antipsychotics were classified as appropriate medications for BPD. Antidepressants and other psychotropic medications in the absence of antimanic agents were classified as inappropriate for the treatment of BPD. In the case of BPD, 12-month treatment was assessed separately among respondents with 12-month BPD and lifetime but not 12-month BPD (i.e., maintenance treatment). Appropriateness of medication was examined separately for those in treatment with a psychiatrist and general medical provider.

LIFETIME AND 12-MONTH PREVALENCE

Prevalence estimates of DSM-IV MDD in the total NCS-R sample are 16.2% lifetime and 6.6% in the 12 months before the interview. These are equivalent to national population projections of approximately 33 million U.S. adults with lifetime MDD and 13 million with 12-month MDD (Kessler et al. 2003b). These estimates are intermediate between those in earlier large-scale U.S. surveys (Blazer et al. 1994, Weissman et al. 1991) and very similar to estimates in a separate national survey carried out at about the same time as the NCS-R (Hasin et al. 2005). The NCS-R estimates are likely to be more accurate than those in these other surveys in that the concordance between CIDI and SCID diagnoses in the NCS-R is higher than in these or other community epidemiological surveys carried out over the past two decades (Kessler et al. 1998b, Wittchen 1994). We attribute this improved accuracy to the fact that the CIDI was refined for use in the NCS-R to improve the clinical sensitivity of diagnostic assessment. The lower CIDI MDD prevalence estimates in the NCS-R than in the baseline NCS (Blazer et al. 1994) are consistent with the fact that these refinements reduced false positives. Contrary to the recent assertion of critics that prevalence estimates such as these, based on fully structured interviews in a community sample, substantially overestimate the prevalence of clinically significant disorders (Narrow et al. 2002), our comparison of CIDI with SCID prevalence estimates shows that, if anything, the CIDI underestimates the lifetime prevalence of clinician-diagnosed major depressive episodes, while only marginally overestimating 12-month prevalence.

Lifetime prevalence estimates of BPD are 1.0% for BP-I, 1.1% for BP-II, and 2.4% for subthreshold BPD (4.4% overall), equivalent to nearly 9 million U.S. adults. Twelve-month prevalence estimates are 0.6% for BP-I, 0.8% for BP-II, and 1.4% for subthreshold BPD (2.8% overall), equivalent to more than 5 million U.S. adults (Merikangas et al. 2007). The BP-I and BP-II prevalence estimates are consistent with estimates from earlier population-based studies (Angst 2004, Bauer & Pfennig 2005, Pini et al. 2005, Tohen & Angst 2002, Waraich et al. 2004, Weissman et al. 1996, Wittchen et al. 2003), with the exception of an implausibly high lifetime prevalence estimate of BP-I (3.3%) using a measure with no evidence of clinical validity in another recent national survey of the United States (Grant et al. 2005). It is noteworthy that the NCS-R clinical reappraisal study confirmed the much lower NCS-R BP-I prevalence estimate. The NCS-R definition of subthreshold BPD, in comparison, is more restrictive than the definitions proposed by clinical researchers (Akiskal & Benazzi 2005, Akiskal et al. 2000, Angst 1998, Angst et al. 2003) due to the fact that no information was included in the survey on brief episodes that could be assessed in more flexible semistructured clinical interviews. This means that the NCS-R subthreshold BPD prevalence estimates are likely to be lower bound estimates, although they are broadly consistent with the results of two large community epidemiological surveys in Europe (Regeer et al. 2004, Szadoczky et al. 1998).

AGE-OF-ONSET DISTRIBUTIONS

Retrospective AOO reports were obtained using a special question series designed to stimulate active memory search and to bound recall inaccuracy (Simon & VonKorff 1995). Experimental research has shown that this question sequence yields responses with a much more plausible AOO distribution than do standard AOO questions (Knauper et al. 1999). The AOO distribution was then generated using the two-part actuarial method (SAS Institute 2001) for each DSM-IV disorder assessed in the survey (Kessler et al. 2005). Median AOO (i.e., the fiftieth percentile on the AOO distribution) of MDD is 32, with an interquartile range (IQR; i.e., the years between the twenty-fifth and seventy-fifth percentiles of the AOO distribution) of 25 years (between ages 19 and 44). Median AOO of BPD is somewhat earlier for BP-I (18) and BP-II (20) than subthreshold BPD (22), with an IQR of roughly two decades for all three types of BPD (from the late teens through the late thirties). It is noteworthy that median AOO is much later for mood disorders than for anxiety disorders (age 11) or impulse-control disorders (age 11). AOO is also less concentrated in a narrow age range for mood disorders than for impulse-control disorders or most anxiety disorders. For example, the IQR is only 8 years for any impulse-control disorder (ages 7–15), 7 years for specific phobia (ages 5–12), and 7 years for social phobia (ages 8–15).

These AOO distribution estimates are consistent with those reported in previous epidemiological surveys (Christie et al. 1988, World Health Organ. Int. Consort. Psychiatr. Epidemiol. 2000) both for mood disorders themselves and in findings that anxiety disorders, impulse-control disorders, and substance disorders have earlier AOOs than mood disorders. However, we are aware of no previous attempt to examine the temporal concentration of AOO or to highlight the concentration of onset ages for most disorders in a very narrow time span. It is also striking, in light of evidence reported below on the strong comorbidities of mood disorders with other DSM-IV disorders, that the upper bounds of the AOO IQRs for disorders with narrow ranges are all quite early: age 15 for impulse-control disorders and for anxiety disorders with narrow IQRs and age 27 for substance disorders. These are opposite the patterns found for almost all chronic physical disorders, where conditional risk increases with age and the upper bound of the IQR is in late middle age or old age (Murray & Lopez 1996).

The finding that comorbid disorders typically have an earlier age of onset than mood disorders is also consistent with prospective family studies of at-risk children (Loeber et al. 1988, Warner et al. 1999). Although this finding implies that temporally primary disorders are risk factors for the subsequent first onset of mood disorders, it is less clear whether this is because these earlier disorders are causal risk factors or, alternatively, because they are markers of other more fundamental causes. If they were causal risk factors, we would expect that their successful treatment before the onset of secondary mood disorders would reduce the risk of subsequent mood disorders occurring. This would not be the case if the earlier disorders were risk markers. We are aware of no experimental studies that have evaluated the effect of early treatment of primary anxiety or impulse control disorders (ICDs) on the prevention of subsequent mood disorders. However, two intriguing findings in the baseline NCS are consistent with the prediction that such interventions might be successful. The first is that active anxiety disorders are more powerful predictors of the subsequent onset of MDD than are remitted anxiety disorders (Kessler et al. 1998a). The second is that the risk of subsequent major depression among survey respondents with prior panic disorder is lower for those who receive treatment for their panic than for those who do not (Goodwin & Olfson 2001). It is noteworthy that the second of these findings runs counter to the obvious noncausal interpretation of the first finding: that persistent panic is a severity marker rather than a causal risk factor for later MDD. If this noncausal interpretation were true, we would expect to find that survey respondents who received treatment for their panic would have a higher risk of subsequent MDD than those whose panic was untreated due to the selection bias for the most severe cases to have the highest probability of seeking treatment. The fact that the opposite pattern exists suggests that the causal interpretation has some plausibility and that early treatment of primary anxiety might be a neglected opportunity for the prevention of MDD and possibly also of BPD.

PERSISTENCE

Persistence, indirectly indicated by the ratio of 12-month prevalence to lifetime prevalence, is higher for BP-I (63.3%) and BP-II (73.2%) than for subthreshold BPD (59.5%), and lowest for MDD (40.7%). The same pattern is found for retrospectively reported number of years in episode (means of 10.3 BP-I, 11.6 BP-II, 6.8 subthreshold BPD, and 5.8 for MDD) and number of lifetime episodes (77.6 BP-I, 63.6 BP-II, 31.8 subthreshold BPD, and 8.5 for MDD). More detailed analysis (results available on request from first author) showed that low persistence of subthreshold BPD is limited to cases without a history of MDE.

The finding that the ratio of 12-month CIDI MDD prevalence to lifetime prevalence is approximately 40% is broadly consistent with the finding of ratios between one-third and one-half in most previous epidemiological surveys carried out throughout the world (Andrade et al. 2003, Weissman et al. 1996). These ratios, in turn, are indirectly consistent with both retrospective reports in cross-sectional community surveys (Kessler et al. 1996, Weissman et al. 1991) and prospective assessments in a small number of community (Angst & Merikangas 1997, Murphy et al. 1984) and clinical (Keller 1985) samples, all of which suggest that MDD is typically an episodically chronic-recurrent disorder. The much higher estimates of persistence of BPD are consistent with prospective studies in clinical samples and with family studies (Fisfalen et al. 2005, Kupka et al. 2005). These results, consistent with the recommendation of the recent Surgeon General's Report on Mental Health (U.S. Department of Health and Human Services 1999), suggest that MDD and BPD should be classified as chronic diseases, along with such physical diseases as cancer, diabetes, and heart disease.

COMORBIDITY

Nearly three-fourths of respondents with lifetime MDD also met criteria for at least one of the other DSM-IV/CIDI disorders assessed in the NCS-R (Kessler et al. 2003b). This includes 59.0% with at least one lifetime comorbid anxiety disorder, 31.9% with at least one lifetime comorbid ICD, and 24.0% with at least one lifetime comorbid substance use disorder. Lifetime comorbidity is even higher among respondents with 12-month MDD, implying that comorbid MDD is more persistent (i.e., more likely to be either chronic or recurrent) than pure MDD. Approximately two-thirds (65.2%) of respondents with 12-month MDD met criteria for at least one other 12-month disorder, with comorbid anxiety disorders (57.5%) again more common than either comorbid substance use disorders (8.5%) or comorbid ICDs (20.8%). Comparison of retrospective age of onset reports shows that MDD is temporally primary (i.e., reported to have started at an earlier age) in relation to all other comorbid disorders in only 12.4% of lifetime cases and 12.2% of 12-month cases, although temporal priority is much more common in cases of comorbidity with substance use disorders (41.3%–49.2%) than with either anxiety disorders (13.7%–14.6%) or ICDs (17.9%–20.9%).

The vast majority of NCS-R respondents with a history of either threshold (i.e., BP-I or BP-II; 97.7%–95.8%) or subthreshold (88.4%) BPD also met criteria for another lifetime DSM-IV/CIDI disorder (Merikangas et al. 2007). The extent of comorbidity is consistently somewhat higher for threshold than for subthreshold BPD. Included here are 63.1%–86.7% of respondents with lifetime BPD who have a history of at least one lifetime comorbid anxiety disorder, 56.1%–71.2% with at least one lifetime comorbid ICD, and 35.5%–60.3% with at least one lifetime comorbid substance use disorder. As with MDD, lifetime comorbidity is even higher among respondents with 12-month BPD, implying that comorbid BPD is more persistent (i.e., more likely to be either chronic or recurrent) than pure MDD. Comparison of retrospective age of onset reports shows that BPD is temporally secondary (i.e., reported to have started at a later age) in relation to all other comorbid disorders in the vast majority of cases.

A comparison of odds ratios (ORs) for the associations of MDD and BPD across the range of comorbid conditions considered in the NCS-R analysis finds little evidence of strong variation. In other words, the strength of association of mood disorders with other DSM-IV disorders is relatively constant across the range of anxiety, impulse-control, and substance use disorders. The main exceptions are higher ORs of MDD with generalized anxiety disorder and panic disorder than with other comorbid conditions and a stronger OR of BPD with obsessive-compulsive disorder than with other comorbid conditions. By far the higher ORs involving both MDD and BPD are those with a number of comorbid disorders rather than with a type of the latter disorders. Mood disorders are especially highly associated with the existence of three or more other hierarchy-free DSM-IV/CIDI disorders. This "multimorbidity" (Angst et al. 2000) (i.e., comorbidity with multiple conditions) is suggestive of disturbances in multiple regulatory systems and should be a topic for future research.

The finding that MDD is highly comorbid with anxiety and substance disorders is consistent with previous epidemiological research (Kessler 1997, Merikangas et al. 1996). Although there is much less epidemiological evidence about comorbidity between MDD and ICD in community samples, significant MDD-ICD comorbidity has been documented in clinical studies (Lejoyeux et al. 2002, Zimmerman et al. 2002). It is noteworthy that even though comorbid ICD is often thought to be more strongly related to BPD than to MDD (McElroy et al. 1996), the NCS-R found strong comorbidity between ICD and MDD. This could reflect either factors broader than those responsible for BPD or the existence of what has recently been called a "soft bipolar spectrum" in which comorbid ICD among patients with MDD represents a marker of bipolar susceptibility. The notion of a soft bipolar spectrum underlying MDD-ICD comorbidity implies that comorbid ICD is a risk marker for the subsequent onset of mania or hypomania and is a possibility that needs to be evaluated in future prospective epidemiological studies.

The finding that BPD has extremely high comorbidity with other DSM-IV disorders is consistent with prior clinical (Brown 2005, Strakowski & DelBello 2000) and population-based (Grant et al. 2005, Keller 2006, Mitchell et al. 2004, Pini et al. 2005, Regier et al. 1990) studies, although comorbidity with substance use disorders was more prominently featured in previous studies. The higher comorbidity found in the NCS-R with anxiety and impulse-control disorders was less consistently studied in previous research (Freeman et al. 2002, MacKinnon et al. 2002). Despite the higher disorder-specific comorbidity noted above of threshold BPD than of subthreshold BPD, it is interesting to note that comorbidity with at least one other disorder was found to be nearly as common among subthreshold (88.4%) as threshold (95.8%–97.7%) cases.

CLINICAL SEVERITY

Although a great deal of research has examined the clinical severity of patients in treatment, little is known about the clinical severity of community cases. This is an issue of considerable interest in light of the high estimated prevalence of mood disorders in community surveys and the suspicion of some critics that these prevalence estimates are exaggerated. Thirty-eight percent of NCS-R respondents with 12-month MDD were classified as being seriously–severely depressed based on QIDS assessments, while the remaining 62.0% of cases were classified as mildly–moderately depressed (Kessler et al. 2003b). Even higher proportions of cases with 12-month MDE related to BPD were rated serious–severe. This was true for not only MDE associated with BP-I (where 70.5% of cases were rated serious–severe) and BP-II (84.0%), but also subthreshold BPD (46.4%).

YMRS ratings of the 12-month episode severity of mania/hypomania placed the majority of cases in the severe range for BP-I (70.2%) and BP-II (55.4%) and a minority for subthreshold BPD (31.5%), with almost all of the remainder for threshold BPD and a majority of those for subthreshold BPD in the mild–moderate range (Merikangas et al. 2007).

The finding that more than one-third of 12-month community cases of MDD were rated serious–severe on a standard clinical rating scale is indirectly consistent with a growing body of evidence that major depression is one of the most seriously impairing of all chronic conditions (Wang et al. 2003b). The fact that even higher proportions of MDE associated with BPD were rated serious–severe is consistent with evidence that the depressive episodes of people with BPD are, on average, more severe than those of people with MDD. The finding that the proportions of depressive episodes rated severe were higher for BP-II than BP-I is also consistent with previous research (Judd & Akiskal 2003b). Perhaps the more striking result regarding clinical severity, though, is that a higher proportion of depressive episodes associated with subthreshold BPD than MDD were rated serious–severe. This finding, coupled with the finding that nearly one-third of subthreshold BPD hypomanic episodes were classified severe and with the finding that most of the remainder of subthreshold cases were classified mild–moderately severe, strongly argues for the clinical significance of subthreshold BPD.

SEVERITY OF ROLE IMPAIRMENT

The NCS-R analyses documented substantial role impairments associated with both MDD (Kessler et al. 2003b) and BPD (Merikangas et al. 2007) in the areas of work, household responsibilities, social life, and personal relations based on assessments with the Sheehan disability scales. As with clinical severity, the results show that subthreshold BPD is associated with as much, if not more, role impairment than MDD, arguing for the significance of subthreshold BPD.

As reviewed in more detail elsewhere (Kessler et al. 2006b), most research on mood disorders and role impairment focuses on days out of role among people in the workforce. This focus is a natural one from a healthcare policy perspective, as employer-sponsored plans account for the vast majority of all health insurance in the United States and the authors of cost-of-illness studies generally aim to make an argument to these employer-purchasers that human capital investments in expanded treatment of mood disorders would be cost-effective from the employer perspective. However, these studies have largely focused on MDE to the exclusion of mania or hypomania and have failed to distinguish episodes of MDE due to MDD and BPD (Greenberg et al. 1993, 1996, 2003; Rice & Miller 1993). Although several recent cost-of-illness studies (Begley et al. 2001, Das Gupta & Guest 2002, Wyatt & Henter 1995) and reviews (Dean et al. 2004, Kleinman et al. 2003) have focused on the costs of BPD, none has presented comparative information on the workplace costs of MDD and BPD.

An NCS-R analysis of the workplace costs of mood disorders attempted to address this gap in previous research by examining the prevalence and workplace costs of mood disorders in the U.S. civilian labor force (Kessler et al. 2006b). Work performance was assessed with the World Health Organization Health and Work Performance Questionnaire (HPQ) (Kessler et al. 2003a, 2004b), a self-report instrument that combines information about absenteeism (missed days of work) and presenteeism (low performance while at work transformed to lost workday equivalents) into a summary measure of overall lost workdays in the year of interview. Information about salary was used to transform the measures of lost work performance from a time metric to a salary metric for purposes of estimating human capital loss associated with mood disorders.

The analysis showed that MDD and BPD are both associated with significant lost work performance, with annualized estimates of 27.2 excess lost workdays per worker with MDD and 65.5 excess lost workdays per worker with BPD. Disaggregation showed that absenteeism, although important to this total, was less important than presenteeism. This means that workers with mood disorders both miss more days of work than workers in the same jobs having the same sociodemographic profiles but without a mood disorder and, even more importantly, that workers with mood disorders are substantially less productive on days when they are at work than are workers without mood disorders. Projections of individual-level associations to the total U.S. civilian labor force based on information about disorder prevalence and salaries of workers with mood disorders yield estimates of 225.0 million workdays and $36.6 billion salary-equivalent lost productivity per year associated with MDD and 96.2 million lost workdays and $14.1 billion salary-equivalent lost productivity per year associated with BPD.

The finding that both BPD and MDD are both associated with substantial losses in work performance is broadly consistent with other surveys of workplace costs (Calabrese et al. 2003, Dean et al. 2004, Greenberg et al. 2003, Kleinman et al. 2003, Wang et al. 2003b). The estimated annual population-level workplace cost of MDD is in the range of the two other recent studies that estimated the workplace costs of MDE—$31.0 billion (Stewart et al. 2003) and $51.5 billion (Greenberg et al. 2003). The larger of these two is probably upwardly biased because it is based on an analysis of days out of role (i.e., including weekends) rather than days out of work. No previous estimates of the population-level workplace cost of BPD are available to compare to the NCS-R estimate.

Roughly three-fourths of employed NCS-R respondents with 12-month BPD had depressive episodes in the 12 months before interview (63.1% who also had manic-hypomanic episodes and 11.1% who had only depressive episodes). Persistence (days in depressive episodes in the 365 days before interview) was found consistently to be higher in BPD (mean: 134.0–164.0 across the bipolar spectrum; median: 90–150) than MDD (mean: 98.1; median: 60; $z = 2.7$, $p = 0.010$). The individual-level elevation of lost work performance in BPD was consistently higher among respondents with 12-month MDE than only manic-hypomanic episodes. Furthermore, BPD with MDE was consistently associated with significantly more lost work performance than MDD.

The finding that BPD is associated with substantially more lost work performance than MDD at the individual level is not unexpected in light of the greater severity of BPD than MDD, although aggregate impairment is greater for MDD than BPD because of the higher prevalence of the former than latter disorder. Perhaps more surprising is the finding that the higher individual-level impairment of BPD than MDD is due largely to MDE being more impairing in the context of BPD than MDD rather than to mania-hypomania being more impairing than MDE. The finding that mania-hypomania in the absence of MDE is associated with significantly less work impairment than BPD with MDE is consistent with the observation in a prospective patient study that functional impairment is associated with variation in depressive symptoms but not manic symptoms (Bauer et al. 2001).

An important practical problem related to the finding that MDE in BPD is the syndrome associated with most impairment is that MDE due to BPD is sometimes incorrectly treated as if it is due to MDD (Hirschfeld 2004, Judd & Akiskal 2003a). This problem is exacerbated by the fact that people with BPD report considerably more distress due to their depressive than to their manic symptoms (Calabrese et al. 2003). Antidepressant medications, of course, can trigger the onset of mania among patients with MDE due to BPD.

This issue, though, involves the consideration of treatment, a topic that we turn to next.

TREATMENT

Slightly more than half (56.7%) of NCS-R respondents with 12-month MDD received some type of treatment in the 12 months before their interview. The specialty sector was involved in the highest proportion of these cases (54.9%) and the human services sector in the lowest proportion (16.4%) (Kessler et al. 2003b). Treatment met conventional criteria for adequacy based on minimal concordance with published treatment guidelines, however, in only 41.7% of cases. This means that no more than 20.9% of all people with 12-month MDD (i.e., 36.9% of the 56.7% in treatment) received adequate treatment. Although a higher proportion of serious–severe (72.4%) than mild–moderate (47.1%) 12-month NCS-R cases received treatment, severity was not significantly related either to the sector in which treatment was received or to the adequacy of treatment. Sector of treatment, however, was found to be related to treatment adequacy, with a significantly higher 62.3% of patients treated in the specialty mental health sector versus 42.4% of patients treated in the general medical sector receiving adequate treatment.

Treatment of 12-month BPD was higher than treatment of MDD: 67.3% BP-I, 65.8% BP-II, and 36.7% subthreshold BPD. Nonpsychiatrist mental health professionals were the most common providers (35.4% BP-I, 33.8% BP-II, and 20.6% subthreshold BPD). Multisector treatment was the norm, with a 1.7-sector mean. As with MDD, a significantly higher proportion of cases in specialty (45.0%) than general medical (9.0%) treatment received appropriate medication. A significantly higher proportion of cases in general medical (73.1%) than specialty (43.4%) treatment received inappropriate medication. A significant gradient was found in the proportion of all 12-month cases (ignoring whether they received treatment) that received appropriate medication: 25.0% BP-I, 15.4% BP-II, and 8.1% subthreshold BPD. The proportion receiving inappropriate medication was also higher for BP-I (38.7%) and BP-II (38.9%) than for subthreshold BPD (23.8%). The opposite pattern was found for the proportion receiving no medication (36.3% BP-I, 45.7% BP-II, and 68.1% subthreshold BPD). A significant gradient also was found in the proportion of lifetime cases without a 12-month episode (ignoring whether they received 12-month treatment) that received appropriate maintenance medication: 17.9% BP-I, 15.6% BP-II, and 3.2% subthreshold BPD. The proportion of all lifetime cases that received inappropriate medication was also higher for BP-I (35.3%) than BP-II (24.5%) or subthreshold BPD (21.5%). The opposite pattern was found for the proportion receiving no medication (46.8% BP-I, 59.9% BP-II, and 75.3% subthreshold BPD).

The results document serious problems in the treatment of people with mood disorders in the United States. Increasing use of some modalities, most notably pharmacotherapies and physician-administered psychotherapies (Kessler et al. 2003b; Olfson et al. 2002a,b; Wang et al. 2000), has generated hope that mental disorders are now being treated much more effectively than in the past. The NCS-R results suggest that such optimism is premature. Mental health service use for mood disorders remains disturbingly low: a substantial proportion of cases did not receive any care in the prior year, and many of those who successfully accessed health care failed to get adequate treatment according to established treatment guidelines. These results are broadly consistent with those of other studies of treatment quality for mood disorders (Blanco et al. 2002; Wang et al. 2000, 2002; Young et al. 2001).

The frequent use of treatments with uncertain benefit is striking. This is especially worrisome for complementary-alternative treatments (e.g., energy healers, massage therapists), which account for a substantial minority of all visits for the treatment of mood disorders despite a paucity of data supporting their efficacy (Eisenberg et al. 1993, 1998; Hypericum Depression Trial Study Group 2002; Kessler et al. 2001b,c; Wang et al. 2003a; Weaver 1995). A challenge for the providers of conventional services is to determine why complementary-alternative treatment has such great appeal and whether legitimate aspects related to this appeal (e.g., a greater orientation to patient-centered care) can be adopted by conventional mental health care providers to increase the attractiveness of evidence-based treatments.

On the positive side, the proportion of NCS-R respondents with mood disorders who reported 12-month mental health service use is considerably higher than found a decade earlier in the baseline NCS (Kessler et al. 1999) and a decade before that in the ECA study (Regier et al. 1993). By far the greatest part of this expansion, though, occurred in the general medical sector. General medical doctors act as gatekeepers responsible for initiating mental health treatments themselves and for deciding who to triage for specialty care (Forrest 2003, Trude & Stoddard 2003). Increasing awareness of mental disorders on the part of primary care physicians, coupled with an increase in consumer demand stimulated by direct-to-consumer advertising, have probably also played roles in this growth (Kessler & Wang 1999, Kroenke 2003, Simon et al. 1999, Spitzer et al. 1999). However, the fact that only a small minority of patients treated in the general medical sector receives minimally adequate care makes these trends concerning. Reasons for the low rate of treatment adequacy are unclear, but presumably involve both provider (e.g., competing demands, inadequate reimbursements for treating mental disorders, less training and experience in treating mental disorders) and patient factors (e.g., worse compliance with treatments than in mental health specialty sectors) (Klinkman 1997, Pincus et al. 2003, Williams 1998, Williams et al. 1999).

OVERVIEW

This brief review of NCS-R results shows clearly that mood disorders are highly prevalent, highly persistent, and highly impairing. We have seen that although mood disorders are currently treated much more commonly than in the past, they are still substantially undertreated. We also presented evidence regarding the relatively high prevalence and significance of subthreshold bipolar disorders, a series of syndromes of growing interest among specialists in research on the bipolar spectrum (Angst et al. 2003, Judd & Akiskal 2003b). Parallel information was not reviewed on the MDD spectrum, including recurrent brief depression (Pezawas et al. 2005) and minor depression (Judd et al. 2003), as subthreshold MDD has not yet been examined in the NCS-R. A great many other topics in the descriptive epidemiology of mood disorders were not covered in this review that need to be noted here in light of the fact that they have been reviewed elsewhere. Among the most important of these are information on child and adolescent mood disorders (Kessler et al. 2001a), risk and protective factors for the onset and persistence of mood disorders (Goodwin & Jamison 1990, Gotlib & Hammen 2002), sociodemographic correlates of mood disorders (Kessler et al. 2003b, Merikangas et al. 2007), and barriers to obtaining treatment (Wang et al. 2005).

WMH: World Mental Health Survey Initiative of the World Health Organization

FUTURE DIRECTIONS

We also need to know much more than we currently do about time-space variation in the prevalence and correlates of mood disorders. The World Health Organization's World Mental Health (WMH) Survey Initiative is an exciting new undertaking that is addressing this issue by carrying out coordinated nationally representative surveys like the NCS-R in more than 30 countries throughout the world (**http://www.hcp.med.harvard.edu/wmh**). A number of WMH lines of work deal with mood disorders. Perhaps the most fascinating of these is the attempt to study time-space variation in the association between gender and major depression. The goal here is to determine whether the female preponderance consistently found in Western countries exists throughout the world and whether the magnitude of this association changes over time in specific countries as the roles of women change with the modernization of the country.

We also need to increase our understanding of mood disorders epidemiology using genetically informative epidemiological study designs. Important work along these lines has been carried out in regional studies (Kendler & Prescott 2006), but this needs to be expanded both geographically and conceptually. Epidemiological designs that collect DNA also hold great promise (Caspi et al. 2003) and will almost certainly be used more often in the future. Indeed, a number of the WMH surveys mentioned in the previous paragraph are collecting DNA from all respondents in order to create a repository for future genetic epidemiological studies.

A great deal of interest currently exists in using epidemiological research to help refine the diagnostic criteria for mood disorders in the DSM and ICD diagnostic systems (Zimmerman et al. 2006). This interest is motivated by the fact that both these diagnostic systems are scheduled for major updates at the end of this decade (Helzer & Hudziak 2002, Schachter et al. 2002). Epidemiological data such as those in the NCS-R can be of great value in evaluating the implications of proposed changes in diagnostic criteria. However, in order to maximize usefulness in this way, the epidemiological surveys need to include questions and skip pattern rules that facilitate the analysis of proposed diagnostic changes. This was done in the NCS-R as well as in the WMH surveys. We consequently anticipate that considerable research on diagnostic criteria will emerge from these surveys over the next decade.

Finally, as we learn more and more about risk factors for and social consequences of mood disorders, we will need to increase the extent to which epidemiological studies are blended with quasi-experimental and experimental policy interventions. Kling and his associates (2007), for example, evaluated the effects of neighborhood disorganization on the mental health of residents by carrying out an epidemiological survey of low-income single mothers who applied for housing vouchers allocated by the Department of Housing and Urban Development on the basis of a lottery. Half of the applicants were randomly selected to receive the vouchers, creating a unique opportunity to study neighborhood effects on the mental health of high-risk children. Experimental manipulations of this sort embedded in larger epidemiological surveys have enormous potential to expand our understanding of the correlates of mood disorders as well as of other mental disorders. Experiments of nature could be used in this same way. For example, Costello and her associates (2003) used the opening of a casino on an American Indian reservation midway between the two waves of an epidemiological survey to evaluate the impact of increased parental income on child mental health. A great many experiments of nature exist that could be used in a similar way to expand our understanding of the environmental determinants of mood disorders.

SUMMARY POINTS

1. Mood disorders are highly prevalent.
2. Mood disorders are highly persistent.
3. Mood disorders are highly impairing.

4. Subthreshold bipolar disorders are considerably more common and impairing than is generally recognized.
5. Although mood disorders are currently treated much more commonly in the United States than in the past, they are still substantially undertreated both in the sense that many people with mood disorders are not receiving treatment and also in the sense that many of the people with mood disorders in treatment receive suboptimal treatment.

ACKNOWLEDGMENTS

This article represents a review of previously published results from the National Comorbidity Survey Replication (NCS-R). Portions of this paper appeared previously in Kessler et al. (2003) and are reproduced here with the permission of the publisher. Sources include: for the epidemiology of major depressive disorder, Kessler et al. (2005); for the lifetime prevalence and age-of-onset distributions of DSM-IV disorders, Kessler et al. (2005); for the prevalence, severity, and comorbidity of twelve-month DSM-IV disorders, Wang et al. (2005) and Kessler et al. (2006a). The NCS-R is supported by the National Institute of Mental Health (U01-MH60220) with supplemental support from the National Institute of Drug Abuse, the Substance Abuse and Mental Health Services Administration, the Robert Wood Johnson Foundation (grant #044780), and the John W. Alden Trust. The views and opinions expressed in this report are those of the authors and should not be construed to represent the views of any of the sponsoring organizations, agencies, or the U.S. government. A complete list of NCS publications and the full text of all NCS-R instruments can be found at **http://www.hcp.med.harvard.edu/ncs.** The NCS-R is carried out in conjunction with the World Health Organization World Mental Health (WMH) Survey Initiative, which is supported by the John D. and Catherine T. MacArthur Foundation, the Pfizer Foundation, the U.S. Public Health Service (1R13MH066849, R01-MH069864, and R01 DA016558), Eli Lilly and Company, GlaxoSmithKline, Ortho-McNeil Pharmaceutical, Inc., and the Pan American Health Organization. A complete list of WMH publications and instruments can be found at **http://www.hcp.med.harvard.edu/wmhcidi.**

LITERATURE CITED

Akiskal HS, Benazzi F. 2005. Optimizing the detection of bipolar II disorder in outpatient private practice: toward a systematization of clinical diagnostic wisdom. *J. Clin. Psychiatry* 66:914–21

Akiskal HS, Bourgeois ML, Angst J, Post R, Moller H, Hirschfeld R. 2000. Re-evaluating the prevalence of and diagnostic composition within the broad clinical spectrum of bipolar disorders. *J. Affect. Disord.* 59(Suppl. 1):S5–30

American Psychiatric Association. 1994. *Diagnostic and Statistical Manual of Mental Disorders, Fourth Edition*. Washington, DC: Am. Psychiatr. Assoc.

Andrade L, Caraveo-Anduaga JJ, Berglund P, Bijl RV, Dragomericka E, et al. 2003. The epidemiology of major depressive episodes: results from the International Consortium of Psychiatric Epidemiology (ICPE) surveys. *Int. J. Methods Psychiatr. Res.* 12:3–21

Angst J. 1998. The emerging epidemiology of hypomania and bipolar II disorder. *J. Affect. Disord.* 50:143–51

Angst J. 2004. Bipolar disorder—a seriously underestimated health burden. *Eur. Arch. Psychiatry Clin. Neurosci.* 254:59–60

Angst J, Gamma A, Benazzi F, Ajdacic V, Eich D, Rossler W. 2003. Toward a redefinition of subthreshold bipolarity: epidemiology and proposed criteria for bipolar-II, minor bipolar disorders and hypomania. *J. Affect. Disord.* 73:133–46

Angst J, Merikangas K. 1997. The depressive spectrum: diagnostic classification and course. *J. Affect. Disord.* 45:31–39; discussion 39–40

Angst J, Sellaro R, Merikangas KR. 2000. Depressive spectrum diagnoses. *Comp. Psychiatry* 41:39–47

Bauer M, Pfennig A. 2005. Epidemiology of bipolar disorders. *Epilepsia* 46(Suppl. 4):8–13

Bauer MS, Kirk GF, Gavin C, Williford WO. 2001. Determinants of functional outcome and healthcare costs in bipolar disorder: a high-intensity follow-up study. *J. Affect. Disord.* 65:231–41

Begley CE, Annegers JF, Swann AC, Lewis C, Coan S, et al. 2001. The lifetime cost of bipolar disorder in the US: an estimate for new cases in 1998. *Pharmacoeconomics* 19:483–95

Blanco C, Laje G, Olfson M, Marcus SC, Pincus HA. 2002. Trends in the treatment of bipolar disorder by outpatient psychiatrists. *Am. J. Psychiatry* 159:1005–10

Blazer DG, Kessler RC, McGonagle K, Swartz M. 1994. The prevalence and distribution of major depression in a national community sample: the National Comorbidity Survey. *Am. J. Psychiatry* 151:979–86

Brown ES. 2005. Bipolar disorder and substance abuse. *Psychiatr. Clin. North Am.* 28:415–25

Burke KC, Burke JDJ, Rae DS, Regier DA. 1991. Comparing age at onset of major depression and other psychiatric disorders by birth cohorts in five U.S. community populations. *Arch. Gen. Psychiatry* 48:789–95

Calabrese JR, Hirschfeld RM, Reed M, Davies MA, Frye MA, et al. 2003. Impact of bipolar disorder on a U.S. community sample. *J. Clin. Psychiatry* 64:425–32

Caspi A, Sugden K, Moffitt TE, Taylor A, Craig IW, et al. 2003. Influence of life stress on depression: moderation by a polymorphism in the 5-HTT gene. *Science* 301:386–89

Christie KA, Burke JDJ, Regier DA, Rae DS, Boyd JH, Locke BZ. 1988. Epidemiologic evidence for early onset of mental disorders and higher risk of drug-abuse in young adults. *Am. J. Psychiatry* 145:971–75

Comstock GW, Helsing KJ. 1976. Symptoms of depression in two communities. *Psychol. Med.* 6:551–63

Costello EJ, Mustillo S, Erkanli A, Keeler G, Angold A. 2003. Prevalence and development of psychiatric disorders in childhood and adolescence. *Arch. Gen. Psychiatry* 60:837–44

Das Gupta R, Guest JF. 2002. Annual cost of bipolar disorder to U.K. society. *Br. J. Psychiatry* 180:227–33

Dean BB, Gerner D, Gerner RH. 2004. A systematic review evaluating health-related quality of life, work impairment, and healthcare costs and utilization in bipolar disorder. *Curr. Med. Res. Opin.* 20:139–54

Eisenberg DM, Davis RB, Ettner SL, Appel S, Wilkey SA, et al. 1998. Trends in alternative medicine use in the United States, 1990–1997: results of a follow-up national survey. *JAMA* 280:1569–75

Eisenberg DM, Kessler RC, Foster C, Norlock FE, Calkins DR, Delbanco TL. 1993. Unconventional medicine in the United States. Prevalence, costs, and patterns of use. *N. Engl. J. Med.* 328:246–52

First MB, Spitzer RL, Gibbon M, Williams JBW. 2002. *Structured Clinical Interview for DSM-IV Axis I Disorders, Research Version, Non-patient Edition (SCID-I/NP)*. New York: Biometr. Res., NY State Psychiatr. Inst.

Fisfalen ME, Schulze TG, DePaulo JRJ, DeGroot LJ, Badner JA, McMahon FJ. 2005. Familial variation in episode frequency in bipolar affective disorder. *Am. J. Psychiatry* 162:1266–72

Forrest CB. 2003. Primary care in the United States. Primary care gatekeeping and referrals: effective filter or failed experiment? *Br. Med. J.* 326:692–95

Freeman MP, Freeman SA, McElroy SL. 2002. The comorbidity of bipolar and anxiety disorders: prevalence, psychobiology, and treatment issues. *J. Affect. Disord.* 68:1–23

Goodwin FK, Jamison KR. 1990. *Manic-Depressive Illness*. New York: Oxford Univ. Press

An encyclopedic review of the worldwide literature on all aspects of bipolar disorders.

Goodwin R, Olfson M. 2001. Treatment of panic attack and risk of major depressive disorder in the community. *Am. J. Psychiatry* 158:1146–48

Gotlib IH, Hammen CL, ed. 2002. *Handbook of Depression*. New York: Guilford

An excellent review of the literature on depressive disorders.

Gracious BL, Youngstrom EA, Findling RL, Calabrese JR. 2002. Discriminative validity of a parent version of the Young Mania Rating Scale. *J. Am. Acad. Child Adolesc. Psychiatry* 41:1350–59

Grant BF, Stinson FS, Hasin DS, Dawson DA, Chou SP, et al. 2005. Prevalence, correlates, and comorbidity of bipolar I disorder and Axis I and II disorders: results from the National Epidemiologic Survey on Alcohol and Related Conditions. *J. Clin. Psychiatry* 66:1205–15

Greenberg PE, Kessler RC, Birnbaum HG, Leong SA, Lowe SW, et al. 2003. The economic burden of depression in the United States: How did it change between 1990 and 2000? *J. Clin. Psychiatry* 64:1465–75

The most recent synthesis of information on the societal costs of depression, putting the annual costs of depression in the United States at a staggering $83 billion.

Greenberg PE, Kessler RC, Nells TL, Finkelstein SN, Berndt ER. 1996. Depression in the workplace: an economic perspective. In *Perspectives in Psychiatry: Selective Serotonin Reuptake Inhibitors, Second Edition. Advances in Basic Research and Clinical Practice*, ed. JP Feighner, WF Boyer, pp. 327–63. New York: Wiley

Greenberg PE, Stiglin LE, Finkelstein SN, Berndt ER. 1993. The economic burden of depression in 1990. *J. Clin. Psychiatry* 54:405–18

Haro JM, Brugha TS, de Girolamo G, Kessler RC, Lepine JP. 2007. Validity of the Composite International Diagnostic Interview in the WHO World Mental Health Surveys. *Int. J. Methods Psychiatr. Res.* In press

Hasin DS, Goodwin RD, Stinson FS, Grant BF. 2005. Epidemiology of major depressive disorder: results from the National Epidemiologic Survey on Alcoholism and Related Conditions. *Arch. Gen. Psychiatry* 62:1097–106

Helgason T. 1964. Epidemiology of mental disorders in Iceland. *Acta Psychiatr. Scand.* 40:115–32

Helzer JE, Hudziak JJ, eds. 2002. *Defining Psychopathology in the 21st Century: DSM-V and Beyond*. Washington, DC: Am. Psychiatr. Press

Hettema JM, Prescott CA, Kendler KS. 2003. The effects of anxiety, substance use and conduct disorders on risk of major depressive disorder. *Psychol. Med.* 33:1423–32

Hirschfeld RM. 2004. Bipolar depression: the real challenge. *Eur. Neuropsychopharmacol.* 14(Suppl. 2):S83–88

Hypericum Depression Trial Study Group. 2002. Effect of *hypericum perforatum* (St. John's wort) in major depressive disorder: a randomized controlled trial. *JAMA* 287:1807–14

Judd LL, Akiskal HS. 2003a. Depressive episodes and symptoms dominate the longitudinal course of bipolar disorder. *Curr. Psychiatry Rep.* 5:417–18

An important report from the Collaborative Psychobiology of Depression Study that followed bipolar patients over many years and documented that their time in depressive episodes was much greater than their time in manic-hypomanic episodes.

Judd LL, Akiskal HS. 2003b. The prevalence and disability of bipolar spectrum disorders in the US population: reanalysis of the ECA database taking into account subthreshold cases. *J. Affect. Disord.* 73:123–31

Judd LL, Akiskal HS, Schettler PJ, Coryell W, Maser J, et al. 2003. The comparative clinical phenotype and long-term longitudinal episode course of bipolar I and II: a clinical spectrum or distinct disorders? *J. Affect. Disord.* 73:19–32

Judd LL, Akiskal HS, Schettler PJ, Endicott J, Maser J, et al. 2002. The long-term natural history of the weekly symptomatic status of bipolar I disorder. *Arch. Gen. Psychiatry* 59:530–37

Judd LL, Akiskal HS, Zeller PJ, Paulus M, Leon AC, et al. 2000. Psychosocial disability during the long-term course of unipolar major depressive disorder. *Arch. Gen. Psychiatry* 57:375–80

Keller MB. 1985. Chronic and recurrent affective disorders: incidence, course and influencing factors. In *Chronic Treatments in Neuropsychiatry*, ed. D Kemali, G Racagni, pp. 111–20. New York: Raven

Keller MB. 2006. Prevalence and impact of comorbid anxiety and bipolar disorder. *J. Clin. Psychiatry* 67(Suppl. 1):5–7

Kendler KS, Prescott CA. 2006. *Genes, Environment, and Psychopathology*. New York: Guilford

An important synthesis of results from the most prominent existing program of population genetic twin-family research on the epidemiology of common mental disorders.

Kessler RC. 1995. Epidemiology of psychiatric comorbidity. In *Textbook in Psychiatric Epidemiology*, ed. MT Tsuang, M Tohen, GEP Zahner, pp. 179–97. New York: Wiley

Kessler RC. 1997. The prevalence of psychiatric comorbidity. In *Treatment Strategies for Patients with Psychiatric Comorbidity*, ed. S Wetzler, WC Sanderson, pp. 23–48. New York: Wiley

Kessler RC, Abelson J, Demler O, Escobar JI, Gibbon M, et al. 2004a. Clinical calibration of DSM-IV diagnoses in the World Mental Health (WMH) version of the World Health Organization (WHO) Composite International Diagnostic Interview (WMHCIDI). *Int. J. Methods Psychiatr. Res.* 13:122–39

Kessler RC, Akiskal HS, Ames M, Birnbaum H, Greenberg P, et al. 2006a. Prevalence and effects of mood disorders on work performance in a nationally representative sample of U.S. workers. *Am. J. Psychiatry* 163(9):1561–68

Kessler RC, Akiskal HS, Angst J, Guyer ME, Hirschfeld RMA, et al. 2007. Validity of the Assessment of Bipolar Spectrum Disorders in the WHO CIDI 3.0. *J. Affect. Disord.* In press

Kessler RC, Akiskal HS, Angst J, Hirschfeld R, Merikangas K, et al. 2006b. The workplace costs of mood disorders: bringing bipolar spectrum disorders into the equation. *J. Health Product.* 1:3–8

Kessler RC, Ames M, Hymel PA, Loeppke R, McKenas DK, et al. 2004b. Using the World Health Organization Health and Work Performance Questionnaire (HPQ) to evaluate the indirect workplace costs of illness. *J. Occup. Environ. Med.* 46:S23–37

Kessler RC, Avenevoli S, Ries Merikangas K. 2001a. Mood disorders in children and adolescents: an epidemiologic perspective. *Biol. Psychiatry* 49:1002–14

Kessler RC, Barber C, Beck A, Berglund P, Cleary PD, et al. 2003a. The World Health Organization Health and Work Performance Questionnaire (HPQ). *J. Occup. Environ. Med.* 45:156–74

Kessler RC, Berglund P, Demler O, Jin R, Koretz D, et al. 2003b. The epidemiology of major depressive disorder: results from the National Comorbidity Survey Replication (NCS-R). *JAMA* 289:3095–105

The most recent and definitive data on the descriptive epidemiology of major depression in the United States.

Kessler RC, Berglund P, Demler O, Jin R, Walters EE. 2005. Lifetime prevalence and age-of-onset distributions of DSM-IV disorders in the National Comorbidity Survey Replication. *Arch. Gen. Psychiatry* 62:593–602

Kessler RC, Davis RB, Foster DF, Van Rompay MI, Walters EE, et al. 2001b. Long-term trends in the use of complementary and alternative medical therapies in the United States. *Ann. Intern. Med.* 135:262–68

Kessler RC, Merikangas KR. 2004. The National Comorbidity Survey Replication (NCS-R): background and aims. *Int. J. Methods Psychiatr. Res.* 13:60–68

Kessler RC, Nelson CB, McGonagle KA, Liu J, Swartz M, Blazer DG. 1996. Comorbidity of DSM-III-R major depressive disorder in the general population: results from the U.S. National Comorbidity Survey. *Br. J. Psychiatry* 168:17–30

Kessler RC, Soukup J, Davis RB, Foster DF, Wilkey SA, et al. 2001c. The use of complementary and alternative therapies to treat anxiety and depression in the United States. *Am. J. Psychiatry* 158:289–94

Kessler RC, Stang PE, Wittchen HU, Ustun TB, Roy-Byrne PP, Walters EE. 1998a. Lifetime panic-depression comorbidity in the National Comorbidity Survey. *Arch. Gen. Psychiatry* 55:801–8

Kessler RC, Ustun TB. 2004. The World Mental Health (WMH) survey initiative version of the World Health Organization (WHO) Composite International Diagnostic Interview (CIDI). *Int. J. Methods Psychiatr. Res.* 13:93–121

Kessler RC, Wang PS. 1999. Screening measures for behavioral health assessment. In *SPM Handbook of Health Assessment Tools*, ed. G Hyner, K Peterson, J Travis, J Dewey, J Foerster, E Framer, pp. 33–40. Pittsburgh, PA: Soc. Prospect. Med.

Kessler RC, Wittchen HU, Abelson JM, McGonagle K, Schwarz N, et al. 1998b. Methodological studies of the Composite International Diagnostic Interview (CIDI) in the U.S. National Comorbidity Survey. *Int. J. Methods Psychiatr. Res.* 7:33–55

Kessler RC, Zhao S, Katz SJ, Kouzis AC, Frank RG, et al. 1999. Past year use of outpatient services for psychiatric problems in the National Comorbidity Survey. *Am. J. Psychiatry* 156:115–23

Khan AA, Jacobson KC, Gardner CO, Prescott CA, Kendler KS. 2005. Personality and comorbidity of common psychiatric disorders. *Br. J. Psychiatry* 186:190–96

Kleinman L, Lowin A, Flood E, Gandhi G, Edgell E, Revicki D. 2003. Costs of bipolar disorder. *Pharmacoeconomics* 21:601–22

Kling JR, Liebman JB, Katz LF. 2007. Experimental analysis of neighborhood effects. *Econometrica.* In press

Klinkman MS. 1997. Competing demands in psychosocial care. A model for the identification and treatment of depressive disorders in primary care. *Gen. Hosp. Psychiatry* 19:98–111

Knauper B, Cannell CF, Schwarz N, Bruce ML, Kessler RC. 1999. Improving the accuracy of major depression age of onset reports in the U.S. National Comorbidity Survey. *Int. J. Methods Psychiatr. Res.* 8:39–48

Kroenke K. 2003. Patients presenting with somatic complaints: epidemiology, psychiatric comorbidity and management. *Int. J. Methods Psychiatr. Res.* 12:34–43

Kupka RW, Luckenbaugh DA, Post RM, Suppes T, Altshuler LL, et al. 2005. Comparison of rapid-cycling and nonrapid-cycling bipolar disorder based on prospective mood ratings in 539 outpatients. *Am. J. Psychiatry* 162:1273–80

Lejoyeux M, Arbaretaz M, McLoughlin M, Ades J. 2002. Impulse control disorders and depression. *J. Nerv. Ment. Dis.* 190:310–14

Leon AC, Olfson M, Portera L, Farber L, Sheehan DV. 1997. Assessing psychiatric impairment in primary care with the Sheehan Disability Scale. *Int. J. Psychiatry Med.* 27:93–105

Lin TY. 1953. A study of incidence of mental disorders in Chinese and other cultures. *Psychiatry* 16:315–35

Loeber R, Farrington DP, Stouthamer-Loeber M, Van Kammen WB. 1988. *Antisocial Behavior and Mental Health Problems: Explanatory Factors in Childhood and Adolescence*. Mahwah, NJ: Erlbaum

MacKinnon DF, Zandi PP, Cooper J, Potash JB, Simpson SG, et al. 2002. Comorbid bipolar disorder and panic disorder in families with a high prevalence of bipolar disorder. *Am. J. Psychiatry* 159:30–35

Mattisson C, Bogren M, Nettelbladt P, Munk-Jorgensen P, Bhugra D. 2005. First incidence depression in the Lundby Study: a comparison of the two time periods 1947–1972 and 1972–1997. *J. Affect. Disord.* 87:151–60

McElroy SL, Pope HG, Keck PEJ, Hudson JI, Phillips KA, Strakowski SM. 1996. Are impulse-control disorders related to bipolar disorder? *Comp. Psychiatry* 37:229–40

Merikangas KR, Akiskal HS, Angst J, Greenberg PE, Hirschfeld RMA, et al. 2007. Lifetime and 12-month Prevalence of Bipolar Spectrum Disorder in the National Comorbidity Survey Replication. *Arch. Gen. Psychiatry.* In press

The most recent and definitive data on the descriptive epidemiology of bipolar disorders in the United States.

Merikangas KR, Angst J, Eaton WW, Canino G, Rubio-Stipec M, et al. 1996. Comorbidity and boundaries of affective disorders with anxiety disorders and substance misuse: results of an international task force. *Br. J. Psychiatry* 168:58–67

Mitchell PB, Slade T, Andrews G. 2004. Twelve-month prevalence and disability of DSM-IV bipolar disorder in an Australian general population survey. *Psychol. Med.* 34:777–85

Morrow RH, Hyder AA, Murray CJ, Lopez AD. 1998. Measuring the burden of disease. *Lancet* 352:1859–61

Murphy JM, Horton NJ, Laird NM, Monson RR, Sobol AM, Leighton AH. 2004. Anxiety and depression: a 40-year perspective on relationships regarding prevalence, distribution, and comorbidity. *Acta Psychiatr. Scand.* 109:355–75

Murphy JM, Sobol AM, Neff RK, Olivier DC, Leighton AH. 1984. Stability of prevalence: depression and anxiety disorders. *Arch. Gen. Psychiatry* 41:990–97

Murray CJL, Lopez AD. 1996. *Global Health Statistics*. Cambridge, MA: Harvard Univ. Press

Narrow WE, Rae DS, Robins LN, Regier DA. 2002. Revised prevalence estimates of mental disorders in the United States: using a clinical significance criterion to reconcile 2 surveys' estimates. *Arch. Gen. Psychiatry* 59:115–23

Olfson M, Marcus SC, Druss B, Elinson L, Tanielian T, Pincus HA. 2002a. National trends in the outpatient treatment of depression. *JAMA* 287:203–9

Olfson M, Marcus SC, Druss B, Pincus HA. 2002b. National trends in the use of outpatient psychotherapy. *Am. J. Psychiatry* 159:1914–20

Olfson M, Marcus SC, Wan GJ, Geissler EC. 2004. National trends in the outpatient treatment of anxiety disorders. *J. Clin. Psychiatry* 65:1166–73

Paykel ES, Abbott R, Morriss R, Hayhurst H, Scott J. 2006. Sub-syndromal and syndromal symptoms in the longitudinal course of bipolar disorder. *Br. J. Psychiatry* 189:118–23

Pezawas L, Angst J, Kasper S. 2005. Recurrent brief depression revisited. *Int. Rev. Psychiatry* 17:63–70

Pincus HA, Hough L, Houtsinger JK, Rollman BL, Frank RG. 2003. Emerging models of depression care: multi-level ('6 P') strategies. *Int. J. Methods Psychiatr. Res.* 12:54–63

Pini S, de Queiroz V, Pagnin D, Pezawas L, Angst J, et al. 2005. Prevalence and burden of bipolar disorders in European countries. *Eur. Neuropsychopharmacol.* 15:425–34

Regeer EJ, ten Have M, Rosso ML, Hakkaart-van Roijen L, Vollebergh W, Nolen WA. 2004. Prevalence of bipolar disorder in the general population: a reappraisal study of the Netherlands Mental Health Survey and Incidence Study. *Acta Psychiatr. Scand.* 110:374–82

Regier DA, Farmer ME, Rae DS, Locke BZ, Keith SJ, et al. 1990. Comorbidity of mental disorders with alcohol and other drug abuse. Results from the Epidemiologic Catchment Area (ECA) study. *JAMA* 264:2511–18

Regier DA, Narrow WE, Rae DS, Manderscheid RW, Locke BZ, Goodwin FK. 1993. The de facto U.S. Mental and Addictive Disorders Service System: Epidemiologic Catchment Area prospective 1-year prevalence rates of disorders and services. *Arch. Gen. Psychiatry* 50:85–94

Rice DP, Miller LS. 1993. The economic burden of affective disorders. *Adv. Health Econ. Health Serv. Res.* 14:37–53

Robins LN, Helzer JE, Croughan JL, Ratcliff KS. 1981. National Institute of Mental Health Diagnostic Interview Schedule: its history, characteristics and validity. *Arch. Gen. Psychiatry* 38:381–89

Robins LN, Regier DA, eds. 1991. *Psychiatric Disorders in America: The Epidemiologic Catchment Area Study*. New York: Free Press. 449 pp.

Rush AJ, Trivedi MH, Ibrahim HM, Carmody TJ, Arnow B, et al. 2003. The 16-Item Quick Inventory of Depressive Symptomatology (QIDS), clinician rating (QIDS-C), and self-report (QIDS-SR): a psychometric evaluation in patients with chronic major depression. *Biol. Psychiatry* 54:573–83

SAS Institute. 2001. *SAS/STAT Software: Changes and Enhancements, Release 8.2*. Cary, NC: SAS Publ.

Schachter MF, Kupfer DJ, Regier DA, First MB. 2002. *A Research Agenda for DSM-V*. Washington, DC: Am. Psychiatr. Assoc. Press

Simon GE, VonKorff M. 1992. Reevaluation of secular trends in depression rates. *Am. J. Epidemiol.* 135:1411–22

Simon GE, VonKorff M. 1995. Recall of psychiatric history in cross-sectional surveys: implications for epidemiologic research. *Epidemiol. Rev.* 17:221–27

Simon GE, VonKorff M, Piccinelli M, Fullerton C, Ormel J. 1999. An international study of the relation between somatic symptoms and depression. *N. Engl. J. Med.* 341:1329–35

Spitzer RL, Kroenke K, Williams JB. 1999. Validation and utility of a self-report version of PRIME-MD: the PHQ primary care study. Primary Care Evaluation of Mental Disorders. Patient Health Questionnaire. *JAMA* 282:1737–44

Stewart WF, Ricci JA, Chee E, Hahn SR, Morganstein D. 2003. Cost of lost productive work time among US workers with depression. *JAMA* 289:3135–44

Strakowski SM, DelBello MP. 2000. The co-occurrence of bipolar and substance use disorders. *Clin. Psychol. Rev.* 20:191–206

Susser E, Schwartz S, Morabia A, Bromet EJ. 2006. *Psychiatric Epidemiology: Searching for the Causes of Mental Disorders*. New York: Oxford Univ. Press

Szadoczky E, Papp Z, Vitrai J, Rihmer Z, Furedi J. 1998. The prevalence of major depressive and bipolar disorders in Hungary. results from a national epidemiologic survey. *J. Affect. Disord.* 50:153–62

Tohen M, Angst J. 2002. Epidemiology of bipolar disorder. In *Textbook in Psychiatric Epidemiology*, ed. M Tsuang, M Tohen, pp. 427–44. New York: Wiley

Trude S, Stoddard JJ. 2003. Referral gridlock: primary care physicians and mental health services. *J. Gen. Intern. Med.* 18:442–49

U.S. Dep. Health Human Serv. 1999. *Mental health: a report of the Surgeon General*. Rockville, MD: U.S. Dep. Health Human Serv., Subst. Abuse Mental Health Serv. Admin., Cent. Mental Health Serv., Natl. Inst. Health, Natl. Inst. Mental Health

Wang PS, Berglund PA, Kessler RC. 2000. Recent care of common mental disorders in the United States: prevalence and conformance with evidence-based recommendations. *J. Gen. Intern. Med.* 15:284–92

Wang PS, Berglund PA, Kessler RC. 2003a. Patterns and correlates of contacting clergy for mental disorders in the United States. *Health Serv. Res.* 38:647–73

Wang PS, Demler O, Kessler RC. 2002. Adequacy of treatment for serious mental illness in the United States. *Am. J. Public Health* 92:92–98

Wang PS, Lane M, Olfson M, Pincus HA, Wells KB, Kessler RC. 2005. Twelve-month use of mental health services in the U.S.: results from the National Comorbidity Survey Replication (NCS-R). *Arch. Gen. Psychiatry* 62:629–40

Wang PS, Simon GE, Kessler RC. 2003b. The economic burden of depression and the cost-effectiveness of treatment. *Int. J. Methods Psychiatr. Res.* 12:22–33

Waraich P, Goldner EM, Somers JM, Hsu L. 2004. Prevalence and incidence studies of mood disorders: a systematic review of the literature. *Can. J. Psychiatry* 49:124–38

Warner V, Weeisman MM, Mufson L, Wickramaratne PJ. 1999. Grandparents, parents, and grandchildren at high risk for depression: a three generation study. *J. Am. Acad. Child Adolesc. Psychiatry* 38:289–96

Weaver AJ. 1995. Has there been a failure to prepare and support parish-based clergy in their role as frontline community mental health workers: a review. *J. Pastoral Care* 49:129–47

Weissman MM, Bland RC, Canino GJ, Faravelli C, Greenwald S, et al. 1996. Cross-national epidemiology of major depression and bipolar disorder. *JAMA* 276:293–99

Weissman MM, Livingston Bruce M, Leaf PJ, Florio LP, Holzer CI. 1991. Affective disorders. In *Psychiatric Disorders in America: The Epidemiologic Catchment Area Study*, ed. LN Robins, DA Regier, pp. 53–80. New York: Free Press

Williams JBW. 1998. Competing demands: Does care for depression fit in primary care? *J. Gen. Intern. Med.* 13:137–39

Williams JWJ, Rost K, Dietrich AJ, Ciotti MC, Zyzanski SJ, Cornell J. 1999. Primary care physicians' approach to depressive disorders. Effects of physician specialty and practice structure. *Arch. Fam. Med.* 8:58–67

Wittchen HU. 1994. Reliability and validity studies of the WHO Composite International Diagnostic Interview (CIDI): a critical review. *J. Psychiatr. Res.* 28:57–84

Wittchen HU, Mhlig S, Pezawas L. 2003. Natural course and burden of bipolar disorders. *Int. J. Neuropsychopharmacol.* 6:145–54

World Health Organ. Int. Consort. Psychiatr. Epidemiol. 2000. Cross-national comparisons of the prevalences and correlates of mental disorders. *Bull. World Health Organ.* 78:413–26

Wyatt RJ, Henter I. 1995. An economic evaluation of manic-depressive illness—1991. *Soc. Psychiatry Psychiatr. Epidemiol.* 30:213–19

Young AS, Klap R, Sherbourne CD, Wells KB. 2001. The quality of care for depressive and anxiety disorders in the United States. *Arch. Gen. Psychiatry* 58:55–61

Young RC, Biggs JT, Ziegler VE, Meyer DA. 1978. A rating scale for mania: reliability, validity and sensitivity. *Br. J. Psychiatry* 133:429–35

Zimmerman M, Chelminski I, McDermut W. 2002. Major depressive disorder and Axis I diagnostic comorbidity. *J. Clin. Psychiatry* 63:187–93

Zimmerman M, McGlinchey JB, Young D, Chelminski I. 2006. Diagnosing major depressive disorder introduction: an examination of the DSM-IV diagnostic criteria. *J. Nerv. Ment. Dis.* 194:151–54

Stimulating the Development of Drug Treatments to Improve Cognition in Schizophrenia

Michael F. Green

Semel Neuropsychiatric Institute, Geffen School of Medicine, University of California, Los Angeles, California 90095, and Mental Illness Research, Education and Clinical Center, VA Greater Los Angeles Healthcare System, Los Angeles, California 90073; email: mgreen@ucla.edu

Annu. Rev. Clin. Psychol. 2007. 3:159–80

First published online as a Review in Advance on January 5, 2007

The *Annual Review of Clinical Psychology* is online at http://clinpsy.annualreviews.org

This article's doi:
10.1146/annurev.clinpsy.3.022806.091529

1548-5943/07/0427-0159$20.00

Key Words

neurocognition, MATRICS, FDA, NIMH

Abstract

Cognitive impairment in schizophrenia is a core feature of the illness (i.e., not a result of clinical symptoms or drug treatments) that is related to the daily functioning of patients. Because schizophrenia is associated with poor community functioning, there is considerable interest in finding treatments to improve cognition in schizophrenia in the hopes that such improvement will yield functional benefits. Before the U.S. Food and Drug Administration could consider granting approval to any new drug for improving cognition in schizophrenia, it was first necessary to achieve consensus on the measurements and methods that would be used in clinical trials, as well as neuropharmacological targets. The U.S. National Institute of Mental Health launched an initiative to help address these obstacles to drug approval (MATRICS). This initiative has generated several additional follow-up initiatives including a clinical trial network and consensus projects for other clinical targets, such as negative symptoms. This review describes how an area that was primarily of academic interest (cognition in schizophrenia) became a focus of public health concerns and drug-development policy.

Contents

INTRODUCTION

In the past few years, we have seen a broad convergence on the problem of developing new drugs to treat cognitive impairment in schizophrenia. The effort is unusual in that it required substantial input from highly diverse entities, including academia, the pharmaceutical industry, and the federal government. Another unusual aspect of this effort is that it intended to create a pathway to approve drugs to treat a completely new clinical target. This review summarizes how cognition in schizophrenia was elevated from a limited academic consideration to a broader public health problem and how people with widely ranging expertise worked together to make it an accepted treatment goal.

SCIENTIFIC BACKGROUND

An initial question is how cognition in schizophrenia came to be viewed as an important treatment target. Three key lines of investigation have provided the rationale. First, the cognitive impairments in schizophrenia are considered to be core features of the illness. Second, the impairments are related to how well patients with schizophrenia function in daily life. Third, an emerging neuropharmacology of cognition can provide guidance for new types of medications. I briefly discuss each of these factors below.

Cognition as a Core Feature of Schizophrenia

The cognitive deficits associated with schizophrenia encompass a wide range of domains. Based on a careful literature review and consensus meetings sponsored by the National Institute of Mental Health (NIMH), several cognitive domains were selected as important to assess in all treatment studies of cognition in schizophrenia: speed of processing, attention/vigilance, working memory, verbal learning, visual learning, reasoning and problem solving, and social cognition (Nuechterlein et al. 2004). Although there is considerable variability in the pattern of deficits across subjects, there is an identified modal neurocognitive profile that is characterized by larger deficits (in the range of 1.5 standard deviations) in verbal learning and vigilance, and lesser impairments in visual organization abilities and vocabulary (Heinrichs & Zakzanis 1998). Other studies have supported the relatively large deficits in verbal memory compared with other domains, but the disorder is associated with impairments in nearly all domains (Saykin et al. 1991).

Cognitive impairments are relatively common in schizophrenia, with estimates that 90% of patients have clinically meaningful deficits in at least one cognitive domain and 75% have deficits in at least two (Palmer et al. 1997). Even these relatively high rates of impairment may be underestimates, and almost all schizophrenia patients may have illness-associated performance deficits, even those who perform in the normal range. Such interpretations are based on findings of consistent deficits in patients when they are compared with their unaffected monozygotic twins (Goldberg et al. 1990) or when compared with estimates of expected levels based on premorbid functioning (Kremen et al. 2000).

One of the most important conceptual developments in schizophrenia over the past two decades is that cognitive impairment has become seen as a core feature, meaning that these impairments are not secondary or derivative of other aspects of schizophrenia, such as medications or psychotic symptoms of hallucinations and delusions. Several lines of evidence indicate that cognitive deficits are core features of schizophrenia (Braff 1993, Gold 2004, Gold & Green 2004, Nuechterlein et al. 1994).

1. The time course of cognitive impairment is quite different from that of clinical symptoms. Many patients demonstrate cognitive or intellectual impairments before the onset of psychotic symptoms and other clinical features (Cornblatt et al. 1992, 1999; Davidson et al. 1999; Niendam et al. 2003; Nuechterlein 1983; Reichenberg et al. 2002).
2. Milder cognitive impairment can be detected in first-degree relatives of schizophrenic patients who have no evidence of psychosis (Asarnow et al. 2002; Cannon et al. 1994, 2000; Green et al. 1997; Kremen et al. 1994; Snitz et al. 2006). The presence of such deficits in relatives suggests that certain cognitive deficits are likely to be components of genetic vulnerability to schizophrenia.
3. The magnitude of the cognitive impairment is relatively stable across clinical state. On some cognitive measures, the level of impairment shown by patients during a psychotic episode is remarkably similar to that seen when their symptoms are under control or when they are in full remission (Finkelstein et al. 1997, Nuechterlein et al. 1998). Therefore, cognitive impairment can occur with low levels, or complete absence, of clinical symptoms of schizophrenia.
4. The cross-sectional correlations between cognitive performance and ratings of psychotic-symptom severity are typically small (Bilder et al. 2000, Goldberg et al. 1993, Heydebrand et al. 2004, Mohamed et al. 1999, Nieuwenstein et al. 2001). Although the findings for correlations with psychotic symptoms (i.e., hallucinations and delusions) are consistently small, the findings are inconsistent regarding the degree of association with disorganized symptoms (e.g., formal thought disorder), with some studies showing relationships for specific aspects of disorganization (Mohamed et al. 1999, Perry & Braff 1994, Spitzer 1997). Cognitive performance tends to be related to negative symptoms, although the magnitude of the correlations is modest (typically approximately 15% of the variance).
5. Antipsychotic medications have substantial benefits for the psychotic

NIMH: National Institute of Mental Health

symptoms of schizophrenia, but their effects on cognition are much smaller. This pattern is true for both first- and second-generation antipsychotic medications. This discrepancy between clinical and cognitive effects suggests that antipsychotic medications act on different neural systems from those that underlie the cognitive impairments. Differences in the cognitive effects of first- and second-generation medications have been reported, but these differences are rather small compared with the clinical impact of medications on psychotic symptoms (Harvey & Keefe 2001, Woodward et al. 2005). This limited effect on cognition also provides a rationale to search for other types of drugs to manage the cognitive deficits of the illness.

A related question is whether the cognitive deficits in schizophrenia are diagnostically specific. On the one hand, none of the deficits can be considered specific to schizophrenia, as they appear in other disorders as well. On the other hand, the deficits in schizophrenia are clearly distinguishable from those in dementia (Heaton et al. 1994, Zakzanis 1998). Specifically, dementia is characterized by severe deficits in memory retention, which is largely intact in schizophrenia. Cognitive impairment in mood disorders such as depression and bipolar disorder tends to be reduced in magnitude and different in pattern from that seen in schizophrenia, even when patients are out of a mood episode (Altshuler et al. 2004, Buchanan et al. 2005, Fleck et al. 2001, van Gorp et al. 1998). In contrast, the pattern and magnitude of cognitive impairment in schizoaffective disorder are not distinguishable from that of schizophrenia (Buchanan et al. 2005, Evans et al. 1999, Miller et al. 1996), suggesting that any treatment for cognition in schizophrenia is likely helpful in schizoaffective disorder as well.

Cognition and Functional Outcome

The connection between cognition and functional outcome in schizophrenia provided another key line of support for viewing cognition as a treatment target. To put this area in context, it should be emphasized that functional outcome in schizophrenia has been disappointing, to say the least (Hegarty et al. 1994, Helgason 1990, Wiersma et al. 2000). Even with the introduction of antipsychotic medications that largely control psychotic symptoms for the majority of patients, individuals with schizophrenia have considerable difficulty achieving adequate community functioning. Even in the presence of symptom management, troubles persist in activities such as finding a job, forming a network of friends, or living independently. This is why schizophrenia remains one of the largest causes of disability among all illnesses for young adults (Murray & Lopez 1996). Psychotic symptoms are not strong determinants of community functioning; if they were, controlling symptoms would be sufficient for improved outcomes. Hence, other factors must be related to community functioning. Cognitive impairment is one such determinant.

Several literature reviews have shown that, across studies, cognitive deficits have highly consistent relationships to various types of functional outcomes, including community functioning and the ability to acquire skills in psychosocial rehabilitation (Green 1996; Green et al. 2000, 2004a). The strengths of the associations for individual cognitive domains are typically moderate, although relationships with large effects can be found when multiple cognitive domains are combined into composite scores (Green et al. 2000).

Most of the studies in the reviews have been cross-sectional, but a review of prospective studies with a minimum six-month follow-up also showed that measurement of cognitive impairment at one point in time is a reasonable predictor of later community functioning (Green et al. 2004a). Some of the studies found good associations with outcome two to four years after baseline assessment, which is typically considered long enough to see changes in functional status (Dickerson et al. 1999, Friedman et al. 2002b, Gold et al. 2002, Robinson et al. 2004, Stirling et al. 2003).

Taken as a whole, the literature supports connections between cognition and outcome in a general sense, but there are several recurring questions regarding the specificity of the connections. One question is whether some cognitive domains are more strongly related to outcome than other cognitive domains. A second question is whether specific cognitive domains are related to a specific aspect of functioning. At this stage, we do not have good answers to either of these questions. Verbal episodic memory (Green et al. 2000) or speed of processing (Gold et al. 2002) may be particularly important for functional outcome, but at this point, it is difficult to select one domain that is particularly important to outcome. Instead, it appears that, when averaged across subjects, all the cognitive domains studies are related to functioning (Velligan et al. 2000). Similarly, it is currently difficult to draw any clear connections between specific cognitive domains and particular aspects of outcome (e.g., work versus social outcome, skill acquisition versus independent living). In fact, when specific connections are detected, they may change over time, even for the same functional activity. For example, vigilance was much more important than verbal memory in accounting for the level of work performance (12% versus 4% variance explained) in the first half of a structured vocational program (Bryson & Bell 2003). However, the pattern was reversed for the second half of the program, with verbal memory more important than vigilance (11% versus 6%), suggesting that familiarity with the tasks changed the type of cognitive demands.

The connections between cognitive performance and functioning are not diagnostically specific to schizophrenia, as similar relationships exist in neurological disorders (including multiple sclerosis and HIV infection) (Rao et al. 1991, van Gorp et al. 1999). In fact, these deficits are associated with functioning in normal aging (Moritz et al. 1995). Considerably fewer data exist for other psychiatric disorders, but the emerging findings suggest that similar relationships are present for bipolar disorder (Dickerson et al. 2004, Martínez-Arán et al. 2004). The possibility remains that distinct patterns of relationships will characterize different disorders, possibly owing to differences in the nature of the daily tasks. For example, verbal memory may be particularly important for social functioning in schizophrenia, but executive functions may be more important in bipolar disorder (Laes & Sponheim 2006).

Although the linkages between cognition and functioning are well documented at this stage, little is known about the mechanisms through which the linkages exist. Several studies are proposing and testing intermediate variables that may provide steps linking cognition and functioning (see **Figure 1**). If the mediating variables are included, direct connections between cognition and functioning may or may not remain. One such mediating step may be social cognition. Social cognition research in schizophrenia has explored several areas, including social perception, theory of mind, emotion processing, social knowledge, and attributional bias (Green et al. 2005, Penn et al. 1997). Several recent studies using structural equation modeling and path analysis have demonstrated that measures of social cognition (i.e., emotion perception and social perception) act as mediators between basic (nonsocial) cognition and functional outcome (Brekke et al. 2005, Sergi et al. 2006, Vauth et al. 2004). Measures of functional capacity have also been considered potential mediators. Functional capacity refers to an individual's capacity for performing key tasks of daily living, such as whether a person can maintain a social conversation, prepare a meal, take public transportation, or manage their medications (McKibbin et al. 2004). Assessments of functional capacity are simulated activities and do not rely on observing the individual in the community. Good performance on a

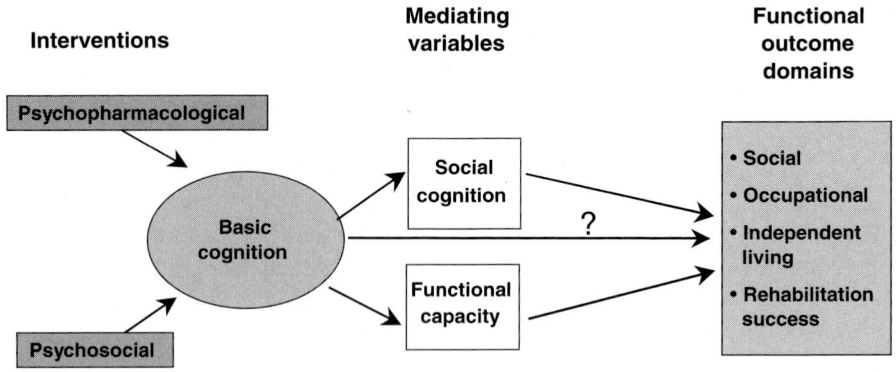

Figure 1

Cognition, mediating variables, and functional outcome.

functional capacity task means that a person can perform the task in the community, but it does not guarantee that he or she will perform the tasks in the community. Such tasks are likely related to both basic neurocognition and functional outcome, and hence may be key mediators (Bowie et al. 2006).

The Neuropharmacology of Cognition in Schizophrenia

The neuropharmacology of cognition was another line of research that helped provide a foundation for drug development in this area. There is considerable activity and interest, from both academia and the pharmaceutical industry, in identifying novel drugs that can improve cognition. These drug-discovery efforts often start with an intention to find drugs for dementia or mild cognitive impairment, but if there is an incentive (i.e., possibility of a new market), these efforts can be directed to other disorders with cognitive impairment, including schizophrenia.

Before considering novel drugs for improving cognition in schizophrenia, an initial question is whether such cognition-enhancing drugs already exist. For example, there have been substantial efforts to determine whether the newer (second-generation) antipsychotic medications have cognitive benefits. Studies in this literature have typically found that second-generation medications have cognitive benefits when compared with first-generation medications that act selectively at the dopamine 2 receptor (Harvey & Keefe 2001, Woodward et al. 2005). However, the size of this difference is modest (in the range of 0.2–0.4 standard deviations). Interestingly, several more recent studies tend to show smaller differences between medications than earlier studies (Keefe et al. 2006b, Purdon et al. 2000). Generally, the studies have become larger and better controlled over time, so the smaller effect sizes may be more representative. In addition, more recent studies with smaller effect sizes sometimes use lower doses of the first-generation medication. Hence, the size of the difference of cognitive effects between first- and second-generation medications may depend partly on the dosage of the first-generation medication (Green et al. 2002). If we accept that there are cognitive differences between first- and second-generation medications, the interpretation remains ambiguous. One could interpret differences either to mean that second-generation medications have cognitive benefits (above a cognitive baseline) or that first-generation medications are more cognitively impairing (Carpenter & Gold 2002). This question is currently unresolved and actively debated.

Even those who are enthusiastic about the cognitive advantages of second-generation antipsychotic medications do not think that cognitive effects of these drugs are sufficient for meaningful improvement. After all, none of the second-generation medications was developed with cognition in mind. Hence, if they had true cognition-enhancing properties, it would be a lucky accident. There is now broad agreement that other drugs are needed to achieve meaningful gains.

We can consider drugs that were developed for dementia, as such drugs may be beneficial for schizophrenia as well. The first drugs approved for dementia stimulate acetylcholine by blocking its breakdown (i.e., acetylcholinesterase inhibitors). Among these dementia drugs, one (donepezil) has been examined in several controlled studies in schizophrenia (Erickson et al. 2005, Freudenreich et al. 2005, Friedman et al. 2002a, Tugal et al. 2004). The results are not encouraging with three studies clearly negative and one study with mixed results. Newer drugs for dementia act on different mechanisms and may provide more promising results. However, the results so far are not encouraging and perhaps not surprising, as there is little reason to assume that the pathophysiology of dementia overlaps with that of schizophrenia. Based on these studies, there is strong interest in seriously considering other neuropharmacological mechanisms for cognition-enhancing drugs for schizophrenia.

One of the key goals of the NIMH-MATRICS Initiative (described below) was to identify the most promising neuropharmacological targets for new cognition-enhancing drugs for schizophrenia. To this end, a large, broad-based consensus meeting at NIMH rated the degree of enthusiasm from experts in this area for various neuropharmacological targets. A special issue of *Psychopharmacology* (volume 174, issue 1) was based on this consensus meeting. At the meeting and in the theme issue, experts made their best case in support of particular neuropharmacological targets (e.g., the dopamine D1 receptor, glutamatergic receptors). The experts included both clinical and preclinical researchers, and they based their arguments on both human and animal data.

Table 1 Promising neuropharmacological targets for cognition enhancement in schizophrenia (from the MATRICS Consensus Meeting)

Neuropharmacological target	Number of nominations
Alpha-7 nicotinic receptor agonists	31
D1 receptor agonists	30
AMPA glutamatergic receptor agonists	14
Alpha-2 adrenergic receptor agonists	14
NMDA glutamatergic receptor agonists	12
Metabotropic glutamate receptor agonists	12
Glycine reuptake inhibitors	8
M1 muscarinic receptor agonists	7
GABA A R subtype selective agonists	5

Table 1 contains a tally from the experts at the consensus meeting of the most promising candidates (they were able to vote for more than one). A glance at the voting reveals the large diversity of interest in the various targets and compounds. Small-scale, and somewhat encouraging, studies have already been conducted in schizophrenia that target the glutamatergic NMDA (*N*-methyl-D-aspartic acid) receptor (Coyle & Tsai 2004), as well as the glutamatergic AMPA (alpha-amino-3-hydroxy-5-methyl-4-isoxazole propionic acid) receptor (Goff et al. 2001). Enthusiasm was high for other targets, including the dopamine D1 receptor (Goldman-Rakic et al. 2004) and the alpha-7 nicotinic receptor (Martin et al. 2004), based largely on the strength of animal models. It is safe to say that there is no shortage of promising targets. Of course, the challenge is finding suitable compounds that act, ideally in a selective fashion, on these targets.

NMDA: *N*-methyl-D-aspartic acid

AMPA: alpha-amino-3-hydroxy-5-methyl-4-isoxazole propionic acid

FDA: Food and Drug Administration

OBSTACLES TO DEVELOPING DRUGS TO IMPROVE COGNITION IN SCHIZOPHRENIA

View from the Food and Drug Administration

One of the key roles for the U.S. Food and Drug Administration (FDA) for any new claim is to decide if the clinical target is appropriate. In most cases, the target is a distinct disease or syndrome (e.g., depression, anxiety, schizophrenia). In some cases, the target is a nonspecific symptom, such as pain or fever. In a few cases, however, an indication (i.e., a claim) for a drug was given for treatment of a symptom specific to a disorder. This situation, which is most relevant to cognition in schizophrenia, happened twice recently in psychiatry: One drug was approved for agitation in schizophrenia (ziprasidone) and another for suicidality in schizophrenia (clozapine).

This latter situation, approving a drug for a symptom of a disorder, is complex because it raises concerns that a claim is pseudospecific, which can lead to FDA disapproval. Pseudospecificity is a key concept for FDA decision making, and it refers to a claim for a drug that is overly narrow, for example, a claim that a drug works for a subgroup of individuals with a disorder (e.g., that a drug treats depression in women) or that it works for a particular aspect of an illness (e.g., a drug specifically for the treatment of hallucinations) (Laughren 2003). The FDA views such overly narrow claims as providing an unwarranted promotional advantage for the drug. Hence, before one can start to think about drugs for cognitive impairment in schizophrenia, one confronts the possibility that efforts can be preempted by pseudospecificity, depending on the FDA's view of cognition in schizophrenia.

There were two concerns related to pseudospecificity that, if not satisfactorily addressed, would have undermined the effort. One was whether the cognitive impairment in schizophrenia was sufficiently different from the clinical symptoms. If cognitive impairment was closely connected to psychotic symptoms, it should respond to treatments for psychotic symptoms, and drug development in this area should continue to focus on newer antipsychotic medications. If cognition and psychotic symptoms were part of the same constellation, then any claims of treating cognition would be pseudospecific. The data mentioned above indicating that cognitive impairment is a core feature of illness were convincing in this regard, and the concern was alleviated. A second concern was whether the cognitive impairment in schizophrenia is diagnostically specific to schizophrenia, or if cognitive impairment is a generic condition, similar to fever. If it was generic, then any claim for cognitive impairment in schizophrenia would be pseudospecific. The answer to this concern was more nuanced. At one level, no particular cognitive deficit is diagnostically specific because many other disorders and neurological conditions have cognitive impairment. Conversely, the pattern of cognitive impairment in schizophrenia is quite distinct from that of dementia (Buchanan et al. 2005). Because of the distinct cognitive profile and time course, in addition to presumed differences in pathophysiology of the two disorders, there was no reason to believe that cognitive impairment is generic and that drugs approved for dementia would be valuable for schizophrenia. With such concerns addressed, it was possible to move on to address other obstacles.

Challenges to Receiving FDA Approval for Cognition in Schizophrenia as a New Clinical Target

Although there is no shortage of promising approaches to enhancing cognition in schizophrenia (see **Table 1**), moving from promising targets to promising new drugs requires a firm commitment from the pharmaceutical industry. However, no drug has been approved by the FDA for this purpose (Marder & Fenton 2004). Several issues were identified that needed resolution before the FDA would consider approval for a drug for cognition in schizophrenia. First, there was no consensus regarding how to measure outcome. Hence, a critical prerequisite for establishing the efficacy of a procognitive agent in schizophrenia is the definition of cognition that can be used as an end point in clinical trials. The FDA had previously received inquiries from companies that were seeking approval of potential cognition-enhancing compounds. However, the companies each used different definitions and measurements of cognition, a situation that the FDA found unacceptable. The FDA regulatory process demanded that an end point in a clinical trial not be selected for the convenience of a single company or academic group but rather reflect a broadly based consensus grounded in evidence that the measures under consideration are reliable, valid, and clinically meaningful. In essence, the situation was similar to the classic prisoner's dilemma in that no one could receive approval for any drug until everyone first made a concession and mutually cooperated to identify a single consensus outcome measure (Marder & Fenton 2004).

There were other significant barriers to drug development for cognition in schizophrenia. For example, there was no consensus regarding the appropriate clinical trial design to evaluate drugs for treating cognitive deficits. Issues such as subject-selection criteria, phase of illness, length of the trials, and ways to manage potential drug-drug interactions were unresolved. Another obstacle was the lack of consensus regarding the best approaches for identifying promising compounds. A consensus regarding appropriate neuropharmacological targets and animal models was needed to guide screening of compounds at the preclinical stage.

The Role of NIMH in Establishing Consensus in Key Areas

In essence, there was a logjam. Cognition in schizophrenia was increasingly viewed as a serious public health problem by NIMH and clinicians owing to its relationships to outcome and its distinctiveness from psychotic symptoms. In addition, the pharmaceutical industry had considerable interest in discovering and developing cognition-enhancing drugs. However, there were obstacles that effectively prohibited any drug from receiving FDA approval. In the absence of a clear pathway for FDA approval, the pharmaceutical industry was understandably unwilling to make a substantial investment in cognition-enhancing agents for schizophrenia.

As a way to unblock this logjam, NIMH used its convening authority and launched MATRICS (Measurement and Treatment Research to Improve Cognition in Schizophrenia). This initiative, awarded through a competitive application process to the University of California at Los Angeles, was charged with developing a mechanism by which cognition-enhancing drugs for schizophrenia could be marketed for that purpose. The goal of MATRICS was to build a pathway that would lead to drug approval.

MATRICS: Measurement and Treatment Research to Improve Cognition in Schizophrenia

The mandate of MATRICS was to hold consensus meetings to decide on the methods and measures that would be used to evaluate promising new drugs so they could receive approval for cognition enhancement in schizophrenia. The expectation was that once a pathway to drug approval was constructed, the pharmaceutical industry would travel it. MATRICS sponsored consensus meetings that brought together representatives of industry, academia, and government to address the key barriers.

DECISIONS FROM NIMH-MATRICS REGARDING MEASUREMENT AND CLINICAL TRIAL DESIGN

Approaches to Reaching Consensus

The development of a consensus involved a complex process that started with selecting individuals representing divergent interests to be part of the consensus-building process. In addition, consensus building also required managing potential sources of bias such as firmly held academic positions or financial conflicts of interest. In MATRICS, success in reaching consensus was not defined by an outcome in which all participants fully agreed with each decision from the group's deliberations. Instead, consensus

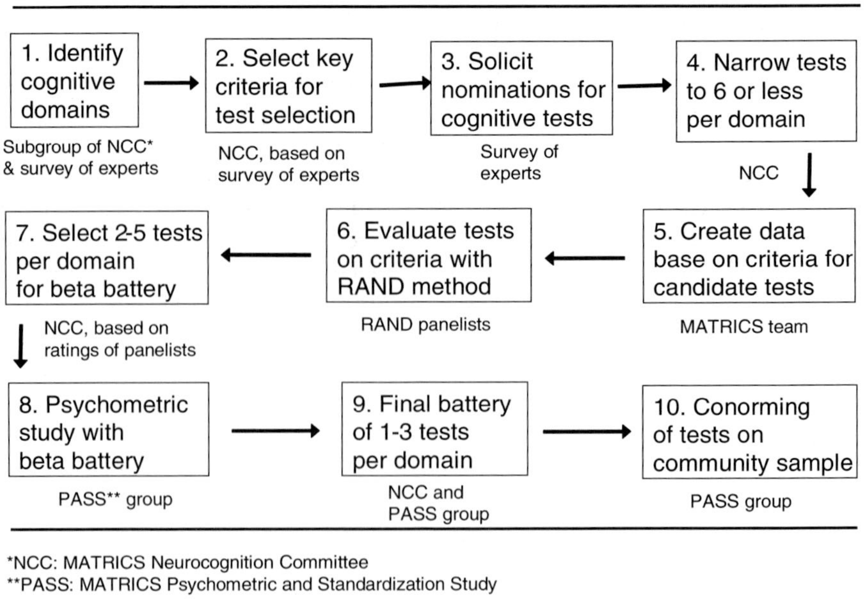

Figure 2

Steps to NIMH-MATRICS Consensus Cognitive Battery.

was defined by success in creating a process that participants agreed was fair and grounded in the best-available scientific data (Marder & Fenton 2004). In addition to a series of large, broad-based consensus meetings, the MATRICS group approached the challenge of developing a consensus cognitive battery by adopting a structured consensus-building process developed by the RAND Corporation (Fitch et al. 2001). Arriving at a consensus battery involved several steps that are described briefly below and shown in **Figure 2**.

Measurement of Cognition for Clinical Trials: MATRICS Consensus Cognitive Battery

Because the lack of a consensus cognitive battery was a serious obstacle for the development of new drugs, an essential product of the NIMH-MATRICS Initiative was a consensus cognitive battery that would provide a standard outcome measure for all clinical trials of cognition-enhancing drugs for schizophrenia. To select the consensus cognitive battery, a thorough multistep process was generated and then carried out with oversight from the MATRICS Neurocognition Committee. **Figure 2** depicts the steps in sequence and the relevant groups responsible for each step. Each step is fully described elsewhere (Green et al. 2004b, Nuechterlein & Green 2006), and a brief summary is provided here.

Step one involved the identification of cognitive domains. There was a clear message from the MATRICS consensus meetings that the battery should assess cognition at the level of individual cognitive domains, as opposed to only a cognitive summary score. Therefore, it was first necessary to determine which cognitive domains should be represented in the MATRICS battery. Although there is a large literature on the nature of cognitive deficits in schizophrenia, there had never been any consensus on how to divide the cognitive deficits into key domains. Hence, one task for MATRICS was to form a group to carefully review the literature and recommend key separable cognitive domains (Nuechterlein et al. 2004). Based on the literature review and subsequent discussions at a consensus meeting, the following domains were selected for the consensus cognitive battery: speed of processing, attention/vigilance, working memory, verbal learning, visual learning, reasoning and problem solving, and social cognition.

Step two involved the selection of key criteria for test selection. Based on interviews with experts about the relative importance of various criteria (Kern et al. 2004) and subsequent discussion at a consensus conference, four key criteria were selected (Green et al. 2004b).

1. *High test-retest reliability.* Test-retest reliability was the highest rated test criterion among the surveyed experts as this property is critical for detecting changes with treatment (Kern et al. 2004, Kraemer 1991).
2. *High utility as a repeated measure.* It was considered desirable to select measures that do not have a substantial practice effect, or if they do, the degree of improvement in performance with repeated administrations is not so large that performance at follow-up approaches ceiling and has reduced variability.
3. *Demonstrated relationship to functional outcome.* For evaluating candidate cognitive tests, priority was given to tests that demonstrated a relationship to some aspect of functional outcome (e.g., work and social outcome, independent living).
4. *Demonstrated tolerability and practicality.* Tolerability refers to the view of the test from the examinee's perspective, including the length of the test, unusual degree of difficulty, or excessive repetitiveness. Practicality refers to the view of the test from the administrator's perspective, including ease of test set-up, staff training, administration, and scoring.

Steps three and four involved the narrowing of a large number of nominated tests to a more tractable (n = 36) number that could be evaluated through a consensus method, known as the RAND Panel method (shown in steps five and six). For the RAND Panel method (Fitch et al. 2001), a large and comprehensive database for each of the 36 tests was created for each of the criteria of test selection (test-retest reliability, utility as a repeated measure, relationship to functional outcome, and practicality/tolerability). The information was sorted, tabulated, and compiled into a large database (available at **http://www.matrics.ucla.edu**). This comprehensive review constituted the database for rankings at the RAND Panel. The RAND Panel comprised 14 panelists of diverse areas of expertise. The RAND panelists independently examined the database compiled in step five and rated each candidate test on each of the essential criteria. Ratings were made independently prior to an in-person meeting, and any discrepancies were resolved following discussion at the meeting. Based on ratings from the RAND Panel, the MATRICS Neurocognition Committee selected 20 tests for the beta version of the battery, with 2–5 tests per cognitive domain (step seven).

MCCB: MATRICS Consensus Cognitive Battery

The remaining steps required a new data collection. MATRICS sponsored a five-site Psychometrics and Standardization Study (MATRICS-PASS) that was conducted in two phases. The first phase (step eight) directly compared the tests in the beta version of the battery on their psychometric properties (including test-retest and practice effects), relationships to functional outcome, and practicality/tolerability. This psychometric study included 176 schizophrenia patients tested at baseline and at a four-week follow-up. Based on the results from this study, the MATRICS Neurocognition Committee carefully compared tests within each cognitive domain and voted their ranking of tests (step nine). Based on this review of data from MATRICS-PASS, the Committee selected the tests that comprise the MATRICS Consensus Cognitive Battery (MCCB) (**Table 2**).

The second phase of MATRICS-PASS involved 300 standardization subjects tested at

Table 2 MATRICS Consensus Cognitive Battery

Domain	Test
Speed of processing	Brief Assessment of Cognition in Schizophrenia (BACS)—Symbol Coding Trail Making A
	Category Fluency (Animal Naming)
	Trail Making A
Attention/vigilance	Continuous Performance Test—Identical Pairs
Working memory (nonverbal)	Wechsler Memory Scale (WMS)-III—Spatial Span
Working memory (verbal)	University of Maryland—Letter-Number Span
Verbal learning	Hopkins Verbal Learning Test—Revised
Visual learning	Brief Visuospatial Memory Test—Revised
Reasoning and problem solving	Neuropsychological Assessment Battery (NAB)—Mazes
Social cognition	Mayer-Salovey-Caruso Emotional Intelligence Test (MSCEIT)—Managing Emotions

the same five sites that were drawn from the community through survey-sampling methods and stratified on age, gender, and education (step ten). These data were used to establish a common metric for each of the individual tests, for the seven cognitive domains, and for the overall cognition composite score. Essentially, this final step provided conorming of the tests in the final battery, and it served as the basis for the computerized scoring system for the MCCB.

How to Establish Meaningfulness in Outcomes: The Use of Coprimary Measures

One of the most complicated, and unexpected, questions in this process was whether improvement of cognition by itself should be sufficient for FDA approval. On the surface, it might appear that if a drug improves cognition, it deserves approval for cognition improvement. The FDA, however, sometimes requires improvements in two types of clinical trial outcomes for approval, one of which is considered to be functionally meaningful. Such a requirement for improvement on two types of measures is referred to as a requirement for coprimary end points. A coprimary requirement occurs for dementia drugs in which treatment-related effects need to be observed on a cognitive measure and also a global measure of functioning.

On the one hand, improvement on a well-developed cognitive performance measure is probably the most reliable and sensitive way to determine whether a drug improves cognition. On the other hand, small but statistically significant changes on cognitive performance measures alone may not be sufficient evidence of patient improvement for drug approval. In other words, it may have insufficient face validity. Although face validity carries little weight in psychological science, it is a consideration for drug approval. This importance stems from a concern about the acceptance of a new drug by patients and prescribing clinicians. In addition, the FDA understandably wants to justify its approval decisions with easily understood evidence of patient improvement. Based on these considerations, the FDA indicated that approval of a new cognition-enhancing drug for schizophrenia would require a functionally meaningful coprimary measure. So, where does one find such a measure?

One possible coprimary measure would be an assessment of community functioning. However, change in community status, such as work and social outcome, is a distant target and having such a requirement would set a high bar for approval for several reasons. For example, we know that intervening variables (e.g., social cognition) act between measures of cognition and functional outcome (Brekke et al. 2005, Sergi et al. 2006,

Vauth et al. 2004). These intervening variables would make it more difficult to see the functional benefits of cognition-enhancing effects because any improvements would need to influence successive steps. Along these lines, improvements in cognition would be expected to take a long time to translate into functional improvements, based on the delays in improved functioning seen for intensive psychosocial interventions (Brekke et al. 1997). In addition, any changes in daily functioning would depend on nonbiological factors that are typically well beyond the control of clinical trial studies, including the availability of psychosocial rehabilitation, social support networks, local employment rates, and training opportunities. Hence, there was concern that a requirement for changes in community status as a coprimary outcome variable may be too stringent and would lead to the failure of drugs to gain approval, even if they improve cognitive performance measures. Alternative coprimary measures that might change more directly with cognitive improvement include standardized tests of functional capacity or interview-based assessments of cognition.

Functional capacity was mentioned above and refers to an individual's capacity for performing key tasks of daily living. It can be measured with tests that assess whether a person can maintain a social conversation, prepare a meal, take public transportation, or manage their medications (Bellack et al. 1994, McKibbin et al. 2004). Good performance on a measure of functional capacity does not mean that a person will perform the tasks in the community, but it does mean that the person could perform the task in the community if he or she had the opportunity and the willingness. Because performance on measures of functional capacity do not depend on social and community factors, they are likely to occur more closely in time with treatment-related changes in underlying cognition compared with changes in community functioning.

The correlations between functional capacity measures and cognitive performance are fairly consistent and suggest a good correspondence between the underlying cognitive skills and the simulated activities (Addington & Addington 1999, Bellack et al. 1994, Klapow et al. 1997). There are fewer data to link functional capacity to community functioning. A recent study showed that measures of functional capacity act as mediating variables between cognitive performance and outcome in schizophrenia (Bowie et al. 2006), similar to the pattern mentioned above for social cognition. Hence, measures of functional capacity appear to be appropriate for clinical trials of cognition-enhancing drugs in schizophrenia because of their face validity and their pattern of correlations with cognitive performance and functional outcome.

Another possible avenue for coprimary measures is to consider interview-based assessments of cognitive abilities. This approach presents a challenge because most of the data show that individuals (healthy subjects as well as patients) are poor at estimating their own performance abilities (Dunning et al. 2004, Mortiz et al. 2004). Some recent cognitive assessment interviews have been developed for use with psychotic patients and their caregivers that might have advantages over previously used assessments. Such measures are now starting to be evaluated in studies of schizophrenia (Keefe et al. 2006a).

Figure 3 illustrates some of the concepts mentioned above (Green et al. 2004a). The coprimary measures being considered represent a middle ground in that they are presumed to be closer to the biological processes affected by drugs than community status, but also more proximal to community functioning than the performance measures.

Finding a suitable indicator that is functionally meaningful remains a huge challenge for approving drugs for cognition in schizophrenia. This area presents a daunting range of conceptual, measurement, and practical challenges (Bellack et al. 2006). To help address these challenges, NIMH has launched a new program to develop and validate measures of functioning that can be used in the

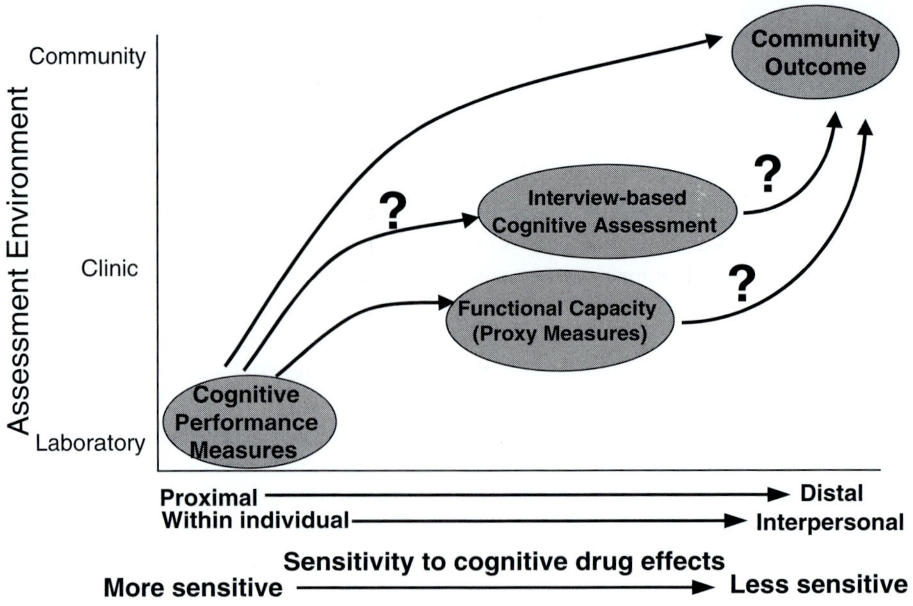

Figure 3

Key linkages for cognition and functional outcome. The *x* axis represents a dimension running from proximal, within-subject factors to distal, social factors. The dimension also reflects differences in how sensitive the outcome measure might be to cognition-enhancing effects of drugs. The *y* axis represents locations of assessments ranging from less to more ecological (e.g., the cognitive-performance laboratory to the community). Arrows on the figure show well-supported linkages, and arrows with question marks are those that are not clearly established.

context of clinical trials with psychotic patients. This will be an area of intense activity over the next several years.

NEXT STEPS: CLINICAL TRIALS AND CONSENSUS

The NIMH-MATRICS Initiative generated a flurry of activities that were stimulated by the initial consensus meetings. A clinical trials network has been launched by NIMH, essentially to field-test the products of MATRICS in actual trials. Other follow-up activities have consisted of consensus meetings on a variety of specific topics, including negative symptoms of schizophrenia, social cognition in schizophrenia, standardization and psychometrics of cognitive neuroscience measures, and the development and validation of coprimary measures for clinical trials. The clinical trial network and one example of a follow-up consensus process (negative symptoms) are briefly described here.

Pilot Clinical Trial Network

As a way to utilize the products of MATRICS, the NIMH established a clinical trials network called Treatment Units for Research on Neurocognition and Schizophrenia (TURNS). The network was awarded through a competitive application process. TURNS is a network of seven research sites located at academic centers that is dedicated to identifying, obtaining, and testing the efficacy of new drugs to improve cognition in schizophrenia. This network will validate the clinical trial methodology recommended by MATRICS (Buchanan et al. 2005) by conducting two or three NIMH-supported trials. The trials will be proof-of-concept studies and will be modest in size (e.g., 40–50 subjects per group). One or two additional pharmacodynamic/pharmacokinetic studies will also be conducted for drugs that are earlier in development. Pharmaceutical and biotechnology companies nominate drugs that they think have promise for cognition enhancement based on available data (typically both preclinical and limited human data). TURNS investigators decide which compounds to study based on careful review of the materials submitted by the companies. After four years of NIMH support, the network should be self-sufficient with federal, foundation, or industry support for subsequent trials.

The compounds nominated for study in the TURNS network act on many of the neuropharmacological targets listed in **Table 1**, including alpha-7 nicotinic, D1, GABA A, and glycine. The first drug to be evaluated in TURNS is expected to be an ampakine (a positive modulator of the glutamate AMPA receptor). Interest in drugs that affect the AMPA receptor grows out of theoretical work on the basis of long-term memory and encouraging preclinical data from animal models of learning (Hampson et al. 1998, Staubli et al. 1994). A small preliminary study with a weaker ampakine administered to schizophrenia patients yielded generally encouraging results but was limited by its small sample size (Goff et al. 2001). Hence, TURNS will provide a more rigorous test (with a larger study and more potent compound) of an ampakine in schizophrenia.

TURNS was designed to be a fast track for evaluating potentially efficacious compounds. Such standing networks for clinical trials are common for testing drugs in other areas of medicine but are not typical for psychiatric disorders. Studies in psychiatry typically use a less efficient system in which each trial has its own particular set of performance sites. The first TURNS trials began in the fall of 2006.

TURNS: Treatment Units for Research on Neurocognition and Schizophrenia

Negative Symptoms in Schizophrenia

Negative symptoms in schizophrenia include features such as blunted affect, anhedonia, asociality, and reduction in speech. Typically the negative symptoms form two different clusters of symptoms: one for diminished expression (e.g., reduced facial and verbal expressivity and reduced verbal outcome) and another for anhedonia and asociality (e.g., decreased social engagement, diminished interest) (Blanchard & Cohen 2006). In some respects, negative symptoms and cognitive impairment in schizophrenia are similar: They are both relatively unresponsive to the current medications, and they are both related to functional outcome. They also have modest overlap, usually in the range of 15% shared variance. The two constructs differ in one key respect: Negative symptoms are an accepted clinical target and part of the definition of schizophrenia. But similar to cognition, negative symptoms are considered to be an unmet need for the illness that has not responded adequately to existing interventions, and there is no approved drug for negative symptoms.

To stimulate drug development for negative symptoms in schizophrenia, many of the same steps need to be taken as described above for cognitive impairment. For example, there would need to be consensus on the definition of negative symptoms, the measure of negative symptoms that would serve as an end point in clinical trials, and the type of trial design (e.g., subject selection, phase of illness, length of trial, drug interactions). The FDA has not taken a position on whether a functional coprimary measure will be required for a drug to receive a claim for treatment for negative symptoms (Bellack et al. 2006, Laughren & Levin 2006), and it is seeking addition input on this question. From the FDA's perspective, the need for a coprimary measure is less obvious than it was for cognition because negative symptoms are an accepted and readily observed feature of schizophrenia. A reduction in negative symptoms would have more face validity and improvement in cognitive performance.

To address these issues, a series of meetings following from MATRICS were held to reach consensus on some of these issues (Kirkpatrick

2006). The resulting discussions were recently published in a special issue of *Schizophrenia Bulletin* (volume 32, issue 2). Aside from definitional issues, this effort has led to the development and field-testing of a new scale for negative symptoms, one designed to detect change in clinical trials. Similar to the situation with cognition, the expectation is that once a pathway for FDA approval is worked out, it will attract interest and investment from the pharmaceutical industry.

Integration with Psychosocial Interventions

This review discusses how cognition in schizophrenia has become an accepted target for psychopharmacological intervention. Because the focus of this chapter is on drug development, nonpharmacological interventions for cognition (such as cognitive remediation) are not mentioned. This omission should not be viewed as dualistic thinking or as a preference of one approach versus another. On the contrary, nonpharmacological intervention has been a recurring topic in the context of drug development for cognition. One reason is that recent efforts to improve cognition in schizophrenia through retraining methods have shown promise (Kurtz et al. 2001, Twamley et al. 2003, Wexler & Bell 2005). In fact, retraining methods are presently the only reliable way we have to improve cognitive performance in schizophrenia. A second reason is that, so far, the primary evidence for cognitive improvement leading to functional benefits comes from nonpharmacological approaches. For example, two groups have recently reported that cognitive retraining coupled with standard vocational rehabilitation yielded greater benefits than vocational rehabilitation alone (McGurk et al. 2005, Wexler & Bell 2005).

A final reason for considering nonpharmacological interventions in the context of drug development is the growing realization that cognition-enhancing drugs will do little good if they act in isolation. To see the full effects of drug treatments, it is likely patients will need to be actively engaged in learning or training. By analogy, the performance-enhancing drugs at the root of professional sports scandals only provide benefits to the user in the context of rigorous physical exercise and training. Similarly, the benefits of cognition-enhancing drugs likely will be seen in the context of mental exercise and training. Although it is expected that the cognition-enhancing effects of drugs will be seen on highly reliable cognition-performance measures, translation of these benefits to community functioning may require an active training and learning environment (e.g., psychosocial rehabilitation, cognitive remediation). Hence, one of the unforeseen benefits of the recent concentration on developing new drugs for cognition is likely to be a renewed focus on nonpharmacological approaches that will serve as complementary interventions.

SUMMARY

This review summarizes several recent developments in the area of cognition in schizophrenia and activities designed to stimulate the development of new drugs to improve cognition. Cognitive impairment in schizophrenia is common, it is a core feature of the illness, and it is a determinant of the daily functioning of patients. There has been strong interest in finding treatments to improve cognition in schizophrenia, but before a drug could be approved for this purpose, it was first necessary to achieve consensus on several key questions, including the measurements and methods that would be used in clinical trials. The NIMH launched one initiative to address obstacles to drug approval and to identify promising neuropharmacological targets (MATRICS), and it introduced a clinical trial network (TURNS) to field-test the products of MATRICS in trials in this area. Other initiatives are underway for other clinical targets, including negative symptoms. This chapter describes how developments in experimental psychopathology have moved and expanded the view of cognition in schizophrenia to be seen as a separate aspect of illness from clinical symptoms, a determinant of functional outcome, a target for intervention, a focus of public health concerns, and finally an area of drug development.

LITERATURE CITED

Addington J, Addington D. 1999. Neurocognitive and social functioning in schizophrenia. *Schizophr. Bull.* 25:173–82

Altshuler LL, Ventura J, van Gorp WG, Green MF, Theberge DC, Mintz J. 2004. Neurocognitive function in clinically stable men with bipolar I disorder or schizophrenia and normal control subjects. *Biol. Psychiatry* 56:560–69

Asarnow RF, Nuechterlein KH, Subotnik KL, Fogelson D, Torquato R, et al. 2002. Neurocognitive impairments in nonpsychotic parents of children with schizophrenia and attention deficit hyperactivity disorder: the UCLA Family Study. *Arch. Gen. Psychiatry* 59:1053–60

Bellack AS, Green MF, Cook JA, Fenton W, Harvey PD, et al. 2006. Assessment of community functioning in people with schizophrenia and other severe mental illnesses: a white paper based on an NIMH-sponsored workshop. *Schizophr. Bull.* In press

Bellack AS, Sayers M, Mueser K, Bennett M. 1994. Evaluation of social problem solving in schizophrenia. *J. Abnorm. Psychol.* 103:371–78

Bilder RM, Goldman RS, Robinson D, Reiter G, Bell L, et al. 2000. Neuropsychology of first-episode schizophrenia: initial characterization and clinical correlates. *Am. J. Psychiatry* 157:549–59

Blanchard JJ, Cohen AS. 2006. The structure of negative symptoms within schizophrenia: implications for assessment. *Schizophr. Bull.* 32:238–45

Bowie CR, Reichenberg A, Patterson TL, Heaton RK, Harvey PD. 2006. Determinants of real-world functional performance in schizophrenia subjects: correlations with cognition, functional capacity, and symptoms. *Am. J. Psychiatry* 163:418–25

Braff D. 1993. Information processing and attention dysfunctions in schizophrenia. *Schizophr. Bull.* 19:233–59

Brekke JS, Kay DD, Kee KS, Green MF. 2005. Biosocial pathways to functional outcome in schizophrenia. *Schizophr. Res.* 80:213–25

Brekke JS, Long JD, Nesbitt N, Sobel E. 1997. The impact of service characteristics from community support programs for persons with schizophrenia: a growth curve analysis. *J. Consult. Clin. Psychol.* 65:464–75

Bryson G, Bell MD. 2003. Initial and final work performance in schizophrenia: cognitive and symptom predictors. *J. Nerv. Mental Dis.* 191:87–92

Buchanan RW, Davis M, Goff D, Green MF, Keefe RSE, et al. 2005. A summary of the FDA-NIMH-MATRICS workshop on clinical trial design for neurocognitive drugs for schizophrenia. *Schizophr. Bull.* 31:5–19

Cannon TD, Eyler-Zorrilla L, Shtasel D, Gur RC, Marco EJ, et al. 1994. Neuropsychological functioning in siblings discordant for schizophrenia and healthy volunteers. *Arch. Gen. Psychiatry* 51:651–61

Cannon TD, Huttunen MO, Lonnqvist J, Tuulio-Henriksson A, Pirkola T, et al. 2000. The inheritance of neuropsychological dysfunction in twins discordant for schizophrenia. *Am. J. Hum. Genet.* 67:369–82

Carpenter WT, Gold JM. 2002. Another view of therapy for cognition in schizophrenia. *Biol. Psychiatry* 51:969–71

Cornblatt B, Lenzenweger MF, Dworkin R, Erlenmeyer-Kimling L. 1992. Childhood attentional dysfunction predicts social deficits in unaffected adults at risk for schizophrenia. *Br. J. Psychiatry* 161:59–64

Cornblatt B, Obuchowski M, Roberts S, Pollack S, Erlenmeyer-Kimling L. 1999. Cognitive and behavioral precursors of schizophrenia. *Dev. Psychopathol.* 11:487–508

Coyle JT, Tsai G. 2004. The NMDA receptor glycine modulatory site: a therapeutic target for improving cognition and reducing negative symptoms in schizophrenia. *Psychopharmacology* 174:32–38

Davidson M, Reichenberg A, Rabinowitz J, Weiser M, Kaplan Z, Mark M. 1999. Behavioral and intellectual markers for schizophrenia in apparently healthy male adolescents. *Am. J. Psychiatry* 156:1328–35

Dickerson F, Boronow JJ, Ringel N, Parente F. 1999. Social functioning and neurocognitive deficits in outpatients with schizophrenia: a 2-year follow-up. *Schizophr. Res.* 37:13–20

Dickerson FB, Boronow JJ, Stallings CR, Origoni AE, Cole S, Yolken RH. 2004. Association between cognitive functioning and employment status of persons with bipolar disorder. *Psychiatr. Serv.* 55:54–58

Dunning D, Heath C, Suls JM. 2004. Flawed self-assessment: implications for health, education, and the workplace. *Psychol. Sci. Public Interest* 5:69–106

Erickson SK, Schwarzkopf SB, Palumbo D, Badgley-Fleeman J, Smirnow AM, Light GA. 2005. Efficacy and tolerability of low-dose donepezil in schizophrenia. *Clin. Neuropharmacol.* 28:179–84

Evans JD, Heaton RK, Paulsen JS, McAdams LA, Heaton SC, Jeste DV. 1999. Schizoaffective disorder: a form of schizophrenia or affective disorder? *J. Clin. Psychiatry* 60:874–82

Finkelstein JRJ, Cannon TD, Gur RE, Gur RC, Moberg P. 1997. Attentional dysfunctions in neuroleptic-naive and neuroleptic-withdrawn schizophrenic patients and their siblings. *J. Abnorm. Psychol.* 106:203–12

Fitch K, Bernstein SJ, Aguilar MD, Burnand B, LaCalle JR, et al. 2001. *The RAND/UCLA Appropriateness Users Manual.* Santa Monica, CA: RAND Inst.

Fleck DE, Sax KW, Strakowski SM. 2001. Reaction time measures of sustained attention differentiate bipolar disorder from schizophrenia. *Schizophr. Res.* 52:251–59

Freudenreich O, Herz L, Deckersbach T, Evins AE, Henderson DC, et al. 2005. Added donepezil for stable schizophrenia: a double-blind, placebo-controlled trial. *Psychopharmacology* 181:358–63

Friedman JI, Adler DN, Howanitz E, Harvey PD, Brenner G, et al. 2002a. A double blind placebo controlled trial of donepezil adjunctive treatment to risperidone for the cognitive impairment of schizophrenia. *Biol. Psychiatry* 51:349–57

Friedman JI, Harvey PD, McGurk SR, White L, Parrella M, et al. 2002b. Correlates of change in functional status of institutionalized geriatric schizophrenic patients: focus on medical comorbidity. *Am. J. Psychiatry* 159:1388–94

Goff DC, Leahy L, Berman I, Posever T, Herz L, et al. 2001. A placebo-controlled pilot study of the ampakine CX516 added to clozapine in schizophrenia. *J. Clin. Psychopharmacol.* 21:484–87

Gold JM. 2004. Cognitive deficits as treatment targets in schizophrenia. *Schizophr. Res.* 72:21–28

Gold JM, Goldberg RW, McNary SW, Dixon L, Lehman AF. 2002. Cognitive correlates of job tenure among patients with severe mental illness. *Am. J. Psychiatry* 159:1395–401

Gold JM, Green MF. 2004. Neurocognition in schizophrenia. In *Comprehensive Textbook of Psychiatry*, ed. BJ Sadock, VA Sadock, pp. 1436–48. Baltimore, MD: Lippincott, Williams & Wilkins

Goldberg TE, Gold JM, Greenberg R, Griffin S. 1993. Contrasts between patients with affective disorders and patients with schizophrenia on a neuropsychological test battery. *Am. J. Psychiatry* 150:1355–62
Goldberg TE, Ragland JD, Torrey EF, Gold JM, Bigelow LB, Weinberger DR. 1990. Neuropsychological assessment of monozygotic twins discordant for schizophrenia. *Arch. Gen. Psychiatry* 47:1066–72
Goldman-Rakic PS, Castner SA, Svensson TS, Siever LJ, Williams GV. 2004. Targeting the dopamine D1 receptor in schizophrenia: insights for cognitive dysfunction. *Psychopharmacology* 174:3–16
Green MF. 1996. What are the functional consequences of neurocognitive deficits in schizophrenia? *Am. J. Psychiatry* 153:321–30
Green MF, Kern RS, Braff DL, Mintz J. 2000. Neurocognitive deficits and functional outcome in schizophrenia: Are we measuring the "right stuff"? *Schizophr. Bull.* 26:119–36
Green MF, Kern RS, Heaton RK. 2004a. Longitudinal studies of cognition and functional outcome in schizophrenia: implications for MATRICS. *Schizophr. Res.* 72:41–51
Green MF, Marder SR, Glynn SM, McGurk SR, Wirshing WC, et al. 2002. The neurocognitive effects of low-dose haloperidol: a two-year comparison with risperidone. *Biol. Psychiatry* 51:972–78
Green MF, Nuechterlein KH, Breitmeyer B. 1997. Backward masking performance in unaffected siblings of schizophrenia patients: evidence for a vulnerability indicator. *Arch. Gen. Psychiatry* 54:465–72
Green MF, Nuechterlein KH, Gold JM, Barch DM, Cohen J, et al. 2004b. Approaching a consensus cognitive battery for clinical trials in schizophrenia: the NIMH-MATRICS conference to select cognitive domains and test criteria. *Biol. Psychiatry* 56:301–7
Green MF, Olivier B, Crawley JN, Penn DL, Silverstein S. 2005. Social cognition in schizophrenia: recommendations from the MATRICS New Approaches Conference. *Schizophr. Bull.* 31:882–87
Hampson RE, Rogers G, Lynch G, Deadwyler SA. 1998. Facilitative effects of the ampakine CX516 on short-term memory in rats: enhancement of delayed-nonmatch-to-sample performance. *J. Neurosci.* 18:2740–47
Harvey PD, Keefe RSE. 2001. Studies of the cognitive change in patients with schizophrenia following novel antipsychotic treatment. *Am. J. Psychiatry* 158:176–84
Heaton R, Paulsen JS, McAdams LA, Kuck J, Zisook S, et al. 1994. Neuropsychological deficits in schizophrenics: relationship to age, chronicity, and dementia. *Arch. Gen. Psychiatry* 51:469–76
Hegarty JD, Baldessarini RJ, Tohen M, Waternaux C, Oepen G. 1994. One hundred years of schizophrenia: a meta-analysis of the outcome literature. *Am. J. Psychiatry* 151:1409–16
Heinrichs RW, Zakzanis KK. 1998. Neurocognitive deficit in schizophrenia: a quantitative review of the evidence. *Neuropsychology* 12:426–45
Helgason L. 1990. Twenty years' follow-up of first psychiatric presentation for schizophrenia: What could have been prevented? *Acta Psychiatr. Scand.* 81:231–35
Heydebrand G, Weiser M, Rabinowitz J, Hoff AL, DeLisi LE, Csernansky JG. 2004. Correlates of cognitive deficits in first episode schizophrenia. *Schizophr. Res.* 68:1–9
Keefe RSE, Poe M, Walker TM, Kang JW, Harvey PD. 2006a. The Schizophrenia Cognition Rating Scale: an interview-based assessment and its relationship to cognition, real-world functioning, and functional capacity. *Am. J. Psychiatry* 163:426–32
Keefe RSE, Young CA, Rock SL, Purdon SE, Gold JM, Breier A. 2006b. One-year double-blind study of the neurocognitive efficacy of olanzapine, risperidone, and haloperidol in schizophrenia. *Schizophr. Res.* 81:1–15

Kern RS, Green MF, Nuechterlein KH, Deng BH. 2004. NIMH-MATRICS survey on assessment of neurocognition in schizophrenia. *Schizophr. Res.* 72:11–19

Kirkpatrick B. 2006. Editor's introduction: theme issue on negative symptoms? *Schizophr. Bull.* 32:212–13

Klapow JC, Evans J, Patterson TL, Heaton RK, Koch WL, Jeste DV. 1997. Direct assessment of functional status in older patients with schizophrenia. *Am. J. Psychiatry* 154:1022–24

Kraemer HC. 1991. To increase power without increasing sample size. *Psychopharmacol. Bull.* 27:217–24

Kremen WS, Seidman J, Pepple JR, Lyons MJ, Tsuang MT, Faraone SV. 1994. Neuropsychological risk indicators for schizophrenia: a review of family studies. *Schizophr. Bull.* 20:103–19

Kremen WS, Seidman LJ, Faraone SV, Toomey R, Tsuang MT. 2000. The paradox of normal neuropsychological function in schizophrenia. *J. Abnorm. Psychol.* 109:743–52

Kurtz MM, Moberg PJ, Gur RC, Gur RE. 2001. Approaches to cognitive remediation of neuropsychological deficits in schizophrenia: a review and meta-analysis. *Neuropsychol. Rev.* 11:197–210

Laes JR, Sponheim SR. 2006. Does cognition predict community function only in schizophrenia? A study of schizophrenia patients, bipolar affective disorder patients, and community control subjects. *Schizophr. Res.* 84:121–31

Laughren T, Levin R. 2006. Food and Drug Administration perspective on negative symptoms in schizophrenia as a target for a drug treatment claim. *Schizophr. Bull.* 32:220–22

Laughren TP. 2003. Comorbid mood disorders and medical illness: a Food and Drug Administration perspective. *Biol. Psychiatry* 54:195–99

Marder SR, Fenton WS. 2004. Measurement and treatment research to improve cognition in schizophrenia: NIMH MATRICS initiative to support the development of agents for improving cognition in schizophrenia. *Schizophr. Res.* 72:5–10

Martin LF, Kem WR, Freedman R. 2004. α-7 nicotinic receptor agonists: potential new candidates for the treatment of schizophrenia. *Psychopharmacology* 174:54–64

Martínez-Arán A, Vieta E, Colom F, Torrent C, Sánchez-Moreno J, et al. 2004. Cognitive impairment in euthymic bipolar patients: implications for clinical and functional outcome. *Bipolar Disord.* 6:224–32

McGurk SR, Mueser KT, Pascaris A. 2005. Cognitive training and supported employment for persons with severe mental illness: one-year results from a randomized controlled trial. *Schizophr. Bull.* 31:898–909

McKibbin CL, Brekke JS, Sires D, Jeste DV, Patterson TL. 2004. Direct assessment of functional abilities: relevance to persons with schizophrenia. *Schizophr. Res.* 72:53–67

Miller LS, Swanson-Green T, Moses JA, Faustman WO. 1996. Comparison of cognitive performance in RDC-diagnosed schizoaffective and schizophrenic patients with the Luria-Nebraska neuropsychological battery. *J. Psychiatr. Res.* 30:277–82

Mohamed S, Paulsen JS, O'Leary DS, Arndt S, Andreasen NC. 1999. Generalized cognitive deficits in schizophrenia. *Am. J. Psychiatry* 156:749–54

Moritz DJ, Kasl SV, Berkman LF. 1995. Cognitive functioning and the incidence of limitations in activities of daily living in an elderly community sample. *Am. J. Epidemiol.* 141:41–49

Mortiz S, Ferahli S, Naber D. 2004. Memory and attention performance in psychiatric patients: lack of correspondence between clinician-rated and patient-rated functioning with neuropsychological test results. *J. Int. Neuropsychol. Soc.* 10:623–33

Murray CJL, Lopez AD, eds. 1996. *The Global Burden of Disease*. Boston, MA: Harvard School Public Health

Niendam TA, Bearden CE, Rosso IM, Sanchez LE, Hadley T, et al. 2003. A prospective study of childhood neurocognitive functioning in schizophrenic patients and their siblings. *Am. J. Psychiatry* 160:2060–62

Nieuwenstein MR, Aleman A, de Haan EHF. 2001. Relationship between symptom dimensions and neurocognitive functioning in schizophrenia: a meta-analysis of WCST and CPT studies. *J. Psychiatr. Res.* 35:119–25

Nuechterlein KH. 1983. Signal detection in vigilance tasks and behavioral attributes among offspring of schizophrenic mothers and among hyperactive children. *J. Abnorm. Psychol.* 92:4–28

Nuechterlein KH, Asarnow RF, Subotnik KL, Fogelson DL, Ventura J, et al. 1998. Neurocognitive vulnerability factors for schizophrenia: convergence across genetic risk studies and longitudinal trait/state studies. In *Origins and Development of Schizophrenia: Advances in Experimental Psychopathology*, ed. MF Lenzenweger, RH Dworkin, pp. 299–327. Washington, DC: Am. Psychol. Assoc.

Nuechterlein KH, Barch DM, Gold JM, Goldberg TE, Green MF, Heaton RK. 2004. Identification of separable cognitive factors in schizophrenia. *Schizophr. Res.* 72:29–39

Nuechterlein KH, Dawson ME, Green MF. 1994. Information-processing abnormalities as neuropsychological vulnerability indicators for schizophrenia. *Acta Psychiatr. Scand.* 90:71–79

Nuechterlein KH, Green MF. 2006. *MATRICS Consensus Cognitive Battery*. Los Angeles, CA: MATRICS Assessment

Palmer BW, Heaton RK, Paulsen JS, Kuck J, Braff D, et al. 1997. Is it possible to be schizophrenic yet neuropsychologically normal? *Neuropsychology* 11:437–46

Penn DL, Corrigan PW, Bentall RP, Racenstein JM, Newman L. 1997. Social cognition in schizophrenia. *Psychol. Bull.* 121:114–32

Perry W, Braff DL. 1994. Information-processing deficits and thought disorder in schizophrenia. *Am. J. Psychiatry* 151:363–67

Purdon SE, Jones BDW, Stip E, Labelle A, Addington D, et al. 2000. Neuropsychological change in early phase schizophrenia during 12 months of treatment with olanzapine, risperidone, and haloperidol. *Arch. Gen. Psychiatry* 57:249–58

Rao SM, Leo GJ, Ellington L, Nauertz T. 1991. Cognitive dysfunction in multiple sclerosis. II. Impact on employment and social functioning. *Neurology* 41:692–96

Reichenberg A, Weiser M, Rabinowitz J, Caspi A, Schmeidler J, et al. 2002. A population-based cohort study of premorbid intellectual, language, and behavioral functioning in patients with schizophrenia, schizoaffective disorder, and nonpsychotic bipolar disorder. *Am. J. Psychiatry* 159:2027–35

Robinson DG, Woerner MG, McMeniman M, Mendelowitz A, Bilder RM. 2004. Symptomatic and functional recovery from a first episode of schizophrenia or schizoaffective disorder. *Am. J. Psychiatry* 161:473–79

Saykin AJ, Gur RC, Gur RE, Mozley PD, Mozley LH, et al. 1991. Neuropsychological function in schizophrenia: selective impairment in memory and learning. *Arch. Gen. Psychiatry* 48:618–24

Sergi MJ, Rassovsky Y, Nuechterlein KH, Green MF. 2006. Social perception as a mediator of the influence of early visual processing on functional status in schizophrenia. *Am. J. Psychiatry* 163:448–54

Snitz BE, MacDonald AW, Carter CS. 2006. Cognitive deficits in unaffected first-degree relatives of schizophrenia patients: a meta-analytic review of putative endophenotypes. *Schizophr. Bull.* 32:179–94

Spitzer M. 1997. A cognitive neuroscience view of schizophrenic thought disorder. *Schizophr. Bull.* 23:29–50

Staubli U, Rogers G, Lynch G. 1994. Facilitation of glutamate receptors enhances memory. *Proc. Nat. Acad. Sci. USA* 91:777–81

Stirling J, White C, Lewis S, Hopkins R, Tantam D, et al. 2003. Neurocognitive function and outcome in first-episode schizophrenia: a 10-year follow-up of an epidemiological cohort. *Schizophr. Res.* 65:75–86

Tugal Ö, Yazici KM, Yagcioglu AEA, Gögüs A. 2004. A double-blind, placebo controlled, cross-over trial of adjunctive donepezil for cognitive impairment in schizophrenia. *Int. J. Neuropsychopharmacol.* 7:117–23

Twamley EW, Jeste DV, Bellack AS. 2003. A review of cognitive training in schizophrenia. *Schizophr. Bull.* 29:359–82

van Gorp WG, Altshuler L, Theberge DC, Wilkins J, Dixon W. 1998. Cognitive impairment in euthymic bipolar patients with and without prior alcohol dependence: a preliminary study. *Arch. Gen. Psychiatry* 55:41–46

van Gorp WG, Baerwald JP, Ferrando SJ, McElhiney MC, Rabkin JG. 1999. The relationship between employment and neuropsychological impairment in HIV infection. *J. Int. Neuropsychol. Soc.* 6:534–39

Vauth R, Rusch N, Wirtz M, Corrigan PW. 2004. Does social cognition influence the relation between neurocognitive deficits and vocational functioning in schizophrenia? *Psychiatry Res.* 128:155–65

Velligan DI, Bow-Thomas C, Mahurin R, Miller AL, Halgunseth LC. 2000. Do specific neurocognitive deficits predict specific domains of community function in schizophrenia? *J. Nerv. Mental Dis.* 188:518–24

Wexler BE, Bell MD. 2005. Cognitive remediation and vocational rehabilitation for schizophrenia. *Schizophr. Bull.* 31:931–41

Wiersma D, Wanderling J, Dragomirecka E, Ganev K, Harrison G, et al. 2000. Social disability in schizophrenia: its development and prediction over 15 years in incidence cohorts in six European centres. *Psychol. Med.* 30:1155–67

Woodward ND, Purdon SE, Meltzer HY, Zald DH. 2005. A meta-analysis of neuropsychological change to clozapine, olanzapine, quetiapine, and risperidone in schizophrenia. *Int. J. Neuropsychopharmacol.* 8:457–72

Zakzanis KK. 1998. Quantitative evidence for neuroanatomic and neuropsychological markers in dementia of the Alzheimer's type. *J. Clin. Exp. Neuropsychol.* 20:259–69

Dialectical Behavior Therapy for Borderline Personality Disorder

Thomas R. Lynch,[1] William T. Trost,[2] Nicholas Salsman,[3] and Marsha M. Linehan[4]

[1]Departments of Psychology & Neurosciences and Psychiatry & Behavioral Sciences, Duke University and Duke University Medical Center, Durham, North Carolina 27710; email: lynch011@mc.duke.edu

[2]Psychiatric and Psychological Associates, Durham, North Carolina 27704; email: williamttrost@gmail.com

[3]Department of Psychology, University of Washington, Seattle, Washington 98195; email: salsman@brtc.psych.washington.edu

[4]Department of Psychology, University of Washington, Seattle, Washington 98195; email: linehan@brtc.psych.washington.edu

Annu. Rev. Clin. Psychol. 2007. 3:181–205

First published online as a Review in Advance on December 8, 2006

The *Annual Review of Clinical Psychology* is online at http://clinpsy.annualreviews.org

This article's doi:
10.1146/annurev.clinpsy.2.022305.095229

1548-5943/07/0427-0181$20.00

Key Words

intentional self-injury, suicide, DBT, emotion regulation, mindfulness

Abstract

Since the introduction of Linehan's treatment manuals in 1993, dialectical behavior therapy (DBT) has been widely disseminated throughout multiple therapeutic settings and applied to a variety of diagnoses. The enthusiasm with which it was embraced by clinicians early on led some to question whether DBT's popularity was outstripping its empirical foundation. Most of the specific concerns raised regarding DBT's early empirical base have been meaningfully addressed in subsequent randomized controlled trials. This review provides a brief introduction to DBT, followed by a critical appraisal of empirical support for the treatment and a discussion of current research trends.

Contents

DBT: dialectical behavior therapy

BPD: borderline personality disorder

Dialectic: the development of two opposing positions (the thesis and antithesis) that are resolved through formation of a synthesis

INTRODUCTION

Following the publication of Linehan's (1993a,b) treatment manuals and the first intensive training for therapists outside of the University of Washington in 1992, dialectical behavior therapy (DBT) for the treatment of borderline personality disorder (BPD) has grown increasingly popular among clinicians, patients, and mental health advocate groups. However, excitement generated by new treatments should correspond with the empirical data supporting the efficacy of the new approach. In an attempt to align enthusiasm with empiricism, several reviewers comprehensively critiqued the body of existent DBT research in a special section of *Clinical Psychology: Science and Practice* (Levendusky 2000, Scheel 2000, Swenson 2000, Turner 2000b, Westen 2000, Widiger 2000). The goals of this review are to continue with this approach by conservatively scrutinizing the status of DBT research and evaluating the rigor with which criticisms of prior research have been addressed to date.

Prior to any careful review of an existing treatment literature, it is useful to define the necessary elements required for an intervention to be classified as representative of the treatment. These issues are particularly important considering the growing number of adaptations developed based on DBT. For our review, we focused primarily on randomized controlled trials (RCTs), and we used criteria for study inclusion based in part on a currently ongoing meta-analytic study of DBT (S. McMain, personal communication). Consequently, we included studies if they met the following criteria: (*a*) At least one of the treatment arms was DBT or described as cognitive behavior therapy and based on treatment protocols specified in Linehan's (1993a,b) books. (*b*) The DBT treatment must have included individual therapy sessions, a formal skills-training group, a therapist consultation team, and some form of coaching (typically telephone for outpatient care), and/or the function associated with each of these modes was addressed in some fashion (e.g., individual therapy conducted over the telephone). (*c*) DBT treatment length must have been at least six months for outpatient programs and at least two months for inpatient treatments. (*d*) Outcome measures must have included at least one scaled measure of self-injury. (*e*) The study specifically states that it is an RCT, or a review of methodology reveals that the study meets RCT criteria (random assignment of subjects to two or more treatment groups). We also report whether the study included measures of adherence. For RCT studies using DBT in non-BPD populations, we used the same criteria with the exception that a measure of self-harm was not required.

Using this as our definitional criteria, we note that DBT has garnered considerably greater empirical evidence for its efficacy in treating BPD since the critiques in 2000, warranting designation as well-established when utilizing criteria outlined by the Division 12 Task Force (Chambless & Hollon 1998). To be considered well-established according to this criteria, a treatment must have demonstrated efficacy in at least two rigorous RCTs with superiority over placebo control conditions or another bona fide treatment (Chambless & Ollendick 2001). At this time, DBT has been evaluated and found to be efficacious for the treatment of BPD in seven well-designed RCTs conducted across four independent research teams (Koons et al. 2001; Linehan et al. 1991, 1993, 1994, 1999, 2002, 2006b; Turner 2000a; Verheul et al. 2003). In addition, it has demonstrated efficacy in RCTs for chronically depressed older adults (Lynch et al. 2003), older depressed adults with comorbid personality disorder (Lynch et al. 2006b), and eating-disordered individuals (Safer et al. 2001, Telch et al. 2001).

In this chapter, we first briefly review the principles and strategies associated with DBT treatment and adherence measures used in treatment studies. Next, we critically review findings from RCTs for BPD and other DBT adaptations that have been published. We then mention published DBT studies that were not RCTs (e.g., quasi-experimental design, open trial). Finally, we outline future directions for research.

Randomized controlled trial (RCT): controls for factors that jeopardize internal validity (history, maturation of participants, testing, instrumentation, statistical regression, selection, and experimental mortality)

Biosocial theory: the transaction between an invalidating rearing environment and a biological tendency toward emotional vulnerability produce a dysregulation in the client's emotional system

OVERVIEW OF DIALECTICAL BEHAVIOR THERAPY TREATMENT APPROACHES

DBT was originally developed as a treatment for people who meet criteria for BPD, particularly those who are highly suicidal. Since then, DBT has been reformulated and conceptualized as a treatment for multidiagnostic treatment-resistant populations. DBT draws its principles from behavioral science, dialectical philosophy, and Zen practice. The therapy balances acceptance and change, with the overall goal of helping patients not only to survive, but also to build a life worth living. In addition, DBT explicitly helps therapists avoid becoming burned out, as often happens in the treatment of behaviors associated with BPD or multidiagnostic cases.

A guiding principle of DBT is summarized in the biosocial theory elucidated by Linehan. Briefly, the biosocial theory of BPD asserts that the client's emotional and behavioral dysregulation are elicited and reinforced by the transaction between an invalidating rearing environment and a biological tendency toward emotional vulnerability (Linehan 1993a). Practically speaking, this theory encourages DBT therapists to view client behaviors as natural reactions to environmental reinforcers. This theory also informs treatment, which focuses on shaping and reinforcing more adaptive behaviors while also providing clients with a validating environment.

Table 1 Interventions that serve the five functions of dialectical behavior therapy

Function	Example interventions
1. Enhance capabilities	Behavioral skills training, modeling, behavioral rehearsal, psychoeducation, coaching and feedback, homework
2. Increase motivation	Behavioral assessment, chain analysis, contingency management, exposure-based strategies, cognitive modification
3. Enhance generalization to the natural environment	Phone and email consultation, homework, in vivo interventions, client review of therapy tapes
4. Structure the environment	Case management, family or marital interventions
5. Enhance therapist capabilities and motivation to treat effectively	Weekly consultation team meeting, treatment manuals, supervision, continuing education

Intentional self-injury: nonfatal, intentional self-harm resulting in tissue damage, illness, or risk of death or ingestion of drugs or other substances with clear intent to cause bodily harm or death

In DBT, therapists pay particularly close attention to the factors that maintain dysfunctional behaviors, such as reinforcers of self-injurious behavior and aversive consequences of more effective behavior. Whereas behavioral principles focus on changing ineffective behavior, a great challenge in treating individuals with BPD is to balance the efforts to change with acceptance and validation. In general, a dialectical philosophy, which synthesizes an initial proposition or thesis that is opposed by a contradictory antithesis, helps to provide this balance. For example, an organizing assumption dialectically considers clients to radically be doing the best that they can while at the same time recognizing that they need to do better and behave more effectively.

In the case of BPD, one of the most frequent dialectical tensions is that a behavior, such as self-injury behavior, is both functional (it helps the patient reduce distress in the short term) and dysfunctional (the self-injury produces negative effects on health and interpersonal functioning in the long term, and is associated with the risk of suicide). The dialectical tension is resolved by finding the synthesis, by seeking to find what is being left out of the thesis and antithesis (e.g., validating the need to relieve distress while helping the client utilize skills that function to reduce stress and the long-term negative consequences of repeated self-injury). The middle path approach of dialectics is an inherent feature of Zen, and DBT utilizes these principles in an effort to help clients behave more effectively and live more balanced lives.

Functions and Modes of Dialectical Behavior Therapy

DBT is a comprehensive treatment designed to serve five functions (see **Table 1**) through interventions delivered in four modes of therapy. The first mode of therapy involves a traditional dyadic relationship between the client and his or her individual therapist. The individual DBT therapist takes primary responsibility for a client's treatment by overseeing progress toward therapy goals, integration of therapy modes, and management of life-threatening behaviors and crises. Individual DBT therapy is organized around the following target hierarchy: (*a*) eliminating life-threatening behaviors including suicide attempts and intentional self-injury, (*b*) eliminating therapy-interfering behavior including nonattendance or not doing homework, and (*c*) ameliorating behaviors and factors leading to decreased quality of life including homelessness, drug dependence, or other severe axis I disorders.

The second mode of therapy, skills training, is a more didactic intervention that teaches clients four primary skill sets: mindfulness, distress tolerance, emotion regulation, and interpersonal effectiveness. Mindfulness primarily has to do with the quality of awareness that an individual brings to the present experience. Mindfulness practice often involves letting go of attachments and becoming one with current experience, without judgment or any effort to change what is. At the same time, mindfulness involves the use of skillful means and the finding of a middle path between extremes or polarities. Skills taught in this module include observing, describing, fully participating, being nonjudgmental, focusing on one thing in the present moment, and being effective over being right. Distress-tolerance training attempts to equip clients with a range of specific methods aimed at improving the client's capacity to tolerate aversive situations, feelings, or thoughts; to survive crises; and to radically accept that which cannot be changed. Emotion-regulation training tends to be more change focused and includes specific methods designed to identify what emotion is being experienced, to decide whether the emotion is justified or fits the current circumstances, and then to learn ways to modulate the emotion if the client decides he or she would like to change his or her emotional experience. Finally, interpersonal effectiveness training is designed to help clients interact with others in ways that allow them to improve relationships while simultaneously maintaining their own personal values and self-respect.

A third mode of therapy in DBT, skills generalization, focuses on helping clients integrate the skills and principles taught in DBT into real-life situations. In practice, this usually translates into telephone contact outside of normal therapy hours (i.e., coaching calls). These calls are typically brief interactions focused on helping clients apply specific skills in specific circumstances.

The fourth mode of therapy employed in DBT is a consultation team designed to support the therapists in working with difficult clients. The teams serve several important functions, including reducing therapist burnout, providing therapy for the therapist, improving phenomenological empathy for clients, and providing consultation for individual therapists or group skills trainers regarding specific client difficulties.

The goal of the treatment approaches outlined above can be distilled down into the following process: the reduction of ineffective action tendencies linked with dysregulated emotions (Chapman & Linehan 2006). The core problem in BPD is hypothesized to not be excessively intense emotions, but instead the pervasive habitual breakdown of the patient's cognitive, behavioral, and emotional regulation systems when he or she experiences intense emotions (Linehan 1993b). Consequently, the primary goal of treatment is to help the patient to engage in functional, life-enhancing behavior, even when intense emotions are present. For example, mindfulness skills and opposite action (i.e., behaving opposite to the action urges of an unjustified emotion) are hypothesized to work by encouraging nonreinforced engagement with emotionally evocative stimuli, while blocking dysfunctional escape, avoidance behaviors, or other ineffective responses to intense emotions (Lynch et al. 2006a).

Four Stages of Dialectical Behavior Therapy

DBT is a flexible treatment that varies in its approach depending on the client's current level of disorder. This tailoring of approach to the client's current needs can be roughly operationalized into four stages of treatment. A patient engaging in imminently dangerous or deadly behaviors, such as suicidal behaviors or severe heroin addiction, enters DBT at the first stage of treatment. Treatment during this stage is focused on eliminating the most severely disabling and dangerous behaviors. Once behavioral dysfunction is under control, patients move to stage two of treatment, which focuses on shifting from quiet desperation to emotional experiencing. Stage two may include helping clients experience emotions after a lifetime of avoiding emotions or inhibited grieving associated with posttraumatic stress disorder. Stage three addresses problems in living, such as uncomplicated axis I disorders, career problems, and marital problems. Finally, stage four involves helping the client develop the capacity for freedom and joy. Treatment targets in stage four may include working on reducing feelings of emptiness or loneliness and increasing experiences associated with feeling complete. Stage one targets are the focus of most of the empirical research available on DBT to date.

However, the ultimate goal of DBT is to provide a comprehensive treatment designed to help clients at all levels of psychological distress achieve optimal functioning.

Therapy Adherence in Dialectical Behavior Therapy

There is no agreed upon approach for conducting manipulation checks in psychotherapy outcome studies (Am. Psychiatr. Assoc. 2001). In addition, in a review of the literature, only approximately 26% of recently completed psychotherapy outcome studies even used specific treatment protocols, less than half these studies reported therapist training, and only 13% documented therapist competence (Luborsky et al. 1997). Including ratings of adherence in intervention research is important, however, because adherence provides information about the purity and dose of a treatment that is received. Additionally, adherence ratings allow researchers to examine interventions that are specific to a particular treatment modality and those that are common to multiple treatment modalities. In DBT-specific treatment, protocols have been developed and validated, and rating systems have been established to examine adherence to treatment protocols (Linehan & Korslund 2003). In contrast to adherence, competence ratings provide a qualitative assessment of therapist skill in providing the prescribed elements of the treatment, and this type of rating is typically employed by experts using videotaped sessions (Miller & Binder 2002). However, measures of competence also should take into account contextual issues, such as the stage in therapy, patient difficulty, and presenting problems (Waltz et al. 1993).

The DBT rating instrument generates a single item index of DBT adherence and subscale scores for the 12 DBT strategy domains. The rating scale comprises 66 items reflective of the major DBT strategies, each operationalized with behaviorally defined anchor points in the corresponding DBT adherence strategy manual (Linehan & Korslund 2003). Anchor points for each item range between 0 and 5. Each item is scored according to an expert judgment-scoring algorithm based on the DBT adherence strategy manual. Conditions for scoring in the form of if-then rules take into account the necessity and sufficiency of each strategy given the context of the session and the prescriptions/proscriptions of the DBT treatment manual. Scores of above 3.9 indicate an adherent session. Inter-rater reliabilities of mean scores of the strategy items range from 0.78 to 0.83. Correlations between the mean score of the items and the global rating range from 0.89 to 0.99 (Linehan & Korslund 2003).

Of the RCTs for BPD reviewed here, all but Turner (2000a) included measures of adherence monitoring using the scale developed by Linehan and Korslund. No studies report competence ratings as this type of rating scale has yet to be developed. Obtaining ratings of adherence can be an expensive proposition, as it requires a reliably trained therapist expert in DBT to watch and code a session in real time. Consequently, it is recommended that researchers budget and plan for how they will obtain reliable ratings of adherence during the early stages of study development. In an effort to maximize the number of sites that have adherence rating ability, the Linehan team recently trained a small group of DBT researchers from institutions outside the University of Washington (UW) in the DBT adherence scale. There are currently nine reliable coders: four at the UW, one in private practice, one in New York City, one in Canada, one in the Netherlands, and one in Spain (K. Korslund, personal communication). All coding is coordinated through the UW regardless of the coder's physical location. Several other groups of coders are in training presently (both in the United States and abroad). However, more raters need to be trained to facilitate DBT research. That said, a significant strength of the existing approach is that a reliable measure has been developed, and expert raters using the measure are tested to reliability on an ongoing basis. Given this measure's strength, it is unlikely that the field would benefit from the development of additional or alternative adherence measures. On the contrary, use of multiple scales would make comparisons across studies more difficult. Thus, at least for now, it is probably best to consider the UW scale as the gold standard.

RANDOMIZED CONTROLLED TRIALS OF DIALECTICAL BEHAVIOR THERAPY FOR BORDERLINE PERSONALITY DISORDER

Linehan et al. 1991, 1993, 1994

Linehan and colleagues at the UW undertook the first major RCT of DBT, which resulted in three published manuscripts examining different aspects of the data (Linehan et al. 1991, 1993, 1994). As this study has been reviewed in detail elsewhere (Robins & Chapman 2004, Scheel 2000), we only discuss it briefly here (see **Table 2** for a summary of RCTs). The study involved 44 subjects with BPD and a history of recent and repeated intentional self-injury and/or suicide attempts who were randomized to either DBT (N = 22) or treatment as usual (TAU) in the community (N = 22). The results indicated several statistically and clinically significant advantages for DBT over TAU. These included substantially greater reductions in intentional self-injury rate and associated medical risk, total psychiatric inpatient hospital days, treatment dropout, self-rated anger, and greater improvements in global and social role functioning among DBT clients (Linehan et al. 1991, 1993, 1994). Both groups improved similarly on measures of suicidal ideation (SI) and depression.

Certainly, this original study represented a seminal achievement. However, it was an early efficacy study of an as-yet unproven treatment. As such, it does suffer from some of the methodological limitations that are typical of such studies. These include small sample size and limited ability to control for nonspecific factors in the comparison treatment such as the intensity, stability, and affordability of therapy and the amount of training and supervision received by therapists. In addition, two subjects assigned to the DBT condition were not included in some of the final statistical analyses because they dropped out after four or fewer sessions. Although this is methodologically appropriate in many cases, particularly where statistical power is limited by small sample size, it is relatively less informative than the gold-standard intent-to-treat (ITT) analysis, in which all subjects who are randomized to a treatment condition are included in all analyses regardless of whether they actually received the treatment.

Secondary analyses of the data in which many of these issues are statistically controlled for have been reported and indicate that the advantages found for DBT are maintained even when these factors are taken into account (see Linehan et al. 1991, 1993, 1994). However, although reassuring, such post-hoc analyses do not provide a true substitute for a priori experimental control. Fortunately, since the completion of this original study, six additional and more methodologically refined RCTs have been published that examine the use of DBT for treatment of BPD or BPD comorbid with substance abuse and substantially address these issues.

TAU: treatment as usual

SI: suicidal ideation

Koons et al. 2001

An independent research team at Duke University (Koons et al. 2001) compared outpatient DBT with TAU for borderline women veterans being treated at the Durham Veterans Affairs Medical Center. This study attempted to replicate Linehan's original findings as well as examine DBT's efficacy with a less severely afflicted group of patients. The researchers hypothesized that lower symptomatic acuity would allow a shift in treatment focus from imminently life-threatening behaviors to treatment targets lower on the therapeutic hierarchy, including depression,

Table 2 Summary of randomized controlled trials of dialectical behavior therapy (DBT)

Treatments (number of patients)	Inclusion criteria	Length	Main effects	Reference(s)
Trials of DBT for BPD				
DBT (N = 24) versus community mental health TAU (N = 22)	BPD + suicide attempt in past 8 weeks + one other in past 5 years Female	1 year	ISI frequency and medical risk, treatment retention, emergency/inpatient treatment, anger, social and global adjustment	Linehan et al. 1991, 1993, 1994
DBT (N = 12) versus TAU (N = 16)	BPD + current drug dependence Female	1 year	Illicit drug use, social and global adjustment, treatment retention	Linehan et al. 1999
DBT + LAAM (N = 11) versus CVT + 12-step + LAAM (N = 12)	Females with BPD + current opiate dependence	1 year	Opiate use	Linehan et al. 2002
DBT-oriented (N = 12) versus CCT (N = 12)	BPD + referral from emergency services for suicide attempt	1 year	ISI/suicide attempts, impulsiveness, anger, depression, global adjustment, inpatient treatment	Turner 2000a
DBT (N = 10) versus Veterans Administration TAU (N = 10)	BPD Female	6 months	ISI/suicide attempts (trend), hopelessness, suicidal ideation, depression, anger expression	Koons et al. 2001
DBT (N = 31) versus TAU (N = 33)	BPD Female	1 year	ISI/suicide attempts (trend), treatment retention, self-damaging impulsivity	van den Bosch et al. 2002, 2005; Verheul et al. 2003
DBT (N = 52) versus CTBE (N = 51)	BPD + recent and recurrent self-injury Female	1 year	Suicide attempts, treatment retention, emergency and inpatient treatment	Linehan et al. 2006b
Trials of DBT modifications for non-BPD diagnoses				
DBT + MED (N = 17) versus MED alone (N = 17)	Age ≥60 Current major depression	28 weeks	Remission at 6-month follow-up	Lynch et al. 2003
DBT + MED (N = 21) versus MED alone (N = 14)	Age ≥55 + personality disorder Current depressive symptoms Nonresponse to MED trial	24 weeks	Interpersonal sensitivity, interpersonal aggression, depression (trend)	Lynch et al. 2006b
Modified DBT skills training (N = 14) versus wait list (N = 15)	Females age 18–65 Binge/purge at least once per week for 12 weeks	20 weeks	Binge episodes, binge days, eating in response to aversive emotions (trend)	Safer et al. 2001
Modified DBT skills training (N = 22) versus wait list (N = 22)	Females age 18–65 Binge eating disorder	20 weeks	Binge episodes; binge days; anger; concerns about weight, body shape, and eating	Telch et al. 2001

BPD, borderline personality disorder; CCT, client-centered therapy; CTBE, community treatment by psychotherapy experts in suicide and BPD; CVT, comprehensive validation therapy; ISI, intentional self-injury; LAAM, levo-alpha-acetylmethadol; MED, antidepressant pharmacotherapy; TAU, treatment as usual.

hopelessness, anxiety, anger, and dissociation. Twenty-five patients were randomized [13 DBT, 12 TAU with 20 completing the study (10 in each group)]. All five dropouts cited transportation difficulties as the reason for discontinuing treatment and were removed from all analyses except for treatment retention. Alterations were made to Linehan's original inclusion criteria such that a history of intentional self-injury was not required and subjects with antisocial personality disorder were excluded. All subjects met DSM-III-R criteria for BPD at study entry, and 40% had a recent history of self-injurious behavior. Reflecting the lower acuity of these subjects, treatment duration was reduced from 12 months to 6 months, and weekly group skills-training sessions were reduced from 180 minutes to 90 minutes. Aside from these modifications, standard DBT was delivered according to Linehan's original (1993a,b) protocol. The TAU comparison condition was actually a somewhat enhanced version of usual treatment at the Veterans Affairs Medical Center and involved weekly 60-min individual psychotherapy sessions, referral to various psychosocial groups as appropriate, and regular medication-management visits.

Despite the small sample size, results pointed strongly to the superiority of DBT across a number of treatment outcomes. DBT was statistically superior to TAU on four outcomes (hopelessness, depression, anger expression, and SI) as measured by group multiplied by time interaction over the treatment period. On four other variables, the DBT group showed either significant improvement (dissociation and unexpressed anger) or a strong trend toward improvement (hospitalizations, intentional self-injury), whereas the TAU group did not. Both groups showed similar significant reductions in interviewer-rated depression scores and SCID-II borderline symptoms, whereas interviewer-rated anxiety symptoms were unimproved by either intervention.

Although this study suffered from some of the same limitations described for Linehan's original study (e.g., small sample size, no ITT analysis, multiple end points increasing risk of type I error), it also incorporated several methodological improvements, most notably in regard to the TAU comparison condition. Specifically, the TAU and DBT conditions were essentially identical in terms of treatment setting, treatment affordability and availability, availability of expert therapist supervision, and institutional prestige. Concerns regarding multiple end points with such a small sample are valid but are perhaps partly allayed when we consider that DBT was significantly superior to TAU on more than one-third of the outcomes assessed despite the small sample size and was numerically superior to TAU on over two-thirds of the outcomes. In addition, the majority of DBT subjects met criteria for clinically meaningful improvement on six of the seven variables for which this could be defined a priori, whereas this was true for TAU subjects on only two of the seven.

CCT: client-centered therapy.

Turner 2000a

A second independent research team led by Turner compared a modified version of DBT with client-centered therapy (CCT) in the treatment of BPD. The DBT treatment regimen included several substantial modifications to standard DBT. First, psychodynamic principles were introduced into the treatment to "conceptualize patients' behavioral, emotional, and cognitive relationship schema" (Turner 2000a, p. 415). Second, to minimize between-group differences in total hours of therapeutic contact, the DBT condition included no formal skills-training group. Instead, DBT skills were taught during individual therapy sessions. Despite the treatment modifications, we chose to include this study in our review as it met the definition of a DBT trial according to our criteria as outlined in the introduction. In addition, it represents an important contribution to the DBT treatment literature because it was the first RCT examining DBT in a nonacademic setting and the first to employ a structured, theory-driven comparison treatment.

A local emergency room referred potential subjects after they were seen for a suicide attempt. All subjects met full DSM-III criteria for BPD according to standardized interview. Subjects with psychosis, bipolar disorder, mental retardation, or an organic mental disorder were excluded; however, unlike most other DBT RCTs, both men and women were included. Thirty-three of 62 potential subjects met study criteria and consented to participate. Of these, 7 dropped out prior to randomization and an additional 2 dropped out after learning treatment assignment, leaving a modified ITT sample of 24 (12 in each group; 19 women and 5 men). The subjects tended to be young (average age 22, with a range of 18 to 27), and 83% carried a diagnosis of nonnicotine substance abuse.

The active comparator, CCT, was based on a treatment model developed by Carkuff. CCT emphasizes "empathic understanding of the patient's sense of aloneness and providing a supportive atmosphere for individuation" (Turner 2000a, p. 416). Therapeutic interpretation and confrontation were generally proscribed in CCT. Whenever possible, CCT clients were seen twice weekly (three times weekly in case of crisis). Frequency of individual therapy for DBT was not specifically mentioned. Both treatments lasted for 12 months, and a total of six group sessions were offered to all participants over the course of the year. The group format was focused loosely around traditional DBT skills training, but there was no mention of the specific skills addressed.

The same four clinicians delivered both treatments. The therapists had an average of 22 years experience and reported backgrounds in family systems, client-centered, and psychodynamic treatments. Instruction in DBT consisted of five lectures and 12 90-minute training sessions over three months. Although the therapists were generally familiar with CCT, each attended a weekly educational seminar for 12 weeks in an effort to control for effects of the DBT training course. Each therapist attended two weekly group supervision sessions: a DBT supervision group led by the author and a CCT supervision group led by the senior clinic therapist. Group supervision focused on improving treatment adherence by reviewing videotaped sessions. No formal adherence ratings were reported.

Although subjects in both treatments tended to improve, the results strongly favored DBT over CCT. Significant between-group differences were found for all three primary outcomes, representing composite measures of suicidality, affective dysregulation, and global mental health functioning. Secondary analyses of individual measures revealed significant between-group differences favoring DBT on rates of suicide and intentional self-injury, depression, SI, hospitalization days, a global score on a brief psychiatric rating scale, impulsiveness, and anger.

As noted above, the Turner study has several characteristics that weaken its status as an authentic DBT study. Perhaps most controversial in this respect is the incorporation of some psychodynamic principles into the DBT condition. In addition, although the mention of weekly supervision to promote adherence is somewhat reassuring, there is no mention of what sort of formal training the DBT supervisor (Turner) had obtained, and no formal adherence rating was used. Although these concerns are valid and might justifiably exclude this study from a formal meta-analysis of DBT RCTs, they may also be viewed as evidence that therapists who accept DBT assumptions and make a sincere effort to apply DBT can achieve beneficial results.

Van den Bosch et al. 2002, 2005; Verheul et al. 2003

A third independent research team led by Verheul, van den Bosch, and colleagues compared standard DBT with TAU for the treatment of women with BPD who were attending community psychiatry and substance-abuse clinics in Amsterdam (van den Bosch et al. 2002,

2005; Verheul et al. 2003). The study was the first large-scale RCT of standard DBT undertaken in a nonacademic setting. Subjects were mostly referred from psychiatric and addiction treatment centers, and each referring provider was required to sign a letter stating that he or she was willing to treat the patient for 12 months if the patient was assigned to the control condition. Subjects referred by a general practitioner or self-referred were required to obtain a similar letter from a psychiatrist or psychologist prior to acceptance into the study.

The comparison condition was a true TAU condition. The setting was similar between groups, but the treatments differed in several other ways. Treatment intensity was substantially higher in the DBT condition and consisted of the full DBT program as described by Linehan et al. (1993). Subjects assigned to TAU, by contrast, "attended generally no more than two sessions per month" (Verheul et al. 2003, p. 136). Between-group differences in clinician characteristics were not explicitly addressed but may have been important as well. DBT therapists (4 psychiatrists and 12 clinical psychologists) may have had more overall education than TAU therapists (a mix of psychiatrists, psychologists, and social workers) and were probably more enthusiastic about the treatment given that the DBT therapists were volunteers, whereas the TAU therapists were the same clinicians who had originally referred subjects for potential treatment elsewhere. DBT therapists also received intensive training and supervision that were not provided to TAU therapists. Although these differences are notable, they are also typical for a comparison of a new treatment with TAU and demonstrate that DBT can be applied in nonacademic community settings. In light of significant limitations, however, it is probably best to interpret the results conservatively.

A total of 94 subjects were referred, of whom 64 were randomized to either DBT ($N = 31$) or TAU ($N = 33$). Two subjects in each group dropped out prior to the first session, and an additional two subjects in the DBT group dropped out after attending only one session. Analyses were performed on a modified ITT sample excluding these six subjects (27 DBT, 31 TAU). Despite high treatment dropout from the TAU condition, 78% of all assessments were completed with no difference between groups. Significant differences in outcomes between groups were evident. Subjects assigned to DBT had significantly greater reductions in self-mutilating and self-damaging impulsive behaviors and were significantly more likely to stay in treatment than TAU subjects. Fewer DBT subjects attempted suicide (2 out of 27 versus 8 out of 31), but this difference was not statistically significant (Fisher's exact $p = 0.0871$). Post-hoc analyses employing a severity factor (defined by a median split on lifetime number of parasuicidal acts) found that DBT's advantage over TAU for treating suicidal and self-mutilating behavior was most pronounced among severely afflicted subjects. DBT was not associated with a differential reduction in prescription psychotropic medication use. Unfortunately, the study did not present data regarding the use of crisis services, depression/anxiety ratings, SI, or global functioning. A follow-up assessment six months after treatment ended found that the superior gains associated with DBT were maintained, although DBT's advantage was less pronounced than it was immediately post-treatment.

A secondary objective of this study was to examine the efficacy of DBT among borderline subjects with active substance abuse and dependence diagnoses. The study found DBT to be equally effective for subjects with and without substance dependence in terms of reducing target behaviors (i.e., intentional self-injury, self-mutilation). However, generalization of improvements to nontarget behaviors (i.e., substance abuse) appeared to be limited. Analysis of 10 variables reflecting substance misuse found only one significant difference between groups (group multiplied by time treatment effect for alcohol use) (van den Bosch et al. 2002, 2005).

CVT: comprehensive validation therapy

Recognizing the importance of treating substance-abuse issues among borderline patients, Linehan's group undertook the first significant modification of standard DBT in the mid-1990s. Specific modifications were based largely on early clinical experiences with substance-abusing clients and included (*a*) more aggressively targeting treatment dropout by introducing a set of attachment strategies and increasing the positive emotional valence of therapy, (*b*) encouraging patients with opiate and stimulant addictions to use replacement pharmacotherapy, and (*c*) providing targeted case management to address issues related to housing, finances, and the legal system. Their work culminated in the creation of a treatment manual for comorbid BPD and substance disorder in 1997 (Linehan & Dimeff 1997).

Linehan et al. 1999

Results of the first randomized trial of the modified treatment were published in 1999 (Linehan et al. 1999). This trial compared DBT with community TAU and involved 28 women with comorbid BPD and substance-use disorder. Using a minimization procedure to match for age, severity of dependence, readiness to change, and Global Assessment Functioning score, the investigators assigned 12 subjects to DBT and 16 to TAU. They ran analyses on both the ITT sample and the treated sample, defined as those subjects in either group who attended more than six sessions and for whom outcome assessments beyond pretreatment were available (N = 18; 7 DBT, 11 TAU).

Results from the ITT analyses indicated an advantage for DBT in terms of treatment retention (7 out of 12 DBT versus 3 out of 16 TAU; Fisher's exact $p = 0.0497$). Included among DBT dropouts was one subject who died during the study, apparently as the result of an accidental overdose. Among subjects who attended at least one session (11 DBT, 11 TAU), a nonsignificant trend favoring better retention in DBT was seen (4 out of 11 DBT versus 8 out of 11 TAU). The primary drug-use outcome was based on structured interviews at baseline and at 4, 8, 12, and 16 months. ITT analyses using one-tailed t-tests indicated significant advantages for DBT on this measure for the treatment year overall as well as at the 4- and 16-month assessments. Treatment-effect size estimates at all time points were in the moderate to large range per Cohen's (1988) recommendations, possibly indicating that the study was underpowered to detect a clinically significant difference between treatments. Urine drug screens were only performed on a maximum of six occasions (once at each assessment and once at random during the study). Urine-drug-screen results tended to favor DBT at all time points according to ITT analysis, nearly reaching statistical significance at 4 and 16 months. Estimated between-groups effect sizes for this outcome were generally small to moderate. No between-groups differences emerged for intentional self-injury, anger, global adjustment, or social adjustment during treatment, but significant differences favoring DBT were found for social adjustment and global adjustment at 4 months post-treatment. Interestingly, better adherence to DBT protocol may have produced better results, as indicated by a post-hoc analysis revealing that adherent DBT therapist-client dyads had a higher proportion of negative urinalyses throughout the study.

Linehan et al. 2002

Building on the results of the 1999 study, a follow-up study compared DBT with a highly structured control condition for the treatment of comorbid BPD and opiate dependence (Linehan et al. 2002). Women who met DSM-IV criteria for both disorders were randomly assigned to DBT or a combination of comprehensive validation therapy and a structured 12-step program (CVT + 12-step). The CVT + 12-step control condition was designed to more thoroughly control for the influence of nonspecific treatment variables on treatment outcome. Essentially, CVT represents only the acceptance side of the acceptance/change dialectic that underlies DBT. As such, CVT therapists employ all of the validation techniques used in DBT, but they do not use cognitive-behavioral change techniques, give overt advice, or actively direct the therapy session beyond insisting that drug use be brought up at least once. To control for group-therapy hours, the study required that CVT subjects attend a weekly Narcotics Anonymous "12 and 12" meeting conducted by the two CVT therapists who were also recovering addicts. As part of the 12-step program, subjects in this condition were also encouraged to meet with an NA sponsor weekly.

The DBT protocol was essentially identical to the one used in the 1999 study, except that an additional 30-minute individual skills-training session was offered to DBT clients to control for the weekly 12-step sponsor meetings in the control group. Women in both groups received opiate replacement therapy throughout the study. Twenty-four women were randomized (12 to each arm). One subject was subsequently dropped from the DBT condition after it was discovered that she did not meet inclusion criteria, leaving a modified ITT sample of 23 for analyses. Significant decreases in opiate use were evident in both treatment arms, and primary outcomes analyses found no significant differences between groups on the main measures of drug use and parasuicidal behavior. Secondary analyses revealed a significantly lower proportion of opiate-positive drug screens among DBT clients over the course of the treatment, primarily resulting from some rebound in drug use among CVT clients over the last four months of treatment. An additional finding of interest was that self-report of drug use was significantly more accurate in the DBT group as corroborated by thrice weekly urine drug screens throughout treatment. Remarkably, not a single subject dropped out of the CVT group over the entire 12 months of treatment. This was attributed to the supportive and validating environment fostered by CVT.

The results of this study reinforce the importance of controlling for nonspecific treatment factors in therapy trials, and they perhaps also speak to concerns regarding the empirical rigor with which DBT has been evaluated. The control treatment here was not a so-called paper tiger designed to emphasize DBT's effectiveness while providing some semblance of experimental control. Instead, CVT + 12-step was both efficacious and skillfully executed, as evidenced by the remarkable 100% retention rate of clients who have historically been difficult to keep in treatment. The increasing sophistication of the control conditions used in DBT trials also reflects a guiding principle that has been embraced by Linehan and others examining DBT, which holds that subject safety and well-being must be of paramount concern.

CTBE: community treatment by experts in suicide and borderline personality disorder

Linehan et al. 2006b

In the largest and most rigorously controlled RCT of DBT to date, Linehan et al. (2006b) compared standard DBT with community treatment by experts (CTBE). This study was designed to replicate the results of the original study while controlling for a wide range of potential confounds not specifically addressed in that study. Subjects in the two groups were matched according to total number of lifetime suicide attempts and nonsuicidal self-injuries combined, number of psychiatric hospitalizations, history of bona fide suicide attempts versus nonsuicidal self-injury only, age, and presence of negative prognostic factors (severe depression and severely impaired interviewer-assessed global functioning). The comparator condition (CTBE) was carefully designed to control for a variety of nonspecific treatment effects, including treatment availability; ease of obtaining and traveling to the first appointment; hours of individual psychotherapy offered; institutional prestige associated with treatment; and therapist factors including gender, allegiance to treatment offered, formal education (i.e., doctoral versus master's degree), clinical experience, and availability of supervision and group clinical consultation.

Subjects were women between the ages of 18 and 45 who met DSM-IV diagnostic criteria for BPD and who had attempted suicide and/or self-injured at least once in the past eight weeks and twice in the past five years. Potential subjects were excluded if they had a psychotic disorder, bipolar disorder, mental retardation, a seizure disorder requiring medication, or if treatment was mandated. One-hundred and eleven subjects were randomized to either DBT (60) or CTBE (51). Eight DBT training cases and two CTBE pilot subjects were not included in the analyses, leaving a final ITT sample of 101 (52 DBT, 49 CTBE).

CTBE therapists were nominated by local mental health leaders based on reputation for expertise with especially difficult and chronically suicidal clients. Of 94 therapists nominated, 38 were selected for the study and 25 accepted at least one study client. To avoid cross-contamination of treatment techniques, only therapists who described their treatment approach as nonbehavioral or mostly psychodynamic were selected for the CTBE condition. To optimize therapist allegiance to the delivered treatment, CTBE therapists were instructed to provide the dose and type of therapy that they felt was most appropriate for the client, with the single requirement that individual therapy be offered at least once per week. To control for both the effects of the DBT therapist consultation team and client expectations linked to institutional prestige, all CTBE therapists were encouraged to attend a weekly group supervision session led by the training director of the Seattle Psychoanalytic Society. To ensure optimal treatment affordability and availability in both conditions, CTBE therapists were paid with study funds, and the study coordinator helped clients contact therapists and arrange transportation to the first meeting.

Standard DBT was administered by 16 therapists who were nominated by colleagues based on their potential to be good DBT therapists. Of the 16, 8 had no prior DBT exposure, and 5 were either graduate students or postdoctorates. DBT training consisted of 45 hours of training followed by supervised practice, and therapists were hired after being rated to adherence on six out of eight consecutive training case sessions. The two groups of therapists were matched according to education (i.e., doctoral versus master's degree) and gender. However, therapists in the CTBE group had significantly more experience than did DBT therapists on average.

Although subjects in both conditions showed substantial improvements, the DBT group generally exhibited better treatment response, particularly on outcomes related to behaviors specifically targeted by treatment. Subjects assigned to DBT were half as likely to attempt suicide as those assigned to CTBE (23.1% with at least one suicide attempt in DBT versus 46% in CTBE; $p = 0.01$). A similar, although not statistically significant, advantage was seen when considering only nonambivalent suicide attempts (5.8% in DBT versus 13.3% in CTBE; $p = 0.18$). Among subjects who did engage in self-injurious or suicidal behaviors, ratings of medical risk associated with these behaviors were significantly lower in the DBT group. Although no significant difference was found for nonsuicidal self-injury between groups, a greater reduction was documented for the DBT group as indicated by an estimated between-group treatment effect size of 0.49 ("moderate" effect per Cohen 1988). Subjects receiving DBT also used significantly fewer crisis services (e.g., psychiatric emergency room visits and inpatient admissions) than subjects assigned to CTBE. Although a significant difference was seen for all psychiatric emergency room visits and admissions in general, it was especially evident when considering only emergency room visits and admissions due to SI. During the treatment year, CTBE subjects were twice as likely as DBT subjects to visit the emergency room for SI (33.3% CTBE versus 15.6% DBT) and three times as likely to be admitted for SI (35.6% CTBE versus 9.8% DBT) (Linehan et al. 2006b).

Consistent with prior studies, subjects in DBT were also significantly less likely to change therapists or drop out of treatment. Both groups improved significantly and similarly on measures of depression, hopelessness, suicidality, and reasons for living. No measured outcomes favored CTBE.

RANDOMIZED CONTROLLED TRIALS OF DIALECTICAL BEHAVIOR THERAPY FOR CLIENTS WITH OTHER DIAGNOSES

Dialectical Behavior Therapy for Depression and Other Personality Disorders

Several RCTs have examined applications of DBT for populations other than individuals with BPD. In one such pilot study, Lynch et al. (2003) randomly assigned 34 adults over the age of 60 in a current major depressive episode to either an antidepressant medication alone condition or an antidepressant medication plus a modified form of DBT condition. The modified form of DBT consisted of 28 weeks of a skills-training group as well as six months of weekly 30-minute phone contact with an individual therapist, followed by three months of once every two weeks and three months of once every three weeks 30-minute phone contact. Phone contacts in the first six months focused on review of diary cards and problem-solving difficulties with applying skills, whereas phone contacts in the second six months focused on use of skills to prevent depression relapse. Those in the DBT condition showed significantly greater improvements than those in the medication-alone condition in areas including self-rated depression at treatment end and interviewer-rated depression scores at six-month follow-up. Post-treatment interviewer ratings of depression indicated that 71% of clients in the DBT condition met criteria for remission, whereas only 47% of clients on medication alone met remission criteria. Furthermore, at a six-month follow-up evaluation, clients in the DBT condition had significantly higher remission rates (75%) than those in the medication-only condition (31%). Clients in the DBT condition also had significant improvement on measures of adaptive coping and dependency, whereas those in the medication-alone condition did not. The authors hypothesize that the improvements in these areas reduce vulnerability to depression.

The main objective of this first study (Lynch et al. 2003) was to determine the feasibility of a group intervention with a skills orientation for older adults. Encouraged by these findings, a second randomized clinical trial was conducted to apply standard DBT (both group and individual) to older adults with major depression and personality disorder with the goal of modifying the DBT specifically for this population (Lynch et al. 2006b).

In this second study, 35 adults over the age of 55 with personality disorders and comorbid depressive symptoms were randomly assigned to either 24 weeks of medication management alone or 24 weeks of medication management plus standard DBT. The DBT condition included in-person weekly individual sessions and group skills training. Those in the DBT condition showed significantly greater decreases in interpersonal sensitivity and interpersonal aggression compared with medication alone. Additionally, assessment at the time point corresponding with the end of the DBT skills group indicated that 71% of clients in the DBT condition met criteria for remission of depression, whereas only 50% of those in the medication-alone condition met criteria for remission. Clients in both conditions showed significant reductions on standardized, clinician-administered ratings of depression, with a nonsignificant difference favoring DBT seen at end of treatment and follow-up assessments. Nine clients in the DBT condition and seven clients in the medication-alone condition no longer met diagnostic criteria for personality disorder after treatment completion. Moderate effect sizes on several variables suggest that this study may have been underpowered to detect significant differences between conditions.

As mentioned above, a major goal of this second study was to modify standard DBT, and a major impetus for the modifications came from the clinical observation that older adults were generally fairly adept at emotion regulation but had substantial difficulty embracing the new perspectives and behavioral changes important for healing. These observations sparked development of a new form of the biosocial theory for this population that retains the basic tenets of the original theory (e.g., maladaptive behavior produced through interaction of biological predisposition and environmental shaping) but recasts the fundamental dialectic as being between rigidity (fixed mind) and openness to experience (fresh mind). In addition to those skills taught in standard DBT, new skills in this modification emphasize reducing rigid mindsets, increasing openness to new experience, and reconciling events over the life course through reviewing past events and generating forgiveness.

Dialectical Behavior Therapy for Eating Disorders

Two RCTs have also examined DBT for eating disorders. Safer et al. (2001) randomly assigned 29 women with at least one binge-and-purge incident per week over the previous three months to either 20 weeks of wait-list control or to a modified form of DBT. The adapted DBT condition conceptualized binge-and-purge behaviors as attempts at emotion regulation and therefore involved weekly individual therapy sessions focusing on teaching alternative emotion-regulation skills. Clients in the DBT condition had significantly greater reductions in binge episodes and purge episodes than those in the control condition. Significantly more subjects in the DBT condition than in the control condition were abstinent from binge-and-purge behaviors at the end of 20 weeks (28.6% versus 0%). Five additional DBT subjects reduced their bingeing and purging episodes by 88% and 89%, respectively. The DBT condition had a dropout rate of 0%. Although not statistically significant, moderate effect sizes favoring DBT were found for negative affect overall and eating due to anger/frustration, anxiety, and depression. In a second study, Telch et al. (2001) randomly assigned 44 women meeting full DSM-IV research criteria for binge eating disorder either to a wait-list control condition or to a modified 20-week DBT skills group. The group met weekly for two hours and included units on core mindfulness skills, distress tolerance, and emotion-regulation skills. At the end of the 20 weeks, significantly more of those in the DBT condition than in the control condition (89% versus 12.5%) were abstinent from binge eating episodes for at least four weeks. Additionally, those in the DBT condition had significantly fewer binge days, binge episodes, weight concerns, shape concerns, eating concerns, and lower urges to eat when angry than those in the control condition. More studies with larger numbers of subjects are needed to further examine the effectiveness of these adaptations of DBT for treating problematic eating behaviors.

Quasi-Experimental Studies

A number of nonrandomized, quasi-experimental studies have examined DBT (see **Table 3**). Two controlled but nonrandomized studies show promise for adaptations of DBT with suicidal adolescents with BPD symptoms in both outclient settings (Rathus & Miller 2002) and inpatient settings (Katz et al. 2004). Other quasi-experimental studies have suggested beneficial effects of DBT in adult inpatient units (Barley et al. 1993, Bohus et al. 2000), in forensic settings (McCann et al. 2000, Trupin et al. 2002), and in females with binge eating disorder (Telch et al. 2000). However, although these studies may indicate interesting directions for future research, conclusions that can be drawn from them are limited. RCTs are needed to establish these adaptations of DBT as empirically supported therapies.

Table 3 Summary of quasi-experimental studies of dialectical behavior therapy (DBT)

Treatment(s)	Participants	Length	Main effects	Reference
Adapted inpatient DBT (N = 31) versus waiting list with community TAU (N = 19)	Women with BPD	12 weeks	Group comparisons: depression, anxiety, interpersonal functioning, social adjustment, global psychopathology, and self-mutilation	Bohus et al. 2004
Adapted DBT (N = 29) versus supportive-dynamic therapy + family therapy (N = 82)	Adolescent inpatients in depression/suicide program; those with suicide attempt and ≥3 BPD criteria assigned to DBT	12 weeks	Group comparisons: treatment retention, psychiatric hospitalization Pre-/post-DBT comparison: suicidal ideation, general psychiatric symptoms, BPD symptoms	Rathus & Miller 2002
Adapted DBT (N = 32) versus TAU (N = 30)	Adolescent inpatients with suicide attempt or ideation	2 weeks	Group comparisons: problem behavior on the ward	Katz et al. 2004
Pre-/postincorporation of DBT onto adult inpatient unit (N = 130)	Consecutive admissions during transition from psychodynamic to DBT + psychodynamic treatment	Average stay 106 days	Pre-/postincorporation of DBT: mean monthly self-harm rate on the unit	Barley et al. 1993
Adapted adult inpatient DBT (N = 24)	Females with BPD + ≥2 suicide attempts and/or ISI incidents in 2 years	Average stay 94 days	Pre-/postincorporation of DBT: self-harm behaviors, depression, dissociation, anxiety, global stress	Bohus et al. 2000
Adapted DBT (N = 21) versus TAU (N = 14)	Inpatients on adult forensic unit with at least three BPD criteria	20 months	Depressed and hostile mood, paranoia, psychotic behaviors, maladaptive coping, adaptive coping, staff burn-out (trend)	McCann et al. 2000
Adapted DBT	Inpatient adolescent females on a forensic unit	Variable	Pre-/postincorporation of DBT: behavioral problems; staff use of restrictive punishments; participation in therapeutic, educational, and vocational services	Trupin et al. 2002
Adapted DBT for binge eating disorder (N = 11)	Females age 18–65 with binge eating disorder	20 weeks	Pre-/postincorporation of DBT: binge episodes, binge days	Telch et al. 2000

BPD, borderline personality disorder; ISI, intentional self-injury; TAU, treatment as usual.

GENERAL ISSUES

One issue that has reverberated throughout the BPD and personality disorder research field has been a concern as to whether DBT can be successfully translated to the community settings that serve many of the individuals it was designed to treat. Recent developments immediately suggest that this issue may be less relevant. To date five independent research labs have conducted DBT RCTs showing positive between-group effects (Koons et al. 2001; Lynch et al. 2003, 2006b; Safer et al. 2001; Telch et al. 2001; Turner 2000a; Verheul et al. 2003), suggesting clearly that the efficacy of the treatment is not dependent on specific people or organizations. Two of these RCTs (i.e., Turner 2000a, Verheul et al. 2003) were conducted in nonacademic community clinics, indicating that dissemination of DBT to community settings is both feasible and effective. Further support for DBT's generalizability comes from multiple published pre-/postdesign and nonrandomized controlled studies (Brassington & Krawitz 2006, Bohus et al. 2004, Comtois et al. 2007, Katz et al. 2004, McCann et al. 2000, Rathus & Miller 2002, Trupin et al. 2002) and from unpublished data from community clinics across the country that have been compiled by Behavioral Tech, LLC, a training company focused on the dissemination of evidence-based treatments (L. Dimeff, personal communication).

Additional issues that may impact generalizability include at least three primary characteristics that can distinguish between academic research and treatment programs in which treatments are developed and the community treatment programs in which they are disseminated: to clients, counselors, and settings. A major strength of DBT is that it is explicitly designed to treat clients who typically present for treatment in community treatment programs (e.g., highly symptomatic individuals with a high degree of psychiatric comorbidity). Accordingly, participants in the RCTs described above included heterogeneous samples of individuals with high axis I and II comorbidity. Overall, additional research in applying DBT in real-world settings is needed, and this includes an evaluation of the effects training has on changing therapist behavior.

An additional concern regarding DBT research has been the influence of allegiance effects on outcome (Westen 2000). Despite criticisms regarding the importance of allegiance to therapy outcome (e.g., Chambless 2002), it is reasonable to conclude that allegiance effects on psychotherapy outcomes may influence what treatment wins (Luborsky et al. 1999). How well has DBT dealt with this issue? The most representative outcome study that systematically controlled for allegiance effects has been a study comparing DBT with CTBE (Linehan et al. 2006b). In this study, the CTBE therapists were nominated by community mental health leaders and were considered experts in treating difficult clients. The content of the treatment provided by them was not prescribed by the research study or interfered with, and institutional prestige was controlled for by having the base of operations for CTBE at the Seattle Psychoanalytic Society and Institute. In addition, therapists were told to provide the treatment they had the greatest allegiance to (i.e., the treatment they thought would work best), and there were no differences between conditions in expectancies. Thus, it is reasonable to conclude that allegiance was high in CTBE.

CURRENT DEVELOPMENTS AND FUTURE DIRECTIONS

The accumulated data clearly indicate that DBT is an effective treatment for BPD. Across studies, DBT has resulted in reductions in several problems associated with BPD, including self-injurious behavior, suicide attempts, SI, hopelessness, depression, and bulimic behavior. Nonetheless, further advances in the treatment of this complex disorder are needed. The question now involves how best to move the field forward.

Are Direct Comparisons with Other Borderline Personality Disorder Treatments Needed?

In our opinion, a so-called horse-race study in which another multicomponent treatment is systematically compared with DBT does not appear warranted at this point. To date there have been only two other RCTs for treatment of BPD. The first was Bateman & Fonagy's (1999) study of a psychodynamic partial hospital program, but this has not been replicated either by the authors or in a second independent lab. Interested readers may refer to a special issue of the *Journal of Personality Disorders* (volume 16, issue 2) that was devoted to the American Psychiatric Association's (2001) practice guidelines for the treatment of BPD and addresses weaknesses of research examining psychoanalytically informed treatments (e.g., Sanderson et al. 2002). The second RCT was the Giesen-Bloo et al. (2006) study of schema-focused therapy versus transference-focused psychotherapy, but again this has not been replicated. Thus, there is currently no other well-established treatment for BPD that would allow comparison with DBT, and the treatments referenced above were of much longer duration than standard DBT, which mitigates direct comparisons. Assuming that the efficacy of another treatment for BPD can be firmly established, it is still not entirely clear that a direct comparison with DBT would represent a wise use of resources. This is not to say that such a comparison might not provide useful information. Rather, the argument against a direct comparison study in this case rests more on whether it is practical or even logistically feasible owing to the large sample size that would be required, and the inherently complex nature of the disorder and, thus, of the treatments being compared. The likely incremental gains from such a study would not offset, in our opinion, the tremendous costs.

Dismantling Studies and Testing Mechanisms of Change

From our perspective, a more appropriate and cost-effective approach would involve determining what makes effective treatments work and using that information to improve patient outcomes. Accordingly, an important goal of current DBT research is to identify the essential features of the treatment to improve its efficacy, efficiency, and generalizability. The recent work of Linehan and others (Lynch et al. 2006a) reflects commitment to this goal. One approach to this problem involves assessing the degree to which DBT strategies are used in non-DBT comparison treatments to determine which strategies and factors are unique to DBT and, thus, might explain its greater efficacy. The rigorous comparison conditions used in recent DBT trials constitute a first step toward identifying these factors. The findings thus far, particularly from the comparison of DBT with CTBE, suggest that superior results obtained with DBT cannot be solely attributed to therapist expertise, experience, gender, and allegiance; institutional prestige; availability of supervision and affordable treatment; assistance to connect with therapist; hours of individual therapy; or other nonspecific factors. A slightly different approach to this issue involves the systematic rating of specific therapist behaviors in individual sessions. Such a study is currently under way in conjunction with a multisite study (Duke University, Principal Investigator T.R. Lynch; University of Washington, Principal Investigator M.M. Linehan) comparing DBT with an established, manualized treatment for substance abuse (individual and group drug counseling) in the treatment of comorbid BPD and heroin dependence. However, although this line of inquiry can tell us which factors do not account for DBT's efficacy, it is relatively less informative regarding which elements of DBT do make it exceptionally effective.

Efforts to further define the relative importance of different aspects of DBT are underway. One current approach involves comparing standard DBT with modified or dismantled forms in which one or more treatment elements are missing. For example, the individual impact of skills training has been assessed in two published RCTs and one unpublished report. Both published studies were adaptations of DBT that included skills training as the primary intervention with some features of individual therapy built into the treatment (Lynch et al. 2003, Telch et al. 2001). Results suggested that skills training alone with minimal individual therapy contact may be helpful for less severe disorders (e.g., eating disorders, chronic depression). However, the nonpublished report (Linehan 1993a, p. 25) found that the outcomes for 11 clients who received DBT skills training in addition to non-DBT individual therapy were no better than 8 clients receiving non-DBT individual therapy only. This suggests that skills training may be an important component of the full treatment package, especially for more severely affected populations.

A related dismantling study is currently ongoing at UW (P.I. Linehan). In this study, women with BPD and histories of suicidal and other self-injurious behaviors are randomly assigned to one of three treatment conditions: (*a*) standard DBT, (*b*) individual therapy plus activity support group, in which the DBT skills-training group is replaced by a structured weekly group activity and DBT skills are not taught in individual therapy, or (*c*) DBT skills training plus case management, which includes no individual DBT therapy.

Preliminary research regarding the relative importance of change versus acceptance strategies in DBT has also been undertaken. The study comparing DBT with CVT + 12-step for treatment of comorbid BPD and substance dependence (Linehan et al. 2002) represents the first step in this direction. Results of that study suggest that validation strategies may be critical for preventing dropout among subjects with comorbid BPD and substance dependence (Linehan et al. 2002). We cannot draw firm conclusions regarding the importance of change strategies from that study, however, as change strategies were included in the control condition as part of the structured 12-step intervention. In another study, Shearin & Linehan (1992) examined individual sessions and found that a combination of change and validation strategies was important. Specifically, sessions in which clients rated therapists as maintaining a balance between change and validation strategies were associated with greater reductions of parasuicidal behavior and ideation relative to sessions during which the therapist was rated as purely accepting or change focused.

Future studies must be designed in which a strong association between the mechanism of action and both pretreatment variables and post-treatment variables can be demonstrated. Additionally, future studies should use multiple measurement points to determine both a gradient (dosage effect) as well as a time line (i.e., changes in the mechanism of action precede changes in outcome). Finally, the proposed mechanism of action must stand up to tests of plausibility and coherence. In other words, there must be a credible explanation for how and why the mechanism results in change. Theory, then, is an important overarching element in the testing of mechanisms of action. The more assessment periods that are included, the more fine grained the analysis of gradient and time line can be.

Based on the data accumulated thus far, Lynch et al. (2006a) have posited several mechanisms of action specific to DBT that distinguish this treatment from other behavioral interventions. For example, based on the dialectical change theory, the authors suggest that a dialectical focus with a synthesis of change and acceptance strategies may be an important mechanism of action in DBT. They suggest that strategies specific to DBT used in both individual sessions (e.g., utilizing commitment strategies, focusing on DBT skills such as opposite action, and high therapist self-disclosure) and group skills training (e.g., mindfulness skills, emotion-regulation skills, interpersonal effectiveness skills, and self-respect effectiveness skills) may account for significant clinical change.

In addition to the initiatives mentioned above, ongoing research includes evaluation of adaptations of DBT to non-BPD diagnoses, mediator/moderator studies, and basic research examining the theoretical precepts of DBT (e.g., biosocial theory; see Linehan et al. 2006a for a review).

CONCLUSION

The primary purpose of this review was to conservatively scrutinize the status of DBT research and evaluate the rigor with which criticisms of prior research have been addressed to date. Using the criteria for manualized treatments established by Chambless & Hollon (1998), we found that the current literature quickly reveals that DBT is the only treatment for BPD considered well established or efficacious and specific. However, despite its strong empirical foundation, a number of gaps do remain in the DBT literature. These include a relative paucity of RCTs involving male or minority clients and little information on the relative importance of DBT's different components to treatment outcomes. In addition, although preliminary attempts to apply DBT to diagnoses other than BPD have been promising, these applications should still generally be considered experimental pending further evidence from RCTs. Once it is known that a treatment is efficacious, the next task is to improve the treatment further by enhancing its efficiency and efficacy (Linehan et al. 1999). This phase of treatment development includes component and process-analytic studies, dismantling studies, analysis of response predictors, and large-sample effectiveness research in community settings. We hope that this review provides the impetus for others to expand research efforts into these new domains and continue a tradition based on empirical observation to maximize the likelihood that the treatment helps those it was designed to help.

SUMMARY POINTS

1. DBT has been reformulated and conceptualized as a treatment for multidiagnostic treatment-resistant populations. It has been evaluated and found to be efficacious for the treatment of BPD in seven well-controlled RCTs conducted across four independent research teams.
2. Treatment approaches can be distilled down into the following process: the reduction of ineffective action tendencies linked with dysregulated emotions. However, studies examining specific mechanisms of change need further development.
3. There is a reliable measure of treatment adherence that generates a single item index of DBT adherence and subscale scores for the 12 DBT strategy domains. Dissemination of the treatment may be slowed by an overreliance on the UW site for adherence ratings. However, until a convincing argument can be made that a new adherence scale is needed, it is probably best to consider the UW scale as the gold standard.
4. DBT has demonstrated efficacy in RCTs for chronically depressed older adults, older depressed adults with comorbid personality disorder, and eating-disordered individuals. Although preliminary attempts to apply DBT to diagnoses other than BPD have been promising, these applications should still generally be considered experimental pending further evidence from RCTs.
5. DBT can be successfully conducted outside of UW as evidenced by the positive outcomes from independent research teams, adherence ratings of therapists, and community treatment involvement. Allegiance effects have been recently controlled for in a rigorous randomized trial (Linehan et al. 2006a).

FUTURE ISSUES

1. Future research should focus on component and process-analytic studies, dismantling studies, and studies designed to analyze response predictors.
2. New adaptations of DBT require further testing using evidence from RCTs.

3. Research should emphasize inclusion of males and minority populations in future studies to enhance treatment generalizability.
4. Future research should examine factors that enhance translation of the treatment into community settings, and large-sample effectiveness research in community settings should be conducted to test this.

ACKNOWLEDGMENTS

The authors thank Linda Dimeff and Kathryn Korslund for their extremely helpful editorial comments and assistance, as well as Sammy Banawan for his contributions to the literature search and manuscript organization.

LITERATURE CITED

Am. Psychiatr. Assoc. 2001. *Practice Guideline for the Treatment of Patients With Borderline Personality Disorder*. Washington, DC: Am. Psychiatr. Assoc.

Barley WD, Buie SE, Peterson EW, Hollingsworth AS, Griva M, et al. 1993. Development of an inpatient cognitive-behavioral treatment program for borderline personality disorder. *J. Personal. Disord.* 7:232–40

Bateman A, Fonagy P. 1999. Effectiveness of partial hospitalization in the treatment of borderline personality disorder: a randomized controlled trial. *Am. J. Psychiatry* 156:1563–69

Bohus M, Haaf B, Simms T, Limberger M, Schmahl C, et al. 2004. Effectiveness of inpatient dialectical behavioral therapy for borderline personality disorder: a controlled trial. *Behav. Res. Ther.* 42:487–99

Brassington J, Krawitz R. 2006. Australasian dialectical behavior therapy pilot outcome study: effectiveness, utility and feasibility. *Australas. Psychiatry*. In press

Campbell DT. 1957. Factors relevant to the validity of experiments in social settings. *Psychol. Bull.* 54:297–312

Chambless DL. 2002. Beware the dodo bird: the dangers of overgeneralization. *Clin. Psychol.* 9:13–16

Chambless DL, Hollon SD. 1998. Defining empirically supported therapies. *J. Consult. Clin. Psychol.* 66:7–18

Chambless DL, Ollendick TH. 2001. Empirically supported psychological interventions: controversies and evidence. *Annu. Rev. Psychol.* 52:685–716

Chapman AL, Linehan MM. 2005. Dialectical behavior therapy for borderline personality disorder. In *Borderline Personality Disorder*, ed. M. Zanarini, pp. 211–42. Boca Raton, FL: Taylor & Francis

Cohen J. 1988. *Statistical Power Analysis for the Behavioral Sciences*. Hillsdale, NJ: Erlbaum. Rev. ed. 474 pp.

Comtois KA, Elwood L, Holdcraft LC, Simpson TL, Smith WR. 2007. Effectiveness of dialectical behavior therapy in a community mental health center. *Cogn. Behav. Pract.* In press

Giesen-Bloo J, van Dyck R, Spinhoven P, van Tilburg W, Dirkson C, et al. 2006. Outpatient psychotherapy for borderline personality disorder: randomized trial of schema-focused therapy vs transference-focused psychotherapy. *Arch. Gen. Psychiatry* 63:649–58

Katz LY, Cox BJ, Gunasekara S, Miller AL. 2004. Feasibility of dialectical behavior therapy for suicidal adolescent inpatients. *J. Am. Acad. Child Adolesc. Psychiatry* 43:276–82

Koons CR, Robins CJ, Tweed J, Lynch TR, Gonzalez AM, et al. 2001. Efficacy of dialectical behavior therapy in women veterans with borderline personality disorder. *Behav. Therapy* 32:371–90

Levendusky PG. 2000. Dialectical behavior therapy: so far so soon. *Clin. Psychol.* 7:99–100

Linehan M, Armstrong HE, Suarez A, Allmon D, Heard HL. 1991. Cognitive-behavioral treatment of chronically parasuicidal borderline patients. *Arch. Gen. Psychiatry* 48:1060–64

Linehan MM. 1993a. *Cognitive-Behavioral Treatment of Borderline Personality Disorder*. New York: Guilford

Linehan MM. 1993b. *Skills Training Manual For Treating Borderline Personality Disorder*. New York: Guilford

Linehan MM, Bohus M, Lynch TR. 2006a. Dialectical behavior therapy for pervasive emotion dysregulation: theoretical and practical underpinnings. In *Handbook of Emotion Regulation*, ed. J Gross. New York: Guilford. In press

Linehan MM, Comtois KA, Murray AM, Brown MZ, Gallop RJ, et al. 2006b. Two-year randomized controlled trial and follow-up of dialectical behavior therapy vs therapy by experts for suicidal behaviors and borderline personality disorder. *Arch. Gen. Psychiatry* 62:1–10

Linehan MM, Dimeff LA. 1997. *Dialectical Behavior Therapy Manual of Treatment Interventions for Drug Abusers with Borderline Personality Disorder*. Seattle: Univ. Wash.

Linehan MM, Dimeff LA, Reynolds SK, Comtois KA, Welch SS, et al. 2002. Dialectical behavior therapy versus comprehensive validation therapy plus 12-step for the treatment of opioid dependent women meeting criteria for borderline personality disorder. *Drug Alcohol Depend.* 67:13–26

Linehan MM, Heard HL, Armstrong HE. 1993. Naturalistic follow-up of a behavioral treatment for chronically parasuicidal borderline patients. *Arch. Gen. Psychiatry* 50:971–74

Linehan MM, Korslund KE. 2003. *Dialectical Behavior Therapy Adherence Manual*. Seattle: Univ. Wash.

Linehan MM, Schmidt H, Dimeff LA, Craft JC, Kanter J, Comtois KA. 1999. Dialectical behavior therapy for patients with borderline personality disorder and drug dependence. *Am. J. Addict.* 8:279–92

Linehan MM, Tutek DA, Heard HL, Armstrong HE. 1994. Interpersonal outcome of cognitive behavioral treatment for chronically suicidal borderline patients. *Am. J. Psychiatry* 151:1771–76

Luborsky L, Barber JP, Siqueland L, McLellan ET, Woody G. 1997. Establishing a therapeutic alliance with substance abusers. *NIDA Res. Monogram* 165:233–44

Luborsky L, Diguer L, Seligman DA, Rosenthal R, Krause ED, et al. 1999. The researcher's own therapy allegiances: a "wild card" in comparisons of treatment efficacy. *Clin. Psychol.* 6:95–106

Presents findings from the first major RCT of DBT for borderline personality disorder; demonstrated DBT's efficacy for reducing intentional self-injury.

Describes the development and theory of DBT, with detailed review of techniques used and tips for clinical application.

Includes specific worksheets and exercises for group skills training; applicable to both individual and group sessions.

Discusses DBT techniques aimed at improving emotion regulation and the importance of emotion regulation in BPD and other disorders.

Describes results of study designed to replicate/extend findings of landmark 1991 study using larger sample and meticulous control of nonspecific treatment factors.

Proposes hypothesized mechanisms of change associated with DBT techniques including mindfulness, validation, opposite action, and dialectics.

Lynch TR, Chapman AL, Rosenthal MZ, Kuo JR, Linehan M. 2006a. Mechanisms of change in dialectical behavior therapy: theoretical and empirical observations. *J. Clin. Psychol.* 62:459–80

Lynch TR, Cheavens JS, Cukrowicz KC, Thorp SR, Bronner LL, Beyer JL. 2006b. Treatment of older adults with co-morbid depression and personality disorder: a dialectical behavior therapy approach. *Int. J. Geriatr. Psychiatry.* Publ. online Nov 10. DOI: 10.1002/gps.1703

Lynch TR, Morse JQ, Mendelson T, Robins CJ. 2003. Dialectical behavior therapy for depressed older adults: a randomized pilot study. *Am. J. Geriatr. Psychiatry* 11:33–45

McCann RA, Ball EM, Ivanoff A. 2000. DBT with an inpatient forensic population: the CMHIP forensic model. *Cogn. Behav. Pract.* 7:447–56

Miller SJ, Binder JL. 2002. The effects of manual-based training on treatment fidelity and outcome: a review of the literature on adult individual psychotherapy. *Psychother. Theory Res. Pract.* 39:184–98

Rathus JH, Miller AL. 2002. Dialectical behavior therapy adapted for suicidal adolescents. *Suicide Life Threat. Behav.* 32:146–57

Robins CJ, Chapman AL. 2004. Dialectical behavior therapy: current status, recent developments, and future directions. *J. Personal. Disord.* 18:73–89

Safer DL, Telch CF, Agras W. 2001. Dialectical behavior therapy for bulimia nervosa. *Am. J. Psychiatry* 158:632–34

Sanderson C, Swenson C, Bohus M. 2002. A critique of the American psychiatric practice guideline for the treatment of patients with borderline personality disorder. *J. Personal. Disord.* 16:122–29

Scheel KR. 2000. The empirical basis of dialectical behavior therapy: summary, critique, and implications. *Clin. Psychol.* 7:68–86

Shearin EN, Linehan MM. 1992. Patient-therapist ratings and relationship to progress in dialectical behavior therapy for borderline personality disorder. *Behav. Ther.* 23:730–41

Swenson CR. 2000. How can we account for DBT's widespread popularity? *Clin. Psychol.* 7:87–91

Telch CF, Agras W, Linehan MM. 2000. Group dialectical behavior therapy for binge eating disorder: a preliminary uncontrolled trial. *Behav. Ther.* 31:569–82

Telch CF, Agras W, Linehan MM. 2001. Dialectical behavior therapy for binge eating disorder. *J. Consult. Clin. Psychol.* 69:1061–65

Trupin EW, Stewart DG, Beach B, Boesky L. 2002. Effectiveness of dialectical behavior therapy program for incarcerated female juvenile offenders. *Child Adolesc. Ment. Health* 7:121–27

Turner RM. 2000a. Naturalistic evaluation of dialectical behavior therapy-oriented treatment for borderline personality disorder. *Cogn. Behav. Pract.* 7:413–19

Turner RM. 2000b. Understanding dialectical behavior therapy. *Clin. Psychol.* 7:95–98

van den Bosch LMC, Koeter MWJ, Stijnen T, Verheul R, van den Brink W. 2005. Sustained efficacy of dialectical behavior therapy for borderline personality disorder. *Behav. Res. Ther.* 43:1231–41

van den Bosch LMC, Verheul R, Schippers GM, van den Brink W. 2002. Dialectical behavior therapy of borderline patients with and without substance use problems: implementation and long-term effects. *Addict. Behav.* 27:911–23

Verheul R, van den Bosch LM, Koeter MW, De Ridder MA, Stijnen T, van den Brink W. 2003. Dialectical behavior therapy for women with borderline personality disorder: 12-month, randomised clinical trial in The Netherlands. *Br. J. Psychiatry* 182:135–40

Waltz J, Addis ME, Koerner K, Jacobson NS. 1993. Testing the integrity of a psychotherapy protocol: assessment of adherence and competence. *J. Consult. Clin. Psychol.* 61:620–30

Westen D. 2000. The efficacy of dialectical behavior therapy for borderline personality disorder. *Clin. Psychol.* 7:92–94

Widiger TA. 2000. The science of dialectical behavior therapy. *Clin. Psychol.* 7:101–3

A Meta-Analytic Review of Eating Disorder Prevention Programs: Encouraging Findings

Eric Stice,[1] Heather Shaw,[2] and C. Nathan Marti[3]

[1]Oregon Research Institute, Eugene, Oregon 97403; email: estice@ori.org

[2]Department of Psychology, [3]Department of Educational Administration, University of Texas at Austin, Austin, Texas 78712; email: shaw@psy.utexas.edu, n.marti@forum.cc.utexas.edu

Annu. Rev. Clin. Psychol. 2007. 3:207–31

First published online as a Review in Advance on December 6, 2006

The *Annual Review of Clinical Psychology* is online at http://clinpsy.annualreviews.org

This article's doi:
10.1146/annurev.clinpsy.3.022806.091447

1548-5943/07/0427-0207$20.00

Key Words

risk factors, eating disorder, prevention interventions, meta-analysis, effect sizes

Abstract

This meta-analytic review found that 51% of eating disorder prevention programs reduced eating disorder risk factors and 29% reduced current or future eating pathology. Larger effects occurred for programs that were selected (versus universal), interactive (versus didactic), multisession (versus single session), solely offered to females (versus both sexes), offered to participants over 15 years of age (versus younger ones), and delivered by professional interventionists (versus endogenous providers). Programs with body acceptance and dissonance-induction content and without psychoeducational content and programs evaluated in trials using validated measures and a shorter follow-up period also produced larger effects. Results identify promising programs and delineate sample, format, and design features associated with larger effects, which may inform the design of more effective prevention programs in the future.

Contents

SIGNIFICANCE

Eating pathology, including threshold and subthreshold anorexia nervosa, bulimia nervosa, and binge eating disorder, is one of the more prevalent psychiatric problems for females, is marked by chronicity and relapse, results in impaired psychosocial functioning, and is associated with elevated risk for suicide (Fairburn et al. 2000, Lewinsohn et al. 2000, Newman et al. 1996). Eating pathology also increases the risk for future depressive disorders, anxiety disorders, substance abuse, health problems, and obesity (Johnson et al. 2002, Stice et al. 1999). Accordingly, much effort has been devoted to developing and evaluating prevention programs for this pernicious problem. This review summarizes effect sizes for eating disorder prevention programs that have been evaluated in controlled trials and investigates sample, intervention, and design features that are associated with larger intervention effects.

Effect size: measure of the strength of the relation between two variables used in meta-analyses (usually correlation coefficient, *r*, or Cohen's *d*)

Risk factor: a variable that has been shown to prospectively predict some subsequent pathological outcome

EMPIRICALLY ESTABLISHED RISK FACTORS

Interventionists typically seek to reduce established risk factors for eating pathology based on the logic that this should decrease current and future eating disturbances. For the present review, we focus on risk factors that have been supported by multiple prospective studies conducted by independent research groups. Elevated perceived pressure to be thin from family, peers, and the media, internalization of the thin-ideal espoused for women by western culture, body mass, body dissatisfaction, and negative affect have predicted future eating pathology in multiple studies (e.g., Field et al. 1999, Killen et al. 1996, Stice 2001, Wertheim et al. 2001, Wichstrom 2000). Randomized experiments have found that interventions that reduce thin-ideal internalization, body dissatisfaction, and negative affect result in consequent reductions in eating disorder symptoms (e.g., Bearman et al. 2003, Burton et al. 2007, Rosen et al. 1995, Stice et al. 2006c), providing evidence that these may be causal risk factors. Although dieting has predicted future eating pathology in multiple prospective studies (e.g., Field et al. 1999, Killen et al. 1996), experiments have found that assignment to a low-calorie weight-loss diet, versus a waitlist control condition, results in decreased bulimic symptoms in normal-weight young women, overweight women, obese binge-eating women, and women with threshold and subthreshold bulimia nervosa (Burton & Stice 2006, Goodrick et al. 1998, Klem et al. 1997, Presnell & Stice 2003). It appears that the inconsistent findings emerged because the prospective studies used invalid measures of dietary restraint (Stice et al. 2004a). Unfortunately, we know little about risk factors that are specific to anorexia nervosa, bulimia nervosa, or binge eating disorder.

POTENTIAL MODERATORS OF INTERVENTION EFFECTS

A unique feature of meta-analysis is that it permits an examination of moderators associated with variation in effect sizes, which may reveal aspects of the participants, intervention, and research design that are associated with the strongest intervention effects. This information may increase the yield of future prevention efforts by identifying the conditions under which optimal prevention effects occur. We investigated several potential moderators of intervention effects that were selected based on theory, prior findings, and clinical experience.

PARTICIPANT FEATURES

Risk Status of Participants

There is evidence that universal prevention programs that target everyone in a sampling frame produce smaller effects than selected interventions that target only those at high risk for eating pathology. Several universal eating disorder prevention programs have been more effective for high-risk participants than for the full sample (Buddeberg-Fischer et al. 1998, Killen et al. 1993, Stewart et al. 2001, Taylor et al. 2006, Weiss & Wertheim 2005). High-risk individuals may be more motivated to engage in prevention programs, which may result in greater benefits. In addition, low-risk individuals may have less room for improvement on the outcomes. Thus, we hypothesized that intervention effects would be larger for selected programs versus universal programs. Because the key distinction between selected and universal programs is that the former are offered to high-risk individuals, we use the term "risk status of participants" to refer to this variable.

Moderator: study characteristics thought to be associated with variation in effect sizes

Meta-analysis: a study that combines results of several studies to understand sample, intervention, and design features associated with variations in effect sizes

Participant Sex

Females are at much higher risk for eating pathology than are males (Newman et al. 1996). Thus, females might be expected to be more likely to engage in eating disorder prevention programs than males. The low base rate of eating pathology in males may also produce a floor effect that makes it difficult to observe intervention effects. Thus, we hypothesized that intervention effects would be stronger for females than for males.

Participant Age

Prospective studies suggest that eating pathology is most likely to emerge between the ages of 15 and 19 in adolescent girls and that the rates of eating pathology are very low during early adolescence. Prevention programs may be most effective when delivered during

Dissonance induction: a social-psychological approach wherein participants engage in counterattitudinal exercises, which results in dissonance between the original and the new attitudes that produces an attitudinal shift toward the new perspective

the developmental period when the pathological condition emerges. Younger adolescents might also possess limited insight, given that their abstract reasoning skills are still developing, which may constrain their ability to benefit from interventions. There might also be a floor effect because the rates of eating pathology are low during early adolescence. Thus, we hypothesized that prevention programs would produce larger effects for middle- to late-adolescent participants relative to preadolescent and early-adolescent participants.

INTERVENTION FEATURES

Session Format

Substance abuse prevention programs with an interactive format have been found to produce larger intervention effects than didactic programs (Tobler et al. 2000). Participants in interactive programs may show greater intervention effects because this format helps them engage in the program content, which facilitates attitudinal and behavioral change. Interactive programs are also more likely to have participants apply the skills taught in the intervention, which should facilitate skill acquisition. Thus, we predicted that interactive programs would be more effective than didactic programs.

Type of Interventionist

It has been suggested that prevention programs are more effective when delivered by dedicated interventionists versus teachers or other endogenous providers who work in school settings (Baranowski et al. 2002). Theoretically, endogenous providers are not able to devote as much time to providing interventions as dedicated interventionists because the former have other responsibilities (e.g., teaching). Dedicated interventionists are also typically able to provide the intervention several times per school year, allowing them to develop and refine their presentation strategies, whereas endogenous providers typically only deliver the intervention once per year. Finally, endogenous providers rarely receive the amount of specialized training and detailed supervision provided to dedicated interventionists. Thus, we hypothesized that intervention effects will be significantly larger for programs delivered by dedicated interventionists versus endogenous providers.

Number of Sessions

Researchers have concluded that brief single-session eating disorder prevention interventions, typically one hour in length, are insufficient to produce lasting attitudinal and behavioral change (Martz & Bazzini 1999). Multisession interventions may allow participants to reflect on intervention material between sessions, thereby maximizing internalization of program tenants. Multisession interventions also give participants a chance to try new skills and then return to the group for troubleshooting advice. We hypothesize that intervention effects would be stronger for longer multiple-session interventions than for briefer interventions.

Program Content

Intervention content should also influence whether a program produces effects. Interventions that target established risk factors for eating pathology should be more effective than those that focus on nonestablished risk factors. More generally, prior trials suggest that psychoeducational content is ineffective in producing behavioral change (Larimer & Cronce 2002). We hypothesized that programs that focused on increasing resistance to sociocultural pressures for thinness, body satisfaction, self-esteem, and healthy weight management skills, as well as programs that use dissonance-induction techniques to reduce thin-ideal internalization, will produce larger intervention effects than programs without this content. Conversely, we expect that programs focusing on stress and coping skills will be associated with weaker effects because these variables are not established eating disorder risk factors. We also hypothesized that psychoeducational programs would be associated with smaller effects.

METHODOLOGICAL FEATURES

Use of Validated Measures

It has been suggested that use of unreliable measures may result in an underestimation of intervention effects in prevention trials (Kalichman et al. 1996). Reliable and valid measures should be better able to detect intervention effects because they are more sensitive. We hypothesized that trials that used validated outcome measures would observe larger intervention effects than trials that used unvalidated measures.

Length of Follow-up

Given that intervention effect sizes tend to fade over follow-up, follow-up effect size might be inversely correlated with length of follow-up. Accordingly, we hypothesized that interventions with longer follow-up periods would have smaller follow-up effect sizes than those with shorter follow-up periods.

METHODS

Sample of Studies

To retrieve published and unpublished articles, a computer search was performed on *PsychInfo*, *MedLine*, *Dissertation Abstracts*, and *Cumulative Index to Nursing and Allied Health Literature* for the years 1980–2006 (through April) using the following keywords: eating disorder, eating pathology, anorexia, anorexic, bulimia, bulimic, binge eating, prevention, preventive, and intervention. We also reviewed the tables of content for journals that commonly publish articles in this area (e.g., *International Journal of Eating Disorders*), examined the reference sections of all identified articles, review chapters, and books, and requested copies of unpublished trials from established prevention researchers. We focused solely on prevention programs that were evaluated in controlled trials. We included trials in which participants were randomly assigned to an intervention or to a minimal-intervention, placebo, waitlist, or assessment-only control condition. We also included trials in which some relevant comparison group was used (e.g., matched controls) in a quasi-experimental design. Eighteen studies without minimal-intervention, placebo, waitlist, or assessment-only control groups were excluded. Although the use of waitlist or assessment-only control groups does not permit one to rule out the possibility that any observed effects are due to expectancies or demand characteristics, because only six trials used minimal-intervention or placebo control conditions, we did not require these types of control conditions. We focused exclusively on studies that tested whether the change in the outcomes over time was significantly greater in the intervention group versus the control group. Studies that only tested for significant changes within condition were not included because this type of analysis does not test whether the reductions in the intervention condition are significantly greater than the reductions in the control condition. Authors of prevention trials that did not test for significant differences in change in the outcomes across conditions were asked if they could provide the results of such analyses. Of 10 authors contacted, 3 provided the requested results so that their findings could be included (the other 7 trials were excluded). Eight studies that did not include both pretest and posttest data were excluded because it is not possible to model change in the outcomes with this type of design. One study that did not collect information to allow the authors to pair pretest and posttest data was excluded because it is not possible to model change with unmatched data. In total, we excluded 12 studies because they did not test for differential change across conditions.

Effect Size Estimation Procedures

We calculated effect sizes for measures of eating pathology and established risk factors for eating pathology. We included outcomes that were examined in at least 15 trials to ensure a sufficient power to detect effect size moderators. We included body mass, thin-ideal internalization, body dissatisfaction, dieting, and negative affect because these factors have predicted subsequent onset of eating pathology in prospective risk factor studies (Stice 2002). The correlation coefficient (*r*) was selected as the index of effect size because of its similar interpretation across different combinations of interval, ordinal, and nominal variables. If effect sizes were reported in Cohen's *d*, we converted them to *r* with the formula provided by Rosenthal (1991). If effects were reported as odds ratios, they were converted to *r* with the formula provided by Lipsey & Wilson (2001). If no effect sizes were reported, we generated them by calculating Cohen's *d* with the means and standard deviations reported in the article, which were then converted to *r* using the Rosenthal formula, or we reconstituted the data using weighted probability values to estimate a χ^2 test that provided an odds ratio, which was then converted to *r* using the Lipsey and Wilson formula. If these options were not possible, we estimated effect sizes from the exact *p*-values reported by the authors using the formula provided by Rosenthal (1991). If *p*-values were not reported, they were generated from the test statistics (e.g., *F*) and degrees of freedom. If these options were not possible, effect sizes were requested from the authors. Of the 32 authors contacted, 20 provided the requested effect sizes. Despite these efforts, we were unable to generate effect sizes for the nonsignificant intervention effects from 12 trials. As the best estimate of missing nonsignificant effect sizes is zero (Rosenthal 1991), we assumed an $r = 0.00$ for these missing effects. Only 8% of the effect sizes examined in this meta-analysis were set to zero because they were missing. We calculated separate effect sizes for intervention effects at posttest and at follow-up (averaging across all available follow-ups) to capture acute and long-term effects. When multiple measures of an outcome were used, effect sizes were calculated for the scale with the most evidence of reliability and validity. Effect sizes were usually from analyses that used all available data (completer analysis) because this was the most common approach.

Coding of Effect Size Moderators

We considered interventions delivered to all participants in intact classrooms and trials that do not mention the intervention objective during recruitment (e.g., body acceptance) to be universal programs (coded 0). Interventions that screened participants for a risk factor or that used recruitment strategies that implicitly screened participants, such as advertisements for a body acceptance class, were considered to be selected programs (coded 1). We tested whether interventions offered solely to females (coded 1) were more effective than those offered solely to males or those offered to both sexes (coded 0). Participant age was coded 1 if the mean age of the sample was 15 years old or greater, and 0 if the mean age was below 15 years of age. Session format was coded such that 1 = interactive program and 0 = didactic program. Interventionist was coded such that 1 = professional interventionist and 0 = endogenous provider (e.g., school counselor). Number of sessions was coded such that one-shot interventions = 0 and multisession interventions = 1. We created nonorthogonal content variables that reflected whether each program focused on seven content areas. Program content, including psychoeducational content, sociocultural resistance skills, body acceptance, healthy weight control skills, dissonance-induction procedures, self-esteem enhancement, and stress/coping skills were coded such that 1 = present and 0 = absent. Trials that used measures with established reliability and validity (minimum requirement was evidence of internal consistency greater than 0.70 and test-retest coefficients greater than 0.60 or evidence of predictive validity) for at least 50% of the outcomes were coded as having used validated measures (coded 1) and the remaining were coded as having used nonvalidated measures (coded 0). Trials with less than a year of follow-up were coded = 1 and those with a longer follow-up were coded = 0.

The first author coded effect sizes and the second author coded the moderators, but consulted each other when questions regarding the coding of particular studies arose. Although this consensus approach allowed for a refinement of the coding system and served to increase inter-rater agreement, it did not lend itself to the calculation of intercoder agreement.

RESULTS

We identified 66 published and unpublished studies that met the inclusion criteria, in which 51 eating disorder prevention programs were evaluated in 68 separate controlled trials (11 programs were evaluated in more than one trial, 9 trials evaluated 2 or 3 interventions simultaneously, and 2 reports described the results from 2 separate trials). In total, this resulted in 81 separate effect sizes estimates for eating disorder prevention programs. These effect sizes are reported in **Table 1**.

Average Intervention Effect Sizes

For each outcome, we calculated the weighted average random effect size. Pearson's *r*'s were converted to *z* scores (Hedges & Olkin 1985) and the SPSS macro developed by Lipsey & Wilson (2001) was used to estimate the overall inverse variance weighted average effect size for random effects models. **Table 2** reports the average effect sizes (*r*) for the intervention versus the control group, which were small to moderate in magnitude. Effect sizes reflect analyses performed on the entire samples used in these studies; effects for high-risk subgroups are not reported here because the few studies that conducted such analyses focused on different high-risk subgroups. Overall, 26 (51%) of the prevention programs resulted in significant reductions in at least one established risk factor for eating pathology, and 15 (29%) of the prevention programs resulted in significant reductions in eating pathology, including evidence that certain interventions both reduce extant eating pathology and prevent increases in eating pathology that were observed in control groups. However, there were a wide variety of intervention effects, which suggests that it is important to examine factors that moderated the effect sizes observed across interventions.

Moderators of Intervention Effects

We tested for significant heterogeneity in the effect sizes with the random effects *Q*-test using the SPSS macro (Lipsey & Wilson 2001). In the event of significant heterogeneity, we tested whether the moderators were related to observed effect sizes with the random effects SPSS macro (Lipsey & Wilson 2001) for inverse variance weighted regression. Moderators were first examined in separate univariate regression models to investigate the univariate relations between moderators and effect sizes that were not complicated by colinearity. Moderators that showed significant effects in the univariate models were then entered in a multivariate model to estimate the unique effect of each moderator controlling for the effects of the other moderators with significant effects. Finally, we tested whether there was significant residual heterogeneity in effect sizes after the moderators were entered into the multivariate models. This process was conducted separately for posttest effects and long-term effects. The overall tests of heterogeneity and results from the univariate models are presented in **Table 2**.

Body mass. There was significant heterogeneity in the effect sizes for body mass at posttest. However, there was insufficient

Table 1 Effect sizes for eating disorder prevention interventions

Study	Body mass	Thin-ideal internalization	Body dissatisfaction	Dieting	Negative affect	Eating pathology
(Austin et al. 2005)	—	—	—	—	—	0.00 (0.09)
(Baranowski et al. 2001)	—	—	0.29 (0.11)	0.40*(0.38*)	0.19 (0.14)	0.19 (0.14)
(Becker et al. 2005) Dissonance	—	0.12* (0.14*)	0.26* (25*)	0.26* (0.25*)	—	0.30* (0.32*)
(Becker et al. 2005) Psychoeducational	—	0.06 (0.07)	0.22* (0.26)*	0.24* (0.25)*	—	0.28* (0.32)*
(Bearman et al. 2003)	—	—	0.39* (0.27*)	0.13 (0.11)	0.38* (0.28*)	0.22* (0.20*)
(Brown et al. 2004)	—	—	−0.04 (0.00)	0.18* (0.00)	—	0.02 (0.00)
(Buddeberg-Fischer et al. 1998)	—	—	—	—	—	0.05
(Butters & Cash 1987)	—	—	0.50*	—	0.59*	—
(Celio et al. 2000) Computer	—	—	0.29* (0.17)	0.30* (0.47*)	—	0.26 (0.18)
(Celio et al. 2000) Class	—	—	0.13 (0.27)	0.11 (0.23)	—	0.12 (0.05)
(Chase 2001)	—	0.10 (0.08)	0.14* (0.11)	0.21* (0.20*)	0.14 (0.02)	0.00 (0.00)
(Dalle-Grave et al. 2001)	—	—	0.10 (0.08)	0.01 (0.00)	0.02 (0.01)	0.21 (0.10)
(Dworkin & Kerr 1987) Cognitive therapy	—	—	0.21*	—	0.18*	—
(Dworkin & Kerr 1987) Cognitive behavior therapy	—	—	0.34*	—	0.31*	—
(Elliot et al. 2004)	—	0.08*	0.01	0.07*	—	—
(Favaro et al. 2005)	0.02	—	—	0.14	—	0.19
(Franko 1998)	—	0.31	0.20	—	—	0.15
(Franko et al. 2005)	—	0.20*	0.07*	0.00	—	0.10
(Groesz & Stice 2006) Normal dieting	—	—	0.40*	0.36*	—	0.28*
(Groesz & Stice 2006) Many small meals	—	—	0.40*	0.33*	—	0.25*
(Jerome 1987)	—	—	0.00	0.00	—	0.00
(Jerome 1991)	—	—	0.00	0.00	0.00	0.00
(Kaminski et al. 1996)	—	0.55* (0.44*)	0.55* (0.56*)	0.43* (0.44*)	0.47* (0.55*)	—
(Kater et al. 2002) Girls	—	0.06	0.10	—	0.05	—
(Kater et al. 2002) Boys	—	0.08	0.06	—	0.11	—
(Killen et al. 1993)	0.00	—	0.00	(0.00)	0.00	0.00 (0.00)
(Kusel 1999)	—	0.20 (0.00)	0.21* (0.00)	0.25* (0.00)	0.22* (0.00)	0.00 (0.00)
(Low et al. 2006) Student Bodies program w/moderator	0.00 (0.00)	(0.00)	0.00 (0.16)	—	—	−0.10 (0.12)
(Low et al. 2006) Student Bodies program w/o moderator	0.00 (0.00)	(0.00)	0.00 (0.33*)	—	—	0.15 (0.54*)

(Continued)

Table 1 (*Continued*)

Study	Body mass	Thin-ideal internalization	Body dissatisfaction	Dieting	Negative affect	Eating pathology
(Low et al. 2006) Student Bodies program, no discussion	0.00 (0.00)	(0.00)	0.00 (0.19)	—	—	0.19 (0.20)
(Mann et al. 1997)	0.15 (0.11)	—	0.03 (0.21)	−0.22 (0.03)	0.03 (0.08)	−0.09 (0.07)
(Martz & Bazzini 1999)	(0.01)	(0.08)	(0.00)	(0.08)	—	—
(Martz & Bazzini 1999)	(0.00)	(0.08)	(0.06)	(0.13)	—	—
(Matusek et al. 2004) Dissonance	—	0.42*	0.00	—	—	0.30*
(Matusek et al. 2004) Healthy weight	—	0.42*	0.00	—	—	0.30*
(McCabe et al. 2006)	—	—	0.00	—	0.03	
(McVey & Davis 2002)	—	—	−0.07	—	—	−0.02
(McVey et al. 2004)	—	—	0.13* (0.15*)	0.15* (0.14*)	0.15* (0.13*)	0.17* (0.10)
(McVey et al. 2003)	—	—	0.23* (0.23*)	0.17* (0.27*)	—	0.18* (0.27*)
(Moreno & Thelen 1993)	—	—	—	—	—	—
(Moreno & Thelen 1993)	—	—	—	—	—	—
(Mutterperl et al. 2002)	0.03 (0.03)	0.01	—	—	—	0.06 (0.06)
(Nebel 1995)	—	—	0.05	—	0.07	0.21*
(Neumark-Sztainer et al. 1995)	0.09 (0.13*)	—	0.03 (0.03)	0.09 (0.07)	0.00 (0.05)	0.15* (0.15*)
(Neumark-Sztainer et al. 2000)	—	0.05 (0.14*)	0.10 (0.06)	0.07 (0.04)	—	0.03 (0.05)
(Nicolino et al. 2001)	—	(0.15)	(0.02)	(0.20)	(0.08)	—
(O'Dea & Abraham 2000)	(−0.11*)	0.02 (0.13*)	0.14* (0.05)	0.03 (0.05)	0.05 (0.05)	0.05 (0.05)
(Outwater 1990)	—	—	0.08 (0.08)	—	0.01 (0.01)	—
(Paxton 1993)	(0.03)	(0.10)	(0.05)	(0.13)	(0.04)	(0.17)
(Presnell et al. 2003)	0.40*	—	—	0.12	0.20	0.32*
(Richman 1993)	—	—	0.24*	0.00	—	0.05
(Richman 1997)	—	—	0.15* (0.07)	0.11* (0.05)	—	0.03 (0.08)
(Rosen et al. 1989)	—	—	0.50* (0.32*)	—	—	—
(Santonastaso et al. 1999)	(0.01)	—	(0.14)	—	(0.11)	(0.10)
(Shepard 2001)	—	0.04 (0.04)	0.03 (0.02)	—	—	0.13 (0.11)
(Smolak et al. 1998a)	—	(0.18*)	(−0.05)	(0.00)	—	—
(Smolak et al. 1998b)	—	(0.00)	(−0.05)	(0.00)	—	—
(Steiner-Adair et al. 2002)	—	0.00 (0.00)	0.00 (0.00)	0.00 (0.00)	—	—
(Stewart et al. 2001)	—	—	0.11* (0.06)	0.19* (0.08*)	0.06 (0.04)	0.12* (0.10*)
(Stice et al. 2006a)	0.35* (0.35*)	0.29* (0.25*)	0.13 (0.30*)	0.01 (0.32*)	0.12 (0.09)	0.29* (0.34*)
(Stice et al. 2006b)	—	0.25* (0.09)	0.23* (0.08)	0.25* (0.11)	0.18* (0.12)	0.27* (0.15)
(Stice et al. 2000)	—	0.40* (0.43*)	0.46* (0.42*)	0.36 (0.27)	0.42* (0.32)	0.37* (0.37*)
(Stice & Ragan 2002)	0.32*	0.38*	0.25*	0.31*	0.14	0.34*

(*Continued*)

Table 1 *(Continued)*

Study	Body mass	Thin-ideal internalization	Body dissatisfaction	Dieting	Negative affect	Eating pathology
(Stice et al. 2006) Dissonance	0.05 (0.15*)	0.31* (0.17*)	0.28* (0.30*)	0.18* (0.18*)	0.23* (0.11)	0.17* (0.16*)
(Stice et al. 2006) Healthy weight	0.12 (0.12)	0.20* (0.21*)	0.16* (0.24*)	0.05 (0.13)	0.16* (0.04)	0.20* (0.17*)
(Stice et al. 2003) Dissonance	—	0.24 (0.15)	0.23 (0.13)	0.17 (0.09)	0.27* (0.26*)	0.23* (0.21*)
(Stice et al. 2003) Healthy weight	—	0.25 (0.20)	0.12 (0.15)	0.06 (0.13)	0.34* (0.23*)	0.31* (0.22*)
(Taylor et al. 2006)	0.00 (−0.02)	—	0.38* (0.21)*	—	0.08 (0.10)	0.11* (0.06)
(Varnado et al. 2001) Girls	—	0.43*	—	0.05	0.06	0.28*
(Varnado et al. 2001) Boys	—	0.21*	—	0.10	0.31*	0.12
(Wade et al. 2003) Media	—	—	0.16 (0.06)	0.18 (0.03)	0.03 (0.17)	—
(Wade et al. 2003) Esteem	—	—	0.05 (0.05)	0.03 (0.00)	0.11 (0.07)	—
(Weiss & Wertheim 2005)	—	0.00	0.03	0.00	0.06	0.02
(Winzelberg et al. 1998)	0.11 (0.22)	—	0.32* (0.31*)	—	—	0.10 (0.20)
(Winzelberg et al. 2000)	—	—	0.17 (0.35*)	—	—	0.16 (0.23)
(Wiseman et al. 2004)	—	—	—	0.00	0.00	—
(Withers et al. 2002)	—	—	0.04 (0.03)	0.00 (0.00)	—	—
(Wolf-Bloom 1998)	—	0.04	0.07	—	0.01	0.01
(Zabinski et al. 2004)	0.00 (0.00)	—	0.25* (0.16)	—	0.00 (0.27*)	—
(Zabinski et al. 2001)	0.07	—	0.01	—	—	—

Note: Effect sizes for pre-effects to post-effects are presented first; effect sizes for pre-analyses to follow-up analyses are presented in parentheses when relevant. A dash indicates that we did not estimate the models because there was no significant heterogeneity in effects.

variability in self-esteem content and stress/coping content for these moderators to be examined. Significantly smaller effects occurred for programs with psychoeducational content ($Mr = 0.06$, $p < 0.05$) than those without this content ($Mr = 0.19$, $p < 0.001$). Programs emphasizing sociocultural resistance skills ($Mr = 0.02$, n.s.) had significantly smaller effects than programs without this content ($Mr = 0.17$, $p < 0.001$). Intervention effects were significantly larger in programs that focused on body acceptance ($Mr = 0.14$, $p < 0.001$) versus those that did not ($Mr = 0.01$, n.s.). In the multivariate model, the effect for sociocultural resistance skills content ($z = -2.26$, $p < 0.05$) remained significant. There was no significant heterogeneity of effect size in this multivariate model (χ^2 [14] = 17.20, n.s.). Because there was no significant heterogeneity of effect sizes for body mass at follow-up, it was not appropriate to test for moderators of effect size in univariate or multivariate models.

Thin-ideal internalization. There was significant heterogeneity of effect sizes for thin-ideal internalization at posttest. A univariate model indicated that selected programs produced significantly larger decreases in thin-ideal internalization ($Mr = 0.24$, $p < 0.001$) than universal programs ($Mr = 0.10$, $p < 0.05$). Significantly larger effects were observed for trials focusing on participants over age 15 ($Mr = 0.23$, $p < 0.001$) than for trials focusing on younger

Table 2 Overall average effect sizes, overall tests of heterogeneity, and univariate effects for moderators

Study	Body mass	Thin-ideal internalization	Body dissatisfaction	Dieting	Negative affect	Eating pathology
Overall models						
Average effect size (r)	0.10*** (0.04)	0.18*** (0.14***)	0.14*** (0.11***)	0.12*** (0.09***)	0.12*** (0.09)	0.13*** (0.13***)
Test of heterogeneity (x2)	37.3** (22.3)	93.1*** (30.41)	196.80*** (74.71**)	99.09*** (64.49**)	81.91*** (29.23)	112.05*** (66.99**)
Moderators						
Risk status of participants	1.11 (—)	2.77** (—)	5.26*** (6.13***)	4.19*** (4.97***)	4.71*** (—)	5.71*** (4.18***)
Sex	0.98 (—)	1.27 (—)	0.82 (2.82**)	1.50 (2.29*)	1.01 (—)	1.53 (1.30)
Age	1.44 (—)	2.29* (—)	2.44* (4.38***)	1.76 (3.22**)	2.32* (—)	3.22** (2.83**)
Session format	1.76 (—)	0.54 (—)	2.40* (2.21*)	2.67** (2.54**)	2.18* (—)	3.21** (2.33**)
Interventionist	1.06 (—)	1.75 (—)	2.35* (3.17**)	2.09* (1.97*)	2.29* (—)	1.79 (0.84)
One-shot intervention	−0.11 (—)	−0.65 (—)	1.74 (−0.20)	3.15** (0.36)	1.95 (—)	1.14 (0.06)
Psychoeducational content	−2.60** (—)	−2.18* (—)	−4.71*** (−1.43)	−3.17** (−1.11)	−5.53*** (—)	−4.07*** (−2.53**)
Sociocultural content	−4.17*** (—)	−0.29 (—)	−0.69 (−1.02)	0.27 (−0.32)	−0.98 (—)	−0.33 (−0.03)
Healthy weight content	−0.72 (—)	0.74 (—)	−1.05 (−0.18)	0.15 (0.02)	−0.71 (—)	−0.10 (−0.64)
Stress and coping content	NA	−2.05* (—)	−0.81 (−0.55)	−0.31 (0.20)	−0.38 (—)	−0.53 (−0.29)
Self-esteem content	NA	−0.35 (—)	−0.87 (−0.69)	−1.12 (−0.03)	−1.03 (—)	−1.48 (−0.96)
Body enhancement content	−2.08* (—)	2.82** (—)	1.73 (0.98)	1.96 (2.29*)	2.07* (—)	1.29 (0.81)
Dissonance content	−0.57 (—)	2.22** (—)	2.10* (1.38)	2.78** (1.80)	2.39** (—)	3.11** (2.44*)
Validated measures	0.51 (—)	2.23* (—)	1.65 (2.68**)	1.33 (1.55)	0.82 (—)	1.40 (0.76)
Length of follow-up	— (—)	— (—)	— (−0.25)	— (0.90)	— (—)	— (2.45*)

* = 0.05, ** = 0.01, *** = 0.001.

Note: Effects for moderators for pre to post-analyses (z-scores) are presented first; effects for moderators for pre-analyses to follow-up analyses are presented in parentheses when relevant. A dash indicates that we did not estimate the models because there was no significant heterogeneity in effects. NA indicates that the models did not converge because of the limited number of effect sizes for body mass index.

participants ($Mr = 0.11, p < 0.05$). Programs with psychoeducational content ($Mr = 0.14$, $p < 0.001$) had significantly smaller effects than those that did not ($Mr = 0.25$, $p < 0.001$). Intervention effects were significantly larger in programs that focused on body acceptance ($Mr = 0.28$, $p < 0.001$) versus those that did not ($Mr = 0.13$, n.s.). Studies that focused on stress and coping skills ($Mr = 0.07$, n.s.) showed significantly smaller effects than programs without this focus ($Mr = 0.21$, $p < 0.001$). Intervention effects were significantly larger for programs with dissonance content ($Mr = 0.28$, $p < 0.001$) relative to those without this content ($Mr = 0.15$, $p < 0.001$). Interventions produced significantly larger effect sizes for thin-ideal internalization in trials that used validated measures ($Mr = 0.22$, $p < 0.001$) than in trials that used unvalidated measures ($Mr = 0.06$, n.s.). No moderators remained significant in the multivariate model; however, the residual variance did not differ from zero (χ^2 [19] $= 30.68$, $p < 0.05$), which indicates that these moderators accounted for the variability in effect sizes. Because there was no significant heterogeneity of effect sizes for thin-ideal internalization at follow-up, we did not test for moderators of effect size.

Body dissatisfaction. There was significant heterogeneity of effect sizes for body dissatisfaction at posttest. A univariate model indicated that selected programs produced significantly larger decreases in body dissatisfaction ($Mr = 0.22$, $p < 0.001$) than universal programs ($Mr = 0.06$, $p < 0.001$). Significantly larger effects were observed for trials focusing on participants over age 15 ($Mr = 0.18$, $p < 0.001$) than for trials focusing on younger participants ($Mr = 0.08$, $p < 0.001$). Interactive programs produced significantly larger decreases in body dissatisfaction ($Mr = 0.16$, $p < 0.001$) than studies that used didactic programs ($r = 0.06$, $p < 0.01$). Programs administered by an interventionist ($Mr = 0.18$, $p < 0.001$) had significantly larger effects than those administered by endogenous providers ($Mr = 0.09$, $p < 0.001$). Programs with psychoeducational content ($Mr = 0.09$, $p < 0.001$) had significantly smaller effects than those with no psychoeducational content ($Mr = 0.25$, $p < 0.001$). Intervention effects were significantly larger for programs with dissonance content ($Mr = 0.24$, $p < 0.001$) relative to those without this content ($Mr = 0.13$, $p < 0.001$). In the multivariate model with the five moderators that showed significant univariate effects, the effects for selected versus universal programs ($z = 3.50$, $p < 0.001$), participant age ($z = -1.97$, $p < 0.05$), and psychoeducational content ($z = -2.15$, $p < 0.05$) remained significant. There was no significant residual heterogeneity in effect sizes (χ^2 [48] $= 49.53$, n.s.) when these six predictors were entered into the model.

There was significant heterogeneity of effect sizes for body dissatisfaction at follow-up. A univariate model indicated that selected programs produced significantly larger decreases in body dissatisfaction ($Mr = 0.19$, $p < 0.001$) than universal programs ($Mr = 0.05$, $p < 0.001$). Significantly larger decreases in body dissatisfaction were observed for interventions offered to female-only samples ($Mr = 0.13$, $p < 0.001$) than for interventions offered to samples containing males ($Mr = 0.03$, n.s.). Significantly larger effects were observed for trials focusing on participants over age 15 ($Mr = 0.16$, $p < 0.001$) than for trials with participants with an average age under 15 ($Mr = 0.05$, $p < 0.001$). Interactive programs produced significantly larger decreases in body dissatisfaction ($Mr = 0.12$, $p < 0.001$) than studies that used didactic programs ($Mr = 0.04$, n.s.). Interventions administered by trained professionals ($Mr = 0.14$, $p < 0.001$) had significantly larger effects than those administered by endogenous providers ($Mr = 0.05$, $p < 0.01$). Interventions produced significantly larger effects in trials that used validated measures ($Mr = 0.12$, $p < 0.001$) than in trials that used unvalidated measures ($Mr = 0.03$, n.s.). In the multivariate model with the seven variables that showed significant univariate effects, only the effect for selected versus universal focus ($z = 3.43$, $p < 0.001$) remained significant. There was no significant residual heterogeneity in effect sizes (χ^2 [39] = 33.36, n.s.) when these seven predictors were entered into the model.

Dieting. There was significant heterogeneity of effect sizes for dieting at posttest. A univariate model indicated that selected programs ($Mr = 0.20$, $p < 0.001$) produced significantly larger decreases in dieting than universal programs ($Mr = 0.06$, $p < 0.01$). Interactive programs produced significantly larger effects ($Mr = 0.14$, $p < 0.001$) than didactic programs ($r = 0.02$, n.s.). Interventions delivered by an interventionist ($Mr = 0.15$, $p < 0.001$) had significantly larger effect sizes than those delivered by endogenous providers ($Mr = 0.07$, $p < 0.05$). Multisession programs produced significantly larger effects ($Mr = 0.14$, $p < 0.001$) than single-session programs ($Mr = -0.05$, n.s.). Programs with psychoeducational content ($Mr = 0.09$, $p < 0.001$) had significantly smaller effects than those that did not ($Mr = 0.20$, $p < 0.001$). Intervention effects were significantly larger for programs with dissonance content ($Mr = 0.25$, $p < 0.001$) relative to those without this content ($Mr = 0.11$, $p < 0.001$). In the multivariate model, effects for selected programs ($z = 2.03$, $p < 0.05$), trained interventionist ($z = 2.49$, $p < 0.05$), and multisession programs ($z = 2.60$, $p < 0.01$) remained significant. There was no significant residual heterogeneity in effect sizes (χ^2 [34] = 40.26, n.s.) when these predictors were entered into the model.

There was significant heterogeneity of effect sizes for dieting at follow-up. A univariate model indicated that selected programs ($Mr = 0.18$, $p < 0.001$) produced significantly larger decreases in dieting than universal programs ($Mr = 0.04$, $p < 0.01$). Significantly larger effects were observed for interventions offered to female-only samples ($Mr = 0.11$, $p < 0.001$) than for interventions offered to samples containing males ($Mr = 0.03$, n.s.). Significantly larger effects were observed for trials focusing on participants over age 15 ($Mr = 0.14$, $p < 0.001$) than for trials focusing on younger participants ($Mr = 0.05$, $p < 0.01$). Interactive programs produced significantly larger effects ($Mr = 0.11$, $p < 0.001$) than studies that used didactic programs ($r = 0.03$, n.s.). Prevention programs administered by an interventionist ($Mr = 0.12$, $p < 0.001$) had significantly larger effects than those administered by endogenous providers ($Mr = 0.06$, $p < 0.01$). Intervention effects were significantly larger in programs with a body acceptance component ($Mr = 0.13$, $p < 0.001$) versus those without ($Mr = 0.05$, $p < 0.01$). Selected program was the only moderator effect that remained significant ($z = 2.76$, $p < 0.01$) in the multivariate model; there was no significant residual heterogeneity in effect sizes (χ^2 [30] = 34.45, n.s.) when these predictors were entered simultaneously.

Negative affect. There was significant heterogeneity of effect sizes for negative affect at posttest. A univariate model indicated that selected programs produced significantly larger decreases in negative affect ($Mr = 0.20$, $p < 0.001$) than did universal programs ($Mr = 0.06$, $p < 0.001$). Significantly larger effects were observed for trials focusing on participants over age 15 ($Mr = 0.16$, $p < 0.001$) than for trials focusing on younger participants ($Mr = 0.06$, $p < 0.001$). Interactive programs produced significantly larger effects ($Mr = 0.13$, $p < 0.001$) than didactic programs ($Mr = 0.03$, n.s.). Programs delivered by an interventionist ($Mr = 0.16$, $p < 0.001$) had significantly larger effects than those delivered by endogenous providers ($Mr = 0.07$, $p < 0.01$). Programs with psychoeducational content ($Mr = 0.06$, $p < 0.001$) produced significantly smaller effects than programs without this content ($Mr = 0.21$, $p < 0.001$). Intervention effects were significantly larger in programs that focused on body acceptance ($Mr = 0.15$, $p < 0.001$) versus those that did not

($Mr = 0.07$, $p < 0.001$). Intervention effects were significantly larger for programs with dissonance content ($Mr = 0.21$, $p < 0.001$) relative to those without this content ($Mr = 0.10$, $p < 0.001$). In the multivariate model, more of the univariate effects remained significant. There was no significant residual heterogeneity in effect sizes (χ^2 [26] = 33.14, n.s.) when all seven predictors were entered simultaneously. Because there was no significant heterogeneity of effect sizes for negative affect at follow-up, it was not appropriate to test for moderators of effect size in univariate or multivariate models.

Eating pathology. There was significant heterogeneity of effect sizes for eating pathology at posttest. A univariate model indicated that selected programs produced significantly larger decreases in eating pathology ($Mr = 0.21$, $p < 0.001$) than universal programs ($Mr = 0.06$, $p < 0.001$). Significantly larger effects were observed for trials focusing on participants over age 15 ($Mr = 0.17$, $p < 0.001$) than for trials focusing on younger participants ($Mr = 0.07$, $p < 0.001$). Interactive programs produced significantly larger effects ($Mr = 0.16$, $p < 0.001$) than did didactic programs ($Mr = 0.03$, n.s.). Significantly smaller effects occurred for programs with psychoeducational content ($Mr = 0.10$, $p < 0.001$) than those without this content ($Mr = 0.22$, $p < 0.001$). Intervention effects were significantly larger for programs with dissonance content ($Mr = 0.25$, $p < 0.001$) relative to those without this content ($Mr = 0.11$, $p < 0.001$). In the multivariate model with the four variables that showed significant univariate effects, the effects for selected programs ($z = 2.43$, $p < 0.05$) and program format ($z = 2.47$, $p < 0.05$) remained significant. There was no significant residual heterogeneity in effect sizes (χ^2 [45] = 49.87, n.s.) when these six predictors were entered into the model.

There was significant heterogeneity of effect sizes for eating pathology at follow-up. A univariate model indicated that selected programs produced significantly larger decreases in eating pathology ($Mr = 0.19$, $p < 0.001$) than universal programs ($Mr = 0.07$, $p < 0.001$). Significantly larger effects were observed for trials focusing on participants over age 15 ($Mr = 0.16$, $p < 0.001$) than for trials focusing on younger participants ($Mr = 0.08$, $p < 0.001$). Interactive programs produced significantly larger effects ($Mr = 0.14$, $p < 0.001$) than did didactic programs ($Mr = 0.04$, n.s.). Programs that contained psychoeducational content ($Mr = 0.11$, $p < 0.001$) had significantly smaller effects than those without this content ($Mr = 0.19$, $p < 0.001$). Intervention effects were significantly larger for programs with dissonance content ($Mr = 0.21$, $p < 0.001$) relative to those without this content ($Mr = 0.11$, $p < 0.001$). Programs that had a follow-up period of less than one year ($Mr = 0.15$, $p < 0.001$) exhibited significantly larger effect sizes than those with a longer follow-up period ($Mr = 0.07$, $p < 0.001$). In the multivariate model with the six variables that showed significant univariate effects, none of the moderators were significant predictors individually. There was no significant residual heterogeneity in effect sizes (χ^2 [31] = 38.20, n.s.) when these five predictors were entered into the model.

DISCUSSION

Summary of Average Effect Sizes

This meta-analytic review found that 51% of eating disorder prevention programs reduced eating disorder risk factors and that 29% reduced current or future eating pathology. The overall percentage of prevention programs that produced effects for eating pathology compares favorably to the success rates of prevention programs for other public health problems, including obesity (21%; Stice et al. 2006d) and HIV (22%; Logan et al. 2002). Although it is encouraging that the average effect sizes were at least statistically significant, given that early eating disorder prevention programs were unsuccessful at reducing risk factors for eating disorders or eating pathology, the average effects were small. Fortunately, the individual effect sizes from the prevention trials ranged from nonexistent to large, and the moderation analyses identified several factors that were associated with larger effects. Certain prevention programs produced very promising effects. For example, a number of interventions have produced medium-sized effects for eating pathology that persisted through follow-up (e.g., Becker et al. 2005, Low et al. 2006). Other programs reduced risk for onset of threshold or subthreshold eating disorders (Stice et al. 2004b, Taylor et al. 2006). One program reduced risk for future onset of both eating disorder symptoms and obesity and resulted in improved psychosocial functioning and reduced mental health care utilization (Stice et al. 2006c).

Summary of Effect Size Moderators

Risk status of participants. Selected programs produced larger intervention effects than did universal programs for five out of the six outcomes. It was noteworthy that only selected interventions prevented the future increases in eating pathology observed in control groups because this suggests that the effects are not merely resulting because the programs decrease initial elevations in eating disturbances. Mirroring the pattern of findings across studies, several universal prevention programs were more effective for subgroups of high-risk participants than for the full sample (Buddeberg-Fischer et al. 1998, Killen et al. 1993, Stewart et al. 2001, Stice et al. 2004b, Weiss & Wertheim 2005). Meta-analytic reviews have found that selected prevention programs produce larger effects than universal prevention programs for obesity and depression (Horowitz & Garber 2006, Stice et al. 2006d). The distress that characterizes high-risk individuals may motivate them to engage more effectively in the prevention program and the lower levels of eating pathology in unselected samples may attenuate intervention effects.

Participant sex. Intervention effects were significantly larger for programs that focused solely on females versus those that included males, but only for two of the six outcomes. Theoretically, effects are more pronounced for females because the elevated body image and eating disturbances that occur for this sex may motivate them to engage more effectively in the intervention and because there may be floor effects for samples containing males.

Participant age. Intervention effects were significantly larger for samples in which participants were over, versus under, 15 year of age for five of the six outcomes. Interventions may be more effective for the former because they were delivered during the period of greatest risk for emergence of eating disturbances, because younger adolescents may have limited insight, or because of a floor effect caused by the low levels of eating pathology during early adolescence.

Program format. Intervention effects were significantly stronger for interactive versus didactic programs for four of the six outcomes. Other prevention researchers have concluded that psychoeducational interventions are less effective than interventions that actively engage participants and teach new skills (Larimer & Cronce 2002). We posit that an interactive format helps participants engage in the program, which likely facilitates acquisition of concepts and promotes attitudinal and behavioral change.

Type of interventionist. Prevention programs delivered by trained interventionists were more effective than those delivered by endogenous providers (e.g., teachers) for three of the six outcomes. Effects may be smaller for endogenous providers because they have other responsibilities that make it difficult to deliver the prevention program with fidelity, have fewer opportunities to practice intervention delivery relative to trained interventionists, and do not receive as much specialized training and detailed supervision. This finding suggests that prevention programs that have emerged as efficacious may not be effective when delivered under ecologically valid conditions by endogenous providers.

Number of sessions. Results provided limited support for the hypothesis that brief single-session programs would be less effective than longer multisession programs, in that the latter only produced significantly stronger intervention effects for one of the six outcomes. We had postulated that multisession interventions might produce stronger effects because it is useful for participants to reflect on intervention material between sessions and because intersession periods give them a chance to try new skills and return to the group for troubleshooting advice.

Program content. Certain program content was associated with intervention effects, but other content was not (e.g., content focusing on healthy weight control skills and self-esteem). Psychoeducational content was associated with weaker effects for all six outcomes, providing support for the assertion that psychoeducational content is ineffective in producing behavioral change (Larimer & Cronce 2002). There was also evidence that interventions focusing on body acceptance were more effective than programs without this focus. This effect may have emerged because body dissatisfaction increases risk for a variety of problems, including unhealthy dieting, negative affect, and eating-disordered behavior (e.g., vomiting for weight control) and that a reduction in body dissatisfaction results in decreases in these downstream disturbances. Programs with dissonance-induction content designed to reduce thin-ideal internalization produced larger effects for thin-ideal internalization, body dissatisfaction, dieting, negative affect, and eating pathology than did programs without this content, providing support for the utility of this attitudinal change approach. Sociocultural content was associated with smaller effects for body mass, and a stress and coping focus was associated with weaker effects for thin-ideal internalization, but the effects of these moderators was limited. It is important to note, however, that the content of the 15 programs that produced intervention effects for eating pathology varied dramatically, including programs that focused on promoting self-esteem, stress management skills, body acceptance, healthy weight control behaviors, and critical analysis of the thin-ideal, which suggests that there are multiple methods to successfully prevent eating pathology or that nonspecific factors account for much of the intervention effects.

Use of validated measures. There was some support for the hypothesis that intervention effects would be larger for trials that used validated outcome measures, but only for two of the six outcomes. Presumably, validated measures are more sensitive in detecting intervention effects. Results imply that researchers should only use measures with established reliability and validity for the population under study.

Length of follow-up. There was little support for the expectation that prevention trials with longer follow-ups would produce weaker effects, in that follow-up length only moderated the effects of one of the six outcomes examined. This finding probably emerged because prevention effects tend to fade over time, which may be unavoidable given the ubiquitous sociocultural pressures for thinness in our culture.

CAVEATS OF MODERATOR ANALYSES

First, because our power to detect moderators was limited by the fact that we only had a moderate number of effect sizes for certain outcomes, null findings should be interpreted with caution. Second, evidence that a moderator is associated with intervention effect sizes does not establish causality. It is possible that a particular effect is due to some other variable that was not modeled (e.g., perhaps the prevention programs for those under the age of 15 are less effective because they are less likely to target causal risk factors). Third, many of the conclusions regarding moderators of intervention effects are based on theoretical considerations rather than on direct empirical evidence. For instance, although we posit that selected programs produce large effects because the distress that may characterize high-risk samples leads them to engage more effectively in the program content, no trials have directly confirmed this speculation.

POSITIVE FEATURES OF THE EATING DISORDER PREVENTION LITERATURE

A number of positive developments have occurred in the eating disorder prevention field. First, several prevention programs have reduced current and future eating disorder symptoms, which has been an elusive goal. Second, the positive effects of certain eating disorder prevention programs have now been replicated in multiple trials conducted by the same lab (*Girl Talk*, McVey et al. 2003; *Student Bodies*, Taylor et al. 2006) and some have been replicated by trials conducted by independent labs (*Body Project*, Stice et al. 2006c; *Healthy Weight*, Stice et al. 2006c). Third, several prevention programs have now been found to significantly outperform active alternative interventions (*Body Project*, *Healthy Weight*). Thus, a handful of prevention programs can now be considered empirically established prevention programs (e.g., efficacious interventions). Fourth, certain prevention programs have been shown to be effective when delivered by endogenous providers under ecologically valid conditions (*Body Project; Girl Talk; Planet Health*, Austin et al. 2005; *Weigh to Eat*, Neumark-Sztainer et al. 1995) and can be considered to be effective interventions. Finally, select prevention programs have produced intervention effects for both eating pathology and obesity (*Planet Health*, *Healthy Weight*), which is desirable because programs that impact multiple public health problems are more desirable from a dissemination perspective than those that just impact a single problem.

NEGATIVE FEATURES OF THE EATING DISORDER PREVENTION LITERATURE

There are also several areas of concern regarding the eating disorder prevention literature. First, even the effect sizes for the most promising programs could be larger, which suggests that it will be vital to explore methods of producing larger and more persistent effects. It is our impression that greater use of persuasion principles from social psychology may prove useful in this regard, but other alternatives should also be explored, such as the use of booster sessions, adjunctive bibliotherapy, or school-wide interventions that challenge unhealthy norms.

Second, few studies have examined the mediators that account for intervention effects, which is vital for testing the intervention theory specific to each program and for exploring the effects of nonspecific factors. The fact that several interventions did not produce significantly stronger effects than minimal-intervention control conditions (e.g., Celio et al. 2000, Mutterperl & Sanderson 2002, Nicolino et al. 2001; but see also Becker et al. 2007, Dworkin & Kerr 1987, Rosen et al. 1989, Stice et al. 2006c) suggests that nonspecific factors should be examined as potential mediators. Refinement of the theory regarding factors that mediate intervention effects may facilitate the design of more effective interventions.

Third, only a handful of studies have examined moderators of intervention effects (e.g., Taylor et al. 2006). These types of analyses may provide important information regarding the types of participants who show the best response to extant prevention programs and suggest future directions for designing programs for those who do not respond to current interventions.

Fourth, randomized prevention trials offer a unique opportunity to provide experimental tests of etiologic theory. Prevention programs that focus on reducing a sole putative risk factor provide a strong test of the effect of that factor on eating pathology, particularly when a placebo control condition is used to control for nonspecific factors. Experimental tests of etiologic theory are vital because there is always a possibility that some confounding variable explains the relation between a risk factor and future eating pathology from prospective studies. For example, it was noteworthy that three of the interventions that reduced eating disorder symptoms *increased* dietary restriction (Groesz & Stice 2006, Presnell & Stice 2003, Stice et al. 2006c)—a variable that is widely accepted to be a risk factor for eating pathology. These results suggest the need for refinement of one of the most widely accepted etiologic risk factors for eating pathology. In addition, trials indicating that a program reduced a putative risk factor, but not eating disorder symptoms, might suggest that said risk factor is not a causal risk factor.

Fifth, there are a number of general methodological limitations of this literature. Many prevention trials did not include a control group, which makes it impossible to separate the effects of the intervention from the effects from the passage of time, regression to the mean, or measurement artifacts. Virtually all trials have not used placebo or alternative intervention control groups, making it impossible to separate intervention effects from effects arising from nonspecific factors, demand characteristics, or expectancies. Numerous eating disorder prevention trials did not include a measure of eating disorder symptoms or diagnoses, which limits what can be learned from these trials. Few prevention programs have been evaluated in effectiveness trials that attempt to determine whether these interventions are effective when endogenous providers are responsible for recruitment of participants and intervention delivery. It was also worrisome that many researchers did not test for differential change in outcomes across intervention condition, which is essential for the proper interpretation of intervention effects. Finally, many researchers did not report effect sizes, which makes it difficult for readers to properly interpret the findings.

CONCLUSIONS AND DIRECTIONS FOR FUTURE RESEARCH

This review revealed that a number of promising eating disorder prevention programs have been developed. Several have decreased current eating pathology and the risk for future increases in eating pathology. The majority decreased risk factors for eating pathology. Certain intervention effects persisted as long as two years and were superior to minimal-intervention control conditions. The heterogeneity in the content of the successful programs implies that there may be several approaches to preventing eating disturbances, but it appeared that successful programs often decreased attitudinal risk factors and promoted healthier weight control behaviors. There was evidence that larger intervention effects occurred for programs that were selected (versus universal), interactive (versus didactic), multisession (versus single-session), solely offered to females (versus both sexes), offered to participants over age 15 (versus younger participants), and delivered by professional interventionists (versus endogenous providers). Further, programs with body acceptance and dissonance-induction content and without psychoeducational content and programs evaluated in trials using validated measures and a shorter follow-up period also produced larger effects.

We hope that the next generation of eating disorder prevention trials will build upon these promising emerging results and will address the limitations of extant programs and trials. It would be useful for future studies to refine the most efficacious interventions in an effort to increase the yield of these programs. It will also be important to conduct more detailed examinations of mediators and moderators of intervention effects. Another vital direction will be to begin conducting effectiveness trials that evaluate whether interventions produce effects when delivered under ecologically valid conditions and to conduct studies that begin to elucidate barriers to successful dissemination of the most promising interventions. It will be important to conduct independent replications of the most promising prevention trials. Greater attention should also be devoted to developing general prevention techniques that are independent of the specific content of the intervention, such as strategic self-presentation, motivational interviewing, and other persuasion techniques from social psychology. We believe that a commitment to methodologically rigorous and programmatic studies will allow the next generation of studies to bring us closer to the goal of reducing the prevalence of eating disorders.

SUMMARY POINTS

1. This meta-analysis identified moderators of eating disorder prevention programs that produced the largest intervention effects.
2. Programs that tended to produce larger intervention effects were selective, interactive, multisession, offered only to females, offered to participants over age 15, delivered by professional interventionists, incorporated body acceptance and dissonance-induction content, evaluated in trials using validated measures, lacked psychoeducational content, and had a shorter follow-up period.
3. There are several empirically established eating disorder prevention programs, some of which have also been shown to be effective when delivered by endogenous providers under ecologically valid conditions.
4. Some of these prevention programs have produced intervention effects for both eating pathology and obesity, which is promising from a public health standpoint.

FUTURE DIRECTIONS

1. Programs need to be further refined to produce larger intervention effects. Adopting social psychological persuasion principles, using booster sessions, adjunctive bibliotherapy, or school-wide interventions that challenge unhealthy norms are possible directions to take to reach this goal.
2. Additional research is needed to elucidate the mediators of intervention effects, which is crucial for testing intervention theories specific to each program and for exploring the effects of nonspecific factors.
3. Randomized prevention trials that manipulate individual risk factors and use placebo comparison groups to control for nonspecific factors are needed to rule out the possibility that the relation between a risk factor and future eating pathology from prospective research is due to a confounding variable.

4. Effectiveness trials that are delivered under ecologically valid conditions and that can elucidate barriers to successfully disseminating promising interventions are needed.
5. The development of general prevention techniques that are independent of the content of the intervention is also needed.

ACKNOWLEDGMENTS

Preparation of this manuscript was supported by research grants (MH/DK61957 and MH70699) from the National Institutes of Health. We are grateful to Krista Heim and Emily Wade for their assistance with the preparation of this article. Thanks also go to the numerous authors who were kind enough to provide effect sizes or conduct additional analyses when requested.

LITERATURE CITED

Describes a school-based obesity prevention trial (Planet Health) that produced effects for eating disorder symptoms and weight-control behaviors.

Austin SB, Field AE, Wiecha J, Peterson KE, Gortmakerer SL. 2005. The impact of a school-based obesity prevention trial on disordered weight-control behaviors in early adolescent girls. *Arch. Pediatr. Adolesc. Med.* 159:225–30

Baranowski MJ, Hetherington MM. 2001. Testing the efficacy of an eating disorder prevention program. *Int. J. Eat. Disord.* 29:119–24

Baranowski T, Cullen K, Nicklas T, Thompson D, Baranowski J. 2002. School-based obesity prevention: a blueprint for taming the epidemic. *Am. J. Public Health* 26:486–93

Bearman SK, Stice E, Chase A. 2003. Effects of body dissatisfaction on depressive and bulimic symptoms: a longitudinal experiment. *Behav. Ther.* 34:277–93

Becker CB, Smith L, Ciao AC. 2005. Reducing eating disorder risk factors in sorority members: a randomized trial. *Behav. Ther.* 36:245–54

Becker CB, Smith LM, Ciao AC. 2006. Peer facilitated eating disorders prevention: a randomized effectiveness trial of cognitive dissonance and media advocacy. *J. Couns. Psychol.* 53(4) 550–55

Bruning-Brown JB, Winzelberg AJ, Abascal LB, Taylor CB. 2004. An evaluation of an internet-delivered eating disorder prevention program for adolescents and their parents. *J. Adolesc. Health* 35:290–96

Buddeberg-Fischer B, Klaghofer R, Gnam G, Buddeberg C. 1998. Prevention of disturbed eating behaviour: a prospective intervention study in 14- to 19-year-old Swiss students. *Acta Psychiatr. Scand.* 98:146–55

Burton E, Stice E. 2006. Evaluation of a healthy-weight treatment program for bulimia nervosa: a preliminary randomized trial. *Behav. Res. Ther.* 44:1727–38

Burton EM, Stice E, Bearman SK, Rohde P. 2007. An experimental test of the affect-regulation model of bulimic symptoms and substance use: an affective intervention. *Int. J. Eat. Disord.* In press

Butters JW, Cash T. 1987. Cognitive-behavioral treatment of women's body-image dissatisfaction. *J. Consult. Clin. Psychol.* 55:889–97

Celio A, Winzelberg A, Wilfley D, Eppstein-Herald D, Springer E, et al. 2000. Reducing risk factors for eating disorders: comparison of an internet- and classroom-delivered psychoeducational program. *J. Consult. Clin. Psychol.* 68:650–57

Chase AK. 2001. *Eating disorder prevention: an intervention for at-risk college women*. Unpubl. dissert., Univ. Texas, Austin

Dalle Grave RD, De Luca L, Campello G. 2001. Middle school primary prevention program for eating disorders: a controlled study with a twelve-month follow-up. *Eat. Disord.* 9:327–37

Dworkin SH, Kerr BA. 1987. Comparison of interventions for women experiencing body image problems. *J. Couns. Psychol.* 34:136–40

Elliot DL, Goldberg L, Moe EL, DeFrancesco CA, Durham MB, Hix-Small H. 2004. Preventing substance use and disordered eating: initial outcomes of the ATHENA (Athletes Targeting Healthy Exercise and Nutrition Alternatives) Program. *Arch. Pediatr. Med.* 158:1043–49

Fairburn CG, Cooper Z, Doll HA, Norman PA, O'Connor ME. 2000. The natural course of bulimia nervosa and binge eating disorder in young women. *Arch. Gen. Psychol.* 57:659–65

Favaro A, Zanetti T, Huon G, Santonastaso P. 2005. Engaging teachers in an eating disorder prevention intervention. *Int. J. Eat. Disord.* 38:73–77

Field AE, Camargo CA, Taylor CB, Berkey CS, Colditz GA. 1999. Relation of peer and media influences to the development of purging behaviors among preadolescent and adolescent girls. *Arch. Pediatr. Adolesc. Med.* 153:1184–89

Franko DL. 1998. Secondary prevention of eating disorders in college women at risk. *Eat. Disord.* 6:29–40

Franko DL, Mintz LB, Villapiano M, Green TC, Mainelli D, et al. 2005. Food, mood, and attitude: reducing risk for eating disorders in college women. *Health Psychol.* 24:567–78

Goodrick GK, Poston WS, Kimball KT, Reeves RS, Foreyt JP. 1998. Nondieting versus dieting treatments for overweight binge-eating women. *J. Consult. Clin. Psychol.* 66:363–68

Groesz LM, Stice E. 2006. An experimental test of the effects of dieting on bulimic symptoms: the impact of eating episode frequency. *Behav. Res. Ther.* 45:49–62

Hedges LV, Olkin I. 1985. *Statistical Methods for Meta-Analysis*. Orlando, FL: Academic

Horowitz JL, Garber J. 2006. The prevention of depressive symptoms in children and adolescents: a meta-analytic review. *J. Consult. Clin. Psychol.* 74:401–15

Jerome LW. 1987. *Primary intervention for bulimia: the evaluation of a media presentation for an adolescent population*. Unpubl. thesis, Kent, OH: Kent State Univ.

Jerome LW. 1991. *Primary intervention for bulimia: the evaluation of a media presentation for an adolescent population*. Unpubl. dissert., Kent, OH: Kent State Univ.

Johnson JG, Cohen P, Kasen S, Brook JS. 2002. Eating disorders during adolescence and the risk for physical and mental disorders during early adulthood. *Arch. Gen. Psychiatry* 59:545–52

Kalichman SC, Carey MP, Johnson BT. 1996. Prevention of sexually transmitted HIV infection: a meta-analytic review of the behavioral outcome literature. *Ann. Behav. Med.* 18:6–15

Kaminski PL, McNamara K. 1996. A treatment for college women at risk for bulimia: a controlled evaluation. *J. Couns. Dev.* 74:288–94

Kater KJ, Rohwer J, Londre K. 2002. Evaluation of an upper elementary school program to prevent body image, eating, and weight concerns. *J. School Psychol.* 72:199–204

Killen JD, Taylor CB, Hammer L, Litt I, Wilson DM, et al. 1993. An attempt to modify unhealthful eating attitudes and weight regulation practices of young adolescent girls. *Int. J. Eat. Disord.* 13:369–84

Killen JD, Taylor CB, Hayward C, Haydel KF, Wilson DM, et al. 1996. Weight concerns influence the development of eating disorders: a 4-year prospective study. *J. Consult. Clin. Psychol.* 64:936–40

Klem ML, Wing RR, Simkin-Silverman L, Kuller LH. 1997. The psychological consequences of weight gain prevention in healthy, premenopausal women. *Int. J. Eat. Disord.* 21:167–74

Kusel AB. 1999. *Primary prevention of eating disorders through media literacy training of girls.* Unpubl. dissert., San Diego, CA: Calif. School Prof. Psychol.

Larimer ME, Cronce JM. 2002. Identification, prevention, and treatment: a review of individual-focused strategies to reduce problematic alcohol consumption by college students. *J. Stud. Alcohol* S14:148–63

Lewinsohn PM, Striegel-Moore RH, Seeley JR. 2000. Epidemiology and natural course of eating disorders in young women from adolescence to young adulthood. *J. Am. Acad. Child Adolesc. Psychol.* 39:1284–92

Lipsey MW, Wilson DB. 2001. *Practical Meta-Analysis.* Thousand Oaks, CA: Sage

Provides an easy-to-understand introduction to meta-analytic procedures.

Logan TK, Cole J, Leukefeld C. 2002. Women, sex, and HIV: social and contextual factors, meta-analysis of published interventions, and implications for practice and research. *Psychol. Bull.* 128:851–85

Low KG, Charanasomboon S, Lesser J, Reinhalter K, Martin R, et al. 2006. Effectiveness of a computer-based interactive eating disorder prevention program at long-term follow-up. *Eat. Disord.* 14:17–30

Mann T, Nolen-Hoeksema S, Huang K, Burgard D, Wright A, Hanson K. 1997. Are two interventions worse than none? Joint primary and secondary prevention of eating disorders in college females. *Health Psychol.* 16:215–25

Martz D, Bazzini D. 1999. Eating disorders prevention programming may be failing: evaluation of two one-shot programs. *J. Coll. Student Dev.* 40:32–42

Matusek JA, Wendt SJ, Wiseman CV. 2004. Dissonance thin-ideal and didactic healthy behavior eating disorder prevention programs: results from a controlled trial. *Int. J. Eat. Disord.* 36:376–88

McCabe MP, Ricciardelli LA, Salmon J. 2006. Evaluation of a prevention program to address body focus and negative affect among children. *J. Health Psychol.* 11:589–98

McVey GL, Davis R. 2002. A program to promote positive body image: a 1-year follow-up assessment. *J. Early Adolesc.* 22:96–108

McVey GL, Davis R, Tweed S, Shaw BF. 2004. An evaluation of a school-based program designed to promote positive body image and self-esteem: a replication study. *Int. J. Eat. Disord.* 36:1–11

McVey GL, Lieberman M, Voorberg N, Wardrope D, Blackmore E. 2003. School-based peer support groups: a new approach to the prevention of disordered eating. *Eat. Disord. J. Prev.* 11:187–95

Describes a model eating disorder prevention program promoting critical media use, body acceptance, and healthy weight; finds effects for eating disorder symptoms.

Moreno AB, Thelen MH. 1993. A preliminary prevention program for eating disorders in a junior high school population. *J. Youth Adolesc.* 22:109–24

Mutterperl JA, Sanderson CA. 2002. Mind over matter: internalization of the thinness norm as a moderator of responsiveness to norm misperception education in college women. *Health Psychol.* 21:519–23

Nebel MA. 1995. *Prevention of disordered eating among college women: a clinical intervention.* Unpubl. dissert., Univ. Ariz., Tucson

Neumark-Sztainer D, Butler R, Palti H. 1995. Eating disturbances among adolescent girls: evaluation of a school-based primary prevention program. *J. Nutr. Educ.* 27:24–31

Presents an example of an excellent first-generation psychoeducational prevention program that reduced risk for onset of future binge-eating onset.

Neumark-Sztainer D, Sherwood NE, Coller T, Hannan PJ. 2000. Primary prevention of disordered eating among preadolescent girls: Feasibility and short-term effect of a community-based intervention. *J. Am. Diet. Assoc.* 100:1466–73

Newman DL, Moffitt TE, Caspi A, Magdol L, Silva PA, Stanton WR. 1996. Psychiatric disorder in a birth cohort of young adults: prevalence, comorbidity, clinical significance, and new case incidence from ages 11 to 21. *J. Consult. Clin. Psychol.* 64:552–62

Nicolino JC, Martz DM, Curtin L. 2001. Evaluation of a cognitive-behavioral therapy intervention to improve body image and decrease dieting in college women. *Eat. Behav.* 2:353–62

O'Dea JA, Abraham S. 2000. Improving the body image, eating attitudes, and behaviors of young male and female adolescents: a new educational approach that focuses on self-esteem. *Int. J. Eat. Disord.* 28:43–57

Outwater AD. 1990. *An intervention project to improve body image and self-esteem in 6th grade boys and girls as a potential prevention against eating disorders.* Unpubl. dissert., Union Inst., Cincinnati, OH

Paxton SJ. 1993. A prevention program for disturbed eating and body dissatisfaction in adolescent girls: a 1 year follow-up. *Health Educ. Res.* 8:43–51

Presnell K, Stice E. 2003. An experimental test of the effect of weight-loss dieting on bulimic pathology: tipping the scales in a different direction. *J. Abnorm. Psychol.* 112:166–70

Richman RD. 1993. *Primary prevention of eating disorders: a pilot program.* Unpubl. thesis, Simon Fraser Univ., Br. Columbia

Richman RD. 1997. *Preventing eating disorders; promoting healthy attitudes and behaviors: a school-based program.* Unpubl.dissert., Simon Fraser Univ., Br. Columbia

Rosen JC, Orosan P, Reiter J. 1995. Cognitive behavior therapy for negative body image in obese women. *Behav. Ther.* 26:25–42

Rosen JC, Saltzberg E, Srebnik D. 1989. Cognitive behavior therapy for negative body image. *Behav. Ther.* 20:393–404

Rosenthal R. 1991. *Meta-Analytic Procedures for Social Research.* Thousand Oaks, CA: Sage

Santonastoso P, Zanetti T, Ferrara S, Olivotto MC, Magnavita N, Savaro A. 1999. A preventive intervention program in adolescent school girls: a longitudinal study. *Psychother. Psychosom.* 68:46–50

Shepard RE. 2001. *The body and soul program: evaluation of a peer educator-led eating disorder education and prevention program.* Unpubl. dissert., Univ. Oregon, Eugene

Smolak L, Levine M, Schermer F. 1998a. A controlled evaluation of an elementary school primary prevention program for eating problems. *J. Psychosom. Res.* 44:339–53

Smolak L, Levine M, Schermer F. 1998b. Lessons from lessons: an evaluation of an elementary school prevention program. In *The Prevention of Eating Disorders*, ed. W Vandereyeken, G Noordenbos, pp. 137–72. London: Athlone

Steiner-Adair C, Sjostrom L, Franko DL, Pai S, Tucker R, et al. 2002. Primary prevention of risk factors for eating disorders in adolescent girls: learning from practice. *Int. J. Eat. Disord.* 32:401–11

Stewart DA, Carter JC, Drinkwater J, Hainsworth J, Fairburn CG. 2001. Modification of eating attitudes and behavior in adolescent girls: a controlled study. *Int. J. Eat. Disord.* 29:107–18

Stice E. 2001. A prospective test of the dual pathway model of bulimic pathology: mediating effects of dieting and negative affect. *J. Abnorm. Psychol.* 110:124–35

Stice E. 2002. Risk and maintenance factors for eating pathology: a meta-analytic review. *Psychol. Bull.* 128:825–48

Stice E, Cameron R, Killen JD, Hayward C, Taylor CB. 1999. Naturalistic weight reduction efforts prospectively predict growth in relative weight and onset of obesity among female adolescents. *J. Consult. Clin. Psychol.* 67:967–74

Stice E, Fisher M, Lowe MR. 2004a. Are dietary restraint scales valid measures of acute dietary restriction? Unobtrusive observational data suggest not. *Psychol. Assess.* 16:51–59

Stice E, Fisher M, Martinez E. 2004b. Eating disorder diagnostic scale: additional evidence of reliability and validity. *Psychol. Assess.* 16:60–71

Stice E, Killen JD, Hayward C, Taylor CB. 1998. Age of onset for binge eating and purging during adolescence: a four-year survival analysis. *J. Abnorm. Psychol.* 107:671–75

Stice E, Mazotti L, Weibel D, Agras WS. 2000. Dissonance prevention program decreases thin-ideal internalization, body dissatisfaction, dieting, negative affect, and bulimic symptoms: a preliminary experiment. *Int. J. Eat. Disord.* 27:206–17

Stice E, Orjada K, Tristan J. 2006a. Trial of a psychoeducational eating disturbance intervention for college women: a replication and extension. *Int. J. Eat. Disord.* 39:233–39

Stice E, Ragan J. 2002. A controlled evaluation of an eating disturbance psychoeducational intervention. *Int. J. Eat. Disord.* 31:159–71

Stice E, Rohde P, Bohon C, Heim K. 2006b. *A Randomized Effectiveness Trial of a Dissonance-Based Eating Disorder Prevention Program.* In preparation

Stice E, Shaw H. 2004. Eating disorder prevention programs: a meta-analytic review. *Psychol. Bull.* 130:206–27

Stice E, Shaw H, Burton E, Wade E. 2006c. Dissonance and healthy weight eating disorder prevention programs: a randomized efficacy trial. *J. Consult. Clin. Psychol.* 74:263–75

Presents prevention trial findings that dissonance and healthy-weight groups both led to reduced binge eating and obesity onset as well as to service utilization.

Stice E, Shaw H, Marti CN. 2006d. A meta-analytic review of obesity prevention programs for children and adolescents: the skinny on interventions that work. *Psychol. Bull.* 132:667–91

Stice E, Trost A, Chase A. 2003. Healthy weight control and dissonance-based eating disorder prevention programs: results from a controlled trial. *Int. J. Eat. Disord.* 33:10–21

Taylor CB, Bryson S, Luce KH, Cunning D, Celio A, et al. 2006. Prevention of eating disorders in at-risk college-age women. *Arch. Gen. Psychiatry* 63:881–88

Describes a computer-based intervention to prevent eating disorder onset in high-risk groups; this Internet-based intervention also reduced weight and shape concerns.

Tobler NS, Roona MR, Ochshorn P, Marshall DG, Streke AV, Stackpole KM. 2000. School-based adolescent drug prevention programs: 1998 meta-analysis. *J. Primary Prev.* 20:275–336

Varnado-Sullivan PJ, Zucker N, Williamson DA, Reas D, Thaw J, Netemeyer SB. 2001. Development and implementation of the Body Logic Program for adolescents: a two-stage prevention program for eating disorders. *Cogn. Behav. Pract.* 8:248–59

Wade TD, Davidson S, O'Dea JA. 2003. A preliminary controlled evaluation of a school-based media literacy program and self-esteem program for reducing eating disorder risk factors. *Int. J. Eat. Disord.* 33:371–83

Weiss KR, Wertheim EH. 2005. An evaluation of a primary prevention program for disordered eating in adolescent girls: examining responses of high- and low-risk girls. *Eat. Disord.* 13:143–56

Wertheim EH, Koerner J, Paxton S. 2001. Longitudinal predictors of restrictive eating and bulimic tendencies in three different age groups of adolescent girls. *J. Youth Adolesc.* 30:69–81

Wichstrom L. 2000. Psychological and behavioral factors unpredictive of disordered eating: a prospective study of the general adolescent population in Norway. *Int. J. Eat. Disord.* 28:33–42

Winzelberg AJ, Eppstein D, Eldredge KL, Wilfley D, Dasmahapatra R, et al. 2000. Effectiveness of an internet-based program for reducing risk factors for eating disorders. *J. Consult. Clin. Psychol.* 68:346–50

Winzelberg AJ, Taylor CB, Sharpe T, Eldredge KL, Dev P, Constantinou PS. 1998. Evaluation of a computer-mediated eating disorder intervention program. *Int. J. Eat. Disord.* 24:339–49

Wiseman CV, Sunday SR, Bortolotti F, Halmi KA. 2004. Primary prevention of eating disorders through attitudinal change: a two-country comparison. *Eat. Disord.* 12:241–50

Withers GF, Twigg K, Wertheim EH, Paxton SJ. 2002. A controlled evaluation of an eating disorders primary prevention videotape using the elaboration likelihood model of persuasion. *J. Psychosom. Res.* 53:1021–27

Wolf-Bloom MS. 1998. *Using media literacy training to prevent body dissatisfaction and subsequent eating problems in early adolescent girls.* Unpubl.dissert., Univ. Cincinnati, OH

Zabinski KJ, Calfas KJ, Gehrman CA, Wilfley DE, Sallis JF. 2001. Effects of a physical activity intervention on body image in university seniors: Project GRAD. *Ann. Behav. Med.* 23:247–52

Zabinski MF, Wilfley DE, Calfas KJ, Winzelburg AJ, Taylor CB. 2004. An interactive psychoeducational intervention for women at risk of developing an eating disorder. *J. Consult. Clin. Psychol.* 72:914–19

Sexual Dysfunctions in Women

Cindy M. Meston and Andrea Bradford

Department of Psychology, University of Texas at Austin, Austin, Texas 78712; email: meston@psy.utexas.edu

Annu. Rev. Clin. Psychol. 2007. 3:233–56

First published online as a Review in Advance on October 12, 2006

The *Annual Review of Clinical Psychology* is online at http://clinpsy.annualreviews.org

This article's doi:
10.1146/annurev.clinpsy.3.022806.091507

1548-5943/07/0427-0233$20.00

Key Words

women's sexuality, orgasm, desire, arousal, sexual pain

Abstract

In this article, we summarize the definition, etiology, assessment, and treatment of sexual dysfunctions in women. Although the *Diagnostic and Statistical Manual of Mental Disorders*, fourth edition (DSM-IV-TR) is our guiding framework for classifying and defining women's sexual dysfunctions, we draw special attention to recent discussion in the literature criticizing the DSM-IV-TR diagnostic criteria and their underlying assumptions. Our review of clinical research on sexual dysfunction summarizes psychosocial and biomedical management approaches, with a critical examination of the empirical support for commonly prescribed therapies and limitations of recent clinical trials.

Contents

INTRODUCTION

NHSLS: National Health and Social Life Survey (see Laumann et al. 1994)

In the past decade, a number of pivotal events in the field of women's sexuality have increased our knowledge of psychological contributors to female sexual dysfunction. One of these events was the publication of *The Social Organization of Sexuality* by Laumann et al. (1994), which presented the results of the National Health and Social Life Survey (NHSLS) of 1410 men and 1749 women aged 18 to 59 years who were given comprehensive interviews about their sexuality. Based on the survey, it was reported that a shocking 43% of women in America experience sexual concerns. This report evoked criticisms for labeling what was defined as sexual "problems" in the survey interviews as sexual "dysfunctions" in the results, with the concern being that the high-prevalence statistic would contribute to the medicalization of women's sexuality and lead to overprescribing drugs to treat psychological issues (e.g., Bancroft 2002a, Tiefer 1996). Although this is a valid concern for women with sexual problems that are not clinically diagnosable, on the opposite end of the spectrum is the percentage of women in that figure who would meet clinical diagnosis for sexual dysfunction. For those women, the NHSLS proved beneficial in spreading the word about women's sexual concerns. The increased discourse and awareness of the extent of women's sexual dysfunctions has undoubtedly helped many women with sexual concerns feel more comfortable talking about their sexual concerns and, perhaps, justified and/or motivated them to seek help. Clinicians in the field of sexuality are now, more than ever, faced with the challenge of effectively diagnosing the many women who present with sexual dysfunctions and offering them the best available treatment options.

The *Diagnostic and Statistical Manual of Mental Disorders*, fourth edition (DSM-IV-TR; Am. Psychol. Assoc. 2000), classifies sexual dysfunctions into disorders of desire (e.g., affecting thoughts about sex or motivation to engage in sexual activity), arousal (affecting psychological and physiological excitement in response to sexual stimulation), orgasm (delayed, diminished, or absent "peak" intensity of sexual pleasure or sensation), and pain (i.e., genital or pelvic pain occurring before, during, or after sexual activity). In the past decade, three International Consensus Conferences gathered experts in the field of women's sexuality for discussion of the definition and classification of female sexual dysfunctions. The most recent of these consisted of four meetings during 2002 and 2003, and was composed of an international, multidisciplinary group of 13 experts from five countries. The result of these consensus conferences was the glaring realization that the DSM-IV-TR and the *International Statistical Classification of Disease and Related Health Problems* (ICD10) definitions of female sexual dysfunction are unsatisfactory. As noted in the conference publication (Basson et al. 2003), this stems in part from the problematic conceptualization of women's sexual response cycle. That is, the DSM-IV-TR and ICD10 definitions of women's sexual dysfunction are based on a model more characteristic of men than of women (Masters & Johnson 1966, Kaplan 1979), with the assumed sequential stages of desire, arousal, and orgasm. The panel challenged several assumptions underlying the DSM-IV-TR and ICD10 definitions of women's sexual dysfunctions and provided a revised classification system (Basson et al. 2003), which is discussed below in this article. Hopefully, the revised definitions will aid future research on women's sexual dysfunctions by better delineating the clinical realities of women's sexuality and by helping clinicians to minimize inappropriate classification and pathologizing of women.

Undeniably, the introduction of sildenafil (Viagra) in 1998 for male erectile disorder, and the subsequent investigation of vasodilator drugs for women's sexual dysfunction, has had an enormous impact on psychological research on women's sexuality. Two findings that emerged from the many clinical trials of sildenafil and similar drugs in women warrant mention here. First is the finding of a substantial placebo effect of up to about 40% in women with sexual problems (e.g., Basson et al. 2002), and second is the finding that these drugs often increased physiological sexual arousal in women without showing a comparable increase in psychological sexual arousal (Basson et al. 2002, Laan et al. 2002). The former of these findings points to the powerful influence that factors such as expectancies for improvement, enrolling in a study about sexuality, talking to a professional about sexual concerns, and/or monitoring sexual responses can have on women's sexual response. Future research is now needed to parse the potential contribution of each of these nonspecific factors to improved sexual functioning and explore how these beneficial elements might be applied in therapeutic settings. The second finding, which we note in the pharmacological treatment of female sexual arousal disorder (FSAD) section in this article, is the lack of a clinically meaningful drug influence on psychological sexual arousal in women, despite increases in genital engorgement with vasodilator drugs. This finding, which contrasts the high correspondence between self-report and physiological sexual arousal with vasodilator drug use in men, highlights the limitations of applying a male template to study women's sexual concerns.

FSAD: female sexual arousal disorder

HSDD: hypoactive sexual desire disorder

In this article, we review current conceptualizations and treatments of the major sexual dysfunctions in women, with a focus on recent empirical and theoretical advances. In particular, we refer to the results of recent epidemiological and clinical studies and to the recommendations of the consensus panel on the classification of women's sexual dysfunctions (Basson et al. 2003).

FEMALE SEXUAL DESIRE AND AROUSAL DISORDERS

Definitions and Epidemiology

Hypoactive sexual desire disorder (HSDD) is defined in the DSM-IV-TR as persistent or recurrent deficient (or absent) sexual fantasies and desire for sexual activity that causes marked distress or interpersonal difficulty. The clinical judgment is made taking into consideration factors that affect sexual functioning, such as age and the context of the person's life. The disorder is subtyped into lifelong versus acquired and generalized versus situational.

A primary criticism of the DSM-IV-TR definition of HSDD made by the consensus panel is the characterization of sexual fantasies as being a primary trigger for sexual behavior. Although engaging in sexual fantasy may be characteristic of women in new relationships, research suggests that spontaneous sexual thoughts or fantasies occur far less frequently among sexually healthy women in longer-term relationships (e.g., Cawood & Bancroft 1996). Moreover, women report a wide range of triggers or cues leading to sexual interactions that are not addressed in the DSM-IV-TR criteria, such as the desire to experience tenderness/appreciation for and by the partner, and the need to feel desirable. As noted above, the DSM-IV-TR criteria are based on early models of sexual response outlined by Masters & Johnson (1966) and amended by Kaplan (1979) in which desire is assumed to precede arousal and orgasm in a linear, sequential manner. Clinical experience indicates, however, that oftentimes arousal precedes desire in women. For example, a woman may not necessarily feel a desire to engage in sexual activity but, if approached, she may be "receptive" to sexual activity and, once engaged, she may then experience a desire for further sexual activity. To address these issues, the consensus panel suggested HSDD be defined as absent or diminished feelings of sexual interest or desire, absent sexual thoughts or fantasies, and a lack of responsive desire (i.e., unwilling or uninterested in engaging in sexual activity when approached). Motivations for attempting to become sexually aroused are scarce or absent. The lack of interest is considered to be beyond a normative lessening with life cycle and relationship duration.

Distinguished from a passive lack of sexual thoughts and/or behaviors is an aversion to sexual situations that is marked by anxiety or disgust, suggesting a phobia-like reaction to sexual behavior. The DSM-IV-TR differentiates this pattern of behavior from HSDD and terms it "sexual aversion disorder," defined as the "persistent or recurrent extreme aversion to, and avoidance of, all (or almost all) genital sexual contact with a sexual partner," causing distress or interpersonal difficulty. The disorder is further categorized by course (lifelong versus acquired) and specificity (situational versus generalized) of symptoms. Under the current definition of the disorder, a woman who engages in sexual activity in spite of anxiety or disgust (e.g., to satisfy a sexual partner) would not meet the avoidance criterion for sexual aversion disorder. The international consensus panel suggested a definition of the disorder (Basson et al. 2003) that emphasizes the appraisal of sexual contact rather than behavior as the hallmark feature of the disorder: "extreme anxiety and/or disgust at the anticipation of or attempt to have any sexual activity." Although sexual aversion disorder is generally not considered rare, surveys of sexual problems seldom assess for symptoms of sexual aversion, and prevalence estimates are not available.

Female sexual arousal disorder (FSAD) is defined in the DSM-IV-TR as a persistent or recurrent inability to attain or to maintain until completion of sexual activity an adequate genital lubrication-swelling response of sexual excitement that causes marked distress or interpersonal difficulty. As with HSDD, FSAD is subtyped into lifelong versus acquired and generalized versus situational. The DSM-IV-TR definition of FSAD focuses exclusively on a genital response when, in fact, women's sexual arousal includes various components including sexual excitement, a sense of being sexually awakened, and other physiological changes such as breast/nipple sensations (Basson et al. 2003). Moreover, vaginal lubrication appears to be an immediate "reflexive" response to any sexual stimuli—whether desired and enjoyed or not, and it does not always correlate closely with a woman's subjective experience of feeling "sexually turned on." For these reasons, the international consensus panel suggested the following three subtypes of FSAD (Basson et al. 2003):

1. Subjective sexual arousal disorder, which refers to the absence of or markedly diminished feelings of sexual arousal (sexual excitement and sexual pleasure) from any type of sexual stimulation. Vaginal lubrication or other signs of physical response still occur.
2. Genital sexual arousal disorder, which is often seen in women with autonomic nerve damage and in some estrogen-deficient women, refers to absent or impaired genital sexual arousal (e.g., minimal vulval swelling or vaginal lubrication from any type of sexual stimulation and reduced sexual sensations from caressing genitalia). Subjective sexual

excitement still occurs from nongenital sexual stimuli.

3. Combined genital and subjective arousal disorder, which is the most common clinical presentation and is usually comorbid with lack of sexual interest.

In addition to these three FSAD subtypes, the consensus committee also suggested including what they termed "persistent sexual arousal disorder." Often seen by clinicians conducting sex therapy, this previously undefined syndrome consists of spontaneous, intrusive, and unwanted genital arousal in the absence of sexual interest and desire. Any awareness of subjective arousal is typically, but not invariably, unpleasant. The arousal is unrelieved by one or more orgasms and the feelings of arousal persist for hours or days (Basson et al. 2003).

Desire concerns are the most frequently reported sexual complaint among women. Based on findings from a large national survey, Laumann et al. (1999) reported 31% of U.S. women experienced a lack of interest in sex for at least several months during the prior year. Findings from a clinic-based study indicated a 29% lifetime prevalence rate of low sexual desire in women. Difficulties with lubrication have been noted in 8%–15% of all women and 21%–31% of sexually active women (for review, see Lewis et al. 2004). The incidence is higher among women of peri- or postmenopausal years, with one study reporting that 44% of postmenopausal women experience persistent or recurrent lubrication problems (Rosen et al. 1993).

HSDD and FSAD often present together, and FSAD rarely presents alone. With regard to the latter, several theorists have suggested that the majority of female sexual difficulties reflect disruptions in sexual arousal. Orgasm is impossible without arousal, and a lack of arousal commonly leads to a lack of desire simply because sexual activity is not enjoyable or reinforcing. Even sexual pain disorders may be intricately linked to a lack of sufficient sexual arousal. Intercourse without lubrication can be painful, and repeated intercourse without arousal may cause vulvar infections, chronic irritation, and may even lead to secondary vaginismus, fear of sex, or the avoidance of sexual activity altogether.

Etiologic Factors

Biological factors. Several lines of evidence point to a link between women's sexual desire and levels of sex steroid hormones, particularly androgens and estrogens. In women, these hormones are produced in the adrenal glands and ovaries via two metabolic pathways. Disorders of ovarian function and of the hypothalamic-pituitary-adrenal axis interfere with these processes and have been associated with reduced sexual desire and problems with sexual arousal (for review, see Guay & Spark 2006). Sexual problems have also been described in connection to menopause, during which decreased ovarian function results in lower estrogen production. Recent epidemiological studies indicate that "surgical menopause" induced by oophorectomy (surgical removal of the ovaries) is a more prominent risk factor for HSDD than is natural menopause, particularly among younger cohorts (Dennerstein et al. 2006, Leiblum et al. 2006).

It is well established that estrogen is necessary to maintain the structure and function of vaginal tissue. Estrogen deficiencies may result in genital arousal problems related to reduced vaginal lubrication and atrophy of vaginal tissue. Androgens have been implicated more commonly in the maintenance of sexual desire and mood, although there is some physiological evidence that androgens also enhance the function of vaginal tissue. However, there is controversy about the relative importance of androgens among the many other factors contributing to women's sexual desire. Past research findings suggest substantial individual differences in responsiveness to androgens (for review, see Bancroft 2002b). Further complicating the picture is the fact that androgens are aromatized to estrogens in the body, and treatment with estrogen can suppress the production of androgens. The bioavailability of both estrogens and androgens is affected by levels of sex hormone–binding globulin, which itself can be affected by hormonal treatment (Basson et al. 2005, Guay & Spark 2006). Thus, sexual function disturbances related to sex hormone levels can be endogenous or iatrogenic.

Individual differences in hormonal profiles and responsiveness to androgen treatment complicate the development of clinical recommendations for androgen supplementation. Despite widespread clinical interest in androgen treatment, studies have not established a broadly generalizable relationship between endogenous androgens and sexual function. Among mid-life women, two longitudinal studies (Dennerstein et al. 2006, Gerber et al. 2005) and a cross-sectional study (Santoro et al. 2005) have found no meaningful relationship between testosterone levels and sexual function. On the other hand, Guay et al. (2004) reported significantly lower levels of adrenal androgens among premenopausal women with sexual complaints compared to those with no sexual complaints. Given individual differences in endocrine physiology, as well as the fact that hormones are but one of many influences on sexual function, further studies using relatively large sample sizes are necessary to draw general conclusions about the relationship of androgens and other sex hormones to women's desire and arousal.

Problems with sexual desire and arousal are associated with several types of pharmacological treatments that affect various neurotransmitter and hormone levels. Some of the most commonly cited classes of drugs believed to impair sexual desire and arousal include serotonergic drugs (e.g., selective serotonin reuptake inhibitors, or SSRIs), some antiadrenergic drugs (e.g., beta-blockers), and selective estrogen receptor modulators. In addition to prescription drug side effects, other iatrogenic sexual side effects, many associated with cancer treatment (e.g., radical hysterectomy, radiation therapy), may cause substantial impairment (for a discussion of sexuality and cancer, see Krychman et al. 2006).

The influence of general health status on sexual desire and arousability is often overlooked in theoretical discussions but is worthy of mention. Fatigue, pain, and mood disturbance caused by chronic illness can contribute to substantial declines in sexual function. In a large population-based study of postmenopausal women, low sexual desire was associated with poorer health on all but one of the domains of the widely used SF-36 health status measure (Leiblum et al. 2006). Physical activity also appears to play a role in sexual function (Dennerstein & Lehert 2004, Gerber et al. 2005) and should be more carefully investigated as a predictor of sexual well-being.

Psychological factors. Beliefs and attitudes about sexuality acquired over the course of sexual development can influence sexual desire and sexual response across the life span. Women who internalize passive gender roles or negative attitudes toward sexuality may be at greater risk of experiencing sexual problems (Nobre & Pinto-Gouveia 2006, Sanchez et al. 2005). Among lesbian and bisexual women, internalized homophobia may negatively affect intimacy between partners (Otis et al. 2006). Women with a history of sexual mistreatment may associate sexual activity with punishment, shame, guilt, and loss, and may be hesitant to enter into relationships (van Berlo & Ensink 2000).

Mood and anxiety disorders have been associated with sexual desire and arousal difficulties and should be ruled out prior to sexuality-focused treatment. Anxiety that is relatively specific to sexual concerns plays an important role in the etiology of sexual arousal problems. Barlow (1986) proposed that the cognitive distraction of performance anxiety directs attention from sexual to nonsexual cues, interfering with arousal. Whereas in men performance anxiety usually pertains to attaining and maintaining an erection, in women "performance" concerns may be directed at other attributes such as perceived sexual attractiveness. Consistent with this view, studies of women indicate that self-consciousness about body image and sexual desirability predict sexual esteem, sexual assertiveness, and sexual function (Dove & Wiederman 2000, Wiederman 2000).

Although factors within the individual woman may contribute to sexual desire and arousal difficulties, it is valuable to conceptualize these problems in the context of the relationship with the sexual partner. The clinician should always consider the possibility that a woman's lack of enthusiasm for sex is a perfectly normal reaction to problems such as poor sexual knowledge or skill on the part of her partner, a highly restricted sexual repertoire, or a lack of sexual activities that are stimulating and pleasurable to the woman. A more extreme, though not uncommon, scenario is when sexual problems develop concomitantly with sexual problems in the partner. Although previous research has identified partner sexual dysfunction as a frequent reason that women avoid sexual activity, the influence of the partner's sexual problems has received relatively little study until recently. Women involved with men who have premature ejaculation or erectile dysfunction are at increased risk for sexual desire and arousal problems. Interestingly, Goldstein et al. (2005) reported that pharmacologic treatment of male erectile dysfunction was associated with improved sexual desire, arousal, and satisfaction among their female partners.

Problems of sexual desire are often conceptualized as "desire discrepancies" between sexual partners to avoid pathologizing the partner who desires sex less often. Whereas individual-centered models of sexual desire may attribute between-partner differences to factors such as personality, hormone levels, and other components of each partner's "innate" sexual drive, systemic theories focus on the function of desire differences in maintaining the power and emotional balance of the relationship. Schnarch (1991) points out the vulnerability inherent in openly desiring a partner, which may be too anxiety provoking if a perceived threat to the relationship or loss of power is at stake.

Feminist perspectives on low sexual desire among women in heterosexual relationships place the couple dynamic in a larger sociocultural context wherein men's desires are valued and women's desires are either minimized or denied (Richgels 1992). Wanting to be desired, to be the object of men's sexual attraction, is culturally reinforced, and deviations from male-centric sexual scripts are socially rejected. In this context, the very notion of a mere desire discrepancy between partners becomes suspect. Hare-Mustin (1991) argues that the pretense of gender parity in the relationship "transform[s] inequality into personality differences or into men's and women's different essential natures." Applied to sexuality, a forced categorization of innate high (normal) and low (pathological) sexual desire is a simplification that obfuscates the considerably thornier issues of gender inequality. Careful assessment may reveal maladaptive gender roles that maintain sexual problems even within ostensibly egalitarian relationships.

Assessment

Comprehensive assessment of women's sexual dysfunction includes a detailed clinical interview to gather information on the presenting problem, on the woman's sexual and relationship history, her psychosocial history, and her medical history. **Table 1** presents an overview of the types of questions that should be included in the interview for all sexual disorders (expanded upon and adapted from Basson et al. 2004, Brandenburg & Schwenkhagen 2006, Perelman 2006). Questions pertaining to the assessment of specific disorders are mentioned separately in the text.

When HSDD is suspected, further questioning about the context of the problem should focus on situations or cues that might have stimulated the woman's interest in sex in

Table 1 General psychosocial and sexual assessment

I. Presenting problem	
a. Nature of the problem	Description of the difficulty in the woman's words Other or secondary sexual problems Past history of sexual problems
b. Degree of distress	What do the symptoms mean for her? What has her reaction been? How has the problem affected the sexual relationship?
c. Lifelong versus acquired	When was the onset? What is her belief about the cause(s) of the change? What has the progression been since the onset?
d. Situational versus generalized	How has it been with other partners? How is it when she is alone? Does she experience the difficulty all the time or only under certain circumstances? Are there any situations or contexts in which the problem *does not* occur?
e. Frequency	How often does the problem occur? Has the frequency of the problem changed over time?
f. Partner sexual problems or concerns	
g. Partner reaction	How has the partner responded to the problem? What does the partner think the cause of the problem is?
h. History of treatment	What prior treatments (including self-help) has she attempted? What was the outcome?
II. Sexual and relationship history	
a. Sexual history	First sexual experiences Family attitudes toward sex History of sexual violence or trauma
b. Relationship history	What have past relationships been like? Nature and duration of current relationship Marital/cohabitation status History of partner abuse/violence
c. Psychosocial history	Cultural, religious, family-of-origin, and/or societal beliefs or values that may influence sexual function Work/finance Children Other life stressors
III. Health history	
a. Psychological/psychiatric history	Mood and anxiety disorders Psychotic disorders Eating disorders and body image disturbance Substance use
b. Medical history	Sexually transmitted infections (e.g., human immunodeficiency virus) Cancer (esp. breast cancer and gynecological cancers) Disease or surgery of the reproductive organs Neurological disorders (e.g., multiple sclerosis) Endocrine disorders (e.g., diabetes, hypothyroidism, hyperprolactinemia) History of spinal cord or traumatic brain injury
c. Current medication use	

the past. If a woman endorses certain "turn-ons," it is useful to determine whether these cues or fantasies are absent from her life, fail to interest her any longer, or have been self-censored because they are unacceptable to her for some reason. A candid discussion of the woman's attraction to and feelings toward her partner are useful as well. Frequency of sexual activity in and of itself should not be considered indicative of a sexual desire problem (or lack thereof), as the desire for sex is only one of a multitude of factors informing the choice to be sexual.

Assessment of arousal problems should focus both on the mental and genital components of the woman's sexual arousal, for example:

1. How mentally excited does she become in various sexual situations: when alone (e.g., reading erotica), when stimulating her partner, and when her partner stimulates her?
2. Does she experience genital sensations (e.g., tingling, swelling, pulsing)?
3. Is genital lubrication completely absent, is it inadequate, or does it disappear?

In addition to the clinical interview, a number of validated measures have been published that may serve as adjuncts for understanding the level of sexual functioning the woman is experiencing and for monitoring treatment changes. These include the Brief Index of Sexual Functioning for Women (Taylor et al. 1994), the Changes in Sexual Functioning Questionnaire (Clayton et al. 1997), the Derogatis Interview for Sexual Functioning (Derogatis 1979), the Female Sexual Function Index (Rosen et al. 2000), the Cues for Desire Scale (McCall & Meston 2006), and the Sexual Satisfaction Scale (Meston & Trapnell 2005) (for review of validated measures, see Meston & Derogatis 2002). Questionnaires that specifically address relationship issues include the Dyadic Adjustment Scale (Spanier 1976), the Relationship Beliefs Scale (Fletcher & Kininmonth 1992), and the Locke-Wallace Marital Adjustment Test (Locke & Wallace 1959).

It is generally recommended that the woman be referred for a full general physical examination for all complaints of sexual function (for detail, see Stewart 2006). In addition to ruling out or identifying various medical factors, the exam serves to educate women about their anatomy and what is normal or problematic. If a hormonal problem is suspected, assays for prolactin, total testosterone, free testosterone, sex hormone–binding globulin, dihydroepiandrosterone, estrogens, and cortisol may be warranted to rule out endocrine disorders. Although diagnostic laboratories routinely provide reference values for these hormones, there is controversy as to what differentiates "normal," "low," and "deficient" hormonal states (Guay & Spark 2006). Hormone deficiencies are defined primarily by symptoms rather than specific quantitative cutoff points (e.g., Bachmann et al. 2002).

Treatment

Psychological. The psychological treatment literature focuses primarily on HSDD, with little apparent work directed specifically at FSAD. However, the sex therapy techniques pioneered by Masters & Johnson (1970) remain in widespread use among clinicians treating all types of sexual disorders. At the core of traditional Masters & Johnson's sex therapy is an emphasis on sexuality education, partner communication skills, and sensate focus exercises. Cognitive-behavioral techniques may be useful when traditional sex therapy and education alone are not effective or appropriate. Studies of cognitive-behavioral treatments for HSDD have, in fact, included traditional sex therapy components such as sensate focus. These therapies are distinguished in large part by cognitive techniques used to challenge beliefs that undermine sexual desire and arousal, such as unrealistic expectations of performance, self-consciousness, and even the notion that one is innately dysfunctional. Evidence from the relatively few systematic trials of psychotherapy for HSDD show varying levels of efficacy for both traditional sex therapy and cognitive-behavioral therapy (for review, see Brotto 2006). Limitations of the psychological treatment literature include heterogeneity of treatment methods, limiting the comparability of studies, and experimental designs that preclude the analysis of separable treatment components. Evidence to support the efficacy of psychodynamic, systemic, and other types of treatment is at the level of clinical case reports. Well-defined manualized treatment protocols and rigorous experimental designs are needed to conduct large, replicable clinical trials.

Medical. The U.S. Food and Drug Administration (FDA) approved the EROS clitoral therapy device (Urometrics, St. Paul, MN) for use in women with FSAD following a noncontrolled study showing that the device, which increases vasocongestion through suction, increased vaginal lubrication, sensation, orgasm, and overall sexual satisfaction (Billups et al. 2001).

A series of recent studies have focused largely on the efficacy of transdermal testosterone among surgically menopausal women who are receiving concomitant estrogen therapy (e.g., Buster et al. 2005, Simon et al. 2005). These studies have found statistically significant improvement in primary and/or secondary outcome endpoints relative to placebo. However, the size of the effects and the nature of the endpoints themselves invite scrutiny. In one study, efficacy was declared on the basis of an average difference of about one "sexually satisfying activity" per four weeks between active treatment and placebo groups (Simon et al. 2005). Although this difference was statistically significant, the clinical meaningfulness of this and similar results is highly questionable (see Althof et al. 2005 for a discussion of regulatory influences on clinical trial endpoints in pharmaceutical trials). To date, transdermal testosterone has failed to appear on the market in light of concerns about long-term safety and treatment effects that are difficult to interpret as indicators of clinical utility.

Relatively few clinical trials have investigated the efficacy of nonhormonal pharmacological treatments specific to HSDD, although drug development efforts continue to target low sexual desire. Two compounds showing initial evidence of efficacy are mentioned here. Bupropion, sometimes used to counteract sexual dysfunction secondary to SSRI treatment, caused a modest improvement in sexual interest and arousal among nondepressed premenopausal women (Segraves et al. 2001) and among premenopausal women complaining of low sexual desire (Segraves et al. 2004). Results of a double-blind, crossover, placebo-controlled trial of apomorphine also suggested some clinical benefit associated with daily use in premenopausal women with HSDD and FSAD (Caruso et al. 2004). Although further study is required to understand the effects of these drugs, their central dopaminergic activity (bupropion as a reuptake inhibitor and apomorphine as an agonist) appears to be key. Animal models (e.g., Pfaus et al. 1995) and human genetic research (Ben Zion et al. 2006) implicate central dopamine pathways in regulating sexual motivation and reinforcement of sexual behavior.

To date, there are no FDA-approved pharmacological treatments for sexual arousal disorders. Most commonly, FSAD treatments involve the administration of topical lubricants that help to mask the impairment in vaginal lubrication associated with FSAD, but are ineffective in enhancing genital/clitoral blood flow or genital sensations that often accompany FSAD. Since the enormous success of using phosphodiesterase inhibitors (sildenafil, tadalafil, vardenafil) for treating male erectile dysfunction, a number of pharmaceutical companies have examined whether these and similar vasodilator drugs may also be effective for treating women's arousal concerns. Many of these drugs involve adrenergic and/or nitric oxide systems. Sexual stimulation leads to nitric oxide production that in turn stimulates the release of guanylate cyclase. Guanylate cyclase converts guanosine triphosphate to cGMP, and cGMP produces relaxation of the smooth muscles of the penile arteries and corpus cavernosum, resulting in increased blood flow into the penis. Drugs such as sildenafil inhibit the metabolism of cGMP, thus prolonging its action. Some evidence suggests that a comparable event may occur in women. Nitric oxide is produced in clitoral tissue and, with the exception that the clitoris does not contain a subalbugineal layer (which contributes to the rigidity of the penis), the anatomy of the clitoris is similar to that of the penis.

Results from a limited number of placebo-controlled studies suggest that phosphodiesterase inhibitors may be effective for treating difficulties with perceptions of physical sensations and physiological aspects of FSAD (e.g., improved genital sensation, vaginal lubrication, satisfaction with intercourse, clitoral sensitivity), particularly among postmenopausal women with FSAD (e.g., Basson & Brotto 2003, Berman et al. 2003). Among premenopausal women with FSAD, one placebo-controlled study indicated increased self-reported sexual arousal, orgasm, sexual fantasy, intercourse, and enjoyment of sexual activity with sildenafil (Caruso et al. 2001). Findings from comparable studies also suggest that vasodilator drugs can enhance blood flow into women's genital tissue and perceptions of genital responses. However, more often than not, sexual interest and psychological arousal are not comparably enhanced (Basson & Brotto 2003, Basson et al. 2002, Kaplan et al. 1999, Laan et al. 2002). This suggests that women may be estimating their degree of sexual arousal according to standards other than genital cues. That is, for women, external stimulus information such as relationship satisfaction, mood state, and sexual scenarios may play a more important role in assessing feelings of sexual desire and arousal than do internal physiological cues. If this is the case, drugs that target increasing vasocongestion are likely to be most effective in women with genital sexual arousal disorder whose primary complaint is decreased genital responding, experienced as decreases in lubrication and/or feelings of vaginal fullness or engorgement. This would most likely be women who are postmenopausal, who have undergone oophorectomy, or who suffer from arterial vascular problems. If a drug increases vaginal engorgement to the extent that it is detected and labeled as a "sexual feeling," for some women this may also enhance feelings of more general, psychological arousal.

FEMALE ORGASMIC DISORDER

FOD: female orgasmic disorder

Definitions and Epidemiology

The DSM-IV-TR defines female orgasmic disorder (FOD) as the persistent or recurrent delay in, or absence of, orgasm following a normal sexual excitement phase. As with HSDD, to meet criteria for FOD, the disturbance must cause marked distress or interpersonal difficulty. The diagnosis of FOD should be based on the clinician's judgment that the woman's orgasmic capacity is less than would be reasonable for her age, sexual experience, and the adequacy of sexual stimulation she receives. The DSM-IV-TR subtypes FOD as lifelong versus acquired and generalized versus situational. Although not stated in the DSM-IV-TR, the clinical consensus is that a woman who can obtain orgasm during intercourse with manual stimulation but not intercourse alone would not meet criteria for clinical diagnosis unless she is distressed by the frequency of her sexual response.

Most studies refer to orgasm problems in women as either "primary orgasmic dysfunction" or "secondary orgasmic dysfunction." In general, the term "primary orgasmic dysfunction" is used to describe women who report never having experienced orgasm under any circumstances, including masturbation. According to the DSM-IV-TR, this would refer to those women who meet criteria for lifelong and generalized FOD. Secondary orgasmic dysfunction relates to women who meet criteria for situational and/or acquired FOD. By definition, this encompasses a heterogeneous group of women with orgasm difficulties. For example, it could include women who were once orgasmic but are now so only infrequently; women who are only able to obtain orgasm in certain contexts, by engaging in certain types of sexual activity, or with certain partners. This lack of specificity in the definition of secondary orgasmic dysfunction often makes interpretation of outcome studies using this definition somewhat limited.

Also confusing in the literature, and for the clinician trying to determine diagnoses, is the fact that the definition of orgasm itself is often vague. A recent article cataloguing definitions of orgasm included more than 25 comprehensive definitions written by different authors (see Mah & Binik 2001). The following definition of female orgasm was derived by the committee on female orgasm, presented at the International Consultation on Urological Diseases in Official Relationship with the World Health Organization, Paris, 2003:

> An orgasm in the human female is a variable, transient peak sensation of intense pleasure, creating an altered state of consciousness, usually accompanied by involuntary, rhythmic contractions of the pelvic, striated circumvaginal musculature often with concomitant uterine and anal contractions and myotonia that resolves the sexually-induced vasocongestion (sometimes only partially), usually with an induction of well-being and contentment (Meston et al. 2004, p. 785).

Based on findings from the NHSLS (Laumann et al. 1994), orgasmic problems are the second most frequently reported sexual problems in U.S. women, with 24% of women reporting a lack of orgasm in the past year for at least several months or more. This percentage is comparable to clinic-based data. Orgasmic problems were noted by 29% of 329 healthy women (ages 18–73) who attended an outpatient gynecological clinic (Rosen et al. 1993) and by 23% of 104 women (18–65+) attending a U.K. general practice clinic (Read et al. 1997).

Etiologic Factors

Biological. Orgasms can be induced via erotic stimulation of a variety of genital and nongenital sites including the clitoris, vagina, other areas of the vulva, and the breasts/nipples, or via mental imagery, fantasy, or hypnosis. Consciousness is not an essential requirement for orgasm, given orgasms have been noted to occur during sleep. Cases of "spontaneous orgasm" have occasionally been described in the psychiatric literature where no obvious sexual stimulus can be ascertained (Polatin & Douglas 1953). Certain psychotropic drugs have infrequently been reported to induce spontaneous orgasms in women. Compared with preorgasm levels of sexual arousal, the brain areas activated during orgasm in women include the paraventricular nucleus of the hypothalamus, the periaqueductal gray of the midbrain, the hippocampus, and the cerebellum.

Although there is no known biological cause of FOD, a number of medical conditions lead to orgasm difficulties in women, and side effects of a number of pharmacological treatments include impairments in orgasm function. The worst drug offenders appear to be those that increase serotonergic activity (e.g., antidepressants; paroxetine, fluoxetine, sertraline) or decrease dopaminergic activity (e.g., antipsychotics). The degree to which the former of these influences orgasm appears to be dependent upon which serotonin receptor subtype they activate/inhibit. For example, the antidepressant nefazodone has been reported to produce fewer sexual side effects in women (Feiger et al. 1996) than many of the earlier generation of SSRIs. Nefazodone increases serotonin activity in general while simultaneously inhibiting serotonin activity at the serotonin$_2$ receptor, which may possibly lead to an increase in dopamine and norepinephrine, neurotransmitters reported to facilitate sexual behavior.

Given that, under most circumstances, a certain level of sexual arousal is necessary for orgasm to occur, any of the factors described above that inhibit arousal can also impair orgasm. Women with spinal cord injuries in the sacral region of the spinal cord, which interferes with the sacral reflex arc, show difficulty attaining orgasm (Sipski et al. 2001). Data from human and animal studies led Whipple et al. (1996) to suggest that the vagus nerve connecting the cervix to the brain is key in maintaining the ability of patients with spinal cord injuries to experience orgasm. Women with spinal cord injuries at the mid-thoracic area and below were able to achieve orgasm 52% of the time in a laboratory study, compared with 100% in healthy controls (Sipski et al. 1995).

Psychological. Age, education, religion, personality, and relationship issues are the psychosocial factors most commonly discussed in relation to female orgasmic ability. Laumann et al. (1994) reported the youngest group of women (18–24 years) surveyed showed rates of orgasm lower than those of the older groups for both orgasm with a partner and orgasm during masturbation. This may be explained in terms of age differences in sexual experience. Substantial differences were also noted between education level and ability to attain orgasm during masturbation, but not with a partner. Approximately 87% of women with an advanced degree reported "always" or "usually" attaining orgasm during masturbation compared with 42% of women with a high school education. These findings were explained as the better-educated women having more liberal views on sexuality and being more likely to seek pleasure as a goal of sexual activity.

A negative relation between high religiosity and orgasmic ability in women is frequently reported in the clinical literature. Possibly, the more religious a person, the more likely they are to experience guilt during sexual activity. Feasibly, guilt could impair orgasm via a number of cognitive mechanisms, in particular distraction processes. A relation between improved orgasmic ability and decreased sexual guilt has also been reported (Sholty et al. 1984). Laumann et al. (1994) reported a substantially higher proportion (79%) of women with no religious affiliation reported being orgasmic during masturbation compared with religious groups (53%–67%).

Relationship factors such as marital satisfaction and adjustment, happiness, and stability have been related to orgasm consistency, quality, and satisfaction in women (for review, see Mah & Binik 2001). These findings are correlational in nature. Clearly, a satisfying marital relationship is not necessary for orgasm, particularly given that rates of orgasm consistency in women are higher during masturbation than with a partner (Laumann et al. 1994). A satisfying marital relationship most likely promotes orgasmic function via increased communication regarding sexually pleasurable activity, decreased anxiety, and enhancement of the subjective and emotional qualities of orgasm (Mah & Binik 2001). In an extensive investigation of background and personality variables and women's orgasm, Fisher (1973) found few significant associations.

Assessment

General psychological and sexual assessment questions are listed in **Table 1**. Additional specific questions pertaining to FOD include:

1. Is orgasm absent, delayed, or of reduced intensity?
2. What is the woman's frequency of masturbation?
3. How often does she experience sexual fantasy?

Treatment

Psychological. Directed masturbation (DM) has been shown to be an empirically valid, efficacious treatment for women diagnosed with primary anorgasmia (for review, see Meston et al. 2004). This treatment uses cognitive behavioral therapy techniques to educate a woman about her body and the sensations she is able to elicit while manually stimulating herself. DM involves several stages that build upon one another. First, the woman engages in a visual exploration

DM: directed masturbation

of her body, using a mirror and educational material depicting female genital anatomy. Following visual and manual identification of the sensitive genital areas that elicit pleasure, the woman is instructed to apply targeted manual stimulation to these regions. The use of topical lubricants, vibrators, and erotic videotapes are often incorporated into the exercises. Once the woman is able to attain orgasm alone, her partner is usually included in the sessions in order to desensitize her to displaying arousal and orgasm in his presence, and to educate the partner on how to provide her with effective stimulation (for a detailed guide to DM, please refer to Heiman & LoPicollo 1988).

Allowing a woman to explore her body on her own is beneficial because it eliminates several factors that may be barriers to orgasm, including anxiety that may be associated with the presence of a partner. The amount and intensity of sexual stimulation is directly under the woman's control and therefore she is not reliant upon her partner's knowledge or her ability to communicate her needs to her partner. A number of studies report DM is highly successful for treating primary anorgasmia in a variety of treatment modalities including group, individual, couples therapy, and self-directed masturbation training (bibliotherapy) (for review, see Meston 2006). Using therapist DM training, Heinrich (1976) reported a 100% success rate for treating primary anorgasmia at two-month follow-up. The study was a controlled comparison of therapist-directed group masturbation training, bibliotherapy, and wait-list control.

Few controlled studies have examined the exclusive effects of DM for treating secondary anorgasmia. Fichen et al. (1983) compared minimal therapist contact bibliotherapy with a variety of techniques including DM and found no change in orgasmic ability. For women with secondary anorgasmia who are averse to touching their genitals, DM may be beneficial. If, however, the woman is able to attain orgasm alone through masturbation but not with her partner, issues relating to communication, anxiety reduction, trust, and ensuring the woman is receiving adequate stimulation either via direct manual stimulation or engaging in intercourse using positions designed to maximize clitoral stimulation may prove more beneficial.

Anxiety reduction techniques such as systematic desensitization and sensate focus are often used to treat orgasm difficulties, usually in combination with other techniques such as sexual techniques training, DM, sex education, communication training, bibliotherapy, and Kegel exercises. Across studies, women have reported decreases in sexual anxiety and, occasionally, increases in frequency of sexual intercourse and sexual satisfaction with systematic desensitization, but substantial improvements in orgasmic ability have not been noted (Meston et al. 2004). Similarly, of the few controlled studies that have included sensate focus as a treatment component, none have reported notable increases in orgasmic ability. These findings suggest that, in most cases, anxiety does not appear to play a causal role in FOD, and anxiety reduction techniques are best suited for anorgasmic women only when sexual anxiety is coexistent.

Other behavioral techniques used to treat FOD that warrant mention include sex education, communication training, and Kegel exercises. Communication training could enhance orgasmic ability by teaching individuals to better express their sexual needs to their partner. Kegel exercises (Kegel 1952), designed to strengthen the pubococcygeous muscle, could feasibly facilitate orgasm by increasing vascularity to the genitals, thus enhancing arousal, or by helping the woman become more aware and comfortable with her genitals. Although the independent contribution of these techniques for treating FOD has not been adequately assessed, an extensive review of the literature suggests these techniques may serve as beneficial adjuncts to therapy (Meston et al. 2004).

Medical. To date, no pharmacological treatments for FOD have been found to be more effective than placebo (for a review of pharmacological treatments, see Meston et al. 2004). There is a high incidence of adverse sexual side effects, including inhibited or delayed orgasm, noted with antidepressant treatment. If the patient is taking selective serotonin reuptake inhibitors and the orgasmic difficulties seem to coincide with the onset of the drug treatment, clinicians may recommend a change in prescription to an antidepressant that also affects dopamine and norepinephrine levels. These include bupropion, nefazodone, and moclobemide.

SEXUAL PAIN DISORDERS

Definitions and Epidemiology

The DSM-IV-TR identifies two sexual pain disorders, vaginismus and dyspareunia. Under the DSM-IV-TR definition, the key criterion for the diagnosis of vaginismus is a persistent or recurrent involuntary spasm of the outer third of the vagina that interferes with sexual intercourse. Two particular aspects of this definition are worthy of comment and scrutiny. First, it is clear that contraction of the pelvic floor musculature can prevent vaginal penetration, but recent empirical work has demonstrated that vaginal spasms are neither sensitive nor specific to women who report difficulty with vaginal penetration (Reissing et al. 2004). Furthermore, although vaginismus is classified as a pain disorder and appears to be associated with genital pain in most cases (ter Kuile et al. 2005), the DSM-IV-TR diagnostic criteria do not specify that pain must be present to receive the diagnosis. These criticisms were noted in the report of the most recent international consensus conference on female sexual dysfunction classification (Basson et al. 2003), which recommended a revised definition of vaginismus as follows:

> Persistent difficulties to allow vaginal entry of a penis, a finger, and/or any object, despite the woman's expressed wish to do so. There is a variable involuntary pelvic muscle contraction, (phobic) avoidance and anticipation/fear/experience of pain. Structural or other physical abnormalities must be ruled out/addressed.

In contrast to the DSM-IV-TR criteria, the proposed definition of vaginismus does not specify a muscle spasm localized exclusively to the vagina. The definition also emphasizes features of the disorder that suggest etiological mechanisms similar to those of anxiety disorders.

Dyspareunia is a broad term used to describe genital pain associated with sexual activity that causes distress or interpersonal difficulty. Though not a formal aspect of the definition, dyspareunia is typically described as either superficial (e.g., associated with the vulva and/or vaginal entrance) or deep (perceived in the abdomen or internal organs, often associated with penile thrusting); most cases fall into the former category. The DSM-IV-TR distinguishes dyspareunia from genital pain caused "exclusively" by vaginismus, lack of lubrication, or a medical condition. In practice, this criterion may be limiting and difficult to establish, as the cause of genital pain is not always implicated exclusively in its maintenance. Accordingly, the international consensus committee recommended a more inclusive revision of the definition as follows: "Persistent or recurrent pain with attempted or complete vaginal entry and/or penile vaginal intercourse" (Basson et al. 2003). Some researchers have further argued that vaginismus and dyspareunia overlap in clinical presentation to the extent that it is questionable to regard them as distinct disorders (de Kruiff et al. 2000, Reissing et al. 1999).

Because many epidemiological studies exclude questions about vaginismus, the prevalence of the disorder is not well established, though it is estimated to be between 1% and 6% (Lewis et al. 2004). More data are available on the epidemiology of dyspareunia, although estimates vary depending on geographical location and setting (Weijmar Schultz et al.

VVS: vulvar vestibulitis syndrome

2005). In one of the largest prevalence surveys to date, Laumann et al. (1999) reported that approximately 16% of American women reported persistent or recurrent sexual pain in the past year, with older age associated with a lower likelihood of sexual pain. These results are consistent with those of a large epidemiological survey conducted in France in which 5% of women endorsed sexual intercourse pain "often" and 19% endorsed intercourse pain "some of the time" (cited in Binik et al. 1999). In a community-based survey of 303 women, 12% reported a chronic history of pain provoked by *any* genital contact (Harlow et al. 2001).

Etiology

Biological. Although vaginal spasm does not appear to be a reliable indicator of vaginismus, increased pelvic muscle tone and greater muscle weakness may distinguish sexual pain conditions with and without vaginal penetration difficulties (Reissing et al. 2004). Genital pain may result from a variety of medical conditions and anatomical variations that should be ruled out by medical examination. Superficial pain may be a symptom of dermatological disorders affecting the external genitalia, vaginal atrophy, anatomical variations, urinary tract infections, injury, and other diseases and infections of the vulva. Deep pain may result from uterine fibroids, endometriosis, urinary disease, and ovarian disease, among other conditions (for review, see Weijmar Schultz et al. 2005).

Clinical observation and research suggests that the majority of women with superficial dyspareunia show a reliable symptom pattern that includes sensitivity to touch and pressure of the vulvar vestibule, a region of the female external genitalia that includes the tissues surrounding the vaginal and urethral openings. There is erythema in the sensitive region, and touch or pressure evokes a sharp, burning pain (Pukall et al. 2005). Known as vulvar vestibulitis syndrome (VVS), this disorder is considered separate from other pain syndromes of the vulva not attributable to infection, injury, etc. The etiology of VVS is uncertain, but several lines of research support evidence of a physiological sensitivity of the vulvar vestibule. Women with VVS often have a history of yeast infections and may have had significant hormonal events in adolescence, including early onset of menstruation and early use of oral contraceptives (Pukall et al. 2005). Vulvodynia is diagnosed when pain is not specific to the vulvar vestibule and is not attributable to other identifiable pathology. Less is known about the etiology of this disorder.

Regardless of origin, pain may persist after its initial provocation via a number of mechanisms, including psychological and neurological changes. When conceptualized as a pain disorder rather than a sexual disorder (Binik et al. 1999), sexual pain shares many etiological similarities with chronic low back pain and other chronic pain syndromes. To attempt to isolate psychogenic and physiological components of chronic pain maintenance is a dubious exercise, as they are integral to one another. Sensitization of peripheral and central nervous pathways governing pain is thought to accompany psychological reactions that exacerbate the experience of pain (Weijmar Schultz et al. 2005).

Psychological. Elevated rates of comorbid anxiety disorders and higher trait anxiety have been found across subtypes of sexual pain disorders. Studies of women with dyspareunia and VVS also suggest greater erotophobia and negative attitudes toward sexuality in these populations (Weijmar Schultz et al. 2005). However, not all women with sex-related anxiety experience sexual pain, and the mechanisms by which anxiety contributes to the onset of a pain disorder are not well understood. Preliminary evidence implicates anxiety as a potentially important maintaining factor in sexual pain. Payne et al. (2005) found that women with VVS reported hypervigilance for sexual pain. Other research suggests that women with VVS catastrophize intercourse-related pain, but not pain in general (Pukall et al. 2002).

Research to date has not clearly identified a psychological "profile" associated with sexual pain disorders, and the direction of causality between sexual pain and psychological symptoms is likely to be complex. In addition to anxiety symptoms and erotophobia, studies have reported increased depressive symptoms, hostility, and psychotic features, albeit somewhat inconsistently, across the sexual pain disorders (for review of psychological features associated with sexual pain disorders, see Weijmar Schultz et al. 2005). Although a history of sexual trauma is commonly suspected as an etiological factor in the sexual pain disorders, sexual trauma has been linked only to vaginismus in the empirical literature, and the data to support this association are inconsistent (Weijmar Schultz et al. 2005).

Not surprisingly, sexual pain conditions are frequently associated with other sexual problems, notably sexual arousal difficulties. Genital changes during sexual arousal include increased vaginal lubrication and elevation of the uterus. When these changes do not occur, coitus may result in friction, tearing, and overstimulation of internal genital structures, leading to pain. Some theorists have speculated that a lack of genital sexual arousal is a key etiological factor in sexual pain conditions. Over time, reduced sexual arousal and fear of pain are thought to become conditioned responses to sexual situations. Although laboratory studies suggest no essential impairment of genital arousal responses associated with sexual pain disorders, whether sexual pain is a conditioned response has yet to be established empirically.

Assessment

In all cases of persistent sexual pain, a cooperative multidisciplinary assessment is warranted to take into account the array of possible medical and psychophysiological factors that contribute to the development, maintenance, or experience of pain. Assessment of genital pain by a physician and, ideally, a physical therapist will inform the diagnosis and course of treatment. In addition to a general psychosocial and sexual history, the psychological assessment should ascertain the following:

1. The location, quality, intensity, and duration of the pain.
2. The circumstances in which pain is noticeable, including both sexual and nonsexual situations.
3. The woman's perception of muscle tension in sexual and nonsexual situations.
4. Changes the woman (and her partner) have made to sexual activity to limit or control pain.
5. The degree to which the woman experiences sexual arousal in sexual situations, both with regard to subjective excitement and to genital sensations and lubrication.
6. The woman's motivation for and expectations of treatment, especially for therapies that involve direct contact with the genitals.

CBT: cognitive-behavioral therapy

Treatment

Psychological. Recent investigations have supported the efficacy of cognitive-behavioral therapy (CBT) for sexual pain syndromes in women. Cognitive interventions for sexual pain disorders typically focus on alleviating anxiety (e.g., decatastrophizing pain) and normalizing alternative forms of sexual activity (e.g., nonpenetrative sex) to enhance sexual pleasure. Bergeron et al. (2001) found that eight sessions of group CBT for VVS was associated with significantly reduced genital pain from pre- to post-treatment, with 39% of women endorsing great improvement or complete pain relief at the six-month follow-up interval. Ter Kuile and Weijenborg (2006) also reported reduced genital pain associated with a 12-session trial of group CBT for women with VVS. The CBT interventions in these studies comprised sexuality education, identifying and correcting maladaptive cognitions, and systematic desensitization exercises designed to facilitate vaginal penetration over time in a gradual manner. The additive benefit of any of these given components to treatment outcomes has yet to be studied.

The use of systematic desensitization has a relatively long history in the treatment of sexual pain disorders, particularly vaginismus, but has surprisingly little empirical support. In the context of sex therapy, systematic desensitization exercises are assigned for homework and entail relaxation coupled with gradual habituation to vaginal touch and penetration, usually beginning with the woman's fingers or artificial devices specifically designed for this purpose. Although a recent clinical trial of CBT for lifelong vaginismus included systematic desensitization as a treatment component (ter Kuile et al. 2006), the efficacy of systematic desensitization alone is unclear.

Psychophysiological. Glazer et al. (1995), observing a relationship between VVS and abnormal responding of the pelvic floor musculature (see also White et al. 1997), developed a novel treatment approach using electromyography combined with visual feedback provided by an electronic instrument. The treatment is designed to reduce hypertonicity and increase the strength and stability of the pelvic floor. Since the development of this treatment, biofeedback has been incorporated successfully into several clinical trials. Women receiving treatment are trained to use the electromyography sensor and biofeedback device in the clinic and then asked to complete a standard pelvic floor training protocol at home twice per day. The protocol consists of pelvic floor contraction exercises of various durations (e.g., short contractions versus long "endurance" contractions, all performed at maximum intensity) separated by prescribed rest periods. Clinical trial data indicate that the pelvic floor training approach significantly reduces VVS pain and may occasionally eliminate it altogether (Bergeron et al. 2001, Glazer et al. 1995, McKay et al. 2001). However, treatment success rates in these trials have varied considerably, and further study is needed to assess the acceptability and effectiveness of this treatment on a broad scale.

Collaboration with a physical therapist can enhance psychophysiological treatment with hands-on techniques informed by expertise on the muscular and connective tissue of the pelvic floor. For example, a physical therapist can incorporate specific massage and stretching techniques to correct muscle tone and improve mobilization, prescribe exercises for the pelvic floor and nearby muscle groups, and strengthen the pelvic floor by means of electrical stimulation (Rosenbaum 2005).

Medical/surgical. Topical anesthetics and other medications are sometimes used to alleviate genital pain in the short term, but no evidence supports the use of topical treatments in long-term management of sexual pain disorders. Likewise, limited data are available to support the use of antidepressants and anticonvulsants for pain relief (Weijmar Schultz et al. 2005). When clients do not respond to psychosocial and physical therapies, surgical treatment may be considered. In studies of women with VVS, removal of vulvar vestibular tissue has been shown to significantly reduce or completely alleviate genital pain among the majority of recipients (Goldstein & Goldstein 2006). As surgery does entail some degree of risk, surgical treatment should be considered an alternative after less invasive therapies have failed.

The selection of appropriate criteria by which to judge the success of any sexual pain disorder treatment is complicated. Because many women with sexual pain disorders are unable to experience genital contact or penetration, investigators have rated treatment efficacy in part by the proportion of women who are able to resume (or initiate) sexual activity by the end of treatment. However, being *able* to have sex does not mean that discomfort is no longer present, nor that sex is necessarily enjoyable. Thus, in evaluating any treatment outcome, it is vital to consider improvements in self-reported genital pain as well as improvements in sexual function (e.g., sexual desire and arousal).

CONCLUSION

Spurred by the profitability of sildenafil (Viagra) and similar treatments for male erectile disorder, an unprecedented influx of industry-sponsored grants promoted basic and clinical research on women's sexual function in the late 1990s and into this decade. Although recent studies have yielded important insights into women's sexual function, the clinical utility of biomedical treatments for women's sexual problems is limited. At present, it seems unlikely that medical therapies provided without substantial education and counseling will successfully address the most common sexual concerns that women face. Although the literature describes several well-articulated psychosocial theories of women's sexual dysfunction, translating theory to practice is problematic. Manualized treatment protocols lend themselves well to clinical investigation but are relatively uncommon in sex therapy. Evaluating the psychological treatment literature is also difficult because of the multicomponent, multimodal nature of many treatments. Few studies have attempted to evaluate the efficacy of separate treatment components.

Rather than adopting or eschewing an exclusively medical or psychosocial model of sexuality, trends in the recent clinical literature point to an increasingly nuanced view of women's sexual problems. Translating the prominently touted "biopsychosocial" viewpoint into empirical hypotheses and assessable treatment methods, however, remains a considerable challenge.

SUMMARY POINTS

1. Existing conceptualizations of women's sexual function are based largely on a model that proposes discrete, sequential phases of sexual response. Recent work questions the utility of this model for explaining women's sexual experiences and clinical presentation.
2. Assessment of women's sexual problems should reflect a biopsychosocial perspective, taking into account cultural, developmental, psychosocial, and health-related contexts.
3. Medical treatments for women's sexual dysfunction have largely failed to outperform placebo treatment but may be useful in specific clinical subgroups.
4. Despite widespread clinical acceptance in many cases, few psychosocial treatments for women's sexual dysfunction are empirically supported. Little is known about which treatment components are most effective.

LITERATURE CITED

Althof SE, Dean J, Derogatis LR, Rosen RC, Sisson M. 2005. Current perspectives on the clinical assessment and diagnosis of female sexual dysfunction and clinical studies of potential therapies: a statement of concern. *J. Sex. Med.* 2(Suppl. 3):146–53

Summarizes the conclusions of an international panel of experts assembled to review and critique the diagnosis and assessment of sexual dysfunction, particularly in clinical trial outcome measurement.

Am. Psychol. Assoc. 2000. *Diagnostic and Statistical Manual of Mental Disorders*. Washington, DC: Am. Psychol. Assoc. 4th ed., text rev.

Bachmann G, Bancroft J, Braunstein G, Burger H, Davis S, et al. 2002. Female androgen insufficiency: the Princeton consensus statement on definition, classification, and assessment. *Fertil. Steril.* 77:660–65

Bancroft J. 2002a. The medicalization of female sexual dysfunction: the need for caution. *Arch. Sex. Behav.* 31:451–55

Bancroft J. 2002b. Sexual effects of androgens in women: some theoretical considerations. 2002. *Fertil. Steril.* 77(Suppl. 4):55–59

Barlow DH. 1986. Causes of sexual dysfunction: the role of anxiety and cognitive interference. *J. Consult. Clin. Psychol.* 54:140–48

Basson R, Brotto LA. 2003. Sexual psychophysiology and effects of sildenafil citrate in oestrogenised women with acquired genital arousal disorder and impaired orgasm: a randomized controlled trial. *BJOG* 110:1014–24

Basson R, Brotto LA, Laan E, Redmond G, Utian WH. 2005. Assessment and management of women's sexual dysfunctions: problematic desire and arousal. *J. Sex. Med.* 2:291–300

Basson R, Leiblum S, Brotto L, Derogatis L, Fourcroy J, et al. 2003. Definitions of women's sexual dysfunction reconsidered: advocating expansion and revision. *J. Psychosom. Obstet. Gynecol.* 24:221–29

Summarizes the recommendations of an international multidisciplinary panel convened to review and modify existing definitions of women's sexual dysfunction.

Basson R, McInnes R, Smith MD, Hodgson G, Koppiker N. 2002. Efficacy and safety of sildenafil citrate in women with sexual dysfunction associated with female sexual arousal disorder. *J. Womens Health Gend. Based Med.* 11:367–77

Basson R, Weijmar Shultz WCM, Binik YM, Brotto LA, Eschenbach DA, et al. 2004. Women's sexual desire and arousal disorders and sexual pain. See Lue et al. 2004, pp. 851–974

Full report from the committee on women's desire, arousal, and pain disorders convened for the Second International Consultation on Erectile and Sexual Dysfunctions.

Ben Zion IZ, Tessler R, Cohen L, Lerer E, Raz Y, et al. 2006. Polymorphisms in the dopamine D4 receptor gene (DRD4) contribute to individual differences in human sexual behavior: desire, arousal and sexual function. *Mol. Psychiatry* 11:782–86

Bergeron S, Binik YM, Khalifé S, Pagidas K, Glazer HI, et al. 2001. A randomized comparison of group cognitive-behavioral therapy, surface electromyographic feedback, and vestibulectomy in the treatment of dyspareunia resulting from vulvar vestibulitis. *Pain* 91:297–306

Berman JR, Berman LA, Toler SM, Gill J, Haughie S. 2003. Safety and efficacy of sildenafil citrate for the treatment of female sexual arousal disorder: a double-blind, placebo controlled study. *J. Urol.* 170:2333–38

Billups KL, Berman L, Berman J, Metz ME, Glennon ME, Goldstein I. 2001. A new nonpharmacological vacuum therapy for female sexual dysfunction. *J. Sex Marital Ther.* 27:435–41

Binik YM, Meana M, Berkley K, Khalife S. 1999. The sexual pain disorders: Is the pain sexual or is the sex painful? *Annu. Rev. Sex Res.* 10:210–35

Brandenburg U, Schwenkhagen A. 2006. Sexual history. See Goldstein et al. 2006, pp. 343–46

Brotto LA. 2006. Psychologic-based desire and arousal disorders: treatment strategies and outcome results. See Goldstein et al. 2006, pp. 441–48

Buster JE, Kingsberg SA, Aguirre O, Brown C, Breaux JG, et al. 2005. Testosterone patch for low sexual desire in surgically menopausal women: a randomized trial. *Obstet. Gynecol.* 105:944–52

Caruso S, Agnello C, Intelisanò G, Farina M, Di Mari L, Cianci A. 2004. Placebo-controlled study on efficacy and safety of daily apomorphine SL intake in premenopausal women affected by hypoactive sexual desire disorder and sexual arousal disorder. *Urology* 63:955–59

Caruso S, Intelisano G, Lupo L, Agnello C. 2001. Premenopausal women affected by sexual arousal disorder treated with sildenafil: a double-blind, cross-over, placebo-controlled study. *BJOG* 108:623–28

Cawood EH, Bancroft J. 1996. Steroid hormones, the menopause, sexuality and well-being of women. *Psychol. Med.* 26:925–36

Clayton AH, McGarvey EL, Clavet GJ. 1997. The Changes in Sexual Functioning Questionnaire (CSFQ): development, reliability and validity. *Psychopharmacol. Bull.* 33:731–45
de Kruiff ME, ter Kuile MM, Weijenborg PT, van Lankveld JJ. 2000. Vaginismus and dyspareunia: Is there a difference in clinical presentation? *J. Psychosom. Obstet. Gynecol.* 21:149–55
Dennerstein L, Koochaki P, Barton I, Graziottin A. 2006. Hypoactive sexual desire disorder in menopausal women: a survey of Western European women. *J. Sex. Med.* 3:212–22
Dennerstein L, Lehert P. 2004. Women's sexual functioning, lifestyle, mid-age, and menopause in 12 European countries. *Menopause* 11(Suppl.):778–85
Derogatis LR, Melisaratos N. 1979. The Derogatis Interview for Sexual functioning (DISF/DISF-SR): an introductory report. *J. Sex Marital Ther.* 23:291–304
Dove NL, Wiederman MW. 2000. Cognitive distraction and women's sexual functioning. *J. Sex Marital Ther.* 26:67–78
Feiger A, Kiev A, Shrivastava RK, Wisselink PG, Wilcox CS. 1996. Nefazodone versus sertraline in outpatients with major depression: focus on efficacy, tolerability, and effects on sexual function and satisfaction. *J. Clin. Psychiatry* 57(Suppl. 2):53–62
Fichen CS, Libman E, Brender W. 1983. Methodological issues in the study of sex therapy: effective components in the treatment of secondary orgasmic dysfunction. *J. Sex Marital Ther.* 9:191–202
Fisher S. 1973. *The Female Orgasm*. New York: Basic Books
Fletcher GJO, Kininmonth LA. 1992. Measuring relationship beliefs: an individual differences scale. *J. Res. Personal.* 26:371–97
Gerber JR, Johnson JV, Bunn JY, O'Brien SL. 2005. A longitudinal study of the effects of free testosterone and other psychosocial variables on sexual function during the natural traverse of menopause. *Fertil. Steril.* 83:643–48
Glazer HI, Rodke G, Swencionis C, Hertz B, Young AW. 1995. Treatment of vulvar vestibulitis syndrome with electromyographic biofeedback of pelvic floor musculature. *J. Reprod. Med.* 40:283–90
Goldstein AT, Goldstein I. 2006. Sexual pain disorders within the vulvar vestibule: current techniques. See Goldstein et al. 2006, pp. 587–96
Goldstein I, Fisher WA, Sand M, Rosen RC, Mollen M, et al. 2005. Women's sexual function improves when partners are administered vardenafil for erectile dysfunction: a prospective, randomized, double-blind, placebo-controlled trial. *J. Sex Med.* 2:819–32
Goldstein I, Meston CM, Davis SR, Traish AM, eds. *Women's Sexual Function and Dysfunction: Study, Diagnosis, and Treatment*. New York: Taylor & Francis
Guay AT, Spark R. 2006. Pathophysiology of sex steroids in women. See Goldstein et al. 2006, pp. 218–27
Guay A, Jacobson J, Munarriz R, Traish A, Talakoub L, et al. 2004. Serum androgen levels in healthy premenopausal women with and without sexual dysfunction: Part B: reduced serum androgen levels in healthy premenopausal women with complaints of sexual dysfunction. *Int. J. Impot. Res.* 16:121–29
Hare-Mustin RT. 1991. Sex, lies, and headaches: the problem is power. See *Women and Power: Perspectives for Therapy*, ed. TJ Goodrich, pp. 63–85. New York: Norton
Harlow BL, Wise LA, Stewart EG. 2001. Prevalence and predictors of chronic lower genital tract discomfort. *Am. J. Obstet. Gynecol.* 185:545–50
Heiman JR, LoPiccolo J. 1988. *Becoming Orgasmic: A Sexual and Personal Growth Program for Women*. New York: Prentice Hall. Rev. exp. ed.
Heinrich AG. 1976. *The effect of group- and self-directed behavioral-educational treatment of primary orgasmic dysfunction in females treated without their partners*. PhD thesis. Boulder: Univ. Colorado

Kaplan HS. 1979. *Disorders of Sexual Desire*. New York: Brunner/Mazel

Kaplan SA, Reis RB, Kohn IJ, Ikequichi EF, Laor E, et al. 1999. Safety and efficacy of sildenafil in postmenopausal women with sexual dysfunction. *Urology* 53:481–86

Kegel AH. 1952. Sexual functions of the pubococcygeus muscle. *West. J. Surg. Obstet. Gynecol.* 60:521–24

Krychman ML, Amsterdam A, Carter J. 2006. Cancer, sexuality and sexual expression. See Goldstein et al. 2006, pp. 636–43

Laan E, van Lunsen RHW, Everaerd W, Riley A, Scott E, Boolell M. 2002. The enhancement of vaginal vasocongestion by sildenafil in healthy premenopausal women. *J. Womens Health Gend. Based Med.* 11:357–65

Laumann EO, Gagnon JH, Michael RT, Michaels S. 1994. *The Social Organization of Sexuality: Sexual Practices in the United States*. Chicago: Univ. Chicago Press

Laumann EO, Paik A, Rosen RC. 1999. Sexual dysfunction in the United States: prevalence and predictors. *JAMA* 281:537–44

Leiblum SR, Koochaki PE, Rodenberg CA, Barton IP, Rosen RC. 2006. Hypoactive sexual desire disorder in postmenopausal women: US results from the Women's International Study of Health and Sexuality (WISHeS). *Menopause* 13:46–56

Lewis RW, Fugl-Meyer KS, Bosch R, Fugl-Meyer AR, Laumann O, et al. 2004. Definitions, classification, and epidemiology of sexual dysfunction. See Lue et al. 2004, pp. 39–72

Locke H, Wallace K. 1959. Short marital adjustment and prediction tests: their reliability and validity. *Marriage Fam. Living* 2:251–55

Lue TF, Basson R, Rosen R, Giuliano F, Khoury S, Montorsi F, eds. 2004. *Sexual Medicine: Sexual Dysfunctions in Men and Women*. Paris: Health Publ.

Mah K, Binik YM. 2001. The nature of human orgasm: a critical review of major trends. *Clin. Psychol. Rev.* 21:823–56

Masters WH, Johnson VE. 1966. *Human Sexual Response*. Boston, MA: Little, Brown

Masters WH, Johnson VE. 1970. *Human Sexual Inadequacy*. Boston, MA: Little, Brown

McCall KM, Meston CM. 2006. Cues resulting in desire for sexual activity in women. *J. Sex. Med.* 3:838–52

McKay E, Kaufman RH, Doctor U, Berkova Z, Glazer H, Redko V. 2001. Treating vulvar vestibulitis with electromyographic biofeedback of pelvic floor musculature. *J. Reprod. Med.* 46:337–42

Meston CM. 2006. Female orgasmic disorder: treatment strategies and outcome results. See Goldstein et al. 2006, pp. 449–61

Meston CM, Derogatis LR. 2002. Validated instruments for assessing female sexual function. *J. Sex. Marital Ther.* 28:155–64

Meston CM, Hull E, Levin RJ, Sipski M. 2004. Women's orgasm. See Lue et al. 2004, pp. 783–849

Full report from the committee on women's orgasm convened for the Second International Consultation on Erectile and Sexual Dysfunctions.

Meston CM, Trapnell P. 2005. Development and validation of a five-factor sexual satisfaction and distress scale for women: the Sexual Satisfaction Scale for Women (SSS-W). *J. Sex. Med.* 2:66–81

Nobre PJ, Pinto-Gouveia J. 2006. Dysfunctional sexual beliefs as vulnerability factors for sexual dysfunction. *J. Sex. Res.* 43:68–75

Otis MD, Rostosky SS, Riggle EDB, Hamrin R. 2006. Stress and relationship quality in same-sex couples. *J. Soc. Pers. Relat.* 23:81–99

Payne KA, Binik YM, Amsel R, Khalife S. 2005. When sex hurts, anxiety and fear orient attention towards pain. *Eur. J. Pain* 9:427–36

Perelman MA. 2006. Psychosocial history. See Goldstein et al. 2006, pp. 336–42

Pfaus JG, Damsma G, Wenkstern D, Fibiger HC. 1995. Sexual activity increases dopamine transmission in the nucleus accumbens and striatum of female rats. *Brain Res.* 693:21–30

Polatin P, Douglas DE. 1953. Spontaneous orgasm in a case of schizophrenia. *Psychoanal. Rev.* 40:17–26

Pukall CF, Binik YM, Khalife S, Amsel R, Abbott FV. 2002. Vestibular tactile and pain thresholds in women with vulvar vestibulitis syndrome. *Pain* 96:163–75

Pukall CF, Payne KA, Kao A, Khalife S, Binik YM. 2005. Dyspareunia. See *Handbook of Sexual Dysfunction*, ed. R Balon, RT Segraves, pp. 249–72. New York: Taylor & Francis

Read S, King M, Watson J. 1997. Sexual dysfunction in primary medical care: prevalence, characteristics and detection by the general practitioner. *J. Public Health Med.* 19:387–91

Reissing ED, Binik YM, Khalife S. 1999. Does vaginismus exist? A critical review of the literature. *J. Nerv. Ment. Dis.* 187:261–74

Reissing ED, Binik YM, Khalife S, Cohen D, Amsel R. 2004. Vaginal spasm, pain, and behavior: an empirical investigation of the diagnosis of vaginismus. *Arch. Sex. Behav.* 33:5–17

Richgels PB. 1992. Hypoactive sexual desire in heterosexual women: a feminist analysis. *Women Ther.* 12:123–35

Rosen RC, Brown C, Heiman JR, Leiblum S, Meston CM, et al. 2000. The Female Sexual Function Index (FSFI): a multidimensional self-report instrument for the assessment of female sexual function. *J. Sex Marital Ther.* 26:191–208

Rosen RC, Taylor JF, Leiblum S, Bachman GA. 1993. Prevalence of sexual dysfunction in women: results of a survey study of 329 women in an outpatient gynecological clinic. *J. Sex Marital Ther.* 19:171–88

Rosenbaum TY. 2005. Physiotherapy treatment of sexual pain disorders. *J. Sex Marital Ther.* 31:329–40

Sanchez DT, Crocker J, Boike KR. 2005. Doing gender in the bedroom: investing in gender norms and the sexual experience. *Personal. Soc. Psychol. Bull.* 31:1445–55

Santoro N, Torrens J, Crawford S, Allsworth JE, Finkelstein JS, et al. 2005. Correlates of circulating androgens in mid-life women: the study of women's health across the nation. *J. Clin. Endocrinol. Metab.* 90:4836–45

Schnarch DM. 1991. Politics of sexual desire and the nature of wanting. See *Constructing the Sexual Crucible: An Integration of Sexual and Marital Therapy*, pp. 270–305. New York: Norton

Segraves RT, Clayton A, Croft H, Wolf A, Warnock J. 2004. Bupropion sustained release for the treatment of hypoactive sexual desire disorder in premenopausal women. *J. Clin. Psychopharmacol.* 24:339–42

Segraves RT, Croft H, Kavoussi R, Ascher JA, Batey SR, et al. 2001. Bupropion sustained release (SR) for the treatment of hypoactive sexual desire disorder (HSDD) in nondepressed women. *J. Sex Marital Ther.* 27:303–16

Sholty MJ, Ephross PH, Plaut SM, Fischman SH, Charnas JF, Cody CA. 1984. Female orgasmic experience: a subjective study. *Arch. Sex. Behav.* 13:155–64

Simon J, Braunstein G, Nachtigall L, Utian W, Katz M, et al. 2005. Testosterone patch increases sexual activity and desire in surgically menopausal women with hypoactive sexual desire disorder. *J. Clin. Endocrinol. Metab.* 90:5226–33

Sipski ML, Alexander CJ, Rosen RC. 1995. Orgasm in women with spinal cord injuries: a laboratory-based assessment. *Arch. Phys. Med. Rehabil.* 76:1097–102

Sipski ML, Alexander CJ, Rosen RC. 2001. Sexual arousal and orgasm in women: effects of spinal cord injury. *Ann. Neurol.* 49:35–44

Spanier GB. 1976. Measuring dyadic adjustment: new scales for assessing the quality of marriage and similar dyads. *J. Marriage Fam.* 38:15–28

Stewart EG. 2006. Physical examination and female sexual dysfunction. See Goldstein et al. 2006, pp. 347–55

Taylor JF, Rosen RC, Leiblum SR. 1994. Self-report assessment of female sexual function: psychometric evaluation of the Brief Index of Sexual Function for Women. *Arch. Sex. Behav.* 23:627–43

Ter Kuile MM, van Lankveld JJ, de Groot ED, Melles R, Neffs J, Zandbergen M. 2006. Cognitive-behavioral therapy for women with lifelong vaginismus: process and prognostic factors. *Behav. Res. Ther.* In press

Ter Kuile MM, Van Lankveld JJ, Vlieland CV, Willekes C, Weijenborg PT. 2005. Vulvar vestibulitis syndrome: an important factor in the evaluation of lifelong vaginismus? *J. Psychosom. Obstet. Gynecol.* 26:245–49

Ter Kuile MM, Weijenborg PTM. 2006. A cognitive-behavioral group program for women with vulvar vestibulitis syndrome (VVS): factors associated with treatment success. *J. Sex Marital Ther.* 32:199–213

Tiefer L. 1996. The medicalization of sexuality: conceptual, normative, and professional issues. *Annu. Rev. Sex Res.* 7:252–82

van Berlo W, Ensink B. 2000. Problems with sexuality after sexual assault. *Annu. Rev. Sex Res.* 11:235–57

Weijmar Schultz W, Basson R, Binik Y, Eschenbach D, Wesselmann U, Van Lankveld J. 2005. Women's sexual pain and its management. *J. Sex. Med.* 2:301–16

White G, Jantos M, Glazer H. 1997. Establishing the diagnosis of vulvar vestibulitis. *J. Reprod. Med.* 42:157–60

Wiederman MW. 2000. Women's body image self-consciousness during physical intimacy with a partner. *J. Sex Res.* 37:60–68

Whipple B, Gerdes CA, Komisaruk BR. 1996. Sexual response to self-stimulation in women with complete spinal cord injury. *J. Sex Res.* 33:231–40

Relapse and Relapse Prevention

Thomas H. Brandon,[1] Jennifer Irvin Vidrine,[2] and Erika B. Litvin[1]

[1]Department of Psychology, University of South Florida, and the H. Lee Moffitt Cancer Center & Research Institute, Tampa, Florida 33620-7200; email: brandont@moffitt.usf.edu, litvineb@moffitt.usf.edu

[2]Department of Health Disparities Research, The University of Texas M.D. Anderson Cancer Center, Houston, Texas 77030-4009; email: JIrvinVidrine@mdanderson.org

Annu. Rev. Clin. Psychol. 2007. 3:257–84

First published online as a Review in Advance on October 12, 2006

The *Annual Review of Clinical Psychology* is online at http://clinpsy.annualreviews.org

This article's doi:
10.1146/annurev.clinpsy.3.022806.091455

1548-5943/07/0427-0257$20.00

Key Words

behavior change, recurrence, addiction, efficacy

Abstract

Most psychological disorders and problem behaviors are characterized by very high rates of postremittance relapse. Thus, advances in the long-term efficacy of psychological interventions require understanding the causes and processes of relapse, with the ultimate goal of developing strategies that reduce the probability of relapse. Existing psychological theory and interventions relevant to relapse and relapse prevention (RP) are reviewed, with a focus on addictive behaviors. The past two decades have produced increased attention toward the relapse problem and important advances in the conceptualization of relapse (i.e., as a process rather than a discrete event). Further progress will require the translation of basic theory into applied theory, the development of integrative theories of relapse, and the design and testing of theory-based, multimodal RP interventions.

Contents

INTRODUCTION

It ain't over till it's over.

–*Yogi Berra*

Although he was probably referring to baseball rather than behavior change, Mr. Berra's insight concisely captures a conundrum within our own field of play—when can we be confident that improvement in a maladaptive behavior, or psychological syndrome, is stable? Conversely, when, if ever, does the risk of relapse become insignificant? And more interesting, what predicts or causes relapse? And how can the risk of relapse be reduced?

Relapse is a characteristic of all behavioral disorders and, unfortunately, the prevalence of relapse is quite high for most of them. Given that the ultimate goal of nearly all interventions is permanent or at least long-term behavior change, relapse is a significant threat to treatment efficacy. Over the past two decades, considerable research attention has been directed toward understanding the causes of relapse and developing relapse-prevention (RP) interventions. In this article, we provide an overview of this work, with a focus on theories and interventions that have already proven to be influential as well as those that we believe hold particular promise. To do this, we draw primarily from the domain of addictive behaviors. This reflects not only our own research background, but also the fact that attention to relapse and RP was initially driven by addiction research, and the majority of work on relapse continues to derive from this area.

Definitions: What Is Relapse?

Melanie T. received behavioral therapy for pathological gambling that primarily manifested as monthly binges in Atlantic City where she would typically lose several thousands of dollars. Following therapy, Melanie abstained from all forms of gambling for 16 weeks, but when her state's lotto jackpot reached $40 million, she went to the convenience store and bought $20 worth of lottery tickets.

Did Melanie T. relapse? This vignette exemplifies many of the definitional challenges associated with the study of relapse. Issues involved with answering that question include: Given the history and frequency of her problem behavior, was Melanie truly in remission after only 16 weeks of abstinence? If so, should the purchase of lottery tickets (less severe than her gambling binges, and much more normative) be considered a full relapse, a minor setback (a "slip" or "lapse"), or neither? Conversely, was her period of abstinence of sufficient duration that she could have been considered as recovered rather than merely in remission? And if so, should her lotto purchase then be considered a recurrence of her problem rather than a relapse?

The terminology introduced in the previous paragraph has not been used consistently within clinical psychology. In an attempt at standardization, at least with respect to depression, a task force of the 1988 MacArthur Foundation Research Network on the Psychobiology of Depression recommended that remission be defined as a relatively brief, asymptomatic period. A relapse is a return of symptoms after a remission. These symptoms are thought to be part of the original episode. A remission that exceeds some specified duration is considered a recovery, which can last indefinitely. A recurrence is a return of symptoms during recovery and is thought to signal a new episode of illness (Frank et al. 1991).

In contrast, behavioral researchers have traditionally defined relapse as any return of the problem behavior (e.g., first drink) or symptoms after a period of initial remission (e.g., Hunt et al. 1971). Consistent with a medical or disease model, this binary conceptualization treats relapse as a static, discrete event or end state (Donovan 1996, Marlatt 1985, Miller 1996). This definition of relapse has been criticized for equating single, brief "slips" with full-blown relapse. Aside from masking significant variability in process and outcomes, such a conceptualization may be self-fulfilling if a patient believes that a slip is equivalent to a full relapse (Marlatt 1985). Furthermore, for disorders and behaviors that fall on a continuum of severity or frequency, such as depression or overeating, defining relapse as a discrete event is more difficult and probably inappropriate (Miller 1996, Wing 2000).

To address these criticisms of the binary model, researchers have broadened the terminology they use to describe outcomes and have moved toward conceptualizing relapse as a dynamic process that ultimately results in a return of previous behavior patterns (Marlatt 1985). The addiction field has also largely embraced Marlatt's distinction between an initial lapse and a full relapse. Although this conceptualization has led to improved research design and greater attention to changes that occur after an initial lapse, it has complicated the task of operationally defining relapse. Maisto et al. (2003) demonstrated how choosing different cutoff points to define relapse to alcohol use can substantially change the estimated relapse rate. In actuality, however, there is likely to be considerable covariance between various definitions of lapse and relapse such that, for example, they produce similar estimates of the relative efficacy of different treatments (Piasecki 2006).

Attempts to standardize this terminology for particular disorders and problem behaviors (e.g., Frank et al. 1991, Hughes et al. 2003) have helped to reduce variation and facilitate comparisons among studies. Unfortunately, these consensus definitions often lack empirical support or theoretical justification, and the thresholds remain largely arbitrary at this point (Frank et al. 1991, Ockene et al. 2000). Despite the risk of oversimplifying complex outcome data, there remains a need for construct validation of the operational definitions used to describe the relapse process.

Assessment Issues

The definitional difficulties described above are each associated with assessment challenges. Despite the now-dominant conceptualization of relapse as a process that begins prior to the first behavioral violation and continues beyond it (Marlatt 1985), relapse has nearly always been assessed as a discrete event. To assess relapse as a process will require dynamic, repeated measurement of multiple variables, such as the frequency and intensity of the target behavior (e.g., number of drinks/day), cognitive and affective indices, level of functioning, and downstream consequences of the behavior change (Donovan 1996). Similarly, examining the causes of relapse will also require dynamic assessment across multiple classes of variables, including stable, distal variables; intermediate, background variables; and proximal precipitants (Piasecki et al. 2002, Shiffman et al. 1986). A reliance on retrospective recall of the target behavior as well as the precipitating factors, which introduces risks of a variety of recall biases, has also limited the assessment of relapse as a process. More recently, real-time assessment techniques have emerged such as ecological momentary assessment (EMA; Shiffman et al. 1997b), which may involve participants inputting data into handheld computers in response to either random prompts or the occurrence of specified behaviors (e.g., smoking a cigarette). Although this technique also has its drawbacks, it has already proven fruitful in identifying immediate precipitants of relapse episodes and in tracking the progression from lapse to relapse (Shiffman et al. 2006).

The Clinical Problem

For nearly four decades, the ubiquity and consistency of relapse to addiction has been symbolized by a graph illustrating similar relapse curves for heroin, alcohol, and tobacco use after completion of a treatment program (Hunt et al. 1971). The graph suggested that common processes underlie relapse across disorders, and Hunt et al. deserve credit for highlighting the need for more research on RP. Nevertheless, the definitional and assessment issues described above form the basis for several valid criticisms directed toward the graph, including the use of a rigid, binary definition of relapse (Miller 1996); the curves' elevation and slope as dependent on the relapse criteria employed (Miller 1996); and that negative deceleration is an inherent characteristic of survival curves that does not directly implicate any particular relapse process (Litman et al. 1979, Sutton 1979).

Despite advances in treatment and the advent of more liberal definitions of maintenance that allow lapses, the problem of relapse continues to pervade the field of clinical psychology. **Table 1** illustrates reported relapse rates from representative studies across a variety of addictive behaviors and other psychological disorders. Note that randomized controlled trials of specific treatments may produce somewhat lower relapse rates and individuals who meet operational criteria

Table 1 Comparison of relapse rates for different disorders and problem behaviors

Relapse rates				
Disorder/behavior	**Relapse definition**	**Relapse rate**	**Follow-up period**	**Citation**
Alcohol use	First drink	92%	1 year	Miller et al. 1996
Alcohol use	First heavy drinking day	80%	1 year	Miller et al. 1996
Tobacco use (self-quitters)	Any use	~95%–98%	6–12 months	Hughes et al. 2004
Tobacco use (pharmacotherapy)	Any use	84%	1 year	Medioni et al. 2005
IV drug use	Any use	75%	Up to 10 years	Shah et al. 2006
Heroin use	Any use	86%	1 year	Darke et al. 2005
Weight loss	Varied	~80%	Up to 5 years	Wing & Phelan 2005
Major depression	New episode after 8-week recovery	85%	Up to 15 years	Mueller et al. 1999
Panic disorder (no agoraphobia)	2 weeks of symptoms after 8-week recovery	56%	Up to 12 years	Bruce et al. 2005
Generalized anxiety disorder	2 weeks of symptoms after 8-week recovery	45%	Up to 12 years	Bruce et al. 2005
Social phobia	2 weeks of symptoms after 8-week recovery	39%	Up to 12 years	Bruce et al. 2005
Obsessive-compulsive disorder	1 week of symptoms after 8-week recovery	48%	2 years	Eisen et al. 1999
Anorexia	Varied	30%–50%	1 year	Pike 1998

for relapse may not necessarily have returned to previous levels of impairment. For example, although Miller et al. (1996) reported a 12-month relapse rate of 92% following treatment for alcohol problems, the average number of drinks per week declined from 86 to 19.

Further inspection of **Table 1** indicates that relapse tends to occur much faster for drug use (usually within days or months) than for other psychological disorders (often years). However, this difference is partially an artifact of the criteria used to define both initial remission and relapse, generally on the scale of days for drug use and weeks or months for other psychological disorders. Furthermore, relapse rates are sometimes confounded with initial recovery rates. For example, some anxiety disorders may have lower relapse rates in part because they also have lower rates of initial recovery (Bruce et al. 2005).

THEORIES OF RELAPSE

Numerous reviews of relapse to different behaviors have emphasized various consistent predictor variables (e.g., self-efficacy, coping skills, negative affect, disorder severity). In contrast, the present review is organized around relevant theories, which often include roles for these same predictor variables. There is no doubt, however, that each theory reviewed below is grossly insufficient in explaining the phenomenon of relapse to behavioral disorders. Relapse—much like the original etiology of these disorders—is clearly multidetermined both within and across individuals. The modest percentages of variance accounted for by each theory are no doubt less than additive, because the theories often address overlapping processes at multiple levels of explanation. Nevertheless, these theories represent our best bet at advancing our understanding of behavioral relapse, and of eventually developing targeted, theory-based interventions. Space limitations required that we be selective, so we focus on theories that appear most likely to yield behavioral interventions.

Learning Theories

Classical conditioning. Both retrospective and real-time reports have repeatedly indicated that initial episodes of postcessation substance use (i.e., lapses) tend to occur primarily in settings previously paired with substance use (Marlatt 1996, Shiffman 1982). This observation is consistent with the notion that stimuli repeatedly paired with substance use eventually become conditioned stimuli (CSs) that can elicit conditioned responses (CRs) that, in turn, are subjectively perceived as cravings for the substance. In this manner, classical conditioning may contribute to both the maintenance of substance use as well as to relapse. For example, a cocaine addict in remission may encounter spilled sugar on the counter of a diner and experience conditioned cravings that propel him to seek out and use cocaine again. Indeed, it has been suggested that the anticipated heroin epidemic among U.S. troops returning from Vietnam never occurred because, after they returned home, the troops no longer encountered the cues associated with their heroin use (Siegel 1999).

Supporting this classical conditioning model is much laboratory-based research on human cue-reactivity, which has demonstrated that exposure to substance-related stimuli produces self-reported cravings and physiological responses [heart rate, skin conductance, localized brain activity (Childress et al. 1999)]. Cue-reactivity has been studied extensively over a wide range of addictive substances (Carter & Tiffany 1999) and has recently been applied to other areas, such as eating disorders (Carter et al. 2002), food craving (Rodriguez et al. 2005), gambling (Grusser et al. 2005), and trauma (Karl et al. 2004). Stimuli that have produced reactivity include both exteroceptive cues, such as drug paraphernalia, and interoceptive cues, such as affective states (Litt et al. 1990, Payne et al. 1991); cognitions (Bradizza et al. 1994), for example, knowing that a drug is available (Juliano & Brandon 1998); and the initial onset effects of a drug (McDonald & Siegel

2004). The latter has particular implications for explaining the progression from an initial lapse to subsequent use.

These findings are consistent with animal studies, such as those that show increases in drug self-administration in the presence of conditioned stimuli (Caggiula et al. 2002, Schenk & Partridge 2001). Importantly, several studies have demonstrated that alcohol and smoking cue reactions can be predictive of drug relapse (e.g., Abrams et al. 1988, Cooney et al. 1997, Niaura et al. 1989), although there has been little consistency to date with respect to the particular cue-reactivity indices or relapse criteria identified.

Based on classical conditioning theory, repeated exposure to the CSs should extinguish the conditioned reactivity and reduce the risk of cue-elicited relapse. Extinction trials may be deliberate, as with cue exposure therapy (reviewed below), or may occur incidentally via naturalistic exposure (e.g., seeing other people drink alcohol, walking through a casino, smelling cigarette smoke). Once extinction occurs, the mechanisms associated with relapse shift to factors that reestablish conditioned responding to the CSs. Animal research suggests that extinction does not erase the conditioned association, but instead creates a competing inhibitory association that is highly context-dependent (Bouton 2002). Consequently, conditioned responding can resume through processes such as renewal (if the CS appears in a context other than the extinction context) or reinstatement (reexposure to the unconditioned stimulus, such as with an initial lapse).

There are several formal theories of drug use and relapse based on classical conditioning, including conditioned withdrawal theory (Wikler 1948), which emphasized cues associated with drug withdrawal rather than drug use; conditioned compensatory response theory (Siegel 1975), which describes CSs as cues paired with drug use, but CRs as opposite in direction to the direct drug effects, resulting in withdrawal-like symptoms; and appetitive motivation theory (Stewart et al. 1984), which describes iso-directional CSs that prime cravings for additional use. An evaluation of these competing theories is beyond the scope of this review, but importantly they share the prediction that drug-related cues produce CSs that are subjectively experienced as cravings and that motivate drug use and relapse. Moreover, classical conditioning has been incorporated into a range of other contemporary theories as described below (e.g., Niaura et al. 1988, Robinson & Berridge 1993, Tiffany 1990), including instrumental conditioning models.

Instrumental conditioning. Particularly within the area of addictive behaviors, instrumental theories of use and relapse have prospered. The historically dominant theories have emphasized negative reinforcement, i.e., drug use to obtain relief from unpleasant withdrawal symptoms or other aversive states. More recently, positive reinforcement models have gained prominence.

Theories of negative reinforcement can be divided into four overlapping categories (Eissenberg 2004). Withdrawal-based models posit that drug use is maintained via relief of the signs and symptoms of withdrawal, an unpleasant temporary state associated with abrupt abstinence from most addictive drugs. These models appear to have limited direct relation to drug relapse because the duration of the withdrawal syndrome is typically only a matter of days for most drugs, although recent advances in studying individual, temporal differences in withdrawal suggest that for some individuals the duration may be much longer and indeed be predictive of relapse (Piasecki et al. 2003).

The relevance of withdrawal to relapse is extended via models that incorporate classical conditioning, as noted above (Siegel 1983, Wikler 1948). In these models, CSs that elicit withdrawal-like CRs can motivate relapse long after unconditioned withdrawal has abated. Siegel's model of conditioned compensatory responses has enjoyed much empirical support from both animal studies and human studies. In this model, a stimulus that reliably predicts drug administration comes to initiate a compensatory response that serves to counter the direct, unconditioned effect of the drug, preserving homeostasis. Indeed, in laboratory settings, stimuli that had been paired with drug administration later elicit CRs that are counterdirectional to the unconditioned, direct drug effects. For example, CRs to morphine cues include tachycardia, hyperalgesia, hypothermia, and hyperactivity, versus the unconditioned morphine effects of bradycardia, analgesia, hyperthermia, and hypoactivity, respectively (Siegel 1983). Yet the degree to which conditioned compensatory responses actually elicit natural relapse is unknown.

Self-medication models state that drug use is motivated by the drive to alleviate negative psychological states. Although one psychodynamic model posits links between specific disorders and drugs of abuse (Khantzian 1985), the more general version is that individuals use substances to regulate their affect—particularly to avoid or alleviate negative affect. Though intuitively appealing, it has proven challenging to delineate the parameters under which drug use alleviates negative affect and, in turn, negative affect motivates drug use (e.g., Kassel et al. 2003, Sayette 1993, Shiffman et al. 2002, Steele & Josephs 1990).

Finally, opponent-process models emphasize that chronic drug use resets reward thresholds, which then alters the reinforcement potential of further drug use. Although an early opponent-process model had great influence on the conceptualization of addiction (Solomon & Corbit 1974), George Koob's reward allostasis model currently dominates this category (Koob et al. 2004, Koob & Le Moal 1997). According to this model, initial drug use produces a neurobiological decrease in the hedonic set point, or reward threshold, which makes additional drug use and other positively valenced stimuli more rewarding. Continued use, however, produces a more enduring increase in the hedonic set point, such that positive stimuli seem less rewarding and neutral stimuli are perceived as unpleasant (Eissenberg 2004). A downward spiral of further increasing set-point change (allostasis) is thought to underlie drug dependence and drive relapse via progressively more potent negative reinforcement mechanisms.

The modest and complex associations between negative affect and self-administration, and stronger evidence supporting positive reinforcement, or appetitive, models of drug dependence (see below) have tempered enthusiasm for negative reinforcement models (Robinson & Berridge 2003). However, many of the shortcomings of negative reinforcement models are addressed by a recent reconceptualization of negative affect motivation that posits preconscious perception of interoceptive cues and suggests that avoidance and escape of negative affect states primarily motivate drug use and relapse (Baker et al. 2004). Despite the theoretical ambiguity, retrospective reports consistently indicate that negative affect accounts for a significant proportion of initial lapses (Brandon et al. 1990, Maisto et al. 1995, Marlatt & Gordon 1980), as have recent real-time assessments with smokers (Shiffman 2005, Shiffman et al. 1996b). Finally, animal studies have also demonstrated that a stressor can produce reinstatement of drug self-administration (Shaham et al. 2000).

Positive reinforcement models of drug use have gained influence in recent years in response to the aforementioned perceived shortcomings of the negative reinforcement models. Contradicting withdrawal-based models, Stewart et al. (1984) demonstrated that a priming dose of a drug (or a drug-paired CS) reinstates self-administration in animals who had previously received extinction training. Indeed, reinstatement could be triggered by direct injection of opiates or amphetamines into the mesolimbic dopamine system. Baker et al. (1986) expanded this model to include a "positive affect urge network" that is activated by not only drug per se but also by positive affect states or relevant conditioned stimuli. The effect of a priming dose on reinstatement appears to model human progression from lapse to relapse. Subsequent animal research indicated that reinstatement was maximized when the priming dose was response-contingent, which suggests that relapse is not driven purely by pharmacological mechanisms (Leri & Stewart 2002), although see Tiffany & Conklin (2002) for a critique of the animal model of relapse. Other influential appetitive theories include the Psychomotor Stimulant Theory (Wise & Bozarth 1987) and the Incentive Sensitivity Theory (Robinson & Berridge 2000). The former posits that drugs are addicting because they produce psychomotor activation (positive affect) via stimulation of the medial forebrain bundle. Thus, drugs are sought after primarily to achieve this rewarding effect. In contrast, Robinson & Berridge (2000) noted a disconnect between drug users' desire for a drug and their subjective pleasure from it and proposed separate neural mechanisms responsible for drug "wanting" versus "liking." Specifically, they posit that repeated drug use produces neural sensitization of brain reward systems (ventral dopamine systems) associated with incentive motivation ("wanting"). This sensitization produces pathological craving that is primarily triggered by classically conditioned drug-paired stimuli, accounting for relapse.

Trait/Individual-Difference Theories

Another class of theories emphasizes relatively enduring characteristics of the drug user, although learning mechanisms may play a role in the development of these traits. We discuss three trait-based models of relapse below.

Negative affectivity. We mentioned above negative affect states as motivating drug use and relapse. Therefore, to the degree that the frequency and magnitude of negative affect varies across individuals, it represents a trait (variously labeled negative affectivity, neuroticism, or depression-proneness) that should be predictive of all phases of drug use, from initiation through relapse. And indeed, that appears to be the case. For example, among smokers, self-reported endorsement of negative affect motivations to smoke is predictive of relapse (Pomerleau et al. 1978), individuals scoring higher on measures of negative affectivity have poorer long-term outcomes following cessation (Zelman et al. 1992), and smokers with clinical levels of depression (or history of depression) are less likely to achieve and sustain abstinence (Anda et al. 1990, Covey 1999). In fact, negative affectivity has been found to be more predictive of smoking relapse than measures of physical dependence (Kenford et al. 2002). The association between negative affectivity and relapse appears to hold across substances, moderated by stressors and coping skills (Wills 1990).

Task persistence/distress tolerance. These two terms likely refer to the same construct—or to highly related ones. The general notion is that individuals differ in the degree to which they are able to tolerate psychological and physical distress, and thus the degree to which they are able to persist in tasks that cause such distress. Moreover, it is assumed that cessation from substance dependence is distressful (due to withdrawal symptoms, negative affect, etc.), yet requires considerable persistence. Several studies have now found an association between behavioral measures of task persistence/distress tolerance and substance use and cessation. Quinn et al. (1996) drew upon learned industriousness (LI) theory (Eisenberger 1992) to hypothesize that nonsmokers would persist on two frustrating tasks (solving anagrams and tracing polygons in a mirror) longer than would smokers. According to LI theory, and supported by considerable animal research, reinforcement of effortful behavior on a task produces LI and increases the effort an organism will expend on a range of other tasks. Quinn and colleagues (1996) reasoned that smoking was a low-effort behavior, and thus it would be attractive to individuals who are low in LI. Moreover, smoking would itself serve as further low-effort training; in contrast, cessation usually requires a high degree of effort. As hypothesized, smokers were less persistent than were nonsmokers on both behavioral tasks. A subsequent prospective study found that pretreatment persistence in mirror tracing was predictive of both short-term and long-term outcomes of a smoking cessation clinic (Brandon et al. 2003). Meanwhile, Brown et al. (2002) found that that individuals who had successfully abstained from smoking in the past showed greater distress tolerance (persistence in mental arithmetic and breath holding) than those with little previous cessation success. Subsequent studies have reported similar findings with pathological gamblers (Daughters et al. 2005c) and substance abusers (Daughters et al. 2005b), and have also found that low persistence on the mental arithmetic task and a computerized version of mirror tracing predicted treatment dropout from a residential substance abuse program (Daughters et al. 2005a). Thus, there is accumulating evidence that performance on persistence tests is associated with performance in abstaining from substance abuse.

Cognitive/social learning variables. Social learning theory (Bandura 1977) has had significant influence upon contemporary conceptualization of addictive behaviors (see Maisto et al. 1999). Two of Bandura's constructs—outcome expectancies and self-efficacy—have been particularly influential and have been included in most of the integrative models of relapse described below. The study of expectancies (if-then hypotheses about the world) preceded social learning theory (e.g., Tolman 1932) and has been extended beyond it (e.g., Goldman 1999). However, the basic notion is that individuals' expectations (conscious or unconscious) about the outcomes of their behaviors influence their motivation to engage in those behaviors. For example, a drinker's expectancies that alcohol relieves stress or eases socializing may motivate him or her to drink, whether or not alcohol actually produces these effects. Indeed, expectancies may influence some perceived effects of drug consumption more than the pharmacological actions of the substances themselves (Juliano & Brandon 2002, Kirsch 1985, Marlatt & Rohsenow 1980). Expectancies have traditionally been assessed via self-report questionnaires, and magnitude of positive expectancies has been predictive of every phase of substance use, from initiation through poorer treatment outcome and relapse (Brown 1985, Copeland et al. 1995, Wetter et al. 1994). The second construct, self-efficacy, refers to beliefs regarding one's ability to perform a given goal-oriented behavior, which are also posited to affect the motivation to engage in that behavior. Simple, self-report measures of self-efficacy regarding maintaining abstinence are among the most robust predictors of long-term outcome (Burleson & Kaminer 2005, Condiotte & Lichtenstein 1981, McKay et al. 1993). Building upon findings on self-efficacy and outcome expectancies measured at a single point in time, recent EMA research found that daily changes in cessation self-efficacy and outcome expectancies predicted smoking lapse the next day, and subsequent relapse (Gwaltney et al. 2005).

General Self-Regulatory Theories

Three relevant theories can be categorized as based upon notions of self-regulation: behavioral economics, resource depletion, and automaticity.

Behavioral economics. Behavioral economics is the application of economic theory to behavior analysis (Madden 2000). Bickel & Marsch (2001) review two major concepts in behavioral economics that have implications for relapse and RP: inelasticity of drug demand and discounting of delayed reinforcers. The former refers to the experimental observation that drugs are not exempt from the classic law of supply and demand, but consumption of drugs is less responsive to price changes than consumption of other reinforcers. That is, drug users will choose alternative reinforcers to drugs, but only when the price of drugs is very high relative to the price of the alternatives (e.g., Johnson & Bickel 2003). Reinforcers that are only available after a delay are "discounted" (subjectively worth less) compared with immediate reinforcers of equal value, and this discounting rate varies among individuals. Those who tend to prefer smaller, immediate rewards are said to be more impulsive than those who tend to prefer larger, delayed rewards. Numerous studies have shown that drug users are more impulsive than are nonusers when given a series of choices between immediate and delayed rewards (e.g., Bickel et al. 1999, Kirby et al. 1999, Petry 2001). In this model, a drug-dependent individual who ceases drug use has chosen the delayed benefits of abstinence (e.g., long-term health) over the immediate reward of drug use. Over time, as drug cravings increase or when an opportunity to use drugs arises, preference may shift to drug use, resulting in relapse. This "preference reversal" has been demonstrated in a variety of experiments with both animals and humans, including one study with drug users (Bickel & Marsch 2001). Research is needed to examine whether magnitude of delay discounting is predictive of treatment outcome and relapse.

Resource-depletion model of self-control. Whereas behavioral economics focuses on impulsivity, another general self-regulatory model targets its opposite, self-control. Self-control requires overriding or inhibiting urges, thoughts, and behaviors (i.e., cravings for a drug) that conflict with long-term goals, social norms, or other rules (i.e., desire to abstain, health). To explain why self-control often fails (i.e., why relapse occurs), Baumeister and colleagues have developed the theory of ego depletion, also called the strength or resource model of self-regulation (Muraven & Baumeister 2000). According to this theory, self-control works like a muscle, in that all acts of self-control draw upon a common resource, with a limited capacity that varies among individuals. In the short term, acts of self-control temporarily deplete this resource until time and rest restore it, whereas in the long term, self-control strength may increase through repeated "exercise." Increasing motivation can also help compensate for depletion (Muraven & Slessareva 2003).

More recently, the model has been applied specifically to addictive behaviors, such as alcohol use (Baumeister 2003), with the idea that abstention or cessation requires the consumption of self-control resources and that relapse may occur when self-control is depleted, either from the effort to maintain abstinence itself or from other tasks requiring self-control. For example, Muraven et al. (2002) offered an incentive to male social drinkers to limit beer consumption during a taste test. As predicted, they found that participants who were randomly assigned another task requiring self-control (suppressing their thoughts of a white bear) showed reduced ability to moderate their drinking, compared with participants asked to solve arithmetic problems (not requiring self-control). Similar results have been shown for other problem behaviors such as spending money (Vohs & Faber 2004) and eating fattening foods (Vohs & Heatherton 2000).

Automaticity. Tiffany (1990) proposed a cognitive processing model of drug craving that posits that drug-taking behavior becomes largely automatized (i.e., under little conscious control) in the experienced user. According to the model, craving arises in the user attempting to abstain when he or she is confronted with stimuli associated with drug use, which interrupts automatic action plans and requires controlled cognitive processing. Relapse occurs when controlled processing is insufficient to impede the automatic drug-use action plan. An extreme example of such "absentminded relapse" would be when an individual is not even initially aware that he or she has used a drug, although there is likely a continuum of conscious awareness. Tiffany

(1990) proposes that the association between negative affect and relapse exists because negative affect evokes controlled processing that competes with the controlled processes required to interrupt the automated action plan. This model has influenced much research, but it has not been fully evaluated. It may apply primarily to drug use that does indeed involve very frequent repetitive behaviors, such as cigarette smoking, and be less applicable to most illicit drug use that requires more controlled, deliberate behaviors to acquire and administer the drug while avoiding detection. Predictions of the model have received moderate support. For example, dual-task paradigms have revealed that cigarette craving is associated with poorer performance on other controlled processing tasks, such as simple reaction time, under certain conditions (Cepeda-Benito & Tiffany 1996, Juliano & Brandon 1998, Sayette & Hufford 1994). Also, an EMA study of smoking lapse found that 6% of lapses could be categorized as absentminded (Catley et al. 2000).

Integrative Theories/Models of Relapse

The theories and models described above for the most part each deal with a particular mechanism thought to influence relapse. In addition, few of the models focus on relapse per se, but instead have some implications for relapse. In contrast, there exist integrative models of the relapse process itself that reflect primarily a social learning perspective.

Marlatt's original model. No model of relapse, or prescription for RP, has been more influential than that of G. Alan Marlatt and his colleagues. Marlatt & Gordon's (1985) edited volume has guided much of the field for more than two decades. The primary theoretical innovations of their conceptualization of relapse were (*a*) the aforementioned distinction between a lapse and relapse, and (*b*) the delineation of a specific cognitive-behavioral model of the relapse process, as reproduced in **Figure 1**. Perusal of the figure will reveal

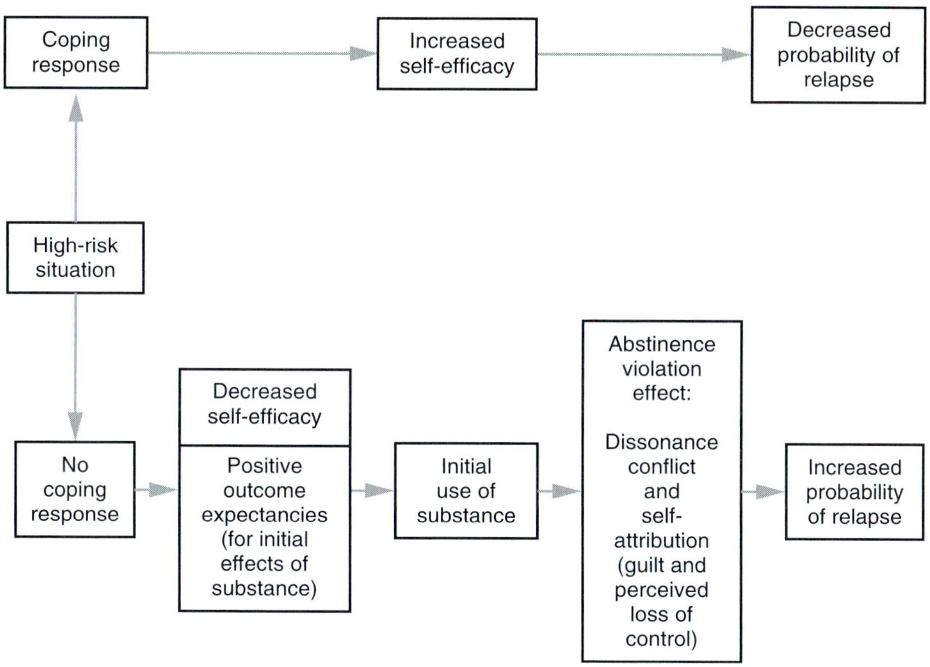

Figure 1

Marlatt's (1985) cognitive-behavioral model of relapse. From *Relapse Prevention: Maintenance Strategies in the Treatment of Addictive Behavior* (p. 38) by Marlatt & Gordon 1985, New York: Guilford. Copyright 1985 by The Guilford Press. Reprinted with permission.

many of the constructs discussed above. According to the model, the process of potential relapse is precipitated by a high-risk situation. These are inter- and intrapersonal conditions that include negative affect and conditioned stimuli. Failure to execute adequate coping responses is thought to lead to reduced self-efficacy and increased positive expectancies about the substance or activity, which in turn are likely to produce the initial lapse. The probability of progressing to a full relapse depends on an individual's response to the initial lapse. Marlatt termed a common but maladaptive response, the "abstinence violation effect" (AVE), which is characterized by dichotomous thinking ("I've blown it all") produced by cognitive dissonance (conflict and guilt) and self-attribution of failure (Marlatt 1985). The AVE produces a shift in self-perception extremes from absolute self-control to absolute loss of control, which provides the self-justification for progressing to full relapse.

Strengths of this model include its face validity and correspondence with clinical reports as well as its sequential specificity. The individual constructs (cues, affect, coping, self-efficacy, expectancies) have received much empirical support over the past 20 years with respect to their associations with clinical outcomes, as reviewed above. Unfortunately, however, given the clinical influence of the model and its corresponding intervention, there has been relatively little research on the model as a whole or on the causal sequence of cognitive and behavioral elements. Some studies, however, have examined the hypothesized relationships between adjacent links in the model, such as the antecedents and consequences of the AVE. Considerable evidence from both retrospective reports and EMA studies indicates that AVE-like reactions to lapsing do occur (Brandon et al. 1990, Carels et al. 2004, Shiffman et al. 1997a). The evidence is less consistent with respect to whether AVE magnitude is related to subsequent outcome, such as progression to relapse. Studies using participants' retrospective reports of the lapse tend to support the model (e.g., Curry et al. 1987, Grilo & Shiffman 1994, Stephens et al. 1994), whereas studies that have collected real-time (EMA) data have found little support for the hypothesized predictors of the AVE (Shiffman et al. 1997a) and no relationship between AVE variables and progression to relapse (Shiffman et al. 1996a).

In summary, the original Marlatt model of relapse deserves considerable credit for altering the conception of relapse itself from a discrete event or outcome to a process, for providing a rich account of the relapse process, and for instigating much research into that process. But evidence for much of the model is lacking. The model has also received criticism for excluding certain variables shown to predict relapse (e.g., social support, withdrawal, craving), which has led to a revision that is described below.

Other integrative models. Although no other relapse model has had the influence of Marlatt's original model, several others are noteworthy. The most specified of the alternative models was proposed by Niaura et al. (1988). They proposed a dynamic regulatory feedback system whereby contextual cues, moderated by affect state, produced urges, physiologic activation, and positive outcome expectancies, which in turn were linked to coping and attributions about control. These constructs all fed into self-efficacy expectations, which were inversely related to the probability of a lapse and then relapse. The model is complex and contains multiple feedback loops, yet it has been criticized for its omissions and logical inconsistencies, such as having self-efficacy as the sole final determinant of drug use (Tiffany 1995).

Other models of relapse have acknowledged the difficulty in postulating specific causal chains instead taking the broader approach of identifying various classes of contributory variables. For example, Marlatt's new, dynamic reformulated model (Witkiewitz & Marlatt 2004) is based on the interaction of tonic processes (distal risks, such as family history and dependence; cognitive processes, such as self-efficacy and outcome expectancies; and physical withdrawal), high-risk situations (contextual factors), and phasic processes (coping behaviors, affective state, substance use behaviors, and the AVE). The general direction of causality is from the tonic processes to the phasic processes, with the interaction of high-risk situations, and with multiple feedback loops. Another example is Shiffman et al. (1986), who described relapse proneness as the summative effects of slowly changing background variables (e.g., stress, personality traits, dependence) and acute events (e.g., specific stressors and other high-risk situations). A lapse is thought to occur in this model when total relapse proneness at any time surpasses a certain threshold, and relapse occurs when relapse proneness surpasses a higher threshold. Abstinence is resumed when relapse proneness once again falls below threshold. Piasecki et al. (2002) used the Shiffman et al. (1986) framework to propose three specific additive factors that contribute to relapse-proneness: physiological withdrawal, stressors/temptations, and cessation fatigue. Fatigue may be a function of resource depletion (Baumeister 2003), and unlike the first two factors, it is postulated to increase over time, contributing to relatively late lapse and relapse.

Conclusions Regarding Theories of Relapse

1. Although more than two decades have passed since Marlatt shifted the conceptualization of relapse from a discrete dichotomous outcome to a process, it is still often treated as the former, particularly with respect to measuring and reporting treatment effects. From the process perspective, it makes little sense to report continuous abstinence as the only criterion for a successful treatment. Such a practice also inhibits the continued study of the relapse process itself (see Shiffman 2006).
2. Addictions are chronic relapsing disorders, yet we tend to treat them as acute disorders. By analogy, we often treat addictions as if they were bacterial infections that are responsive to a single course of therapy and that do not require long-term monitoring once remission has occurred. Instead, a better model may be diabetes, which demands ongoing monitoring and treatment adjustments, when necessary. Indeed, other psychological disorders, such as anxiety and depression, are already more likely to be conceptualized in this manner. Neither remission nor relapse are viewed as end states, but rather as data informing decisions about the need for treatment adjustments.
3. There is a need for better animal models of relapse. Although animal research has been informative, an animal model does not yet exist that approaches the complexity and volitional aspects of human substance abuse and relapse (Li 2000, Tiffany & Conklin 2002).
4. Recent integrative theories of relapse have shied away from highly specific causal models (e.g., Marlatt 1985, Niaura et al. 1988) toward broader models that categorize classes of risk variables. Perhaps this is the most defendable approach toward integrating all known relapse-related variables into a single model. However, such a risk-adverse strategy comes at a cost: Scientific progress occurs best through the testing and rejection of specific theories. It is not necessary that an integrative model be fully comprehensive. For example, models such as resource depletion, task persistence/distress tolerance, negative affectivity, and classical conditioning lend themselves to integration into a single learning-based model.
5. To date there has been little differentiation in relapse models between individuals who make behavioral changes

on their own versus those who receive treatment, and there have been few, if any, treatment-specific models of relapse. That is, different treatments may be associated with different relapse processes. This is an avenue for further exploration.

6. Finally, the review of relapse models introduces the question of whether these addiction-focused models have relevance for relapse to other psychological disorders. To date, the various operational definitions of relapse used across disorders have hindered the direct comparison of their relapse processes. Yet it seems likely that some of the models applied to addiction (e.g., classical conditioning, resource depletion) would have wide relevance. It is also likely, though, that some relapse-related models and variables identified for other disorders (e.g., expressed emotion for psychotic disorders; Butzlaff & Hooley 1998) may fit within the general models of relapse discussed above. It may be fruitful to search for common processes underlying relapse across disorders.

RELAPSE PREVENTION INTERVENTIONS

Marlatt's Relapse Prevention Intervention

The wide acceptance of RP as an explicit treatment goal can be credited to Marlatt and colleagues, who described the core components of an RP program based on their model of relapse (Marlatt & Gordon 1985). Due to its dominance in the field, much of our review focuses on this approach. Marlatt's RP has several components, targeting the various elements of the hypothesized relapse process, as represented by the lower branch of **Figure 1**. These range from training in anticipating and avoiding high-risk situations at the distal end of the relapse process, to preparing patients for the possibility of a lapse and inoculating them from experiencing the AVE at the proximal end of the proposed process. Other elements of the intervention include self-efficacy enhancement exercises, education designed to reduce positive outcome expectancies about the initial effects of re-engaging in the targeted behavior, and more general lifestyle modification. However, reflecting the prominence of coping in the relapse model, the key component of RP involves training patients in coping skills that can be activated in high-risk situations and when they are tempted to lapse. A strong emphasis is placed on learning from past lapse and relapse experiences.

Since the RP model of Marlatt and colleagues was first introduced more than 20 years ago, interventions based on the model have taken many different forms. RP interventions were originally developed to augment primary treatments for substance abuse. However, RP has been increasingly used for the treatment of other disorders (particularly other impulse-control problems, such as gambling, eating disorders, and sexual behaviors). They have also become more frequently used as the primary treatment program per se, targeting initial behavior change, rather than as an adjuvant therapy targeting only relapse. This shift no doubt reflects the fuzzy definitional distinction between unsuccessful behavior change versus relapse, as well as the fact that some components of RP interventions that are critical to the prevention of relapse are also key in facilitating initial behavior change (e.g., anticipating high-risk situations, coping). Thus, today RP interventions may be delivered as a component of a primary treatment intended to facilitate an initial change in behavior, as an adjuvant to the primary therapy with a focus on maintaining behavior change, or as a stand-alone treatment delivered to patients who have already remitted. They may be delivered individually, in group format, or via self-help materials. Existing evidence suggests that modality in which RP interventions are delivered has little impact on treatment outcomes (Irvin et al. 1999).

Efficacy of RP. Principles of RP have been incorporated into a variety of treatments for a range of addictive behaviors, although the greatest number of clinical trials has involved smoking cessation. Particular elements of RP, such as training in coping skills, have been found to be effective. That is, RP interventions have proven efficacious in instilling coping skills (Davis & Glaros 1986, Hall et al. 1984, Zelman et al. 1992), and the utilization of coping skills enhances the likelihood of achieving and maintaining abstinence (Fiore et al. 2000, Zelman et al. 1992). The overall efficacy of comprehensive RP interventions has been more difficult to evaluate. In a qualitative review of controlled clinical trials, Carroll (1996) concluded that strong evidence existed for Marlatt-based RP when compared with no-treatment control conditions, but there was less consistent support for the efficacy of RP compared with discussion controls or comparison treatments. Carroll (1996) found the strongest support for RP when it was applied to smoking cessation. Another qualitative review that focused on smoking cessation also reported mixed findings regarding the efficacy of RP (Curry & McBride 1994).

There have been two recent meta-analyses of RP. Irvin et al. (1999) evaluated the efficacy of Marlatt-based RP across substance use disorders in a meta-analytic review based on 26 controlled trials representing a sample of 9504 participants. These authors found a significant overall effect size of $r = 0.14$ for reduction in substance use, and a much larger effect of $r = 0.48$ for improving overall psychosocial functioning. Treatment effects were strongest for alcohol ($r = 0.37$) and polysubstance use ($r = 0.27$), and weaker for smoking ($r = 0.09$), but all three were significant. The effect was not significant for cocaine, but only three studies were included. The most recent meta-analysis focused solely on smoking (Lancaster et al. 2006) and included 42 studies of controlled trials with at least six months of follow-up, most of which used skills training approaches. Separate analyses were conducted based on whether participants were randomized before or after they achieved cessation, and on the population studied (e.g., pregnant/postpartum, hospital inpatients, military personnel, aided and unaided abstainers). Although odds ratios were generally positive, they were small, and no significant effects were found for behavioral interventions. These findings are surprising in light of the strong meta-analytic evidence for the efficacy of interventions consistent with RP for smoking cessation reported in the U.S. Public Health Service's Clinical Practice Guideline (Fiore et al. 2000). These disparate findings may be the result of the Lancaster et al. (2006) analysis using a more conservative strategy in evaluating outcomes. Note also that a wide range of treatment modalities was collapsed in these analyses, most interventions were low intensity (i.e., brief meetings, written materials, or telephone contacts), and the included studies were not limited to Marlatt-based interventions.

Self-help RP interventions. Self-help interventions targeting relapse have been most commonly utilized in the area of smoking cessation. Although the overall efficacy of self-help interventions for smoking cessation has been marginal (Fiore et al. 2000), those focused on preventing relapse have demonstrated greater efficacy. A large early study found that inclusion of an American Lung Association manual on maintaining abstinence significantly improved upon self-help materials focusing solely on cessation (Davis et al. 1984). More recently Brandon and colleagues (2000, 2004) conducted two randomized, controlled trials of a self-help relapse prevention intervention for ex-smokers who had quit on their own prior to study enrollment. The first study found that eight RP booklets (based largely on the principles of Marlatt) mailed to self-quit ex-smokers over the course of one year reduced relapse by two-thirds among recent quitters. The follow-up study indicated that efficacy was due to the content of the booklets rather than to the frequency of contact made with participants via the repeated mailings. Moreover, the intervention was found to be highly cost-effective relative to other public health interventions.

Other RP Interventions

Although interventions based on Marlatt's original RP model (Marlatt 1985) clearly dominate the literature, many other approaches have been attempted. The simplest, usually atheoretical, approach to maintaining behavior change has been to extend treatment, i.e., to add "booster sessions." It is difficult to evaluate this approach due to the vast differences in treatment content, frequency, duration, population, and target behavior across studies. However, in a qualitative review of booster sessions, Whisman (1990) concluded that they have been moderately successful, although there is also some evidence that they may simply delay, rather than prevent, relapse (e.g., Brandon et al. 1987). Other, more highly specified RP therapies are reviewed below.

Cue exposure therapy. Cue exposure treatment is based on classical conditioning theory, as reviewed above. The rationale is that repeated exposure to drug-related stimuli without reinforcement will facilitate extinction of conditioned responses to these stimuli. Relatively few controlled studies have tested the efficacy of cue exposure therapies in treating addictive disorders, and findings have been mixed. Kadden (2001) reviewed published trials of cue exposure treatments for alcohol dependence and concluded that cue exposure therapy may have some value as a treatment approach for alcohol dependence. His assessment was based on findings that although cue exposure treatment failed to prevent relapse to alcohol use, it was effective in reducing the severity of drinking following an initial lapse (Drummond & Glautier 1994, Monti et al. 1993, Rohsenow et al. 2001).

Conklin & Tiffany (2002) conducted a meta-analytic review of the efficacy of cue exposure treatment for addictive disorders including alcohol, cocaine, opiate, and nicotine dependence. Their analysis was based on the results of nine studies and revealed no significant overall treatment effect for the efficacy of cue exposure treatment in reducing or preventing relapse to substance use. Taken together these findings suggest that existing cue exposure therapies have little to no efficacy in substantially reducing or preventing relapse to problematic substance use. This conclusion is disappointing, given that the theoretical principles upon which cue exposure therapy is based appear to have considerable merit. Conklin & Tiffany (2002) and others (e.g., Brandon 2001) have, therefore, called for a refinement of cue exposure therapies driven by contemporary research and theory on extinction.

As reviewed above, Bouton (2002) has found that extinction learning is highly context dependent, and renewal occurs when an organism is exposed to CSs in a context other than the extinction context. This may account for the poor performance of cue exposure therapies to date. One promising approach to improving the generalization of extinction involves aiding the organism's retrieval of the extinction memory by presenting a cue that was present during extinction (Brooks 2000). Collins & Brandon (2002) tested this phenomenon in humans (heavy social drinkers) and found that the presence of such an extinction cue (a novelty pencil) significantly reduced craving and salivation to alcohol cues presented in a novel context following extinction. Thus, these findings provided preliminary evidence to suggest that providing patients with a portable stimulus associated with extinction, such as a token (or even a cognitive cue), may be useful in improving the generalizability and efficacy of cue exposure therapies.

Gorski's CENAPS model. The model of relapse prevention developed by Terrence Gorski is a comprehensive approach to preventing relapse to alcohol or other substance use following completion of primary treatment (Gorski & Miller 1982). Key components of Gorski's Center for Applied Sciences (CENAPS) model include assessment, identification, and management of warning signs for relapse, planning for recovery, and early intervention training for relapse. Central to the model is the concept of a 37-step progression of "warning signs" that predict proximity to a relapse. Although the model has achieved considerable popularity and anecdotal support among clinical treatment providers over the past 25 years, very little empirical research on the efficacy of the model exists (Miller & Harris 2000). However, Miller & Harris (2000) found that Gorski's warning signs did predict the occurrence of lapses and relapses, but the signs did not emerge in progression as predicted. Rather, the warning signs appeared to reflect that "general depression" and "demoralization" were associated with relapse to alcohol, consistent with negative affectivity models. Thus, the CENAPS model of relapse may add little to what is already documented within the relapse literature. However, the intervention itself awaits empirical evaluation.

Mindfulness-based treatment. Mindfulness-based treatments represent a novel cognitive-behavioral approach that may hold promise for the prevention of relapse. Mindfulness reflects an intentional allocation of attention to cognitions, emotions, perceptions, and sensations that occur on a moment-to-moment basis. Specifically, mindfulness reflects the purposeful control of attention and can be learned through intensive training in meditation (Kabat-Zinn 1994, Marlatt & Kristeller 1999). Treatment involves helping individuals to increase their awareness of cognition, affect, and sensations in the present moment; training individuals to change the way they relate to these; and facilitating the ability to disengage attention and respond to these as they arise. Proponents of the model (Marlatt 1994, Witkiewitz et al. 2005) have argued that mindfulness-based interventions may be especially relevant to the prevention of relapse because they directly target affective (e.g., stress, negative affective states) and cognitive (e.g., urges, apparently irrelevant decisions) mechanisms underlying relapse to addictive behaviors. Although studies testing the efficacy of mindfulness in treating substance abuse have not yet been published, a recent meta-analytic review of the efficacy of mindfulness-based interventions revealed moderate effects (mean $d = 0.59$) for other psychological problems (e.g., stress, pain, anxiety-related disorders, eating disorders, depression), at follow-up points ranging from three months to four years (Baer 2003). Moreover, a multicenter randomized trial found that mindfulness-based cognitive therapy significantly reduced relapse to major depression over a one-year follow-up (Teasdale et al. 2000). Thus, this approach appears worthy of additional study.

Contingency management. As discussed above, a behavioral economics approach to preventing relapse would recommend increasing the availability of alternative reinforcers. Contingency management (CM) treatments provide clients with vouchers or other reinforcers in exchange for biochemically verified abstinence. Because these programs require frequent monitoring to verify clients' abstinence, they are most commonly employed in outpatient treatment programs for heroin and cocaine users (e.g., Higgins et al. 1994, Silverman et al. 1996), but they have also been used to treat nicotine (Donatelle et al. 2004) and alcohol dependence (e.g., Petry et al. 2000). CM programs are often instituted to help prevent relapse after clients have been maintained on methadone for several weeks. Although they are generally very effective in the short term, most participants relapse once the program is discontinued, usually after three to six months (e.g., Silverman et al. 1996). Recently, longer-term CM treatments that last one to three years have been developed (Silverman et al. 2002), and in a few studies, positive effects of CM have been detected through up to 15 months of postintervention follow-up (Higgins et al. 2000, Preston et al. 2002). To improve the efficacy of CM at preventing relapse after the reinforcers are withdrawn, Marlatt (2001) has suggested combining CM and RP training.

Pharmacotherapy

Although this review focuses on behavioral interventions, pharmacotherapies are increasingly used to treat and prevent relapse to addictive behaviors and other disorders. The evidence suggests that they can have a powerful effect on treatment outcomes, particularly when used as an adjunct to behavioral interventions for relapse prevention (Welsh & Liberto 2001). Pharmacological approaches designed to prevent relapse differ widely and are often specific to particular classes of substances of abuse. However, they can be divided into two broad categories: (*a*) those intended to reduce relapse through extending treatment effects instrumental in the initial achievement of cessation, and (*b*) those that have mechanisms of action with particular relevance to relapse. The former category includes agonist, or substitution, therapies, such as methadone maintenance and nicotine replacement, for the treatment of opiate and tobacco dependence, respectively. Both of these pharmacotherapies have demonstrated efficacy. The latter category includes aversives and antagonists. Disulfiram (Antabuse), has been FDA approved as an aversive treatment of alcohol dependence since 1951. It is intended to prevent relapse by creating intense physical discomfort (e.g., flushing, tachycardia, hypotension, nausea) upon the consumption of alcohol, via the accumulation of acetaldehyde. The anticipation of this reaction inhibits relapse to alcohol. Disulfiram appears to be effective among those who adhere to the drug regimen, but adherence itself remains a barrier to treatment (Suh et al. 2006). Antagonists represent a class of pharmacotherapies that attenuates the reinforcing effects of substance use. In theory, they should contribute to extinction of drug use when taken prior to cessation. And once a lapse occurs, the attenuated reinforcement should inhibit the reinstatement processes reviewed above. The prototypical antagonist is naltrexone for the treatment of opiate dependence and, more recently, alcohol dependence. Efficacy findings with both substances are mixed, but the overall efficacy appears to be positive for treating alcohol dependence (Streeton & Whelan 2001) and less clear for opiate dependence. A recent addition to the smoking cessation armamentarium is varenicline, a partial nicotine receptor agonist, which received FDA approval in 2006. It should produce both agonist (reducing withdrawal and craving) and antagonist (reducing reinforcement following a lapse) effects. Initial efficacy findings are positive. Most relevant was the efficacy of an extended 12-week course of varenicline (versus placebo) for individuals who had already achieved initial abstinence with the drug, suggesting its utility at maintaining tobacco abstinence (Tonstad et al. 2006). It was not clear from the results the degree to which the agonist versus antagonist effects contributed to the efficacy in that rates of recovery from a lapse were not reported.

Conclusions Regarding Relapse Prevention Interventions

1. Interventions based on Marlatt's original model of RP have had the most profound impact on changing the way addictive disorders are conceptualized and treated. RP interventions have typically comprised treatment strategies that correspond to elements of the model, but few interventions have captured the full RP model.
2. Although considerable empirical research has supported the efficacy of interventions based on the RP model, outcomes associated with RP have not

proven to be superior to outcomes of other active treatment approaches.

3. Self-help interventions based on RP have demonstrated efficacy in preventing relapse to smoking among self-quitting smokers. The efficacy of similar interventions should be tested for other substances of abuse and perhaps other disorders with high rates of both spontaneous remission and relapse.
4. Interventions intended to prevent relapse to substance use based on cue exposure therapy appear to have little efficacy in reducing or preventing relapse to problematic substance use. Refinement of cue exposure therapies driven by contemporary theory and research on extinction may be useful in enhancing their efficacy.
5. Treatments based on Gorski's model of relapse prevention have been widely accepted among the treatment community. The lack of empirical research on the efficacy of the approach is troubling and should be rectified.
6. Pharmacotherapies have demonstrated powerful effects on the achievement and maintenance of abstinence from substance use, particularly when used as adjuncts to behavioral interventions intended to prevent relapse.
7. Promising future directions include novel treatments, such as mindfulness-based therapy, as well as treatments linked to the theories of relapse reviewed above. For example, contingency management approaches are consistent with principles derived from behavior economic theory. Also, findings on task persistence/distress tolerance suggest treatments based on general effort training (Eisenberger 1992) or specific abstinence-related training via either partial reinforcement schedules (Quinn et al. 1996) or requiring progressively longer periods of abstinence (Brown et al. 2005).
8. Although the distinction between a lapse and relapse was an important theoretical advance, few behavioral interventions have truly drawn upon this distinction. The pragmatic barriers to timely intervention after a lapse might today be overcome through technology, such as portable telecommunication devices.

FINAL CONCLUSIONS

Over the past 20 years we have seen the recognition of both the problem of relapse and the potential of RP, such that today most credible treatments devote some attention to the maintenance of behavior change. However, the importance of RP has yet to be fully appreciated. Given the high rate of relapse for most psychological problems, preventing relapse is arguably at least as important as producing initial behavior change. Yet there is still a relatively slow rate of progress in the development of theories, research paradigms, or interventions dedicated to relapse and RP.

The first step is the advancement of theory. Although we identified in this review several theoretical directions with potential, greater effort is required to translate basic research (on learning, affect, neuroscience, etc.) into applied theory. Moreover, there is a need for integrated theories that can be exposed to risk of refutation. There also remains a need for the development of novel RP interventions that are based on explicated theory, and the therapies that are already in use must be subject to empirical test. Finally, there is a need for theory-based interventions that incorporate pharmacotherapy and behavioral strategies. Today, these two approaches are often used in isolation or in combination with additive effects at best. The potential synergism between pharmacotherapy and behavioral approaches is not being exploited.

In summary, relapse theory, research, and intervention have been making slow progress that does not reflect the magnitude of the relapse problem. It is our hope that we will soon see renewed investment and accelerated progress in this vital area, taking advantage of advances in technology as well as basic theory and research. Quoting Yogi Berra again: "The future ain't what it used to be."

ACKNOWLEDGMENTS

Preparation of this paper was supported by National Cancer Institute grant R01CA94256 and American Cancer Society Grant RSGPB CPPB-109035 to Thomas H. Brandon, and National Center for Chronic Disease Prevention and Health Promotion grant K01DP000086 to Jennifer Irvin Vidrine. We thank Tim Baker, Alan Marlatt, Roger Peters, and Katie Witkiewitz for their helpful comments.

LITERATURE CITED

Abrams DB, Monti PM, Carey KB, Pinto RP, Jacobus SI. 1988. Reactivity to smoking cues and relapse: two studies of discriminant validity. *Behav. Res. Ther.* 26:225–33

Anda RF, Williamson DF, Escobedo LG, Mast EE, Giovino GA, Remington PL. 1990. Depression and the dynamics of smoking. A national perspective. *JAMA* 264:1541–45

Baer RA. 2003. Mindfulness training as a clinical intervention: a conceptual and empirical review. *Clin. Psychol. Sci. Pract.* 10:125–43

Baker TB, Morse E, Sherman JE. 1986. The motivation to use drugs: a psychobiological analysis of urges. *Nebr. Symp. Motiv.* 34:257–323

Baker TB, Piper ME, McCarthy DE, Majeskie MR, Fiore MC. 2004. Addiction motivation reformulated: an affective processing model of negative reinforcement. *Psychol. Rev.* 111:33–51

Reformulation of the negative reinforcement model of drug addiction. Posits that escape and avoidance of negative affect are central.

Bandura A. 1977. *Social Learning Theory*. Englewood Cliffs, NJ: Prentice-Hall

Baumeister RF. 2003. Ego depletion and self-regulation failure: a resource model of self-control. *Alcohol Clin. Exp. Res.* 27:281–84

Describes the resource-depletion model of self-control and its relevance to addictive behaviors.

Bickel WK, Marsch LA. 2001. Toward a behavioral economic understanding of drug dependence: delay discounting processes. *Addiction* 96:73–86

Bickel WK, Odum AL, Madden GJ. 1999. Impulsivity and cigarette smoking: delay discounting in current, never, and ex-smokers. *Psychopharmacology (Berl.)* 146:447–54

Bouton ME. 2002. Context, ambiguity, and unlearning: sources of relapse after behavioral extinction. *Biol. Psychiatry* 52:976–86

Reviews the role of context in extinction, its implications regarding the mechanisms of learned associations, and its relevance to relapse.

Bradizza CM, Stasiewicz PR, Maisto SA. 1994. A conditioning reinterpretation of cognitive events in alcohol and drug cue exposure. *J. Behav. Ther. Exp. Psychiatry* 25:15–22

Brandon TH. 2001. Behavioral tobacco cessation treatments: yesterday's news or tomorrow's headlines? *J. Clin. Oncol.* 19:64–68S

Brandon TH, Collins BN, Juliano LM, Lazev AB. 2000. Preventing relapse among former smokers: a comparison of minimal interventions through telephone and mail. *J. Consult. Clin. Psychol.* 68:103–13

Brandon TH, Herzog TA, Juliano LM, Irvin JE, Lazev AB, Simmons VN. 2003. Pretreatment task persistence predicts smoking cessation outcome. *J. Abnorm. Psychol.* 112:448–56

Demonstrates in a prospective study that persistence on a simple behavioral task (mirror tracing) is predictive of short-term and long-term smoking cessation.

Brandon TH, Meade CD, Herzog TA, Chirikos TN, Webb MS, Cantor AB. 2004. Efficacy and cost-effectiveness of a minimal intervention to prevent smoking relapse: dismantling the effects of amount of content versus contact. *J. Consult. Clin. Psychol.* 72:797–808

Brandon TH, Tiffany ST, Obremski KM, Baker TB. 1990. Postcessation cigarette use: the process of relapse. *Addict. Behav.* 15:105–14

Brandon TH, Zelman DC, Baker TB. 1987. Effects of maintenance sessions on smoking relapse: delaying the inevitable? *J. Consult. Clin. Psychol.* 55:780–82

Brooks DC. 2000. Recent and remote extinction cues reduce spontaneous recovery. *Q.J. Exp. Psychol. B* 53:25–58

Brown RA, Lejuez CW, Kahler CW, Strong DR. 2002. Distress tolerance and duration of past smoking cessation attempts. *J. Abnorm. Psychol.* 111:180–85

Brown RA, Lejuez CW, Kahler CW, Strong DR, Zvolensky MJ. 2005. Distress tolerance and early smoking lapse. *Clin. Psychol. Rev.* 25:713–33

Brown SA. 1985. Reinforcement expectancies and alcoholism treatment outcome after a one-year follow-up. *J. Stud. Alcohol* 46:304–8

Bruce SE, Yonkers KA, Otto MW, Eisen JL, Weisberg RB, et al. 2005. Influence of psychiatric comorbidity on recovery and recurrence in generalized anxiety disorder, social phobia, and panic disorder: a 12-year prospective study. *Am. J. Psychiatry* 162:1179–87

Burleson JA, Kaminer Y. 2005. Self-efficacy as a predictor of treatment outcome in adolescent substance use disorders. *Addict. Behav.* 30:1751–64

Butzlaff RL, Hooley JM. 1998. Expressed emotion and psychiatric relapse: a meta-analysis. *Arch. Gen. Psychiatry* 55:547–52

Caggiula AR, Donny EC, Chaudhri N, Perkins KA, Evans-Martin FF, Sved AF. 2002. Importance of nonpharmacological factors in nicotine self-administration. *Physiol. Behav.* 77:683–87

Carels RA, Douglass OM, Cacciapaglia HM, O'Brien WH. 2004. An ecological momentary assessment of relapse crises in dieting. *J. Consult. Clin. Psychol.* 72:341–48

Carroll KM. 1996. Relapse prevention as a psychosocial treatment: a review of controlled clinical trials. *Exp. Clin. Psychopharmacol.* 4:46–54

Carter BL, Tiffany ST. 1999. Meta-analysis of cue-reactivity in addiction research. *Addiction* 94:327–40

Carter FA, Bulik CM, McIntosh VV, Joyce PR. 2002. Cue reactivity as a predictor of outcome with bulimia nervosa. *Int. J. Eat. Disord.* 31:240–50

Catley D, O'Connell KA, Shiffman S. 2000. Absentminded lapses during smoking cessation. *Psychol. Addict. Behav.* 14:73–76

Cepeda-Benito A, Tiffany ST. 1996. The use of a dual-task procedure for the assessment of cognitive effort associated with cigarette craving. *Psychopharmacology (Berl.)* 127:155–63

Childress AR, Mozley PD, McElgin W, Fitzgerald J, Reivich M, O'Brien CP. 1999. Limbic activation during cue-induced cocaine craving. *Am. J. Psychiatry* 156:11–18

Collins BN, Brandon TH. 2002. Effects of extinction context and retrieval cues on alcohol cue reactivity among nonalcoholic drinkers. *J. Consult. Clin. Psychol.* 70:390–97

Condiotte MM, Lichtenstein E. 1981. Self-efficacy and relapse in smoking cessation programs. *J. Consult. Clin. Psychol.* 49:648

Conklin CA, Tiffany ST. 2002. Applying extinction research and theory to cue-exposure addiction treatments. *Addiction* 97:155–67

Review and meta-analysis of cue-exposure treatment for addictions. Recommends greater attention to contemporary learning theory.

Cooney NL, Litt MD, Morse PA, Bauer LO, Gaupp L. 1997. Alcohol cue reactivity, negative-mood reactivity, and relapse in treated alcoholic men. *J. Abnorm. Psychol.* 106:243–50

Copeland AL, Brandon TH, Quinn EP. 1995. The Smoking Consequences Questionnaire-Adult: measurement of smoking outcome expectancies of experienced smokers. *Psychol. Assess.* 7:484–94

Covey LS. 1999. Tobacco cessation among patients with depression. *Prim. Care* 26:691–706

Curry S, Marlatt G, Gordon JR. 1987. Abstinence violation effect: validation of an attributional construct with smoking cessation. *J. Consult. Clin. Psychol.* 55:145–49

Curry SJ, McBride CM. 1994. Relapse prevention for smoking cessation: review and evaluation of concepts and interventions. *Annu. Rev. Public Health* 15:345–66

Darke S, Ross J, Teesson M, Ali R, Cooke R, et al. 2005. Factors associated with 12 months continuous heroin abstinence: findings from the Australian Treatment Outcome Study (ATOS). *J. Subst. Abuse Treat.* 28:255–63

Daughters SB, Lejuez CW, Bornovalova MA, Kahler CW, Strong DR, Brown RA. 2005a. Distress tolerance as a predictor of early treatment dropout in a residential substance abuse treatment facility. *J. Abnorm. Psychol.* 114:729–34

Daughters SB, Lejuez CW, Kahler CW, Strong DR, Brown RA. 2005b. Psychological distress tolerance and duration of most recent abstinence attempt among residential treatment-seeking substance abusers. *Psychol. Addict. Behav.* 19:208–11

Daughters SB, Lejuez CW, Strong DR, Brown RA, Breen RB, Lesieur HR. 2005c. The relationship among negative affect, distress tolerance, and length of gambling abstinence attempt. *J. Gambl. Stud.* 21:363–78

Davis AL, Faust R, Ordentlich M. 1984. Self-help smoking cessation and maintenance programs: a comparative study with 12-month follow-up by the American Lung Association. *Am. J. Public Health* 74:1212–17

Davis JR, Glaros AG. 1986. Relapse prevention and smoking cessation. *Addict. Behav.* 11:105–14

Donatelle R, Hudson D, Dobie S, Goodall A, Hunsberger M, Oswald K. 2004. Incentives in smoking cessation: status of the field and implications for research and practice with pregnant smokers. *Nicotine Tob. Res.* 6(Suppl. 2):S163–79

Donovan DM. 1996. Assessment issues and domains in the prediction of relapse. *Addiction* 91(Suppl.):S29–36

Drummond DC, Glautier S. 1994. A controlled trial of cue exposure treatment in alcohol dependence. *J. Consult. Clin. Psychol.* 62:809–17

Eisen JL, Goodman WK, Keller MB, Warshaw MG, DeMarco LM, et al. 1999. Patterns of remission and relapse in obsessive-compulsive disorder: a 2-year prospective study. *J. Clin. Psychiatry* 60:346–51

Eisenberger R. 1992. Learned industriousness. *Psychol. Rev.* 99:248–67

Eissenberg T. 2004. Measuring the emergence of tobacco dependence: the contribution of negative reinforcement models. *Addiction* 99(Suppl. 1):5–29

Fiore MC, Bailey WC, Cohen SJ, Dorfman SF, Goldstein MG, et al. 2000. *Treating Tobacco Use and Dependence: Clinical Practice Guideline*. Rockville, MD: U.S. Dept. Health Human Serv., Public Health Serv.

Frank E, Prien RF, Jarrett RB, Keller MB, Kupfer DJ, et al. 1991. Conceptualization and rationale for consensus definitions of terms in major depressive disorder. Remission, recovery, relapse, and recurrence. *Arch. Gen. Psychiatry* 48:851–55

Goldman MS. 1999. Expectancy operation: cognitive-neural models and architectures. In *How Expectancies Shape Experience*, ed. I Kirsch, pp. 41–63. Washington, DC: Am. Psychol. Assoc.

Gorski TT, Miller M. 1982. *Counseling for Relapse Prevention.* Independence, MO: Harald House Independ. Press

Grilo CM, Shiffman S. 1994. Longitudinal investigation of the abstinence violation effect in binge eaters. *J. Consult. Clin. Psychol.* 62:611–19

Grusser SM, Plontzke B, Albrecht U. 2005. Pathological gambling. An empirical study of the desire for addictive substances. *Nervenarzt* 76:592–96

Gwaltney CJ, Shiffman S, Balabanis MH, Paty JA. 2005. Dynamic self-efficacy and outcome expectancies: prediction of smoking lapse and relapse. *J. Abnorm. Psychol.* 114:661–75

Hall SM, Rugg D, Tunstall C, Jones RT. 1984. Preventing relapse to cigarette smoking by behavioral skill training. *J. Consult. Clin. Psychol.* 52:372–82

Higgins ST, Budney AJ, Bickel WK, Foerg FE, Donham R, Badger GJ. 1994. Incentives improve outcome in outpatient behavioral treatment of cocaine dependence. *Arch. Gen. Psychiatry* 51:568–76

Higgins ST, Wong CJ, Badger GJ, Ogden DE, Dantona RL. 2000. Contingent reinforcement increases cocaine abstinence during outpatient treatment and 1 year of follow-up. *J. Consult. Clin. Psychol.* 68:64–72

Hughes JR, Keely J, Naud S. 2004. Shape of the relapse curve and long-term abstinence among untreated smokers. *Addiction* 99:29–38

Hughes JR, Keely JP, Niaura RS, Ossip-Klein DJ, Richmond RL, Swan GE. 2003. Measures of abstinence in clinical trials: issues and recommendations. *Nicotine Tob. Res.* 5:13–25

Hunt WA, Barnett LW, Branch LG. 1971. Relapse rates in addiction programs. *J. Clin. Psychol.* 27:455–56

Irvin JE, Bowers CA, Dunn ME, Wang MC. 1999. Efficacy of relapse prevention: a meta-analytic review. *J. Consult. Clin. Psychol.* 67:563–70

The most comprehensive meta-analysis of Marlatt-based RP interventions.

Johnson MW, Bickel WK. 2003. The behavioral economics of cigarette smoking: the concurrent presence of a substitute and an independent reinforcer. *Behav. Pharmacol.* 14:137–44

Juliano LM, Brandon TH. 1998. Reactivity to instructed smoking availability and environmental cues: evidence with urge and reaction time. *Exp. Clin. Psychopharmacol.* 6:45–53

Juliano LM, Brandon TH. 2002. Effects of nicotine dose, instructional set, and outcome expectancies on the subjective effects of smoking in the presence of a stressor. *J. Abnorm. Psychol.* 111:88–97

Kabat-Zinn J. 1994. *Wherever You Go, There You Are: Mindfulness Meditation in Everyday Life.* New York: Hyperion

Kadden RM. 2001. Behavioral and cognitive-behavioral treatments for alcoholism: research opportunities. *Addict. Behav.* 26:489–507

Karl A, Malta LS, Alexander J, Blanchard EB. 2004. Startle responses in motor vehicle accident survivors: a pilot study. *Appl. Psychophysiol. Biofeedback* 29:223–31

Kassel JD, Stroud LR, Paronis CA. 2003. Smoking, stress, and negative affect: correlation, causation, and context across stages of smoking. *Psychol. Bull.* 129:270–304

Kenford SL, Smith SS, Wetter DW, Jorenby DE, Fiore MC, Baker TB. 2002. Predicting relapse back to smoking: contrasting affective and physical models of dependence. *J. Consult. Clin. Psychol.* 70:216–27

Khantzian EJ. 1985. The self-medication hypothesis of addictive disorders: focus on heroin and cocaine dependence. *Am. J. Psychiatry* 142:1259–64

Kirby KN, Petry NM, Bickel WK. 1999. Heroin addicts have higher discount rates for delayed rewards than non-drug-using controls. *J. Exp. Psychol. Gen.* 128:78–87

Kirsch I. 1985. Response expectancy as a determinant of experience and behavior. *Am. Psychol.* 40:1189–202

Koob GF, Ahmed SH, Boutrel B, Chen SA, Kenny PJ, et al. 2004. Neurobiological mechanisms in the transition from drug use to drug dependence. *Neurosci. Biobehav. Rev.* 27:739–49

Koob GF, Le Moal M. 1997. Drug abuse: hedonic homeostatic dysregulation. *Science* 278:52–58

Lancaster T, Hajek P, Stead LF, West R, Jarvis MJ. 2006. Prevention of relapse after quitting smoking: a systematic review of trials. *Arch. Intern. Med.* 166:828–35

Leri F, Stewart J. 2002. The consequences of different "lapses" on relapse to heroin seeking in rats. *Exp. Clin. Psychopharmacol.* 10:339–49

Li TK. 2000. Clinical perspectives for the study of craving and relapse in animal models. *Addiction* 95:S55–60

Litman GK, Eiser JR, Taylor C. 1979. Dependence, relapse and extinction: a theoretical critique and a behavioral examination. *J. Clin. Psychol.* 35:192–99

Litt MD, Cooney NL, Kadden RM, Gaupp L. 1990. Reactivity to alcohol cues and induced moods in alcoholics. *Addict. Behav.* 15:137–46

Madden GJ. 2000. A behavioral economics primer. In *Reframing Health Behavior Change with Behavioral Economics*, ed. WK Bickel, RE Vuchinich, 1:3–26. Mahwah, NJ: Erlbaum

Maisto SA, Carey KB, Bradizza CM. 1999. Social learning theory. In *Psychological Theories of Drinking and Alcoholism*, ed. K Leonard, HT Blane, pp. 106–63. New York: Guilford. 2nd ed.

Maisto SA, McKay JR, O'Farrell TJ. 1995. Relapse precipitants and behavioral marital therapy. *Addict. Behav.* 20:383–93

Maisto SA, Pollock NK, Cornelius JR, Lynch KG, Martin CS. 2003. Alcohol relapse as a function of relapse definition in a clinical sample of adolescents. *Addict. Behav.* 28:449–59

Marlatt GA. 1985. Relapse prevention: theoretical rationale and overview of the model. In *Relapse Prevention*, ed. GA Marlatt, JR Gordon, pp. 3–70. New York: Guilford

Marlatt GA. 1994. Addiction, mindfulness, and acceptance. In *Addiction and Acceptance*, ed. S Hayes, N Jacobson, V Folette, M Dougher, pp. 175–97. Reno, NV: Context Press

Marlatt GA. 1996. Taxonomy of high-risk situations for alcohol relapse: evolution and development of a cognitive-behavioral model. *Addiction* 91(Suppl.):S37–49

Marlatt GA. 2001. Integrating contingency management with relapse prevention skills: comment on Silverman et al. 2001. *Exp. Clin. Psychopharmacol.* 9:33–34

Marlatt GA, Gordon JR. 1980. Determinants of relapse: implications for the maintenance of behavior change. In *Behavioral Medicine: Changing Health Lifestyles*, ed. PO Davidson, SM Davidson, pp. 410–52. New York: Brunner/Mazel

Marlatt GA, Gordon JR, eds. 1985. *Relapse Prevention: Maintenance Strategies in the Treatment of Addictive Behaviors*. New York: Guilford

A historically important volume that described the full cognitive-behavioral model of relapse and its associated RP intervention.

Marlatt GA, Kristeller JL, eds. 1999. *Mindfulness and Meditation*. Washington, DC: Am. Psychol. Assoc. 293 pp.

Marlatt GA, Rohsenow DJ. 1980. Cognitive processes in alcohol use: expectancy and the balanced-placebo design. In *Advances in Substance Abuse: Behavioral and Biological Research*, ed. NK Mello, pp. 159–99. Greenwich, CT: Aijai Press

McDonald RV, Siegel S. 2004. Intra-administration associations and withdrawal symptoms: morphine-elicited morphine withdrawal. *Exp. Clin. Psychopharmacol.* 12:3–11

McKay JR, Maisto SA, O'Farrell TJ. 1993. End-of-treatment self-efficacy, aftercare, and drinking outcomes of alcoholic men. *Alcohol Clin. Exp. Res.* 17:1078

Medioni J, Berlin I, Mallet A. 2005. Increased risk of relapse after stopping nicotine replacement therapies: a mathematical modelling approach. *Addiction* 100:247–54

Miller WR. 1996. What is a relapse? Fifty ways to leave the wagon. *Addiction* 91(Suppl.):S15–27

An interesting discussion of the conceptual challenges associated with defining relapse.

Miller WR, Harris RJ. 2000. A simple scale of Gorski's warning signs for relapse. *J. Stud. Alcohol* 61:759–65

Miller WR, Westerberg VS, Harris RJ, Tonigan JS. 1996. What predicts relapse? Prospective testing of antecedent models. *Addiction* 91(Suppl.):S155–72

Monti PM, Rohsenow DJ, Rubonis AV, Niaura RS, Sirota AD, et al. 1993. Cue exposure with coping skills treatment for male alcoholics: a preliminary investigation. *J. Consult. Clin. Psychol.* 61:1011–19

Mueller TI, Leon AC, Keller MB, Solomon DA, Endicott J, et al. 1999. Recurrence after recovery from major depressive disorder during 15 years of observational follow-up. *Am. J. Psychiatry* 156:1000–6

Muraven M, Baumeister RF. 2000. Self-regulation and depletion of limited resources: Does self-control resemble a muscle? *Psychol. Bull.* 126:247–59

Muraven M, Collins RL, Nienhaus K. 2002. Self-control and alcohol restraint: an initial application of the self-control strength model. *Psychol. Addict. Behav.* 16:113–20

Muraven M, Slessareva E. 2003. Mechanisms of self-control failure: motivation and limited resources. *Personal. Soc. Psychol. Bull.* 29:894–906

Niaura RS, Abrams DB, Demuth B, Pinto R, Monti P. 1989. Responses to smoking-related stimuli and early relapse to smoking. *Addict. Behav.* 14:419–28

Niaura RS, Rohsenow DJ, Binkoff JA, Monti PM, Pedraza M, Abrams DB. 1988. Relevance of cue reactivity to understanding alcohol and smoking relapse. *J. Abnorm. Psychol.* 97:133–52

Ockene JK, Emmons KM, Mermelstein RJ, Perkins KA, Bonollo DS, et al. 2000. Relapse and maintenance issues for smoking cessation. *Health Psychol.* 19:17–31

Payne TJ, Schare ML, Levis DJ, Colletti G. 1991. Exposure to smoking-relevant cues: effects on desire to smoke and topographical components of smoking behavior. *Addict. Behav.* 16:467–79

Petry NM. 2001. Delay discounting of money and alcohol in actively using alcoholics, currently abstinent alcoholics, and controls. *Psychopharmacology (Berl.)* 154:243–50

Petry NM, Martin B, Cooney JL, Kranzler HR. 2000. Give them prizes, and they will come: contingency management for treatment of alcohol dependence. *J. Consult. Clin. Psychol.* 68:250–57

Piasecki TM. 2006. Relapse to smoking. *Clin. Psychol. Rev.* 26:196–215

Piasecki TM, Fiore MC, McCarthy DE, Baker TB. 2002. Have we lost our way? The need for dynamic formulations of smoking relapse proneness. *Addiction* 97:1093–208

Piasecki TM, Jorenby DE, Smith SS, Fiore MC, Baker TB. 2003. Smoking withdrawal dynamics: II. Improved tests of withdrawal-relapse relations. *J. Abnorm. Psychol.* 112:14–27

Pike KM. 1998. Long-term course of anorexia nervosa: response, relapse, remission, and recovery. *Clin. Psychol. Rev.* 18:447–75

Pomerleau O, Adkins D, Pertschuk M. 1978. Predictors of outcome and recidivism in smoking cessation treatment. *Addict. Behav.* 3:65–70

Preston KL, Umbricht A, Epstein DH. 2002. Abstinence reinforcement maintenance contingency and one-year follow-up. *Drug Alcohol Depend.* 67:125–37

Quinn EP, Brandon TH, Copeland AL. 1996. Is task persistence related to smoking and substance abuse? The application of learned industriousness theory to addictive behaviors. *Exp. Clin. Psychopharmacol.* 4:186–90

Robinson TE, Berridge KC. 1993. The neural basis of drug craving: an incentive-sensitization theory of addiction. *Brain Res. Brain Res. Rev.* 18:247–91

Robinson TE, Berridge KC. 2000. The psychology and neurobiology of addiction: an incentive-sensitization view. *Addiction* 95(Suppl. 2):S91–117

Robinson TE, Berridge KC. 2003. Addiction. *Annu. Rev. Psychol.* 54:25–53

Rodriguez S, Fernandez MC, Cepeda-Benito A, Vila J. 2005. Subjective and physiological reactivity to chocolate images in high and low chocolate cravers. *Biol. Psychol.* 70:9–18

Rohsenow DJ, Monti PM, Rubonis AV, Gulliver SB, Colby SM, et al. 2001. Cue exposure with coping skills training and communication skills training for alcohol dependence: 6- and 12-month outcomes. *Addiction* 96:1161–74

Sayette MA. 1993. An appraisal-disruption model of alcohol's effects on stress responses in social drinkers. *Psychol. Bull.* 114:459–76

Sayette MA, Hufford MR. 1994. Effects of cue exposure and deprivation on cognitive resources in smokers. *J. Abnorm. Psychol.* 103:812–18

Schenk S, Partridge B. 2001. Influence of a conditioned light stimulus on cocaine self-administration in rats. *Psychopharmacology (Berl.)* 154:390–96

Shah NG, Galai N, Celentano DD, Vlahov D, Strathdee SA. 2006. Longitudinal predictors of injection cessation and subsequent relapse among a cohort of injection drug users in Baltimore, MD, 1988–2000. *Drug Alcohol Depend.* 83:147–56

Shaham Y, Erb S, Stewart J. 2000. Stress-induced relapse to heroin and cocaine seeking in rats: a review. *Brain Res. Brain Res. Rev.* 33:13–33

Shiffman S. 1982. Relapse following smoking cessation: a situational analysis. *J. Consult. Clin. Psychol.* 50:71–86

Shiffman S. 2005. Dynamic influences on smoking relapse process. *J. Personal.* 73:1715–48

Shiffman S. 2006. Reflections on smoking relapse research. *Drug Alcohol Rev.* 25:15–20

Shiffman S, Gwaltney CJ, Balabanis MH, Liu KS, Paty JA, et al. 2002. Immediate antecedents of cigarette smoking: an analysis from ecological momentary assessment. *J. Abnorm. Psychol.* 111:531–45

Shiffman S, Hickcox M, Paty JA, Gnys M, Kassel JD, Richards TJ. 1996a. Progression from a smoking lapse to relapse: prediction from abstinence violation effects, nicotine dependence, and lapse characteristics. *J. Consult. Clin. Psychol.* 64:993–1002

Shiffman S, Hickcox M, Paty JA, Gnys M, Kassel JD, Richards TJ. 1997a. The abstinence violation effect following smoking lapses and temptations. *Cogn. Ther. Res.* 21:497–523

Shiffman S, Hufford M, Hickcox M, Paty JA, Gnys M, Kassel JD. 1997b. Remember that? A comparison of real-time versus retrospective recall of smoking lapses. *J. Consult. Clin. Psychol.* 65:292–300

Shiffman S, Paty JA, Gnys M, Kassel JA, Hickcox M. 1996b. First lapses to smoking: within-subjects analysis of real-time reports. *J. Consult. Clin. Psychol.* 64:366–79

One of the first studies using EMA technology to study the process of relapse.

Shiffman S, Scharf DM, Shadel WG, Gwaltney CJ, Dang Q, et al. 2006. Analyzing milestones in smoking cessation: illustration in a nicotine patch trial in adult smokers. *J. Consult. Clin. Psychol.* 74:276–85

Shiffman S, Shumaker SA, Abrams DB, Cohen S, Garvey A, et al. 1986. Task Force 2: models of smoking relapse. *Health Psychol.* 5:13–27

Siegel S. 1975. Evidence from rats that morphine tolerance is a learned response. *J. Comp. Physiol. Psychol.* 89:498–506

Siegel S. 1983. Classical conditioning, drug tolerance, and drug dependence. In *Research Advances in Alcohol and Drug Problems*, ed. RG Smart, FB Glaser, Y Israel, H Kalant, RE Popham, W Schmidt, pp. 207–46. New York: Plenum

Siegel S. 1999. Drug anticipation and drug addiction: the 1998 H David Archibald lecture. *Addiction* 94:1113–24

Silverman K, Higgins ST, Brooner RK, Montoya ID, Cone EJ, et al. 1996. Sustained cocaine abstinence in methadone maintenance patients through voucher-based reinforcement therapy. *Arch. Gen. Psychiatry* 53:409–15

Silverman K, Svikis D, Wong CJ, Hampton J, Stitzer ML, Bigelow GE. 2002. A reinforcement-based therapeutic workplace for the treatment of drug abuse: three-year abstinence outcomes. *Exp. Clin. Psychopharmacol.* 10:228–40

Solomon RL, Corbit JD. 1974. An opponent-process theory of motivation. I. Temporal dynamics of affect. *Psychol. Rev.* 81:119–45

Steele CM, Josephs RA. 1990. Alcohol myopia. Its prized and dangerous effects. *Am. Psychol.* 45:921–33

Stephens RS, Curtin L, Simpson EE, Roffman RA. 1994. Testing the abstinence violation effect construct with marijuana cessation. *Addict. Behav.* 19:23–32

Stewart J, de Wit H, Eikelboom R. 1984. Role of unconditioned and conditioned drug effects in the self-administration of opiates and stimulants. *Psychol. Rev.* 91:251–68

Streeton C, Whelan G. 2001. Naltrexone, a relapse prevention maintenance treatment of alcohol dependence: a meta-analysis of randomized controlled trials. *Alcohol Alcohol.* 36:544–52

Suh JJ, Pettinati HM, Kampman KM, O'Brien CP. 2006. The status of disulfiram: a half of a century later. *J. Clin. Psychopharmacol.* 26:290–302

Sutton SR. 1979. Interpreting relapse curves. *J. Consult. Clin. Psychol.* 47:96–98

Teasdale JD, Segal ZV, Williams JMG, Ridgeway VA, Soulsby JM, Lau MA. 2000. Prevention of relapse/recurrence in major depression by mindfulness-based cognitive therapy. *J. Consult. Clin. Psychol.* 68:615–23

Tiffany ST. 1990. A cognitive model of drug urges and drug-use behavior: role of automatic and nonautomatic processes. *Psychol. Rev.* 97:147–68

Tiffany ST. 1995. The role of cognitive factors in reactivity to drug cues. In *Addictive Behaviour: Cue Exposure Theory and Practice*, ed. D Drummond, ST Tiffany, S Glautier, B Remington, pp. 137–65. West Sussex, UK: Wiley

Tiffany ST, Conklin CA. 2002. The promise and pitfalls of animal and human models of relapse: comment on Leri and Stewart 2002. *Exp. Clin. Psychopharmacol.* 10:361–63

Tolman EG. 1932. *Purposive Behavior in Animals and Man*. New York: Appleton-Century-Crofts

Tonstad S, Tonnesen P, Hajek P, Williams KE, Billing CB, et al. 2006. Effect of maintenance therapy with varenicline on smoking cessation: a randomized controlled trial. *JAMA* 296:64–71

Vohs KD, Faber RJ. 2004. To buy or not to buy? Self-control and self-regulatory failure in purchase behavior. In *Handbook of Self-Regulation: Research, Theory, and Applications*, ed. RF Baumeister, KD Vohs, pp. 509–24. New York: Guilford

Vohs KD, Heatherton TF. 2000. Self-regulatory failure: a resource-depletion approach. *Psychol. Sci.* 11:249–54

Welsh CJ, Liberto J. 2001. The use of medication for relapse prevention in substance dependence disorders. *J. Psychiatr. Pract.* 7:15–31

Wetter DW, Smith SS, Kenford SL, Jorenby DE, Fiore MC, et al. 1994. Smoking outcome expectancies: factor structure, predictive validity, and discriminant validity. *J. Abnorm. Psychol.* 103:801–11

Whisman MA. 1990. The efficacy of booster maintenance sessions in behavior therapy: review and methodological critique. *Clin. Psychol. Rev.* 10:155–70

Wikler A. 1948. Recent progress in research on the neurophysiologic basis of morphine addiction. *Am. J. Psychiatry* 105:329–38

Wills TA, ed. 1990. *Stress and Coping Factors in the Epidemiology of Substance Use*. New York: Plenum. 409 pp.

Wing RR. 2000. Cross-cutting themes in maintenance of behavior change. *Health Psychol.* 19:84–88

Wing RR, Phelan S. 2005. Long-term weight loss maintenance. *Am. J. Clin. Nutr.* 82:222–25S

Wise RA, Bozarth MA. 1987. A psychomotor stimulant theory of addiction. *Psychol. Rev.* 94:469–92

Witkiewitz K, Marlatt GA. 2004. Relapse prevention for alcohol and drug problems: That was Zen, this is Tao. *Am. Psychol.* 59:224–35

Review and reformulation of Marlatt's cognitive-behavioral model of relapse.

Witkiewitz K, Marlatt GA, Walker D. 2005. Mindfulness-based relapse prevention for alcohol and substance use disorders. *J. Cogn. Psychother*. 19:211–28

Zelman DC, Brandon TH, Jorenby DE, Baker TB. 1992. Measures of affect and nicotine dependence predict differential response to smoking cessation treatments. *J. Consult. Clin. Psychol.* 60:943–52

Marital and Family Processes in the Context of Alcohol Use and Alcohol Disorders

Kenneth E. Leonard[1,2] and Rina D. Eiden[1,3]

[1]Research Institute on Addiction, [2]Department of Psychiatry, and [3]Department of Pediatrics & Psychology, State University of New York, Buffalo, New York 14203; email: leonard@ria.buffalo.edu, eiden@ria.buffalo.edu

Annu. Rev. Clin. Psychol. 2007. 3:285–310

First published online as a Review in Advance on December 6, 2006

The *Annual Review of Clinical Psychology* is online at http://clinpsy.annualreviews.org

This article's doi:
10.1146/annurev.clinpsy.3.022806.091424

1548-5943/07/0427-0285$20.00

Key Words

parental behavior, intimate partner violence, child development, family violence

Abstract

Alcohol use is often part of the fabric of marriage and family life, and although it is associated with certain positive effects, excessive drinking and alcohol disorders can exert a negative effect on the marital development and on the development of children in the context of the family. This review considers evidence that alcohol influences and is influenced by marital/family processes, including transitions into marriage and parenthood, marital satisfaction, marital violence, parenting, and child development. The review discusses the importance of antisocial behavior and the need to examine women's drinking, and the joint impact of men's and women's drinking on marital/family processes. The review highlights the lack of studies in certain key areas, including the link between discordant drinking and violence and marital satisfaction, the role of alcohol in child neglect, and the potential role of marital conflict as a mediator or moderator of the relationship between alcohol and child functioning.

Contents

INTRODUCTION

Alcohol presents two faces to the family. One face is that of a beneficial and healthful beverage that fosters warmth and intimacy. The other face is that of a potentially hazardous potion that jeopardizes one's family through conflict, violence, and deprivation. In a recent study of problem drinkers and their partners, we asked the partners what they liked and disliked about the drinking of the alcoholic partner. While some partners had nothing positive to say, others described positive relationship effects such as "opens up his feelings to me," "he gets more sensitive and pays more attention to me," and "he is also very giving and says nice things to me." These same women also reported negative relationship effects like "more flirtatious with women," "usually makes him moody or irritable," and "bad mood/frightens me." In understanding the interrelationship between alcohol and family functioning, we are confronted with this dual nature, and the impact of this is often a more heterogeneous picture than we imagine. In this review, we examine the interrelationships between drinking and alcoholism on one hand and marriage and family processes on the other hand, touching both on the positive and negative aspects, as well as on heterogeneity of alcohol effects.

COMMON RESEARCH PROBLEMS

Researchers addressing alcohol and family functioning face several methodological challenges. The first is the changing nature of the family. Several demographic trends have created a multiplicity of family structures that complicate the study of family processes (Bumpass 2004). Increasing proportions of individuals do not marry, but more than half of younger adults have cohabitated without marriage. The age of marriage and the likelihood of entering marriage with a child have increased. After a long period of increase, the likelihood of divorce has stabilized at about

50%. Fertility has decreased and the age of childbearing has generally increased. More than one-third of children are born to unmarried mothers, and more than half of all children will live in a single-parent household for some time. The consequence of these trends is the tremendous diversity of family structures and caregiving arrangements among families. In longitudinal studies, there are multiple transitions without a clear developmental sequence. The problem is further complicated by the fact that alcohol disorders are associated with family structures and the likelihood of transitioning to alternate family structures.

The second challenge is that excessive drinking and alcohol disorders are knotted together with other family disturbances. Alcoholics often have comorbid psychiatric disorders, and the interrelationship among these disorders is not always clearly understood (Kessler et al. 1997). These comorbid disorders may have independent impacts on family processes, but also may modify the expression of alcoholism within the family. Moreover, in the context of the family, the alcoholic's intimate partner may have psychiatric disorders, either independently or associated with the partner's alcoholism. Under these circumstances, disentangling the unique aspects of alcoholism on family processes is difficult.

The third challenge concerns the sampling of alcoholic or excessive-drinking families. Such families are often recruited from families in which one person has sought treatment. This often occurs at the insistence of an intimate partner (Cunningham et al. 1994) and may be less likely if the partner also is an excessive drinker (Kelly et al. 2004). It is possible that, relative to the population of alcoholic couples, couples recruited from clinical settings may have more marital commitment, but also may be less likely to have a partner who also has an alcohol disorder. Alternatively, alcohol-involved families may be recruited from the community, either through assessments of potential participants or through advertising specifically for such individuals. Given the prevalence of a current alcohol disorder and the potential recruitment biases, couples recruited in this manner may show less severe alcohol problems, fewer comorbid disorders, and perhaps less marital distress. Because we cannot assess the full population of alcoholic couples, some of these potential sample differences are speculative. Nonetheless, the primary issue is that the different sampling methods have the potential to identify alcoholic couples with quite different characteristics.

Intimate partner violence: behaviors that involve physical aggression from one person to a partner in an intimate relationship, including less severe items such as pushing, grabbing, and shoving as well as more severe items such as hitting with a fist and beating up

Alcohol problems: social, legal, or interpersonal consequences that occur while drinking (e.g., arrested for DWI, violent behavior) or are attributed to acute or chronic consumption (e.g., lost friends due to drinking, damaged health)

TRANSITIONS TO MARRIAGE AND PARENTHOOD

Does Alcohol Influence the Timing of Marriage?

Excessive drinking could influence the timing of marriage in two different ways. First, the acute impact of alcohol on decision-making and particularly sexual decision making, or the influence of more chronic heavy use on educational attainment, could necessitate the early assumption of adult roles. On the other hand, individuals involved in a pattern of excessive drinking may have an impaired ability to form an intimate relationship, be unwilling to commit to a marital relationship, or be viewed as an undesirable partner. From this perspective, excessive drinking could delay marriage. Studies have found that drinking patterns are associated with early marriages (Newcomb & Bentler 1985), delayed marriages (Fu & Goldman 1996), a decreased likelihood of an "on-time" marriage (Forthofer et al. 1996), and are unrelated to marriage (Bachman et al. 1997). Certain methodological factors could influence which of these effects would be identified. These include the age range of the participants at baseline, the severity of the alcohol variable for that age, and the age at follow-up. Leonard & Rothbard (1999) suggested that excessive drinking could be associated with early marriages for some individuals, possibly because of its comorbidity with antisocial behavior, and with delayed marriage for others; however, the field still awaits more definitive research.

Excessive or heavy drinking: a pattern of alcohol consumption that exceeds normative levels and is considered to be hazardous, in terms of either the total amount of consumption over an extended time period (i.e., average drinks per day over the last month) or the frequent consumption of large amounts at one time

Alcohol diagnosis or disorder: a maladaptive pattern of physical, behavioral, and experiential symptoms that are indicative of impairments in functioning and/or physical or psychological dependence. This term encompasses both alcohol abuse and alcohol dependence (or alcoholism) and is usually assessed with specific criteria or is assumed because the individual has presented for treatment for alcoholism

Do Transitions into Marriage/Parenthood Impact Drinking?

The transition to marriage. The literature regarding changes in excessive drinking over marriage and parenthood transitions is more consistent. Alcohol consumption, particularly excessive drinking, declines over the transition to marriage (Miller-Tutzauer et al. 1991), and this is not due to other transitions such as becoming a parent or completing one's education (Bachman et al. 1997). This "marriage effect" is also observed before marriage among men and women who report being engaged to marry and appears to stabilize within two years after marriage. The strongest findings are observed in large general population studies of young adults that assess drinking annually or biannually.

Very little research has addressed why the transition to marriage leads to reduced excessive drinking. The most systematic work in this regard is by Bachman et al. (2002), in an expansion of their earlier work. Using data from Monitoring the Future, a large, longitudinal study of youth, these investigators examined changes in religiosity, social-recreational activities, friends' alcohol use, and normative views of alcohol use and found evidence that all of these were impacted by marriage. Structural equation models suggested that reductions in binge drinking were completely mediated by decreased "evenings out" and increased "disapproval of occasional heavy drinking" for both men and women. The model was examined for the total quantity of alcohol consumed in the last 30 days, and the results were largely comparable.

Some research has examined factors that might qualify the relationship between the transition to marriage and drinking reductions. However, much of this evidence is equivocal. For example, studies have found the marriage effect only for women, only for men, or for both men and women (Leonard & Rothbard 1999). Most of the research has focused on young adult participants, and few researchers have examined the marriage effect later in life. Bogart et al. (2005) found the marriage effect for marriages that occurred under 20 years old, and for marriages occurring in the 20s, which is developmentally normative. It is unclear whether marriage later in the 30s has the same protective effect. Some evidence suggests that the marriage effect may be stronger for European Americans in the United States than among African Americans (Curran et al. 1998, Mudar et al. 2002).

Several studies have shown that marriage serves as a protective factor even among those with serious alcohol problems. Chilcoat & Breslau (1996) assessed approximately 1000 young adult members of a health maintenance organization at age 21–30 and reinterviewed them three and a half years later. Among single subjects with no initial alcohol problems, those who married were less likely (8.6%) to experience an alcohol symptom at follow-up than single subjects who remained single (15.7%). Among subjects who had an alcohol diagnosis at baseline, the remission rate was higher among those who married (76.5%) than among those who remained single (46%). Dawson et al. (2006) reported on participants who had a lifetime diagnosis of alcohol dependence. Controlling for sociodemographic factors, alcoholism severity, and other disorders, entry into a first marriage increased the likelihood of nonabstinent recovery, but did not increase the likelihood of abstinent recovery.

The transition to parenthood. Only a handful of studies have examined women's drinking from conception to the postnatal period. These studies have documented marked decreases in women's drinking from prepregnancy to pregnancy, and a marked increase in drinking from pregnancy to the postnatal period. Others have reported significant declines during pregnancy and a marked increase to or above prepregnancy levels by 8 to

12 months postpregnancy (Fried et al. 1985, Homish 2004). Data from the Monitoring the Future project also indicate dramatic decreases in frequency of heavy drinking in the past two weeks, from baseline to pregnancy status for both men and women (Bachman et al. 1997). Other mediating factors, such as living arrangements, employment status, and marital status, did not account for this dramatic decrease in alcohol consumption from prepregnancy to pregnancy for women, but did explain the decrease in heavy drinking for men. Thus, although there was some reduction in heavy drinking among men that was associated with having a pregnant spouse, this reduction was explained primarily by the general condition of being married rather than the pregnancy status of the spouse.

These data also indicate an association between being a parent and reductions in frequency of drinking and frequency of heavy drinking from prepregnancy among both men and women. This association was not explained by marital status for frequency of drinking, but was explained by marital status for frequency of heavy drinking. There were reductions in both alcohol variables for single mothers, but not for single fathers (Bachman et al. 1997). Data from this study were obtained at two-year intervals over two decades. Thus, they describe general changes occurring over much longer periods, unlike the longitudinal data regarding increases in women's drinking after delivery described above.

Do Transitions Out of Marriage Impact Drinking?

Given that the transition into marriage is associated with reduced drinking, it is reasonable to hypothesize that the transition out of marriage would be associated with increased drinking. Cross-sectional studies indicate that divorced men and women are more likely to be excessive drinkers than are single men and women. However, as we discuss below, such an association could arise from excessive drinking playing a role in divorce. Consequently, longitudinal studies, particularly studies that can accurately place the temporal position of the divorce, are most informative. Two studies are particularly noteworthy. Bachman et al. (1997) found that the transition from marriage to divorce led to increases in the percentage of both men and women who were classified as heavy drinkers. Temple et al. (1991) conducted a meta-analysis of 12 longitudinal studies conducted in Europe, Canada, and the United States and reported that "for the younger age group, and for both sexes, not getting married and becoming unmarried are associated with increased typical quantity per occasion at follow-up" (p. 1279). These effects were homogeneous across all 12 studies. Moreover, it is not simply that individuals appear to drink more after divorce. They also appear to experience more alcohol-related problems (Chilcoat & Breslau 1996, Horwitz et al. 1996). As with the reduction in excessive drinking in the transition into marriage, there are various explanations concerning the increase in drinking over the transition out of marriage. It is important to recognize that entirely different explanations may account for these symmetrical effects. Several important changes occur with divorce, such as the diminution of family responsibilities (depending on the presence of children and the custody arrangements) and the restructuring of the social network and patterns of socializing that could be responsible for the increased drinking. Unfortunately, as with the transition into marriage, little empirical work exists that attempts to address the processes underlying the divorce transition.

Despite the strong support for increased drinking after divorce, there is one interesting and somewhat discordant finding. Wilsnack et al. (1991) found that married women who were problem drinkers at an earlier assessment were at a reduced risk for alcohol problems at follow-up if they had separated or divorced between assessments. This suggests that divorce among problem-drinking women may reduce the risk of alcohol problems, possibly by removing them from a heavy-drinking or stress-inducing partner.

Assortative mating: nonrandom selection of intimate partner, usually viewed in terms of similarity or concordance with respect to some specific characteristic

PARTNER'S DRINKING AND ALCOHOLISM

Assortative Mating

Alcoholics are more likely to be married to other alcoholics than would be expected by random pairing of individuals (Jacob & Bremer 1986). Although this is labeled "assortative mating," these studies do not differentiate between spousal influence, assortative mating, and differential divorce. In fact, although considerable research documents spousal similarity, even as early as immediately prior to marriage (Leonard & Eiden 1999), few studies directly address whether an individual's drinking pattern has a prospective influence on the selection of a spouse. Yamaguchi & Kandel (1993) found evidence of similarity between husbands and wives in terms of adolescent substance use, suggesting that the men and women had selected spouses whose drinking histories were similar. Labouvie (1996), in analyses of the two cohorts of the Rutgers Health and Human Development Study, reported that respondents' alcohol use at age 21–24 was predictive of spouses' alcohol use seven years later. These findings, although not definitive, are generally supportive of an assortative mating process. It is important not to overstate the extent of this process. A categorical examination (Mudar et al. 2001) found that among couples with a man who was not a heavy drinker, 7% of women were heavy drinkers. In contrast, among couples with a heavy-drinking man, 25% of the women were heavy drinkers. Moreover, 58% of heavy-drinking women were in a couple with a man who was not a heavy drinker. Hence, although there is strong evidence of similarity, it is clear that there are many couples in which husbands and wives have quite different drinking patterns.

Spousal Influence

The clearest evidence of spousal influence is observed among treatment studies in which alcoholics are more likely to return to drinking if their spouse is a drinker (e.g., Moos et al. 1990). In a more recent example, McAweeney et al. (2005) followed alcoholic men and their wives recruited from the community for nine years. One of the predictors of husband recovery was whether the wife had an alcoholic disorder at baseline. In addition, there was evidence that husband recovery had a salutary effect on the alcohol problems of the wife, indicative of reciprocal effects of husband and wife drinking on each other's recovery.

Few studies address the possibility of spousal-influenced drinking in community samples. In a sample of newlyweds, Leonard & Eiden (1999) found evidence in SEM analyses that husband drinking before marriage was longitudinally predictive of wife drinking in the first year of marriage, controlling for wife premarital drinking and husband drinking in the first year of marriage. In an independent sample of newlyweds, Leonard & Mudar (2004) replicated this association, but also found evidence that after the first year of marriage, wife's heavy drinking was longitudinally predictive of husband's heavy drinking. This study also examined factors that might promote spousal influence. We hypothesized that a husband's influence on his wife's drinking over the transition to marriage might reflect an interdependency process and a desire to maintain or consolidate their relationship. Our results suggested that husband-to-wife influence over the transition to marriage was stronger among women who were more highly dependent, reported fewer friends, and believed that alcohol had a positive impact on relationships. However, it is important to note that this effect was only observed over the marital transition, and was not observed from the first to the second year of marriage.

DRINKING AND ALCOHOLISM AS INFLUENCES ON MARITAL PROCESSES

Intimate Partner Violence

Distal drinking patterns and intimate partner violence. Excessive alcohol consumption and alcohol problems are robust correlates of men's violence toward women. The relationship has been observed in case-control studies of partner homicides and injured women seen in an emergency room. The relationship has been observed in other health care settings including primary health care, family practice clinics, prenatal clinics, and rural health clinics. It has also been found in large random samples of the general population and in random samples focused on specific minority populations (see Leonard 2002 for review). In a meta-analysis of this literature, Lipsey et al. (1997) reported an effect size of 0.22 for the association of chronic alcohol use and intimate partner violence (IPV), suggesting that the risk of violence among moderate to heavy drinkers is twice that of nondrinkers and light drinkers. However, the risk may be even higher among the very heavy drinkers. Recently, O'Leary & Schumacher (2003) utilized two nationally representative data sets to examine the full range of drinking and to determine whether the relationship represented a linear or threshold effect. Although they found weak evidence of linearity, they concluded, "the difference between high or binge drinking and more moderate levels of drinking appears to be an important threshold with regard to IPV" (p. 1582).

In contrast to men's drinking, the relationship between women's drinking and IPV is less well-established. Given the association between women and men's drinking, studies that control for men's drinking are the most pertinent. Across community samples, several studies have failed to find a relationship between women's drinking and IPV controlling for men's drinking (Kaufman Kantor & Asdigian 1997, Leonard & Senchak 1996), possibly because of the small number of very-heavy-drinking women, while other studies have found a relationship (Kaufman Kantor & Straus 1989, Schafer et al. 2004). In the Schafer et al. study, approximately 1600 European American, African American, and Hispanic couples were interviewed in 1995 and again in 2000. For both European American and African American couples, men's alcohol problems were associated with male-to-female violence, and female alcohol problems were associated with female-to-male violence. Studies of clinical samples of alcoholic or violent women are strongly supportive of a relationship. Similar to the findings of Schafer et al. (2004), Stuart et al. (2006) studied men and women arrested for IPV and found that perpetrators' alcohol problems were associated with their frequency of IPV, and the partners' alcohol problems were associated with the frequency of their IPV toward the identified perpetrator, for both male and female perpetrators.

IPV: intimate partner violence

Although research addressing women's drinking has usually controlled for the effects of partner's drinking, two recent studies suggest that the configuration of couple's drinking patterns are important predictors of IPV. Quigley & Leonard (2000) found that husband and wife excessive drinking in the first year of marriage interacted to prospectively predict violence over the next two years. The interaction indicated that IPV was more likely for excessive-drinking husbands with light-drinking wives. Leadley et al. (2000) found that discrepant drinking patterns were associated with IPV after controlling for heavy drinking. It may be that excessive drinking is not as contentious when both partners are heavy drinkers in contrast to couples with discordant drinking patterns. It is also plausible that drinking together serves a positive relationship function for concordant heavy drinkers, but not for discordant couples. This is an issue to which we return below.

Alcohol use and IPV following treatment. A growing number of longitudinal analyses suggest that changes in drinking behavior after treatment are predictive of changes in violence. O'Farrell and colleagues have conducted the majority of research in this area focused on alcohol. In a key study, O'Farrell and associates (2004) observed that alcoholic men involved in a combined alcoholism and behavioral couples therapy (ABCT) program reduced their IPV from the year before to the two years after treatment and that this effect was apparent primarily among alcoholics in remission. In addition, these changes were observed for both male aggression and female aggression, and for verbal aggression, overall physical violence, and severe violence. Finally, the extent of involvement in ABCT predicted subsequent partner violence, with some evidence that this effect was mediated by improved relationship functioning and reduced problem drinking. Because these studies used treatments that included ABCT, the reduced violence may be the effect of reduced alcohol consumption in the context of acquiring behavioral relationship skills. However, subsequent research has clarified this issue. O'Farrell et al. (2003) and Stuart et al. (2003) found reductions in husband-to-wife violence among male alcoholics receiving only treatment for alcoholism, and posttreatment violence was associated with fewer days of abstinence. Interestingly, one recent study focused on men who were court referred for treatment for IPV. Jones & Gondolf (2001) assessed the frequency of drunkenness among 308 male batterers for several times over a one-year period. Controlling for severe psychopathology and a previous arrest for nondomestic violence, the frequency of drunkenness was associated with IPV recidivism, with increases observed among men who reported being drunk 2–3 times per month in the time period that the recidivism occurred.

ABCT: alcoholic behavioral couples therapy

Proximal alcohol use and IPV. Although the relationship between men's drinking and IPV is well established, there is controversy as to whether the relationship reflects a direct causal relationship or whether it is spurious or indirect. This controversy stems primarily from the difficulties in establishing causality in psychological research rather than from conflicting data. Three sources of data provide support for a causal hypothesis. The first is experimental studies of alcohol and laboratory aggression, a topic beyond the scope of this chapter. The other two sources are studies of alcohol and marital interactions and event-based studies.

Experimental designs are often considered the strongest for inferring causality. In the context of alcohol and IPV, the primary difficulty with such an experiment is the development of a dependent variable that reflects aggression but that is also ethically acceptable. Marital interaction studies focus on negative verbal behavior in the context of a marital conversation. Although negative verbal behavior is not physical aggression, research has shown that, independent of marital distress, couples who have engaged in IPV display greater negativity in marital interactions than couples who have not engaged in such violence (e.g., Leonard & Roberts 1998a). Moreover, verbal aggression is longitudinally predictive of experiencing and perpetrating subsequent IPV (Schumacher & Leonard 2005). Several studies have examined the impact of alcohol on marital interactions. Leonard & Roberts (1998a) asked aggressive and nonaggressive husbands and their wives to discuss an important conflict, and then to discuss their most serious conflict after the husbands had received no alcohol, an active placebo, or an intoxicating dose of alcohol. Alcohol led to increased husband problem solving and increased husband and wife negativity relative to placebo and no alcohol. Aggressive and nonaggressive couples were equally influenced by alcohol. Similar studies have been conducted with alcoholics. Despite some inconsistent findings, these studies tend to support the hypothesis that alcohol increases negative interactions among alcoholics and their spouses, but not among control husbands and spouses (Jacob & Krahn 1988). It is of interest that this increase in negativity may occur only among alcoholics with antisocial features (Jacob et al.

2001). In an interesting extension of these studies, Haber & Jacob (1997) examined the influence of alcohol on the marital interactions of couples in which the husband, wife, or both were alcoholic. Alcohol was associated with lower negativity among couples in which only the wife was alcoholic, but higher negativity among couples in which both were alcoholic. In short, although there have been some discrepant findings, the administration of alcohol in the context of marital conflict appears to increase the expression of negative affect and behavior, even when both members of the couple are alcoholic.

One of the major advances in our understanding of acute alcohol consumption and IPV has been the use of event-based techniques. Two general approaches have been used. In a between-subjects approach, participants who have experienced an IPV event are compared with individuals who have experienced a less serious event (e.g., verbal aggression) controlling for stable dispositional variables (e.g., hostility) that differ between the participants and situational characteristics that differ between the events. In a within-subjects approach, an IPV event is compared with a less serious event collected from the same participant, with statistical controls for situational factors differing between the events. This approach can be extended to diary data that record the occurrence/nonoccurrence of IPV daily and link this to alcohol use on each day.

Event-based research has found that acute alcohol consumption is associated with both the occurrence and severity of IPV. The relationship has been found with between-subjects designs, within-subjects designs, and diary studies, and by men's reports, women's reports, and combined reports. It has been found in studies of community samples (Leonard & Quigley 1999), criminal justice surveys (Martin & Bachman 1997), and detailed studies of alcoholics and batterers in treatment (Fals-Stewart 2003). Studies that have examined both men's and women's drinking found largely uniform support for a relationship between men's drinking and IPV, but reported equivocal findings with respect to women's drinking. Several specific findings are worth highlighting. The amount of alcohol consumed prior to the violence is often quite substantial. Murphy et al. (2005) reported the husband consumed 13–14 drinks prior to IPV but 8–10 prior to verbal aggression events. In addition, Fals-Stewart (2003) found that the violence was most likely to occur within four hours after drinking. Finally, the event-based approach has been utilized to examine moderators of the proximal association of men's drinking and IPV. Fals-Stewart et al. (2005) tested antisocial personality disorder (ASPD) as a potential moderator in the context of a multiple-thresholds model of IPV. Among clinical samples of men who had previously engaged in IPV, alcohol consumption was associated with the occurrence of nonsevere violence for men who did not meet criteria for ASPD. For men with ASPD, proximal alcohol use did not increase the likelihood of nonsevere violence, but it did increase the likelihood of severe violence.

Marital Satisfaction and Stability

Heavy drinking and alcoholism are widely accepted as causes of marital problems and dissolution. In early studies, husband's alcohol use was one of the common reasons given for the breakup of the marriage (Levinger 1966). Similarly, among couples presenting for marital therapy, heavy drinking among the men is very common and is often a source of disagreements (Halford & Osgarby 1993). In an extensive review of the literature, Marshal (2003) found that studies with sufficient variability in measures of alcohol consumption and sample sizes reported significant negative correlations between alcohol consumption and marital satisfaction. He also found considerable evidence that alcoholics in treatment and their spouses have lower levels of marital satisfaction than appropriate groups, and that the marital interaction of alcoholics and their spouses were also indicative of poor marital functioning. One recent study (Floyd et al. 2006) found that hostile marital interactions were observed among couples with an antisocial alcoholic husband. Interestingly, positive interaction behaviors were highest among couples who were concordant for alcoholism (either both or neither had a diagnosis) and lowest among couples consisting of an alcoholic husband and a nonalcoholic wife.

It seems obvious that excessive drinking and alcoholism would have a detrimental impact on marital quality and, if unresolved, could result in marital separations and divorce. Although it seems implausible that there should be no causal influence, the nature and strength of that causal influence are not clear, nor is it clear whether there are any moderating factors. There are several key aspects to consider. First, as noted earlier, excessive drinking and alcohol disorders often co-occur with other disorders, such as antisocial personality and depression. For example, Whisman (1999) found that any mood, anxiety, or substance use disorder was associated with poor marital satisfaction for both women and men. However, after controlling for other disorders, neither alcohol nor drug use disorders were associated with marital satisfaction. Second, very few longitudinal studies have examined this issue, and the results are not entirely consistent. In a 1981 probability sample of women in which heavier drinkers were oversampled, wives' reports of husbands' drinking at baseline predicted wives' distrust and lack of support from husbands five years later (Wilsnack & Wilsnack 1990). In contrast, in a sample of newlyweds, Leonard & Roberts (1998b) observed that decreases in marital quality over the first year of marriage were predicted by husbands' average daily alcohol consumption, husbands' problem drinking, and wives' problem drinking at the time of marriage. However, only wives' problem drinking remained a significant predictor after controlling for sociodemographic factors, personality factors, and perceived conflict behaviors. Recently, Kearns-Bodkin & Leonard (2005) used longitudinal growth curve analyses to examine the relationship between frequent excessive drinking and marital satisfaction over a three-year period. Contrary to our expectations, we did not observe any longitudinal influence of husband or wife heavy drinking on declines in marital satisfaction or vice versa. However, there were significant correlations between one partner's change in alcohol involvement and the spouse's change in marital quality; steeper declines in drinking were associated with less steep declines in partner's marital quality.

A final key aspect is that, similar to studies of IPV, very few studies actually assess both husband and wife alcohol use and consider the possibility that the combination of husband and wife drinking may predict relationship quality. Specifically, research suggests that discrepant drinking patterns are related to marital functioning. In a community sample of married couples, McLeod (1993) found that couples who were concordant on lifetime alcohol dependence reported more positive marriages in comparison with discordant couples. Mudar et al. (2001) observed that newlywed couples with concordant heavy drinking had marital satisfaction scores that were comparable to couples with concordant nonheavy drinking, and that both of these groups had higher marital satisfaction than did couples with discordant drinking patterns. Homish & Leonard (2007) have found that the discrepancy between husband and wife heavy drinking is longitudinally predictive of lower scores on marital satisfaction. Finally, Ostermann et al. (2005) have found that discrepant drinking was prospectively predictive of the probability of divorce. It may be that excessive drinking is not as contentious among couples in which both partners are heavy drinkers, in contrast to couples in which one partner is not a heavy drinker. It is also plausible that drinking together serves as a positive relationship event for concordant heavy drinkers but not for discordant couples.

MARITAL FUNCTIONING AS AN INFLUENCE ON ALCOHOLISM

Marital Satisfaction as an Influence on Drinking

Marital problems create stress, and some individuals might increase their drinking in response. However, there are few empirical studies of this issue. In community samples, only two studies have examined this. Whisman et al. (2006) examined almost 1700 married men and women without a current alcohol disorder. Over 12 months, baseline marital dissatisfaction predicted the occurrence of an alcohol disorder after controlling for lifetime alcohol disorders, although separate analyses by gender could not be conducted. Testa & Leonard (2001) studied IPV as a predictor of drinking among women. After controlling for sociodemographic variables, initial relationship satisfaction, and verbal aggression, wives who experienced IPV during the first year of marriage reported a greater frequency of heavy drinking episodes.

In contrast to community samples, there is clear evidence that marital distress has an adverse impact on drinking among alcoholics in treatment. Couples who fail to complete conjoint alcoholism treatment have lower levels of commitment to the marriage (Epstein et al. 1994). Men in more satisfying marriages are more likely to have successful treatment outcomes (Maisto et al. 1998, Moos et al. 1990, Orford et al. 1975). Some data that suggest that verbal criticism may be a significant factor. O'Farrell et al. (1998b) examined expressed emotion (EE), which includes verbal criticism and overinvolvement. Alcoholics with high-EE spouses at the beginning of treatment had worse outcomes over the 12-month follow-up period than alcoholics with low-EE spouses.

Treating the Marriages of Alcoholics

If couples with better marriages do better after alcoholism treatment, it seems reasonable to hypothesize that the efficacy of alcohol treatment could be enhanced by coupling it with marital therapy. Seminal work, conducted by O'Farrell et al. (1985) and McCrady et al. (1986), reported promising effects for adding ABCT to alcoholism treatment, with respect to both marital functioning and drinking outcomes. This work and subsequent research by these two teams demonstrated that (*a*) the improvement was not simply due to including the spouse in the treatment context; (*b*) the improvement was observed primarily in ABCT and not other marital therapies; (*c*) the advantages of ABCT could be observed at two years after treatment, and (*d*) ABCT had an overall positive cost/benefit ratio (Epstein & McCrady 1998). Although less data are available for women's alcoholism, ABCT has been shown to be effective for both male and female alcoholics. More recently, this research has focused on two different issues: enhancing the long-term efficacy of ABCT for alcoholism and utilizing intimate relationships to foster and support treatment entry.

EE: expressed emotion

RP: relapse prevention

The efficacy of ABCT, like most therapies, dissipates with time. Moreover, couples with more severe marital problems, as well as more severe alcohol problems, are the most likely to relapse (O'Farrell et al. 1992). Two studies have assessed the value of additional relapse prevention (RP) sessions following standard ABCT for alcoholism. McCrady et al. (2004) found that four RP sessions did not lead to better marital or drinking outcomes in contrast to standard ABCT or ABCT with linkage to Alcoholics Anonymous. In contrast, O'Farrell et al. (1998a) found that 15 additional RP sessions led to better marital outcomes for 18 months after RP. For couples with very low pretreatment marital satisfaction, the RP sessions led to more days of abstinence than did ABCT alone. One potential explanation for the different findings is that O'Farrell et al. had 15 RP sessions over a one-year period, whereas McCrady et al. only had four, with three of the four occurring within six months post treatment.

Recent work has also focused on helping family members behave and cope more

CRT: community reinforcement treatment

FAE: fetal alcohol effects

FASD: fetal alcohol spectrum disorders

Fetal alcohol syndrome (FAS): a developmental disability that includes central nervous system deficits, growth deficits, and a distinctive pattern of facial anomalies

effectively when an alcoholic family member will not seek treatment. Sisson & Azrin (1986) developed a treatment for the family members of alcoholics that focused on avoiding violence, reinforcing sobriety, not reinforcing drinking, and strengthening the alcoholic's motivation for treatment. Miller et al. (1999) further developed this community reinforcement treatment (CRT) and conducted a clinical trial in which significant others (e.g., wives, parents) were randomly assigned to one of three conditions: (*a*) CRT; (*b*) an alternative approach designed to facilitate involvement with Al-Anon; or (*c*) the Johnson Institute Intervention, which was centered around a family/group confrontation of the alcoholic. All three approaches had a positive effect on the functioning of the significant others, but the CRT led more of the alcoholics to seek treatment than the other two approaches. Recently, Rychtarik & McGillicuddy (2005) evaluated two approaches for women with an alcoholic partner: a coping skills approach and an Al-Anon approach. This study found that involvement in either the Spouse Coping Intervention or the Al-Anon facilitation program led to improvements in spouse functioning and reductions in husband drinking. Of importance, a strong interaction was observed that suggested women who had experienced IPV had lower depression and had partners with fewer drinks per drinking day in the Spouse Coping Intervention relative to the Al-Anon facilitation program.

DEVELOPMENTAL OUTCOMES AMONG CHILDREN OF ALCOHOLIC PARENTS

Maternal Alcohol Use

The most significant consequence of chronic heavy maternal alcohol use during pregnancy is fetal alcohol syndrome (FAS). Children are diagnosed with FAS when they have central nervous system deficits (e.g., cognitive and/or behavioral problems), growth deficits, and a distinctive pattern of facial anomalies. Although many children with FAS have low IQ scores (below 70), a number of children with FAS perform in the low-average to average range. Compared to children with similar IQ or behavioral issues, FAS children exhibit consistent difficulties in arithmetic, executive function, and social-emotional development (Howell et al. 2006, Olson et al. 1998). A number of children exposed to heavy maternal alcohol use exhibit some but not all of the FAS features, and thus have fetal alcohol effects (FAE; Coles et al. 1997). These children tend to have higher IQ scores than those with FAS, although scores are still in the low-average to average range. They also have a broad spectrum of deficits ranging from facial anomalies and congenital abnormalities to neurodevelopmental and social-emotional problems. More recently, the term "fetal alcohol spectrum disorders" (FASD) has been used to collectively refer to children with FAS and FAE. In addition to chronic heavy alcohol use, some consistent, although small, effects on children's arithmetic abilities and school functioning have been reported as a consequence of maternal binge drinking during pregnancy, even before pregnancy recognition. Although the effects of chronic heavy alcohol exposure have been well documented, the effects of more moderate drinking during pregnancy have been the subject of more debate. Some studies have noted subtle effects on learning and behavior at relatively low levels of exposure (e.g., Jacobson & Jacobson 2002). Others have noted an interaction of alcohol exposure and maternal age on child outcomes, with children of older alcohol-exposed mothers at higher risk for negative outcomes (e.g., Streissguth et al. 1980). Children with developmental disabilities have significant effects on family functioning, including increased parental stress, lower support, higher parental depression, and higher parenting problems in response to difficult child behavior. These may be exacerbated among alcohol-exposed children raised by biological parents, who may continue to have problems with alcohol in the postnatal period.

Children of Alcoholics Literature

The relatively large literature on children of alcoholics focuses primarily on children of alcoholic fathers, and maternal alcohol problems, when present, are generally nested within fathers' alcohol problems. These studies range from infancy to adulthood and focus on a range of outcomes, including temperamental antecedents to alcohol problems, socialization experiences, behavior problems, substance use among peers, variables related to alcohol use such as expectancies, age of onset, smoking, and alcohol use, as well as problem drinking and transition to adulthood. Several models for increased vulnerability among children of alcoholics have been proposed, including the risk for substance abuse problems among children of alcoholics (see Sher 1991, Zucker 2006). Early research demonstrated associations between paternal alcoholism and externalizing and internalizing behavior problems (Sher 1991) and the subsequent development of substance use, alcohol problems, and alcoholism (e.g., Jacob & Windle 2000). Theoretical discussions on children of alcoholics have suggested that one pathway to greater substance use problems is via the association between fathers' alcoholism and difficult temperament in infancy, to poor behavioral undercontrol and greater externalizing problems in early childhood, to conduct disorder in middle childhood, to higher antisocial behavior and substance abuse in adolescence and adulthood (Tarter et al. 1999, Zucker 2006). These discussions have also emphasized the importance of gene x environment interactions or interactions of temperamental vulnerability and environmental risk in predicting child outcomes as a function of parental alcohol problems (Jacob et al. 2003, Tarter et al. 1999, Zucker 2006). In this view, temperamental predispositions may be activated only in the presence of environmental stress. As noted in a recent review (Zucker 2006), eight different longitudinal studies have provided consistent evidence that externalizing and internalizing problems are developmental precursors to substance use disorders in adolescence. However, longitudinal studies examining such pathways from conception or infancy have been few in number. Until recently, the majority of studies began in early adolescence with the goal of tracking substance use trajectories. The literature has also been plagued by treatment samples with generalizability issues, lack of consideration of comorbid risk factors, and lack of focus on process variables, although more recent longitudinal studies have used sophisticated methodologies to address these issues (see Zucker 2006).

The few studies focusing on early childhood trajectories indicate that children of alcoholics, especially those with two parents with an alcohol problem, deviate from more normative trajectories for externalizing behavior problems. For instance, Edwards et al. (2006) reported that children of nonalcoholics followed a developmental trajectory of increasing aggressive behavior from 18 months to 3 years, a peak at age 3, and a sharp decline from age 3 to 4. However, children of two parents with an alcohol problem did not exhibit the normative decline from 3 to 4 years of age. In addition, cumulative family risk (other parental psychopathology, family conflict, and negative parenting) was predictive of higher aggression at 18 months of age, and trajectories varied by child gender. Similarly, Loukas et al. (2003) examined trajectories of disruptive behavior from preschool to early adolescence among sons of alcoholic and nonalcoholic parents. Although disruptive behavior declined from preschool to age 12, sons of alcoholic fathers were consistently higher in disruptive behavior than were sons of nonalcoholics and this association remained after controlling for maternal alcohol problems, family conflict, and child temperament. Finally, Hussong et al. (2005) reported that girls of alcoholic fathers had lower social competence at age 6 than girls of nonalcoholic fathers on both self-reports and teacher reports, but did not differ at age 15, primarily due to decreases in social competence among girls of

Internalizing behavior problems: feelings of depression, sadness, anxiety, and social withdrawal

Externalizing behavior problems: a combination of physical aggression, acting out behaviors, oppositional or defiant behaviors, and engagement with illegal activities

Trajectories: the shape or nature of change in a given variable or construct over time

nonalcoholic fathers. Thus, although the association between parents' alcohol problems and early risk outcomes such as behavior problems is more consistent and suggests deviations from normative trajectories beginning between 3 and 4 years of age, results regarding positive aspects of social development such as social competence are not as clear.

Although few longitudinal studies have focused on early childhood antecedents of the pathways to risk among children of alcoholics, several have examined trajectories of substance use beginning in early adolescence, as well as predictors and consequences of these trajectories. These studies have used sophisticated analytic frameworks to examine longitudinal changes in alcohol-related outcomes in adolescence, from adolescence to adulthood, and within adulthood (see Chassin et al. 2004). Despite considerable variability in age of participants and the dependent measures, results indicate three to four specific trajectories including an early-onset/heavy-use group, a moderate/experimental/developmentally limited group, and a low-risk/low-use group. Across these studies, a family history of alcohol problems is consistently linked to the early-onset/heavy-use trajectory. Individual difference variables such as negative emotionality and low self-regulation have also been predictive of the early-onset/heavy-use trajectory (e.g., Chassin et al. 2004). One persistent question is the role of comorbid parental psychopathology such as depression and antisociality in predicting substance abuse trajectories among children of alcoholics. Using a prospective design, Chassin et al. (1991) reported that parents' alcohol problems were uniquely predictive of adolescent alcohol involvement and internalizing problems, parents' antisocial behavior was uniquely predictive of drug use and externalizing problems, and parents' affective disorder was uniquely predictive of internalizing problems. Thus, the results regarding the association between fathers' alcoholism and risky trajectory for alcohol involvement are quite consistent and remain even after including comorbid risk factors in model testing.

Many studies have assessed parental alcohol problems at a single point and have failed to consider that alcohol problems tend to fluctuate, with periods of remission and relapse. Studies of variations in child outcomes with fluctuations in parents' alcohol problems over time are few in number. Moss et al. (1997) reported that children with fathers who recovered from substance use during the first six years of the child's life were no different from controls by adolescence. Similarly, Moos & Billings (1982) found children of recovered alcoholics to be similar to controls on both family environment and child outcomes, with the exception of child depression, whereas children of relapsed alcoholics had poorer family environment and emotional functioning. DeLucia et al. (2001) specifically tested the hypothesis that parental recovery from alcohol problems may be associated with improvements in parenting, leading to better child outcomes. Contrary to expectations, parenting and child outcomes did not change over time as a function of fathers' alcohol trajectories over a three-year period, and this result was consistent across reporters (father or child) and for multiple-outcome variables. In summary, the temporal associations between fathers' alcohol problems or alcohol consumption and parenting or child outcomes have not been studied extensively and have produced mixed results, with more recent studies specifically testing variations over time producing largely null results. Large longitudinal data sets using more recent advances in statistical analyses of parallel processes may be better able to answer this question.

PARENTING BEHAVIOR AMONG ALCOHOLICS

Few studies have examined dynamic associations between parenting behavior and parents' alcohol problems, and there are gaps in the literature during critical developmental periods such as transition to school and onset of puberty. Beginning in infancy, data from an ongoing longitudinal study indicated that parents' alcohol problems were significantly associated with lower positive involvement and sensitivity, and higher negative affect longitudinally, so that fathers who met diagnoses for alcohol problems at infant age of 12 months behaved more negatively with their children at 24 months, as did their partners (Eiden et al. 2004a). The toddler age (about 24 months) may be developmentally salient because of the increase in infant negative behavior at this age and the change in parenting requirements from nurturance to a combination of nurturance and limit setting. It is possible that the longitudinal associations between fathers' alcohol problems and fathers' parenting are particularly significant at 24 months, because of this change in child behavior, resulting in an increase in negativity among alcoholic fathers and their partners. Thus, the associations between fathers' alcoholism and parenting behavior may not be apparent until there are significant demands on parents to modulate their behavior in response to negative child behavior. Similarly, Whipple et al. (1995) reported that alcoholic fathers displayed lower dyadic synchrony and engagement during play interactions with their 3- to 5-year-old sons. Few studies have examined parent-child interactions among school-aged children as a function of parents' alcohol problems and nested risk factors. A number of studies have examined parenting among adolescent children of alcoholics, although only a handful (discussed below) have used observational methodologies. Jacob et al. (1991) compared families with alcoholic fathers, depressed fathers, and control fathers during dyadic and triadic conflict discussions both with and without alcohol. Nondistressed fathers displayed greater positive affect and problem-solving compared with the other two groups. Alcohol effects were apparent only in triadic interactions. Fathers were found to engage in more problem-solving behavior under the influence of alcohol compared with the no-alcohol condition. Jacob et al. (2000) examined dinnertime conversations of families with antisocial alcoholic fathers as well as those with nonalcoholic fathers. Families of antisocial alcoholics displayed lower positivity, but also lower disagreements and instrumentality. The authors interpreted these findings as perhaps reflecting higher disengagement among antisocial alcoholic fathers and their families in naturalistic settings. In addition to the association between parents' alcohol problems and parenting, a series of studies has used experimental paradigms to demonstrate child effects on parenting behavior. Parents who were exposed to a child confederate exhibiting deviant behaviors consumed more alcohol during interactions with this child confederate in comparison with parents exposed to normal child behavior (see Pelham & Lang 1999). This series of studies suggests that there may be a circular loop between parents' alcoholism, children's behavior problems, and parenting, with bidirectional influences between parents and children. Alcoholic parents are at higher risk for having children with behavior problems, and children's behavior problems may increase parental stress and lead to more drinking.

A number of studies have examined the link between parents' alcohol problems and child maltreatment (see Leonard 2002) and noted clear associations between these constructs. However, studies examining the association between parents' alcohol problems and child maltreatment are fraught with methodological challenges that do not permit causal inferences. In an extensive review of the literature linking child abuse and neglect with parents' alcohol problems, Leonard (2002) noted that although a number of studies are methodologically sophisticated, involving large samples, clear definitions of alcohol problems and child abuse, and differentiation between different types of abuse, there remain a number of methodological and theoretical issues that need to be addressed. Primary among them is the need for theoretical models elucidating the processes underlying the relationship between parents' alcohol abuse and child maltreatment. Such models will need to examine potentially different processes underlying the association between alcohol abuse and child neglect versus other forms of maltreatment. Recent advances in the measurement of child neglect (e.g., Child Neglect Scale, Multidimensional Neglectful Behavior Scale) may lead to further developments in this area. A second problem is that the majority of data in this area are derived from agency reports. Previous studies have demonstrated that poor, minority families are more likely to be reported to Child Protective Services (CPS) and children are more likely to be placed out of home quickly, remain in the system longer, and receive more intensive and punitive services (e.g., Church et al. 2005). Thus, data derived from these sources are likely to be significantly biased. Another issue noted in the previous review was the need for a developmental orientation. Maltreatment of younger children may have a different etiology and consequence than maltreatment of older children. The gender of the parent with the alcohol problem was identified as also being important for advancing research in this area. There is some suggestion in the literature that maternal alcohol problems may be a more salient predictor of impaired protection of the child from negative external influences such as a predatory male, whereas paternal alcoholism may be a more salient predictor of physical or sexual abuse. Finally, a clearer understanding of temporal precedence of alcoholism before maltreatment occurs is important for understanding causal influences. This can only occur if alcoholism is viewed separately from other forms of parental psychopathology including other substance abuse, and if studies move away from lifetime measures of both maltreatment and alcoholism.

MARITAL AND PARENTING PROCESSES AS MEDIATORS OR MODERATORS OF OUTCOMES

The adverse developmental outcomes observed among children of alcoholics may arise from a variety of different sources. As noted above, some of the cognitive and behavioral problems may occur because of prenatal alcohol use, as well as the use of other substances (e.g., tobacco, marijuana) common among women who drink heavily during pregnancy. In addition, some of the outcomes may reflect genetic influences associated with parental alcoholism and comorbid disorders. From a family process perspective, our major interest is in whether marital conflict or parenting behavior mediate, or possibly moderate, the outcomes observed in these families.

Considerable research has investigated whether marital conflict has an adverse impact on children, but only two studies have examined the role of marital conflict as a potential mediator of the associations between parents' alcohol problems and child outcomes. Using a community sample with primarily subclinical levels of alcohol problems, Keller et al. (2005) reported that parents' alcohol problems predicted higher marital conflict, higher marital conflict was associated with more ineffective parenting, and this in turn was associated with higher child behavior problems among kindergarten children. El-Sheikh & Flanagan (2001) reported that marital conflict mediated the association between maternal alcohol problems and children's externalizing symptoms among elementary school–aged children. However, when considered in the same model with maternal depression and parent-child conflict, parent-child conflict was the most significant mediator of the link between parents' alcohol problems and children's behavior problems. Both studies used cross-sectional designs. Studies using longitudinal data and incorporating measures of other parental risk factors, such as depression and antisocial behavior, in model testing may be better able to address this issue.

Several theorists note that the association between parents' alcohol problems and child outcomes are mediated or moderated by the quality of the environment, including both parent and peer influences (Windle 1994). Indeed, results from the Minnesota Twin Family Study indicated that parent-child relationships and peer deviance accounted for 77% of the variance in substances used by age 14 (Walden et al. 2004). In one longitudinal study beginning in infancy, parental warmth/sensitivity during play interactions in the infant/toddler period mediated the association between fathers' current alcohol problems and children's self-regulation at age 3 (effortful control and internalization of parental rules) (Eiden et al. 2004b, 2006). Data from the Michigan Longitudinal Study indicated that parents' negative affect expression mediated the association between child temperament at 3–5 years and externalizing behavior problems at 6–8 years among antisocial alcoholic families, but not among low-risk families (Wong et al. 1999). Studies with adolescent samples have reported that fathers' monitoring and family stress partially mediated the association between fathers' alcoholism and children's substance use trajectories in adolescence (Chassin et al. 1996). Although a consistent picture seems to be emerging regarding parenting as a mediator of outcomes, the literature is by no means unequivocal. Other studies have failed to find that the association between parent alcohol problems and child outcomes is even partially mediated by parenting (e.g., Barnow et al. 2002). This may be due to differences in sample characteristics, child age, measurement of substance use and parenting, and longitudinal versus cross-sectional designs. Shared method variance has been a problem in this literature because parent reports have often been used to measure parenting, parents' alcohol problems, and child outcomes. Studies with adolescents have partially mitigated this problem by including child reports of parenting and using multimethod assessments of child outcomes.

With regard to potential moderating effects, there is a general theme in the literature that the quality of the relationship with the nonalcoholic parent may buffer the impact of the alcoholic parent on child outcomes. Few studies have systematically examined this hypothesis, and fewer still have used prospective designs. Moreover, although this general idea has been investigated for some time, most studies have not used adequate statistical analyses to examine interaction effects, or true moderation. In one of the few studies using a prospective design and observational measures of the parent-child relationship, Edwards et al. (2006) reported that among 2- and 3-year-old children of alcoholic fathers, those with secure attachment relationships with their mothers had significantly lower externalizing behavior problems compared with children who had insecure attachment relationships with their mothers. A similar pattern was noted for internalizing behavior at 3 years of age. The results are similar to those reported by Moser & Jacob (1997). Results from this study, using an adolescent sample and observations of parent-child interactions, indicated that higher amounts of positivity expressed by the nonalcoholic mother with an alcoholic partner were associated with fewer child behavior problems. These results support the hypothesis that the modifying effect of a protective factor may only be apparent in the presence of adversity or risk (Rutter 1987, Werner 1986). In contrast, El-Sheikh & Buckhalt (2003) reported that children's perceived attachment to mother and father interacted with parents' problem drinking to predict 6- to 12-year-old children's social problems such that even among children with secure attachment to mother, parents' problem drinking was associated with higher social problems. However, the same study reported that family cohesion and adaptability has a buffering effect on the relationship between parents' alcohol problems and children's internalizing and externalizing problems among school-age children (El-Sheikh & Buckhalt 2003). Other longitudinal studies with adolescent samples have failed to find a buffering effect of parenting on the impact of parents' alcohol problems on child outcomes (Curran & Chassin 1996).

SUMMARY

Several important issues are apparent throughout the alcohol and family process literature, including the critical role of antisocial behavior patterns, the necessity of examining the configuration of both husband (father) and wife (mother) drinking patterns, and the clear necessity of utilizing designs that can examine bidirectional effects between drinking behavior and family processes.

It is clear that heavy drinking and alcohol problems are linked to antisocial behavior throughout the adolescent and adult years. Adolescents who are excessive drinkers appear to enter marriage early, primarily the result of the relationship of drinking and adolescent antisocial behaviors. The entry into marriage results in reduced drinking, in part through the adoption of social norms about excessive drinking and marriage. Although research has not addressed this issue specifically, it may be that individuals with antisocial characteristics would be less likely to adopt maritally congruent drinking roles and reduce their drinking. Studies of marital satisfaction and stability have not specifically examined alcohol and antisociality together. However, there is evidence that alcohol increases negative marital behaviors among alcoholics with antisocial characteristics, and studies of IPV suggest that antisociality and closely related factors moderate the association between alcohol and IPV. Together, these findings would suggest that alcohol and antisociality could have a strong impact on marital stability. In the area of parenting behavior, there is some evidence of differential behaviors between antisocial and nonantisocial alcoholics, as well as evidence that the developmental outcomes of children of antisocial alcoholics are worse in comparison with those of nonantisocial alcoholics, although whether this represents additive effect or moderation is unclear. These findings suggest an interleaving between heavy drinking and antisociality that together could have a very disruptive effect on the marriage and that could be involved in the intergenerational transmission of these two problems. These findings should create an impetus for studies of alcohol and family processes to actively investigate the role of subtypes of alcoholism in these processes, a call that was made by McCrady & Epstein (1995) more than 10 years ago and that is only slowly being heeded.

Although considerable research has examined family functioning among families in which the husband is alcoholic, much less research is focused on families in which the wife is an alcoholic or heavy drinker beyond the prenatal period. This is especially critical given evidence that although alcohol consumption decreases dramatically during pregnancy, there is a marked increase in drinking after delivery. There is also growing evidence that it is important to study husband and wife alcoholism jointly. Couples in which both are frequent heavy drinkers or have a lifetime diagnosis of alcohol disorder appear to have high levels of marital satisfaction, a phenomenon that prospectively may protect against marital dissatisfaction and divorce. In terms of IPV, the association is less clear. Leadley et al. (2000) suggests that heavy drinking is associated with increased IPV, but that discrepant drinking is independently associated with increased IPV. In terms of marital interactions, McAweeney found positive marital interactions among concordant alcoholics, but Haber & Jacob (1997) found that the most verbal negativity was displayed by concordant alcoholics. In terms of parenting, one study suggests the negative effects of parental alcoholism are more evident in couples in which both are alcoholic, and one study indicates that children from two alcoholic parents have a riskier developmental trajectory for aggressive behavior. These results suggest the possibility that concordant alcoholism may be associated with more stable marriages, and possibly less conflictual marriages, but have worse effects on the children. These findings lead us to argue for research that examines the configuration of couples in terms of drinking rather than research that simply examines the main effects of husband and wife drinking on family processes.

It is clear that studies must take a broader view of alcohol and family processes. We have reviewed studies that address marital violence, satisfaction, and stability, as well as parental dysfunction and the impact of alcoholism on the children. However, most research focuses on the impact of alcohol on one of these issues. Studies that address alcohol and the interrelationships among these marital/family domains are rare. Although marital satisfaction, IPV, and parenting behaviors are linked, studies focusing on alcohol have often treated these separately. Consequently, although a substantial literature indicates links between marital conflict, parenting, and child outcome, there are few such studies of these links in the alcohol field. In broadening our approach, other issues need to be examined. At several points, our review touched on potential bidirectional effects with respect to alcohol and marital/family processes. There is considerable evidence that heavy drinking leads to marital and family conflict. Moreover, negative emotions and interpersonal interactions often lead to relapses among alcoholics, and it seems likely that stress generated by marital/family conflict could motivate continued drinking. Few studies have specifically addressed this issue.

In our culture, and in many others, the consumption of alcohol is not an isolated event. It is woven into the fabric of marriage and family life. Through our shared experiences, we have developed expectations regarding whether and how drinking can have positive effects. We believe that alcohol enhances social situations and that it increases interpersonal warmth and intimacy. In family celebrations, alcohol is used symbolically to wish for health, long life, and prosperity. As a culture, we have also developed rules, both explicit and implicit, that serve to enhance the positive effects of drinking and to minimize the negative effects. Close interpersonal and family relationships serve important functions in communicating and monitoring these rules. As a young and extraordinarily dynamic society, these rules can sometimes be weak and contradictory, and the role of these relationships is all the more important. Given the vast changes in family development that we have seen in the past several decades, it is clear that research is vital in addressing the role of marital/family processes in heavy drinking and alcoholism and in developing approaches to strengthen these processes in the face of these cultural changes in the nature of the family.

SUMMARY POINTS/FUTURE ISSUES

1. Marital and family transitions exert an influence both with respect to excessive drinking and the development of alcohol disorders, although the effect is strongest close to the transition.
2. Excessive drinking and alcohol disorders adversely affect marital satisfaction and stability, although this impact is observed primarily among couples with discordant patterns of consumption.
3. A strong association exists between excessive alcohol consumption and the occurrence of intimate partner violence, and although there continues to be controversy over the causal status, the evidence is supportive of a contributing role of acute heavy consumption in the occurrence of violence.

4. By treating the marriage in conjunction with alcoholism, Alcoholic Behavioral Couples Treatment appears to lead to improved drinking outcomes and greater marital satisfaction and has a salutary effect on intimate partner violence.
5. The association between parents' alcohol problems and child maltreatment has been well documented, but these studies have methodological problems that do not allow for causal inferences. In particular, although child neglect is the most common form of maltreatment, problems of definition and measurement have been rampant. Recent advances in measurement of child neglect should allow for more sophisticated study designs, including designs that allow causal inferences.
6. Alcoholic parents are at higher risk for having children with behavior problems, and children's behavior problems may increase parental stress and lead to more drinking, but more research is needed to firmly document the link between parental stress and drinking.
7. A large number of studies have documented the effects of marital conflict on child functioning. Given the effects of alcohol on marriage, future studies should use longitudinal designs to examine the potential role of marital processes as mediators or moderators of the association between parents' alcohol problems and child outcomes.
8. The early developmental trajectories of children of alcoholics leading to risk or resilience are still unclear. Although behavioral undercontrol is cited as an early milestone signifying a trajectory of increasing risk, this construct is not well defined and is not a developmentally salient indicator of risk until the preschool years. Better understanding of neonatal and infancy predictors of behavioral undercontrol and more cohesive definition of this construct would facilitate longitudinal research attempting to understand developmental pathways to risk and resilience among children of alcoholics.

ACKNOWLEDGMENTS

Preparation of this chapter was supported in part by National Institute on Alcohol Abuse and Alcoholism grants R37AA009922 to Kenneth Leonard and R01AA10042 to Rina Eiden.

Largest, most extensive report on the longitudinal impact of young adult transitions, including engagement, marriage, parenthood, and divorce as well as other transitions that are not family specific.

LITERATURE CITED

Bachman JG, O'Malley PM, Schulenberg JE, Johnston LD, Bryant AL, Merline AC, eds. 2002. *The Decline of Substance Use in Young Adulthood: Changes in Social Activities, Roles, and Beliefs*. Mahwah, NJ: Erlbaum. 307 pp.

Bachman JG, Wadsworth KN, O'Malley PM, Johnston LD, Schulenberg JD. 1997. *Smoking, Drinking, and Drug Use in Young Adulthood: The Impacts of New Freedoms and New Responsibilities*. Mahwah, NJ: Erlbaum. 241 pp.

Barnow S, Schuckit MA, Lucht M, John U, Freyberger HJ. 2002. The importance of a positive family history of alcoholism, parental rejection and emotional warmth, behavioral problems and peer substance use for alcohol problems in teenagers: a path analysis. *J. Stud. Alcohol* 63:305–15

Bogart LM, Collins RL, Ellickson PL, Martino SC, Klein DJ. 2005. Effects of early and later marriage on women's alcohol use in young adulthood: a prospective analysis. *J. Stud. Alcohol* 66:729–37
Bumpass LL. 2004. Social change and the American family. *Ann. NY Acad. Sci* 1038:213–19
Chassin L, Curran PJ, Hussong AM, Colder CR. 1996. The relation of parent alcoholism to adolescent substance use: a longitudinal follow-up study. *J. Abnorm. Psychol.* 105:70–80
Chassin L, Flora DB, King KM. 2004. Trajectories of alcohol and drug use and dependence from adolescence to adulthood: the effects of familial alcoholism and personality. *J. Abnorm. Psychol.* 113:483–98
Chassin L, Rogosch F, Barrera M. 1991. Substance use and symptomatology among adolescent children of alcoholics. *J. Abnorm. Psychol.* 100:449–63
Chilcoat HD, Breslau N. 1996. Alcohol disorders in young adulthood: effects of transitions into adult roles. *J. Health Soc. Sci.* 37:339–49
Church WT II, Gross ER, Baldwin J. 2005. Maybe ignorance is not always bliss: the disparate treatment of Hispanics within the child welfare system. *Child. Youth Serv. Rev.* 27:1279–92
Coles CD, Platzman KA, Raskind-Hood CL, Brown RT, Falek A, Smith IE. 1997. A comparison of children affected by prenatal alcohol exposure and attention deficit, hyperactivity disorder. *Alcohol Clin. Exp. Res.* 21:150–61
Cunningham JA, Sobell LC, Sobell MB, Gaskin J. 1994. Alcohol and drug abusers' reasons for seeking treatment. *Addict. Behav.* 19:691–96
Curran PJ, Chassin L. 1996. A longitudinal study of parenting as a protective factor for children of alcoholics. *J. Stud. Alcohol* 57:305–13
Curran PJ, Muthen BO, Harford TC. 1998. The influence of changes in marital status on developmental trajectories of alcohol use in young adults. *J. Stud. Alcohol* 59:647–58
Dawson DA, Grant BF, Stinson FS, Chou PS. 2006. Maturing out of alcohol dependence: the impact of transitional life events. *J. Stud. Alcohol* 67:195–203
DeLucia C, Belz A, Chassin L. 2001. Do adolescent symptomatology and family environment vary over time with fluctuations in paternal alcohol impairment? *Dev. Psychol.* 37:207–16
Edwards EP, Eiden RD, Leonard KE. 2006. Behavior problems in 18- to 36-month-old children of alcoholic fathers: secure mother-infant attachment as a protective factor. *Dev. Psychopathol.* 18:395–407
Eiden RD, Edwards EP, Leonard KE. 2004a. Predictors of effortful control among children of alcoholic and nonalcoholic fathers. *J. Stud. Alcohol* 65:309–19
Eiden RD, Edwards EP, Leonard KE. 2006. Children's internalization of rules of conduct: role of parenting in alcoholic families. *Psychol. Addict. Behav.* 20(3):305–15
Eiden RD, Leonard KE, Hoyle RH, Chavez F. 2004b. A transactional model of parent-infant interactions in alcoholic families. *Psychol. Addict. Behav.* 18:350–61
El-Sheikh M, Buckhalt JA. 2003. Parental problem drinking and children's adjustment: attachment and family functioning as moderators and mediators of risk. *J. Fam. Psychol.* 17:510–20
El-Sheikh M, Flanagan E. 2001. Parental problem drinking and children's adjustment: family conflict and parental depression as mediators and moderators or risk. *J. Abnorm. Child Psychol.* 29:417–32
Epstein EE, McCrady BS. 1998. Behavioral couples treatment of alcohol and drug use disorders: current status and innovations. *Clin. Psychol. Rev.* 18:689–711.

Extensively reviews research with respect to ABCT, describing much of the history, rationale, and future directions for combining alcoholism treatment with marital treatment.

Epstein EE, McCrady BS, Miller KJ, Steinberg M. 1994. Attrition from conjoint alcoholism treatment: Do dropouts differ from completers? *J. Subst. Abuse* 6:249–65
Fals-Stewart W. 2003. The occurrence of partner physical aggression on days of alcohol consumption: a longitudinal diary study. *J. Consult. Clin. Psychol.* 71:41–52

Reports on a diary study of men's drinking and the occurrence of IPV. In addition to establishing that alcohol consumption was associated with the occurrence of male to female IPV, it introduces a multiple thresholds model for understanding moderators of the alcohol-IPV relationship and applies this to antisocial personality as a moderator.

Focuses on positive aspects of development using statistically sophisticated methodology and multimethod assessments to examine developmental trajectory of social competence among children of alcoholic and nonalcoholic parents.

Fals-Stewart W, Leonard KE, Birchler GR. 2005. The occurrence of male-to-female intimate partner violence on days of men's drinking: the moderating effects of antisocial personality disorder. *J. Consult. Clin. Psychol.* 73:239–48.

Floyd FJ, Cranford JA, Daugherty MK, Fitzgerald HE, Zucker RA. 2006. Marital interaction in alcoholic and nonalcoholic couples: alcoholic subtype variations and wives' alcoholism status. *J. Abnorm. Psychol.* 115:121–30

Forthofer MS, Kessler RC, Story AL, Gotlib IH. 1996. The effects of psychiatric disorders on the probability and timing of first marriage. *J. Health Soc. Behav.* 37:121–32

Fried PA, Barnes MV, Drake ER. 1985. Soft drug use after pregnancy compared to use before and during pregnancy. *Am. J. Obstet. Gynecol.* 151:787–92

Fu H, Goldman N. 1996. Incorporating health into models of marriage choice: demographic and sociological perspectives. *J. Marriage Fam.* 58:740–58

Galanter M. 1997. *Recent Developments in Alcoholism, Vol. 13: Alcohol and Violence: Epidemiology, Neurobiology, Psychology, Family Issues*. New York: Plenum

Haber JR, Jacob T. 1997. Marital interactions of male versus female alcoholics. *Fam. Proc.* 36:385–402

Halford WK, Osgarby SM. 1993. Alcohol abuse in clients presenting with marital problems. *J. Fam. Psychol.* 6:245–54

Homish GG. 2004. Antenatal psychosocial risk and protective factors associated with postpartum comorbid depressive symptomatology and alcohol use. *Dissert. Abstr. Int. Sect. B Sci. Eng.* 64(7-B):3184

Homish GG, Leonard KE. 2007. The drinking partnership and marital satisfaction: the longitudinal influence of discrepant drinking. *J. Cons. Clin. Psychol.* In press

Horwitz AV, White HR, Howell-White S. 1996. Becoming married and mental health: a longitudinal study of a cohort of young adults. *J. Marriage Fam.* 5:895–907

Howell KK, Lynch ME, Platzman KA, Smith GH, Coles CD. 2006. Prenatal alcohol exposure and ability, academic achievement, and school functioning in adolescence: a longitudinal follow-up. *J. Pediatr. Psychol.* 31:116–26

Hussong AM, Zucker RA, Wong MM, Fitzgerald HE, Puttler LI. 2005. Social competence in children of alcoholic parents over time. *Dev. Psychol.* 41:747–59.

Jacob T, Bremer DA. 1986. Assortative mating among men and women alcoholics. *J. Stud. Alcohol* 47:219–22

Jacob T, Haber JR, Leonard KE, Rushe R. 2000. Home interactions of high and low antisocial male alcoholics and their families. *J. Stud. Alcohol* 61:72–80

Jacob T, Krahn GL. 1988. Marital interactions of alcoholic couples: comparison with depressed and nondistressed couples. *J. Consult. Clin. Psychol.* 56:73–79

Jacob T, Krahn GL, Leonard KE. 1991. Parent-child interactions in families with alcoholic fathers. *J. Consult. Clin. Psychol.* 59:176–81

Jacob T, Leonard KE, Haber RH. 2001. Family interactions of alcoholics as related to alcoholism type and drinking condition. *Alcohol. Clin. Exp. Res.* 25:835–43

Jacob T, Waterman B, Heath A, True W, Bucholz KK, et al. 2003. Genetic and environmental effects on offspring alcoholism: new insights using an offspring-of-twins design. *Arch. Gen. Psychiatry* 60:1265–72

Jacob T, Windle M. 2000. Young adult children of alcoholic, depressed and nondistressed parents. *J. Stud. Alcohol* 61:836–44

Jacobson JL, Jacobson SW. 2002. Effects of prenatal alcohol exposure on child development. *Alcohol Res. Health* 26:282–86

Jones AS, Gondolf EW. 2001. Time-varying risk factors for reassault among batterer program participants. *J. Fam. Violence* 16:345–59

Kaufman Kantor G, Asdigian N. 1997. When women are under the influence: Does drinking or drug use by women provoke beatings by men? See Galanter 1997, pp. 315–36

Kaufman Kantor G, Straus MA. 1989. Substance abuse as a precipitant of wife abuse victimizations. *Am. J. Drug Alcohol Abuse* 15:173–89

Kearns-Bodkin JN, Leonard KE. 2005. Alcohol involvement and marital quality in the early years of marriage: a longitudinal growth curve analysis. *Alcohol. Clin. Exp. Res.* 29:2123–34

Keller PS, Cummings EM, Davies PT. 2005. The role of marital discord and parenting in relations between parental problem drinking and child adjustment. *J. Child Psychol. Psychiatry* 46:943–51

Kelly S, Epstein EE, McCrady BS. 2004. Pretreatment attrition from couple therapy for male drug abusers. *Am. J. Drug Alcohol Abuse* 30:1–19

Kessler RC, Crum RM, Warner LA, Nelson CB, Schulenberg J, Anthony JC. 1997. Lifetime co-occurrence of DSM-III-R alcohol abuse and dependence with other psychiatric disorders in the National Comorbidity Survey. *Arch. Gen. Psychiatry* 54:313–21

Labouvie E. 1996. Maturing out of substance abuse: selection and self-correction. *J. Drug Issues* 26:457–76

Leadley K, Clark CL, Caetano R. 2000. Couples' drinking patterns, intimate partner violence, and alcohol-related partnership problems. *J. Subst. Abuse* 11:253–63

Leonard KE. 2002. Alcohol and substance abuse in marital violence and child maltreatment. In *The Violence and Addiction Equation: Theoretical and Clinical Issues in Substance Abuse and Relationship Violence*, ed. C Wekerle, A Wall, pp.194–219. Philadelphia, PA: Brunner/Mazel.

Critiques studies of alcohol and child maltreatment with sections highlighting methodological issues, offers suggestions for future directions, and provides a detailed review and critique of studies of alcohol and marital violence.

Leonard KE, Eiden RD. 1999. Husbands and wives drinking: unilateral or bilateral influences among newlyweds in a general population sample. *J. Stud. Alcohol Suppl.* 13:130–38

Leonard KE, Mudar P. 2004. Husbands influence on wives' drinking: testing a relationship motivation model in the early years of marriage. *Psychol. Addict. Behav.* 18:340–49

Leonard KE, Quigley BM. 1999. Drinking and marital aggression in newlyweds: an event-based analysis of drinking and the occurrence of husband marital aggression. *J. Stud. Alcohol* 60:537–45

Leonard KE, Roberts LJ. 1998a. The effects of alcohol on the marital interactions of aggressive and nonaggressive husbands and their wives. *J. Abnorm. Psychol.* 107:602–15

Leonard KE, Roberts LJ. 1998b. Marital aggression, quality and stability in the first year of marriage. In *The Developmental Course of Marital Dysfunction*, ed. TN Bradbury, pp. 44–73. New York: Cambridge Univ. Press

Leonard KE, Rothbard JC. 1999. Alcohol and the marriage effect. *J. Stud. Alcohol Suppl.* 13:139–46.

Comprehensively reviews factors underlying differences in drinking patterns among married, single, and divorced couples and the inferential problems created by a variety of basic design features of the studies.

Leonard KE, Senchak M. 1996. Prospective prediction of husband marital aggression within newlywed couples. *J. Abnorm. Psychol.* 105:369–80

Levinger G. 1966. Sources of marital dissatisfaction among applicants for divorce. *Am. J. Orthopsychiatry* 36:803–7

Lipsey MW, Wilson DB, Cohen MA, Derzon JH. 1997. Is there a causal relationship between alcohol use and violence? A synthesis of evidence. See Galanter 1997, pp. 245–82

Loukas A, Zucker RA, Fitzgerald HE, Krull JL. 2003. Developmental trajectories of disruptive behavior problems among sons of alcoholics: effects of parent psychopathology, family conflict, and child undercontrol. *J. Abnorm. Psychol.* 112:119–31

Maisto SA, McKay JR, O'Farrell TJ. 1998. Twelve-month abstinence from alcohol and long-term drinking and marital outcomes in men with severe alcohol problems. *J. Stud. Alcohol* 59:591–98

Marshall MP. 2003. For better or for worse? The effects of alcohol use on marital functioning. *Clin. Psychol. Rev.* 23:959–97

Martin SH, Bachman R. 1997. The relationship of alcohol to injury in assault cases. See Galanter 1997, pp. 41–56

McAweeney MJ, Zucker RA, Fitzgerald HE, Puttler LI, Wong MM. 2005. Individual and partner predictors of recovery from alcohol-use disorder over a nine-year interval: findings from a community sample of alcoholic married men. *J. Stud. Alcohol* 66:220–28

McCrady BS, Epstein EE. 1995. Directions for research on alcoholic relationships: marital- and individual-based models of heterogeneity. *Psychol. Addict. Behav.* 9:157–66

McCrady BS, Epstein EE, Kahler CW. 2004. Alcoholics Anonymous and relapse presentation as maintenance strategies after conjoint behavioral alcohol treatment for men: 18-month outcomes. *J. Consult. Clin. Psychol.* 72:870–78

McCrady BS, Noel NE, Abrams DB, Stout RL, Nelson HF, Hay WM. 1986. Comparative effectiveness of three types of spouse involvement in outpatient behavioral alcoholism treatment. *J. Stud. Alcohol* 47:459–67

McLeod JD. 1993. Spouse concordance for alcohol dependence and heavy drinking: evidence from a community sample. *Alcohol. Clin. Exp. Res.* 17:1146–55

Miller WR, Myers RJ, Tonigan JC. 1999. Engaging the unmotivated in treatment for alcohol problems: a comparison of three strategies for intervention through family members. *J. Consult. Clin. Psychol.* 67:688–97.

Unique approach to the problem of motivating alcoholics to seek treatment. This study examines the effects of three different approaches that involve significant others, many of whom are spouses of alcoholics.

Miller-Tutzauer C, Leonard KE, Windle M. 1991. Marriage and alcohol use: a longitudinal study of "maturing out". *J. Stud. Alcohol* 52:434–40

Moos RH, Billings AG. 1982. Children of alcoholics during the recovery process: alcoholic and matched control families. *Addict. Behav.* 7:155–63

Moos RH, Finney JW, Cronkite RC, eds. 1990. *Alcoholism Treatment: Context, Process, and Outcome*. New York: Oxford Univ. Press

Moser RP, Jacob T. 1997. Parent-child interactions and child outcomes as related to gender of alcoholic parent. *J. Subst. Abuse* 9:189–208

Moss HB, Clark DB, Kirisci L. 1997. Timing of paternal substance use disorder cessation and effects on problem behaviors in sons. *Am. J. Addict.* 6:30–37

Mudar P, Kearns JN, Leonard KE. 2002. The transition to marriage and changes in alcohol involvement among black couples and white couples. *J. Stud. Alcohol* 63:568–76

Mudar P, Leonard KE, Soltysinski K. 2001. Discrepant substance use and marital functioning in newlywed couples. *J. Consult. Clin. Psychol.* 69:130–34

Murphy CM, Winters J, O'Farrell TJ, Fals-Stewart W, Murphy M. 2005. Alcohol consumption and intimate partner violence by alcoholic men: comparing violent and nonviolent conflicts. *Psychol. Addict. Behav.* 19:35–42

Newcomb MD, Bentler PM. 1985. Changes in drug use from high school to young adulthood: effects of living arrangement and current life pursuit. *J. Appl. Dev. Psychol.* 8:221–46

O'Farrell TJ, Chouquette KA, Cutter HSG. 1998a. Couples relapse prevention sessions after behavioral marital therapy for male alcoholics: outcomes during the three years after starting treatment. *J. Stud. Alcohol* 59:357–71

O'Farrell TJ, Cutter HS, Choquette KA, Floyd FJ. 1992. Behavioral marital therapy for male alcoholics: marital and drinking adjustment during the two years after treatment. *Behav. Therapy* 23:529–49

O'Farrell TJ, Cutter HS, Floyd FJ. 1985. Evaluating behavioral marital therapy for male alcoholics: effects on marital adjustment and communication from before to after treatment. *Behav. Therapy* 16:147–67

O'Farrell TJ, Fals-Stewart W, Murphy M, Murphy CM. 2003. Partner violence before and after individually based alcoholism treatment for male alcoholic patients. *J. Consult. Clin. Psychol.* 71:92–102

O'Farrell TJ, Hooley J, Fals-Stewart W, Cutter HSG. 1998b. Expressed emotion and relapse in alcoholic patients. *J. Consult. Clin. Psychol.* 66:744–52

O'Farrell TJ, Murphy CM, Stephen SH, Fals-Stewart W, Murphy M. 2004. Partner violence before and after couples-based alcoholism treatment for male alcoholic patients: the role of treatment involvement and abstinence. *J. Consult. Clin. Psychol.* 72:202–17.

Comprehensively assesses verbal and physical aggression by both alcoholics and wives and longitudinal follow-ups for two years after treatment. Replicates earlier work by this research team, and begins to assess the processes linking ABCT to reduced IPV.

O'Leary KD, Schumacher JA. 2003. The association between alcohol use and intimate partner violence: linear effect, threshold effect, or both? *Addict. Behav.* 28:1575–85

Olson HC, Feldman JJ, Streissguth AP, Sampson PD, Bookstein FL. 1998. Neuropsychological deficits in adolescents with fetal alcohol syndrome: clinical findings. *Alcohol. Clin. Exp. Res.* 22:1998–2012

Orford J, Gutherie S, Nicholls P, Oppenheimer E, Egert S, Hensman C. 1975. Self-reported coping behavior of wives of alcoholics and its association with drinking outcome. *J. Stud. Alcohol* 36:1254–67

Ostermann J, Sloan FA, Taylor DH. 2005. Heavy alcohol use and marital dissolution in the USA. *Soc. Sci. Med.* 61:2304–16

Pelham WEJ, Lang AR. 1999. Can your children drive you to drink? Stress and parenting in adults interacting with children with ADHD. *Alcohol Res. Health* 23:292–98.

Reviews a series of studies using experimental methodology to examine the potential circular loop between parents' alcoholism, children's behavior problems, and parenting, with bidirectional influences between parents and children. Studies are unique in their methodology and in the focus on child influences on parents' alcohol consumption.

Quigley BM, Leonard KE. 2000. Alcohol and the continuation of early marital aggression. *Alcohol. Clin. Exp. Res.* 24:1003–10

Rutter M. 1987. Psychosocial resilience and protective mechanisms. *Am. J. Orthopsychiatry* 57:316–31

Rychtarik RG, McGillicuddy NB. 2005. Coping skills training and 12-step facilitation for women whose partner has alcoholism: effects on depression, the partner's drinking, and partner physical violence. *J. Consult. Clin. Psychol.* 73:249–61

Schafer J, Caetano R, Cunradi CB. 2004. A path model of risk factors for intimate partner violence among couples in the United States. *J. Interpers. Viol.* 19:127–42

Schumacher JA, Leonard KE. 2005. Husbands' and wives' marital adjustment, verbal aggression, and physical aggression as longitudinal predictors of physical aggression in early marriage. *J. Consult. Clin. Psychol.* 73:28–37

Sher KJ, ed. 1991. *Children of Alcoholics: A Critical Appraisal of Theory and Research*. Chicago, IL: Univ. Chicago Press

Sisson RW, Azrin NH. 1986. Family-member involvement to initiate and promote treatment of problem drinkers. *J. Behav. Therapy Exp. Psychiatry* 17:15–21

Streissguth AP, Barr HM, Martin DC, Herman CS. 1980. Effects of maternal alcohol, nicotine, and caffeine use during pregnancy on infant mental and motor development at 8 months. *Alcohol. Clin. Exp. Res.* 4:152–64

Stuart GL, Meehan JC, Moore TM, Morean M, Hellmuth J, Follansbee K. 2006. Examining a conceptual framework of intimate partner violence in men and women arrested for domestic violence. *J. Stud. Alcohol* 67:102–12

Stuart GL, Ramsey SE, Moore TM, Kahler CW, Farrell LE, et al. 2003. Reductions in marital violence following treatment for alcohol dependence. *J. Interpers. Violence* 18:1113–31

Tarter RE, Vanyukov M, Giancola PR, Dawes MA, Blackson TC, et al. 1999. Etiology of early age onset substance use disorder: a maturational perspective. *Dev. Psychopathol.* 11:657–83

Temple MT, Fillmore KM, Hartka E, Johnstone B, Leino EV, Motoyoski M. 1991. A meta-analysis of change in marital and employment status as predictors of alcohol consumption on a typical occasion. *Br. J. Addict.* 86:1269–81

Testa M, Leonard KE. 2001. Impact of marital aggression on women's psychological and marital functioning in a newlywed sample. *J. Fam. Violence* 16:115–30

Walden B, McGue M, Iacono WG, Burt SA, Elkins I. 2004. Identifying shared environmental contributions to early substance use: the respective roles of peers and parents. *J. Abnorm. Psychol.* 113:440–50

Werner EE. 1986. Resilient offspring of alcoholics: a longitudinal study from birth to age 18. *J. Stud. Alcohol* 47:34–40

Whipple EE, Fitzgerald HE, Zucker RA. 1995. Parent-child interactions in alcoholic and nonalcoholic families. *Am. J. Orthopsychiatry* 65:153–59

Whisman MA. 1999. Marital dissatisfaction and psychiatric disorders: results from the national comorbidity survey. *J. Abnorm. Psychol.* 108:701–6

Whisman MA, Uebelacker LA, Bruce ML. 2006. Longitudinal association between marital dissatisfaction and alcohol use disorders in a community sample. *J. Fam. Psychol.* 20:164–67

Wilsnack SC, Klassen AD, Schur BE, Wilsnack RW. 1991. Predicting onset and chronicity of women's problem drinking: a five-year longitudinal analysis. *Am. J. Public Health* 81:305–18

Wilsnack RW, Wilsnack SC. 1990. *Marital drinking and the quality of marital relationships: patterns from a U.S. longitudinal study*. Paper presented at 35th Int. Inst. Prev. Treat. Alcohol., Int. Counc. Alcohol Addict. Berlin, Germany

Windle M. 1994. Coexisting problems and alcoholic family risk among adolescents. In *Types of Alcoholics: Evidence from Clinical, Experimental, and Genetic Research*, ed. TF Baker, VM Hesselbrock, RE Meyer, W Shoemaker, pp. 157–64. New York: N.Y. Acad.Sci.

Wong MM, Zucker RA, Puttler LI, Fitzgerald HE. 1999. Heterogeneity of risk aggregation for alcohol problems between early and middle childhood: nesting structure variations. *Dev. Psychopathol.* 11:727–44

Yamaguchi K, Kandel DB. 1993. Marital homophily on illicit drug use among young adults: assortative mating or marital influence? *Soc. Forces* 72:505–28

Zucker RA. 2006. Alcohol use and the alcohol use disorders: a developmental-biopsychosocial systems formulation covering the life course. In *Developmental Psychopathology: Risk, Disorder, and Adaptation*, ed. D Cicchetti, D Cohen, pp. 620–56. New York: Wiley.

Thoroughly reviews literature on pathways to development of substance use disorders among children of alcoholics. Highlights importance of a systems approach that incorporates temperamental risk with environmental factors that foster the development of alcohol problems in this population.

Unwarranted Assumptions about Children's Testimonial Accuracy

Stephen J. Ceci,[1] Sarah Kulkofsky,[1] J. Zoe Klemfuss,[1] Charlotte D. Sweeney,[1] and Maggie Bruck[2]

[1]Department of Human Development, Cornell University, Ithaca, New York 14853; email: sjc9@cornell.edu

[2]Department of Psychiatry & Behavioral Sciences, Johns Hopkins University, Baltimore, Maryland 21287

Annu. Rev. Clin. Psychol. 2007. 3:311–28

First published online as a Review in Advance on January 2, 2007

The *Annual Review of Clinical Psychology* is online at http://clinpsy.annualreviews.org

This article's doi:
10.1146/annurev.clinpsy.3.022806.091354

1548-5943/07/0427-0311$20.00

Key Words

suggestibility, open-ended questions, false reports

Abstract

We examine eight unwarranted assumptions made by expert witnesses, forensic interviewers, and legal scholars about the reliability of children's eyewitness reports. The first four assumptions modify some central beliefs about the nature of suggestive interviews, age-related differences in resistance to suggestion, and thresholds necessary to produce tainted reports. The fifth unwarranted assumption involves the influence of both individual and interviewer factors in determining children's suggestibility. The sixth unwarranted assumption concerns the claim that suggested reports are detectable. The seventh unwarranted assumption concerns new findings about how children deny, disclose, and/or recant their abuse. Finally, we examine unwarranted statements about the value of science to the forensic arena. It is important not only for researchers but also expert witnesses and court-appointed psychologists to be aware of these unwarranted assumptions.

INTRODUCTION

In recent years, an increasing number of children have entered the legal system to provide testimony in a broad range of cases. In the United States alone, hundreds of thousands of children are deposed, interviewed, and examined each year as part of civil and family court proceedings, abuse/neglect investigations, and other types of criminal investigations. Before the early 1980s, children rarely were permitted to testify in criminal cases[1] (see Ceci & Bruck 1993, p. 408). Now, however, it is so common that most English-speaking nations have developed special interviewing procedures and techniques to minimize children's discomfort (e.g., video links that allow them to testify remotely, barriers between them and the defendant) and increase the reliability of their statements (e.g., Home Off. Dept. Health 1992, Natl. Soc. Prev. Cruel. Child. Childline 1993, Smith & Goretsky-Elstein 1993).

Given the recent ubiquity of children's participation in forensic matters, it is not surprising that beginning in the 1980s researchers turned their attention to the sensitive issues that arise when children enter the legal arena. This research has made significant contributions to the theoretical and applied science of child development. It has provided new and often surprising insights into the capabilities and weaknesses of children's cognitive, linguistic, social, and emotional development. This research also has dispelled myths or common beliefs about aspects of child development both in and out of the forensic arena. In this review, we first outline how some of the current research has challenged misconceptions about the reliability and credibility of children's statements. Given that many of the issues concerning children in the courtroom revolve around cases of suspected sexual abuse, it is not surprising that having the science accepted in the courtroom has been

[1]An anecdote from the John Grisham novel *The Last Juror* underscores the scientific research. It concerns a cross-examination of a newspaper publisher set in Mississippi in 1970: Attorney: Mr. Traynor, how many cases did you find where children aged five or younger were allowed to testify in a criminal trial? Newspaper Publisher Traynor: None. Attorney: Perfect answer, Mr. Traynor. None. In the history of this state, no child under the age of eleven has ever testified in a criminal trial.

a difficult process. To illustrate this point, we end the article with a misconception of the usefulness of the science to the forensic arena and show how scientists attempt to deal with efforts to keep the current science out of the courtroom.[2]

Unwarranted Assumption 1: Suggestive Interviews Can Be Indexed by the Sheer Number of Leading Questions

The suggestiveness (and thus the risk of eliciting false information) of an interview is not adequately reflected by the number of leading questions. Rather, one must consider how the concept of interview bias plays out in the current interview, as well as in all previous interviews. Interview bias characterizes those interviewers who hold a priori beliefs about what has occurred and mold the interview to maximize disclosures that are consistent with such beliefs. The means by which the bias is communicated to the child goes well beyond the use of misleading questions; other suggestive techniques include providing positive and negative reinforcement (e.g., praising the child for disclosing information consistent with the interviewer's beliefs, criticizing the child or withholding benefits such as trips to the restroom for not disclosing), utilizing peer or parental pressure (e.g., telling the child that his or her friends or parents have already disclosed), creating a negative or accusatory emotional tone (e.g., urging the child to help keep the defendant in jail), and repeating questions or interviews until the child provides a desired answer.

The following testimony of an expert in a trial illustrates this point. She testified that her questioning was not suggestive because technically speaking she did not ask suggestive questions. But as seen from her testimony, her approach is characteristic of interviewer bias:

> I usually say, "Mama talked about that somebody did some bad touching." And that's still pretty open ended. I'm not saying who and I'm not saying exactly what. I'm just introducing the subject. Or I will say, "I see many children, and children come and tell me when bad things happen to them, and I've heard other kids tell me when bad things happen. So it's okay if you want to tell me." (*In the Matter of Riley, Shelby, and Austin Blanchard v. John Blanchard* 2001, p. 876)

A number of studies have demonstrated the negative effects of interviewer bias (see Ceci & Bruck 1995 for a review). In one type of study examining interviewer bias, children witness a staged event and are then interviewed by an individual who is given misinformation about what has occurred. The interviewer is allowed to interview the child in any way he or she deems appropriate; that is, the interviewer is simply told to find out what happened. These studies have found that children who are interviewed by an individual who has been misinformed (or who has a bias) about what has occurred begin to report this misinformation themselves (e.g., Bruck et al. 1999, White et al. 1997). For example, if the interviewer has been misinformed that the child had her knee licked by another child, she ends up getting the child to assent to this false claim (White et al. 1997).

Another set of studies has examined the effects of combining multiple suggestive techniques in eliciting false reports from children. These studies demonstrate that misleading questions asked by a neutral interviewer do not have the same effect as multiple suggestive techniques, implying that misleading questions alone are not sufficient to expose an interviewer's bias. For example, Garven and her colleagues (1998, 2000) examined how the techniques used by investigators in the infamous McMartin Preschool case (*State of Calif. v. Buckey* 1990) can taint children's

[2] In preparing this review, we drew upon several examples from a recent article of ours (Bruck & Ceci 2004), but have gone considerably beyond it.

testimony beyond the damage that misleading information alone can cause. In one study (Garven et al. 2000), the researchers asked kindergarten children to recall details from when a visitor named Paco came to their classroom and read a story, gave out treats, and wore a funny hat. Half the children were given interviews that included misleading questions about plausible events (e.g., Did Paco break a toy?) and about bizarre events (e.g., Did Paco take you to a farm in a helicopter?). Between 5%–13% of the children falsely agreed with the misleading questions. A second group of children was also questioned, but these children were given feedback after their answers to the misleading questions. "No" responses were negatively evaluated, whereas "yes" responses were positively evaluated. For example,

> Interviewer: Did Paco take you somewhere in a helicopter?
> Child: No.
> Interviewer: You're not doing good.
> Interviewer: Did Paco break a toy?
> Child: Yes.
> Interviewer: Great, you're doing excellent now.

This latter group of children provided the desired but false answer to 35% of the plausible questions and to 52% of the bizarre questions. This study demonstrates that a simple count of misleading/leading questions would not reflect the suggestiveness of the interview. It was the added use of selective reinforcement that provided the child with sufficient information about the interviewer's bias—to make "yes" responses for all statements regardless of their plausibility. In a follow-up interview two weeks later, when children were simply asked nonleading questions with no selective reinforcement feedback, the same level of between group differences was obtained. Thus, interviewer bias in a prior interview can produce false reports in a later unbiased/neutral interview. This is an important point to bear in mind when analyzing transcripts of an interview: Just because that particular interview may be neutral, prior interviews may have been suggestive, seeding false claims made in the neutral interview. The bottom line is that the number of leading or suggestive questions deployed in an interview is neither a good index of how suggestive it is, nor a good index of whether prior (nonrecorded) interviews that were more suggestive are responsible for false claims by the child.

Unwarranted Assumption 2: Suggestibility Is Primarily a Problem for Younger Age Groups

The erroneous view that preschool children are the only population vulnerable to suggestion can be found in many experts' testimony. Consider the following example: "Well, in virtually all these studies, two and three-year olds do not do well in suggestibility, and the four and five-year olds. . . [d]o pretty well" (expert testimony by prosecution witness *In the Matter of Riley, Shelby, and Austin Blanchard v. John Blanchard* 2001). "It's true that the sorts of questioning that were asked of the children are not supported by basic research into suggestibility, but these children were all over the age of 6, the cut-off for suggestibility-proneness in scientific studies" (transcript, p. 1441).

This view that only the youngest children are vulnerable to suggestive questioning reflects the disproportionate attention to the study of preschool children at the end of the twentieth century. This practice was directly motivated by forensic concerns. During the 1980s and 1990s, there were a number of high-profile criminal cases in which preschool children's horrific claims about sexual abuse by day-care workers, parents, and other unfamiliar adults were presented to the jury (see descriptions of several of these cases in Ceci & Bruck 1995). Although the case facts showed that these children had been subjected to highly suggestive interviews, at that time there was no relevant body of scientific literature to indicate the risk of these interviewing techniques in producing false allegations about a range of salient events. When researchers began to fill in this empirical void, most of the studies focused on preschoolers, with few examining age-related differences. Those that did include age comparisons usually found ceiling effects for the older children, leading to the conclusion that only preschoolers are suggestible (e.g., Ceci et al. 1987) and that there is little need for concern when older children are subjected to suggestive interviewing practices.

However, the conclusion that suggestibility is minimal among grade-school children and young adults is discrepant with the finding of another body of literature that shows that many of the suggestive techniques used in the child studies also produced tainted reports or memories in adults (e.g., see Loftus 2004). Indeed, much of the earliest work on the malleability of memory was conducted with adults, not young children. For example, in a highly cited study by Loftus & Pickrell (1995), adults ranging in age from 18 to 35 were convinced through a variety of suggestive techniques that that they had been lost in a shopping mall as young children, and they developed elaborate, albeit false memories of these events. Similarly, Hyman and his colleagues have conducted a number of studies whereby through suggestive techniques, college-aged students developed false memories of events, such as spilling a punch bowl at a wedding (e.g., Hyman et al. 1995).

By inference then, one might assume that children in middle childhood must also be quite suggestible, given the knowledge of both the younger children and older groups. Recent evidence supports this view: Susceptibility to suggestion is highly common in middle childhood, and under some conditions, there are small or even no developmental differences. For example, Finnila et al. (2003) staged an event (a version of the Paco visit described in Garven et al. 2000) for two age groups of children (four- and five-year-olds, and seven- and eight-year-olds). One week later, half the children were given a low-pressure interview that contained some misleading questions with abuse themes (e.g., "He took your clothes off, didn't he?"). The other children received a high-pressure interview during which the interviewer told them that their friends had answered the leading questions affirmatively. Children were praised for assenting to the misleading questions, and when they did not assent, the question was repeated. In both the low- and high-pressure conditions, there were no significant age differences, although a significant number (68%) of misleading questions were assented to in the high-pressure condition (see also Bruck et al. 2007, Zaragoza et al. 2001).

Under some conditions, older children are even more suggestible than younger children are (e.g., Ceci et al. 2007, Finnila et al. 2003, Lindberg 1991, Scullin & Ceci 2001, Zaragoza et al. 2001). For example, in a recent study, researchers administered a suggestibility test to four-year-olds and nine-year-olds (Ceci et al. 2007). Children were read a short story that focused on a series of objects. Later children were given misinformation about the objects in the story. Days later, they were asked to recall the objects that were part of the original story. The direction of age differences in suggestibility was predicted by age differences in children's semantic representations of the similarity between the actual and suggested object. For example, compared with younger children, older children were much more likely to erroneously report that there was an egg sandwich in a story in which they actually heard about a cheese sandwich. This is because older children find eggs and cheese to be more similar than younger children do. Similarly, compared with older children, younger children were more likely to report the false suggestion that there was a soda in the story when there was actually milk. Again, this was because younger children perceive milk and soda as more similar than do older children.

These newer findings reshape current views of developmental trends in suggestibility and challenge current conceptualizations of the developmental mechanisms in children's suggestibility. Specifically, current mechanisms that have been touted for children's suggestibility (e.g., theory of mind, social compliance) are commonly known to have developed by the end of the preschool years (Wellman et al. 2001). Clearly, a wider perspective needs to be taken, and skills that develop throughout the childhood years should become the focus of future study (e.g., appreciation of the ramifications of false statements, insight into questioner's motives). The bottom line is that, expert testimony notwithstanding (Bruck & Ceci 2004), all age groups are vulnerable to misleading suggestions, even if preschoolers are disproportionately more vulnerable.

Unwarranted Assumption 3: Multiple Suggestive Interviews Are Needed to Taint a Report; Milder Forms of Suggestion Do Not Produce Tainted Reports

A third scientific misconception concerns the view that it is difficult to implant memories or to taint reports and, therefore, repeated suggestive interviews are required, especially to produce a false report for salient events (e.g., Ceci & Bruck 1995). For example, the expert in the *Matter of Ryan D. Smith* (2001) testified, "[s]uggestions must be repeated for children to incorporate them into their reports" (transcript, p. 886).

We have been as responsible as anyone has for this view because often when we describe our own findings, we report that our methodology involved multiple suggestive interviews of children over time (e.g., Bruck et al. 1995a, Ceci et al. 1994a, Leichtman & Ceci 1995). Although this is a correct description of our own methodology and results, it does not gainsay the many studies that have reported that children can incorporate suggestions about salient events after a single suggestive interview (Bruck et al. 2007, Garven et al. 2000, Thompson et al. 1997). Importantly, the effects of a single interview that produced false reports had powerful and lasting effects: Children's initial false responses to suggestions, which may have reflected social pressure, continued in later interviews even when questioned by different (neutral) interviewers. This enduring pattern may reflect that with time children come to believe that the false suggestion actually happened; in other words, they developed a false belief about a statement they initially realized was false.

Significant tainting and production of false beliefs can also occur with a single mildly suggestive interview. For example, in two studies, Poole & Lindsay (1998, 2001) had parents read their child a brief narrative that outlined the child's previous encounters with a character known as "Mr. Science" at the researchers' laboratory. Unknown to the parent, some of the details in the brief narrative they read to their children were inaccurate and thus were not experienced by their child when they met Mr. Science. Nonetheless, even under these mild conditions, significant numbers of children (four- to eight-year-olds) later told an interviewer that they had experienced the suggested events.

In a similar line of research, Principe and her colleagues (Principe & Ceci 2002, Principe et al. 2006) found that children exposed to rumors by their peers or by overhearing adult conversations were as likely to falsely report being part of the event as those who actually did participate. In one study (Principe & Ceci 2002), a group of children participated in a scripted event that contained two highly salient events (the target activities). The second group included classmates of the first group; these children participated in the same scripted event, but they were not shown the two target events. A third group of children was taken from a different school; similar to the second group, they experienced the scripted activity without the target events. The children were then interviewed in either a neutral or a suggestive manner. Children who were classmates of those who participated in the target event made more false claims alleging that they had viewed the target activities than children who did not view the target events and were from a different school. These data suggest that there was contamination from classroom interactions; children who had not experienced the target events learned of them from their classmates who had, and thus were more likely to assent to false events. In a second study, Principe et al. (2006) found that children who overheard a child talking about a target event (a rabbit that escaped from a magician) were as likely to falsely claim to have seen the event in question as were peers who actually saw it escape. Moreover, in this study, the effect of suggestive questioning did not notably increase their false reports; they were as likely to report falsely if they overheard peers talking about the rabbit, regardless of whether interviewers employed suggestive questions.

So far, we have only focused on the extent to which one exposure to false information can lead to high rates of misreporting about salient events. Some studies directly compare the effects of multiple versus one suggestive interview on children's suggestibility. Evidence suggests that, contrary to common psychological principles, a number of circumstances exist in which one suggestive interview produces the same amount of taint as two or more suggestive interviews. The impact of a second interview depends on the spacing of the interviews from the initial events and from the final interview, and also on the strength of the original memory trace (Marche 1999, Melnyk & Bruck 2004).

In light of these considerations, it is regrettable that expert witnesses create the impression that interviewing methods must be repetitive, egregious, and coercive to taint a child's statement about abuse. In a posttestimonial brief, one expert witness made just such a claim, arguing that short of using what she felt were repetitive, egregiously coercive forms of interviewing, one could expect children's statements to be highly accurate: "[Q]uestioning that is 'merely' suggestive (e.g., occasional leading questions embedded in an interview with neutral and direct questions) yields a 92–100% accuracy rate on abuse-relevant or trauma-relevant questions" (Dalenberg 2000, p. 11). In her words,

> In the Janitor, Sam Stone, and Garven et al. (in press) studies . . . the authors subject children to the following procedures: Repeated affirmative statements that the perpetrator is guilty, not just questions about his acts. Refusals to hear and acknowledge the child's denials of a perpetrator's guilt . . . statements to the child that she is not doing a good job when she says something that the interviewer does not want to hear. Offering of evidence to the child that the perpetrator was guilty (such as telling the child that her mother, or other children, knows that the perpetrator is guilty or that the trauma occurred [as in the Garven studies or Mousetrap studies], or showing the child physical evidence of the crime [as in the Sam Stone study]). Taking the methods of these studies into the sexual abuse arena, the questioner would have affirmatively told R.B. that her father was a sexual abuser, falsely told her that there was physical evidence that she was abused, and then repeatedly, even if she denied a type of abuse each and every time she was queried, asked if her father was angry when he abused her, where he went after he abused her, etc. . . . I see no evidence that the interviewers of R.B. went this far.

Unwarranted Assumption 4: Children's Spontaneous Reports Are Always Accurate

A commonly held belief is that although children's prompted statements may be suspect, their spontaneous statements are generally accurate, and errors only occur when children are asked specific, often misleading questions. Similar to many of the other assumptions, this too made its way into expert testimony. For example, Dr. Constance Dalenberg testified for the prosecution *In the Matter of Riley, Shelby, and Austin Blanchard v. John Blanchard* 2001 that "[s]pontaneous statements are likely to be accurate statements" (transcript, p. 39).

It is true that children tend to be more accurate when asked open-ended questions compared with more directed questioning. This has been recognized since Binet's (1900) earliest studies on children's suggestibility. However, it is not the case that children's spontaneous statements are always accurate statements. When children have been questioned suggestively, the suggestions can taint both what they later spontaneously report as well as their answers to specific questions. For example, the children in Poole & Lindsay's (2001) Mr. Science study, discussed above, were simply asked to describe everything they remembered from interacting with Mr. Science after they had been exposed to a misleading narrative by their parents about the event. A full 21% of the statements children reported were events they had not actually experienced. Furthermore, some of these events included bodily touch, such as Mr. Science putting something yucky in the child's mouth. In a different study, Poole & White (1993) interviewed children about an event that had occurred two years previously. Following the first event the children had been exposed to repeated questions, some of which where misleading. Two years later, 39% of the six-year-olds' (who were four years old at the time of the original event) statements in response to the open-ended request "Tell me what happened" were incorrect. Older children did not fare much better, with 23% of eight-year-olds' and 25% of ten-year-olds' statements being incorrect.

Furthermore, even if children have not been exposed to misleading suggestions, their open-ended recall is still not guaranteed to be accurate. This is especially true if the child is interviewed about a confusing or ambiguous event. For example, Ornstein and colleagues (1998) engaged children in a mock medical exam in which some common features (such as listening to the child's heart) were omitted and atypical features (such as wiping the child's belly button with alcohol) were added. When children were interviewed about the event 12 weeks later, 42% of the four-year-olds and 74% of the six-year-olds spontaneously reported at least one of the common features had occurred even though they had not. In another study, Goodman and her colleagues (1994) interviewed children about a painful genital catheterization procedure. Among the children who were three to four years old, 23% of their free-recall statements were incorrect. Finally, Greenhoot (2000) examined five- and six-year-olds' recall of ambiguous stories, in which the protagonist may have been considered acting prosocially or antisocially. Error rates on open-ended recall ranged between 20%–30%.

Taken together, these studies show that although children's free-recall and spontaneous statements are generally more accurate than their responses to directed questions, free recall is by no means error free.

Unwarranted Assumption 5: Erroneous Suggestions Ineluctably Lead to Erroneous Reports by Children

In the literature on children's suggestibility, it is rare to find a study in which 100% of the children are influenced by 100% of the false suggestions. Although some children easily and readily succumb to suggestive interviews, others remain steadfast in their denial that the suggested events occurred. Mounting evidence from different paradigms and methodologies leads to the conclusion that suggestibility proneness is jointly determined by contextual (factors intrinsic to the interview) and individual (factors intrinsic to the child) differences. Thus, suggestive interviews need not inevitably lead to false reports by children.

For example, Peterson and her colleagues (2004) have demonstrated that in certain contexts (in which an event actually occurred, was strongly encoded, and probably reinforced by family retellings), the provision of misinformation can actually lead to superior memory accuracy. This is because the strong memory stands in stark contrast to the misinformation, thus reinforcing and refreshing it. These researchers conducted an experiment to find out if presenting misleading suggestions to children after they experienced an emergency medical procedure (e.g., setting a broken bone, suturing a laceration, treatment for a dog bite, or treatment for crushed fingers) would taint their recall of that earlier event. The misleading suggestions were presented one year after the medical procedure; children were tested one week later and one year later (i.e., two years after the medical procedure). Contrary to the reasonable assumption that the mere presence of misleading suggestions would inevitably lead to lower accuracy and incorporation of false details, Peterson et al. found that none of the misleading suggestions contaminated the children's reports, especially one year later. How can we reconcile this finding with other findings showing that the passage of time makes it likely that children will incorporate such misleading information into their long-term recalls (e.g., Bruck et al. 1997)? Two aspects to this finding merit attention.

First, the children in Peterson et al.'s study had accurate memories of their medical procedures. Not only were these salient events, but they were rehearsed via family discussions during the intervening year, in the absence of any attempt to taint their recall. Therefore, when one year elapsed and the researchers provided the first misleading suggestions, they were flying into a headwind, trying to overwrite what by then had become strong representations. Imagine trying to alter a child's memory of his or her own name; you could not do it unless you worked on the child relentlessly for long periods. Children's emergency-room experiences may not have been as deeply entrenched as their names, but they were undoubtedly quite entrenched.

Second, many studies showing incorporation of false suggestions in children's reports may have been documenting report inaccuracy rather than alteration of the underlying memory, a suggestion made by Peterson and her colleagues as well. In other words, children may report misinformation for a variety of reasons, including some that have nothing to do with their memory of what actually occurred. For example, they may tell the interviewer the false details that had been suggested because they believe this is what the interviewer expects, rather than because they really believe what they are reporting.

One example from an actual case illustrates both points. In a Jordan, Minnesota, case, Andy Meyers, an 11-year-old child, was removed from the family home and placed across town in an emergency foster placement because his father was suspected of abusing him (see Feher 1987). He steadfastly denied that his parents, or anyone else, had abused him. However, after three months of almost daily interrogations, he finally reported that he had been abused. He claimed that his parents held orgies in the woods and killed babies and then dumped them in a nearby river. His charges, along with those of 39 other children against 24 adults (many of whom were their parents), formed the basis of a long number of indictments that eventually were dropped because of the suggestive manner in which the children had been interviewed. Approximately nine years after making these charges, Andy described his disclosures to a journalist as follows:

> Andy: I finally just said (to investigators) "fine, yeah that happened."
> Journalist: Why did you say "yes" that day?
> Andy: I have no idea. Probably cause I was just sick of being badgered. I didn't think I was ever going home. I mean, I figured if this is gonna be the way life is, I might as well make it a little more tolerable for myself. (Feher 1987, p. 232)

Concerning the role of individual differences, numerous reviews have been published in recent years showing that various factors differentiate children's suggestibility proneness, such as personality and cognitive variables (see Bruck & Melnyk 2004, Bruck et al. 1997, Roebers & Schnieder 2001). For example, there seems to be fairly consistent evidence that children with more advanced language abilities are more resistant to suggestion, whereas children who are more creative are less resistant to suggestion. Other psychological factors such as intelligence, memory abilities, theory of mind, and attachment status have been implicated in distinguishing children who are more versus less likely to fall prey to suggestive influences, although research with these other factors is more equivocal (Bruck & Melnyk 2004).

Recently, Gilstrap & Ceci (2004) have argued that the degree to which children assent to false information in an interview is best predicted by the child's own disposition rather than by the interviewer's use of suggestive techniques. Specifically, they showed that when interviewing children about a gamelike staged event, the best predictor of a child's rate of incorporating false suggestions into his or her report was his or her prior behavior rather than the interviewer's prior behavior. For example, lagged sequential analyses showed that it was possible to predict a child's subsequent answer directly from his or her prior answer, effectively skipping the intervening adult questioning. Although the interviewer's use of misleading questioning still had deleterious effects on the child's accuracy, the results demonstrated that a child's answers were driven at least as much by his or her personal style as by the interviewer's form of questioning. Researchers and expert witnesses need to be aware of these possibilities, although clearly this finding needs to be replicated under more realistic conditions.

One may conclude from this body of literature that although suggestive influences can have a negative impact on the accuracy of a child's statement, these influences do not guarantee inaccuracy in all situations and for all children and, conversely, the absence of these influences does not guarantee accuracy.

Unwarranted Assumption 6: False Reports Produced by Suggestive Interviewing Are Distinguishable from Accurate Reports

Expert witnesses often state that it is easy to detect false reports that are the result of suggestion because such children merely parrot the words of their interrogators or, conversely, that true reports integrate affect into their accounts (e.g., showing appropriate emotions). Consider two claims made by an expert witness in *Oregon v. Ryan Smith*, a criminal case involving alleged sexual abuse:

> Children can only provide information about body sensations if they have experienced the event. If children are suggested information and later repeat this information but include with it sensory information then their reports must be accurate. The child's accusations could not be the result of suggestions that he'd been sodomized because he reported that he could hardly walk back to his classroom. Children would not incorporate this type of detail into their false reports. Their inclusion is another sign the statement is valid. Children who are lying merely parrot suggestions and are easier to detect because they are rehearsed. These children were going beyond anything an adult might have suggested. (transcript, p. 886)

> When children have been coached to talk about sexual abuse, they talk about it in a different way than when it is genuine. Often there is no affect involved, they aren't showing an emotional reactions. They don't show any distress or anything. None of the children in this case talked spontaneously about details to give validity to their allegations. (transcript, p. 819)

However, there is no support for this assertion; in fact, most research to date suggests the contrary.

First, when children are suggestively interviewed, their subsequent narratives include false reports that go beyond what was suggested to them but are consistent with the suggestions (e.g., Bruck et al. 1995a, 2002). For example, Leichtman & Ceci (1995) found that when children were given false suggestions that a person was clumsy, they later generalized this information to make false claims that this individual spilled, ripped, soiled, or broke things during his visit to their classroom.

Second, subjective ratings of children's reports after suggestive interviewing reveal that children who make false reports after being suggestively interviewed appear highly credible to trained professionals in the fields of child development, mental health, and forensics (e.g., Ceci et al. 1994a,c; Leichtman & Ceci 1995); these professionals cannot reliably discriminate between children whose reports are accurate from those whose reports are inaccurate as a result of suggestive interviewing techniques. The children who provided the false reports spoke sincerely and provided accounts laden with emotion and perceptual details.

Even when experts attempt to apply more systematic means to distinguish true from false reports, their decisions are not reliable. Statement validity assessment, and more specifically criterion-based content analysis (CBCA), has been touted as one way to distinguish true from false reports. In CBCA, experts code the witness's statement for the presence of specific contents, such as the presence of peripheral details or mentions of the perpetrator's state of mind. Each of the CBCA criteria is expected to appear more often in true reports than in false reports; thus, every instance that a criterion appears in a child's report increases the likelihood that the report is valid (Raskin & Esplin 1991, Steller & Koehnken 1989). For example, a report that includes reproductions of dialogue, superfluous details, spontaneous corrections, and mentions of the perpetrator's state of mind would be more likely to be considered true than a statement that did not include these characteristics.

There is some limited evidence that CBCA can identify truthful statements from intentional lies (Vrij 2005); however, CBCA cannot distinguish true statements from statements that were developed as the result of suggestive questioning. For example, Stromwell et al. (2004) found no significant differences in CBCA scores for real versus imagined events; CBCA scores correctly predicted 44% of real events and 64% of imagined events (see also Erdmann et al. 2004).

Moving beyond the specific criterion of CBCA, results of several studies (Bruck et al. 2002, Powell et al. 2003, Principe & Ceci 2002, Scullin et al. 2002) reveal that linguistic markers, such as the amount of elaboration or temporal connectivity, do not consistently differentiate true from false narratives that emerge as a result of repeated suggestive interviews. In the Bruck et al. study (2002), analysis of children's narratives of true and false events showed that narratives of the false events actually contained more embellishments (including descriptions and emotional terms) and details than their narratives of the true events. The false narratives also had more spontaneous statements than the true narratives and included more temporal connectors.

Third, one cannot make judgments of reliability based on features of the child's narrative that are known to be true. That is, one cannot conclude that everything in the child's report about abuse by his or her pediatrician must be accurate because he or she correctly described the layout of the pediatrician's office. This is because when children are suggestively interviewed, they often interweave the false suggestions with accurate details about their lives. For example, Hershkowitz (2001) reported the case study of a 10-year-old girl who, as a consequence of her mother's suggestive questioning, falsely reported being the victim of a rape. In reality, the girl had been the victim of a man exposing his genitalia to her. She interwove the details of the actual exposure incident into her detailed false narrative of a rape.

These findings show that reliability and credibility are orthogonal dimensions. Credibility refers only to the degree to which the witness is motivated to tell the truth but not to the accuracy of the witness' statement (Ceci et al. 1995, Kohenken 1989, Poole & Lindsay 1998). Children may appear highly credible (or their interviews may have the characteristics of credible narratives), yet their reports may be unreliable. Children can also be reliable yet not appear credible in the eyes of judges and jurors. Accordingly, one cannot use perceived credibility to judge reliability. However, in the forensic arena, it is crucial for those who make judgments about credibility (i.e., the court) to make these judgments based on the reliability of the report, in other words, details on the degree to which suggestive interviewing was used to elicit the child's statements.

Unwarranted Assumption 7: Children's Disclosures of Traumatic Events Are Delayed, Denied, and Often Recanted

A highly influential assumption is that sexually abused children do not readily disclose abuse because of shame, guilt, and fear. Consequently, there are long delays between abuse and disclosure, and often there is never any disclosure. It has repeatedly been asserted that, when questioned, children will initially deny their abuse, but with repeated questioning, they will slowly divulge its details. It is further claimed that these disclosures are frequently recanted, but with additional support their disclosures will be reinstated. Summit (1983) proposed the most popular embodiment of this model, which is termed the child sexual abuse accommodation syndrome.

Because models of the child sexual abuse accommodation syndrome were not based on empirical data but on clinical intuitions and unsystematically collected observations, we recently reviewed the literature to determine their empirical support (London et al. 2005). We identified ten studies in which adults with documented histories of childhood abuse were asked to recall their disclosures in childhood. Results were consistent; on average only 33% of the adults remembered disclosing the abuse during childhood. These data support the view that sexually abused children are silent about their victimization and delay disclosure for long periods of time. These data are also important in that they support the contention that prevalence data on sexual abuse (which are based on reports to official agencies) greatly underestimate the extent of the problem because so much abuse is not reported.

Although these studies are informative on the issue regarding the delay of reporting, the data are silent on issues of denial and recantation by sexually abused children because the adults in these studies were never asked, "As a child, did anyone ever ask you or question you about abuse?" However, a second set of studies provides some relevant data on this point. We identified 17 studies that examined rates of denial and recantation by sexually abused children who were, in fact, asked directly about being abused when they were assessed or treated at clinics. The rates of denial at assessment interviews were highly variable (4% to 76%) as were the rates of recantation (4% to 27%). We found that the methodological adequacy of each study (sampling procedures, validation of sexual abuse) was related to denial and recantation rates, with the highest rates being associated with the weakest studies. For the six methodologically superior studies, the average rate of denial was only 14%, and the average rate of recantation was only 7%. Thus, sexually abused children do not usually deny or recant the details of their abuse. In other words, although these children do not readily disclose their abuse, if they are asked about it in a structured interview, they will tell, and few will recant.

Even if it is conceded that children will not deny when asked, this does not address the issue of how to elicit disclosures. Even though there are known risks of using leading or specific questions, perhaps these are necessary to elicit reports or details from sexually abused children who are frightened, ashamed, or feeling too guilty to reveal their victimization. A series of studies conducted by Lamb, Sternberg, and colleagues has recently challenged this claim. This team constructed a structured interview protocol and then trained interviewers of suspected child abuse victims in its use. The major characteristic of the protocol is to encourage the child to provide detailed life-event narratives through the guidance of open-ended questions (e.g., "Tell me what happened." "And what happened next?" "And you said it happened at the store. Tell me about the store."). The use of specific questions is allowed only after exhaustive free-recall prompting. Suggestive questions are highly discouraged. In their latest study, Lamb et al. (2003) examined the interviews of 16 trained police officers with 130 children (four to eight years old), all of whom had made allegations of sexual abuse. They found that 83% of all allegations/disclosures were elicited through free-recall questions (78% for preschoolers), and 66% of all children identified the suspect through open-ended question (60% for preschoolers). These data dispel the belief that children need to be bombarded with suggestive techniques to elicit details of their traumatic events; in fact, children can provide detailed information through open-ended prompts, and if a child denies abuse when asked directly, there is no scientifically compelling evidence that the child is in denial. Abused children usually disclose when directly asked.

Unwarranted Assumption 8: Laboratory Research Is Not an Accurate Reflection of Child Witnesses' Experiences in the Real World

The issues and themes in this section do not come from basic researchers in the field of children's suggestibility but instead reflect the concerns and beliefs of expert witnesses and professionals who advocate for sexually abused children. The central theme of the argument is that much of the science (some of which is reviewed above) is not ecologically valid because the science either overestimates children's suggestibility or underestimates the capabilities of the child witness. Research accused of overestimating children's suggestibility has been referred to as new wave to distinguish its investigators from prior cohorts who found children to be less suggestible (Lyon 1999).

The essence of the first argument is that laboratory studies conducted by new-wave researchers yield high rates of suggestibility in children because these researchers employ extreme or coercive tactics that are seldom found in real-world interviews of children. For example, Lyon (1999) wrote,

> In sum, "leading" questions are certainly common in investigative interviews. Yet the new wave's research goes far beyond asking leading questions in assessing children's suggestibility. The limited observational evidence available indicates that the new-wave methods are not, in fact, common investigative techniques. The experimental evidence indicates that such techniques are largely responsible for the impressive demonstrations of suggestibility that the new wave has produced. (Lyon 1999, p. 15)

Following Lyon's views, Dr. Dalenberg's testimony for the prosecution *In the Matter of Riley, Shelby, and Austin Blanchard v. John Blanchard* (2001) reflected her view that in the absence of extremely coercive interviewing tactics, children's statements are highly accurate:

> The children are 95–98% accurate typically—often 100% accurate with abuse-related, misleading questions. When they become inaccurate is in these coercive studies ... in which the children are asked six or seven leading questions in a row, contradicted every time they say something positive, frowned at when they say something positive, shown evidence against the individual, told that other people know the guy is guilty. Those kinds of extremely

Table 1 Some rates of suggestive utterances by forensic interviewers

Study	Mean number of suggestive utterances	% of total utterances
Lamb et al. (1996)	14	8.75
Sternberg et al. (1996)	9.5	9.2
Sternberg et al. (1997)	8.75	8
Sternberg et al. (1999)	7.6	6.5
Hershkowitz (1999)	11	8.8
Orbach et al. (2000)	9.1	10
Overall mean	**9.99**	**8.54**

coercive circumstances are necessary to get children to—to do this. (transcript, p. 39)

Thus, the insinuation among some who come to court is that studies of children's suggestibility are unrealistic because they utilize high-pressure, coercive tactics not found in actual forensic interviews. Proponents of this argument, however, do not present any data to back their claim that the techniques used in the laboratory do not mirror those used in real-world forensic interviews. In fact, in the real world, children are often exposed to similarly highly suggestive questioning (see Ceci & Friedman 2000 for evidence for this claim). **Table 1** reports the average suggestions for a number of field studies of social workers and law-enforcement professionals. As shown, typically between 6.5% and 10% of all field utterances can be classified as suggestive questions. This translates into approximately 10 suggestions per interview. This is more than many laboratory studies have employed that are associated with high rates of suggestibility errors. Thus, research that utilizes frequent suggestive questioning is appropriate for generalization to field-based interviews.

Moreover, most scientific studies producing high rates of suggestibility have not employed coercive or high-pressured techniques such as positive or negative reinforcement or peer pressure. In the majority of these studies, as shown above, children are suggestible even when the interviewer is neutral and supportive. This bears noting because if children succumb to noncoercive questioning that is commonly employed in research, they can be expected to succumb even more so in response to the types of coercive questioning observed in some field-based interviews.

Rather than arguing whether the conditions of a specific study reflect practices in the real world (which are highly variable), it is more logical to argue from the facts of the interviews from a specific case. If a child initially denied abuse and then only gradually disclosed some details after multiple interviews with many suggestive elements, then it is entirely appropriate to use the suggestibility studies of the new wave. For ethical reasons involved in research with children, these studies of children's suggestibility most likely underestimate how a combination of motives, strong suggestions, threats, and inducements that have been documented in actual forensic interviews might lead a child to make an inaccurate report. Thus, the value of the science depends on the specifics of the case to which it is applied. Blanket statements about the practical significance of a study or the relevance of scientific findings are meaningless in the abstract.

CONCLUSION

Despite the substantial advances that developmental forensic researchers have made to both application and theory, there remain misconceptions that border on urban legends. In this review, we unveil eight unwarranted assumptions that in each case have made their way into expert testimony in court cases. We show that the sheer number of leading questions does not indicate the suggestiveness of an interview, and interviewer bias, which may contribute an interviewer's utilization of other suggestive factors, must be taken into account. In addition, young children are not alone in their susceptibility to suggestive techniques; older children and adults can be quite susceptible as well. In addition, extremely coercive techniques are not necessary to produce tainted reports, and furthermore, even free recall is not error free in both younger and older children. At the same time, children will not always report false information if they have been exposed to suggestive techniques; contextual and individual factors are important and must be taken into consideration. However, when a child does produce an erroneous report as a result of suggestive techniques, these reports often appear highly credible, and there is no scientifically established means to distinguish these false reports from true ones. There is also no compelling evidence to support the belief that victims of abuse deny their abuse when they are initially questioned about it, nor do they usually recant, as some have claimed. Thus, arguments in favor of relentlessly pursuing reticent interviewees find no scientific support. Finally, we argue that scientific findings may be quite pertinent to real-world cases of child sexual abuse and should not be ignored by the courts, expert witnesses, or child advocates.

The literature presented above may seem ambiguous or even self-contradictory at some points. For example, on the one hand we show that children may develop false reports in the absence of extreme suggestive techniques, but on the other hand, we review studies showing that extreme techniques do not ineluctably lead to false reports. How should these ambiguities and discrepancies be reconciled to apply the scientific research in actual forensic settings? We suggest practitioners, interviewers, and expert witnesses must take into account the qualifying role of context, and further research must consider how the child may interact in a given context. A child's report, its degree of embellishment of central versus peripheral details, and its narrative coherence and consistency are the product of the full history of the child's involvement with interviewers as well as the child's own particular psychological characteristics. In this regard, it is important to note that tainting misinformation can occur prior to the first officially recorded interview. For example, a child may be interviewed informally by a parent, teacher, social worker, or mental health professional before any formal interviews take place. Even hearsay reports and suggestions from informal sources (e.g., overheard conversations, rumors, and even interactions with others who overheard suggestions) are capable of tainting a child's report, and when this occurs, the tainted report may appear indistinguishable from true reports.

In summary, although tainting of reports is neither easy nor inevitable, it is also not that difficult to accomplish, especially at the hands of a biased interviewer. Researchers and expert witnesses alike must refrain from the temptation to assert specialized knowledge that permits them to determine the reliability of a child's claim, based solely on that child's responses in a neutral interview that may have followed unrecorded suggestive ones. Furthermore, forensic professionals should avoid characterizing a child's testimony as veridical based solely on group norms and averages without giving full consideration to the context of the child's testimony.

LITERATURE CITED

Binet A. 1900. *La Suggestibilité*. Paris: Schleicher Freres

Bruck M, Ceci SJ. 2004. Forensic developmental psychology: unveiling four common misconceptions. *Curr. Direct. Psychol. Sci.* 13:229–32

Bruck M, Ceci SJ, Francoer E. 1999. The accuracy of mothers' memories of conversations with their preschool children. *J. Exp. Psychol. Appl.* 5:89–106

Bruck M, Ceci SJ, Francouer E, Barr R. 1995a. "I hardly cried when I got my shot": influencing children's reports about a visit to their pediatrician. *Child Dev.* 66:193–208

Bruck M, Ceci SJ, Francoeur E, Renick A. 1995b. Anatomically detailed dolls do not facilitate preschoolers' reports of a pediatric examination involving genital touching. *J. Exp. Psychol. Appl.* 1:95–109

Bruck M, Ceci SJ, Hembrooke H. 2002. Nature of true and false narratives. *Dev. Rev.* 22:520–54

Bruck M, London K, Landa R, Goodman J. 2007. Autobiographical memory and suggestibility. *Dev. Psychopathol.* 19:73–95

Bruck M, Melnyk L. 2004. Individual differences in children's suggestibility: a review and synthesis. *Appl. Cogn. Psychol.* 18:947–96

Bruck M, Melnyk L, Ceci SJ. 1997. External and internal sources of variation in the creation of false reports in children. *Learn. Individ. Differ.* 9:289–316

Ceci SJ, Bruck M. 1995. *Jeopardy in the Courtroom.* Washington, DC: Am. Psychol. Assoc.

Ceci SJ, Bruck M. 1993. The suggestibility of children's recollections: an historical review and synthesis. *Psychol. Bull.* 113:403–39

Ceci SJ, Bruck M, Rosenthal R. 1995. Children's allegations of sexual abuse: forensic and scientific issues: a reply to commentators. *Psychol. Public Policy Law* 1:494–520

Ceci SJ, Crotteau-Huffman M, Smith E, Loftus EW. 1994a. Repeatedly thinking about non-events. *Conscious. Cogn.* 3:388–407

Ceci SJ, Friedman RD. 2000. The suggestibility of children: scientific research and legal implications. *Cornell Law Rev.* 86:34–108

Ceci SJ, Loftus EF, Leichtman M, Bruck M. 1994b. The possible role of source misattributions in the creation of false beliefs among preschoolers. *Int. J. Clin. Exp. Hypn.* 42:304–20

Ceci SJ, Loftus EW, Leichtman M, Bruck M. 1994c. The role of source misattributions in the creation of false beliefs among preschoolers. *Int. J. Clin. Exp. Hypn.* 62:304–20

Ceci SJ, Papierno PB, Kulkofsky S. 2007. Representational constraints on children's suggestibility. *Psychol. Sci.* In press

Ceci SJ, Ross D, Toglia M. 1987. Suggestibility of children's memory: psycholegal implications. *J. Exp. Psychol. Gen.* 116:38–49

Erdmann K, Volbert R, Bohm C. 2004. Children report suggested events even when interviewed in a nonsuggestive manner: What are the implications for credibility assessment? *Appl. Cogn. Psychol.* 18:589–611

Feher B. 1987. The alleged molestation victim, the rules of evidence, and the constitution: Should children really be seen and not heard? *Am. J. Crim. Law* 14:227, 231–33

Finnila K, Mahlberga N, Santtilaa P, Sandnabbaa K, Niemib P. 2003. Validity of a test of children's suggestibility for predicting responses to two interview situations differing in their degree of suggestiveness. *J. Exp. Child Psychol.* 85:32–49

Garven S, Wood JM, Malpass R, Shaw JS. 1998. More than suggestion: consequences of the interviewing techniques from the McMartin preschool case. *J. Appl. Psychol.* 83:347–59

Garven S, Wood JM, Malpass RS. 2000. Allegations of wrongdoing: the effects of reinforcement on children's mundane and fantastic claims. *J. Appl. Psychol.* 1:38–49

Gilstrap L, Ceci SJ. 2004. Reconceptualizing children's suggestibility: bidirectional and temporal properties. *Child Dev.* 75:1–14

Goodman GS, Quas JA, Batterman-Faunce JM, Riddlesberger MM, Kuhn J. 1994. Predictors of accurate and inaccurate memories of traumatic events experienced in childhood. *Conscious. Cogn.* 3:269–94

Greenhoot AF. 2000. Remembering and understanding: the effects of changes in underlying knowledge on children's recollections. *Child Dev.* 71:1309–28

Hershkowitz I. 1999. The dynamics of interviews involving plausible and implausible allegations of child sexual abuse. *Appl. Dev. Sci.* 3:86–91

Hershkowitz I. 2001. A case study of child sexual false allegation. *Child Abuse Negl.* 25:1397–411
Home Off. Dept. Health. 1992. *Memorandum of Good Practice on Video Recorded Interviews with Child Witnesses for Criminal Proceedings*. London: Her Majesty's Station. Off.
Hyman IEJ, Husband TH, Billings JF. 1995. False memories of childhood experiences. *Appl. Cogn. Psychol.* 9:181–97
In the Matter of Riley, Austin, and Shelby Blanchard v. John Blanchard. July 2001. Calif. Sup. Ct., CK40772/CK40775
In the Matter of Ryan D. Smith. May 30, 2001. State of Oregon Appelate Ct., #98–0325-JA; A106007
Kohenken G. 1989. Behavioral correlates of statement credibility: theories, paradigms, and results. In *Criminal Behavior and the Justice System: Psychological Perspectives*, ed. H Wegener, F Leosel, J Haisch, pp. 271–89. New York: Springer-Verlag
Lamb ME, Sternberg KJ, Orbach Y, Esplin PW, Stewart H, Mitchell S. 2003. Age differences in young children's responses to open-ended invitations in the course of forensic interviews. *J. Consult. Clin. Psychol.* 71:926–34
Lamb ME, Hershkowitz I, Sternberg KJ, Esplin PW, Hovav M, et al. 1996. Effects of investigative style on Israeli children's responses. *Int. J. Behav. Dev.* 19:627–37
Leichtman MD, Ceci SJ. 1995. The effects of stereotypes and suggestions on preschoolers' reports. *Dev. Psychol.* 31:568–78
Lindberg M. 1991. An interactive approach to assessing the suggestibility and testimony of eyewitness. In *The Suggestibility of Children's Recollections*, ed. J Doris, pp. 47–55. Washington, DC: Am. Psychol. Assoc.
Loftus EF. 2004. Memories of things unseen. *Curr. Direct. Psychol. Sci.* 13:145–47
Loftus EF, Pickrell JE. 1995. The formation of false memories. *Psychiatr. Ann.* 25:720–25
London K, Bruck M, Ceci SJ, Shuman D. 2005. Disclosure of child sexual abuse: What does the research tell us about the ways that children tell? *Psychol. Public Policy Law* 11:194–226
Lyon TD. 1999. The new wave in children's suggestibility research: a critique. *Cornell Law Rev.* 86:1–84
Marche TA. 1999. Memory strength affects reporting misinformation. *J. Exp. Child Psychol.* 73:45–71
Melnyk L, Bruck M. 2004. Timing moderates the effect of repeated suggestive interviewing on children's suggestibility. *Appl. Cogn. Psychol.* 18:613–31
Natl. Soc. Prev. Cruel. Child. Childline. 1993. *The Child Witness Pack*. London: Nat. Soc. Prev. Cruel. Child.
Orbach Y, Hershkowitz I, Lamb ME, Epslin PE, Horowitz D. 2000. Assessing the value of structured protocols for forensic interviews of alleged sexual abuse victims. *Child Abuse Negl.* 24:733–52
Ornstein PA, Merritt KA, Baker-Ward K, Furtado E, Gordon BN, Principe G. 1998. Children's knowledge, expectation, and long-term retention. *Appl. Cogn. Psychol.* 12:387–405
Peterson C, Parsons T, Dean M. 2004. Providing misleading and reinstatement information a year after it happened: effects on long-term memory. *Memory* 12:1–13
Poole DA, Lindsay DS. 1998. Assessing the accuracy of young children's reports: lessons from the investigation of child sexual abuse. *Appl. Prevent. Psychol.* 7:1–26
Poole D, Lindsay DS. 2001. Children's eyewitness reports after exposure to misinformation from parents. *J. Exp. Psychol. Appl.* 7:27–50
Poole DA, White LT. 1993. Two years later: effects of question repetition and retention interval on the eyewitness testimony of children and adults. *Dev. Psychol.* 29:844–53
Powell MB, Jones CH, Campbell C. 2003. A comparison of preschooler's recall of experienced versus nonexperienced events across multiple interviewers. *Appl. Cogn. Psychol.* 17:935–52

Principe GF, Ceci SJ. 2002. "I saw it with my own ears": the influence of peer conversations and suggestive questions on preschoolers' event memory. *J. Exp. Child Psychol.* 83:1–25

Principe GF, Kanaya T, Ceci SJ, Singh M. 2006. Believing is seeing: how rumors can engender false memories in preschoolers. *Psychol. Sci.* 17(3):243–48

Raskin DC, Esplin PW. 1991. Statement validity assessment: interview procedures and content analysis of children's statements of sexual abuse. *Behav. Assess.* 13:265–91

Roebers CM, Schnieder W. 2001. Individual differences in children's eyewitness recall: the influence of intelligence and shyness. *Appl. Dev. Sci.* 5:9–21

Scullin M, Kanaya T, Ceci SJ. 2002. Measurement of individual differences in children's suggestibility across situations. *J. Exp. Psychol. Appl.* 8:233–46

Scullin MH, Ceci SJ. 2001. A suggestibility scale for children. *Personal. Individ. Differ.* 30:843–56

Smith BE, Goretsky-Elstein S. 1993. *The Prosecution of Child Sexual and Physical Abuse Cases.* Washington, DC: Am. Bar Assoc.

State of Calif. v. Buckey. 1990. Sup. Ct., Los Angeles County, #A750900

Steller M, Koehnken G. 1989. Criteria-based statement analysis. In *Psychological Methods in Criminal Investigation and Evidence*, ed. DC Raskin, pp. 217–45. New York: Springer Publ.

Sternberg KJ, Lamb ME, Hershkowitz I. 1996. Child sexual abuse investigations in Israel. *Crim. Justice Behav.* 23:322–37

Sternberg KJ, Lamb ME, Hershkowitz I. 1997. Effects of introductory style on children's abilities to describe experiences of sexual abuse. *Child Abuse Neglect* 21:1130–41

Sternberg KJ, Lamb ME, Esplin PW, Baradaran L. 1999. Using a scripted protocol in investigative interviews: a pilot study. *Appl. Dev. Sci.* 3:70–76

Stromwell LA, Bengtsson L, Leander L, Granhag PA. 2004. Assessing children's statements: the impact of a repeated experience on CBCA and RM ratings. *Appl. Cogn. Psychol.* 18:653–68

Summit R. 1983. The child sexual abuse accommodation syndrome. *Child Abuse Neglect* 7:177–93

Thompson WC, Clarke-Stewart KA, Lepore SJ. 1997. What did the janitor do? Suggestive interviewing and the accuracy of children's accounts. *Law Hum. Behav.* 21:405–26

Vrij A. 2005. Criteria-based content analysis: a qualitative review of the first 37 studies. *Psychol. Public Policy Law* 11:3–41

Wellman HM, Cross D, Watson J. 2001. Meta-analysis of theory-of-mind development: the truth about false belief. *Child Dev.* 72:655–84

White TL, Leichtman MD, Ceci SJ. 1997. The good, the bad, and the ugly: accuracy, inaccuracy, and elaboration in preschoolers' reports about a past event. *Appl. Cogn. Psychol.* 11:S37–54

Zaragoza M, Payment K, Kichler J, Stines L, Drivdahl S. 2001. *Forced confabulation and false memory in child witnesses.* Presented at Bienn. Meet. Soc. Res. Child Dev. Minneapolis, MN

Expressed Emotion and Relapse of Psychopathology

Jill M. Hooley

Department of Psychology, Harvard University, Cambridge, Massachusetts 02138; email: jmh@wjh.harvard.edu

Annu. Rev. Clin. Psychol. 2007. 3:329–52

First published online as a Review in Advance on January 19, 2007

The *Annual Review of Clinical Psychology* is online at http://clinpsy.annualreviews.org

This article's doi: 10.1146/annurev.clinpsy.2.022305.095236

1548-5943/07/0427-0329$20.00

Key Words

families, stress, clinical outcome, schizophrenia, depression

Abstract

Expressed emotion (EE) is a measure of the family environment that predicts worse clinical outcomes for patients with a range of disorders. This article describes the assessment of EE and the evidence linking EE to clinical relapse in patients with psychopathology. This is followed by consideration of the possible explanatory models that might account for the EE-relapse link and a review of the evidence suggesting that EE may play a causal role in the relapse process. The results of studies describing the effect of EE on patients, as well as cross-cultural aspects of the construct, are highlighted. Finally, the possibility that high levels of EE may stress patients by perturbing activity in neural circuits that underlie psychopathology is considered and new directions for EE research are outlined.

Contents

INTRODUCTION

EE: expressed emotion

Rates of relapse are notoriously high for many forms of psychopathology. These relapses are costly and they exact an emotional toll on patients and their families (Almond et al. 2004). The early identification of patients who are at high risk for relapse after remission from an episode of illness is clearly important for both theoretical and practical reasons. Moreover, greater understanding of the factors involved in the relapse process not only holds the potential to inform us about the nature of vulnerability, but also provides information that is essential for the development of new clinical interventions.

Given the strong biological basis of many forms of psychopathology, it may at first seem surprising that one of the most consistent predictors of psychiatric relapse across a broad range of disorders is a measure of the family environment that is called expressed emotion (EE). It is important to keep in mind, however, that psychosocial variables are capable of affecting not only the structure and the functioning of the brain, but also the occurrence or the timing of gene expression (Fish et al. 2004, Kandel 1998, Weaver et al. 2006). Biological, psychological, and social variables have reciprocal influences. A growing body of evidence suggests that these factors interact to affect the onset or clinical course of mental disorders (see Caspi et al. 2003, Tienari et al. 2004).

Before we begin our discussion, one point warrants emphasis. Although this article describes a family variable that has been reliably linked to psychiatric relapse, there is no evidence that families cause disorders such as schizophrenia. Indeed, in a longitudinal study, Tienari and his colleagues (2004) have demonstrated that family difficulties, including high levels of criticism, do not predict the development of schizophrenia in adopted children who have no genetic risk for the disorder. However, when children who are at high genetic risk for the disorder (by virtue of a having a mother with schizophrenia) are adopted into dysfunctional families, they are much more likely to develop schizophrenia later than if they were raised in a more healthy family environment. This suggests that people's genotypes may make them more or less sensitive to certain aspects of their environments (see Caspi et al. 2003). What is particularly exciting about Tienari's work, however, is that when children with a genetic risk for schizophrenia were raised in a well-functioning family, the probability that they would later develop schizophrenia was the same as it was for children who had no genetic risk. This speaks to the protective role healthy families can play, even in the face of high genetic risk.

EXPRESSED EMOTION

Origins and Measurement

The EE construct was developed in the 1960s by George Brown, a British sociologist. In an early study, Brown and his colleagues noted that male patients with schizophrenia did better clinically if they left the hospital to live, not with wives or parents, but with siblings or in lodgings (Brown et al. 1958). This led Brown to consider the possibility that something about family relationships might be important with respect to relapse in schizophrenia. Over the next several years, Brown, working with Michael Rutter, addressed the problem of how to measure the "range of feelings and emotions to be found in ordinary families" (Brown 1985, Brown & Rutter 1966, Rutter & Brown 1966). Of note here is that it was the more commonplace aspects of family relationships that were thought to be important, rather than relationships that were unusual or deeply disturbed. The result was the development of the EE construct (Brown et al. 1972).

Expressed emotion is assessed through a semistructured interview called the Camberwell Family Interview (CFI; see Leff & Vaughn 1985). The interview is named after the Camberwell area of London, which is where the research team was located and where many of the patients and families in the early studies lived. The CFI is conducted with a patient's family member in the absence of the patient. It typically takes 1–2 hours, and it is always audiotaped for later coding. Designed to facilitate a conversation with the relative, the CFI contains questions about the development of the patient's psychiatric difficulties as well as questions about specific symptoms. The CFI also focuses on how the relative deals with difficult situations involving the patient and how the relative gets along with the patient more generally. Ratings of EE are derived not only from what the family member says but also from the voice tone that the relative uses when speaking about the patient.

> **EXPRESSED EMOTION**
>
> Expressed emotion, which is assessed through an interview with a key family member (parent, spouse, etc.), is a measure of how much criticism, hostility, or emotional overinvolvement the relative expresses when speaking about a family member with psychopathology. Although it is measured in an individual, it is thought to reflect disturbances in the organization, emotional climate, and transactional patterns of the entire family system.

CFI: Camberwell Family Interview

EOI: emotional overinvolvement

The key elements of EE are criticism, hostility, and emotional overinvolvement (EOI). Critical remarks reflect obvious dislike or disapproval of some aspect of the patient's behavior (e.g., "He's always sleeping. It's very annoying."). Critical remarks can be rated on the basis of their content or because of a particularly negative voice tone that is used to describe a situation involving the patient. Hostile remarks, like criticism, also reflect dislike or disapproval. However, in the case of hostility there is a more generalized critical attitude and dislike of the patient as a person (e.g., "He's very lazy—he won't do anything unless you make him."). Rejection of the patient is also evidence of hostility. Finally, EOI reflects a dramatic, exaggerated, or overprotective attitude on the part of the relative toward the patient. This is reflected in an intrusive style when dealing with the patient or in the relative's extreme emotional distress during the interview (e.g., "I won't leave him alone if I can avoid it. I worry constantly.").

EOI is more commonly noted in parents than it is in spouses (Goldstein et al. 2002).

After approximately two weeks of training, coders are able to rate the elements of EE quite reliably. Training is important, however. When psychiatrists familiar with the EE construct were asked to guess the EE status (high versus low) of their patients' relatives (with whom they were familiar), they performed no better than chance (King et al. 1994).

Relatives are classified as high in EE if they make an above-threshold number of critical remarks, or show any evidence of hostility, or score high (3 or more) on a 0–5 scale of EOI. However, the most important component of EE is criticism—an observation made by Brown et al. 1972 and repeatedly confirmed by researchers in subsequent studies. For family members of patients with schizophrenia, making six or more critical remarks warrants a high EE classification. For relatives of patients with unipolar depression, however, a lower cutting score (two or three critical remarks) is used. It is also important to note that, in addition to rating criticism, hostility, and EOI, coders also note how much warmth the relative expresses when talking about the patient and how many positive comments he or she makes about the patient. Warmth is rated on a 0–5 scale; for positive comments a frequency count is used. However, neither of these ratings is considered in the overall (high versus low) EE assessment. This is because, in the first prospective study of the association between EE and relapse, very low warmth tended to be associated with high rates of criticism, and very high warmth was associated with high levels of EOI (see Brown et al. 1972). Unfortunately, this has led to a general neglect of the role of warmth in families (see Lopez et al. 2004 for an exception).

On first inspection, the procedures that are used to determine a high- versus low-EE classification may appear somewhat arbitrary. However, the reason that EE is a composite variable based on ratings of criticism, hostility, and EOI is because these scales predicted an increased likelihood of relapse in Brown's seminal study (Brown et al. 1972). Brown did explore the consequences of using different cutting scores for criticism. However, the best separation (based on statistical criteria) between relapsing and nonrelapsing patients came when a cutoff of seven critical comments was used. Vaughn & Leff (1976) subsequently replicated Brown et al.'s results using the original cutting score for criticism, but further refined the classification and reduced the cutoff to six critical remarks, again based on statistical considerations. Because this cutting score has been associated with positive findings in many other studies (see Butzlaff & Hooley 1998), there has been little effort on the part of EE researchers to conduct the kinds of statistical modeling studies that might provide data supporting other approaches.

An inherent assumption in the traditional approach to EE classification is that something is qualitatively different about families who score above or below the specified critical comment threshold. Although many studies have provided empirical support for this assumption, dichotomizing EE (as opposed to using critical comment frequency as a continuous variable) does create problems. First, it gives the impression that low-EE families are experiencing few difficulties and are therefore not in need of any help. As a result, such families are typically not offered family-based treatments or provided with support, even though they may benefit from them (Linszen et al. 1996). Second, adopting a dichotomous classification of EE restricts the range of the variable in statistical analyses. It is therefore perhaps surprising that EE predicts relapse as well as it does. Although the predictive power of (dichotomous) EE and critical comment frequency has not been subjected to any systematic empirical scrutiny, correlations scattered throughout the EE literature do suggest that EE might actually be better as a threshold construct than criticism is as a continuous variable. For example, in a study of relapse in alcohol-abusing patients, O'Farrell et al. (1998) reported that the correlation between critical comments and relapse was 0.31. However, the correlation between EE and relapse was 0.36. Similarly, in Hooley et al.'s (1986) study of relapse in patients with unipolar depression, the correlation between criticism and relapse was not as large as the correlation between EE and relapse ($r = 0.40$ and $r = 0.52$, respectively).

Alternative Measures of EE

The CFI is the gold standard measure for the assessment of EE (Hooley & Parker 2006). The vast majority of the work that has been conducted to validate the EE construct has employed the CFI, and this instrument is undoubtedly the assessment measure of choice. However, the extended period of training (two or more weeks) that is required to learn to rate EE combined with the long duration of the CFI (1–2 hours) and time taken to code the interview (2–3 hours) has led some researchers to seek quicker forms of assessment. Although there is still no fully acceptable alternative, a few instruments warrant mention.

One of the most frequently used alternative measures of EE is the Five Minute Speech Sample (FMSS; Magaña et al. 1986). As its name suggests, the FMSS simply requires the relative to talk about the patient for five uninterrupted minutes. This measure is widely used by researchers studying childhood psychopathology (e.g., Asarnow et al. 1993, Hirshfeldt et al. 1997, Peris & Baker 2000). It has also been employed, with mixed success, in studies involving adult patients with schizophrenia and bipolar disorder (Jarbin et al. 2000, Marom et al. 2002, Tompson et al. 1995, Uehara et al. 1997, Yan et al. 2004). Although coding the FMSS still requires a period of training, one advantage it has over the CFI is that it takes only 5 minutes to administer and about 20 minutes to code. These benefits must be weighed, however, against the tendency of the FMSS to underidentify high-EE relatives (see Hooley & Parker 2006 for a review).

For schizophrenia researchers, two questionnaire measures, the Level of Expressed Emotion Scale (LEE; Cole & Kazarian 1988) and the Family Attitude Scale (FAS; Kavanagh et al. 1997) have some demonstrated validity. For other disorders (e.g., mood disorders, anxiety disorders, and substance abuse), the very short (one question) Perceived Criticism measure (see Hooley & Teasdale 1989) appears to be capable of predicting patients at high risk for poor clinical outcomes. Nonetheless, two recent reviews have concluded that the CFI remains the measure of choice for the assessment of EE (Hooley & Parker 2006, Van Humbeeck et al. 2002).

RELAPSE

Relapse is a measure of outcome that reflects a clinically significant return of symptoms based on an independent assessment with a structured clinical interview. Relapse is not based on rehospitalization, although many patients who do relapse will be admitted to the hospital. This is because rehospitalization can be influenced by other factors, including how willing the family is to manage the patient at home.

FMSS: Five-Minute Speech Sample

EXPRESSED EMOTION AND RELAPSE

Schizophrenia

Efforts to understand the clinical outcomes of patient with schizophrenia provided the original impetus for the development of the EE construct. In light of this, it is perhaps not surprising that the vast majority of work on EE has concerned patients with this disorder. Numerous studies, conducted with patients from all over the world, have repeatedly demonstrated that EE (assessed using the CFI) is a reliable predictor of relapse for schizophrenia. When patients with schizophrenia return home from the hospital to live in family environments that are high in EE, they have a risk of relapse that is more than double that of patients living in low-EE homes. A meta-analysis conducted by Butzlaff &

Hooley (1998) examined 27 prospective outcome studies and resulted in a weighted mean effect size of r = 0.31 for the association between EE and relapse in schizophrenia. Moreover, although EE is a risk factor for relapse even for patients who have recently developed the disorder, patients who have more chronic and long-standing illnesses are at even greater risk of relapse when they live in high-EE home environments.

PTSD: posttraumatic stress disorder

Mood Disorders

At least seven studies have used the CFI to examine the association between family levels of EE and relapse in patients with major mood disorders such as unipolar and bipolar depression. All but one (Hayhurst et al. 1997) have shown a positive association between EE and relapse. The meta-analysis study of Butzlaff & Hooley (1998) reported a weighted mean effect size of r = 0.39 for the association between EE and relapse in depression using a cutting score of two critical comments to define high EE and an effect size of 0.45 when a cutting score of three critical comments was used. Including the data from Hayhurst et al. (1997) reduces this latter effect size to 0.39, which is still highly significant (see Hooley & Gotlib 2000).

It is worth noting that, although the majority of relatives of patients with schizophrenia are parents, most of the relatives of patients with depression tend to be spouses. The fact that EE still predicts relapse when nonbiological relatives are involved and when the diagnosis is not schizophrenia is important. Goldstein et al. (1992) have previously suggested that high EE could be a behavioral manifestation of the schizophrenia genotype that is measured in the biological relatives of patients. If this were the case, it could explain why high levels of EE in family members are associated with greater risk of relapse in patients. However, this genetic model of EE is seriously challenged by data linking EE with relapse in depression and by the finding that high levels of EE in nonbiological relatives (e.g., spouses) are predictive of patient relapse.

Anxiety Disorders

Not all studies that have explored the association between EE and clinical outcome have used relapse as a dependent measure. In studies of patients with anxiety disorders, researchers have examined the role of EE in the prediction of outcome after treatment with behavior therapy.

Tarrier et al. (1999) used the CFI to assess EE in the relatives (mostly spouses) of patients with posttraumatic stress disorder (PTSD). Consistent with the findings for schizophrenia and depression described above, both criticism and hostility were predictive of patients doing less well at post-test after being treated with imaginal exposure. In contrast, Peter & Hand (1988) reported that patients with agoraphobia who lived with spouses who were rated as critical on the CFI had *better* clinical outcomes 1–2 years after a behavioral (exposure) intervention than did patients whose spouses were low on criticism. This rather counterintuitive finding was later replicated in outpatients suffering from either agoraphobia or obsessive-compulsive disorder who were treated with exposure therapy (Chambless & Stetekee 1999). Although criticism was associated with a more positive clinical outcome, patients did not do well when they lived in family environments that were high on hostility (see Chambless & Steketee 1999). Finally, for patients receiving cognitive behavior therapy for social phobia, EE was unrelated to treatment outcome, although there was a trend toward patients with relatives who were rated as high in EOI to do worse (Fogler et al. 2007).

These findings are interesting because they suggest that the impact of criticism may be different for patients with different types of psychopathology. Although patients with schizophrenia, mood disorders, and PTSD tend to fare more poorly in the face of high criticism, this does not seem to be the case for patients with agoraphobia and obsessive-compulsive disorder. Both Chambless & Steketee (1999) and Peter & Hand (1988) have suggested that perhaps critical spouses pressure anxious patients to confront anxiety-provoking stimuli more than would otherwise be the case. By not tolerating avoidance, these critical spouses may actually be helping patients engage in exposure on a routine basis, hence facilitating improvement after treatment. This may not happen for PTSD patients with critical spouses because of the imaginal (versus in vivo) nature of the exposure. It may also not happen when patients are receiving therapy that has a more cognitive focus, as was the case in the study of Fogler et al. (2007).

Eating Disorders

In addition to schizophrenia and anxiety and mood disorders, research into the predictive validity of EE has also included patients with eating disorders or disordered eating patterns. Fischmann-Havstad & Marston (1984) reported that married women who had lost at least 15 pounds over the previous year were more likely to relapse and gain weight again if they lived with spouses who were high in EE (based on three or more critical comments). Higher levels of parental criticism also predicted worse clinical functioning of patients with anorexia nervosa after six months of therapy (LeGrange et al. 1992) and predicted less-favorable outcomes in bulimia nervosa patients at the end of a six-year follow-up (Hedlund et al. 2003). Patients with anorexia nervosa and bulimia nervosa were more likely to drop out of outpatient family treatment prematurely if their parents were high rather than low in EE (Szmukler et al. 1985). An association between EE and reduced treatment compliance was also reported by Flanagan & Wagner (1991) for severely obese patients.

The studies described above vary with respect to the nature of the patients' problems and the type of outcome measure used. However, taken together, the findings suggest that family levels of EE are good predictors of treatment compliance, early treatment outcome, and long-term clinical outcomes for patients with eating disorders or weight problems.

Substance Use Disorders

The first extension of the EE construct to the course of alcoholism was conducted by Fichter et al. (1997). Using a cutting score of four or more critical comments to determine high EE, these researchers noted an association between high levels of EE and more relapses at a six-month follow-up. The number of critical comments made by the family member (most typically a spouse) was also related to a shorter time until relapse occurred. O'Farrell et al. (1998) subsequently reported that male patients who received behavioral marital therapy designed to promote abstinence fared much worse over the course of a one-year follow-up when they lived with a high- versus a low-EE spouse. More specifically, men with high-EE spouses (i.e., those who made more than the median number of six critical comments) were more likely to relapse, had a shorter time to relapse, and spent more days drinking in the 12-month follow-up than did men with low-EE spouses. Finally, in the only study of dually diagnosed patients to date, Pourmand et al. (2005) reported that for patients with both psychosis and substance abuse, EE was the strongest univariate predictor of relapse of all the variables examined.

Personality Disorders

EE is most typically studied in the context of Axis I disorders. However, one study has reported on the association between EE and clinical outcome in patients with an Axis II disorder. Hooley & Hoffman (1999) measured EE in the family members of hospitalized patients who were diagnosed with borderline personality disorder. Patients received follow-up for one-year after they had been discharged from the hospital, and EE was used to predict the clinical outcome of patients during this time. Contrary to prediction, neither criticism nor hostility was associated with how patients did clinically over the follow-up period. Patients whose relatives were critical of them did just as well as patients who had families who made few criticisms. Moreover, patients whose families were rated as high in EOI actually did better than did patients whose families showed low levels of EOI. This was a surprising finding because, for mood disorders and schizophrenia, EOI is typically associated with relapse.

Findings such as these highlight the importance of considering patient factors in understanding the EE-relapse relationship. Although all high-EE relatives are people who express high levels of criticism, hostility, or marked emotional overinvolvement, the ways in which these attitudes and behaviors are perceived and experienced by patients vary. For patients with schizophrenia or mood disorders, high levels of criticism and high levels of EOI are associated with relapse. When the diagnosis is borderline personality disorder, however, criticism is unrelated to relapse and EOI is an indicator of a better longer-term outcome. Understanding how different types of psychopathology moderate the impact and the meaning of critical or overinvolved behaviors on the part of relatives is clearly an important topic for future research.

EVIDENCE OF CAUSALITY

Methodological Issues

In the prototypical EE and relapse study, symptoms are assessed during follow-up using structured clinical interviews. This allows relapse to be determined on the basis of increases in symptom severity. From a methodological perspective, it is important that rehospitalization not be used as a measure of relapse because this could be confounded with EE. For example, if high-EE relatives are less tolerant of symptoms, they may make efforts to have the patient readmitted to the hospital when, under the same clinical circumstances, low-EE relatives might allow the patient to remain at home.

Even with this methodological issue addressed, however, the presence of a reliable correlation between EE in relatives and unfavorable clinical outcomes in patients does not permit us to conclude that EE plays a causal role in the relapse process. Although it is possible that high levels of EE cause vulnerable patients to relapse, it is also plausible to suggest that some of the illness characteristics of relapse-prone patients might engender criticism in family members. If this were the case, EE could be associated with relapse and yet play no causal role.

Even in the very early research studies, investigators were attentive to this possibility. Brown et al. (1972) observed that patients with more severe behavioral or work impairments were more likely to relapse than were patients who had fewer problems in these areas. Patients with more behavioral or occupational difficulties were also more likely to have high-EE relatives. However, even when these factors were statistically controlled, EE remained a significant predictor of patients' clinical outcomes. Subsequent studies that have controlled for potentially important patient variables have further confirmed the independent contribution that is made to relapse by EE (e.g., Nuechterlein et al. 1992).

Intervention Studies Involving EE

Although the question of directionality is not fully resolved, the hypothesis that EE may play a causal role in the relapse process is consistent with the findings of treatment studies. Rates of relapse in patients (who are already taking medications) are greatly reduced when families also receive interventions that are designed to reduce aspects of high-EE behavior (e.g., Hogarty et al. 1991, Leff et al. 1982). Typically, such interventions involve providing relatives with education about the illness as well as improving communication skills and problem solving.

When families receive interventions of this kind, 6- to 12-month relapse rates for patients with schizophrenia are around 12.5% (range 0%–33%) compared with relapse rates averaging 42% (range 17%–61%) for patients whose families do not receive such interventions (Miklowitz & Tompson 2003). There is also evidence that family-based interventions improve clinical outcomes for patients with bipolar disorder (Miklowitz et al. 2003) and anorexia nervosa (Eisler et al. 2000). Family interventions can also be successful when conducted with several families at once rather than in a single-family format (e.g., McFarlane et al. 1995, Schooler et al. 1997).

The success of family-based interventions in reducing patients' relapse rates supports the idea that EE may play a causal role in the relapse process. However, care must be taken to avoid an overly simplistic and unidirectional view of EE (see Hooley et al. 1995 for a review). Family-based interventions may benefit families in many ways, and changes in EE are not always necessary for patients to show clinical improvement (see Miklowitz 2004). That EE is a bidirectional construct is now widely accepted (see Hooley et al. 1995, Hooley & Gotlib 2000). Far from being a construct that blames families, EE is perhaps best regarded as "a measure of a set of *patient-relative relationship problems* that are important for the relapse process" (Hooley et al. 2006b). As Miklowitz (2004) has noted, "EE may reflect disturbances in the organization, emotional climate, and transactional patterns of the entire family system, even if it is only measured in a single caregiver."

WHY DO HIGH-EE ATTITUDES DEVELOP?

The measure of EE that researchers obtain from a single relative almost certainly reflects the product of the interaction between the relative and the patient. Conceptualizing EE in this way thus requires a consideration of the characteristics of relatives that might make them more likely to become critical, hostile, or emotionally overinvolved when they have to cope with a psychiatrically impaired family member. In a similar vein, it also calls for a consideration of the characteristics of patients that might present challenges to relatives and thus engender the development of high-EE attitudes in those who are inclined to respond in this way. This type of formulation allows us to move beyond simple trait-versus-state notions of the EE construct and acknowledges the mutual influences of relatives' characteristics and patient factors in the development of this relational variable.

Patient Factors that Contribute to High-EE Attitudes

It might be expected that relatives would be more critical of patients who are more severely ill or who have more symptoms of psychopathology. However, this is generally not the case (Brown et al. 1972, Cutting et al. 2006, Heikkilä et al. 2002, Hooley et al. 1986, Miklowitz et al. 1988, Nuechterlein et al. 1992, Vaughn & Leff 1976). Levels of psychopathology in patients who have low-EE relatives are quite comparable to levels of psychopathology in patients who have high-EE relatives. EE in relatives is also unrelated to the gender of the patient (Davis et al. 1996). Stated simply, EE does not appear to be a simple reaction to specific characteristics of patients. The fact that two relatives of the same patient can sometimes have different levels of EE is further evidence of this (Weisman et al. 2000).

However, although there is notable absence of consistent findings across studies, some isolated reports do link EE to characteristics of patients. Of course, care needs to be taken to avoid relying on relatives' reports here, because these could be correlated with EE for other reasons (the more overwhelmed and upset relatives are, the more they may report problems). Even so, higher levels of criticism have sometimes been linked to patients showing more aggressive or delinquent behavior (Brown et al. 1972) or being less engaged in productive activities such as work (Bentsen et al. 1998, Brown et al. 1972). There are also reports of patients in high-EE families having worse social functioning (Barrowclough & Tarrier 1990) or showing greater irritability (Karno et al. 1987) as well as manifesting other impairments or difficulties (see Hooley et al. 1995 for a more thorough review). Running counter to this general trend of patients in high-EE families having more problems are the reports of better premorbid adjustment (Linszen et al. 1997) and the higher levels of cognitive functioning in patients from high- versus low-EE homes (Bentsen et al. 1998).

When the EE literature is considered overall, there do not appear to be any reliable and specific clinical differences that discriminate between patients from high- and low-EE families. Instead, what may be important is that patients are experiencing symptoms and showing a decline in their functioning. Families are therefore trying to cope with patients whose behavior, for a variety of reasons, may be more difficult and challenging to manage than it was before. Circumstances such as these demand accommodations from close relatives. The willingness and ability of relatives to make such accommodations may underlie the development of high-EE attitudes.

Characteristics of High-EE Relatives

High- and low-EE relatives differ from each other in ways that may have considerable implications for how they try to manage psychopathology in a close family member. For example, Hooley (1998) has reported that high-EE relatives tend to have a more internal locus of control for their own behavior than do low-EE relatives. In other words, they tend to take an active role in managing their own life problems and difficulties. Low-EE relatives, in contrast, are more fatalistic. Moreover, on self-report measures of personality, high-EE relatives tend to score in ways that suggest they are more conscientious (King et al. 2003) as well as less tolerant and less flexible in their approach to life than are low-EE relatives (Hooley & Hiller 2000). This lack of tolerance may also be self-directed, and could explain Docherty et al.'s (1998) finding of higher levels of self-criticism in high- versus low-EE relatives.

Other researchers note that high-EE relatives report feeling more burdened in the caretaking role than do their low-EE counterparts and experience more distress (Barrowclough & Parle 1997, Scazufca & Kuipers 1996, Tarrier et al. 2002). However, the possible overlap between high-EE behavior and the voicing of subjective distress is important to keep in mind here. Tarrier et al. (2002) failed to find significant associations between EE and levels of salivary cortisol (an objective measure of stress) in the relatives of patients with Alzheimer's disease. Moreover, although high EE was associated with relatives reporting that patients had more symptoms, no patient differences were found across levels of EE when independent clinicians rated symptoms (Tarrier et al. 2002). Taken together, these findings suggest that high levels of EE may serve to identify relatives who are suffering more and experiencing more difficulty in the caretaking role. This may be because, unlike low-EE relatives, they have personalities that make them less able to accept the status quo and because they are inclined to adopt a more hands-on as opposed to a more relaxed coping style.

It warrants mention that high-EE relatives do not have more individual psychopathology than low-EE relatives do. Although it is plausible to suggest that high-EE relatives are more negative in their attitudes toward patients because they have higher levels of depression, no empirical support for this hypothesis has been found. Goldstein et al. (2002) conducted clinical interviews with relatives and examined the association between EE and the presence of current or past DSM-IV psychopathology. There was no evidence of any link. This suggests that personality rather than psychopathology is most important. As Leff & Vaughn presciently noted many years ago:

> A critical response depended less on the degree of the patients' disturbance than on the relative's own personality. If a relative was easy going, he or she tended to adopt a noncritical stance. If a relative was typically tense or moody when stressed, the strain of coping with someone psychiatrically ill could result in feelings of anger. (Leff & Vaughn 1985, p. 67)

Attributions and EE

If high-EE relatives are less tolerant, less flexible, and more confident in their ability to take action to manage problematic situations, what are the implications of this for the patients with whom they live? Hooley (1985) was the first to suggest that high levels of EE (particularly criticism) might be linked to a desire on the part of relatives to get the patient to behave differently and that this might be linked to controlling behavior on the part of the relative. This idea was later developed into a model of EE based on attributions (see Hooley 1987).

Central to the attribution model of EE is the idea that high- and low-EE relatives differ in their underlying beliefs about why patients might be experiencing problems or difficulties and what should be done about it. Even when they accept that the patient has a severe mental illness, high-EE relatives tend to be more likely to believe that more could be done to exert some control (however minimal) over a problematic situation to improve things. Accordingly, they have higher expectations for patients, make more attributions of control in situations involving the patient, and become more frustrated and controlling in their own behavior when patients fail to behave in the ways that relatives think would be helpful.

Empirical tests of this model of EE suggest that it has considerable validity (see Barrowclough & Hooley 2003 for a review). Several investigators have examined the spontaneous speech of the relatives of patients with schizophrenia and coded it for its attribution content. When they were discussing problem situations involving the patient, high-EE relatives of patients with schizophrenia were more likely than low-EE relatives to make attributions to factors they believed were controllable by patients (Barrowclough et al. 1994, 2005; Brewin et al. 1991; Weisman et al. 1993). Similar findings have also been reported for the high-EE relatives of unipolar and bipolar depressed patients (Hooley & Licht 1997, Wendel et al. 2000). Using a self-report measure, Hinrichsen and colleagues (Hinrichsen et al. 2004) have also shown that blaming attributions are associated with high levels of EE in the family members of depressed older adults.

BEHAVIOR OF HIGH- AND LOW-EE RELATIVES

A major assumption in the early research on EE was that the critical attitudes expressed by relatives during the course of a private interview were reflective of their behavior when they interacted with patients. Studies have now demonstrated the concurrent validity of EE for schizophrenia (Hahlweg et al. 1989, Miklowitz et al. 1995), unipolar depression (Hooley 1986), bipolar disorder (Miklowitz et al. 1995), and anxiety disorders (Chambless et al. 2006).

In the typical study, patients and their family members are videotaped during a face-to-face interaction and independent raters subsequently code their behaviors. Using this design, researchers have demonstrated that high-EE relatives are more critical during face-to-face interactions with patients than are low-EE relatives (Hahlweg et al. 1989, Hooley 1986, Miklowitz et al. 1995). They also tend to disagree with patients more readily and they show lower levels of accepting behavior (Hooley 1986). Moreover, not just the relatives are negative. Interactions involving high-EE relatives are characterized by more reciprocal negativity and less positive reciprocity than those involving low-EE relatives (Hahlweg et al. 1989, Hooley 1990, Simoneau et al. 1998). This means that regardless of whether the patient or the relative initiates a negative behavior, a negative interaction sequence is much more likely to be prolonged if a high-EE family member is involved. When interactions involve low-EE family members, however, negative interaction sequences are less likely to start and, once begun, are quickly terminated.

CHANGES IN EE OVER TIME

If EE is a relational construct that signifies problems in the patient-relative relationship, we might expect that EE levels would change over time if the nature of the relationship between the patient and the relative also changes. On the other hand, if certain aspects of temperament or personality underlie the development of high-EE attitudes, we might also expect some stability in EE across time. Stated differently, we might predict that EE would be both a stable and a dynamic construct with some state-like and trait-like properties (Hooley & Gotlib 2000).

The available evidence on the temporal stability of EE is highly consistent with this formulation. EE levels have been shown to decrease after relatives receive family-based interventions (Hogarty et al. 1991, Leff et al. 1982). Moreover, even in the absence of any formal intervention, there can be spontaneous change (Brown et al. 1972, Tarrier et al. 1988a). When EE assessments are repeated 9–12 months after patients have left the hospital (and presumably entered a period of symptomatic improvement), somewhere between 25% and 50% of relatives who were previously classified as high in EE are rated as being low in EE. Changes in the opposite direction (i.e., from low to high EE) also occur, although these are much less frequent.

The fact that EE levels decline when patients are less symptomatic provides support for the idea that relatives' critical attitudes are, at least in part, a response to aspects or correlates of the patients' illnesses. However, there is also some evidence suggesting that the tendency to be critical about patients may have some stability. Hooley and colleagues assessed EE in relatives around the time that patients were admitted to the hospital and again three months after the patient returned home (see Hooley et al. 1995). The mean number of critical remarks that relatives made about patients dropped considerably between the two assessments (11.3 versus 4.3). Nonetheless, there was a high correlation ($r = 0.74$) between how many criticisms relatives made initially and how many they made at the follow-up assessment. This suggests that, although relatives become less critical of patients when patients are doing better, relatives also show stability in terms of how critical they are inclined to be. Put another way, the most critical relatives at the first assessment are still the most critical relatives at the second assessment, even though the number of critical remarks they make overall has declined sharply.

Taken together, the empirical evidence suggests that EE levels can change over time, with relatives tending to be more critical during periods of greater stress and becoming less critical as patients show clinical improvement. In addition to these short-term fluctuations, however, there is also some evidence that families may become more critical over time as a consequence of increased exposure to psychopathology. Using cross-sectional data, Hooley & Richters (1995) compared the number of critical comments made by the relatives of schizophrenia patients who had recently become ill with the number of critical comments made by relatives of patients who had been ill for much longer periods of time. Relatives who had been coping with the illness for less than a year made an average of 4.2 critical comments. In contrast, those who had been coping with the illness for three to five years made an average number of 15 critical remarks during the EE interview.

Although longitudinal studies are clearly needed to examine the issue in a more methodologically rigorous manner, these preliminary findings suggest that there is a developmental component to expressed emotion. Over time, and in the face of chronic exposure to psychopathology, there may well be a tendency for the family climate to deteriorate. This speaks to the importance of early intervention with the families of patients with major mental illnesses.

THEORETICAL SYNTHESIS AND SUMMARY

EE is a complex construct. It is measured in an individual relative of a person with psychopathology. However, EE is a relational variable that reflects important aspects of the patient-relative interaction. EE does not cause psychopathology de novo. However, for people who have a vulnerability to psychopathology, high EE is a well-replicated risk factor for relapse.

EE can also change over time. EE levels show a tendency to decrease over the shorter term (i.e., across illness and recovery periods) but also to increase gradually over the longer term, perhaps as function of continued exposure to psychopathology. This indicates that EE has a reactive component. However, there is also evidence that EE has some trait-like aspects as well.

How can we best understand and organize these rather diverse observations? The most accepted theoretical model to date is the diathesis-stress attribution model of EE (Hooley 1987, Hooley & Gotlib 2000). This holds that certain characteristics of relatives (e.g., internal locus of control, a more inflexible personality style) render them more vulnerable to responding to patients' behavioral difficulties or functional impairments in a manner that is designed to create change. This may be because the personality traits that underlie high-EE attitudes make relatives less willing to tolerate or otherwise accommodate to behaviors they perceive as undesirable. Accordingly, when patients exhibit behaviors that these relatives do not like, they make efforts to get the patient to behave differently.

It is very important to keep in mind that high-EE relatives are not bad or difficult people. In fact, in most of the industrialized world, high-EE attitudes are more normative than are low-EE attitudes (Hooley et al. 1995). Moreover, the impression one gets from conversations with high-EE relatives is that the vast majority of them are highly motivated to help the patient. They are also very involved with the patient's care (van Os et al. 2001). In contrast to low-EE relatives, however, high-EE family members seem to have distinct and definite ideas about what needs to be done to improve the current situation. This may be linked to their more internal locus of control and the more active and problem-solving approach they take when dealing with life's difficulties. The desire to change bad situations and the beliefs that there are things that patients can and should do to effect positive change in their circumstances are thought to be at the heart of why relatives develop critical attitudes.

Although the majority of relatives are initially low in EE, EE levels tend to rise gradually over time. This may be because, over time, the well-intentioned efforts of high-EE relatives to get patients to function better do not lead to the kind of successful outcomes for which they are striving. As a result, it is natural for relatives to become more frustrated, critical, and blaming. The fact that the majority of relatives end up being high in EE over time speaks volumes about the difficulties inherent in trying to cope with psychopathology in a loved one.

CROSS-CULTURAL ASPECTS

The construct of EE has been studied in countries all over the world, including the United Kingdom, the United States, Australia, Denmark, Poland, India, Egypt, Israel, China, Japan, and Iran. EE has also been examined in a number of ethnic minority groups. Space does not permit a full review of the findings from cross-cultural research on EE (see Bhugra & McKenzie 2003 or Hashemi & Cochrane 1999 for reviews). However, a few general comments warrant mention.

As Jenkins & Karno (1992) have observed, culture defines the kinds of behaviors that warrant criticism. In light of this, it is hardly surprising that levels of criticism vary across cultures. Levels of EE are lower in India than they are the United Kingdom and the United States, for example (Leff et al. 1987). Moreover, the majority of relatives of Latino patients with schizophrenia are classified as low rather than high in EE (Weisman et al. 2003). In contrast, Hashemi & Cochrane (1999) reported that 80% of the relatives of British Pakistani patients with schizophrenia were rated as being high EE compared with 45% of white and 30% of British Sikh families. A major difference was how relatives in these different ethnic groups scored on the EE component of emotional overinvolvement. Whereas the modal score for the white and Sikh families was 1 (EOI is rated on a 0–5 scale), the modal score for the Pakistani families was 4. These findings highlight the role of culture in the expression of critical or emotionally overinvolved attitudes. They also speak to the importance of understanding cultural factors before beginning interventions with the families of patients from different ethnic groups.

Culture also appears to moderate the EE-relapse relationship. Although EE has been shown to predict more negative clinical outcomes in samples of schizophrenia patients in places such as Japan (Tanaka et al. 1995), India (Leff et al. 1987), Egypt (Kamal 1995), and Iran (Mottaghipour et al. 2001), the components of EE differ with regard to their predictive validity. In Indian families, for example, the presence of hostility is most associated with relapse (Leff et al. 1987). In Japan, patients who are living in high-EOI homes may be at the greatest risk (see Tanaka et al. 1995). In Egypt, there seems to be no association between EOI and relapse (Kamal 1995). There is also some evidence that patients in Egypt are able to tolerate higher levels of criticism than is typical of patients in Western samples (see Hashemi & Cochrane 1999).

Overall, the available data suggest that the prevalence of high-EE attitudes varies across cultures. Given this, it is not surprising that different cutting scores are often used to define high or low EE in cross-cultural studies. In some ethnic groups, high levels of criticism or emotional overinvolvement may be more culturally accepted than in other minority groups (see Bhugra & McKenzie 2003, Rosenfarb et al. 2004). Nonetheless, there appears to be some general support for the conclusion that the EE-relapse association replicates across cultures. The meaning of EE, however, is likely to be influenced by a broad array of cultural factors (Jenkins & Karno 1992). Understanding the cross-cultural aspects of the construct is now an active research area (Nomura et al. 2005, Yang et al. 2004).

WHY DOES EE PREDICT RELAPSE?

Mechanisms of Action

Prevailing models of the EE-relapse association conceptualize EE as a form of stress for patients. In his early study, Brown speculated that high levels of EE might provide too much stress for patients vulnerable to schizophrenia (Brown et al. 1972). Subsequent discussions of this issue have stayed close to such a formulation (Nuechterlein & Dawson 1984).

The idea that high-EE environments are stressful for patients is supported by the findings from several empirical studies. Depressed patients who are married to high EE spouses report more problems in their relationship than do patients with low-EE spouses (Hooley & Teasdale 1989). In a related vein, Cutting et al. (2006) found that patients with schizophrenia reported feeling more stressed by their interactions with high-EE parents, siblings, spouses, or romantic partners than patients with low-EE relatives or partners did. Kuipers et al. (2006) noted that patients reported feeling more anxious if they had caretakers who were rated as more critical. Patients with schizophrenia also recalled more negative and fewer positive memories of high-EE relatives of than-low EE relatives (Cutting & Docherty 2000).

These empirical observations mesh well with the general perception patients report that high-EE relatives are less tolerant, more intrusive, and have higher expectations than do low-EE relatives (Kazarian et al. 1990). What is interesting is that high-EE relatives also describe themselves as being more behaviorally controlling in their interactions with patients than do low-EE relatives (Hooley & Campbell 2002). The fact that relatives' controlling behaviors also predict relapse in patients with schizophrenia (see Hooley & Campbell 2002) lends further support to the idea that something in the interaction styles of high-EE relatives that may provide too much stress for vulnerable patients.

Care must be taken to avoid overgeneralizations, however. Hooley & Campbell (2002) did not find that controlling behaviors on the part of high-EE relatives predicted relapse in patients with depression. This again highlights the importance of considering characteristics of the patients' underlying psychopathology in any discussion of the mechanisms through which EE is linked to relapse (see Hooley & Gotlib 2000).

Psychophysiological Studies and Patient Arousal

A major assumption with regard to the mechanism of action of EE in schizophrenia is that autonomic hyperarousal mediates the effects of psychosocial stress on a person vulnerable to the disorder and eventually produces relapse (see Tarrier & Turpin 1992). In their efforts to test this hypothesis, researchers have used psychophysiological techniques to measure arousal in patients with schizophrenia during interactions with their high- or low-EE relatives.

In general, the empirical findings are consistent with the idea that interactions with high-EE relatives are more stressful for patients than are interactions with low-EE relatives. Tarrier et al. (1979) measured skin conductance and blood pressure in remitted schizophrenia patients who were tested in their own homes. Psychophysiological data were collected for 15 minutes while patients were in the company of the experimenter and then for 15 minutes after high- or low-EE relatives entered the room. There were no differences between the patients prior to the entry of the relatives. However, after the entry of high-EE relatives, patients showed an increase in diastolic blood pressure; in contrast, after the entry of their low-EE relatives, patients showed a decrease in electrodermal arousal (measured as reduced spontaneous fluctuations in skin conductance). Later testing in a laboratory setting revealed no overall differences between patients with high and low EE relatives for such variables as heart rate, EEG, or electrodermal activity.

Similar results have also been obtained when this kind of experimental design is used with acutely ill patients (Sturgeon et al. 1981, Tarrier et al. 1988b). Although patients in the acute phase of illness generally have higher levels of electrodermal arousal than do patients in remission, the entry of low-EE relatives seems to facilitate habituation to the novel testing situation in both ill and remitted patients. In contrast, the presence of a high-EE relative is associated with continued arousal.

These differences in electrodermal reactivity to high- and low-EE relatives were nicely demonstrated in a single case design involving a 29-year-old male patient who was suffering from schizophrenia (Tarrier & Barrowclough 1984). Skin conductance measurements were taken when the patient was in the presence of a neutral experimenter, alone with his low-EE father, and alone with his high-EE mother. The patient showed a similar number of spontaneous skin conductance

fMRI: functional magnetic resonance imaging

DLPFC: dorsolateral prefrontal cortex

fluctuations when he was talking with the experimenter and when he was with his low-EE father. When in the company of his high-EE mother, however, the patient showed significantly more electrodermal arousal than at any other time.

The data are therefore consistent with the idea that something about the presence of high-EE relatives may be stressful or arousing for patients. The presence of low-EE relatives, on the other hand, may be calming and facilitate habituation to a novel situation. There is also some evidence that patients with schizophrenia and bipolar disorder show increased cardiovascular activity immediately after their relatives direct critical, intrusive, or guilt-inducing comments toward them (Altorfer et al. 1998). Moreover, electrodermal reactivity to the presence of a high-EE relative has been shown to be predictive of later relapse (Sturgeon et al. 1984). Although we are still far from a good understanding of the mechanisms through which EE is linked to relapse, the idea that EE is a form of psychosocial stress that has biological consequences for vulnerable patients is consistent with the available data.

Neuroimaging Approaches

What happens in the brains of healthy people and people vulnerable to psychopathology when they are exposed to criticism? New studies in EE research are now exploring this question using functional magnetic resonance imaging (fMRI). Such approaches are exciting because they provide a bridge between traditional EE research and the growing interest in social cognitive neuroscience.

Using a novel paradigm, Hooley et al. (2005) have collected brain-imaging data from research participants who received brain scans while their mothers were criticizing them. Some of the research participants were healthy controls who had no history of psychopathology. Others were young adults who were fully well but who had previously experienced one or more episodes of clinical depression. While they were lying in the MRI scanner, all of the subjects heard the voice of their own mothers coming through the headphones. In some trials, mothers made remarks that were critical of their offspring. In other trials, mothers made positive and praising comments. Importantly, each comment was individually tailored to be relevant to the particular subject.

What effect did hearing these affectively challenging stimuli have on the research participants? When they were exposed to criticism from their mothers, the healthy controls showed activation of dorsolateral prefrontal cortex (DLPFC), an area of the brain that is involved in cognitive and emotional processing. What was striking about the recovered depressed participants, however, was that they failed to activate DLPFC when they were exposed to criticism.

These findings are interesting because positron emission tomography and fMRI studies have shown abnormal blood flow in depressed patients in multiple prefrontal regions, including DLPFC (Davidson et al. 2002). Hooley et al.'s (2005) findings provide support for the idea that abnormalities in neural pathways involving the DLPFC are associated with vulnerability to depression and that exposure to criticism can lead to perturbations in these neural circuits, even when formerly depressed people are fully well.

CONCLUSIONS AND FUTURE DIRECTIONS

In his pioneering work on the development of the EE construct, Brown (1985) sought to develop a measure that would reflect the feelings and emotions that were characteristic of normal families who were facing the challenge of coping with mental illness. In this regard, he was successful. High levels of EE are normative in industrialized countries. Moreover, people who have high levels of EE have characteristics, such as an internally based locus of control, that are widely valued in modern culture and that probably serve them well in many areas of their lives.

The skills needed to cope with psychopathology in a loved one, however, are not always intuitive or obvious. In some cases, less is more. High-EE relatives, in their efforts to help patients function better, may sometimes try too hard. Over time, well-meaning suggestions may evolve into critical comments and controlling behaviors. The result of this very natural process is a family environment that is stressful for relatives and patients alike.

One clear benefit of EE research is that it has been the catalyst for the development of several types of family-based intervention programs (Leff et al. 1982, McFarlane et al. 1995). These have provided benefits for both patients and relatives. In addition to treatment programs for patients with schizophrenia, psychosocial treatment approaches have now been developed for families of patients with mood disorders (e.g., Miklowitz et al. 2003) and are also being implemented for family members of patients with borderline personality disorder (Hoffman et al. 2005).

Not only has EE research been extended to more and more disorders, but it also has been expanded to include assessments of hospital staff members who interact with patients on a regular basis (e.g., Moore et al. 1992). This is important, not least because it destigmatizes high-EE families. Research of this kind makes it clear that even trained professionals are not immune to the development of high-EE attitudes and behaviors. It also makes the EE construct more clinically relevant for patients who do not reside with their families.

The stress associated with high-EE home environments appears to be a major reason why patients with a range of psychopathological conditions are at increased risk of relapse if they are exposed to critical, hostile, or intrusive family members. Yet the mechanisms through which a psychosocial event like criticism can culminate in a biobehavioral outcome like symptom relapse remain relatively unexplored. By employing challenge paradigms based on the EE construct, researchers are now bringing a decades-old construct into the era of affective neuroscience. Those interested in this psychosocial risk factor are now well positioned to make important contributions to an understanding of the perturbations in neural circuitry that might be implicated in relapse of schizophrenia, depression, and other disorders. Moreover, by exploring the neural correlates of such EE components as criticism and emotional overinvolvement, we may learn much about the links between interpersonal experience and the neurobiology of relapse. We may also learn about the patient factors that moderate the appraisal or processing of affectively charged emotional stimuli leading to more benign or more negative clinical outcomes. Why, for example, does criticism predict relapse in major depression but not in borderline personality disorder, even though the rate of comorbidity between these two disorders is very high? By exploring how healthy people and people with different forms of psychopathology respond to such elements of EE as criticism, emotional overinvolvement, and warmth, researchers may be able to learn much about the neural circuitry that underlies vulnerability to a wide range of psychopathological conditions.

Finally, it warrants mention that EE is a construct that lends itself well to research designs that seek to explore gene x environment interactions. Of interest here is the now-replicated finding that a functional polymorphism in the promoter region of the serotonin transporter (5-HTT) gene renders people more susceptible to depression in the face of stressful life events (Caspi et al. 2003, Wilhelm et al. 2006). Examining the possible consequences of an ongoing stressor such as EE in the context of differential genetic susceptibility to depression is an obvious next step.

SUMMARY POINTS

1. High levels of expressed emotion predict relapse in patients with schizophrenia, mood disorders, eating disorders, posttraumatic stress disorder, and substance abuse disorders. For patients with anxiety disorders receiving exposure treatment, higher levels of criticism may be beneficial, although high levels of hostility are not.
2. High levels of emotional overinvolvement predict better clinical outcome for patients with borderline personality disorder.
3. Expressed emotion (EE) is an independent predictor of relapse even when clinical factors in patients are considered and are statistically controlled.
4. EE is both a reaction to patients' psychopathology as well as a link to characteristics of the relatives themselves. Bidirectional processes are at work in the development of high-EE attitudes. High-EE attitudes also tend to rise over time, probably as a consequence of continued exposure to psychopathology.
5. Interventions that improve family communication and problem solving skills tend to lower EE levels and improve the family environment more generally. Relapse rates in patients are reduced when families receive this kind of help.
6. Interactions between patients and high-EE relatives involve more negative and less positive behavior. This is reciprocal, and it involves the patient as well as the family member.
7. Psychophysiological data show that patients are more aroused when they are interacting with high-EE family members. Patients also report feeling more stressed when they are with high- versus low-EE relatives.
8. New research is using neuroimaging approaches to explore how people who are vulnerable to psychopathology respond to the challenge of being criticized. This research may help us lean more about the neurobiology of relapse. However, the mechanism through which EE and relapse are linked is still unknown.

LITERATURE CITED

Almond S, Knapp M, Francois C, Toumi M, Brugha T. 2004. Relapse in schizophrenia: costs, clinical outcomes and quality of life. *Br. J. Psychiatry* 184:346–51

Altorfer A, Kasermann ML, Hirsbrunner H. 1998. Arousal and communication: 1. The relationship between nonverbal, behavioral, and psychophysiological indices of the stress response. *J. Psychophysiol.* 12:40–59

Asarnow JR, Goldstein MJ, Tompson M, Guthrie D. 1993. One-year outcomes of depressive disorders in child psychiatric in-patients: evaluation of the prognostic power of a brief measure of expressed emotion. *J. Child Psychol. Psychiatry* 34:129–37

Barrowclough C, Hooley JM. 2003. Attributions and expressed emotion: a review. *Clin. Psychol. Rev.* 23:849–980

Barrowclough C, Johnston M, Tarrier N. 1994. Attributions, expressed emotion and patient relapse: an attributional model of relatives' response to schizophrenic illness. *Behav. Ther.* 25:67–88

Barrowclough C, Parle M. 1997. Appraisal, psychological adjustment and expressed emotion in relatives of patients suffering from schizophrenia. *Br. J. Psychiatry* 171:26–30

Barrowclough C, Tarrier N. 1990. Social functioning in schizophrenia patients. I. The effects of expressed emotion and family intervention. *Soc. Psychiatry Psychiatr. Epidemiol.* 25:125–29

Barrowclough C, Ward J, Wearden A, Gregg L. 2005. Expressed emotion and attributions in relatives of schizophrenia patients with and without substance misuse. *Soc. Psychiatry Psychiatr. Epidemiol.* 40:884–91

Bentsen H, Notland TH, Boye B, Munkvold OG, Bjorge H, et al. 1998. Criticism and hostility in relatives of patients with schizophrenia or related psychoses: demographic and clinical predictors. *Acta Psychiatr. Scand.* 97:76–85

Bhugra D, McKenzie K. 2003. Expressed emotion across cultures. *Adv. Psychiatr. Treat.* 9:342–48

Brewin CR, MacCarthy B, Duda K, Vaughn CE. 1991. Attribution and expressed emotion in the relatives of patients with schizophrenia. *J. Abnorm. Psychol.* 100:546–54

Brown GW. 1985. The discovery of expressed emotion: induction or deduction? In *Expressed Emotion in Families*, ed. J Leff, C Vaughn, pp. 7–25. New York: Guilford

Brown GW, Birley JLT, Wing JK. 1972. Influence of family life on the course of schizophrenic disorders: a replication. *Br. J. Psychiatry* 121:241–58

First study to demonstrate the link between family expressed emotion and relapse in patients with schizophrenia.

Brown GW, Carstairs GM, Topping G. 1958. Post hospital adjustment of chronic mental patients. *Lancet* ii:685–89

Brown GW, Rutter M. 1966. The measurement of family activities and relationships: a methodological study. *Hum. Relat.* 19:241–63

Butzlaff RL, Hooley JM. 1998. Expressed emotion and psychiatric relapse. *Arch. Gen. Psychiatry* 55:547–52

A meta-analysis providing the effect sizes associated with the expressed emotion/relapse relationship for schizophrenia, mood disorders, and eating disorders.

Caspi A, Sugden K, Moffitt TE, Taylor A, Craig IW, et al. 2003. Influence of life stress on depression: moderation by a polymorphism in the 5-HTT gene. *Science* 301(5631):386–89

Chambless DL, Floyd F, Rodebaugh TL, Steketee G. 2006. Expressed emotion and familial interaction: a study with agoraphobic and obsessive-compulsive patients and their relatives. Manuscr. submitted

Chambless DL, Steketee G. 1999. Expressed emotion and behavior therapy outcome: a prospective study with obsessive-compulsive and agoraphobic outpatients. *J. Consult. Clin. Psychol.* 67:658–65

Cole JD, Kazarian SS. 1988. The Level of Expressed Emotion Scale: a new measure of expressed emotion. *J. Clin. Psychol.* 44:392–97

Cutting LP, Aakre JM, Docherty NM. 2006. Schizophrenic patients' perceptions of stress, expressed emotion, and sensitivity to criticism. *Schizophr. Bull.* 32:743–50

Cutting LP, Docherty NM. 2000. Schizophrenia outpatients' perceptions of their parents: Is expressed emotion a factor? *J. Abnorm. Psychol.* 109:266–72

Davidson RJ, Pizzagalli D, Nitschke JB, Putnam K. 2002. Depression: perspectives from affective neuroscience. *Annu. Rev. Psychol.* 53:545–74

Davis JA, Goldstein MJ, Nuechterlein KH. 1996. Gender differences in family attitudes about schizophrenia. *Psychol. Med.* 26:689–96

Docherty NM, Cutting LP, Bers SA. 1998. Expressed emotion and differentiation of self in the relatives of stable schizophrenia outpatients. *Psychiatry* 61:269–78

Eisler I, Dare C, Hodes M, Russell G, Dodge E, LeGrande D. 2000. Family therapy for adolescent anorexia nervosa: the results of a controlled comparison of two family interventions. *J. Child. Psychol. Psychiatry* 6:727–36

Fichter MM, Glynn SM, Weyerer S, Liberman RP, Frick U. 1997. Family climate and expressed emotion in the course of alcoholism. *Fam. Process.* 36:203–21

Fischmann-Havstad L, Marston AR. 1984. Weight loss maintenance as an aspect of family emotion and process. *Br. J. Clin. Psychol.* 23:265–71

Fish EW, Shahrokh D, Bagot R, Caldji C, Bredy T, et al. 2004. Epigenetic programming of stress responses through variations in maternal care. *Ann. NY Acad. Sci.* 1036:167–80

Flanagan DA, Wagner HL. 1991. Expressed emotion and panic-fear in the prediction of diet treatment compliance. *Br. J. Clin. Psychol.* 30:231–40

Fogler JM, Tompson MC, Steketee G, Hofmann SG. 2007. Influence of expressed emotion and perceived criticism on cognitive-behavioral therapy for social phobia. *Behav. Res. Ther.* 45(2):235–39

Goldstein MJ, Talovic SA, Nuechterlein KH, Fogelson DL, Subotnik KL, et al. 1992. Family interaction versus individual psychopathology. Do they indicate the same processes in the families of schizophrenics? *Br. J. Psychiatry* 161:98–102

Goldstein TR, Miklowitz DJ, Richards JA. 2002. The relationship between expressed emotion attitudes and individual psychopathology among relatives of bipolar patients. *Fam. Process.* 41:647–59

Hahlweg K, Goldstein MJ, Nuechterlein KH, Magaña AB, Mintz J, et al. 1989. Expressed emotion and patient-relative interaction in families of recent-onset schizophrenics. *J. Consult. Clin. Psychol.* 57:11–18

Hashemi AH, Cochrane R. 1999. Expressed emotion and schizophrenia: a review of studies across cultures. *Int. Rev. Psychiatry* 11:219–24

Hayhurst H, Cooper Z, Paykel ES, Vearnals S, Ramana R. 1997. Expressed emotion and depression. *Br. J. Psychiatry* 171:439–43

Hedlund S, Fichter MM, Quadflieg N, Brandl C. 2003. Expressed emotion, family environment, and parental bonding in bulimia nervosa: a 6-year investigation. *Eat. Weight Disord.* 8:26–35

Heikkilä J, Karlsson H, Taiminen T, Lauerma H, Ilonen T, et al. 2002. Expressed emotion is not associated with disorder severity in first-episode mental disorder. *Psychiatr. Res.* 111:155–65

Hinrichsen GA, Adelstein L, McMeniman M. 2004. Expressed emotion in family members of depressed older adults. *Aging Mental Health* 8:355–63

Hirshfeld DR, Biederman J, Brody L, Faraone SV, Rosenbaum JF. 1997. Associations between expressed emotion and child behavioral inhibition and psychopathology: a pilot study. *J. Am. Acad. Child Adolesc. Psychiatry* 36:205–13

Hoffman PD, Fruzzetti AE, Buteau E, Neiditch ER, Penney D, et al. 2005. Family connections: a program for relatives of persons with borderline personality disorder. *Fam. Process.* 44:217–25

Hogarty GE, Anderson CM, Reiss DJ, Kornblith SJ, Greenwald DP, et al. 1991. Family psychoeducation, social skills training, and maintenance chemotherapy in the aftercare of schizophrenia. *Arch. Gen. Psychiatry* 48:340–47

Hooley JM. 1985. Expressed emotion: a review of the critical literature. *Clin. Psychol. Rev.* 5:119–39

Hooley JM. 1986. Expressed emotion and depression: interactions between patients and high-versus low-expressed emotion spouses. *J. Abnorm. Psychol.* 95:237–46

Hooley JM. 1987. The nature and origins of expressed emotion. In *Understanding Major Mental Disorder: The Contribution of Family Interaction Research*, ed. MJ Goldstein, K Hahlweg, pp. 176–94. New York: Family Process Press

Hooley JM. 1990. Expressed emotion and depression. In *Depression and Families: Impact and Treatment*, ed. GI Keitner, pp. 57–83. Washington, DC: Am. Psychiatr. Press

Hooley JM. 1998. Expressed emotion and locus of control. *J. Nerv. Ment. Dis.* 186:374–78

Hooley JM, Campbell C. 2002. Control and controllability: an examination of beliefs and behavior in high and low expressed emotion relatives. *Psychol. Med.* 32:1091–99

Hooley JM, Gotlib IH. 2000. A diathesis-stress conceptualization of expressed emotion and clinical outcome. *Appl. Prev. Psychol.* 9:135–51

Hooley JM, Gruber SA, Scott LA, Hiller JB, Yurgelun-Todd DA. 2005. Activation in dorsolateral prefrontal cortex in response to maternal criticism and praise in recovered depressed and healthy control participants. *Biol. Psychiatry* 57:809–12

Hooley JM, Hiller JB. 2000. Expressed emotion and personality. *J. Abnorm. Psychol.* 109:40–44

Hooley JM, Hoffman PD. 1999. Expressed emotion and clinical outcome of borderline personality disorder. *Am. J. Psychiatry* 156:1557–62

Hooley JM, Licht DM. 1997. Expressed emotion and causal attributions in the spouses of depressed patients. *J. Abnorm. Psychol.* 106:298–306

Hooley JM, Miklowitz DM, Beach SRH. 2006. Expressed emotion and the DSM-V. In *Relational Processes and DSM-V: Neuroscience, Assessment, Prevention and Intervention*, ed. SRH Beach, M Wamboldt, N Kaslow, RE Heyman, MB First, LG Underwood, D Reiss, pp. 175–91. Washington, DC: Am. Psychiatr. Press

Hooley JM, Orley J, Teasdale JD. 1986. Levels of expressed emotion and relapse in depressed patients. *Br. J. Psychiatry* 148:642–47

Hooley JM. Parker HA. 2006. Measuring expressed emotion: an evaluation of the shortcuts. *J. Fam. Psychol.* 20:386–96

Hooley JM, Richters JE. 1995. Expressed emotion: a developmental perspective. In *Rochester Symposium on Developmental Psychopathology*, ed. D Cicchetti, SL Toth, vol. 6, pp. 133–66. Rochester, NY: Univ. Roch. Press

Hooley JM, Rosen LR, Richters JE. 1995. Expressed emotion: toward clarification of a critical construct. In *The Behavioral High Risk Paradigm in Psychopathology*, ed. G Miller, pp. 88–120. New York: Springer-Verlag

Hooley JM, Teasdale JD. 1989. Predictors of relapse in unipolar depressives: expressed emotion, marital distress, and perceived criticism. *J. Abnorm. Psychol.* 98:229–35

Jarbin H, Grawe RW, Hansson K. 2000. Expressed emotion and prediction of relapse in adolescents with psychotic disorders. *Nord. J. Psychiatry* 54:201–5

Jenkins JH, Karno M. 1992. The meaning of expressed emotion: theoretical issues raised by cross-cultural research. *Am. J. Psychiatry* 149:9–21

Kamal A. 1995. Variables in expressed emotion associated with relapse: a comparison between depressed and schizophrenic samples in an Egyptian community. *Curr. Psychiatry* 2:211–16

Kandel ER. 1998. A new intellectual framework for psychiatry. *Am. J. Psychiatry* 155:457–69

Karno M, Jenkins JH, De La Selva A, Santana F, Telles C, et al. 1987. Expressed emotion and schizophrenic outcome among Mexican-American families. *J. Nerv. Ment. Dis.* 175:143–51

Kavanagh DJ, O'Halloran P, Manicavasagar V, Clark D, Piatkowska O, et al. 1997. The Family Attitude Scale: reliability and validity of a new scale for measuring the emotional climate of families. *Psychiatr. Res.* 70:185–95

Kazarian SS, Malla AK, Cole JD, Baker B. 1990. Comparisons of two expressed emotion scales with the Camberwell Family Interview. *J. Clin. Psychol.* 46:306–9

King S, Lesage AD, Lalonde P. 1994. Psychiatrists' ratings of expressed emotion. *Can. J. Psychiatry* 39:358–60

King S, Ricard N, Richon V, Steiger H, Nelis S. 2003. Determinants of expressed emotion in mothers of schizophrenia patients. *Psychiatr. Res.* 117:211–22

Kuipers E, Bebbington P, Dunn G, Fowler D, Freeman D, et al. 2006. Influence of carer expressed emotion and affect on relapse in non-affective psychosis. *Br. J. Psychiatry* 188:173–79

Leff J, Kuipers L, Berkowitz R, Eberlein-Vries R, Sturgeon D. 1982. A controlled trial of social intervention in the families of schizophrenic patients. *Br. J. Psychiatry* 141:121–34

Leff J, Wig NN, Ghosh A, Bedi H, Menon DK, et al. 1987. Influence of relatives' expressed emotion on the course of schizophrenia in Chandigarh. *Br. J. Psychiatry* 151:166–73

First study to show that expressed emotion predicted relapse in a non-Western culture.

Leff J, Vaughn C. 1985. *Expressed Emotion in Families*. New York: Guilford

LeGrange D, Eisler I, Dare C, Hodes M. 1992. Family criticism and self-starvation: a study of expressed emotion. *J. Fam. Ther.* 14:177–92

Linszen DH, Dingemans PM, Nugter MA, Van der Does AJW, Scholte, et al. 1997. Patient attributes and expressed emotion as risk factors for psychotic relapse. *Schizophr. Bull.* 23:119–30

Linszen DH, Dingemans PM, Van der Does JW, Nugter A, Scholte P, et al. 1996. Treatment, expressed emotion and relapse in recent onset schizophrenic disorders. *Psychol. Med.* 26:333–42

Lopez SR, Nelson HK, Polo AJ, Jenkins JH, Karno M, et al. 2004. Ethnicity, expressed emotion, attributions, and course of schizophrenia: family warmth matters. *J. Abnorm. Psychol.* 11:428–39

McFarlane WR, Lukens E, Link B, Dushay R, Deakins S, et al. 1995. Multiple-family groups and psychoeducation in the treatment of schizophrenia. *Arch. Gen. Psychiatry* 52:679–87

Magaña AB, Goldstein MJ, Karno M, Miklowitz DJ, Jenkins J, et al. 1986. A brief method for assessing expressed emotion in relatives of psychiatric patients. *Psychiatr. Res.* 17:203–12

Marom S, Munitz H, Jones PB, Weizman A, Hermesh H. 2002. Familial expressed emotion: outcome and course of Israeli patients with schizophrenia. *Schizophr. Bull.* 28:731–43

Miklowitz DJ. 2004. The role of family systems in severe and recurrent psychiatric disorders: a developmental psychopathology view. *Dev. Psychopathol.* 16:667–88

Miklowitz DJ, George EL, Richards JA, Simoneau TL, Succath RL. 2003. A randomized study of family-focused psychoeducation and pharmacotherapy in the outpatient management of bipolar disorder. *Arch. Gen. Psychiatry* 60:904–12

Miklowitz DJ, Goldstein MJ, Nuechterlein KH. 1995. Verbal interactions in the families of schizophrenic and bipolar affective patients. *J. Abnorm. Psychol.* 104:268–76

Miklowitz DJ, Tompson MC. 2003. Family variables and interventions in schizophrenia. In *Textbook of Marital and Family Therapy*, ed. GP Sholevar, LD Schwoeri, pp 585–617. Washington, DC: Am. Psychiatr. Publ.

Moore E, Ball RA, Kuipers L. 1992. Expressed emotion in staff working with the long-term adult mentally ill. *Br. J. Psychiatry* 161:802–8

Mottaghipour Y, Pourmand D, Maleki H, Davidian L. 2001. Expressed emotion and the course of schizophrenia in Iran. *Soc. Psychiatry Psychiatr. Epidemiol.* 36:195–99

Nomura H, Inoue S, Kamimura N, Shimodera S, Mino Y, et al. 2005. A cross-cultural study on expressed emotion in carers of people with dementia and schizophrenia: Japan and England. *Soc. Psychiatry Psychiatr. Epidemiol.* 40:564–70

Nuechterlein KH, Dawson ME. 1984. A heuristic vulnerability/stress model of schizophrenic episodes. *Schizophr. Bull.* 10:300–12

Nuechterlein KH, Snyder KS, Mintz J. 1992. Paths to relapse: possible transactional processes connecting patient illness onset, expressed emotion and psychotic relapse. *Br. J. Psychiatry* 161(Suppl. 18):88–96

O'Farrell TJ, Hooley JM, Fals-Stewart W, Cutter HSG. 1998. Expressed emotion and relapse in alcoholic patients. *J. Consult. Clin. Psychol.* 66:744–52

Peris TS, Baker BL. 2000. Applications of the expressed emotion construct to young children with externalizing behavior: stability and prediction over time. *J. Child Psychol. Psychiatry* 41:457–62

Peter H, Hand I. 1988. Patterns of patient-spouse interaction in agoraphobics: assessment by Camberwell Family Interview (CFI) and impact on outcome on self-exposure treatment. *In Panic and Phobias, 2: Treatments and Variables Affecting Course and Outcome*, ed. I Hand, HU Wittchen, pp. 240–51. Berlin: Springer-Verlag

Pourmand D, Kavanagh DJ, Vaughan K. 2005. Expressed emotion as predictor of relapse in patients with comorbid psychoses and substance use disorder. *Aust. N.Z. J. Psychiatry* 39:473–78

Rosenfarb IS, Bellack AS, Aziz N, Kratz KM, Sayers S. 2004. Race, family interactions, and patient stabilization in schizophrenia. *J. Abnorm. Psychol.* 113:109–15

Rutter M, Brown GW. 1966. The reliability and validity of measures of family life and relationships in families containing a psychiatric patient. *Soc. Psychiatry* 1:38

Scazufca M, Kuipers E. 1996. Links between expressed emotion and burden of care in relatives of patients with schizophrenia. *Br. J. Psychiatry* 168:580–87

Schooler NR, Keith SJ, Severe JB, Matthews SM, Bellack AS, et al. 1997. Relapse and rehospitalization during maintenance treatment of schizophrenia: the effect of dose reduction and family treatment. *Arch. Gen. Psychiatry* 54:453–63

Simoneau TL, Miklowitz DJ, Saleem R. 1998. Expressed emotion and interactional patterns in the families of bipolar patients. *J. Abnorm. Psychol.* 107:497–507

Sturgeon D, Turpin G, Kuipers L, Berkowitz R, Leff J. 1981. Psychophysiological responses of schizophrenic patients to high and low expressed emotion relatives. *Br. J. Psychiatry* 138:40–45

Sturgeon D, Turpin G, Kuipers L, Berkowitz R, Leff J. 1984. Psychophysiological responses of schizophrenic patients to high and low expressed emotion relatives: a follow-up study. *Br. J. Psychiatry* 145:62–69

Szmukler GI, Eisler I, Russell GFM, Dare C. 1985. Parental "expressed emotion," anorexia nervosa and dropping out of treatment. *Br. J. Psychiatry* 147:265–71

Tanaka S, Mino Y, Inoue S. 1995. Expressed emotion and the course of schizophrenia in Japan. *Br. J. Psychiatry* 167:794–98

Tarrier N, Barrowclough C. 1984. Psychophysiological assessment of expressed emotion in schizophrenia: a case example. *Br. J. Psychiatry* 145:197–203

Tarrier N, Barrowclough C, Vaughn C, Bamrah JS, Porceddu K, et al. 1988a. The community management of schizophrenia: a controlled trial of a behavioural intervention with families to reduce relapse. *Br. J. Psychiatry* 153:532–42

Tarrier N, Barrowclough C, Porceddu K, Watts S. 1988b. The assessment of physiological reactivity to the expressed emotion of the relative of schizophrenic patients. *Br. J. Psychiatry* 152:618–24

Tarrier N, Barrowclough C, Ward J, Donaldson C, Burns A, et al. 2002. Expressed emotion and attributions in the carers of patients with Alzheimer's disease: the effect on carer burden. *J. Abnorm. Psychol.* 11:340–49

Tarrier N, Sommerfield C, Pilgrim H. 1999. Relatives expressed emotion (EE) and PTSD treatment outcome. *Psychol. Med.* 29:801–11

Tarrier N, Turpin G. 1992. Psychosocial factors, arousal and schizophrenic relapse: the psychophysiological data. *Br. J. Psychiatry* 161:3–11

Tarrier N, Vaughn C, Lader MH, Leff JP. 1979. Bodily reactions to people and events in schizophrenics. *Arch. Gen. Psychiatry* 36:311–15

Thompson MC, Goldstein MJ, Lebell LB, Mintz LI, Marder SR, et al. 1995. Schizophrenic patients' perceptions of their relatives' attitudes. *Psychiatr. Res.* 57:155–67

Tienari P, Wynne LC, Sorri A, Lahti I, Laksy K, et al. 2004. Genotype-environment interaction in schizophrenia-spectrum disorder. *Br. J. Psychiatry* 184:216–22

Demonstrates that, in the absence of genetic risk, even dysfunctional family environments do not lead to the development of schizophrenia.

Uehara T, Yokoyama T, Nakano Y, Ihda S, Goto M, et al. 1997. Characteristics of expressed emotion rated by the Five Minute Speech Sample and relationship with relapse of outpatients with schizophrenia. *Clin. Psychiatry* 39:31–37

Van Humbeeck G, Van Audenhove C, De Hert M, Pieters G, Storms G. 2002. Expressed emotion: a review of assessment instruments. *Clin. Psychol. Rev.* 22:321–41

van Os J, Marcelis M, Germeys I, Graven S, Delespaul P. 2001. High expressed emotion: marker for a caring family? *Comp. Psychiatry* 42:504–7

Vaughn C, Leff J. 1976. The influence of family and social factors on the course of psychiatric illness. *Br. J. Psychiatry* 129:125–37

First independent replication of the expressed emotion/relapse link in schizophrenia. Extended expressed emotion research to unipolar depression.

Weaver ICG, Meaney MJ, Szyf M. 2006. Maternal care effects on the hippocampal transcriptome and anxiety-mediated behaviors in the offspring that are reversible in adulthood. *Proc. Natl. Acad. Sci. USA* 103:343480–85

Weisman AG, Gomes LG, Lopez SR. 2003. Shifting blame away from ill relatives: Latino families' reactions to schizophrenia. *J. Nerv. Ment. Dis.* 191:1–8

Weisman AG, Lopez SR, Karno M, Jenkins J. 1993. An attributional analysis of expressed emotion in Mexican-American families with schizophrenia. *J. Abnorm. Psychol.* 102:601–6

Weisman AG, Nuechterlein KH, Goldstein MJ, Snyder KS. 2000. Controllability perceptions and reactions to symptoms of schizophrenia: a within-family comparison of relatives with high and low expressed emotion. *J. Abnorm. Psychol.* 109:167–71

Wendel JS, Miklowitz DJ, Richards JA, George EL. 2000. Expressed emotion and attributions in the relatives of bipolar patients: an analysis of problem-solving interactions. *J. Abnorm. Psychol.* 109:792–96

Wilhelm K, Mitchell PB, Niven H, Finch A, Wedgewood L, et al. 2006. Life events, first depression onset and the serotonin transporter gene. *Br. J. Psychiatry* 188:210–15

Yan LJ, Hammen C, Cohen AN, Daley SE, Henry RM. 2004. Expressed emotion versus relationship quality variables in the prediction of recurrence in bipolar patients. *J. Affect. Disord.* 83:199–206

Yang LH, Philips MR, Licht DM, Hooley JM. 2004. Causal attributions about schizophrenia in families in China: expressed emotion and patient relapse. *J. Abnorm. Psychol.* 113:592–602

Sexual Orientation and Mental Health

Gregory M. Herek[1] and Linda D. Garnets[2]

[1]Department of Psychology, University of California, Davis, California 95616-8686; email: gmherek@ucdavis.edu

[2]Department of Psychology, University of California, Los Angeles, California 90095; email: lgarnets@ucla.edu

Annu. Rev. Clin. Psychol. 2007. 3:353–75

First published online as a Review in Advance on October 12, 2006

The *Annual Review of Clinical Psychology* is online at http://clinpsy.annualreviews.org

This article's doi:
10.1146/annurev.clinpsy.3.022806.091510

1548-5943/07/0427-0353$20.00

Key Words

gay, lesbian, bisexual, minority stress, sexual stigma

Abstract

This article provides an overview of current psychological research on mental health and sexual orientation, as well as clinical practice with sexual minorities. The historical context for current research questions and controversies is described, and the findings of recent empirical research on psychological well-being and distress among nonheterosexuals are summarized. The minority stress model is used to frame a discussion of stressors unique to sexual minorities and to consider their possible effects on psychological well-being. The possible ameliorative effects of adopting a sexual orientation identity are examined, followed by a discussion of how these ideas translate into contemporary clinical work with sexual minority clients. The review concludes with a brief discussion of priority areas for empirical research and clinical practice.

Contents

INTRODUCTION

Homosexuality has not been classified as a mental illness for more than 30 years. Yet the fact that it was assumed to be a pathology during much of the twentieth century continues to complicate discussions of mental health and sexual orientation. The problem is apparent when beliefs about heterosexuality and homosexuality are contrasted. When psychopathology occurs among heterosexuals, it is not interpreted by the mental health professions or society at large as implicating heterosexuality per se as the cause of the individual's problem, even when it is manifested in sexual thoughts, feelings, and behaviors. Rather, psychological interventions aim to help mentally ill and distressed heterosexuals to live their lives in a fulfilling way, as heterosexuals, fully capable of establishing meaningful intimate relationships with people of the other sex.

By contrast, despite mainstream professional opinion to the contrary, some elements of society still regard homosexuality as pathological and believe that sexual minority adults should try to become heterosexual. Prejudice and discrimination against gay, lesbian, and bisexual people remain widespread. Their perpetrators often seek legitimacy in the argument that homosexuality is "sick," "abnormal," or "unnatural." In this milieu, empirical research revealing differences in psychological health between sexual minorities and heterosexuals can be inappropriately seized upon to argue that homosexuality is indeed an illness that needs to be cured.

Consequently, any discussion of sexual orientation and mental health must be grounded in recognition of the extent and effects of sexual stigma, that is, the stigma historically attached by society to same-sex attraction and minority sexual orientations (Herek 2004). Such stigma has played a central role in shaping the mental health professions' stance toward homosexual behavior and people with minority sexual orientations. Indeed, although sexual stigma has long been expressed through cultural institutions such as the law and religion, much of its legitimacy during the past century derived from homosexuality's status as a psychopathology.

Mindful of this fact, the present review focuses on the mental health of sexual minority individuals. Although it is titled "Sexual Orientation and Mental Health," heterosexuals are discussed mainly as a comparison group. Our purpose in taking this approach is not to discount the mental health needs of heterosexuals, which have long been central in psychological science and the mental health professions. Nor do we intend to problematize sexual minority mental health while assuming heterosexuality to be the gold standard, as was historically done by psychiatrists, psychologists, and society at large. Rather, we hope to advance the discourse about mental health among sexual minorities beyond outdated conceptualizations of homosexuality that were informed more by societal stigma than empirical data, and instead address the topic without pathologizing sexual minority individuals as a class.

In this article, we give an overview of current psychological research on mental health and sexual orientation, as well as clinical practice with sexual minorities. After establishing the historical context for current research questions and controversies, we summarize the findings of recent empirical research on psychological well-being and distress among nonheterosexuals. We then consider how various stressors unique to sexual minorities may affect their psychological well-being, and how adopting a sexual orientation identity might ameliorate the effects of these stressors. Next, we discuss how these ideas translate into contemporary clinical work with sexual minority clients. Finally, we highlight priority areas for empirical research and practice.

HISTORICAL BACKGROUND

Historically speaking, sexual orientation is a fairly new construct. Although heterosexual and homosexual behaviors are ubiquitous across human societies, notions of "the homosexual" and "the heterosexual"—as well as the very idea that individuals can be defined in terms of their sexual attractions and behaviors—emerged in medical discourse only in the nineteenth century. They are usually traced to Karl Maria Benkert's use of "homosexuality" in 1868 in a German-language pamphlet (Dynes 1990, Katz 1995). Benkert also introduced the term "heterosexual" in 1868 but he did not consistently use it as the opposite of homosexual. Instead, he contrasted homosexual with "normalsexual." When heterosexual was first introduced into English in 1892, it referred to people who felt "inclinations to both sexes" (Katz 1995, p. 20), what today would be called bisexuality. However, Richard von Kraft-Ebing's *Psychopathia Sexualis*, translated into English late in the nineteenth century, used "hetero-sexual" to refer to desire for the other sex (Katz 1995, Krafft-Ebing 1900). Not until Freud articulated his conceptualization of homosexuality in the first of his *Three Essays on the Theory of Sexuality*, however, did the modern notion of sexual orientation defined in terms of object choice (i.e., the kind of person or thing toward which the sexual aim is directed) become dominant in psychiatric discourse (Chauncey 1982–1983, Freud 1953).

As Benkert's original usage makes plain, homosexuality was defined from the outset in opposition to normalcy. Stigmatization of homosexuality was always integral to society's construction of sexual orientation. Nevertheless, the modern history of sexual orientation has been characterized by an ongoing dialectic between views of homosexuality as pathological (e.g., Krafft-Ebing 1900) and challenges to its linkage with mental illness (Ellis 1901, Ulrichs 1994). Even Freud, who believed that homosexuality represented a less-than-optimal outcome for psychosexual development, nevertheless asserted in a now-famous 1935 letter that "it is nothing to be ashamed of, no vice, no degradation, it cannot be classified as an illness" (Freud 1951, p. 786).

American psychoanalysts, however, broke with Freud. In contrast to Freud's view that humans are innately bisexual, Rado (1940, 1949) argued that only heterosexuality is natural and that homosexuality is a "reparative" attempt to achieve sexual pleasure when normal heterosexual outlet proves too threatening. Rado's followers proposed various theories about homosexuality's etiology, all of them based on an illness model, that is, the assumption that homosexuality is a sickness (Bieber et al. 1962, Socarides 1968).

Psychoanalysis was the dominant perspective in psychiatry during the mid-twentieth century, and the psychoanalysts' assumption that homosexuality was a pathology permeated U.S. culture (Bayer 1987, Friedman & Downey 1998, Silverstein 1991). During World War II, for example, when the U.S. military incorporated psychiatric screening into its induction process, formal procedures were developed for rejecting gay recruits (Bérubé 1990). After the war, the newly created *Diagnostic and Statistical Handbook of Mental Disorders*, or DSM, listed homosexuality as a sociopathic personality disturbance, along with substance abuse and sexual disorders (Am. Psychiatr. Assoc. 1952). During this era, many psychiatrists set out to "cure" homosexuality; homosexual men and women spent countless hours in psychotherapy in what proved to be, for most, a vain attempt to change their sexual orientation (Friedman & Downey 1998, Haldeman 1991). When psychotherapy did not work, many tried (or were coerced into) more drastic methods, including administration of hormones, aversive conditioning, lobotomy, electroshock, and castration (Katz 1976).

Challenges to the psychiatric orthodoxy emerged around this time. Kinsey's groundbreaking studies of sexuality challenged widespread assumptions by revealing that homosexual behavior and attractions were surprisingly common (Kinsey et al. 1948, Kinsey et al. 1953). An influential comparative study documented the existence of homosexual behavior in many nonhuman species and its acceptance in a large number of human cultures (Ford & Beach 1951).

Against this backdrop, Hooker (1957) first introduced key elements of modern research design into psychological studies of sexual orientation and mental health. Rather than accepting the dominant view of homosexuality as pathology, she treated the question of whether homosexuals and heterosexuals differed in their psychological adjustment as an empirical one. Her landmark study compared a nonclinical sample of homosexuals with a matched heterosexual control group, relying on evaluations of projective test protocols by experts who were unaware of each subject's sexual orientation (Hooker 1957). When the Rorschach experts could not identify the respondents' sexual orientation at a level better than chance and their ratings of homosexual and heterosexual men's adjustment did not differ significantly, Hooker concluded that homosexuality is not inherently associated with psychopathology and is not a clinical entity (Hooker 1957).

In the wake of Hooker's study, other researchers compared the psychological functioning of heterosexuals and homosexuals. In a review of these studies, Gonsiorek (1991) noted several important considerations in evaluating the results, two of which are particularly germane to the present article. First, research outcomes were greatly affected by sampling. Many studies used samples of homosexual individuals who were incarcerated or undergoing psychiatric treatment. Not surprisingly, these participants typically evidenced more psychological problems than did heterosexuals recruited from nonclinical venues. Second, Gonsiorek noted that differences in psychological test scores were often inappropriately interpreted as indicative of pathology in one group. Statistical significance should not be equated with clinical significance, however, because two groups can score differently on such measures and both remain within the normal range of functioning (Gonsiorek 1991). Empirical studies that avoided these and other pitfalls failed to support the notion that homosexuality per se is indicative of psychopathology (Gonsiorek 1991, Hart et al. 1978, Riess 1980).

Nevertheless, the growing body of research data alone proved inadequate for convincing mental health practitioners to repudiate the illness model. Soon after the second edition of the DSM listed homosexuality as a "Sexual Deviation," along with fetishism and pedophilia (Am. Psychiatr. Assoc. 1968), however, the newly emerging movement for gay and lesbian civil rights inspired many sectors of U.S. society to reconsider their long-standing assumptions about homosexuality (Adam 1995). In the face of rapidly changing cultural views about homosexuality, and in recognition that empirical data were lacking to support the illness model, the American Psychiatric Association's Board of Directors voted in 1973 to remove homosexuality from the DSM. Their decision was affirmed by a vote of the Association's membership in 1974. The American Psychological Association (APA) strongly endorsed the psychiatrists' actions, and has since worked intensively to eradicate the stigma historically associated with a homosexual orientation (Conger 1975, Morin & Rothblum 1991).

As this brief history shows, the medical and scientific institutions that provided much of the ideological rationale for stigmatizing homosexuality during the first half of the twentieth century dramatically reversed themselves in 1973. Today the mainstream position among clinicians and researchers is that homosexuality is a normal variant of human sexual expression and is no more inherently associated with psychopathology than is heterosexuality.

CONTEMPORARY RESEARCH ON SEXUAL ORIENTATION AND MENTAL HEALTH

With the advantage of hindsight, it can be seen that debates about the status of homosexuality as a pathology often conflated issues of classification and the definition of mental illness with questions about the prevalence of psychological disorders in a particular population. It was inappropriately assumed that if homosexuals simply evidenced higher rates of psychopathology or psychological distress than did heterosexuals, then homosexuality itself must be an illness (Meyer 2003). Consequently, conducting research on the mental health needs of sexual minority communities always carried the risk of further stigmatizing nonheterosexuals. With the demise of the illness model, such risks have abated, although the research is still at a preliminary stage in important respects. In the section below, we review the current state of the available data.

Preliminary Considerations

Before discussing the findings, it is important to consider four aspects of research design that affect the interpretation of data: sampling strategies, the operational definition of sexual orientation, the operational definition of mental health, and data analysis strategies.

Sampling. As noted above, empirical research conducted within the framework of the illness model often recruited homosexual participants from clinical and incarcerated populations. Later research used community-based samples, which were less biased toward psychopathology but also had limited generalizability. Samples recruited at community festivals, for example, may have been biased toward well-functioning individuals, whereas samples recruited through bars probably overrepresented sexual minority individuals who consumed alcohol. In recent years, researchers have begun to publish studies that use innovative sampling strategies to overcome these limitations. Some large-scale health surveys, for example, have included questions about sexuality or romantic attractions. This has permitted researchers to examine differences in a variety of health indices according to respondents' sexual behavior or identity in national probability samples (e.g., Cochran & Mays 2006, Russell 2006). In other cases, studies conducted with large nonprobability samples that were not initially recruited on the basis of sexual orientation have yielded data on sexual orientation and health (e.g., Case et al. 2004). Still other researchers have collected original data from nonprobability samples of sexual minority adults and their heterosexual siblings, thus permitting group comparisons that control for multiple background variables (e.g., Herrell et al. 1999, Rothblum & Factor 2001). Because the results from these studies are more readily generalizable to the sexual minority population than are data from earlier research with small convenience samples, our discussion focuses on them.

Operational definitions of sexual orientation. Because of sexual stigma, some individuals are unwilling to disclose their homosexual or bisexual orientation to researchers, especially when traditional survey techniques are used (Villarroel et al. 2006). Even when research participants provide accurate information about their sexuality, how they are categorized for purposes of data analysis depends on the operational definition of sexual orientation selected by the researcher. In most empirical research, sexual orientation has been defined in terms of sexual attraction, sexual behavior, or self-labeling as gay, lesbian, or bisexual. Because individuals are not always consistently heterosexual or homosexual across these dimensions (Laumann et al. 1994, Villarroel et al. 2006), research participants who are categorized as heterosexual by one criterion might have been classified as homosexual or bisexual if a different operational definition had been employed. Unfortunately, most published studies have relied on a single dimension for operationalizing sexual orientation. When interpreting the research, therefore, it is always important to consider how sexual orientation was measured and to recognize the potential for misclassification.

Operational definitions of psychological distress. Empirical studies have used a variety of strategies for assessing psychological distress, including structured diagnostic interviews (e.g., Cochran & Mays 2006), self-reports of symptoms using standardized scales or checklists (e.g., Rothblum & Factor 2001), and respondents' subjective ratings of their own level of functioning or distress (e.g., Diamant & Wold 2003). We note three important caveats for interpreting these data. First, as explained above, differences between sexual orientation groups on measures of psychological well-being can be statistically significant without indicating clinically significant differences in functioning. That is, two groups can have reliably different mean scores on a psychological test or symptom inventory yet both be within the normal range of functioning (Gonsiorek 1991). Second, individual items on psychological tests can have different meanings and thus evoke different response patterns from different cultural groups. These variations in response patterns can produce group differences in test scores. Hence, making clinical inferences about sexual minority adults based on predetermined cutoff scores derived from testing heterosexual adults is of questionable validity in the absence of standardization data from gay, lesbian, and bisexual respondents. Such independent validation of psychological tests with sexual minority populations has been rare. Third, sexual minority individuals are more likely than heterosexuals to receive psychotherapy or counseling, regardless of their level of functioning (Cochran & Mays 2006). This often occurs when they first recognize their sexual orientation and begin to disclose it to others (a process referred to as "coming out of the closet" or simply "coming out"). Consequently, they may be more attuned to their own internal states and more able and willing than heterosexuals to report psychological symptoms to researchers (Meyer 2003).

Data analysis strategies. Because a fairly small proportion of the population reports same-sex sexual behavior or identifies as gay, lesbian, or bisexual, the number of nonheterosexual respondents in most general samples is typically small. Some samples include so few nonheterosexual respondents that drawing conclusions from them about sexual minorities is extremely perilous. For example, one longitudinal study based its analyses of sexual orientation and mental health on a sample of 967 adults that included only 7 males and 20 females who were not exclusively or predominantly heterosexual (Fergusson et al. 2005). Even in samples with larger numbers of sexual minority respondents, researchers frequently have had to combine all nonheterosexuals for data analyses to achieve adequate statistical power. In nearly all of the studies discussed below, comparisons were made mainly between (*a*) a heterosexual group comprising respondents who labeled themselves heterosexual or reported a history of exclusively heterosexual behavior and (*b*) a nonheterosexual group comprising individuals who reported having ever engaged in a homosexual act as well as self-identified lesbians, gay men, bisexual women, and bisexual men.[1] With this approach, nonheterosexual subgroups (e.g., bisexuals versus homosexuals) cannot be examined separately, which, as discussed below, may obscure important intergroup differences in mental health.

Empirical Findings

Mindful of these considerations, the main findings from recent empirical research can be summarized. First, regardless of their sexual orientation, most respondents in large-scale epidemiological surveys do not manifest heightened risk for psychopathology, suicidality, substance use, or psychological distress (e.g., Cochran & Mays 2006). Second, nonheterosexuals appear to be at greater risk than heterosexuals for anxiety and mood disorders. This general pattern has been observed among nonheterosexual men (Cochran & Mays 2000a, Cochran et al. 2003, Sandfort et al. 2001) and women (Case et al. 2004, Cochran et al. 2003, Gilman et al. 2001, Sandfort et al. 2001). However, some studies have not found statistically significant differences among sexual orientation groups when relevant demographic factors were statistically controlled (for women: Cochran & Mays 2000a; for men: Cochran & Mays 2000b, Gilman et al. 2001; for women and men: Balsam et al. 2005).

Third, nonheterosexual adults are more likely than are heterosexuals to report past suicidal ideation and attempts (Balsam et al. 2005, Cochran & Mays 2000b, Gilman et al. 2001, Herrell et al. 1999). Self-reported suicidal ideation and attempts are also more common among nonheterosexual (versus heterosexual) adolescents (Russell 2003). Some studies have found a greater risk for male sexual minority youths compared with females (Garofalo et al. 1999, Remafedi et al. 1998), but others have found both nonheterosexual girls and boys to be at higher risk than heterosexuals (Russell & Joyner 2001). Fourth, in comparison with heterosexual women, nonheterosexual women appear to consume alcohol in greater amounts and more frequently (Burgard et al. 2005, Case et al. 2004, Scheer et al. 2003) and may be at greater risk for problems related to alcohol consumption (Cochran et al. 2000, Drabble et al. 2005, Gilman et al. 2001, Sandfort et al. 2001).

FACTORS AFFECTING MENTAL HEALTH AMONG SEXUAL MINORITY POPULATIONS

In summary, the available empirical data suggest that although most nonheterosexual men and women function well, this population may be at heightened risk for some forms of psychopathology, psychological distress, and problems with substance use. Because operational definitions of sexual orientation have differed across studies and most samples have included relatively small numbers of nonheterosexuals, however, these data do not offer many insights into the factors that distinguish the well-functioning majority of sexual minority individuals from those who are distressed. In the present section, we consider possible explanations for the occurrence of psychological problems among sexual minorities.

Since the demise of the illness model, a minority stress model has become the most commonly used framework for conceptualizing mental health among lesbian, gay, and bisexual individuals. It posits that minority group members are at risk for some kinds of psychological problems because they face unique,

[1] In describing research findings, we use the terms "gay," "lesbian," and "bisexual" only when (*a*) respondents' self-labeled sexual orientation was assessed and (*b*) data were reported separately for different sexual minority groups. Because of the variety of different operationalizations across studies, we believe "nonheterosexual" is the most accurate term for collectively characterizing the findings when two or more sexual orientation or sexual behavior groups were combined for purposes of analysis (e.g., self-labeled lesbians and bisexual women; men reporting a history of any homosexual behavior).

chronic stressors as a result of their disadvantaged status in society. These stressors are experienced in addition to the routine stressors encountered by nonminority individuals. Although the minority stress model has not yet been subjected to extensive empirical testing (Meyer 2003), it offers a valuable framework for conceptualizing the experiences of stigmatized groups. It highlights three stress processes: (*a*) external, objectively stressful events and conditions, (*b*) the minority individual's expectations of such events and the vigilance this expectation requires, and (*c*) the minority individual's internalization of negative societal attitudes (Meyer 2003). We use these three categories as a framework for discussing the challenges routinely encountered by sexual minority individuals.

First, sexual minority individuals face a variety of objectively stressful events that heterosexuals do not experience. Because most such events are directly related to the stigmatized status of sexual minorities, our discussion focuses on the effects of sexual stigma. It should be understood, however, that minority groups also face other unique stressors that are not directly caused by stigma (although stigma often plays a role in how those stressors are experienced and understood). For example, the human immunodeficiency virus (HIV) epidemic has been a unique source of stress for sexual minority individuals in the United States because of its disproportionate impact on gay and bisexual men. Many sexual minority men deal with the stress of having HIV disease, and those who are healthy are regularly confronted with the possibility of infection. Many men have experienced the death of a life partner. Sexual minority men and women alike have experienced extensive losses in their personal and social networks resulting from the death of close friends and acquaintances. Indeed, many gay, lesbian, and bisexual individuals experienced the loss of entire communities during the 1980s and 1990s. Such experiences of disease and multiple losses are linked to high levels of psychological distress (Folkman et al. 1996, Martin 1988). Given these effects, the HIV epidemic would have been a source of stress to any community. However, the pervasiveness of sexual stigma exacerbated the stress by impeding society's response to the epidemic and contributing to HIV-related stigma (Herek et al. 1998, Herek & Capitanio 1999).

Sexual stigma also leads to other objectively stressful events. Once their sexual orientation becomes known to others, sexual minority individuals can be subjected to multiple types of "enacted stigma" (Scambler & Hopkins 1986), ranging from personal rejection and ostracism to discrimination and criminal victimization (Herek et al. 1999, Herek & Sims 2007, Mays & Cochran 2001). Experiencing enacted stigma can have serious and enduring psychological consequences. For example, for gay men and lesbians, being the target of antigay violence can be even more traumatic than "routine" criminal victimization; victims of hate crimes manifest heightened levels of depressive symptoms, anxiety, and symptoms of posttraumatic distress compared with sexual minority victims of violent crimes that were not motivated by antigay animus (Herek et al. 1999; see also Huebner et al. 2004, Mills et al. 2004). In one national survey, Mays & Cochran (2001) found that the correlation observed between mental health and sexual orientation was largely explained by nonheterosexuals' experiences with discrimination; when the latter were statistically controlled, heterosexuals and nonheterosexuals did not differ significantly on mental health indicators.

In addition to direct enactments of stigma, sexual minority individuals are also subjected to the effects of institutionalized stigma, or "heterosexism" (Herek et al. 2007). At the time of this writing, for example, same-sex couples are denied the right to marry in all U.S. states except Massachusetts. Being denied the right to marry probably subjects same-sex couples to more stress than heterosexual married couples, has negative consequences for their well-being, and ultimately creates challenges and obstacles to the success of their relationships that are not faced by heterosexual couples (Herek 2006). Sexual stigma also has negative economic effects, especially for gay men, who may earn significantly less than their heterosexual counterparts (Badgett 2001, Herek et al. 2007). Furthermore, because many religious denominations condemn homosexual relationships (Herek et al. 2007), sexual minority individuals are often disenfranchised from religious and spiritual resources that might otherwise ameliorate the effects of stress.

A member of a stigmatized minority group need not be a victim of enacted stigma directly in order to be affected by it. "Felt stigma" refers to an individual's subjective experience of stigma against her or his group, including her or his awareness of stigma's prevalence and manifestations even without having directly experienced enacted stigma (Scambler & Hopkins 1986). Felt stigma is likely to be heightened by societal events in which antigay hostility is made salient, such as highly visible acts of antigay violence (Noelle 2002) and antigay political campaigns (Russell 2000, Russell & Richards 2003).

Felt stigma plays a central role in sexual minority individuals' decision-making about whether and when to disclose their sexual orientation. Making such decisions typically involves weighing the relative costs and benefits of coming out, including others' likely responses to one's sexual orientation and the impact of prejudiced social reactions to one's subjective well-being (Cole 2006, Herek 1996). On the one hand, public revelation that one is not heterosexual can incur enacted stigma. On the other hand, concealing one's sexual minority identity requires constant vigilance regarding the personal information one shares with other people. Many sexual minority individuals adopt a strategy of "rational outness," that is, being as open as possible about their sexual orientation while remaining as closed as necessary to protect themselves against discrimination (Bradford & Ryan 1987, p. 107). The subjective meanings of "as open as possible" and "as closed as necessary," however, differ widely depending on the individual's circumstances and personality factors. For example, whereas many studies have revealed a positive correlation between being out and positive psychological and physical states (e.g., Jordan & Deluty 1998, Morris et al. 2001, Ullrich et al. 2004), this pattern has not been uniformly observed (e.g., Frable et al. 1997), perhaps because individuals who are highly sensitive to social rejection may not benefit from being out of the closet (Cole 2006). Thus, disclosure of one's sexual orientation represents a strategy for managing stigma, but the decisions that a sexual minority individual makes about being out of the closet can also have stressful consequences.

Such decisions can be influenced by the third source of stress identified by the minority stress model: the individual's self-stigmatization as a consequence of accepting society's negative attitudes toward nonheterosexuals. This phenomenon has been variously labeled internalized homophobia, internalized heterosexism, and internalized homonegativity. Mental health practitioners and researchers generally agree that negative feelings about one's own homosexual desires are likely to have important consequences for physical and psychological well-being, including diminished self-esteem, demoralization, depression, increased use of alcohol and drugs, and relationship instability (DiPlacido 1998, Shidlo 1994, Szymanski & Chung 2003, Williamson 2000). To the extent that high levels of internalized stigma lead sexual minority individuals to conceal their sexual orientation beyond what is required to protect themselves from enactments of stigma, it can exacerbate minority stress.

Collective Identity as a Potential Moderator of Minority Stress

The fact that most nonheterosexuals do not manifest high levels of depression, anxiety, suicidality, and substance abuse indicates that they cope successfully with the stress created by stigma. It is appropriate to ask how they do it. Meyer (2003) pointed out that sexual minority individuals draw on both personal and group resources in coping with minority stress. Variations in personal resources reflect individual differences in, for example, resilience, hardiness, and coping styles (e.g., Masten 2001, Ouellette & DiPlacido 2001). By contrast, group resources, as elements of the larger social structure, are potentially available to all sexual minority individuals who have developed a collective identity based on their sexual orientation.

Used in this sense, a collective identity (sometimes referred to as a social identity) involves strong identification with a social group and linkage of one's self-esteem to group membership (Ashmore et al. 2004). Nonheterosexuals whose sexuality is part of a collective sexual orientation identity integrate their sexual feelings, intimate relationships, and affiliations with the sexual minority community into the core of their self-concept. If they encounter enactments of stigma, they are likely to interpret those events as unjust not only from an individual perspective but also because they believe it is wrong to treat anyone differently because of their sexual orientation (Branscombe & Ellemers 1998). Such individuals will have group resources for responding to stigma in addition to their personal coping abilities. By contrast, nonheterosexuals who adopt an assimilationist or individual identity pattern (Fingerhut et al. 2005, McCarn & Fassinger 1996) conceive their sexuality largely in personal terms, discounting the importance of sexual behaviors and desires for defining their sense of self. Without necessarily denying or rejecting their personal same-sex desires, they might distance themselves from or even express hostility toward the gay and lesbian community. If they encounter enactments of sexual stigma, they may object on the grounds that they should be regarded as unique individuals rather than members of a group defined on the basis of sexual orientation. Such people frame their sexuality largely in terms of personal identity, and their resources for responding to stigma are thus largely a function of their personal coping abilities.

Nonheterosexuals who actively participate in a sexual minority community report less psychological distress than those who do not (Lewis et al. 2001, Luhtanen 2003, Mills et al. 2004, Morris et al. 2001). This pattern may occur because a collective identity affords an individual additional resources beyond those available through a purely personal identity. Thus, in comparison with other nonheterosexuals, individuals who adopt a sexual minority identity may be better equipped to cope with minority stress. By identifying and affiliating with similarly stigmatized others, they are able to experience social environments in which they are not stigmatized. In such environments, they can more readily develop a worldview that invalidates negative stereotypes and biases while affirming positive evaluations of the group and its members. This worldview can reduce an individual's level of internalized stigma while fostering a positive collective identity (e.g., Frable et al. 1997). Minority communities can also provide emotional and instrumental support for dealing with stigma and teach survival skills for meeting the challenges created by sexual stigma (e.g., Bowleg et al. 2003, D'Augelli et al. 1987, Ueno 2005). Adopting a collective identity also increases the likelihood that sexual minority individuals will come out to their heterosexual family members, friends, and acquaintances. To the extent that significant others respond favorably, coming out can make additional social support available in the face of societal stigma (e.g., Hershberger & D'Augelli 1995, Luhtanen 2003).

This discussion highlights an important limitation of research that combines all sexual minority respondents into a single "nonheterosexual" group. That undifferentiated category inevitably includes not only individuals with a collective sexual orientation identity, but also those who regard their sexuality in purely personal terms. Indeed, two leading researchers in this area estimated that only half of the individuals who report sexual contact with a same-sex adult actually identify as lesbian, gay, or bisexual (Cochran & Mays 2006). Consistent with this observation, the proportion of adults who identified as gay, lesbian, or bisexual in a 2000 national probability sample was roughly the same as the proportion who reported same-sex behavior but identified as heterosexual (Drabble et al. 2005). If sexual minority individuals with a collective identity experience lower levels of psychological distress than do nonheterosexuals with a purely personal sexual orientation identity, then the group differences in mental health observed in the research described above may be due mainly to heightened distress among the latter.

It is important to recognize that collective identity is not static. The meanings attached to sexuality have changed over the past century (Chauncey 1994) and are likely to continue to change in the future. The political activism of gay, lesbian, and bisexual groups since the 1970s has increased public awareness of sexual minority communities, expanded civil rights protections, and lessened social constraints on the lives of nonheterosexuals (Garnets & Peplau 2006). Consequently, the world in which today's sexual minority youth come to understand their sexual orientation is vastly different from that of previous generations. Indeed, not all manifestations of same-sex sexuality among contemporary youth are adequately accounted for by the labels "gay," "lesbian," and "bisexual" and the identities associated with them (Diamond 2006, Russell 2006, Savin-Williams 2005). Thus, any attempt to understand the role of collective identity in shaping sexual minority mental health must necessarily be grounded in its historical and cultural context.

Moreover, the benefits of collective identity may be offset to some degree by the increased vulnerability to stigma that results from greater visibility. For example, hate-crime victimization is more likely to be experienced by gay, lesbian, and bisexual individuals who are out of the closet (Herek et al. 1999, Huebner et al. 2004). In addition, involvement with the sexual minority community may include exposure to subgroups that engage in maladaptive behaviors, such as alcohol abuse. To the extent that the net benefits of embracing a collective identity outweigh the net costs of visibility, however, individuals who strongly identify as lesbian, gay, or bisexual seem likely to manifest less psychological distress and pathology than individuals whose same-sex attractions and behavior are not part of a collective identity.

Effects of multiple identities. In a complex society, most individuals have multiple collective identities, each of which can assume greater or lesser salience in different situations. When two or more of those identities are stigmatized, an individual may be the target of multiple prejudices in majority group contexts (e.g., as an African American, a woman, and a lesbian) but may also experience prejudice in minority community settings (e.g., sexual prejudice from black heterosexuals, racial prejudice from white lesbians). Individuals with multiple statuses may even have difficulty assessing the source of stigma in a particular situation, as when lesbian victims of hate crimes are uncertain whether they were attacked because of their sexual orientation or their gender (Von Schulthess 1992).

Having multiple minority statuses increases one's chances for experiencing stigma (Diaz et al. 2006, Greene 1994), but integrating multiple identities may enhance a minority individual's overall psychological resilience and increase one's available resources for coping with stigma (Crawford et al. 2002). As children, for example, sexual minority individuals typically are not taught the skills necessary for coping with sexual prejudice. However, members of racial and ethnic minority groups often acquire relevant skills from family members and community elders early in life. To the extent that such skills are transferable from the experience of dealing with racial and ethnic stigma to dealing with sexual stigma, individuals with both a sexual and ethnic minority status may be better prepared than Euro-American sexual minority individuals (Greene 1994). In addition, individuals with multiple identities may be especially resilient to stress because of the greater complexity of their self-concept and their ability to strategically emphasize identities that are socially valued in a specific context (Shih 2004). Thus, sexual minority individuals with multiple minority identities do not necessarily evidence greater psychological distress than do their Euro-American counterparts (e.g., Consolacion et al. 2004) and may even be better equipped to cope with minority stress.

MENTAL HEALTH PRACTICE WITH SEXUAL MINORITIES

Since the demise of the illness model, mental health practitioners have developed new approaches to guide the provision of mental health services to sexual minorities. Consistent with the minority stress model, this gay-, lesbian-, and bisexual-affirmative approach interprets many of the problems experienced by sexual minority individuals as resulting from sexual stigma. It focuses on helping gay men, lesbians, and bisexuals to cope adaptively with the impact of stigma and their minority status. Affirmative practice assists them in understanding and accepting their sexual orientation as a natural part of themselves; helps them develop strategies for coping and forming a positive sense of identity; and teaches them the effect of sexual stigma on psychological functioning (Browning et al. 1991, Division 44/ Committee on Lesbian Gay and Bisexual Concerns Joint Task Force on Guidelines for Psychotherapy with Lesbian Gay and Bisexual Clients 2000 [hereafter Division 44/CLGBC 2000], Eubanks-Carter et al. 2005, Perez et al. 2000). To assist providers, educators, and clinical supervisors, the APA has developed professional and ethical guidelines that articulate best practices and core competencies for affirmative practice with sexual minority clients. These and other resources for reducing bias and knowledge deficits in this area are listed in the Appendix.

Widely promulgated guidelines for psychotherapy with sexual minority clients rely on the minority stress model and recommend that mental health practitioners use a minority stress assessment for identifying the negative impact of sexual stigma and prejudice in the lives of sexual minority individuals (Division 44/CLGBC 2000). In such an assessment, the therapist takes a full history of the client's experiences with enacted stigma and seeks to understand how the client subjectively experiences sexual stigma, as well as the psychological consequences (overt and subtle) of her or his internalization of sexual stigma. This approach is helpful in highlighting the central therapeutic tasks that inform affirmative practice with sexual minority individuals.

As discussed above, enacted and felt stigma contribute to an individual's fear of self-identifying as sexual minority. When clients have experienced direct enactments of stigma, a primary therapeutic task is to deal with the aftermath of the victimization. Enactments of stigma may have an additional impact beyond that of other types of victimization because the clients' sexuality may be directly linked to the heightened sense of vulnerability that normally follows such victimization. Consequently, sexual minority clients who experience enacted stigma often must cope with negative feelings about their sexual orientation identity. The focus of therapy includes assessing the meanings that the person is deriving from her or his experience, her or his feelings about the self, and the degree to which the experience is equated with her or his identity as a sexual minority. In addition, it is important to assess the client's internal and external coping resources (e.g., previously developed coping skills, sources of personal social support, current or potential involvement in community networks) with the goal of building on these resources and assisting the client in developing new ones as needed.

The impact of enacted stigma is likely to be affected by the client's location in the coming-out process. If the stigma experience has "outed" the client (i.e., forced an involuntary, premature disclosure of the client's sexual orientation identity), it may have amplified the feelings of vulnerability, alienation, and exposure that are often encountered during the coming-out process. These feelings warrant exploration in therapy with the aim of separating the victimization experience from the coming-out experience. In addition, the practitioner may assist the client in feeling the positive effects of identity disclosure that also are part of coming out. Individuals who are further along in the coming-out process prior to experiencing enacted stigma have the benefit of being able to balance the victimization experience against positive experiences associated with their minority sexual identity. Even so, they may experience negative feelings about their sexuality as a consequence of enacted stigma. In such cases, the central task of the therapist is to review the bases for the client's past coming-out decisions, with the aim of re-establishing her or his positive identity as a lesbian, gay, or bisexual person (Garnets et al. 1992).

Whereas felt stigma is unavoidable and, as explained above, often provides a basis for adaptive responses to sexual stigma, high levels of it can lead to excessive feelings of personal danger and vulnerability, perceptions of the world as malevolent, and a linkage of these perceptions to one's sexual orientation identity. Consequently, one's sexuality can be experienced as a source of pain and punishment rather than intimacy, love, and community. In this situation, the principal therapeutic challenge for practitioners is to help sexual minority clients to establish trust in the world that is tempered by accurate assessments of the dangers resulting from sexual stigma. Given the real social and physical risks that sexual minority clients must face, helping them to develop a sense of safety is of central importance.

Within this context, helping clients to make realistic decisions about when it is and is not safe to come out is an important therapeutic task. For some clients, perceived dangers or restrictions on coming out in a particular situation may in fact be projected prohibitions due to intrapsychic conflicts about dealing with their own sexual identity. Thus, a therapeutic task is to assist clients in distinguishing their projected fears about their sexual identity from the objective risks of discrimination and victimization. The coming-out process has a highly individualized and personal meaning for everyone who goes through it, and the psychological consequences of coming out are influenced by both personality and situational variables (Cole 2006). Consequently, it is important for therapists to assess the situation of each client rather than adhering rigidly to a goal of progressively increasing openness for all.

Because most individuals have internalized sexual stigma to some extent, feelings of ambivalence, conflict, and discontent about one's sexual attractions and behaviors are common in the course of developing a positive sexual orientation identity (Division 44/CLGBC 2000). It is important for practitioners to recognize the extent to which sexual minority individuals' self-stigmatizing attitudes, feelings, and beliefs influence their symptoms of distress. Internalized stigma is not always conscious and its psychological consequences (e.g., shame, anxiety, depression, low self-esteem) are not always obvious. Clients with negative feelings about their own homosexuality often are in the closet and not well integrated into a sexual minority social network (Gonsiorek 1995, Malyon 1981–1982, Shidlo 1994, Szymanski & Chung 2003). A primary therapeutic task associated with internalized stigma is to assist clients in assessing, confronting, and rejecting the negative conception of minority sexual orientation dictated by society, and transforming it into a positive and viable identity in which their sexuality is well integrated with other parts of the self. This process of forming a positive sexual orientation identity involves refuting the negative stereotypes associated with the cognitive categories of "gay," "lesbian," or "bisexual" and replacing them with positive content.

An example of the consequences of antigay hate crimes illustrates how experiences of enacted stigma can translate into internalized stigma. An antigay attack may be interpreted as a violation of oneself as a gay person; guilt and self-blame may become attached to the individual's sexual orientation, leading to feelings that she or he has been justifiably punished for being gay. This linkage can be harmful because sexual orientation is such an important part of self-identity. Such self-blame can lead to feelings of depression and helplessness, even in individuals who were previously comfortable with their sexual orientation. In such a case, the practitioner's aim is to assist the survivor in cognitively restructuring these false self-attributions about herself or himself and the assault. Specifically, the cognition that "bad things happen because I am gay" should be reformulated to "bad things happen" (Garnets et al. 1992).

Although the affirmative model has become the dominant theoretical approach for psychotherapy with sexual minority clients, it has been slow to be implemented. Empirical research conducted during the 1980s and 1990s found that many clinicians still engaged in practices that sexual minority clients perceived to be biased, insensitive, and unhelpful. Some providers discouraged and demeaned lesbian and gay clients, urged them to become heterosexual, or trivialized and disregarded their intimate relationships, even to the point of refusing to provide therapy to same-sex couples. Some practitioners were uninformed or misinformed about fundamental issues facing sexual minorities, such as the psychological consequences of prejudice and discrimination (Garnets et al. 1991, Liddle 1996). Other studies highlighted weaknesses in training and clinical supervision (Halpert et al. 2006, Murphy et al. 2002, Phillips & Fischer 1998).

These data, in conjunction with observations by practitioners (e.g., Eubanks-Carter et al. 2005), suggest that mental health services for sexual minority clients often may not be comparable to those provided to heterosexuals. Receiving therapy from a psychologist who harbors prejudice or is misinformed about sexual orientation may exacerbate a client's distress. The most dramatic instance of such a problem occurs when a therapist believes that the optimal strategy for sexual minority clients is to attempt to change their sexual orientation (Division 44/CLGBC 2000). Interventions to promote such attempts are variously labeled "conversion therapy," "reparative therapy," or "reorientation therapy" (Bieschke et al. 2006). Whereas individuals may naturally experience changes in their sexual orientation over time (Peplau & Garnets 2000), the human capacity for erotic fluidity does not mean that such change can necessarily be effected by external interventions. Indeed, despite testimonials from individuals who believe they have changed from homosexual to heterosexual (Spitzer 2003), no empirical research has shown that conversion therapies can cause such change (Haldeman 1994, Herek 2003). The available data suggest, however, that such interventions can have negative psychological effects on sexual minority individuals who undergo them (Haldeman 2001, Shidlo & Schroeder 2002), making them ethically questionable regardless of their efficacy (Davison 1991). In recognition of these problems, the APA and the American Psychiatric Association have both adopted official resolutions reaffirming the mainstream position that a homosexual orientation is not pathological and raising ethical concerns about conversion therapy, especially when it is practiced on adolescents (Am. Psychiatr. Assoc. 2000, DeLeon 1998; see also Schneider et al. 2002).

In working with sexual minority clients, practitioners should remember the extent to which internalized stigma may play a central role in creating a person's discomfort with his or her sexual orientation (Davison 1991, Haldeman 1994). When a client is questioning her or his sexuality or is experiencing discomfort related to it, practitioners need to assess the psychological and social contexts in which this questioning and discomfort occur. Such an assessment might include an examination of internal and external pressures on clients to change their sexual orientation, the presence or absence of social support and models of positive sexual minority life, and the extent to which clients associate homosexuality or bisexuality with negative stereotypes and experiences (DeLeon 1998, Schneider et al. 2002).

The effort to articulate best practices for addressing conversion therapies has been part of a broader discussion of the conflicts that can arise among sexual minority individuals with multiple identities. An affirmative perspective encourages clinicians to recognize the particular life experiences and challenges that stem from the varied and often conflicting norms, values, and beliefs associated with sexual minority clients' multiple identities (Division 44/CLGBC 2000). For religious sexual minority individuals, for example, faith and sexuality may constitute conflicting social worlds as a result of religious texts and denominational teachings that condemn homosexuality. Sexual prejudice within religious congregations is another potential source of conflict (Haldeman 2004). Therapists working with this population face the challenge of navigating and respecting multiple identities simultaneously (Miville & Ferguson 2004). The primary therapeutic task is to find integrative solutions that provide self-acceptance and balance the different components of identity (Fischer & DeBord 2006, Morrow et al. 2004).

CONCLUSION

Additional research is needed to further illuminate the mental health needs of sexual minority populations, to identify factors that facilitate their adaptive coping and enhance their psychological resilience, and to assess the efficacy of therapeutic interventions based on an affirmative model. Whereas recent research employing national probability samples represents a new level of sophistication in the empirical study of sexual minority mental health, studies with larger samples and more extensive measures of sexual orientation and identity are needed. Such research will permit better assessment of the extent to which sexual minorities are at heightened risk for different types of psychological distress and how such risk varies by gender and sexual orientation identity, as well as race, ethnicity, age, and other variables. It should also examine predictors of resilience and effective coping among subgroups within the sexual minority population, with the goal of better understanding how adoption of a collective identity, disclosure of one's sexual orientation to others, and involvement in a sexual minority community may ameliorate the effects of minority stress. By testing hypotheses derived from the minority stress model, such research will yield valuable information about the experiences of sexual minorities while also permitting refinement of the model.

In addition, systematic study of the efficacy of specific therapeutic interventions inspired by lesbian-, gay-, and bisexual-affirmative models of psychotherapy is needed. To date, relatively little empirical research has been published in this area (Bieschke et al. 2006). Consequently, recommendations for professional practice have often had to rely on case studies, anecdotal reports, and observations by individual therapists. Although these can be useful sources of insight, large-scale clinical studies will facilitate the development and dissemination of more effective therapeutic techniques.

Although empirical research should be a priority, the mental health professions need not wait for more data before addressing the goal of better integrating affirmative models into clinical education, theory, and practice. Training programs can incorporate current knowledge about the mental health needs of sexual minorities into their coursework, practica, and continuing education. Theories of personality and therapy can be revisited to ensure that they address the experiences of sexual minority individuals. Existing guidelines for affirmative therapy with sexual minorities can be better promulgated among practitioners.

More than three decades ago, the mental health professions made a remarkable reversal in how they regarded homosexuality. Since then, impressive advances have been made in psychology's knowledge about the special vulnerabilities, resources, and strengths of sexual minorities. Nevertheless, we continue to face the challenge of understanding and meeting the mental health needs of sexual minority individuals while working to eradicate sexual stigma.

APPENDIX: RESOURCES FOR PRACTITIONERS

Am. Psychol. Assoc. 1993. Guidelines for providers of psychological service to ethnic, linguistic, and culturally diverse populations. *Am. Psychol.* 48(1):45–48

Am. Psychol. Assoc. 2002. Ethical principles of psychologists and code of conduct. *Am. Psychol.* 57:1060–73

Am. Psychol. Assoc. 2003. Guidelines on multicultural education, training, research, practice, and organizational change for psychologists. *Am. Psychol.* 58:377–402

Biaggio M, Orchard S, Larson J, Petrino K, Mihara R. 2003. Guidelines for gay/lesbian/bisexual-affirmative educational practices in graduate psychology programs. *Prof. Psychol. Res. Pract.* 34:548–54

Makes recommendations for fostering affirmative educational practice with respect to institutional climate and education about sexual minority issues.

Bieschke KJ, Perez RM, DeBord KA. 2006. *Handbook of Counseling and Psychotherapy with Lesbian, Gay, Bisexual, and Transgender Clients.* Washington, DC: Am. Psychol. Assoc.

Reviews best practices in affirmative therapy with lesbian, gay, bisexual, and transgender clients from the perspective of three main themes: (*a*) the definition and practice of affirmative psychotherapy with sexual and gender minority clients; (*b*) the role of a diverse sexual and gender minority community in identity development and social connection; and (*c*) the growing sociopolitical influence of lesbian, gay, bisexual, and transgender communities.

DeLeon PH. 1998. Proceedings of the American Psychological Association, Incorporated, for the legislative year 1997. *Am. Psychol.* 53:882–939

Reports on the Resolution on Appropriate Therapeutic Responses to Sexual Orientation, adopted by the APA Council of Representatives, which stresses the need for practitioners to assess the psychological and social contexts in which questioning or discomfort occurs among clients who are questioning their sexuality or experiencing discomfort related to it.

Division 44/Comm. Lesbian, Gay, Bisexual Concerns Joint Task Force Guidelines Psychother. Lesbian, Gay, Bisexual Clients. 2000. Guidelines for psychotherapy with lesbian, gay, and bisexual clients. *Am. Psychol.* 55(12):1440–51

Presents guidelines to provide practitioners with a frame of reference for the treatment of lesbian, gay, and bisexual clients. It includes basic information and further references in the areas of assessment, intervention, identity, relationships, and the education and training of psychologists.

ACKNOWLEDGMENTS

The authors thank Anne Peplau and Barrie Levy for their helpful comments on earlier drafts of the manuscript, and Jack Dynis for his support and assistance during its preparation.

LITERATURE CITED

Adam BD. 1995. *The Rise of a Gay and Lesbian Movement*. New York: Twayne Publ. Rev. ed.

Am. Psychiatr. Assoc. 1952. *Mental Disorders: Diagnostic and Statistical Manual*. Washington, DC: Am. Psychiatr. Assoc.

Am. Psychiatr. Assoc. 1968. *Diagnostic and Statistical Manual of Mental Disorders*. Washington, DC: Am. Psychiatr. Assoc.

Am. Psychiatr. Assoc. 2000. *Therapies Focused on Attempts to Change Sexual Orientation (Reparative or Conversion Therapies)*. Washington, DC: Am. Psychiatr. Assoc.

Ashmore RD, Deaux K, McLaughlin-Volpe T. 2004. An organizing framework for collective identity: articulation and significance of multidimensionality. *Psychol. Bull.* 130(1):80–114

Badgett MVL. 2001. *Money, Myths, and Change: The Economic Lives of Lesbians and Gay Men*. Chicago: Univ. Chicago Press

Balsam KF, Beauchaine TP, Mickey RM, Rothblum ED. 2005. Mental health of lesbian, gay, bisexual, and heterosexual siblings: effects of gender, sexual orientation, and family. *J. Abnorm. Psychol.* 114:471–76

Bayer R. 1987. *Homosexuality and American Psychiatry: The Politics of Diagnosis*. Princeton, NJ: Princeton Univ. Press

Provides historical and political analysis of the events leading up to the removal of homosexuality from the DSM.

Bérubé A. 1990. *Coming Out Under Fire: The History of Gay Men and Women in World War Two*. New York: Free Press

Bieber I, Dain HJ, Dince PR, Drellich MG, Grand HG, et al. 1962. *Homosexuality: A Psychoanalytic Study*. New York: Basic Books

Bieschke KJ, Paul PL, Blasko KA. 2006. Review of empirical research focused on the experience of lesbian, gay, and bisexual clients in counseling and psychotherapy. In *Handbook of Counseling and Psychotherapy With Lesbian, Gay, Bisexual, and Transgender Clients*, ed. KJ Bieschke, RM Perez, KA DeBord, pp. 293–315. Washington, DC: Am. Psychol. Assoc.

Bowleg L, Huang J, Brooks K, Black A, Burkholder G. 2003. Triple jeopardy and beyond: multiple minority stress and resilience among black lesbians. *J. Lesbian Stud.* 7(4):87–108

Bradford J, Ryan C. 1987. *The National Lesbian Health Care Survey*. Washington, DC: Natl. Lesbian Gay Health Found.

Branscombe NR, Ellemers N. 1998. Coping with group-based discrimination: individualistic versus group-level strategies. In *Prejudice: The Target's Perspective*, ed. JK Swim, C Stangor, pp. 243–66. San Diego, CA: Academic

Browning C, Reynolds AL, Dworkin SH. 1991. Affirmative psychotherapy for lesbian women. *Couns. Psychol.* 19:177–96

Burgard SA, Cochran SD, Mays VM. 2005. Alcohol and tobacco use patterns among heterosexually and homosexually experienced California women. *Drug Alcohol Depend.* 77:61–70

Case P, Austin SB, Hunter DJ, Manson JE, Malspeis S, et al. 2004. Sexual orientation, health risk factors, and physical functioning in the Nurses' Health Study II. *J. Womens Health* 13:1033–47

Chauncey GJ. 1982–1983. From sexual inversion to homosexuality: medicine and the changing conceptualization of female deviance. *Salmagundi* 58–59:114–46

Chauncey GJ. 1994. *Gay New York: Gender, Urban Culture, and the Making of the Gay Male World, 1890–1940*. New York: Basic Books

Cochran SD, Keenan C, Schober C, Mays VM. 2000. Estimates of alcohol use and clinical treatment needs among homosexually active men and women in the U.S. population. *J. Consult. Clin. Psychol.* 68:1062–71

Cochran SD, Mays VM. 2000a. Relation between psychiatric syndromes and behaviorally defined sexual orientation in a sample of the US population. *Am. J. Epidemiol.* 151:516–23

Cochran SD, Mays VM. 2000b. Lifetime prevalence of suicide symptoms and affective disorders among men reporting same-sex sexual partners: results from NHANES III. *Am. J. Public Health* 90:573–78

Cochran SD, Mays VM. 2006. Estimating prevalence of mental and substance-using disorders among lesbians and gay men from existing national health data. In *Sexual Orientation and Mental Health*, ed. AM Omoto, HS Kurtzman, pp. 143–65. Washington, DC: Am. Psychol. Assoc.

Reviews the authors' extensive secondary analyses of data from major national health surveys that included measurement of some aspect of sexual orientation.

Cochran SD, Sullivan JG, Mays VM. 2003. Prevalence of mental disorders, psychological distress, and mental services use among lesbian, gay, and bisexual adults in the United States. *J. Consult. Clin. Psychol.* 71:53–61

Cole SW. 2006. Social threat, personal identity, and physical health in closeted gay men. In *Sexual Orientation and Mental Health*, ed. AM Omoto, HS Kurtzman, pp. 245–67. Washington, DC: Am. Psychol. Assoc.

Reviews the author's program of research on the health consequences of coming out and remaining in the closet.

Conger JJ. 1975. Proceedings of the American Psychological Association, Incorporated, for the year 1974: minutes of the annual meeting of the Council of Representatives. *Am. Psychol.* 30:620–51

Consolacion TB, Russell ST, Sue S. 2004. Sex, race/ethnicity, and romantic attractions: multiple minority status adolescents and mental health. *Cult. Divers. Ethnic Minor. Psychol.* 10:200–14

Reports findings on the association between adolescents' multiple minority statuses and self-reported suicidal thoughts, depression, and self-esteem.

Crawford I, Allison KW, Zamboni BD, Soto T. 2002. The influence of dual-identity development on the psychosocial functioning of African-American gay and bisexual men. *J. Sex Res.* 39:179–89

D'Augelli AR, Collins C, Hart MM. 1987. Social support patterns of lesbian women in a rural helping network. *J. Rural Commun. Psychol.* 8(1):12–22

Davison GC. 1991. Constructionism and morality in therapy for homosexuality. In *Homosexuality: Research Implications for Public Policy*, ed. JC Gonsiorek, JD Weinrich, pp. 137–48. Newbury Park, CA: Sage

DeLeon PH. 1998. Proceedings of the American Psychological Association, Incorporated, for the legislative year 1997. *Am. Psychol.* 53:882–939

Diamant AL, Wold C. 2003. Sexual orientation and variation in physical and mental health status among women. *J. Womens Health* 12:41–49

Diamond LM. 2006. What we got wrong about sexual identity development: unexpected findings from a longitudinal study of young women. In *Sexual Orientation and Mental Health*, ed. AM Omoto, HS Kurtzman, pp. 73–94. Washington, DC: Am. Psychol. Assoc.

Diaz RM, Bein E, Ayala G. 2006. Homophobia, poverty, and racism: triple oppression and mental health outcomes in Latino gay men. In *Sexual Orientation and Mental Health*, ed. AM Omoto, HS Kurtzman, pp. 207–24. Washington, DC: Am. Psychol. Assoc.

DiPlacido J. 1998. Minority stress among lesbians, gay men, and bisexuals: a consequence of heterosexism, homophobia, and stigmatization. In *Stigma and Sexual Orientation: Understanding Prejudice Against Lesbians, Gay Men, and Bisexuals*, ed. GM Herek, pp. 138–59. Thousand Oaks, CA: Sage

Division 44/Comm. Lesbian, Gay, Bisexual Concerns Joint Task Force Guidelines Psychother. Lesbian, Gay, Bisexual Clients. 2000. Guidelines for psychotherapy with lesbian, gay, and bisexual clients. *Am. Psychol.* 55:1440–51

Drabble L, Midanik LT, Trocki K. 2005. Reports of alcohol consumption and alcohol-related problems among homosexual, bisexual and heterosexual respondents: results from the 2000 National Alcohol Survey. *J. Stud. Alcohol* 66:111–20

Dynes WR. 1990. Heterosexuality. In *Encyclopedia of Homosexuality*, ed. WR Dynes, pp. 532–35. New York: Garland

Ellis H. 1901. *Sexual Inversion*. Philadelphia, PA: F.A. Davis
Eubanks-Carter C, Burckell LA, Goldfried MR. 2005. Enhancing therapeutic effectiveness with lesbian, gay, and bisexual clients. *Clin. Psychol. Sci. Pract.* 12:1–18
Fergusson DM, Horwood LJ, Ridder EM, Beautrais AL. 2005. Sexual orientation and mental health in a birth cohort of young adults. *Psychol. Med.* 35:971–81
Fingerhut AW, Peplau LA, Ghavami N. 2005. A dual-identity framework for understanding lesbian experience. *Psychol. Women Q.* 29:129–39
Fischer AR, DeBord K. 2006. Perceived conflicts between sexual and religious diversity affirmation: That's perceived. In *Handbook of Counseling and Psychotherapy With Lesbian, Gay, Bisexual, and Transgender Clients*, ed. KJ Bieschke, RM Perez, KA DeBord, pp. 317–39. Washington, DC: Am. Psychol. Assoc.
Folkman S, Chesney M, Collette L, Boccellari A, Cooke M. 1996. Postbereavement depressive mood and its prebereavement predictors in HIV+ and HIV− gay men. *J. Personal. Soc. Psychol.* 70:336–48
Ford CS, Beach FA. 1951. *Patterns of Sexual Behavior*. New York: Harper & Bros
Frable DES, Wortman C, Joseph J. 1997. Predicting self-esteem, well-being, and distress in a cohort of gay men: the importance of cultural stigma, personal visibility, community networks, and positive identity. *J. Personal.* 65:599–624
Freud S. 1951. A letter from Freud. *Am. J. Psychiatry* 107:786–87
Freud S. 1953/1905. Three essays on the theory of sexuality. In *The Standard Edition of the Complete Psychological Works of Sigmund Freud*, ed. J Strachey, pp. 123–43. London: Hogarth
Friedman RC, Downey JI. 1998. Psychoanalysis and the model of homosexuality as psychopathology: a historical overview. *Am. J. Psychoanal.* 58:249–70
Garnets LD, Hancock KA, Cochran SD, Goodchilds J, Peplau LA. 1991. Issues in psychotherapy with lesbians and gay men: a survey of psychologists. *Am. Psychol.* 46:964–72
Garnets LD, Herek GM, Levy B. 1992. Violence and victimization of lesbians and gay men: mental health consequences. In *Hate Crimes: Confronting Violence Against Lesbians and Gay Men*, ed. GM Herek, KT Berrill, pp. 207–26. Thousand Oaks, CA: Sage
Garnets LD, Peplau LA. 2006. Sexuality in the lives of adult lesbian and bisexual women. In *Lesbian, Gay, Bisexual, and Transgender Aging*, ed. D Kimmel, T Rose, S David, pp. 70–90. New York: Columbia Univ. Press
Garofalo R, Wolf RC, Wissow LS, Woods ER, Goodman E. 1999. Sexual orientation and risk of suicide attempts among a representative sample of youth. *Arch. Pediatr. Adolesc. Med.* 153:487–93
Gilman SE, Cochran SD, Mays VM, Hughes M, Ostrow D, et al. 2001. Risk of psychiatric disorders among individuals reporting same-sex sexual partners in the National Comorbidity Survey. *Am. J. Public Health* 91:933–39
Gonsiorek JC. 1991. The empirical basis for the demise of the illness model of homosexuality. In *Homosexuality: Research Implications for Public Policy*, ed. JC Gonsiorek, JD Weinrich, pp. 115–36. Newbury Park, CA: Sage
Gonsiorek JC. 1995. Gay male identities: concepts and issues. In *Lesbian, Gay, and Bisexual Identities Across the Life Span*, ed. AR D'Augelli, CJ Patterson, pp. 24–47. Cambridge, MA: Oxford Univ. Press
Greene B. 1994. Lesbian women of color: triple jeopardy. In *Women of Color: Integrating Ethnic and Gender Identities in Psychotherapy*, ed. L Comas-Diaz, B Greene, pp. 389–427. New York: Guilford
Haldeman DC. 1991. Sexual orientation conversion therapy for gay men and lesbians: a scientific examination. In *Homosexuality: Research Implications for Public Policy*, ed. JC Gonsiorek, JD Weinrich, pp. 149–60. Newbury Park, CA: Sage

Suggests ways for therapists to provide competent care to lesbian, gay, and bisexual clients by becoming more aware of their attitudes and by learning more about issues that many sexual minority clients face.

Haldeman DC. 1994. The practice and ethics of sexual orientation conversion therapy. *J. Consult. Clin. Psychol.* 62:221–27

Haldeman DC. 2001. Therapeutic antidotes: Helping gay and bisexual men recover from conversion therapies. *J. Gay Lesbian Psychother.* 5(3–4):117–30

Haldeman DC. 2004. When sexual and religious orientation collide: considerations in working with conflicted same-sex attracted male clients. *Couns. Psychol.* 32:691–715

Halpert SC, Reinhardt B, Toohey M. 2006. Affirmative clinical supervision. In *Handbook of Counseling and Psychotherapy With Lesbian, Gay, Bisexual, and Transgender Clients*, ed. KJ Bieschke, RM Perez, KA DeBord, pp. 341–58. Washington, DC: Am. Psychol. Assoc.

Hart M, Roback H, Tittler B, Weitz L, Walston B, et al. 1978. Psychological adjustment of nonpatient homosexuals: critical review of the research literature. *J. Clin. Psychiatry* 39:604–8

Herek GM. 1996. Why tell if you're not asked? Self-disclosure, intergroup contact, and heterosexuals' attitudes toward lesbians and gay men. In *Out in Force: Sexual Orientation and the Military*, ed. GM Herek, J Jobe, R Carney, pp. 197–225. Chicago: Univ. Chicago Press

Herek GM. 2003. Evaluating interventions to alter sexual orientation: methodological and ethical considerations. *Arch. Sex. Behav.* 32:438–39

Herek GM. 2004. Beyond "homophobia": thinking about sexual stigma and prejudice in the twenty-first century. *Sex. Res. Soc. Policy* 1(2):6–24

Herek GM. 2006. Legal recognition of same-sex relationships in the United States: a social science perspective. *Am. Psychol.* 61:607–21

Herek GM, Capitanio JP. 1999. AIDS stigma and sexual prejudice. *Am. Behav. Sci.* 42:1130–47

Herek GM, Chopp R, Strohl D. 2007. Sexual stigma: putting sexual minority health issues in context. In *The Health of Sexual Minorities: Public Health Perspectives on Lesbian, Gay, Bisexual, and Transgender Populations.* ed. I Meyer, M Northridge. New York: Springer. In press

Herek GM, Gillis JR, Cogan JC. 1999. Psychological sequelae of hate crime victimization among lesbian, gay, and bisexual adults. *J. Consult. Clin. Psychol.* 67:945–51

Herek GM, Mitnick L, Burris S, Chesney M, Devine P, et al. 1998. AIDS and stigma: a conceptual framework and research agenda. *AIDS Public Policy J.* 13(1):36–47

Herek GM, Sims C. 2007. Sexual orientation and violent victimization: hate crimes and intimate partner violence among gay and bisexual males in the United States. In *Unequal Opportunity: Health Disparities Among Gay and Bisexual Men in the United States*, ed. RJ Wolitski, R Stall, RO Valdiserri. New York: Oxford Univ. Press. In press

Herrell R, Goldberg J, True WR, Ramakrishnan V, Lyons M, et al. 1999. Sexual orientation and suicidality: a cotwin control study in adult men. *Arch. Gen. Psychiatry* 56:867–74

Hershberger SL, D'Augelli AR. 1995. The impact of victimization on the mental health and suicidality of lesbian, gay, and bisexual youths. *Dev. Psychol.* 31:65–74

Hooker E. 1957. The adjustment of the male overt homosexual. *J. Proj. Tech.* 21:18–31

Huebner DM, Rebchook GM, Kegeles SM. 2004. Experiences of harassment, discrimination, and physical violence among young gay and bisexual men. *Am. J. Public Health* 94:1200–3

Jordan KM, Deluty RH. 1998. Coming out for lesbian women: its relation to anxiety, positive affectivity, self-esteem and social support. *J. Homosex.* 35(2):41–63

Katz JN. 1976. *Gay American History: Lesbians and Gay Men in the U.S.A.* New York: Crowell

Katz JN. 1995. *The Invention of Heterosexuality*. New York: Dutton

Kinsey AC, Pomeroy WB, Martin CE. 1948. *Sexual Behavior in the Human Male*. Philadelphia, PA: Saunders

Kinsey AC, Pomeroy WB, Martin CE, Gebhard PH. 1953. *Sexual Behavior in the Human Female*. Philadelphia, PA: Saunders

Krafft-Ebing RV. 1900. *Psychopathia Sexualis*. Chicago: Keener
Laumann EO, Gagnon JH, Michael RT, Michaels S. 1994. *The Social Organization of Sexuality: Sexual Practices in the United States*. Chicago: Univ. Chicago Press
Lewis RJ, Derlega VJ, Berndt A, Morris LM, Rose S. 2001. An empirical analysis of stressors for gay men and lesbians. *J. Homosex.* 42(1):63–88
Liddle BJ. 1996. Therapist sexual orientation, gender, and counseling practices as they relate to ratings of helpfulness by gay and lesbian clients. *J. Couns. Psychol.* 43:394–401
Luhtanen RK. 2003. Identity, stigma management, and well-being: a comparison of lesbians/bisexual women and gay/bisexual men. *J. Lesbian Stud.* 7(1):85–100
Malyon AK. 1981–1982. Psychotherapeutic implications of internalized homophobia in gay men. *J. Homosex.* 7(2–3):59–69
Martin JL. 1988. Psychological consequences of AIDS-related bereavement among gay men. *J. Consult. Clin. Psychol.* 56:856–62
Masten AS. 2001. Ordinary magic: resilience processes in development. *Am. Psychol.* 56:227–38
Mays VM, Cochran SD. 2001. Mental health correlates of perceived discrimination among lesbian, gay, and bisexual adults in the United States. *Am. J. Public Health* 91:1869–76
McCarn SR, Fassinger RE. 1996. Revisioning sexual minority identity formation: a new model of lesbian identity and its implications. *Couns. Psychol.* 24:508–34
Meyer IH. 2003. Prejudice, social stress, and mental health in lesbian, gay, and bisexual populations: conceptual issues and research evidence. *Psychol. Bull.* 129:674–97
Mills TC, Paul J, Stall R, Pollack L, Canchola J, et al. 2004. Distress and depression in men who have sex with men: the Urban Men's Health Study. *Am. J. Psychiatry* 161:278–85
Miville ML, Ferguson AD. 2004. Impossible "choices": identity and values at a crossroads. *Couns. Psychol.* 32:760–70
Morin SF, Rothblum ED. 1991. Removing the stigma: fifteen years of progress. *Am. Psychol.* 46:947–49
Morris JF, Waldo CR, Rothblum ED. 2001. A model of predictors and outcomes of outness among lesbian and bisexual women. *Am. J. Orthopsychiatry* 71:61–71
Morrow SL, Beckstead AL, Hayes JA, Haldeman DC. 2004. Impossible dreams, impossible choices, and thoughts about depolarizing the debate. *Couns. Psychol.* 32:778–85
Murphy JA, Rawlings EI, Howe SR. 2002. A survey of clinical psychologists on treating lesbian, gay, and bisexual clients. *Prof. Psychol. Res. Pract.* 33:183–89
Noelle M. 2002. The ripple effect on the Matthew Shepard murder: impact on the assumptive worlds of members of the targeted group. *Am. Behav. Sci.* 46:27–50
Ouellette SC, DiPlacido J. 2001. Personality's role in the protection and enhancement of health: where the research has been, where it is stuck, how it might move. In *Handbook of Health Psychology*, ed. A Baum, TA Revenson, JE Singer, pp. 175–93. Mahwah, NJ: Erlbaum
Peplau LA, Garnets LD. 2000. A new paradigm for understanding women's sexuality and sexual orientation. *J. Soc. Issues* 56:329–50
Perez RM, DeBord KA, Bieschke KJ. 2000. *Handbook of Counseling and Psychotherapy With Lesbian, Gay, and Bisexual Clients*. Washington, DC: Am. Psychol. Assoc.
Phillips JC, Fischer AR. 1998. Graduate students' training experiences with lesbian, gay, and bisexual issues. *Couns. Psychol.* 26:712–34
Rado S. 1940. A critical examination of the concept of bisexuality. *Psychosom. Med.* 2:459–67
Rado S. 1949. An adaptational view of sexual behavior. In *Psychosexual Development in Health and Disease*, ed. PH Hoch, J Zubin, pp. 159–89. New York: Grune & Statton
Remafedi G, French S, Story M, Resnick MD, Blum R. 1998. The relationship between suicide risk and sexual orientation: results of a population-based study. *Am. J. Public Health* 88:57–60

Riess BF. 1980. Psychological tests in homosexuality. In *Homosexual Behavior: A Modern Reappraisal*, ed. J Marmor, pp. 296–311. New York: Basic Books

Rothblum ED, Factor R. 2001. Lesbians and their sisters as a control group: demographic and mental health factors. *Psychol. Sci.* 12:63–69

Russell GM. 2000. *Voted Out: The Psychological Consequences of Anti-Gay Politics*. New York: NYU Press

Russell GM, Richards JA. 2003. Stressor and resilience factors for lesbians, gay men, and bisexuals confronting antigay politics. *Am. J. Community Psychol.* 31:313–28

Russell ST. 2003. Sexual minority youth and suicide risk. *Am. Behav. Sci.* 46:1241–57

Russell ST. 2006. Substance use and abuse and mental health among sexual-minority youths: evidence from Add Health. In *Sexual Orientation and Mental Health*, ed. AM Omoto, HS Kurtzman, pp. 13–35. Washington, DC: Am. Psychol. Assoc.

Russell ST, Joyner K. 2001. Adolescent sexual orientation and suicide risk: evidence from a national study. *Am. J. Public Health* 91:1276–81

Sandfort TGM, de Graaf R, Bijl RV, Schnabel P. 2001. Same-sex sexual behavior and psychiatric disorders: findings from the Netherlands mental health survey and incidence study (NEMESIS). *Arch. Gen. Psychiatry* 58:85–91

Savin-Williams RC. 2005. *The New Gay Teenager*. Cambridge, MA: Harvard Univ. Press

Scambler G, Hopkins A. 1986. Being epileptic: coming to terms with stigma. *Soc. Health Illn.* 8:26–43

Scheer S, Parks CA, McFarland W, Page-Shafer K, Delgado V, et al. 2003. Self-reported sexual identity, sexual behaviors and health risks: examples from a population-based survey of young women. *J. Lesbian Stud.* 7(1):69–83

Schneider MS, Brown LS, Glassgold JM. 2002. Implementing the resolution on appropriate therapeutic responses to sexual orientation: a guide for the perplexed. *Prof. Psychol. Res. Pract.* 33:265–76

Provides background information and examples to assist practitioners in implementing APA's Resolution on Appropriate Therapeutic Responses to Sexual Orientation.

Shidlo A. 1994. Internalized homophobia: conceptual and empirical issues in measurement. In *Lesbian and Gay Psychology*, ed. B Greene, GM Herek, pp. 176–205. Thousand Oaks, CA: Sage

Shidlo A, Schroeder M. 2002. Changing sexual orientation: a consumers' report. *Prof. Psychol. Res. Practice* 33:249–59

Shih M. 2004. Positive stigma: examining resilience and empowerment in overcoming stigma. *Ann. Am. Acad. Pol. Soc. Sci.* 591:175–85

Silverstein C. 1991. Psychological and medical treatments of homosexuality. In *Homosexuality: Research Implications for Public Policy*, ed. JC Gonsiorek, JD Weinrich, pp. 101–14. Newbury Park, CA: Sage

Socarides CW. 1968. *The Overt Homosexual*. New York: Grune & Stratton

Spitzer RL. 2003. Can some gay men and lesbians change their sexual orientation? 200 participants reporting a change from homosexual to heterosexual orientation. *Arch. Sex. Behav.* 32:403–17

Szymanski DM, Chung YB. 2003. Internalized homophobia in lesbians. *J. Lesbian Stud.* 7(1):115–25

Ueno K. 2005. Sexual orientation and psychological distress in adolescence: examining interpersonal stressors and social support processes. *Soc. Psychol. Q.* 68:258–77

Ullrich PM, Lutgendorf SK, Stapleton JT, Horowitz M. 2004. Self regard and concealment of homosexuality as predictors of CD4+ cell count over time among HIV seropositive gay men. *Psychol. Health* 19:183–96

Ulrichs KH, Lombardi-Nash MA. 1994. *The Riddle of "Man-Manly" Love: The Pioneering Work on Male Homosexuality*. Buffalo, NY: Prometheus

Villarroel MA, Turner CF, Eggleston E, Al-Tayyib A, Rogers SM, et al. 2006. Same-gender sex in the United States: impact of T-ACASI on prevalence estimates. *Public Opin. Q.* 70:166–96

Von Schulthess B. 1992. Violence in the streets: anti-lesbian assault and harassment in San Francisco. In *Hate Crimes: Confronting Violence Against Lesbians and Gay Men*, ed. GM Herek, KT Berrill, pp. 65–75. Thousand Oaks, CA: Sage

Williamson IR. 2000. Internalized homophobia and health issues affecting lesbians and gay men. *Health Educ. Res.* 15:97–107

Coping Resources, Coping Processes, and Mental Health

Shelley E. Taylor and Annette L. Stanton

Department of Psychology, University of California, Los Angeles, California 90095-1563; email: taylors@psych.ucla.edu, astanton@ucla.edu

Annu. Rev. Clin. Psychol. 2007. 3:377–401

First published online as a Review in Advance on November 6, 2006

The *Annual Review of Clinical Psychology* is online at http://clinpsy.annualreviews.org

This article's doi:
10.1146/annurev.clinpsy.3.022806.091520

1548-5943/07/0427-0377$20.00

Key Words

coping resources and processes, genetic bases of coping, neural bases of coping, coping interventions, stress

Abstract

Coping, defined as action-oriented and intrapsychic efforts to manage the demands created by stressful events, is coming to be recognized both for its significant impact on stress-related mental and physical health outcomes and for its intervention potential. We review coping resources that aid in this process, including individual differences in optimism, mastery, self-esteem, and social support, and examine appraisal and coping processes, especially those marked by approach or avoidance. We address the origins of coping resources and processes in genes, early life experience, and gene-environment interactions, and address neural underpinnings of coping that may shed light on evaluating coping interventions. We conclude by outlining possible intervention strategies for improving coping processes.

Contents

INTRODUCTION

Stress is a negative experience, accompanied by predictable emotional, biochemical, physiological, cognitive, and behavioral accommodations (Baum 1999). Coping is the process of attempting to manage the demands created by stressful events that are appraised as taxing or exceeding a person's resources (Lazarus & Folkman 1984). These efforts can be both action-oriented and intrapsychic; they seek to manage, master, tolerate, reduce, or minimize the demands of a stressful environment (Lazarus & Launier 1978). Coping resources can aid in this process; these resources include relatively stable individual differences in optimism, a sense of mastery, and self-esteem, and in social support. Coping resources, in turn, affect coping processes, specifically ones marked by approach, such as taking direct action or confronting emotional responses to a stressor, and ones marked by avoidance, such as withdrawal or denial. Coping efforts may be adaptive or maladaptive, and the form that coping processes assume affects how successful resolution of a stressor will be.

In this essay, we focus on the origins and effects of coping resources and processes, describing how they develop over the lifespan, how they affect mental and physical health, and whether they can be taught through interventions. Although we focus primarily on mental health, we address physical health outcomes in certain places. The rationale for so doing stems from the strong comorbidities between mental and physical health outcomes and the likelihood that mechanisms relating coping to mental (or physical) health outcomes will have implications for physical (or mental) health as well. In addition, the major stress systems of the body implicate both mental and physical health risks. Stress-related changes in autonomic and neuroendocrine functioning include (*a*) activation of the sympathetic nervous system, which leads to increases in anxiety, heart rate, and blood pressure, among other changes; and (*b*) activation of the hypothalamic-pituitary-adrenal (HPA) axis, which leads to the production of corticosteroids, including cortisol, which are necessary for energy mobilization, but are implicated in both mental (e.g., depression) and physical (e.g., infectious disorders) health risks. Stress inductions have also been associated with changes in proinflammatory cytokine activity (e.g., Dickerson et al. 2004), effects that may be driven, in part, by autonomic and HPA axis activity. Proinflammatory cytokine activity (including interleukin-6 [IL-6] and tumor necrosis factor alpha [sTNFαRII]) is stimulated by stressful conditions and has been tied to negative emotional states, including depression (Maier & Watkins 1998). Although these stress-related multisystem changes are protective in the short term, their chronic activation may negatively affect mental health over time, potentially elevating risk for depression and anxiety disorders and also enhancing risks for physical illnesses, including cardiovascular disease and Type II diabetes (see, e.g., Kiecolt-Glaser et al. 2002 for a review). Coping can intervene between stress and mental and physical health outcomes such as these, and thus merits consideration both as an intrinsically significant process in its own right and as a potential point of intervention for reducing adverse mental and physical health risks of stress. Note that we do not focus on stress-related processes and risk for specific psychological disorders, as these topics have been recently reviewed (e.g., Hammen 2005, Ozer et al. 2003), but rather on psychological outcomes more generally.

The empirical literature on coping is vast. A PsycINFO literature search of scientific journal articles from 2000 through 2005 using "coping" as a keyword generated 5151 documents. In a recent *Annual Review of Psychology* article, Folkman & Moskowitz (2004) reviewed the history of coping research, identified challenges for researchers (e.g., problems in measurement), and highlighted new developments. Commenting on the rapid expansion of research on coping over the past three decades, they noted, as we do, that the construct's "allure is not only as an explanatory concept regarding variability in response to stress, but also as a portal for interventions" (p. 746).

The model that organizes and characterizes our assessment of the origins and consequences of coping appears in **Figure 1**. **Figure 1** may be read both as a lifespan model that moves from the origins of coping resources and processes in early life to health and mental health outcomes later in life, and as a conceptual account of coping that occurs iteratively across episodes of stress. We begin with the characterization of coping resources and processes.[1] We next consider the origins of coping resources and processes in the early environment, genes, and gene-environment interactions. We then consider neural mechanisms, which may link coping resources and processes to downstream mental and physical health outcomes. The literature on the origins of coping in genes, gene-environment interactions, and neural bases of coping is still in its infancy. But, as we note in the conclusions, we believe these directions represent important avenues for future research. Finally, we return to coping processes and resources as portals of intervention and close by posing directions for future study.

COPING RESOURCES

It has long been known that people with a diverse array of mental disorders, including depression, schizophrenia, anxiety disorders, and autism lack coping resources for managing the challenges of daily living. Likewise, chronic psychological distress, which is related to lack of coping resources (Repetti et al. 2002), is implicated in more than half of the DSM-IV axis I disorders and in almost all of the axis II psychiatric disorders (Am. Psychiatr. Assoc. 1994). For example, depression is marked by pessimism, low self-esteem, a low sense of control, and adverse effects on social relationships (Beck 1967). The inability to establish and maintain normal social relations with others is central to autism (Med. Res. Counc. 2001). The onset of schizophrenia is associated with a disruption in an individual's sense of agency and perceived abilities to act intentionally (e.g.,

[1]We here distinguish between coping processes and emotion regulation. The term "coping processes" refers to thoughts and behaviors undertaken to manage the demands of stressful circumstances, which may include emotion regulation efforts. Emotion regulation involves the monitoring, evaluation, control, and expression of emotion, especially in challenging circumstances.

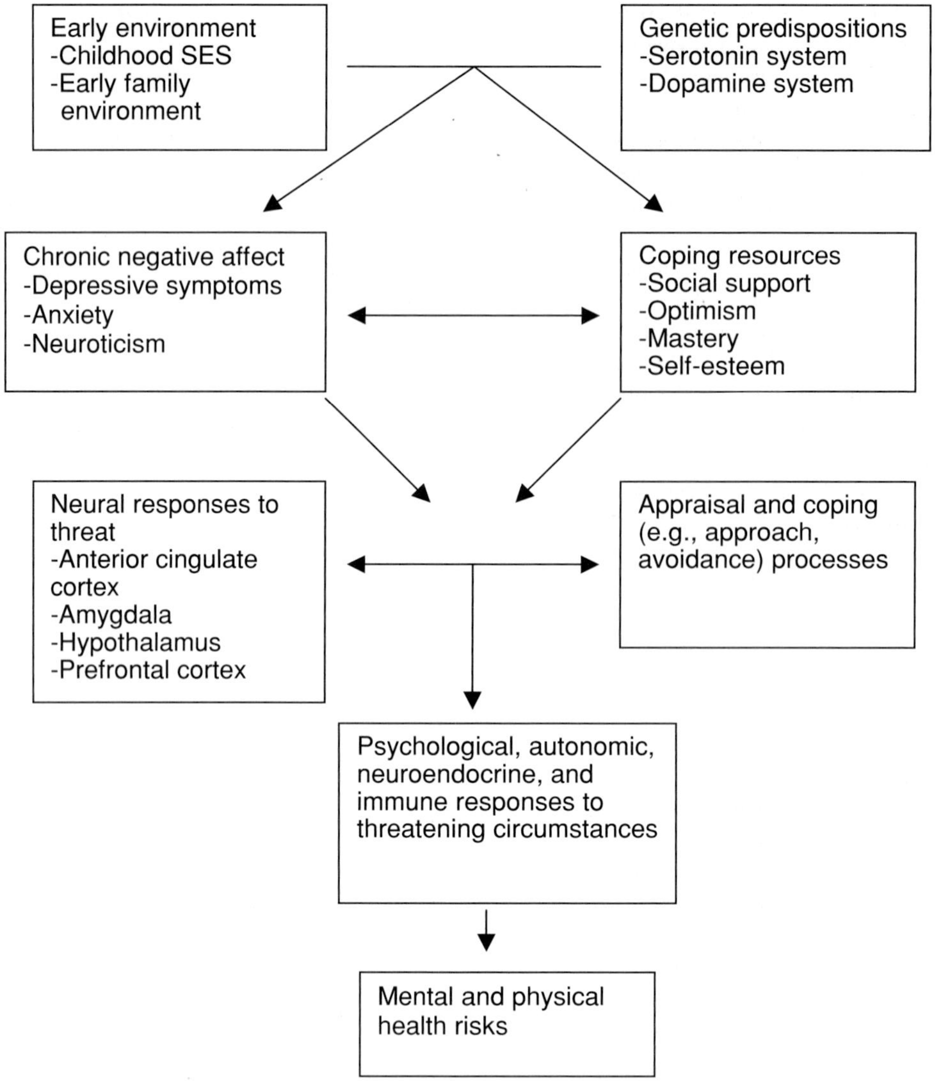

Figure 1

Origins and effects of coping resources.

Frith et al. 2000). The lack of coping resources associated with clinical disorders in some cases may represent symptoms, in other cases, developmental risk factors, and in other instances, risk factors for poor prognosis or recurrence.

Researchers have identified stable individual differences in coping resources that both improve the ability to manage stressful events and are tied to lesser distress and better health outcomes. Among these are optimism, psychological control or mastery, self-esteem, and social support. In addition to their roles as antecedents of specific coping strategies, coping resources can also have direct effects on psychological and physical health.

Optimism refers to outcome expectancies that good things rather than bad things will happen to the self. Dispositional optimism, typically measured by the Life Orientation Test (LOT-R; Scheier et al. 1994), has been tied to a broad array of mental and physical health benefits, including greater psychological well-being (e.g., Kubzansky et al. 2002), faster recovery from illness (Scheier et al. 1989), and a slower course of physical disease (e.g., Matthews et al. 2004) (see Carver & Scheier 2002 for a review). In addition, researchers have examined situation-specific optimistic expectations, which represent a potential target for intervention; they appear to have similar beneficial effects on stress-related mental and physical health outcomes (e.g., Reed et al. 1999).

Personal control or mastery refers to whether a person feels able to control or influence outcomes (Thompson 1981). Studies have shown a relationship between a sense of control and better psychological health (Haidt & Rodin 1999), as well as better physical health outcomes, including lower incidence of coronary heart disease (CHD; Karasek et al. 1982), better self-rated health, better functional status, and lower mortality (Seeman & Lewis 1995). As is true for optimism, situation-specific control expectations, which are often conceptualized as self-efficacy beliefs, are potential intervention targets and appear to have similar beneficial effects on managing stressful events (see Bandura 2006 for a review).

A positive sense of self or high self-esteem is also protective against adverse mental and physical health outcomes. For example, research consistently ties a positive sense of self to lower autonomic and cortisol stress responses (Seeman & Lewis 1995). Higher self-esteem has also been consistently tied to better psychological well-being (e.g., DuBois & Flay 2004), and interventions designed to enhance the self have beneficial effects on both psychological and biological responses to stress (e.g., Creswell et al. 2005).

The question has arisen as to whether these positive coping resources may be the mirror image of negative affectivity, such that people who are low in chronic negative affect have higher optimism, control-related beliefs, or self-esteem essentially by default. An emerging consensus is that although positive coping resources share overlapping variance with negative affectivity, they also account for unique variance in the prediction of mental and physical health outcomes (Scheier et al. 1994; see also Neiss et al. 2005).

Social support, another significant coping resource, is defined as the perception or experience that one is loved and cared for by others, esteemed and valued, and part of a social network of mutual assistance and obligations (Wills 1991). Research consistently demonstrates that social support reduces psychological distress, such as depression or anxiety, during times of stress and promotes psychological adjustment to a broad array of chronically stressful conditions (see Taylor 2007 for a review). Social support also contributes to physical health and survival. For example, Berkman & Syme (1979) found that having a high number of social contacts predicted an average 2.5 increased years of life.

Recent research has tied coping resources to underlying mechanisms that may mediate their effects. For example, Taylor et al. (2003a,b) related a cluster of coping resources including optimism, mastery, self-esteem, and social support to clinical assessments of mental health (Taylor et al. 2003a) and to lower baseline cortisol levels and autonomic responses to challenging tasks in the laboratory (Taylor et al. 2003b). Thus, at least some of the beneficial effects of coping resources may be mediated by the lesser physiological toll that stress exerts among those high in coping resources. Social isolation and loneliness have been related to high stress reactivity and inadequate and inefficient physiological repair and maintenance processes (Hawkley & Cacioppo 2003). In an experimental laboratory investigation, Dickerson et al. (2004) found that a manipulation designed to induce social threat led to an increase in sTNFαRII activity, suggesting that social emotions (in this case, shame and guilt) may be associated with elevations in proinflammatory cytokine activity. These documented immunologic mechanisms may help to explain the relation of social support/isolation to both acute infectious disorders (Cohen et al. 1997) and to chronic emotional disorders implicating proinflammatory cytokine activity, such as depression.

Although the existing research suggests numerous qualifications to these generalizations as a function of type and duration of stressor, coping resources are generally regarded as helpful to managing stress and have both direct effects on mental health as well as indirect effects on mental health via their effects on coping processes and stress-reducing abilities. In particular, evidence suggests that these coping resources may foster more positive appraisals of potentially stressful situations and more approach-related coping (e.g., Scheier et al. 1989).

COPING PROCESSES AND ADJUSTMENT UNDER STRESSFUL CONDITIONS

Coping resources in turn affect coping processes, that is, the specific intrapsychic or behavioral actions that people use for managing stress. In the following section, focusing on recent longitudinal and experimental research, we highlight major findings regarding coping as an explanatory construct in its links to mental and physical health outcomes in adults under stress (for a review of coping in childhood/adolescence, see Compas et al. 2001). We also examine coping processes as proximal mediators of the relations of other psychosocial parameters to stress-related adjustment.

In stress and coping theory (e.g., Lazarus & Folkman 1984), cognitive reappraisal processes regarding a stressful situation are considered important antecedents to coping processes. For example, in a longitudinal study of women seeking treatment for sexual assault, Frazier et al. (2005, Study 1) found that behavioral self-blame for the assault prompted coping through social withdrawal, which in turn predicted heightened distress. Women who perceived high control over their recovery made little use of social withdrawal coping and greater use of cognitive restructuring, which in turn predicted decreased distress. In a meta-analysis of 27 studies on causal attributions and coping with illness, Roesch & Weiner (2001) found that internal, unstable, or controllable attributions were associated with positive adjustment through their relations with greater approach-oriented and emotion-focused coping processes. Stable and uncontrollable illness attributions were associated with maladjustment through avoidant coping. In a meta-analysis of 15 studies on cognitive appraisals and coping in cancer patients, Franks & Roesch (2006) concluded that individuals who appraise their disease as highly threatening are likely to use more problem-focused coping strategies, those who believe their disease has caused harm or loss engage in more avoidance, and those who appraise their experience with cancer as potentially carrying benefits use more problem-focused and approach-oriented coping. Research on coping resources also suggests that at least some of their benefits may operate via appraisals of stressful events as less stressful or as more amenable to change (e.g., Bandura 2006).

Numerous frameworks for delineating coping processes have been advanced (for a review, see Skinner et al. 2003). Coping strategies often are organized according to their intended functions: as directed toward resolving the stressful situation (i.e., problem-focused coping) or palliating event-related distress (i.e., emotion-focused coping; Lazarus & Folkman 1984), or as approaching or avoiding the sources of stress (approach- versus avoidance-oriented coping; Suls & Fletcher 1985). Reflecting a core motivational construct (e.g., Davidson et al. 2000), the approach-avoidance continuum maps easily onto broader theories of biobehavioral functioning. Examples of active and approach-oriented coping are problem solving, seeking social support, and creating outlets for emotional expression. Coping through avoidance includes both cognitive and behavioral strategies. Some approaches, such as spiritual coping, potentially can serve either approach-oriented or avoidance goals.

Coping processes are conceptualized as effective to the extent that they are responsive to personal and situational contingencies (Lazarus & Folkman 1984). The empirical literature reveals that coping through avoidance can be useful in specific situations, particularly those that are short term and uncontrollable (Suls & Fletcher 1985). For example, Heckman et al. (2004) found that upon notification of a questionable mammography result, women's use of cognitive avoidance regarding the potential outcome predicted reduced anxiety after being informed that they did not have breast cancer. Early avoidance can presage longer-term problems when the stressor persists, however. For example, Levine et al. (1987) found that cardiac patients who denied their disease spent fewer days in the coronary care unit and had fewer indications of cardiac dysfunction during hospitalization than did nondeniers. However, deniers were less adherent to exercise training and had more days of rehospitalization in the year after discharge.

As demonstrated in longitudinal research, attempting to avoid thoughts and feelings surrounding persistent stressors predicts elevated distress across such samples as impoverished women (Rayburn et al. 2005), cancer patients (e.g., Stanton & Snider 1993), caregivers for individuals with chronic disease (Billings et al. 2000), hospitalized burn patients (Fauerbach et al. 2002), and individuals coping with terrorist attacks (Silver et al. 2002). Use of avoidance-oriented coping also predicts other important outcomes, including lower medical regimen adherence and subsequently greater viral load in HIV-positive individuals (Weaver et al. 2005), more risky behaviors in HIV-positive injection drug users (Avants et al. 2001), increased physical symptoms among AIDS caregivers (Billings et al. 2000), greater pain (Rosenberger et al. 2004) and compromised recovery of function following surgical procedures (Stephens et al. 2002), and lower likelihood of remission in depressed patients (Cronkite et al. 1998). Suggestive evidence that avoidant coping predicts chronic disease progression and/or mortality also exists for samples with cancer (Epping-Jordan et al. 1994), HIV infection (Leserman et al. 2000), congestive heart failure (Murberg et al. 2004), and rheumatoid arthritis (Evers et al. 2003). Neuroendocrine parameters are associated with avoidant behaviors under stress (e.g., Roelofs et al. 2005, Rosenberger et al. 2004), and passive/avoidant coping during experimentally imposed stress also has been associated with tumor development in animal models (Vegas et al. 2006). Avoidance-oriented coping may preempt more effective coping efforts, involve damaging behaviors (e.g., substance use), or induce intrusion of stress-related thoughts and emotions.

Although findings are less consistent for approach coping, longitudinal research has revealed a link between approach-oriented coping strategies and positive psychological and physical health in stressful circumstances. For example, use of such strategies as positive reappraisal of stressors, social approach, and problem-focused coping predicts an increase in positive affect (Billings et al. 2000). In a daily process study (Keefe et al. 1997), use of coping through relaxation and active efforts to reduce pain contributed to next-day enhanced positive mood and reduced pain in rheumatoid arthritis patients. Use of approach-oriented strategies during military deployment also predicted a reduction in depressive symptoms in Army personnel after the Gulf War (Sharkansky et al. 2000). In adults caring for a family member with dementia, approach-oriented coping was associated with a more vigorous cellular immune response to pathogens at high levels of stress (Stowell et al. 2001) and with lower procoagulant activity under experimentally induced acute stress (Aschbacher et al. 2005).

The fact that approach-oriented coping strategies predict adjustment less consistently than avoidant strategies might be explained by several factors. Some approach-oriented processes, such as problem solving, are not useful for immutable facets of a stressor, but rather are effective only for stressors that are amenable to change (e.g., Park et al. 2001).

Further, avoidance- and approach-oriented strategies may differentially predict negative and positive indicators of stress-related adjustment, with approach-oriented strategies more likely to contribute to positive affect (e.g., Billings et al. 2000). Because maladjustment receives more attention in the coping literature than positive functioning, effective approach-oriented coping processes might be missed in such research.

Coping as a Mediator of Relations Between Psychosocial Parameters and Adjustment

Ways of coping under stressful conditions do not operate on adjustment in isolation, but rather mediate the relations of other psychosocial parameters with adaptive outcomes. Antecedent psychosocial parameters include characteristics of the stressor, the social context, dispositional attributes, and cognitive appraisals. With regard to stressor characteristics, the experience of both distal (e.g., a history of childhood abuse) and proximal (e.g., living in a homeless shelter) relatively uncontrollable stressors predicts greater use of avoidant coping in impoverished women, and avoidance partially mediates their relations with subsequent depressive symptoms (Rayburn et al. 2005). An unsupportive social context also can prompt engagement in avoidance-oriented coping under stress, which in turn predicts an increase in distress in women with breast cancer (Manne et al. 2005a) and poorer adherence and higher viral load in HIV-positive individuals (Weaver et al. 2005). Holahan et al. (1997) found that a positive social context at study entry predicted greater relative use of approach-oriented coping by cardiac patients four years later, which in turn predicted a reduction in depressive symptoms.

Intraindividual factors, including coping resources and cognitive appraisals, also affect coping processes. Some research suggests that people high in optimism (Carver et al. 1993) or with high self-esteem (Aspinwall & Taylor 1992) use less avoidant and more approach coping, which are tied to better mental and physical health. Approach-oriented strategies such as positive reappraisal and active acceptance have been found to mediate the relation of optimism to better adjustment in stressful circumstances (Brissette et al. 2002, Carver et al. 1993).

In sum, mounting evidence suggests that coping processes play an important mediating role between contextual and individual variables and adaptive outcomes. A number of studies have suggested that coping strategies are not simply proxies for coping resources, but rather explain unique variance in adjustment (e.g., Murberg et al. 2002). However, some evidence suggests that coping strategies operate in tandem with other variables to affect outcomes. For example, Lancastle & Boivin (2005) found that low optimism, high trait anxiety, and use of avoidant coping were significant indicators of a latent construct, which predicted women's biological response to infertility treatment (e.g., number of oocytes). Although coping strategies share variance with dispositional and contextual variables, they are likely to provide a more malleable target for intervention.

In addition to their role as mediators, coping processes also can interact with contextual and individual parameters in their contribution to adjustment. For example, cancer patients who experienced low social support in tandem with the greater use of avoidant coping subsequently evidenced more severe symptoms of posttraumatic stress (Jacobsen et al. 2002). Emotionally expressive coping predicted decreased distress and fewer medical appointments for cancer-related morbidities in breast cancer patients high in hope (Stanton et al. 2000).

Newer models for conceptualizing the links among stressful life experiences, coping processes, and mental health outcomes also recognize their potentially reciprocal relations. Hammen's (1991) stress generation hypothesis points to the potential for the experience of depression to engender stressful events, which in turn can exacerbate depressive symptoms. Holahan et al. (2005) recently integrated coping processes into the stress generation model. In a decade-long investigation of 1211 adults aged 55 to 65 years at study entry, avoidance-oriented coping at study entry predicted more chronic and acute life stressors four years later, which in turn predicted an increase in depressive symptoms at ten years. Thus, coping through avoidance played a stress-generating role.

ORIGINS OF COPING RESOURCES AND PROCESSES

The relation of coping resources and processes to stress-related mental and physical health outcomes suggests that understanding their antecedents and consequences is pivotal for intervening to promote successful adjustment. Accordingly, we next turn to origins of coping resources in the early environment, in genetic predispositions, and in their interaction.

Origins of Coping in the Early Environment

Both animal (e.g., Francis et al. 1999) and human (e.g., Repetti et al. 2002) investigations reveal that a harsh early environment affects mental and physical functioning across the lifespan, and research implicates coping in these relations. We focus here on the human literature, but note the important parallels to both rodent (e.g., Liu et al. 1997) and primate (e.g., Suomi 1997) studies. Aspects of early life that have been consistently tied to poor coping include two markers of a stressful or threatening environment, specifically low childhood socioeconomic status (SES) and a harsh early familial environment.

Substantial research links economic adversity (low SES) to mental and physical health disorders (Adler et al. 1999). Low childhood SES predicts exposure to a broad array of early stressful events, including neighborhood conflict, violence exposure, exposure to pathogens, and other chronic stressors (Adler et al. 1999). Socioeconomic status in childhood has been related to problems in the enlistment or use of coping resources, including social support, optimism, mastery, and self-esteem (Adler et al. 1999, Repetti et al. 2002, Taylor & Seeman 1999). For example, there is an SES gradient in pessimism (Taylor & Seeman 1999), suggesting that harsh early life experiences contribute to the development of enduring pessimistic expectations. A sense of personal mastery appears to mitigate mental health risks conferred by low SES; among low-SES individuals with strong beliefs in personal mastery, mental and physical health outcomes are equivalent to those seen in high-SES groups (Lachman & Weaver 1998). To a lesser extent, self-esteem (Adler et al. 1999) shows an SES gradient, and perceived social support has a strong SES gradient (Kessler et al. 1992), such that those of higher SES in childhood and/or adulthood report greater social support resources. Low childhood SES has, in turn, been related to development of psychological distress (Gallo & Matthews 2003) and to a broad array of risk factors for mental and physical health disorders, including depression, anxiety disorders, coronary heart disease, cardiovascular disease, and immune-related disorders (Adler et al. 1999, Hemingway et al. 2003, Owen et al. 2003), although, to date, research has not examined the mediational role of coping in these processes.

Early family environments marked by harsh or conflict-ridden parenting are reliably associated with deficits in offspring coping resources and processes and with difficulty in managing challenging circumstances (see Repetti et al. 2002 for a review). Specifically, research suggests that offspring from harsh family environments may overreact to threatening circumstances, responding aggressively to situations that are only modestly stressful (e.g., Reid & Crisafulli 1990), but may also respond by tuning out or avoiding stressful circumstances, as through behavioral escape/avoidance or substance abuse

(Johnson & Pandina 1991, Valentiner et al. 1994). Poor coping related to early family environment may appear in latent form in early childhood and may contribute to chronic psychological distress and to a lack of coping resources, including optimism, mastery, self-esteem, and social support, in adulthood (Repetti et al. 2002). A harsh family upbringing has been related to higher levels of depression (Repetti et al. 2002); to preclinical risk factors for mental and physical health disorders, including elevated autonomic and cortisol responses to threatening circumstances (Seeman & McEwen 1996); to risk factors for mental and physical health disorders, including C-reactive protein (Taylor et al. 2006a); and to major mental and physical health disorders (Felitti et al. 1998). Thus, the existing literature provides a strong basis for a pathway linking a stressful early childhood to the compromised development of coping resources and processes and to risk for adverse stress-related mental and physical health outcomes.

Genetic Origins of Coping

Although genetic bases of risk for major mental disorders have been explored for more than 15 years, potential genetic contributions to coping have received less empirical attention. Behavioral genetics studies have identified the fact that there are genetic contributions to coping, but not the specific genes that are implicated. Twin studies estimate that approximately 25% of the variance in optimism is genetically based (Plomin et al. 1992). There is moderate genetic influence on self-esteem (e.g., Roy et al. 1995) and a larger genetic contribution to social support (e.g., Kessler et al. 1992). To our knowledge, genetic bases of mastery have not been examined.

At least some of the genetic contribution to effective coping may stem from genetic bases of approach-related behavior underpinned by dopaminergic pathways (Reuter & Hennig 2005). Activity within the dopamine system appears to be involved in regulating emotional responsivity to stressors (Giorgi et al. 2003). For example, the 48 base pair repeat within exon 3 of the DRD4 gene is related to novelty seeking (Ebstein et al. 1996) and to lower anxiety to potentially stressful events (Lakatos et al. 2003) and, thus, is a potential candidate for understanding coping processes. Similarly, COMT is implicated in prefrontal dopamine neural transmission, and the COMT val158met functional polymorphism has been related to positive emotionality and incentive motivation (Reuter & Hennig 2005). The relation of genetic polymorphisms in the dopamine system to executive functioning in the prefrontal cortex (PFC) more generally suggests that coping processes may reduce stress responses via PFC downregulation of activity in brain regions known to be activated in response to threat, including the amygdala, dorsal anterior cingulate cortex, and hypothalamus.

It is also possible that coping resources and processes operate via the moderation of genetic contributors to psychological distress. For example, studies have shown that the short variant of the serotonin transporter gene-linked functional polymorphic region (5-HTTLPR) is related to trait anxiety (Schinka et al. 2004); to depression in conjunction with life stress (e.g., Caspi et al. 2003); to neuroticism (Sen et al. 2004); and to amygdala hyperactivity to threat in healthy people (Hariri et al. 2005). The G allele of the serotonin receptor 1A (5-HT_{1a}) gene has been tied to neuroticism and harm avoidance (Strobel et al. 2003). An SNP in the 5-HTR_{2a} receptor gene has been associated with anxiety-related traits and sociability, and the T allele of the 5-HTR_{2a} is associated with higher activity level and sociability and lower level of anxiety-related traits (Golimbet et al. 2004). The G-1438A polymorphism of the 5-HTR_{2a} receptor gene has been related to introversion and sociality and may thus be related to social support processes. Finally, the monoamine oxidase gene has been tied to impulsivity and impulsive anger among other indicators of poor emotional control in response to stress (Huang et al. 2004).

Efforts to explore the genetic underpinnings of coping are in their infancy. The dopamine and serotonin systems by no means exhaust the bases for exploring genetic contributions to the development of coping resources or their deployment via coping processes. At present, they represent promising points of departure with a basis in the existing literature. Moreover, the existing literature has yet to examine the cumulative impact of multiple risk-related genes or gene-gene interactions as potential bases for the development or deployment of coping efforts.

Gene-Environment Interactions

The effects of genes related to coping resources are likely to be moderated by environmental factors, suggesting possibilities for intervention. Researchers have long suspected that a harsh early family environment may contribute to poor coping and to lifespan risk for mental and physical health disorders, not only directly, but also via gene-environment interactions (Repetti et al. 2002). The fact that the same family characteristics (a harsh, conflict-ridden or chaotic early family environment) appear to fuel such a diverse array of adverse physical and mental health outcomes suggests that a risky early family environment may exacerbate preexisting genetically-based risks (Repetti et al. 2002). Animal studies have also suggested the likelihood that early environment interacts with genetic predispositions to affect behavioral outcomes. For example, maternal behavior moderates genetic risk for serotonergic dysfunction related to serotonin transport (Bennett et al. 2002) and behavioral concomitants of the s allele of the serotonin transporter gene (5-HTTLPR), specifically impulsivity and social competence (Suomi 2003). Thus, family environment may exert a moderating effect on genetically based temperamental susceptibilities to poor coping and its adverse mental health outcomes.

Recent gene-environment interaction studies in humans have found that the relation between the 5-HTTLPR and depression is also moderated by early family environment. Specifically, a recent empirical study (Taylor et al. 2006b) reveals that individuals who grow up in a harsh early family environment or who are experiencing a current stressful environment are significantly more likely to experience depressive symptomatology if they have the s/s genotype of the 5-HTTLPR; however, those with the s/s genotype are significantly less likely to report depressive symptomatology if they are from a more supportive family environment and/or are currently in a nonstressful environment. Coping resources or processes are likely to mediate these effects, as they appear to do in the animal studies, but this link has not yet been made. Nonetheless, studies such as these suggest that there is significant environmental regulation of genetic contributions to susceptibility to adverse stress-related mental and physical health outcomes, with the potential for the quality of the environment to reverse the relation between a genetic risk and an outcome (in this specific instance, depression).

Using twin study methodology, behavioral genetics investigations have estimated the genetic contribution to coping strategies, including problem solving, emotion-focused coping, use of social support, and avoidant coping. Moderate genetic influences have been found for all four (e.g., Kato & Pedersen 2005, Kendler et al. 1991). Both shared and unshared environmental factors appear to contribute to these coping strategies as well (Mellins et al. 1996). However, research is mixed on whether genetic contributions to coping strategies overlap with genetic contributions to more stable coping resources, such as optimism, self-esteem, and other personality factors (Busjahn et al. 1999, Kato & Pedersen 2005).

NEURAL LINKS FROM COPING TO STRESS-RELATED MENTAL AND PHYSICAL HEALTH OUTCOMES

Exactly how coping exerts protective effects on mental and physical health outcomes has been largely unknown. A particular lacuna concerns the neural mechanisms that may underpin these relationships. Knowledge of the neural underpinnings by which coping may exert protective effects on mental and physical health outcomes may suggest not only strategies for coping interventions, but also criteria by which interventions may be evaluated (e.g., Etkin et al. 2005).

Neural Bases of Threat Detection and Coping

Recent research on neural bases of threat detection and emotion regulation help to clarify how stress affects brain functioning and how coping moderates those neural pathways. As noted, the amygdala and the dorsal anterior cingulate cortex (dACC) are associated with threat detection, serving an "alarm" function that mobilizes other neural regions, such as the lateral prefrontal cortex (LPFC) and hypothalamus, to promote adaptive responses to stress. The amygdala is sensitive to environmental cues signaling danger or novelty (e.g., Hariri et al. 2000) and predicts how unpleasant negative stimuli are reported to be (Lane et al. 1997). The dACC also serves as a threat detector, responding to conflict in incoming information (Carter et al. 2000). The dACC especially responds to social distress (Eisenberger et al. 2003).

Once activated, these neural threat detectors set in motion a cascade of responses via projections to the hypothalamus and lateral prefrontal cortex (Davis 1989, LeDoux 1996) aimed at amplifying or attenuating the threat signal and preparing to respond to the threat. Studies have shown connections between neural structures critical to threat detection and the hypothalamus, which is the origin of both sympathetic and HPA responses to threat. The amygdala has dense projections to the hypothalamus (Ghashghaei & Barbas 2002), and the ACC projects to the paraventricular nucleus of the hypothalamus (PVN; Risold et al. 1997), the specific region of the hypothalamus that triggers the cascade of events ultimately leading to cortisol release. Stimulation of both the amygdala and the ACC has also been associated with increases in blood pressure and cortisol levels in both animals and humans (Frankel et al. 1978, Setekleiv et al. 1961).

A neural region that appears critical for regulating the magnitude of these threat responses is the ventrolateral prefrontal cortex (VLPFC) (Hariri et al. 2000, Ochsner et al. 2004). Specifically, activation of the right VLPFC can directly down regulate the activation of the amygdala and dACC (Eisenberger et al. 2003, Hariri et al. 2002, Lieberman et al. 2006). Thus, the VLPFC appears to be a self-regulatory structure that modulates the reactivity of the amygdala and dACC to threat.

The neural bases of threat detection and reaction are important to the study of coping because they provide clues as to how coping resources and processes regulate psychological and biological threat responses. For example, people with strong coping resources may show lower amygdala and/or dACC reactivity to threatening stimuli. Alternatively, people with stronger coping resources may show stronger VLPFC responses to threatening stimuli. A third possibility is that strong coping resources are manifested in the correlation between VLPFC and threat-responsive regions, such as the amygdala or the dACC; a strong negative correlation would be suggestive of better regulation of threat responsivity by the VLPFC.

Although investigations have documented the role of the medial PFC (MPFC) and the left VLPFC in the modulation of pathways contributing to stress responses, the mechanisms have remained elusive. A key neurotransmitter in MPFC functioning is dopamine, and animal research suggests that the MPFC modulates responses to stressful tasks (Spencer et al. 2004). Using functional magnetic resonance imaging (fMRI) methodology, Smolka et al. (2005) reported that the number of COMT met158 alleles in the limbic system (specifically left hippocampus, amygdala, and right thalamus) and connected prefrontal areas (bilateral ventrolateral prefrontal cortex, right dorsolateral prefrontal cortex) were significantly positively correlated with reactivity to unpleasant stimuli. They interpreted these findings to suggest that increased limbic and prefrontal activation elicited by unpleasant stimuli in people with more met alleles may reflect poor emotion regulation. Note that these findings provide suggestive evidence consistent with the hypothesis implicating dopaminergic functioning in coping resources and implicating a negative relation between VLPFC and limbic functioning in the moderation of stress responses via coping resources.

Approach coping processes also link to patterns of brain activity suggesting involvement of dopaminergic pathways. The behavioral activation system (BAS), which is assumed to underlie approach-related coping, is organized largely by the dopaminergic neurotransmitter system and is associated with striatal dopamine projections to areas in the lateral and orbital frontal cortices (Rolls 1996). BAS is associated with goal-directed behavior, a promotion regulatory focus (Amodio et al. 2004), and positive emotions (Davidson et al. 1990), consistent with findings reviewed above on coping processes. By contrast, the behavioral inhibition system (BIS) may underlie avoidant coping. BIS is associated with a neural circuit organized by monoamine neurotransmitter systems, including noradrenergic and serotonergic networks, and their associated neural structures. The heart of the noradrenergic system is the locus coeruleus, located in the brainstem. In humans and monkeys, the locus coeruleus has modulatory noradrenergic effects on the anterior cingulate cortex (ACC) (Berridge & Waterhouse 2003). Polymorphisms in the serotonin transporter gene have also been implicated in ACC function (Canli et al. 2005). Direct links from avoidant coping to ACC functioning via these pathways have not yet been made, however.

Research relating coping resources and processes directly to activity in brain regions is in its infancy. However, one such study (Eisenberger et al. 2007) found that people who interacted regularly with supportive individuals showed diminished dACC and Brodmann's Area (BA8) reactivity to social rejection in an fMRI laboratory task and diminished cortisol reactivity during the Trier Social Stress Task; individual differences in dACC and BA8 activity mediated the relationship between social support and cortisol reactivity. Thus, social support may influence downstream biological stress responses by modulating neurocognitive reactivity to social stressors, which in turn attenuates neuroendocrine stress response. Other coping resources may exert their effects via similar pathways, although this hypothesis has yet to be explored empirically.

Research also suggests that early family environment is related to the neural underpinnings of stress management and coping processes. For example, in a task involving the labeling of emotions pictured in faces, Taylor et al. (2006a) found that young adults who had grown up in supportive families showed expected and relatively modest amygdala reactions to threat cues (fearful/angry faces) and strong activation of the right VLPFC, which was negatively related to amygdala activity; this pattern suggests regulation of limbic response via cortical responses to threatening stimuli. By contrast, young adults from harsh early family environments showed a strong positive correlation between right VLPFC and amygdala activation, suggesting that early family environment may be associated with dysregulation in the neural pathways involved in regulating responses to threat. Research has also begun to integrate genetic and neural bases of threat, with concomitant implications for coping. For example, Hariri et al. (2005) used fMRI to examine the relation of the 5-HTTLPR to amygdala responses to threat-relevant stimuli. As predicted, they found that people carrying the s allele of the 5-HTTLPR had stronger amygdala responses to fearful stimuli in comparison with those homozygous for the l allele.

Multilevel integrative efforts to relate genetic and/or familial origins of coping resources and processes to neural mechanisms that link to both emotional and physiological stress responses are in their infancy. But as these early studies suggest, such an approach can help to flesh out the pathways that relate the origins of coping and coping resources and processes to psychological and biological stress responses. Moreover, mapping such pathways may provide useful clues for intervention, an issue to which we next turn.

PATHWAYS FOR INTERVENTION

On the surface, the likely origins of coping resources in genes and early family environment might suggest dismal prospects for their modification. Recall, though, the evidence indicating substantial influence of the current environment on genetically based risk for depression. In that case, a supportive environment entirely reversed the impact of a genetic risk factor. Thus, modifying coping resources, coping processes, and the current environment would seem to have significant potential for managing stress and avoiding stress-related compromises in mental health. Of course, biological interventions to modify neural function also are relevant, but we do not address that literature here.

Interventions Directed Toward Coping Resources

Although long assumed to be relatively immutable, some coping resources evidence change across the adult life course (Roberts et al. 2006), and there is suggestive evidence that coping resources can change with psychosocial intervention. For example, Chesney et al. (2003) found that optimism increased following coping effectiveness training for HIV-positive men (but changes in optimism in the control group were not assessed). Antoni et al. (2001) found an increase in optimism over time in breast cancer patients following cognitive-behavioral stress management, but not in control group participants.

Another approach to considering psychosocial interventions directed to coping resources is to investigate coping resources or deficits as moderators of intervention effects. For example, Antoni et al. (2001) found that cognitive-behavioral stress management was more effective for women low in optimism than those high in optimism. Psychosocial interventions may also be more effective for women who lack support than for those in highly supportive environments (Helgeson et al. 2000, Manne et al. 2005b). Among individuals undergoing stressful life circumstances, interventions that address specific skills and coping deficits might be more promising than attempts to change personal dispositions directly. The match between the content of an intervention and the recipients' characteristics also requires attention (e.g., Cameron & Nicholls 1998).

Interventions Directed Toward Coping Processes

The large body of research on coping processes as contributors to adaptive outcomes under stress has not seen adequate translation into strategies for psychosocial intervention (Coyne & Racioppo 2000, de Ridder & Schreurs 2001). Some recent trials, however, illustrate the incorporation of findings from this body of work into psychosocial interventions, the impact of cognitive-behavioral interventions for managing stress on coping processes, and the mediating role of coping strategies on intervention outcomes. For example, Folkman et al. (1991) used coping effectiveness training (CET) that involves appraisal training to disaggregate global stressors into specific coping tasks and to distinguish between malleable and immutable aspects of stressors, tailoring application of particular coping strategies to specific stressors, and training to increase effectiveness in selecting and maintaining support resources. In HIV-positive men, CET was successful in improving perceived stress, burnout, and anxiety (but not depressive symptoms) relative to control conditions, and coping self-efficacy mediated intervention effects on the first two outcomes (Chesney et al. 2003). In another trial with HIV-positive men, cognitive-behavioral stress management produced significant reductions in mood disturbance and depressive symptoms relative to a standard care control (Cruess et al. 2002). Improvements were predicted by increases in coping self-efficacy, active coping, and coping through acceptance, and by decreases in dysfunctional attitudes and coping through behavioral disengagement (see Carrico et al. 2006).

Relevant interventions also have been conducted with individuals coping with chronic pain. Incorporating intervention elements based on empirically demonstrated links between specific coping strategies and outcomes in populations with chronic pain, Keefe et al. (2004) found, in a sample of adults with persistent arthritic pain, that spouse-assisted coping skills training combined with exercise training improved physical fitness and strength, pain-related coping attempts, and self-efficacy for controlling arthritis. Rhee et al. (2000) compared stress management training with control conditions in patients with rheumatoid arthritis. Improvements in depressive symptoms and pain were mediated by changes in a composite of coping through pain control and rational thinking, coping self-efficacy, and arthritis-related helplessness. Gil et al. (2000) conducted a pain coping skills intervention and a disease education control condition in African American adults with sickle cell disease. The intervention produced a significant reduction in laboratory pain perception and an increase in coping attempts. Moreover, daily diaries of intervention participants revealed that on days with significant pain during which participants practiced coping strategies, they had fewer major health care contacts (e.g., emergency room visits) than on days during which they did not use the strategies.

Investigations such as these suggest that psychosocial interventions can modify coping strategies and that increases in approach-oriented strategies and decreases in avoidance predict favorable intervention outcomes. A seemingly contradictory finding emerges from a study of couples coping with cancer (Scott et al. 2004), in which couples-based coping training and individual coping training for the patient were compared with a medical education control. The couples intervention was most successful in improving several outcomes. Assessed by totaling the number of coping strategies endorsed, coping efforts decreased in the couples intervention relative to the other conditions. This finding illuminates an important nuance to be considered in intervention research designed to change coping strategies. Active coping efforts are likely no longer to be necessary once they are successful in resolving the stressor. Chronic pain, for example, is likely to require persistent coping efforts, and thus increases in active coping strategies are likely to promote adaptive outcomes (Gil et al. 2000). But when resolution of aspects of a stressor is prompted through active coping, as might occur once cancer treatment is concluded, coping efforts are likely to decrease after intervention.

Interventions Directed Toward Changing Environments

Macro-level environmental factors (e.g., socioeconomic status) are not modified easily through traditional psychosocial interventions. However, in a randomized trial, a program to increase parents' employment and reduce poverty (e.g., employment-contingent earnings supplements, extensive child-care assistance) has been shown to improve children's academic achievement, motivation, and social behavior, particularly for boys, with effects on achievement particularly robust at five-year follow-up (Huston et al. 2005).

More proximal contexts, such as risky family environments, represent promising targets for preventive efforts. Specifically, such interventions as promoting parenting and family management skills in inner-city parents with young children (Tolan et al. 2004), conducting parent-child interaction therapy with physically abusive parents (Chaffin et al. 2004), and enhancing communication skills in adolescents with a history of maltreatment (Wolfe et al. 2003) have produced positive results in randomized trials, although contextual factors can moderate effects (Eron et al. 2002). Most such preventive programs have not examined their effectiveness on the recipients' coping attempts in later stressful contexts; however, such programs have yielded valuable lessons for the design of effective evidence-based prevention programs for families and children (Kumpfer & Alvarado 2003, Weisz et al. 2005).

TOWARD THE FUTURE

Until recently, research on coping was in disarray. In recent years, its bases, structure, origins, and neural underpinnings have begun to come into view. Important directions for future research include an increased understanding of the environmental and genetic inputs to the development of coping resources and processes over the lifespan and continued delineation of the neural and downstream biological mechanisms whereby coping contributes to mental and physical health outcomes. With this knowledge may come additional successful efforts to modify coping with concomitant mental and physical health benefits.

SUMMARY POINTS

1. Coping resources and coping processes affect mental and physical health.
2. Stable individual differences in coping resources such as optimism, personal control or mastery, and a positive sense of self or high self-esteem, as well as high levels of social support, promote effective coping with stress and have direct effects on mental and physical health.
3. Approach-oriented coping strategies have been tied to positive psychological and physical health outcomes in stressful circumstances.
4. Although avoidance coping strategies can be successful for coping with short-term uncontrollable stressors, avoidance coping has generally been tied to increased distress and chronic disease progression and mortality.
5. The beneficial effects of coping resources may be heavily mediated by their relations to approach-oriented coping and negative relations to avoidance coping.
6. Coping resources have their origins not only in genetics but also in the early environment; a nurturant early environment promotes the development of coping resources, and a harsh early environment interferes with it; gene/environment interactions are also implicated in successful coping with stress.
7. The neural pathways in the brain that are implicated in coping are increasingly coming to be understood. In particular, the amygdala and dACC are implicated in threat detection, and regions of the prefrontal cortex are associated with adaptive responses to stress.

8. Interventions implied by these perspectives include ones directed to coping resources, to coping processes, and to the environments within which coping skills develop and coping takes place.

ACKNOWLEDGMENTS

Preparation of this manuscript was supported by NIMH MH56880, NIA AG30309, and NSF 444040-ST-21549 to the first author.

LITERATURE CITED

Adler NE, Marmot M, McEwen BS, Stewart J. 1999. *Socioeconomic Status and Health in Industrial Nations: Social, Psychological, and Biological Pathways*. New York: N.Y. Acad. Sci.

Am. Psychiatr. Assoc. 1994. *Diagnostic and Statistical Manual of Mental Disorders*. Washington, DC: Am. Psychiatric Assoc. 4th ed.

Amodio DM, Shah JY, Sigelman J, Brazy PC, Harmon-Jones E. 2004. Implicit regulatory focus associated with asymmetrical frontal cortical activity. *J. Exp. Soc. Psychol.* 40:225–32

Antoni MH, Lehman JM, Kilbourn KM, Boyers AE, Culvers JL, et al. 2001. Cognitive-behavioral stress management intervention decreases the prevalence of depression and enhances benefit finding among women under treatment for early-stage breast cancer. *Health Psychol.* 20:20–32

Aschbacher K, Patterson TL, von Kanel R, Dimsdale JE, Mills PJ, et al. 2005. Coping processes and hemostatic reactivity to acute stress in dementia caregivers. *Psychosom. Med.* 67:964–71

Aspinwall LG, Taylor SE. 1992. Modeling cognitive adaptation: a longitudinal investigation of the impact of individual differences and coping on college adjustment and performance. *J. Personal. Soc. Psychol.* 63:989–1003

Avants SK, Warburton LA, Margolin A. 2001. How injection drug users coped with testing HIV-seropositive: implications for subsequent health-related behaviors. *AIDS Educ. Prev.* 13:207–18

Bandura A. 2006. Toward a psychology of human agency. *Perspect. Psychol. Sci.* 1:164–80

Baum A. 1999. Stress, intrusive imagery, and chronic distress. *Health Psychol.* 9:653–75

Beck AT. 1967. *Depression: Causes and Treatment*. Philadelphia, PA: Univ. Penn. Press

Bennett AJ, Lesch KP, Heils A, Long JC, Lorenz JG, et al. 2002. Early experience and serotonin transporter gene variation interact to influence primate CNS function. *Mol. Psychiatry* 7:118–22

Berkman LF, Syme SL. 1979. Social networks, host resistance, and mortality: a nine-year followup study of Alameda County residents. *Am. J. Epidemiol.* 109:186–204

Berridge CW, Waterhouse BD. 2003. The locus coeruleus-noradrenergic system: modulation of behavioral state and state-dependent cognitive processes. *Brain Res. Brain Res. Rev.* 42:33–84

Billings DW, Folkman S, Acree M, Moskowitz JT. 2000. Coping and physical health during caregiving: the roles of positive and negative affect. *J. Personal. Soc. Psychol.* 79:131–42

Brissette I, Scheier MF, Carver CS. 2002. The role of optimism in social network development, coping, and psychological adjustment during a life transition. *J. Personal. Soc. Psychol.* 82:102–11

Busjahn A, Faulhaber HD, Freier K, Luft FC. 1999. Genetic and environmental influences on coping styles: a twin study. *Psychosom. Med.* 61:469–75

Cameron LD, Nicholls G. 1998. Expression of stressful experiences through writing: effects of a self-regulation manipulation for pessimists and optimists. *Health Psychol.* 17:84–92

Canli T, Omura K, Haas BW, Fallgatter A, Constable RT, Lesch KP. 2005. Beyond affect: a role for genetic variation of the serotonin transporter in neural activation during a cognitive attention task. *Proc. Natl. Acad. Sci. USA* 102:12224–29

Carrico AW, Antoni MH, Duran RE, Ironson G, Penedo F, et al. 2006. Reductions in depressed mood and denial coping during cognitive behavioral stress management with HIV-positive gay men treated with HAART. *Ann. Behav. Med.* 31:155–64

Carter CS, MacDonald AW, Botvinick MM, Ross LL, Stenger VA, et al. 2000. Parsing executive processes: strategic vs. evaluative functions of the anterior cingulate cortex. *Proc. Natl. Acad. Sci. USA* 97:1944–48

Carver CS, Pozo C, Harris SD, Noriega V, Scheier MF, et al. 1993. How coping mediates the effect of optimism on distress: a study of women with early stage breast cancer. *J. Personal. Soc. Psychol.* 65:375–90

Carver CS, Scheier MF. 2002. Optimism. In *Handbook of Positive Psychology*, ed. CR Snyder, SJ Lopez, pp. 231–43. New York: Oxford Univ. Press

Caspi A, Sugden D, Moffitt TE, Taylor A, Craig IW, et al. 2003. Influence of life stress on depression: moderation by a polymorphism in the 5-HTT gene. *Science* 301:386–89

Chaffin M, Silovsky JF, Funderburk B, Valle LA, Brestan EV, et al. 2004. Parent-child interaction therapy with physically abusive parents: efficacy for reducing future abuse reports. *J. Consult. Clin. Psychol.* 72:500–10

Chesney MA, Chambers DB, Taylor JM, Johnson LM, Folkman S. 2003. Coping effectiveness training for men living with HIV: results from a randomized clinical trial testing a group-based intervention. *Psychosom. Med.* 65:1038–46

Cohen S, Doyle WJ, Skoner DP, Rabin BS, Gwaltney JJM. 1997. Social ties and susceptibility to the common cold. *JAMA* 277:1940–44

Compas BE, Connor-Smith JK, Saltzman H, Thomsen AH, Wadsworth ME. 2001. Coping with stress during childhood and adolescence: problems, progress, and potential in theory and research. *Psychol. Bull.* 127:87–127

Coyne JC, Racioppo MW. 2000. Never the twain shall meet? Closing the gap between coping research and clinical intervention research. *Am. Psychol.* 55:655–64

Creswell JD, Welch WT, Taylor SE, Sherman DK, Gruenewald T, et al. 2005. Affirmation of personal values buffers neuroendocrine and psychological stress responses. *Psychol. Sci.* 16:846–51

Cronkite RC, Moos RH, Twohey J, Cohen C, Swindle R. 1998. Life circumstances and personal resources as predictors of the ten-year course of depression. *Am. J. Community Psychol.* 26:255–80

Cruess S, Antoni MH, Hayes A, Penedo F, Ironson G, et al. 2002. Changes in mood and depressive symptoms and related change processes during cognitive-behavioral stress management in HIV-infected men. *Cogn. Ther. Res.* 26:373–92

Davidson RJ, Ekman P, Saron CD, Senulis JA, Friesen WV. 1990. Approach/withdrawal and cerebral asymmetry: emotional expression and brain physiology: I. *J. Personal. Soc. Psychol.* 58:330–41

Davidson RJ, Jackson DC, Kalin NH. 2000. Emotion, plasticity, context, and regulation: perspectives from affective neuroscience. *Psychol. Bull.* 126:890–909

Davis M. 1989. The role of the amygdala and its efferent projections in fear and anxiety. In *Psychopharmacology of Anxiety*, ed. P Tyrer, pp. 52–79. New York: Oxford Univ. Press

de Ridder D, Schreurs K. 2001. Developing interventions for chronically ill patients: Is coping a helpful concept? *Clin. Psychol. Rev.* 21:205–40

Dickerson SS, Kemeny ME, Aziz N, Kim KH, Fahey JL. 2004. Immunological effects of induced shame and guilt. *Psychosom. Med.* 66:124–31

DuBois DL, Flay BR. 2004. The healthy pursuit of self-esteem: comment on and alternative to the Crocker and Park 2004 formulation. *Psychol. Bull.* 130:415–20

Ebstein RP, Novick O, Umansky R, Priel B, Osher Y, et al. 1996. Dopamine D4 receptor (D4DR) exon III polymorphism associated with the human personality trait of novelty seeking. *Nat. Genet.* 12:78–80

Eisenberger NI, Lieberman MD, Williams KD. 2003. Does rejection hurt? An fMRI study of social exclusion. *Science* 302:290–92

Eisenberger NI, Taylor SE, Gable SL, Hilmert CJ, Lieberman MD. 2007. Neural pathways link social support to attenuated neuroendocrine stress responses. *Psychosom. Med.* In press

Epping-Jordan JE, Compas BE, Howell DC. 1994. Predictors of cancer progression in young adult men and women: avoidance, intrusive thoughts, and psychological symptoms. *Health Psychol.* 13:539–47

Eron L, Huesmann R, Spindler A, Guerra N, Henry D, et al. 2002. A cognitive-ecological approach to preventing aggression in urban settings: initial outcomes for high-risk children. *J. Consult. Clin. Psychol.* 70:179–94

Etkin A, Phil M, Pittenger C, Polan HJ, Kandel ER. 2005. Toward a neurobiology of psychotherapy: basic science and clinical applications. *J. Neuropsychiatry Clin. Neurosci.* 17:145–58

Evers AWM, Kraaimaat FW, Geenen R, Jacobs JWG, Bijlsma JWJ. 2003. Stress-vulnerability factors as long-term predictors of disease activity in early rheumatoid arthritis. *J. Psychosom. Res.* 55:293–302

Fauerbach JA, Heinberg LJ, Lawrence JW, Bryant AG, Richter L, et al. 2002. Coping with body image changes following a disfiguring burn injury. *Health Psychol.* 21:115–21

Felitti VJ, Anda RF, Nordenberg D, Williamson DF, Apitz AM, et al. 1998. Relationship of childhood abuse and household dysfunction to many of the leading causes of death in adults. *Am. J. Prev. Med.* 14:245–58

Folkman S, Chesney M, McKusick L, Ironson G, Johnson DS, et al. 1991. Translating coping theory into intervention. In *The Social Context of Coping*, ed. J Eckenrode, pp. 239–59. New York: Plenum

Folkman S, Moskowitz JT. 2004. Coping: pitfalls and promise. *Annu. Rev. Psychol.* 55:745–74

Francis D, Diorio J, Liu D, Meaney MJ. 1999. Nongenomic transmission across generations of maternal behavior and stress responses in the rat. *Science* 286:1155–58

Frankel RJ, Jenkins JS, Wright JJ. 1978. Pituitary-adrenal response to stimulation of the limbic system and lateral hypothalamus in the rhesus monkey (*Macacca Mulatta*). *Acta Endocrinol. (Copenh.)* 88:209–16

Franks HM, Roesch SC. 2006. Appraisals and coping in people living with cancer: a meta-analysis. *Psychooncology*. In press

Frazier PA, Mortensen H, Steward J. 2005. Coping strategies as mediators of the relations among perceived control and distress in sexual assault survivors. *J. Couns. Psychol.* 52:267–78

Frith CD, Blakemore SJ, Wolpert DM. 2000. Explaining the symptoms of schizophrenia. Abnormalities in the awareness of action. *Brain Res. Rev.* 31:357–63

Gallo LC, Matthews KA. 2003. Understanding the association between socioeconomic status and physical health: Do negative emotions play a role? *Psychol. Bull.* 129:10–51

Ghashghaei HT, Barbas H. 2002. Pathways for emotion: interactions of prefrontal and anterior temporal pathways in the amygdala of the rhesus monkey. *Neuroscience* 115:1261–79

Gil KM, Carson JW, Sedway JA, Porter LS, Schaeffer JJW, et al. 2000. Follow-up of coping skills training in adults with sickle cell disease: analysis of daily pain and coping practice diaries. *Health Psychol.* 19:85–90

Giorgi O, Lecca D, Piras G, Driscoll P, Corda MG. 2003. Dissociation between mesocortical dopamine release and fear-related behaviours in two psychogenetically selected lines of rats that differ in coping strategies to aversive conditions. *Eur. J. Neurosci.* 17:2716–26

Golimbet VE, Alfimova MV, Mitiushina NG. 2004. Polymorphism of the serotonin 2A receptor gene (5HTR2A) and personality traits. *Mol. Biol. (Mosk.)* 38:404–12 (Transl. from Russian)

Haidt J, Rodin J. 1999. Control and efficacy as interdisciplinary bridges. *Rev. Gen. Psychol.* 3:317–37

Hammen C. 1991. Generation of stress in the course of unipolar depression. *J. Abnorm. Psychol.* 100:555–61

Hammen C. 2005. Stress and depression. *Annu. Rev. Clin. Psychol.* 1:293–318

Hariri AR, Bookheimer SY, Mazziotta JC. 2000. Modulating emotional responses: effects of a neocortical network on the limbic system. *Neuroreport* 11:43–48

Hariri AR, Drabant EM, Munoz KE, Kolachana BS, Mattay VS, et al. 2005. A susceptibility gene for affective disorders and the response of the human amygdala. *Arch. Gen. Psychiatry* 62:146–52

Hariri AR, Tessitore A, Mattay VS, Fera F, Weinberger DR. 2002. The amygdala response to emotional stimuli: a comparison of faces and scenes. *Neuroimage* 17:317–23

Hawkley L, Cacioppo J. 2003. Loneliness and pathways to disease. *Brain Behav. Immun.* 17:S98-105

Heckman BD, Fisher EB, Monsees B, Merbaum M, Ristvedt S, et al. 2004. Coping and anxiety in women recalled for additional diagnostic procedures following an abnormal screening mammogram. *Health Psychol.* 23:42–48

Helgeson VS, Cohen S, Schulz R, Yasko J. 2000. Group support interventions for women with breast cancer: Who benefits from what? *Health Psychol.* 19:107–14

Hemingway H, Shipley M, Mullen MJ, Kumari M, Brunner E, et al. 2003. Social and psychosocial influences on inflammatory markers and vascular function in civil servants (the Whitehall II Study). *Am. J. Cardiol.* 92:984–87

Holahan CJ, Moos RH, Holahan CK, Brennan PL. 1997. Social context, coping strategies, and depressive symptoms: an expanded model with cardiac patients. *J. Personal. Soc. Psychol.* 72:918–28

Holahan CJ, Moos RH, Holahan CK, Brennan PL, Schutte KK. 2005. Stress generation, avoidance coping, and depressive symptoms: a 10-year model. *J. Consult. Clin. Psychol.* 73:658–66

Huang Y, Cate SP, Battistuzzi C, Oquendo MA, Brent D, et al. 2004. An association between a functional polymorphism in the monoamine oxidase a gene promoter, impulsive traits and early abuse experiences. *Neuropsychopharmacology* 29:1498–505

Huston AC, Duncan GJ, McLoyd VC, Crosby DA, Ripke MN, et al. 2005. Impacts on children of a policy to promote employment and reduce poverty for low-income parents: New Hope after 5 years. *Dev. Psychol.* 41:902–18

Jacobsen PB, Sadler IJ, Booth-Jones M, Soety E, Weitzner MA, et al. 2002. Predictors of posttraumatic stress disorder symptomatology following bone marrow transplantation for cancer. *J. Consult. Clin. Psychol.* 70:235–40

Johnson V, Pandina RJ. 1991. Effects of family environment on adolescent substance use, delinquency, and coping styles. *Am. J. Drug Alcohol Abuse* 17:71–88

Karasek RA, Theorell T, Schwartz J, Pieper C, Alfredsson L. 1982. Job, psychological factors and coronary heart disease: Swedish prospective findings and U.S. prevalence findings using a new occupational inference method. *Adv. Cardiol.* 29:62–67

Kato K, Pedersen NL. 2005. Personality and coping: a study of twins reared apart and twins reared together. *Behav. Genet.* 35:147–58

Keefe FJ, Affleck G, Lefebvre JC, Starr K, Caldwell DJ, et al. 1997. Pain coping strategies and coping efficacy in rheumatoid arthritis: a daily process analysis. *Pain* 69:35–42

Keefe FJ, Blumenthal J, Baucom D, Affleck G, Waugh R, et al. 2004. Effects of spouse-assisted coping skills training and exercise training in patients with osteoarthritic knee pain: a randomized controlled study. *Pain* 110:539–49

Kendler KS, Kessler RC, Heath AC, Neale MC, Eaves LJ. 1991. Coping: a genetic epidemiological investigation. *Psychol. Med.* 21:337–46

Kessler RC, Kendler KS, Heath AC, Neale MC, Eaves LJ. 1992. Social support, depressed mood, and adjustment to stress: a genetic epidemiological investigation. *J. Personal. Soc. Psychol.* 62:257–72

Kiecolt-Glaser JK, McGuire L, Robles TF, Glaser R. 2002. Emotions, morbidity, and mortality: new perspectives from psychoneuroimmunology. *Annu. Rev. Psychol.* 53:83–107

Kubzansky LD, Wright RJ, Cohen S, Weiss S, Rosner B, et al. 2002. Breathing easy: a prospective study of optimism and pulmonary function in the normative aging study. *Ann. Behav. Med.* 24:345–53

Kumpfer KL, Alvarado R. 2003. Family-strengthening approaches for the prevention of youth problem behaviors. *Am. Psychol.* 58:457–65

Lachman ME, Weaver SL. 1998. The sense of control as a moderator of social class differences in health and well-being. *J. Personal. Soc. Psychol.* 74:763–73

Lakatos K, Nemoda Z, Birkas E, Ronai Z, Kovacs E, et al. 2003. Association of D4 dopamine receptor gene and serotonin transporter promoter polymorphisms with infants' response to novelty. *Mol. Psychiatry* 8:90–97

Lancastle D, Boivin J. 2005. Dispositional optimism, trait anxiety, and coping: unique or shared effects on biological response to fertility treatment? *Health Psychol.* 24:171–78

Lane RD, Reiman EM, Bradley MM, Lang PJ, Ahern GL, et al. 1997. Neuroanatomical correlates of pleasant and unpleasant emotion. *Neuropsychologia* 35:1437–44

Lazarus RS, Folkman S. 1984. *Stress, Appraisal, and Coping*. New York: Springer

Lazarus RS, Launier R. 1978. Stress-related transactions between person and environment. In *Perspectives in Interactional Psychology*, ed. LA Pervin, M Lewis, pp. 87–327. New York: Plenum

LeDoux J. 1996. *The Emotional Brain: The Mysterious Underpinnings of Emotional Life*. New York: Simon & Schuster

Leserman J, Petitto JM, Golden RN, Gaynes BN, Gu H, et al. 2000. Impact of stressful life events, depression, social support, coping, and cortisol on progression to AIDS. *Am. J. Psychiatry* 157:1221–28

Levine J, Warrenburg S, Kerns R, Schwartz G, Delaney R, et al. 1987. The role of denial in recovery from coronary heart disease. *Psychosom. Med.* 49:109–17

Lieberman MD, Eisenberger NI, Crockett MJ, Tom S, Pfeifer JH, Way BM. 2006. Putting feelings into words: affect labeling disrupts amygdala activity to affective stimuli. *Psychological Science*. In press

Liu D, Dorio J, Tannenbaum B, Caldji C, Francis D, et al. 1997. Maternal care, hippocampal glucocorticoid receptors, and hypothalamic-pituitary-adrenal responses to stress. *Science* 277:1659–62

Maier SF, Watkins LR. 1998. Cytokines for psychologists: implications of bi-directional immune-to-brain communication for understanding behavior, mood, and cognition. *Psychol. Rev.* 105:83–107

Manne SL, Ostroff J, Winkel G, Fox K, Grana G. 2005a. Partner unsupportive responses, avoidant coping, and distress among women with early stage breast cancer: patient and partner perspectives. *Health Psychol.* 24:635–41

Manne SL, Ostroff JS, Winkel G, Fox K, Grana G, et al. 2005b. Couple-focused group intervention for women with early stage breast cancer. *J. Consult. Clin. Psychol.* 73:634–46

Matthews KA, Raikkonen K, Sutton-Tyrell K, Kuller LH. 2004. Optimistic attitudes protect against progression of carotid atherosclerosis in healthy middle-aged women. *Psychosom. Med.* 66:640–44

Med. Res. Counc. 2001. *Review of Autism Research. Epidemiology and Causes.* London: Natl. Autistic Soc.

Mellins CA, Gatz M, Baker L. 1996. Children's methods of coping with stress: a twin study of genetic and environmental influences. *J. Child Psychol. Psychiatry* 37:721–30

Murberg TA, Bru E, Stephens P. 2002. Personality and coping among congestive heart failure patients. *Personal. Individ. Differ.* 32:775–84

Murberg TA, Furze G, Bru E. 2004. Avoidance coping styles predict mortality among patients with congestive heart failure: a 6-year follow-up study. *Personal. Individ. Differ.* 36:757–66

Neiss MB, Stevenson J, Sedikides C, Kumashiro M, Finkel EJ, et al. 2005. Executive self, self-esteem, and negative affectivity: relations at the phenotypic and genotypic level. *J. Personal. Soc. Psychol.* 89:593–606

Ochsner KN, Ray RD, Robertson ER, Cooper JC, Chopra S, et al. 2004. For better or for worse: neural systems supporting the cognitive down-and-up-regulation of negative emotion. *Neuroimage* 23:483–99

Owen N, Poulton T, Hay FC, Mohamed-Ali V, Steptoe A. 2003. Socioeconomic status, C-reactive protein, immune factors, and responses to acute mental stress. *Brain Behav. Immun.* 17:286–95

Ozer EJ, Best SR, Lipsey TL, Weiss DS. 2003. Predictors of posttraumatic stress disorder and symptoms in adults: a meta-analysis. *Psychol. Bull.* 129:52–73

Park CL, Folkman S, Bostrom A. 2001. Appraisals of controllability and coping in caregivers and HIV+ men: testing the goodness-of-fit hypothesis. *J. Consult. Clin. Psychol.* 69:481–88

Plomin R, Scheier MF, Bergeman SC, Pedersen NL, Nesselroade JR, et al. 1992. Optimism, pessimism, and mental health: a twin/adoption study. *Personal. Individ. Differ.* 13:921–30

Rayburn NR, Wenzel SL, Elliott MN, Hambarsoomians K, Marshall GN, et al. 2005. Trauma, depression, coping, and mental health service seeking among impoverished women. *J. Consult. Clin. Psychol.* 73:667–77

Reed GM, Kemeny ME, Taylor SE, Visscher BR. 1999. Negative HIV-specific expectancies and AIDS-related bereavement as predictors of symptom onset in asymptomatic HIV-positive gay men. *Health Psychol.* 18:1–10

Reid RJ, Crisafulli A. 1990. Marital discord and child behavior problems: a meta-analysis. *J. Abnorm. Child Psych.* 18:105–17

Repetti RL, Taylor SE, Seeman TE. 2002. Risky families: family social environments and the mental and physical health of offspring. *Psychol. Bull.* 128:330–66

Reuter M, Hennig J. 2005. Association of the functional catechol-o-methlytransferase val158met polymorphism with the personality trait of extraversion. *Neuroreport* 16:1135–38

Rhee SH, Parker JC, Smarr KL, Petroski GF, Johnson JC, et al. 2000. Stress management in rheumatoid arthritis: What is the underlying mechanism? *Arthritis Care Res.* 13:435–42

Risold PY, Thompson RH, Swanson LW. 1997. The structural organization of connections between hypothalamus and cerebral cortex. *Brain Res. Rev.* 24:197–254
Roberts BW, Walton KE, Viechtbauer W. 2006. Patterns of mean-level change in personality traits across the life course: a meta-analysis of longitudinal studies. *Psychol. Bull.* 132:1–25
Roelofs K, Elzinga BM, Rotteveel M. 2005. The effects of stress-induced cortisol responses on approach-avoidance behavior. *Psychoneuroendocrinology* 30:665–77
Roesch S, Weiner B. 2001. A meta-analytic review of coping with illness: Do causal attributions matter? *J. Psychosom. Res.* 41:813–19
Rolls ET. 1996. The orbitofrontal cortex. *Philos. Trans. R. Soc. Lond. B Biol. Sci.* 351:1433–43
Rosenberger PH, Ickovics JR, Epel ES, D'Entremont D, Jokl P. 2004. Physical recovery in arthroscopic knee surgery: unique contributions of coping behaviors to clinical outcomes and stress reactivity. *Psychol. Health* 19:307–20
Roy MA, Neale MC, Kendler KS. 1995. The genetic epidemiology of self-esteem. *Br. J. Psychiatry* 166:813–20
Scheier MF, Carver CS, Bridges MW. 1994. Distinguishing optimism from neuroticism (and trait anxiety, self-mastery, and self-esteem): a re-evaluation of the Life Orientation Test. *J. Personal. Soc. Psychol.* 67:1063–78
Scheier MF, Matthews KA, Owens J, Magovern GJS, Lefebvre RC, et al. 1989. Dispositional optimism and recovery from coronary artery bypass surgery: the beneficial effects on physical and psychological well-being. *J. Personal. Soc. Psychol.* 57:1024–40
Schinka JA, Busch RM, Robichaux-Keene N. 2004. A meta-analysis of the association between the serotonin transporter gene polymorphism (5-HTTLPR) and trait anxiety. *Mol. Psychiatry* 9:197–202
Scott JL, Halford WK, Ward BG. 2004. United we stand? The effects of a couple-coping intervention on adjustment to early stage breast or gynecological cancer. *J. Consult. Clin. Psychol.* 72:1122–35
Seeman M, Lewis S. 1995. Powerlessness, health, and mortality: a longitudinal study of older men and mature women. *Soc. Sci. Med.* 41:517–25
Seeman TE, McEwen BS. 1996. Impact of social environment characteristics on neuroendocrine regulation. *Psychosom. Med.* 58:459–71
Sen S, Villafuerte S, Nesse R, Stoltenberg SF, Hopcian J, et al. 2004. Serotonin transporter and GABA(A) alpha 6 receptor variants are associated with neuroticism. *Biol. Psychiatry* 55:244–49
Setekleiv J, Skaug OE, Kaada BR. 1961. Increase of plasma 17-hydroxycorticosteroids by cerebral cortical and amygdaloid stimulation in the cat. *J. Endocrinol.* 22:119–27
Sharkansky EJ, King DW, King LA, Wolfe J, Erickson DJ, et al. 2000. Coping with Gulf War combat stress: mediating and moderating effects. *J. Abnorm. Psychol.* 109:188–97
Silver RC, Holman EA, McIntosh DN, Poulin M, Gil-Rivas V. 2002. Nationwide longitudinal study of psychological responses to September 11. *JAMA* 288:1235–44
Skinner EA, Edge K, Altman J, Sherwood H. 2003. Searching for the structure of coping: a review and critique of category systems for classifying ways of coping. *Psychol. Bull.* 129:216–69
Smolka MN, Schumann G, Wrase J, Grüsser SM, Flor H, et al. 2005. Catechol-o-methyltransferase val^{158} met genotype affects processing of emotional stimuli in the amygdala and prefrontal cortex. *J. Neurosci.* 25:836–42
Spencer SJ, Ebner K, Day TA. 2004. Differential involvement of rat medial prefrontal cortex dopamine receptors in modulation of hypothalamic-pituitary-adrenal axis responses to different stressors. *Eur. J. Neurosci.* 20:1008–16

Stanton AL, Danoff-Burg S, Cameron CL, Bishop MM, Collins CA, et al. 2000. Emotionally expressive coping predicts psychological and physical adjustment to breast cancer. *J. Consult. Clin. Psychol.* 68:875–82

Stanton AL, Snider PR. 1993. Coping with a breast cancer diagnosis: a prospective study. *Health Psychol.* 12:16–23

Stephens MAP, Druley JA, Zautra AJ. 2002. Older adults' recovery from surgery for osteoarthritis of the knee: psychosocial resources and constraints as predictors of outcomes. *Health Psychol.* 21:377–83

Stowell JR, Kiecolt-Glaser JK, Glaser R. 2001. Perceived stress and cellular immunity: when coping counts. *J. Behav. Med.* 24:323–39

Strobel A, Lesch KP, Jatzke S, Paetzold F, Brocke B. 2003. Further evidence for a modulation of novelty seeking by DRD4 Exon III, 5-HTTLPR, and COMT Val/Met variants. *Mol. Psychiatry* 8:371–72

Suls J, Fletcher B. 1985. The relative efficacy of avoidant and nonavoidant coping strategies: a meta-analysis. *Health Psychol.* 4:249–88

Suomi SJ. 1997. Early determinants of behavior: evidence from primate studies. *Br. Med. Bull.* 53:170–84

Suomi SJ. 2003. Gene-environment interactions and the neurobiology of social conflict. *Ann. NY Acad. Sci.* 1008:132–39

Taylor SE. 2007. Social support. In *Foundations of Health Psychology*, ed. HS Friedman, RC Silver, pp. 145–71. New York: Oxford Univ. Press

Taylor SE, Eisenberger NI, Saxbe D, Lehman BJ, Lieberman MD. 2006a. Neural responses to emotional stimuli are associated with childhood family stress. *Biol. Psychiatry* 60:296–301

Taylor SE, Lehman BJ, Kiefe CI, Seeman TE. 2007. Relationship of early life stress and psychological functioning to adult C-reactive protein in the Coronary Artery Risk Development in Young Adults study. *Biol. Psychiatry* 60:819–24

Taylor SE, Lerner JS, Sherman DK, Sage RM, McDowell NK. 2003a. Portrait of the self-enhancer: well-adjusted and well-liked or maladjusted and friendless? *J. Personal. Soc. Psychol.* 84:165–76

Taylor SE, Lerner JS, Sherman DK, Sage RM, McDowell NK. 2003b. Are self-enhancing cognitions associated with healthy or unhealthy biological profiles? *J. Personal. Soc. Psychol.* 85:605–15

Taylor SE, Seeman TE. 1999. Psychosocial resources and the SES-health relationship. In *Socioeconomic Status and Health in Industrial Nations: Social, Psychological, and Biological Pathways*, ed. N Adler, M Marmot, B McEwen, J Stewart, pp. 210–25. New York: N.Y. Acad. Sci.

Taylor SE, Way BM, Welch WT, Hilmert CJ, Lehman BJ, Eisenberger NI. 2006b. Early family environment, current adversity, the serotonin transporter polymorphism, and depressive symptomatology. *Biol. Psychiatry* 60:671–76

Thompson SC. 1981. Will it hurt less if I can control it? A complex answer to a simple question. *Psychol. Bull.* 90:89–101

Tolan P, Gorman-Smith D, Henry D. 2004. Supporting families in a high-risk setting: proximal effects of SAFEChildren preventive intervention. *J. Consult. Clin. Psychol.* 72:855–69

Valentiner DP, Holahan CJ, Moos RH. 1994. Social support, appraisals of event controllability, and coping: an integrative model. *J. Personal. Soc. Psychol.* 66:1094–102

Vegas O, Fano E, Brain PF, Alonso A, Azpiroz A. 2006. Social stress, coping strategies and tumor development in male mice: behavioral, neuroendocrine and immunological implications. *Psychoneuroendocrinology* 31:69–79

Weaver KE, Llabre MM, Duran RE, Antoni MH, Ironson G, et al. 2005. A stress and coping model of medication adherence and viral load in HIV-positive men and women on highly active antiretroviral therapy (HAART). *Health Psychol.* 24:385–92

Weisz JR, Sandler IN, Durlak JA, Anton BS. 2005. Promoting and protecting youth mental health through evidence-based prevention and treatment. *Am. Psychol.* 60:628–48

Wills TA. 1991. Social support and interpersonal relationships. In *Prosocial Behavior*, ed. MS Clark, pp. 265–89. Newbury Park, CA: Sage

Wolfe DA, Wekerle C, Scott K, Straatman A, Grasley C, et al. 2003. Dating violence prevention with at-risk youth: a controlled outcome evaluation. *J. Consult. Clin. Psychol.* 71:279–91

Cumulative Indexes

Contributing Authors, Volumes 1–3

P

R

S

T

V

W

Y

Z

Chapter Titles, Volumes 1–3

Childhood Disorders

Pervasive Developmental Disorders

Eating Disorders

Obesity

Cognitive Disorders and Lifespan Issues

Mental Disorders in Later Life

Sexual Disorders and Gender Identity Disorder

Sexual Dysfunctions

Substance-Related Disorders

An Introduction to

Powder Metallurgy

F. THÜMMLER

Dr.-Ing.habil., FIM
Professor Emeritus for Materials
University and Nuclear Research Centre
Karlsruhe

and

R. OBERACKER

Dr.-Ing., Central Laboratory
Institute for Ceramics in Mechanical Engineering
University of Karlsruhe

Series Editors
I. JENKINS
and
J.V. WOOD

THE INSTITUTE OF MATERIALS

Book 490

Published in 1993 by
The Institute of Materials
1 Carlton House Terrace
London SW1Y 5DB

British Library Cataloguing-in-Publication Data

Thummler, F.
Introduction to Powder Metallurgy
I. Title II. Oberacker, R.
669

ISBN 0–901716–26–X

Typeset by Dorwyn Ltd, Rowlands Castle, Hants

Printed and bound in Great Britain at
The University Press, Cambridge